"This sure-footed, clear, and stimulating commentary will give students of Genesis new insight and new questions on page after page. It is naturally a radically different work from the previous volume on Genesis in this series by Gerhard von Rad, which has been an exegetical and theological resource for over sixty years. It will thus open the eyes of readers to seeing Genesis anew in light of the way critical theories look at Genesis in the twenty-first century."

—John Goldingay, Senior Professor of Old Testament
and David Allan Hubbard Professor Emeritus
of Old Testament, Fuller Theological Seminary

"David L. Petersen provides readers with an insightful commentary that employs a combination of literary and social-scientific methodologies that have grown out of earlier models of source, tradition, form, and redaction criticism. He reads Genesis as a family narrative that explains how the ancestral family grew into a people in its relationship with G-d within the context of creation, and he points to the role of the *tôlədôt*, "generations," formulas that trace the ancestral family's history throughout the book. Petersen's volume is a worthy successor to the earlier work of Gerhard von Rad."

—Marvin A. Sweeney, Professor of Hebrew Bible,
Claremont School of Theology

"David Petersen's *Genesis* is the work of deep integrative intelligence. Petersen's commentary builds upon historical-critical questions in service of the larger matter of Genesis as literature, a book about family on the way to nationhood. The family is besieged by problems of infertility, domestic violence, and generational power struggles. Resonant with contemporary issues and eminently readable, this commentary is a must for scholars and of interest to a broad audience of readers."

—Kathleen M. O'Connor, William Marcellus McPheeters
Professor Emerita of Old Testament,
Columbia Theological Seminary

“David Petersen presents a fresh and methodologically diverse approach to the book of Genesis. His commentary is informed by recent developments in the study of the Pentateuch and provides an accessible way to read Genesis, not only as a prologue to the Moses story but also as a book in its own right. A more-than-timely replacement of Gerhard von Rad’s predecessor volume in the Old Testament Library!”

—Konrad Schmid, Professor of Hebrew Bible
and Ancient Judaism, University of Zurich

“Petersen’s commentary on Genesis provides a readable evaluation of this foundational book, drawing it together from the perspective of family and geography. His approach is primarily literary with close attention to ancient Near Eastern parallels and text-critical variants. It is a welcome addition to the literature on Genesis and as such will be an asset for scholars, clergy, and those interested in studying the narrative accounts of Israel’s origins.”

—Victor H. Matthews, Professor Emeritus of Old Testament
and retired Dean of the College of Humanities and
Public Affairs, Missouri State University

GENESIS

THE OLD TESTAMENT LIBRARY

David L. Petersen

Genesis
A Commentary

This volume is dedicated to my wife, Sara Joyce Myers

First edition
Published by Westminster John Knox Press
Louisville, Kentucky

25 26 27 28 29 30 31 32 33 34—10 9 8 7 6 5 4 3 2 1

Unless otherwise indicated, translations from Genesis are by the author. Verse numbering in the OT follows the HB, with numbers for English versions following in parentheses or brackets.

Book design by Jennifer K. Cox

Library of Congress Cataloging-in-Publication Data
is on file at the Library of Congress, Washington, DC.

ISBN: 978-0-664-22079-2

CONTENTS

PREFACE

I have been thinking regularly about the book of Genesis for over fifty years, having published my first article devoted to texts in that book in 1973. Those fifty years have seen many changes in the field of Hebrew Bible studies. In the 1970s, source criticism, tradition history, and form criticism undergirded much so-called higher-critical study of the book. That is no longer the case. Attention to redaction criticism, which pushes beyond the division of the text into earlier components, has enriched the field. And, since the early 1970s, a myriad of newer approaches, particularly those informed by literary analysis and social-scientific studies, have become prominent. I hope this commentary not only reflects some of the strengths of earlier approaches, but also incorporates important perspectives that have emerged since the last third of the twentieth century.

I owe a debt of gratitude to innumerable individuals. Perhaps most important are the students with whom I worked at the University of Illinois Urbana-Champaign, Iliff School of Theology, and Emory University. They invariably posed questions that pushed me to think in new ways about familiar texts. And I want to thank colleagues from whom I learned, not only in their publications, but also in sessions at professional meetings of the Chicago Society of Biblical Research, the Society of Biblical Literature, the International Organization for the Study of the Old Testament, the Colloquium for Biblical Research, and the OTFS. I am deeply grateful to William P. Brown, my Old Testament Library editor, who graciously invested so much time and effort on this volume. Finally, I owe a debt of gratitude to colleagues at Westminster John Knox Press—Dan Braden, S. David Garber, and Tina E. Noll—for their careful work on this project. Needless to say, I am responsible for the shortcomings present in it.

February 14, 2024
Fort Collins, CO

ABBREVIATIONS

//	parallel to; Gen 12:3 // Num 24:9; poetic line // parallel poetic line
×	times
AB	Anchor Bible
ABD	*Anchor Bible Dictionary*. Edited by David Noel Freedman. 6 vols. New York: Doubleday, 1992
ABRL	Anchor Bible Reference Library
AfO	*Archiv für Orientforschung*
AIL	Ancient Israel and Its Literature
AnBib	Analecta Biblica
ANE	Ancient Near East(ern)
ATD	Das Alte Testament Deutsch
BCE	before the Common Era
BETL	Bibliotheca Ephemeridum Theologicarum Lovaniensium
BHS	*Biblia Hebraica Stuttgartensia*. Edited by Karl Elliger and Wilhelm Rudolph. Stuttgart: Deutsche Biblegesellschaft, 1983
BibOr	Biblica et Orientalia
BR	*Biblical Research*
BZAW	Beihefte zur Zeitschrift für die alttestamentliche Wissenschaft
c.	century
ca.	circa
ch(s).	chapter(s)
CBQ	*Catholic Biblical Quarterly*
CEB	Common English Bible
DSS	Dead Sea Scrolls
Dtr	Deuteronomistic
ed.	edition
e.g.	*exempli gratia*, for example
et al.	*et alii*, and others
FAT	Forschungen zum Alten Testament

FIOTL	The Formation and Interpretation of Old Testament Literature
FOTL	Forms of Old Testament Literature
FRLANT	Forschungen zur Religion und Literatur des Alten und Neuen Testaments
HALOT	*The Hebrew and Aramaic Lexicon of the Old Testament.* By Ludwig Koehler, Walter Baumgartner, and Johann J. Stamm. Translated and edited under the supervision of Mervyn E. J. Richardson. 4 vols. Leiden: Brill, 1994–99
HBAI	Hebrew Bible and Ancient Israel
HC	Holiness Code (Lev 17–26)
HTR	*Harvard Theological Review*
IBC	Interpretation: A Bible Commentary for Teaching and Preaching
IBHS	*An Introduction to Biblical Hebrew Syntax*. By Michael O'Connor and Bruce K. Waltke. Winona Lake, IN: Eisenbrauns, 1990
ICC	International Critical Commentary
i.e.	*id est*, that is
IECOT	International Exegetical Commentary on the Old Testament
J	Yahwist source
JAOS	*Journal of the American Oriental Society*
JARCE	*Journal of the American Research Center in Egypt*
JBL	*Journal of Biblical Literature*
JCS	*Journal of Cuneiform Studies*
JEA	*Journal of Egyptian Archaeology*
JJS	*Journal of Jewish Studies*
JSOT	*Journal for the Study of the Old Testament*
JSOTSup	Journal for the Study of the Old Testament Supplement Series
JTS	*Journal of Theological Studies*
lit.	literally
LXX	Septuagint
MS(S)	manuscript(s)
MT	Masoretic Text
n(n).	note(s)
NCBC	New Century Bible Commentary
NIDB	*New Interpreter's Dictionary of the Bible*. Edited by Katharine Doob Sakenfeld. 5 vols. Nashville: Abingdon, 2006–2009
NIV	New Internation Version

NJPS	*Tanakh: The Holy Scriptures: The New JPS Translation according to the Traditional Hebrew Text*
NRSV	New Revised Standard Version
NRSVue	New Revised Standard Version Updated Edition
OBO	Orbis Biblicus et Orientalis
OBT	Overtures to Biblical Theology
OTFS	Old Testament Fishing Society
OTL	Old Testament Library
OTR	Old Testament Readings
OTS	Old Testament Studies
P	Priestly source
PTMS	Pittsburgh Theological Monograph Series
SBLDS	Society of Biblical Literature Dissertation Series
SBS	Stuttgarter Bibelstudien
SemeiaSt	Semeia Studies
SHANE	Studies in the History of the Ancient Near East
SHBC	Smyth & Helwys Bible Commentary
SP	Samaritan Pentateuch
SymS	Symposium Series
Syr	Peshitta/Syriac
tg	targum
ThWAT	*Theologisches Wörterbuch zum alten Testament*. Edited by G. Johannes Botterweck and Helmer Ringgren. 10 vols. Stuttgart: Kohlhammer, 1973–77
v(v).	verse(s). Keyed to MT. Alternates within brackets fit English Bibles.
viz.	*videlicet*, namely
vs.	versus
VT	Vetus Testamentum
VTSup	Supplements to Vetus Testamentum
Vulg	Vulgate
WBC	Word Biblical Commentary
WMANT	Wissenschaftliche Monographien zum Alten und Neuen Testament
x	an unspecified person, thing, quantity
YHWH	Represents Hebrew consonants for Yahweh, LORD
ZA	*Zeitschrift für Assyriologie*
ZAW	*Zeitschrift fur die alttestamentliche Wissenschaft*

BIBLIOGRAPHY

Alter, Robert. 1981. *The Art of Biblical Narrative*. New York: Basic Books.

———. 1996. *Genesis: Translation and Commentary*. New York: Norton.

Anderson, Bernhard. 2017. *An Introduction to the Study of the Pentateuch*. T&T Clark Approaches to Biblical Studies. London: Bloomsbury.

Arnold, Bill T. 2009. *Genesis*. NCBC. Cambridge: Cambridge University Press.

Astour, Michael C. 1966. "Political and Cosmic Symbolism in Genesis 14 and Its Babylonian Sources." Pages 65–122 in *Biblical Motifs: Origins and Transformations*. Edited by Alexander Altmann. Cambridge: Harvard University Press.

Baden, Joel S. 2009. "The Tower of Babel: A Case Study in the Competing Methods of Historical and Modern Literary Criticism." *JBL* 128.2:209–24.

Bird, Phyllis A. 1981. "'Male and Female He Created Them': Gen 1:27b in the Context of the Priestly Account of Creation." *HTR* 74.2:129–59.

Blenkinsopp, Joseph. 1982. "Abraham and the Righteous of Sodom." *JJS* 33.1–2:119–32.

———. 1992. *The Pentateuch: An Introduction to the First Five Books of the Bible*. ABRL. New York: Doubleday.

Bloch-Smith, Elizabeth. 1992. *Judahite Burial Practices and Beliefs about the Dead*. JSOTSup 123. Sheffield: Sheffield Academic Press.

Blum, Erhard. 1990. *Studien zur Komposition des Pentateuch*. BZAW 189. Berlin: de Gruyter.

Brett, Mark G. 2000. *Genesis: Procreation and the Politics of Identity*. OTR. London: Routledge.

Brett, Mark G., and Jacob Wöhrle, eds. 2018. *The Politics of the Ancestors: Exegetical and Historical Perspectives on Genesis 12–36*. FAT 124. Tübingen: Mohr Siebeck.

Brown, William P. 1993. *Structure, Role, and Ideology in the Hebrew and Greek Texts of Genesis 1:1–2:3*. SBLDS 132. Atlanta: Scholars Press.

Brueggemann, Walter. 1982. *Genesis*. IBC. Atlanta: John Knox.

Carr, David. 1996. *Reading the Fractures of Genesis: Historical and Literary Approaches*. Louisville: Westminster John Knox.

———. 2020. *The Formation of Genesis 1–11: Biblical and Other Precursors*. New York: Oxford University Press.

———. 2021. *Genesis 1–11*. IECOT. Stuttgart: Kohlhammer.

Clines, David J. A. 2012. "The Failure of the Flood." Pages 74–84 in *Making a Difference: Essays on the Bible and Judaism in Honor of Tamara Cohn Eskenazi*. Edited by David Clines et al. Sheffield: Sheffield Phoenix.

Coats, George W. 1983. *Genesis, with an Introduction to Narrative Literature*. FOTL 1. Grand Rapids: Eerdmans.

Crawford, Sidnie W. 2012. "Genesis in the Dead Sea Scrolls." Pages 353–73 in *The Book of Genesis: Composition, Reception, and Interpretation*. Edited by Craig A. Evans et al. VTSup 152. Leiden: Brill.

Cross, Frank M. 1973. *Canaanite Myth and Hebrew Epic: Essays in the History of the Religion of Israel*. Cambridge: Harvard University Press.

Crüsemann, Frank. 1981. "Die Eigenständigkeit der Urgeschichte. Ein Beitrag zur Diskussion zum den 'Jahwisten.'" Pages 11–29 in *Die Botschaft und die Boten: Festschrift für Hans Walter Wolff zum 70. Geburtstag*. Edited by Jörg Jeremias and Lothar Perlitt. Neukirchen-Vluyn: Neukirchener Verlag.

———. 1996. "Human Solidarity and Ethnic Identity: Israel's Self-Definition in the Genealogical System of Genesis." Pages 57–76 in *Ethnicity and the Bible*. Edited by Mark G. Brett. Leiden: Brill.

Dalley, Stephanie. 1989. *Myths from Mesopotamia: Creation, the Flood, Gilgamesh, and Others*. Oxford: Oxford University Press.

Dozeman, Thomas B., and Konrad Schmid, eds. 2006. *A Farewell to the Yahwist? The Composition of the Pentateuch in Recent European Interpretation*. SymS 34. Atlanta: Society of Biblical Literature.

Emerton, John A. 1971. "Some False Clues in the Study of Genesis 14." *VT* 21.1:24–47.

———. 1988. "The Priestly Writer in Genesis." *JTS* 39.2:381–400.

Evans, Craig A., Joel N. Lohr, and David L. Petersen, eds. 2012. *The Book of Genesis: Composition, Reception, and Interpretation*. VTSup 152. Leiden: Brill.

Eyre, Christopher J. 1984. "Crime and Adultery in Ancient Egypt." *JEA* 70:92–105.

Finkelstein, Israel, and Thomas Römer. 2014. "Comments on the Historical Background of the Abraham Narrative. Between 'Realia' and 'Exegetica.'" *HBAI* 3.1:3–23.

Fishbane, Michael A. 1975. "Composition and Structure in the Jacob Cycle (Gen 25:19–35:22)." *JJS* 26.1:15–38.

Fitzmyer, Joseph A. 1967. Pages 14–15 in *The Aramaic Inscriptions of Sefire*. BibOr 19. Rome: Pontifical Biblical Institute.

Fox, Everett. 1989. "Can Genesis Be Read as a Book?" *Semeia* 46:31–40.

Fox, Michael V. 2001. "Wisdom in the Joseph Story." *VT* 51.1:26–41.

———. 2012. "Joseph and Wisdom." Pages 231–62 in *The Book of Genesis: Composition, Reception, and Interpretation.* Edited by Craig A. Evans et al. VTSup 152. Leiden: Brill.

Fretheim, Terence E. 1994. "Genesis." Pages 319–674 in vol. 1 of *The New Interpreter's Bible*. Edited by L. Keck et al. Nashville: Abingdon.

Galambush, Julie. 2018. *Reading Genesis: A Literary and Theological Commentary*. Reading the Old Testament. Macon, GA: Smyth & Helwys.

Geoghegan, Jeffrey C. 2005. "Additional Evidence for a Deuteronomistic Redaction of the 'Tetrateuch.'" *CBQ* 67.3:405–21.

George, Andrew R. 2005/2006. "The Tower of Babel: Archaeology, History and Cuneiform Texts." *AfO* 51:75–95.

Gertz, Jan Christian. 2012. "The Formation of the Primeval History." Pages 107–35 in *The Book of Genesis: Composition, Reception, and Interpretation.* Edited by Craig A. Evans et al. VTSup 152. Leiden: Brill.

———. 2018. *Das erste Buch Mose, Genesis: Die Urgeschichte Gen 1–11*. ATD 1. Göttingen: Vandenhoeck & Ruprecht.

Gertz, Jan Christian, Bernard M. Levinson, Dalit Rom-Shiloni, and Konrad Schmid, eds. 2016. *The Formation of the Pentateuch: Bridging the Academic Cultures of Europe, Israel, and North America.* FAT 111. Tübingen: Mohr Siebeck.

Gertz, Jan Christian, Konrad Schmid, and Markus Witte, eds. 2002. *Abschied vom Jahwisten: Die Komposition des Hexateuch in der jüngsten Diskussion.* BZAW 315. Berlin: de Gruyter.

Giuntoli, Federico, and Konrad Schmid, eds. 2015. *The Post-Priestly Pentateuch: New Perspectives on Its Redactional Development and Theological Profiles*. FAT 101. Tübingen: Mohr Siebeck.

Goetze, Albrecht. 1938. *The Hittite Ritual of Tunnawi*. New Haven: American Oriental Society.

Golka, Friedemann W. 1978. "Die theologische Erzählungen im Abraham-Kreis." *ZAW* 90.2:186–95.

———. 1999. "Bechorah und Berachah: Erstgeburtsrecht und Segen." Pages 133–44 in *Recht und Ethos im Alten Testament—Gestalt und Wirkung: Festschrift für Horst Seebass zum 65. Geburtstag*. Edited by Stefan Beyerle et al. Neukirchen-Vluyn: Neukirchener Verlag.

Grüneberg, Keith N. 2003. *Abraham, Blessing, and the Nations: A Philological and Exegetical Study of Genesis 12:3 in Its Narrative Context*. BZAW 332. Berlin: de Gruyter.

Gunkel, Hermann. 1964. *The Legends of Genesis: The Biblical Saga and History*. Translated by W. H. Carruth. New York: Schocken Books.

———. 1997. *Genesis*. Translated by Mark Biddle. Mercer Library of Biblical Studies. Macon, GA: Mercer University Press.

Güterbock, Hans Gustav. 1934. "Die historische Tradition und ihre literarische Gestaltung bei Babylonien und Hethitern bis 1200." *ZA* 42:1–91.

Hartenstein, Friedhelm, and Konrad Schmid, eds. 2022. *Farewell to the Priestly Writing? The Current State of the Debate*. AIL 38. Atlanta: Society of Biblical Literature.

Heard, R. Christopher. 2001. *Dynamics of Diselection: Ambiguity in Genesis 12–36 and Ethnic Boundaries in Post-Exilic Judah*. SemeiaSt 39. Atlanta: Society of Biblical Literature.

Helfmeyer, Franz Joseph. 1973–77. "*nsh*." In *ThWAT* 5:481.

Hendel, Ronald S. 1998. *The Text of Genesis 1–11: Textual Studies and Critical Edition*. New York: Oxford University Press.

———. 2012. "Historical Context." Pages 51–81 in *The Book of Genesis: Composition, Reception, and Interpretation*. Edited by Craig A. Evans et al. VTSup 152. Leiden: Brill.

Hensel, Benedikt, ed. 2021. *The History of the Jacob Cycle (Genesis 25–35): The History of the Compilation, the Redaction and the Reception of the Biblical Narrative and Its Historical and Cultural Context*. Archaeology and Bible 4. Tübingen: Mohr Siebeck.

Hiebert, Robert J. V. 2007. "To the Reader of Genesis." Pages 1–6 in *A New English Translation of the Septuagint*. Edited by Albert Pietersma and Benjamin G. Wright. New York: Oxford University Press.

Hiebert, Theodore. 2007. "The Tower of Babel and the Origin of the World's Cultures." *JBL* 126.1:29–58.

Humphreys, W. Lee. 2001. *The Character of God in the Book of Genesis: A Narrative Appraisal*. Louisville: Westminster John Knox.

Jacobsen, Thorkild. 1992. "The Spell of Nudimmud." Pages 403–16 in *Sha'arei Talmon: Studies in the Bible, Qumran, and the Ancient Near East Presented to Shemaryahu Talmon*. Edited by Michael A. Fishbane and Emanuel Tov. Winona Lake, IN: Eisenbrauns.

Jeansonne, Sharon Pace. 1990. "Gen 25:33—The Use of Poetry in the Rebekah Narrative." Pages 145–52 in *The Psalms and Other Studies on the Old Testament*. Edited by Jack C. Knight and Lawrence A. Sinclair. Nashotah, WI: Nashotah House Seminary.

Kaminsky, Joel. 2012. "The Theology of Genesis." Pages 635–56 in *The Book of Genesis: Composition, Reception, and Interpretation*. Edited by Craig A. Evans et al. VTSup 152. Leiden: Brill.

King, Thomas J. 2009. *The Realignment of the Priestly Literature: The Priestly Narrative in Genesis and Its Relation to Priestly Legislation and the Holiness School*. PTMS 102. Eugene, OR: Pickwick.

Köckert, Matthias. 2015. "Gen 20–22 als nach-priesterliche Erweiterung der Vätergeschichte." Pages 157–76 in *The Post-Priestly Pentateuch: New Perspectives on Its Redactional Development and Theological Profiles*. Edited by Federico Giuntoli and Konrad Schmid. FAT 101. Tübingen: Mohr Siebeck.

Kramer, Samuel N. 1968. "The 'Babel' of Tongues: A Sumerian Version." *JAOS* 88.1:108–11.

Leemhuis, Fred. 2002. "Ibrahim's Sacrifice of His Son in the Early Post-Koranic Tradition." Pages 125–39 in *The Sacrifice of Isaac: The Aqedah (Genesis 22) and Its Interpretations*. Edited by Ed Noort and Eibert Tigchelaar. Themes in Biblical Tradition: Jewish and Christian Traditions. Leiden: Brill.

Levenson, Jon D. 1993. *The Death and Resurrection of the Beloved Son: The Transformation of Child Sacrifice in Judaism and Christianity*. New Haven: Yale University Press.

Levin, Christoph. 1993. *Der Jahwist*. FRLANT 157. Göttingen: Vandenhoeck & Ruprecht.

Lohfink, Norbert. 1984. "God the Creator and the Stability of Heaven and Earth." Pages 116–35 in *Theology of the Pentateuch: Themes of the Priestly Narrative and Deuteronomy*. Minneapolis: Fortress.

Margalith, Othniel. 2000. "The Riddle of Genesis 14 and Melchizedek." *ZAW* 112.4:501–8.

Mauss, Marcel. 1954. *The Gift: Forms and Functions of Exchange in Archaic Societies*. Glencoe, IL: Free Press.

McCarthy, Dennis J. 1963. *Treaty and Covenant: A Study in Form in the Ancient Oriental Documents and in the Old Testament*. AnBib 21. Rome: Pontifical Biblical Institute.

McEvenue, Sean E. 1971. *The Narrative Style of the Priestly Writer*. AnBib 50. Rome: Biblical Institute Press.

Meyers, Carol L. 1988. *Rediscovering Eve: Ancient Israelite Women in Context*. New York: Oxford University Press.

Milgrom, Jacob. 1991. *Leviticus 1–16*. AB 3. New York: Doubleday.

———. 2000. *Leviticus 17–22*. AB 3A. New York: Doubleday.

Miller, Patrick D. 1984. "Syntax and Theology in Genesis XII 3a." *VT* 34.4: 472–76.

Moberly, R. W. L. 2009. *The Theology of the Book of Genesis*. Old Testament Theology. Cambridge: Cambridge University Press.

Muffs, Yochanan. 1982. "Abraham the Noble Warrior: Patriarchal Politics and Laws of War in Ancient Israel." *JJS* 33:81–107.

Nicholson, Ernest W. 1998. *The Pentateuch in the Twentieth Century: The Legacy of Julius Wellhausen*. Oxford: Clarendon.

Noth, Martin. 1972. *A History of Pentateuchal Traditions*. Translated by B. Anderson. Englewood Cliffs, NJ: Prentice-Hall.

O'Connor, Kathleen M. 2018. *Genesis 1–25A*. SHBC. Macon: GA: Smyth & Helwys.

Petersen, David L. 1973. "A Thrice-Told Tale: Genre, Theme, and Motif." *BR* 18:30–43.

———. 1976. "The Yahwist on the Flood." *VT* 26:438–46.

———. 1977. "Covenant Ritual: A Traditio-Historical Perspective." *BR* 22:7–18.

———. 1979. "Genesis 6:1–4, Yahweh and the Organization of the Cosmos." *JSOT* 13:47–64.

———. 2005a. "Genesis and Family Values." *JBL* 124:5–23.

———. 2005b. "Polities in Genesis 12–36." Pages 75–88 in *Constituting the Community: Studies on the Polity of Ancient Israel in Honor of S. Dean McBride Jr*. Edited by John T. Strong and Steven S. Tuell. Winona Lake, IN: Eisenbrauns.

———. 2010. "The Genesis of Genesis." Pages 27–40 in *Congress Volume Ljubljana 2007*. Edited by André Lemaire. VTSup 133. Leiden: Brill.

———. 2012. "Blood in the Post-Flood World." Pages 242–50 in *Making a Difference: Essays on the Bible and Judaism in Honor of Tamara Cohn Eskenazi*. Edited by David J. A. Clines et al. Sheffield: Sheffield Phoenix.

———. 2022. "The Priestly Portrayal of Jacob in Genesis." Pages 35–41 in *Historical Settings, Intertextuality, and Biblical Theology: Essays in Honor of Marvin A. Sweeney*. Edited by Hyun Chul Paul Kim, Tyler D. Mayfield, and Hye Kyung Park. FAT 160. Tübingen: Mohr Siebeck.

Petschow, Herbert. 1965. "Die neubabylonische Zwiegesprächsurkunde und Genesis 23." *JCS* 19.4:103–20.

Picardo, Nicholas. 2007. "'Semantic Homicide' and the So-Called Reserve Heads: The Theme of Decapitation in Egyptian Funerary Religion and Some Implications for the Old Kingdom." *JARCE* 43:221–52.

Pury, Albert de. 2006. "The Jacob Story and the Beginning of the Formation of the Pentateuch." Pages 51–72 in *A Farewell to the Yahwist? The Composition of the Pentateuch in Recent European Interpretation*. Edited by Thomas B. Dozeman and Konrad Schmid. SymS 34. Atlanta: Society of Biblical Literature.

———. 2000. "Der priesterschriftliche Umgang mit der Jakobsgeschichte." Pages 33–60 in *Schriftauslegung in der Schrift: Festschrift für Odil Hannes Steck zu seinem 65. Geburtstag*. Edited by Reinhard G. Kratz et al. BZAW 300. Berlin: de Gruyter.

Rad, Gerhard von. 1972. *Genesis*. Translated by John H. Marks. OTL. Philadelphia: Westminster.

Redford, Donald B. 1970. *A Study of the Biblical Story of Joseph (Genesis 37–50)*. VTSup 20. Leiden: Brill.

Rendsburg, Gary B. 1995. "*LĀŚÛAḤ* in Genesis xxiv 63." *VT* 45.4:558–60.

Rendtorff, Rolf. 1961. "Gen 8.21 und die Urgeschichte des Jahwisten." *Kerygma und Dogma* 7.1:69–78.

———. 1990. *The Problem of the Process of Transmission in the Pentateuch*. Translated by John J. Scullion. JSOTSup 89. Sheffield: Sheffield Academic Press.

———. 1993. "Two Kinds of P? Some Reflections on the Occasion of the Publishing of Jacob Milgrom's Commentary on Leviticus 1–16." *JSOT* 60.1:75–81.

Rofé, Alexander. 1990. "An Enquiry into the Betrothal of Rebekah." Pages 27–39 *in Die Hebräische Bibel und ihre zweifache Nachgeschichte: Festschrift für Rolf Rendtorff*. Edited by Erhard Blum et al. Neukirchen: Neukirchener Verlag.

Römer, Thomas. 2006. "The Elusive Yahwist: A Short History of Research." Pages 9–27 in *A Farewell to the Yahwist? The Composition of the Pentateuch in Recent European Interpretation*. Edited by Thomas B. Dozeman and Konrad Schmid. SymS 34. Atlanta: Society of Biblical Literature.

———. 2015. "The Story of Joseph in the Book of Genesis: Pre-P or Post-P?" Pages 185–201 in *The Post-Priestly Pentateuch: New Perspectives on Its Redactional Development and Theological Profiles*. Edited by Federico Giuntoli and Konrad Schmid. FAT 101. Tübingen: Mohr Siebeck.

———. 2016. "How to Date the Pentateuch." Pages 357–70 in *The Formation of the Pentateuch: Bridging the Academic Cultures of Europe, Israel, and North America*. Edited by Jan C. Gertz et al. FAT 111. Tübingen: Mohr Siebeck.

Ru, Yi-ling. 1992. *The Family Novel: Toward a Generic Definition*. American University Studies: Series 19, General Literature 28. New York: Peter Lang.

Ruppert, Lothar. 1972. "Das Motiv der Versuchung durch Gott in vordeuteronomischer Tradition." *VT* 22.1:55–63.

Schmid, Konrad. 2021. "The Neo-Documentarian Manifesto: A Critical Reading." *JBL* 140.3:461–79.

Schmidt, Werner H. 1964. *Die Schöpfungsgeschichte der Priesterschrift: Zur Überlieferungsgeschichte von Genesis 1, 1–2, 4a*. WMANT 17. Neukirchen-Vluyn: Neukirchener.

Scholz, Susanne. 2000. *Rape Plots: A Feminist Cultural Study of Genesis 34*. Studies in Biblical Literature 13. New York: Peter Lang.

Schüle, Andreas. 2005. "Made in the 'Image of God': The Concept of Divine Images in Gen 1–3." *ZAW* 117.1:1–19.

Ska, Jean-Louis. 2006. *Introduction to Reading the Pentateuch*. Translated by Sr. Pascale Dominique. Winona Lake, IN: Eisenbrauns.

———. 2009. "L'appel d'Abraham et l'acte de naissance d'Israël (Genèse 12,1–4a)." Pages 46–66 in *The Exegesis of the Pentateuch: Exegetical Studies and Basic Questions*. FAT 66. Tübingen: Mohr Siebeck.

Skinner, John. 1930. *A Critical and Exegetical Commentary on the Book of Genesis*. ICC. Edinburgh: T&T Clark.

Smith, Mark S. 2002. *The Early History of God: YHWH and Other Deities in Ancient Israel*. 2nd ed. Grand Rapids: Eerdmans.

———. 2010. *The Priestly Vision of Genesis 1*. Minneapolis: Fortress.

Speiser, E. A. 1964. *Genesis*. AB 1. Garden City, NY: Doubleday.

Steinberg, Naomi. 1989. "The Genealogical Framework of the Family Stories in Genesis." *Semeia* 46:41–50.

———. 1993. *Kinship and Marriage in Genesis: A Household Economics Perspective*. Minneapolis: Fortress.

———. 2012. "The World of the Family in Genesis." Pages 279–300 in *The Book of Genesis: Composition, Reception, and Interpretation*. Edited by C. Evans et al. FIOTL 6. Leiden: Brill.

Strong, John T. 2008. "Shattering the Image of God: A Response to Theodore Hiebert's Interpretation of the Story of the Tower of Babel." *JBL* 127.4:625–34.

Sweeney, Marvin A. 2017. *The Pentateuch*. Core Biblical Studies. Nashville: Abingdon.

Toorn, Karel van der. 1996. *Family Religion in Babylon, Syria, and Israel: Continuity and Change in the Forms of Religious Life*. SHANE 7. Leiden: Brill.

Tov, Emanuel. 2012. *Textual Criticism of the Hebrew Bible*. 3rd ed. Minneapolis: Fortress.

Trible, Phyllis. 1978. *God and the Rhetoric of Sexuality*. OBT. Philadelphia: Fortress.

Tucker, Gene M. 1966. "The Legal Background of Genesis 23." *JBL* 85.1:77–84.

Uehlinger, Christoph. 1990. *Weltreich und "eine Rede": Eine neue Deutung der sogenannten Turmbauerzählung (Gen 11:1–9)*. OBO 101. Freiburg: Universitätsverlag.

Vall, Gregory. 1994. "What Was Isaac Doing in the Field (Genesis xxiv 63)?" *VT* 44.4:513–23.

Van Seters, John. 1975. *Abraham in History and Tradition*. New Haven: Yale University Press.

———. 1992. *Prologue to History: The Yahwist as Historian in Genesis*. Louisville: Westminster John Knox.

von Rad. *See* Rad

Warner, Megan. 2018. *Re-Imagining Abraham: A Reassessment of the Influence of Deuteronomism in Genesis*. OTS 72. Leiden: Brill.

Wenham, Gordon. 1987. *Genesis 1–15*. WBC 1. Waco: Word Books.

———. 1994. *Genesis 16–50*. WBC 2. Dallas: Word Books.

Wenin, André, ed. 2001. *Studies in the Book of Genesis: Literature, Redaction and History*. BETL 155. Leuven: Leuven University.

Westbrook, Raymond. 1971. "Purchase of the Cave of Machpelah." *Israel Law Review* 6.1:29–38.

Westermann, Claus. 1980. *Promises to the Fathers: Studies on the Patriarchal Narratives*. Philadelphia: Fortress.

———. 1984. *Genesis 1–11: A Commentary*. Translated by John J. Scullion. Minneapolis: Augsburg.

———. 1985. *Genesis 12–36: A Commentary*. Translated by John J. Scullion. Minneapolis: Augsburg.

———. 1986. *Genesis 37–50: A Commentary*. Translated by John J. Scullion. Minneapolis: Augsburg.

Wilson, Robert R. 1977. *Genealogy and History in the Biblical World*. New Haven: Yale University Press.

Witte, Markus. 1998. *Die biblische Urgeschichte: Redaktions– und theologiegeschichtliche Beobachtungen zu Genesis 1,1–11,26*. BZAW 265. Berlin: de Gruyter.

Wöhrle, Jakob. 2012. *Fremdlinge im eigenen Land: Zum Entstehung und Intention der priesterlichen Passagen der Vätergeschichte*. FRLANT 246. Göttingen: Vandenhoeck & Ruprecht.

Wolde, E. J. van. 2002. "Does *ʿinnâ* Denote Rape? A Semantic Analysis of a Controversial Word." *VT* 52.4:528–44.

Zenger, Erich. 1983. *Gottes Bogen in den Wolken: Untersuchungen zu Komposition und Theologie der priesterschriftlichen Urgeschichte*. SBS. Stuttgart: Katholisches Bibelwerk.

INTRODUCTION

Genesis is a book. That claim might seem odd, but Genesis has rarely been examined and interpreted as a book. Genesis has sometimes been viewed as a collection of diverse sagas (e.g., Gunkel), but little, if any, attention was paid to the collection as a whole. Similarly, Genesis has routinely been construed as a collection of "documents" or "sources," attributed primarily to three different authors or traditions that extended into other books in the Tetrateuch (e.g., Speiser), or beyond (so von Rad). However, such analysis rarely examined the relationship of the sources, especially the extent to which a later source, such as the Priestly source (P), may have been a response to or a critique of an earlier one. Moreover, it was often the case that one source, the Yahwist (J) in the case of von Rad, received special attention. Finally, Genesis has regularly been treated as an entity of three discrete sections: primeval history (Gen 1–11), patriarchal literature (12–36), and the Joseph story (37–50). Such a division does not naturally move to a consideration of the fifty chapters as one literary work. None of these approaches led to an analysis of Genesis as a book.

This situation was primarily a function of the methods being used by those scholars who studied the Hebrew Bible. If one thought about Genesis from a form-critical perspective, then the presence of small stories, genealogies, or myths would receive the lion's share of attention. Similarly, if a scholar approached Genesis from the perspective of the documentary hypothesis, then it would be natural for that individual to focus on the diverse documents present in that book. Indeed, the documentary hypothesis offered yet another rationale for not treating Genesis as a book. The dominant form of the documentary hypothesis insisted that three of the classic sources extended from Genesis through at least Numbers.[1] Therefore Genesis as a literary unit was in principle unimportant if one were focusing on these narrative strands that extended well beyond Genesis. As a result, one would not think that Genesis—or Exodus, for that matter—would exist as a separate piece of literature.

1. For a convenient allocation of the sources in the Pentateuch, see "The Translator's Supplement: Analytical Outline of the Pentateuch," in Noth 1972, 261–76.

There are, however, two elements that hold the book together: (1) a social structure, the family; and (2) the so-called *tôlədôt* (descendants) formula, both of which attest to the importance of family as a unifying element in Genesis (see Arnold 2009, 4–6.) As early as chapter 2, the early account of creation, the book explicitly features the world of the family ("father," "mother," and "wife" in Gen 2:24), an element that continues to the end of the book, even as the family becomes a people. According to the initial chapters of the book, humanity is created to exist within the structure of a family, consisting first of a spousal pair (implicitly in 1:27, explicitly in 2:24) and then growing as progeny are born. The lives of primeval families are recorded in Genesis 3–10: the brothers Cain and Abel, Lamech and his wives, the minor deities marrying human wives, and Noah with his sons.

Then, beginning with Gen 11:27, the families of ancient Israel stem in linear fashion from earlier lineages in the ancient Near East. Three extended families predominate in the family literature (Gen 12–36): Abram/Abraham, Lot, Hagar, Ishmael, Sarai/Sarah, and Isaac; Isaac, Rebekah, Esau, and Jacob; and Jacob, Laban, Rachel, and Leah. From this perspective, the final portion of the book (Gen 37–50) highlights one of Jacob's children, Joseph, and his role in the complex dynamics of Jacob's family with his twelve sons and one daughter (the story concerning Dinah, Jacob's daughter, may be found in ch. 34).

The prominence of family throughout the book is complemented by a redactional device, the *tôlədôt* formula (*tôlədôt* is a plural noun meaning "descendants" or "generations"), which has been used to integrate various portions of the book. The formula comprises the phrase "these are the descendants of x" (Gen 2:4a; 5:1; 6:9; 10:1; 11:10, 27; 25:12, 19; 36:1, 9; 37:2). The formula, normally attributed to a Priestly editor, appears five times in the primeval account, five times in the family literature, and once at the beginning of the Joseph story. And it occurs just before certain descendants are identified. For example, Gen 25:12 reads, "These are the descendants of Ishmael." Immediately thereafter a genealogy provides the names of Ishmael's children. Less typical and more theologically creative is the first occurrence of the formula (Gen 2:4a). The formula identifies the descendants of "the heavens and the earth," which here refers to the humans identified soon thereafter in that chapter. For this author/editor, humans are to be construed as progeny of the world—"the heavens and the earth"—created in Gen 1. In sum, these formulae, brief though they are, reinforce the importance of family and lineage as entities that exist over time through the creation of progeny. The narratives, genealogies, and reports that they introduce depict families with diverse structures. But the constant is the presence of descendants, as well as the complex relationships among them. Genesis is a book about humans in familial life, including its diverse structures and its values.

The *tôlədôt* formula, which points to one generation of a family following another, belongs to the world of genealogies, which are so important in Genesis.

Crüsemann was surely correct when he wrote, “The genealogies, . . . which pervade all of Genesis, form something like the skeleton of this book, a stable framework which holds together and carries all other parts” (1996, 59–60). The *tôlədôt* formulae underscore the importance of these genealogical-familial connections. Steinberg put it well when referring to Gen 12–50: “Genealogy reflects family succession which moves action forward and is the redactional device used by P to organize family history into narrative cycles” (1989, 41).

The book of Genesis concludes with the primary family, the patrilineage of Abraham, being transformed into something other than a family. This transition is presaged by texts such as Gen 12:6; 17:16; 28:13, which look forward to a time when the authors of these verses imagine that Israel will become a nation and that kings will stem from that family. This transformation becomes especially clear as one reaches the end of the book. The notion of the sons of Israel (i.e., of Jacob) now includes the political vocabulary of tribe: “All these are the twelve tribes of Israel” (Gen 49:28). And in the final chapter, those who still reside in Egypt are characterized by yet another political term, “people”: “in order to preserve a numerous people, as he is doing today” (Gen 50:20 NRSV). Though families will reappear in other biblical books (e.g., the family of David), family per se will never have the pride of place that it possesses in this first biblical book.

The Family in Genesis

Genesis is a book that describes humanity through genealogies. According to the structure of vertical genealogies present in the book, all humanity is related to a common source (so, e.g., Gen 5). Over time, humanity grew and became geographically and culturally diverse (Gen 10). Concomitantly, the deity’s interactions with humanity began to narrow, focusing initially on Shem, one of Noah’s sons, then next on his scion in the tenth generation, Terah, and finally on one of his three sons, Abram/Abraham. With this narrowing, the book focuses on a genealogy that branches out among the descendants of Terah and the literature about them.

Beginning with Abram and Sarai, the family encounters challenges to its survival. At the outset, even before they have become immigrants in a foreign land, the genealogist reports that Sarai is infertile, a status that will jeopardize the family’s ability to become “a great nation” (Gen 12:2). After the genealogy in which that report appears, the first story narrates the family confronting the threat from a famine. When Abram and Sarai travel to Egypt, Sarai’s status as a matriarch in Israel is further threatened by being taken into Pharaoh’s household. Once that challenge has been surmounted and the family has returned to the land of Canaan, having survived the famine, Sarai proposes the strategy of polycoity—with Abram having sexual access to both Sarai and her servant

Hagar—to enhance the chances that an heir may be born. With the birth of Ishmael, the strategy proves successful. However, Sarai then has a child, a situation that results in the removal of Hagar and Ishmael from Abram and Sarai's household. (I am indebted to Steinberg's work in this analysis of the family in Genesis [1993]).

The challenge of infertility has been resolved but has resulted in the creation of a potential successor to Abram other than Isaac. The genealogist resolves this problem by reporting that Ishmael marries an Egyptian wife. According to the genealogies in Genesis, an acceptable spouse must come from the patrilineage of Terah (a practice known as patrilineal endogamy). This will hold true for the legitimate heirs of Abraham. Isaac marries Rebekah, the daughter of Betuel, who was the son of Nahor, one of Terah's sons. The same will be true for the wives of Jacob, who were daughters of Laban, the brother of Betuel. Adherence to this system will stop with Judah and Simeon, who marry Canaanite women, and Joseph, who marries an Egyptian wife. This change is consistent with the transition from Israel as a family to Israel as a people at the end of Genesis.

The ensuing generation with Isaac and Rebekah as parents encounters the same problem of infertility, though it is resolved quickly. But a different challenge for the family ensues: the presence of twins. Although Esau is the firstborn, Jacob becomes the heir. The rationale for this deviation from the norm is provided in both narrative and genealogy. In fact, there are two narratives: one that recounts Esau selling his birthright to Jacob, and another recounting that Jacob and Rebekah maneuvered Isaac into granting his blessing to Jacob rather than the expected Esau. If that were not enough, the genealogist reports that Esau married twice outside the patrilineage of Terah, when he selected Judith, a Hittite woman, to be his wife; and when he married Mahalath, the daughter of Ishmael, who was half Egyptian.

The final family, that of Jacob, involves a formal marriage between one man and two wives who are sisters, sororal polygyny. If one possessed only the bare genealogical data without the narratives in Genesis, one might assume that this was a strategy designed to produce an heir when the first daughter to marry was infertile, a rationale used in other cultures where sororal polygyny is practiced. However, the pre-Priestly author offers a story according to which Jacob's marriage to two sisters is a function of Laban's chicanery and a putative custom of having the older daughter be the first to marry. This family also attests to the practice of polycoity, since Jacob has sexual access to the servants of the two sisters.

It is interesting that the polycoity and sororal polygyny were both successful in addressing the problem of fertility. But they also resulted in antagonism between the mothers, a not surprising real-world consequence. And in the family with only one wife, there was even more serious animosity: that between the twins Esau and Jacob. Though the family of Abraham has managed to maintain itself over time, the interpersonal relationships between the women who have borne children to the same man and between siblings, whether twins or not, are fraught.

The existence of the family also faces another challenge: domestic violence. The issue first arises in the primeval history as Cain kills Abel. It reappears in the family literature: in a story likely written by a post-Priestly author, the narrator reports that a father has been commanded by God to kill his own son (Gen 22). This story demonstrates that, in the Israelite mindset, even a parent could endanger the life a child (one is, of course, reminded of Jephthah and his daughter in Judg 11, as well as Saul's threat to Jonathan in 1 Sam 14:44).

Before the narrative involving Abraham and Isaac, Abraham and his nephew Lot find themselves in serious conflict (Gen 13) due to the growth of their flocks and the inability of the area where they are living to accommodate them. Abraham proposes that they move apart, that they distance themselves, so that there is no strife between the two of them. This stratagem of distancing will recur throughout the book.

The dynamics between Jacob and Esau are clearer. Esau hates Jacob because he garnered both his birthright and blessing. As a result, he intends to kill Jacob after Isaac has died. Jacob escapes this fate by traveling to the household of Laban. The narrators provide two rationales for this trip: (1) to find a wife, and (2) to escape Esau's anger. The second involves a strategy to avoid violence: distancing, which was also in play when Sarai told Abram to remove Hagar and Ishmael from their household. This same strategy of distancing will obtain when Jacob anticipates encountering Esau (Gen 32–33). Jacob is worried that Esau still wants to kill him, so he first adopts a strategy of presenting a gift to Esau, an act that, if the gift is accepted, will create an obligation upon Esau (see Mauss 1954). Though Esau did not want to accept the gift, Jacob was successful in convincing him to do so. Later in the narrative, when Esau proposes that he travel with Jacob, Jacob manages to distance himself from Esau in order to avoid the violence that he fears. Jacob adopts two strategies, gifting and distancing, in order to avert violence from the hand of Esau.

The Jacob-Laban narrative (Gen 29–31) presents another moment of potential violence. Jacob and his wives decided, at the deity's behest, to flee from Laban's household and to return to the land of Canaan. When Laban pursued and caught up with them, he told Jacob, "It is in my power to do you harm." But God has appeared to Laban, telling him "not to say a word to Jacob, either good or bad" (31:29). In so doing, the deity has protected Jacob, even as Jacob is trying to distance himself from Laban. Then, at the end of the Jacob-Laban chapters, they make a covenant, one element of which is identifying a boundary—marked by a stela and a pile of stones—that neither of them will cross. Jacob and Laban enact a formal distancing that will prevent any possibility of violence or mistreatment in the future.

The potential for domestic violence is also clearly in play within the Joseph novella. Joseph's brothers want to kill him because of the dreams that he has reported to them and their parents. This potential for fraternal violence was averted when Reuben "distanced" Joseph from his brothers (37:21–22). Soon thereafter, Judah adopted this same strategy of distancing when he proposed to sell Joseph to some Ishmaelite traders (vv. 26–28). Moreover, this same Judah was ready to have his widowed daughter-in-law burned to death because she became pregnant (38:24). He thought she had become a prostitute when, in fact, he himself has unknowingly impregnated her due to her ruse of securing an heir. Here the potential for domestic violence was avoided when Tamar was able to prove to Judah that her actions are defensible. Then a negotiation backed with evidence—the signet that she has acquired from him—between Tamar and Jacob precludes domestic violence.

In sum, throughout the book of Genesis, families confront numerous recurring challenges to their very existence: famine, the search for a proper spouse, infertility, and conflict, even the threat of domestic violence. And, beginning with Abraham and Sarah, the family of three generations adopted various strategies to address these challenges: marrying within the patrilineage of Terah, using various forms of marriage in order to provide for an heir, and distancing in order to prevent domestic violence. Formal agreements, gifting, and negotiation also played a role in keeping members of the family from being killed.

Literary Perspectives

If source-critical discussions of Genesis dominated in the nineteenth and much of the twentieth centuries, literary study of biblical texts provided a new and major lever for the study of Genesis beginning in the latter part of the twentieth century. In its first manifestation, literary study of Genesis focused on the "forms" of literature present in the book. Not surprisingly, such work was called "form criticism." And it involved the attempt to identify the genres present in the book. Analytical categories such as saga and legend belonged to that enterprise. Coats, for example, proposed the following classifications: saga, tale, novella, legend, history, report, fable, etiology, and myth (1983, 5–10). But that exclusive focus on genre later gave way to a broader study of the book. If Genesis were thought to be literature, one could presumably study it, searching for not only genres, but also plot, characterization, and the like. The work of Robert Alter (1996) is exemplary in this regard. This commentary has benefited from such insights.

The book of Genesis presents readers with remarkable literary diversity. The most basic distinction is that between poetry and prose. At the outset, it is important to note that the boundary between Hebrew prose and poetry is not always clear. For example, though the Masoretic Text does not print Gen 1:27

in stichometric fashion (viz., printed out in parallel lines), the NRSV construes these verses to be poetry, though the NJPS translation, following the MT, does not. There is, however, a general consensus that, apart from 1:27 and a few other places, poetry is relatively rare in Genesis. There is only one long poem (Gen 49). Both it and all other poetic texts share one essential feature: they convey direct discourse. If one includes Gen 1:27 in the list, there are fourteen instances of poetry. Of those fourteen, six convey the speech of the deity (Gen 1:27; 3:14–19; 8:22; 9:6; 16:11–12; 25:23) and eight report speech of humans (2:23; 4:23–24; 9:25–27; 14:19–20; 24:60; 27:27–29, 39–40; 49:2–27). In many cases, the presence of poetry highlights the speeches in question. They often come at pivotal points in the respective texts, often near the end or at a high point in a report or narrative. For example, Adam breaks out in poetry when God shows him the woman who has just been created (2:23). Or the pre-Priestly version of the deluge account concludes with a brief poem in the mouth of the deity, affirming that the natural order will perdure (8:22).

Three primary prose genres populate the book: narratives, reports, and genealogies. The latter two require less discussion than does the first. Genealogies are prominent throughout Gen 1–36. They derive from various authorial hands, including both the pre-Priestly and Priestly tradents. Further, there are two basic forms of genealogies: so-called vertical and horizontal (or branching-out) genealogies (see the foundational study of Wilson 1977). A vertical genealogy moves from a progenitor down to someone many generations later. That latter individual garners status or identity by being able to trace descent from an earlier ancestor. Genesis 5 stands as a classic example of a vertical genealogy. Noah, due to his genealogy that traces his origins back to the primal human (through Seth, not Cain), becomes a likely candidate to be the flood survivor. By contrast, a horizontal or branching-out genealogy typically spans few generations but encompasses many individuals in one (or a few) generation(s). The genealogy that lies behind the poetry in Gen 49 involves only one generation, that of Jacob's sons. But it is clear that the genealogy is concerned with their relative statuses. The same may be said for the so-called Table of Nations (Gen 10). That genealogy includes at most four generations, as with the three sons of Noah, their sons, and their grandsons, and in one case, their great grandsons. This genealogy maps the world, reporting, among other things, who is closer and further from the line out of which Israel emerges.

The report is a second type of prose literature. Those texts that I will construe as reports have often been treated as narratives. However, texts such as Gen 9; 15; 17; and 35 include no arc of tension or problem that needs to be resolved. The basic elements of plot are absent. Such prose texts chronicle activity but do not involve a story per se. The making of a covenant is a classic example of what can transpire in a report (Gen 17). Movement from one place to another, replete with itinerary, is another standard topic for a report (Gen 12:4–9). From a source-critical perspective, it is interesting that the Priestly hand is regularly associated with many of these reports.

Narrative prose is more frequent than are either genealogies or reports. Moreover, that prose has been the subject of much analysis, especially by those who worked from the aforementioned form-critical perspective. Early on, Hermann Gunkel argues that the primary literary component present in Genesis was the short *Sage* (1964). (The German noun *Sage* was then translated in English as "legend," an unfortunate rendition, since *legenda*, prose accounts about holy places or people [e.g., Gen 28:10–22], are quite different from the narratives in Genesis that Gunkel analyzed.) Typically ranging from ten to twenty verses, a *Sage* contained few characters, focused on action (verbs were prominent), often involved the family, and had little use for general description (few adjectives). Gunkel maintained that this kind of literature originated in an oral story-telling environment. Over time, *Sagen* (plural for *Sage*) told about an individual were collected, creating so-called cycles of *Sagen*. Hence, one could refer to the cycle of *Sagen* about Abraham or Jacob. Numerous scholars challenged Gunkel's claim that these *Sagen* were the result of oral composition. As a result, the term *Sage* is no longer used prominently in study of Gen 12–36.

Gunkel used the term *Sage* to describe not only the short narratives about the patriarchs and matriarchs; he used it as well to construe the literature in the primeval history, so-called primal legends (in contradistinction to "patriarchal legends," which populate Gen 12–36). This move was unfortunate since there is minimal generic similarity between the literature in Gen 1–11 and that in Gen 12–36. Gunkel himself recognized that there was myth-like material in the early chapters of Genesis, though he, and others, thought it was not "pure myth" (1997, xiii). Based on current definitions of mythographic literature, there is good reason to construe some episodes in Gen 1–9 as mythic literature.

There is yet another literary category relevant for the study of literature: "family literature" (Petersen 2005a, 11–14). For the purposes of this commentary, I refer to Y. Ru (1992), who has identified the genre of a family novel and discerned four critical characteristics: (1) family novels depict a family chronology in a realistic fashion; (2) family novels devote major attention to familial rites within the broader context of traditional communal life; (3) family novels focus on conflicts within the family; and (4) family novels possess a unique form. That form comprises a "long, forward-moving vertical structure," the family chronology, with a horizontal component, intrafamilial relations at any one time. Genesis 12–36 includes all four of these elements. As a result, I use the term "family literature" to describe these chapters (and reserve the term "novella" for Gen 37–50).

Thus far I have suggested a macrogeneric distinction (poetry vs. prose), assayed three basic forms of prose (report, genealogy, and narrative), reviewed scholarly literature regarding several relatively small-scale forms of narrative

(*Sage*, legend), and suggested that portions of Genesis may be construed as family literature. There is, however, one more distinction of critical importance to the study of Genesis. Though Genesis has often been construed as a book having three basic parts, typically primeval history, patriarchal literature, Joseph novella, I maintain that it is preferable think about *four* basic components: primeval history; Abraham and Sarah saga; Jacob, Rachel, and Leah story; and Joseph novella. The chapters devoted to Abraham and his family, on the one hand, and Jacob and his family, on the other hand, are sufficiently different in their literary structure, the nature of the families, and their respective theologies to be viewed as distinct from each other within the book. And it goes without saying that the primeval history and the Joseph novella are even more different from these just-mentioned bodies of literature.

Formation of Genesis

Analysis of the formation of Genesis has been embedded in the broader discussion regarding the origins of the Pentateuch. To a large extent, that discussion has been heavily influenced by source criticism: the notion that the Pentateuch is made up of four different sources or traditions (or "documents," hence the phrase "documentary hypothesis"). Of the four classic sources (J [Yahwist], E [Elohist], D [Deuteronomist], and P [Priestly]), the typical consensus reported that D was primarily to be found in the book of Deuteronomy. Hence, one would expect to find only J, E, and P in the Tetrateuch and especially in Genesis.

The predominant form of the source-critical hypothesis held that these three sources extended throughout the Tetrateuch. If one looks at a standard chart according to which each verse of the Pentateuch is allocated to a source, J, E, and P were to be found in Genesis, Exodus, and Numbers. (Leviticus was attributed entirely to various Priestly hands.) This, at least, was the view that held sway in standard introductions written in the twentieth century and is widely reported in basic works even today.

There were, however, two other versions of the source-critical hypothesis: the supplementary and the fragmentary theories. On the one hand, proponents of the former view maintained that there was one primary form of Israel's origins and that it was supplemented by one and another addition over time. The most significant supplement stemmed from the hands of the Priestly school. However, there was no independent Priestly version of Israel's story. Rather, one and another priest added material to enhance the earlier version. On the other hand, advocates of the fragmentary hypothesis claimed that the overall story reported in Genesis through Deuteronomy developed out of what were originally separate literary complexes. There were no sources (e.g., that of the Yahwist) that extended throughout Genesis, much less on through the Tetrateuch. Nor was there an early primary narrative that lies behind the Tetrateuch.

Rather, those who argue for the fragmentary hypothesis think that, for example, the story about Joseph emerged as something distinct from either that which preceded it and that which followed it. The same may be said for narratives concerning the primal Israelite families and that which transpired at Sinai. These originally distinct "fragments" were later integrated, possibly by the Priestly editors, yielding the form of the Tetrateuch that one reads today. In sum, there were three distinct models by means of which scholars thought about the formation of the Pentateuch: the documentary, supplementary, and fragmentary hypotheses.

In my judgment, it is possible to combine the latter two views. It appears likely that the pre-Priestly material in the primeval history (Gen 1–11) developed independently from the pre-Priestly literature in Gen 12–36. Similarly, the literature associated with Abraham and Jacob each developed in separate fashion. The same may be said for the Joseph novella. It too was not of a piece with the pre-Priestly material elsewhere in Genesis. These large sections can be viewed as "fragments," which were at some point put together to create the book of Genesis. This view of the formation of Genesis relies upon the work of many scholars, but most notably Rolf Rendtorff, who published a seminal study in 1977 that laid the groundwork for much recent work on the formation of the Pentateuch (see the English translation in 1990). In that work, Rendtorff argued that there were no sources that extended across the boundaries of Pentateuchal books. What was thought to be a "J" source was, instead, a series of originally independent literary complexes, such as the primeval history or narratives about Jacob, which were collected and supplemented by what had been known as "P." This notion of "fragments" makes it difficult to think about a narrative strand (e.g., a Yahwistic source) that extends throughout the book, or even between any two of its four parts. I follow Rendtorff's lead in this commentary. (For a recent and comprehensive discussion of these issues, see Carr 2020).

If Rendtorff and others were correct in thinking that Genesis is made up of a series of originally distinct literary collections, then it is natural to ask: who integrated them? One important response to that question has been the Priestly school, a group of authors, who over time synthesized and added to the earlier materials. In some cases, they probably created an alternative version to a text they inherited. This seems to be the situation with the flood narrative. In other cases, they introduced traditions that already existed but had not been used by the pre-Priestly authors, such as the views of the creation of the universe present in Gen 1. But in either case, what the priests introduced may be understood as a supplement to an earlier tradition or text, often offering an alternative or providing a different angle of vision or evaluation of creation, as in Gen 1 and 2, or a different perspective on the character of Jacob. In the latter case, P presents a more "respectable" Jacob than does the basic story. In many ways, P is a challenge to the prior traditions. The Priestly author seems to be inventing an alternative to what has come before. To this extent, Genesis is a book involving differing versions of various traditions (e.g., the significance of the flood, the nature of the Abrahamic covenant, or the character of Jacob).

If one couples a literary assessment with a discussion of P in the formation of the book, it quickly becomes clear that one major difference between the earlier material and P is the absence of narrative material in P. The Priestly literature is replete with long reports (e.g., Gen 1; 17; 23), short notices (11:32), genealogies (Gen 5), and itineraries (11:31), but P creates few if any stories. Moreover, P adds or corrects details in prior narratives, notably in the flood narrative, but offers no narratives of its own. Rendtorff identifies two basic types of Priestly literature in Genesis: (1) chronological notes about the age of a person at one time or that person's lifespan; and (2) "theological" passages that include the name El and the language of blessing: the promise of progeny and land. For the sake of completeness, one may add the *tôlədôt* formulae to the list of Priestly composition in Genesis.[2]

Another important feature of what has been known as P is its composite character. This situation is well-known in another biblical book, Leviticus. There, in chapters that concern all manner of ritual matters that would have been part of the Priestly purview, one may discern two distinct bodies of literature: (1) the one associated with P, as found prominently in the books of Genesis and Exodus; and (2) the so-called Holiness Code (HC). The former is apparent in Lev 1–16; HC is found primarily in chapters 17–26. (For a classic treatment, see Milgrom 1991, 42–52; 2000, 1325–56.) One may therefore ask if what has been designated as P in Genesis is similar to either of the corpora present in Leviticus. On the one hand, for example, the rite of circumcision, which appears prominently in Gen 17, is mentioned only in the P portion of Leviticus (12:3). On the other hand, the notion of a seventh day as having special significance is present in Lev 19:3, 30; 26:2, which belong to the Holiness Code. The notion of that seventh day being "made holy," reflecting the idea of temporal holiness, is similar to the ideas of spatial holiness as found in HC: the land that Israel occupies is holy (see Milgrom 2000, 1353, 1399, who articulates "the doctrine of the 'holy land'"). In sum, what has been known as P in Genesis may well stem from different Priestly groups and their respective theologies, as those are known in Leviticus and elsewhere in the Hebrew Bible.

Of even greater import is the likelihood that the Priestly author(s) responsible for literature in Genesis is (are) different from the Priestly author(s) who wrote and/or collected prescriptive documents elsewhere in the Tetrateuch. Rendtorff argued that a Priestly redactor was responsible for reworking and integrating earlier texts, namely, those concerning the primeval period, especially creation

2. For an insightful analysis of P as an author, see McEvenue 1971. He notes, e.g., the prominence of repetition and an interest in data, such as reports about lifespan or the date of an event.

and the Noachian covenant and the "patriarchal period," with special attention given to Abraham (Rendtorff 1990, 192–194; 1993). More to the point, this activity did not continue beyond the first six chapters of Exodus. That means while one may focus on the "Priestly texts" as a distinct body of literature in Genesis (and Exod 1–6), one does not include texts such as Exod 25–31; 35–40; Leviticus; and Num 1–10.

The Priestly writer in Genesis regularly offers an alternative and challenge to the earlier literature. (On the Priestly writer in Genesis, see Petersen 2010, 39.) Genesis 1 offers a far more positive view of creation than is present in Gen 2–3, especially as creation in the latter devolves in chapter 3. The Priestly version of the flood enhances the scale and length of the flood and makes it more significant by introducing a covenant at its conclusion. Genesis 10, a Priestly text, thinks differently about human and especially linguistic diversity than does Gen 11. Genesis 17 radically revises the picture of the covenant in the early portions of Gen 15. The Priestly writer offers a more favorable portrait of Jacob than does his predecessor.

In considering programmatic issues, "one may discern three ways in which the Priestly material coheres: two covenants integrate the primeval history with the ancestral literature, the Priestly compositor advocates a number of rituals, and the *tôlədôt* formulae integrate both Priestly and pre-Priestly literature throughout Genesis" (Petersen 2010, 34). Noteworthy are the rituals—the Sabbath, the prohibition of consuming blood, and circumcision—all of which could and would have been practiced in exile. The Priestly writers in Genesis are interested in addressing the situation of the postexilic Yahwist communities: those in Egypt, Mesopotamia, and in Syria-Palestine. They describe norms and rituals that could be practiced in all three places. That Priestly texts could derive from such diverse places should not surprise, since priests resided in all three environments: Jeremiah, who came from a priestly lineage in Anathoth but concluded his life in Egypt; Ezekiel, who lived near Nippur (Mesopotamia); and Zechariah, who was likely an exile who had returned to the land.

I now offer some brief comments about the four primary sections of Genesis, each of which derives from a different hand and reflects a different process of composition.

Primeval History

To understand the origins of Gen 1–11, one must place it within the context of other ancient Near Eastern literatures devoted to the primeval period. The most important text for this purpose is the Atrahasis myth, a text that reports both the creation of humanity and the flood as an attempt to annihilate the human race. This account, composed early in the second millennium BCE, would have been known by an Israelite author during the first millennium. In fact, it is difficult to imagine that an Israelite scribe, intending to compose a primeval account appropriate for his culture, could avoid narrating these two episodes together: the creation of humanity and the flood.

As a result, one may hypothesize that Israelites inherited the pattern of creation of humanity and flood from their cultural heritage. That inheritance was enhanced by the addition of narratives regarding Cain and Abel, Lamech, and the sons of God and human women. These all belong to or reflect the primeval period before the flood, which marks the break between that era and the age in which humans now live. The early account included episodes regarding humanity in the postflood period (e.g., the drunken Noah, tower of Babel), narratives that include reference to the entities that Israel knew, such as Canaan and Babylon. The author/compiler of this majestic work created an Israelite primeval history in which one God, YHWH, was responsible for the creation and preservation of humanity.

To these stories, the Priestly author prefixed a report about the origins of the cosmos, one that included a second account of humanity's creation. Moreover, the Priestly author skillfully integrated an alternative version of the flood account, one that magnified its scale and significance. In addition, Priestly hands included a genealogy that offers a new lineage for humanity, one that can be traced to Seth, and a comprehensive genealogy that depicts the progeny of Noah and his sons. The combined early and Priestly texts that follow the flood narrative recount the process by means of which Israel emerges from those who survived the flood.

Family Literature

The family literature of Genesis (chs. 12–36) does not bear the same strong impress of ancient Near Eastern forebears present in chapters 1–11. Here the Israelite authors exercised much freer hands at the outset. At the risk of oversimplification, chapters 12–36 are made up of two basic literatures, those associated with Abraham and Jacob respectively. The account involving Abraham involves a more complex process of growth than does the literature dealing with Jacob. For the purposes of distinguishing the two corpora, I identify an Abraham and Sarah saga in contradistinction to the Jacob, Rachel, and Leah story.

The Abrahamic collection is made up of some early stories focusing on the family and issues germane to its existence: the viability of the family (Gen 12); familial conflict around issues of land and its effects (Gen 13; 19); whether an heir will be born and the complications of polygyny (Gen 16; 18; 21). Apart from the portions devoted to Lot, the primary focus is on Abram/Abraham's immediate family; his wife, Sarai/Sarah; her servant, Hagar; and their two sons. Those narratives have been supplemented by the Priestly hand at several crucial points (Gen 17; 23). Finally, there have been some further additions, often exploring significant theological issues. Westermann (1985, 121–36) characterized some of these as "theological narratives" (Gen 12:1–3; 15:1–6; 18:17–33; 22:1–19). To these, Golka (1978) added Genesis 23–24. Golka correctly noted that not all of the texts were truly narratives. Of these texts, only chapters 22, 23, and 24 are really stories. In addition, though Golka thought each of the traditional Pentateuchal sources was represented in this list, it now is possible to argue that, perhaps with the exception of Gen 23, all these texts stem from post-Priestly hands, from authors interested in exploring the theological implications of various elements in the Abrahamic saga. That some more recent scholars (e.g., Warner 2018) have identified so-called Deuteronomistic elements in the Abrahamic material is consistent with the general thesis that post-Priestly biblical authors have interpolated material into the Abrahamic saga.

Study of post-Priestly additions to the Abrahamic saga has continued unabated. Rofé has made a convincing case that Gen 20 should be dated to the postexilic period (1990). Köckert has argued that Gen 20–22 is, in its entirety, a post-Priestly supplement at the end of the Abrahamic saga. Other sizable post-Priestly literature includes Gen 18, 20, and 22 (see, e.g., Köckert 2015, 157–76). In these chapters, which derive from different authorial hands, authors offer theological reflection occasioned by the earlier literature. For example, the author of Gen 20 offers a rereading of Gen 12:10–20 that wrestles with the question of the "piety" of a foreign ruler. The issue becomes explicit in Gen 20 with reference to "the fear of God" in a foreign land. Both the Priestly and post-Priestly expansions of the Abrahamic saga demonstrate how rich and seminal this biblical figure had become.

Though the origins of the literature regarding Jacob (Gen 25:19–36:43) are no doubt complex, that story in its biblical form involves a "tight" structure. The literature associated with Jacob and Esau occurs as bookends, with the sojourn of Jacob with Laban (chs. 29–31) in the middle. The nocturnal scenes of Jacob at Bethel and Peniel (28:10–22; 32:22–32) stand both immediately before and then after Jacob's time in Paddan-Aram. There is minimal compositional depth. The plot, which might be characterized as flight and return, involves an initial set of scenes in the patrimonial household, flight that includes an encounter with the deity, sojourn in the ancestral land, return that includes another encounter with the deity, and settling in the ancestral land (for a more elaborate version of this structure, see Fishbane 1975, 15–38). Though the story addresses familial issues, they are unlike those in the Abrahamic saga, where the immediate family, especially husband and wife, was front and center. In the Jacob material, fraternal relations and the extended family play a primary role. There is little evidence that any of these crucial episodes belong to a hand other than the pre-Priestly writer. Moreover, there have been minimal additions by the Priestly hand (the most significant is Gen 35:9–15) and no supplements comparable to the post-Priestly theological literature associated with Abraham.

The Joseph Novella

Genesis 37–50, the Joseph novella, stands in marked contrast to the three foregoing bodies of literature. Excluding the Judah and Tamar story (Gen 38), the novella covers thirteen chapters, which is longer than either the Abraham saga or the Jacob story. There is the complex theme of how a family falls apart and then achieves a modicum of restoration. Characters, not only Joseph but also Judah and even Potiphar, are developed. Complex individual scenes make up a larger whole (e.g., ch. 40). There is a consistent literary style throughout. Complex literary techniques such as flashbacks are in play (e.g., 41:9–13). Recurring motifs appear: dreams (chs. 37, 40, 41), a focus on garments (37, 39, 41), and meals/food (37:25; 43:1–2; 43:31–34), and Joseph's weeping (43:30; 45:2; 50:17). The author is interested in describing human emotions and psychological processes (42:21, 28; 43:30; 45:1, 3, 26).

Von Rad noted that the Joseph novella is in some way related to the wisdom tradition present in the Hebrew Bible. For example, Joseph is in trouble when he violates wisdom norms (Prov 16:18). And he succeeds when he follows wisdom norms (Prov 14:35a). Moreover, the novella seems to affirm the theological stances of orthodox wisdom literature (Proverbs), especially that God is in control of human events (Gen 45:5–8; 50:20). And yet God remains hidden from human actors (Prov 20:24; 16:9).

These similarities between the Joseph novella and Israelite wisdom literature need to be read with nuance. Michael Fox writes, "Joseph's wisdom is evident in his ability to interpret dreams, in his practical shrewdness and planning ability, and in his fear of God" (2012, 261). However, Fox also notes that wisdom in these chapters of Genesis is less the result of human analysis and reflection, as is the case in Proverbs, and more the result of God-given knowledge, something shared by the book of Daniel (M. Fox 2001, 26–41).

Ultimately, the ways in which these four bodies of literature were configured into one book remain lost in the proverbial mists of antiquity. Still, the general contours of the formation are reasonably clear: individual stories, reports, and genealogies were collected into groups associated with the primeval history, Abraham, and Jacob. A Priestly hand modified especially the first two (primeval history and Abraham) by adding new literature and, in so doing, competing perspectives about creation, the flood, and the figure of Abraham. Later hands integrated the foregoing by inserting the *tôlədôt* formulae and theological reflections, most notably in Gen 22–24.

Historical Background

Attempts to date the various literatures present in the book have generated no scholarly consensus. (For a comprehensive overview of this topic, see Hendel

2012, 51–81). Some arguments have focused on dating one or another portion of the book (e.g., attempting to date the "patriarch literature"). Appeals to date features such as specific legal customs (e.g., naming a younger son as heir) or religious practices (such as invoking the name "El") have yielded no identifiable period of composition. Other scholars, following one classic form of the documentary hypothesis, have tried to identify the dates of composition for the Yahwist, the Elohist, and the Priestly strands. In the twentieth century, many of those who held to such hypotheses maintained that the Yahwist should be dated to the tenth century BCE and the Elohist to the ninth century. This strategy, however, has foundered following challenges to the very existence of the Yahwistic and Elohistic traditions (see, e.g., Römer 2006, 9–27).

A more recent debate about the dating of Genesis involves an assessment of the language in which Genesis is written. Scholars who study Biblical Hebrew have long observed that many texts in the Hebrew Bible are composed in a similar fashion, such as the Hebrew present in Genesis being virtually identical to that present in the books of Kings. Texts that are more recent, such as Ezra-Nehemiah, present different grammatical features, whether morphological or lexical. Genesis–Kings uses the vocabulary of classical Hebrew, and Ezra-Nehemiah use late Biblical Hebrew, with some Aramaic passages. Since Genesis belongs to the style of classical Hebrew, which was almost certainly used during the monarchic period, some scholars have claimed that much in Genesis should be dated to the preexilic period. However, others have observed that classical Hebrew, like the much later Ecclesiastical Latin, was used long after it was first introduced. So Genesis, though certainly different from Ecclesiastes and (to a lesser extent) Ezra-Nehemiah, could well have been written in the Persian period. Yet discrete elements in the book were likely written in an earlier period. Genesis 49 contains elements of Hebrew written before the so-called classical style (so Hendel 2012, 52–54).

Still, even though it has proved difficult to identify the time during which Genesis was composed, it is possible to maintain that two portions of the book (i.e., the Priestly material and the Joseph novella) were composed during the Persian period. And since the Priestly material was composed in response to earlier material, one must infer that the pre-Priestly material was formulated at an earlier time. Such a judgment implies that some of the primeval history or the family literature was probably composed before the first deportation from Jerusalem in 597 BCE, most likely after the defeat of the Northern Kingdom in 721 BCE. This was a time of cultural ferment when many from the Northern Kingdom moved to Judah, causing significant growth in Jerusalem. Still, attempting to find historical allusions in Genesis to that (ca.) 125-year period is difficult. (Some scholars seek the references to a "tower of Babel" in that historical context [e.g., George 2005–2006, 75–95].) In sum, I agree with the judgments of Thomas Römer: "The most secure date for the existence of

Pentateuchal texts is the Persian period. . . . As for P, a Persian period dating is still the best option" (Römer 2016, 370).

If the Priestly texts in Genesis are rooted relatively early in the Persian period, then the post-Priestly texts are likely to have been added somewhat later, in the fifth or early fourth centuries BCE. Römer has convincingly argued that the story of Joseph is a post-Priestly addition to the book (2015, 185–201). The Joseph narrative, reflecting the experience of exile, was likely written in the early Persian period. However, Römer observes that the Priestly editor never refers to the Joseph material, strongly suggesting that a later editor introduced the narrative into Genesis after the Priestly additions to Genesis had been made. The purpose of the novella is to introduce "a voice from the Diaspora" into the book, which received its final form in the late Persian period.

Nonetheless, rather than fixating on these theoretical dates for composition, it is more important to observe the ways in which much in the book addresses concerns for Yahwistic worshipers during the exilic and postexilic periods, both to those who returned to the land and especially to those who remained in exile, whether in Egypt, Babylon, or elsewhere.

Religious and Theological World

Religious rites and practices feature throughout the book of Genesis, though those present in the family literature (Gen 12–36) are distinct from those in the primeval history and the Joseph novella. In the primeval history, there are overt references to sacrifice (4:3–4; 8:20) in the pre-Priestly narratives. In both cases, animals are sacrificed, though in the first one, there is an offering of agricultural produce as well. The pre-Priestly author also reports that humans began using the name of YHWH before the flood (4:26). By contrast and with the exception of the prohibition of the consumption of blood (9:4), the Priestly author makes no overt claims about the presence of religious practice before the time that God chooses the family of Abraham. As for the latter portion of Genesis, the Joseph novella includes little mention of religious practices. The Priestly writer recounts Jacob commanding his sons to bury him in the cave of Machpelah (49:29–33). Joseph offers a less detailed comment about his funerary rites (50:24), though he was ultimately interred at Shechem (Josh 24:32).

Things are quite different in Gen 12–36 for a variety of reasons. The ancestral family is now in the land of Canaan and living in or near sites that would have been well-known to authors of these literatures. One may make a number of observations. (1) With the exception of the idiosyncratic Gen 14, there is no group of ritual specialists. And even in that chapter, the priest is not a member of the Israelite patrilineage. (2) Ritual sites are often at or near cities (e.g., Bethel in 12:8; 28:18–19; 35:6; Mamre in 13:18; Beersheba in 21:33; Shechem in 33:18–20). (3) Various ritual installations are constructed, especially altars

(12:7–8). Moreover, trees are planted (21:33) or mentioned (12:6; 13:18; 35:1–4) at the aforementioned sites. Stelae are also erected (35:19–20; 28:18, 22). (4) Life-cycle rites are important: circumcision and especially funerary practices. Burials routinely occur at a place owned by the family: Sarah (23:19); Abraham (25:9–10); Isaac (35:27–29), Rebekah, and Leah (49:31), but Rachel is interred near Ephrath (35:19). (5) Manipulation of dietary products: anointing with olive oil (28:18) and the consumption of foodstuffs: bread (31:54) or bread and wine (14:18). (6) Rites involving blood are important: circumcision (ch. 17) and animal sacrifice (15:7–17; 22:13; 31:54). (7) The use of icons is present: teraphim or "household gods" (31:19) and "foreign gods" (35:1–4). (8) Prayer, direct address to the deity, is rare: that of Abraham's servant (24:12–14) and Jacob (32:9–12) are parade examples. The brief report, "Abram . . . invoked the name of YHWH" (12:8; 13:4), suggests that it may have been a well-known practice. Vows, another form of religious discourse, are also present (e.g., 28:20–22). (9) The practice of a tithe is attested for both Abram (14:20) and Jacob (28:22). (10) The piety is conservative. When Jacob is ordered by God to go to Bethel (35:1–4), he requires the members of his family to divest themselves of their "foreign gods" and earrings. Instead of destroying them, he buries them carefully under an oak. This form of respectfully retiring a ritual object no longer in use is common to many cultures and reflects respect for the holy. (For a study of religious rites practiced by families in the ancient Near East, see van der Toorn 1996).

Clearly, ritual sites were important in the world portrayed in the family literature. There is no dominant or central shrine, though Bethel is the most frequently mentioned toponym. Even though many altars are built, reference to sacrifice on them is rare. Some of the practices occur only in post-Priestly texts, namely sacrifice, though 31:54 is an exception, and prayer. There is no reference to the calendrical rituals of the Priestly tradition, nor to the noncalendrical rituals, such as the sin offering. The authors were walking a fine line; on the one hand, they wanted to convey, a world in which the family members were involved in legitimate religious practices; on the other hand, those authors could not portray them enacting religious life as it had been authorized in Sinai covenant.

The overt theological language in Genesis is diverse. And this is true in at least two ways. As early as the first chapters of Genesis, readers encounter "God" (1:1, *ʾĕlōhîm*), YHWH Elohim (2:4b, *yhwh ʾĕlōhîm*), and YHWH (4:1, *yhwh*). These differences have regularly been explained by appeal to the source-critical hypothesis, according to which the Priestly source uses Elohim because the Priestly writer thought that the divine name YHWH had been revealed at Sinai (Exod 6:2–3), and hence it should not appear in his literature until that point. The name YHWH, by contrast, appears in the earlier texts, which up until recently had been labeled J, the Yahwistic account. The dual name

YHWH Elohim was probably used in Gen 2–3 as a way of providing a transition between chapters 1 and 4, where the individual names are used.

The pre-Priestly and Priestly authors, who use these two names, offer differing pictures of the deity. For over a century, standard handbooks have taken the anthropomorphic YHWH in Gen 2–3, who molds humanity from earth and breathes into *ʾādām*'s nostrils, to be in contrast with the transcendent Elohim, who says, "Let there be . . . ," and something is created. Put simply, these two authors have differing ways of understanding the nature and behavior of the deity. More recently, biblical interpreters have used literary-critical perspectives and focused on God as a character, sometimes allowing the distinctions between the authorial hands to stand, including the conception of God in the Priestly source, and other times trying to formulate a composite that incorporates all the literary diversity (see, e.g., Humphreys 2001).

There is, however, another distinction in the way the Israelite deity is understood in Genesis: "the God of the fathers" and "El" (see Cross 1973 and Smith 2002 for a discussion of these two formulations). First, the God of the fathers. Genesis 31 reports that Laban and Jacob make a covenant. During the ceremony, each of them takes an oath by the God of his father. Laban swears by the God of Nahor (brother to Abraham), and Jacob swears by the God of Abraham. Both Laban and Jacob are part of a religious tradition that involves deities associated with a clan. Each clan or lineage identifies a deity with a revered ancestor. In this case, the ancestors are Nahor and Abraham, and the deities would be known, respectively, as the God of Nahor and the God of Abraham. In this case, each person swears by his own clan deity. To make matters more interesting, the text reports that Jacob swears "by the Fear of his father Isaac" (31:53). The noun *paḥad*, often translated as "fear," may well be the proper name of the ancestral god associated especially with Isaac. Similar names appear with Abraham: *māgēn*, or "shield" (Gen 15:1); and with Jacob: *ʾăbîr*, or "bull" (49:24). Over time, these three appellations fall out of use such that Israelites can speak of "the God of your fathers, the God of Abraham, the God of Isaac, and the God of Jacob" (Exod 3:15). Clearly, the book of Genesis reflects the notion of a God who is related to this specific family and hence can be called the God of their fathers, a form of religion apt for a book that focuses on the family.

Elsewhere in Genesis, there is a different vocabulary and form of religion. At least ten texts use the name El when referring to Israel's God in association with particular places: El Elyon, "God Most High," at Jerusalem (14:18–22); El Roi, "God of seeing," at Beer-lahay-roi (16:13); El Shaddai, "God Almighty," at Mamre (13:18; 17:1; 18:1); El Olam, "Everlasting God," at Beersheba (21:33); El Shaddai, "God Almighty," at Beersheba (26:33; 28:3, 10); El Bethel, "God of Bethel," at Bethel (31:13); El Elohe Israel, "God, the God of Israel," at Shechem (33:20); El Bethel, "God of Bethel" (35:7); El Shaddai, "God Almighty," at Bethel (35:11); El Shaddai, "God Almighty," at Luz (48:3). It is noteworthy that most, if not all, of these texts are attributed to the Priestly source. Fortunately, due to the discovery of the Canaanite Ugaritic texts (14th c. BCE), readers now know to whom the name "El" refers.

El was the Canaanite high god. He functioned as creator and judge and officiated from a divine council. And there were other Canaanite gods, including Baal, who was deemed anathema to "orthodox" Yahwistic religion. But there was no such comparable polemic against El. In fact, Israel's God, YHWH, shared traits of El. YHWH, too, was viewed as the creator of heaven and earth. YHWH was also a cosmic judge. And YHWH, like El, presided over a divine council, most notably in 1 Kgs 22, Isa 6, and Job 1–2. The presence of the name El and the epithets associated with him in Genesis suggest that Israelite authors thought it appropriate to use this diction for their God, YHWH. Of particular interest is the presence of epithets for El and the association of these epithets with a city or shrine (see Cross 1973, 47). This suggests at least two things about the Priestly author's mindset: (1) that the name El was associated with an urban shrine, and (2) that the diverse names were due to the way El/YHWH was known at that place. The presence of different epithets in the practice of Marian devotion (e.g., Mary of Lourdes, Our Lady of Almudena) may serve as an analogy. If that analogy holds, there may have been a distinctive image at each of the shrines at which El/YHWH was venerated.

One may therefore conclude that at least two forms of religious discourse are present in Genesis, one involving the god associated with a lineage, and another with a deity known as El. Clearly, both were deemed acceptable by those who composed the book. In fact, a text such as Gen 49:25 demonstrates that a poet could use both of these vocabularies to depict Israel's God: "by the God of your father, who will help you // by Shaddai, who will help you." (The appellation Shaddai is used of El elsewhere in Genesis, as in 17:1.) The presence of such diverse theological language reflects understandings of Israel's early religious history from the perspective of someone writing many centuries after that putative period.

It also remains possible, though risky, to comment about the conceptual theological world present in Genesis. It is risky because all too often categories taken from the world of systematic theology have been inappropriately imported as tools to study religions from the Neo-Assyrian and Persian periods. To avoid this problem at the outset, the reader may use diction present in the text. The most prominent term to appear is "covenant," a word and notion used by the Priestly writer in Gen 9 and 17. (The notion of covenant is also present in Gen 15, a text attributable to multiple authors. See comments.) So, at the outset, one may identify the Priestly author in Genesis with an overt theological interest, as expressed in his theology of covenant.

The Priestly writer presages his version of the flood by announcing that God will make a covenant with Noah (6:18) and then, in the postflood scene in chapter 9, God does such. The covenant exists as a promise that God makes not only to Noah and his family but with all faunal life, as represented by the animals preserved on the ark. In fact, the parties are restated in 9:13 to be God and "the earth." It is a promise that God will never again deploy a flood in an attempt to destroy life on earth; it is to be an "everlasting covenant" (v. 16). Moreover, the covenant has a sign: the (rain)bow that God places in the heavens. The scope of the Noachian covenant is worldwide. Its guarantee for the continuation of "all flesh" holds for all people. Such a promissory note fits the world in which the Priestly author wrote, one in which Yahwists were now living in Egypt and Mesopotamia as well as in Syria-Palestine. God was protecting all of those places and peoples, a sentiment also to be found in the book of Jonah.

The second Priestly covenant occurs in Gen 17. There, God makes a covenant with Abraham. It too involves promises: Abraham will have numerous heirs, so much so that kings and nations will be his descendants. Moreover, God will grant the land of Canaan to his descendants. This dual promise of progeny and land is intended to perdure: regarding his offspring, it will be an "everlasting covenant" (v. 7), and the land will be a "perpetual holding" (v. 8). This covenant, too, includes a sign: the rite of circumcision. However, unlike the Noachian covenant, Abraham has certain responsibilities. He is to be "blameless" (v. 1, the same word the Priestly writer uses to characterize Noah in 6:9), and he along with all the males of his household must be circumcised.

The covenants depicted by the Priestly writer are formal promises; he also records promises of a less formal sort. Many scholars have identified a "theology of promise" in Genesis, one that focuses on the lineage of Terah (e.g., Westermann 1980). Though there has been debate about which element is primary, land or progeny, both are regularly featured together, and both are passed from Abraham to Isaac and thence to Jacob. Such language of covenant and promise is primarily to be found in texts written or edited by priests.

The discourses of covenant and promise are the primary theological categories in the book of Genesis. Yet it is possible to comb through various texts and try to formulate concepts such as a theology of creation or a theology of sin found throughout the book. But these attempts are frequently problematic since they import vocabulary and conceptual categories foreign to the Hebrew text. (However, see Kaminsky 2012, 639–43, for a helpful discussion of "corruption," a topic that in many other studies would be treated under the topic of "sin.") Alternatively, one might focus on the Priestly source and try to summarize the theological perspectives present there. For example, the Priestly author uses the diction of "be fruitful and multiply" ten times in Genesis. No other author in the Hebrew Bible does so (for a discussion, see King 2009, 85–87). This concern about the population growth of humans, and more especially Israelites, is consistent with a restoration of the Yahwistic community after the destruction of Jerusalem in 587 BCE.

To suggest that texts other than those attributable to priests lack theological interest would, of course, be difficult to sustain. As the earlier discussion of the formation of Genesis has suggested, there are two other primary bodies of literature, the early or pre-Priestly texts, such as Gen 2–3 in the primeval account, and the post-Priestly texts, such as Gen 20 and 24. In both literatures, theological issues are worked out within the context of a story. For example, Gen 2–3 offers not only a report about the creation of faunal and human life but also a narrative about how humans will respond to the presence of a certain tree (or trees) and a prohibition that they not eat from one of them. It seems licit to think that the early author of Gen 2–3 is exploring the way in which humans will respond or be related to their God, an issue of significant theological import. Or, in Gen 20, the second of the so-called wife-sister stories, a post-Priestly author addresses a theological question concerning whether Israelites can trust someone when they live in a foreign land. The issue is couched in explicit theological language: "the fear of God." Through narrative and dialogue, the author offers an affirmative answer to this issue, which was of critical importance when Yahwists were forced to live outside the land after the fall of Judah. As these two examples suggest, each narrative or report can raise a discrete or distinctive theological issue. As a result, in this commentary I have often focused on addressing theological issues on a smaller scale, exploring the theological implications of a particular report or story rather than attempting to identify themes that might occur more broadly throughout the book.

Geography

It may seem strange to include reference to geography in an introduction to the book of Genesis. But place looms large in the world of these fifty chapters. In chapters 1–11, authors address a vast scale, "heavens and earth," a cultural map of the world (Gen 11), and a world divided by rivers (2:10–14). On occasion, their vision narrows to a garden in/of Eden (2:8; 3:23), the mountains of Ararat (8:4); and a plain in the land of Shinar (11:2). In Gen 11:27–50:24, the map becomes smaller. At the outset the book refers to Ur of the Chaldeans (Mesopotamia), but Terah soon leaves there and moves to Haran (in Syria, northeast of Damascus). From then on, there is movement between the land of Canaan and into Syria and back again, to Gerar and back again (twice), and to Egypt and back again, with a final trip to Egypt that leaves them outside the land of Canaan at the end of the book.

People and the literature in which they appear are often associated with specific places. In the family literature, Jacob is associated with the cities of Bethel (28:11–22; 35:9–13) and Shechem (33:18–20), as well as the central portion of Israel. There is also a tradition of Jacob residing with Laban in Paddan-Aram (28:2) and Peniel (32:31), which is east of the Jordan River but much closer to Bethel and Shechem than is Paddan-Aram. This stands in contrast with the localities connected with Abraham. He appears more frequently in southern areas or cities, such as Negeb (12:9; 13:1), Gerar (20:1), Mamre and Hebron (13:18; 18:1), Machpelah (23:17), Beersheba (21:31), and, of course, Egypt (12:10). The German word *Ortsgebundenheit*, literally, "bound to a place," reflects that phenomenon. According to the world described in Genesis, Israel's two primary patriarchs belonged to two different regions, each of which would be associated with one of the ensuing nations: Jacob with Israel in the north, and Abraham with Judah in the south. Many scholars think that the literature concerning these two individuals emerged separately in these two regions and that the respective literatures important for the two nations emerged there.

It is also important to recognize that the theologies expressed in the book were also influenced by geography. As the study of El epithets (see above) has shown, El was known by a distinct liturgical name, depending on the place at which a shrine was located. The name El was coupled with a place name, such as El Bethel (Gen 35:7). Moreover, one might infer that the god of father Abraham might have been of special importance in Hebron, whereas the god of father Jacob would have been at home in Shechem.

Even more important than the relationship of individuals or the deity to a specific geographic region is the motif of geographic movement throughout the entire book. This obtains for all four sections. In the primeval history, humanity is forced to leave the garden. In the next chapter, Cain, after killing his brother, is consigned to being "a wanderer on the earth" (4:12, 14). Thereafter, humanity begins to build cities, but the deluge that ensues requires that Noah and his family escape death by floating on the seas (Gen 6–8). The postflood world is one in which humanity settles, but by the end of Gen 11, humanity is scattered "over all the face of the earth."

The family literature begins with Terah migrating from Mesopotamia to Syria. That movement continues when, following God's command, Abram travels to Canaan. Soon after arriving, he moves to Egypt to survive a famine. Subsequently he settles in the land of Canaan, living near Mamre (13:18). But again, he leaves the land, traveling to Gerar (20:1) to seek food during another famine. After returning to the land, he lives near Beersheba (21:32). Later, when Sarah dies, the family has been living near Hebron (23:2); near there, Abraham is able to purchase land for her burial and for later burials. Throughout his life, Abraham is moving not only within the land but away from and back to it.

Jacob's journeys are different, but they also involve movement within and away from the land. In order to survive his brother Esau's murderous wrath and to find an appropriate wife, Jacob leaves the land and goes to Paddan-Aram in Syria, where other members of Terah's patrilineage lived (28:2). On the journey to Syria, Jacob spends time in Bethel (28:19); on the way home with his family and flocks, he stays east of the Jordan at Penuel. From there he leaves for

Shechem, where he purchases land (33:19). After residing in Shechem, God commands Jacob to move to Bethel (35:1) and settle there. However, the family leaves Bethel and moves to Ephrath (35:16), apparently near Bethlehem. Only later are readers told that Jacob's sons are pasturing his livestock near Shechem (37:12). So again, the family literature depicts another patriarch residing outside the land and moving about within it. There is no permanent geographic place except for one plot of land secured by Abraham as a burial plot and a field that Jacob buys.

Like the foregoing individuals, Joseph undertakes several journeys. The first one is against his will: he is taken away from the land of Canaan and sold as a slave in Egypt. While there, he resides in multiple locations, including Potiphar's house, prison, and his own house (44:14). Once he achieves status in Egypt, he is able to travel freely throughout the land (41:46). His second journey is occasioned by the death of his father. He fulfills his father's charge that he be buried in the ancestral cemetery at Machpelah. Once the interment has taken place, Joseph and his family return to their homes and herds in Egypt. (Unlike the family literature, and with the exception of the phrase "the land of Goshen," the Joseph novella does not list many toponyms to identify places where Joseph either resided or visited.)

At the end of the novella, Joseph has been joined by Jacob and his household, that is, emergent Israel. An Israelite writer identifies sixty-six people, "not including the wives of Jacob's sons" (46:26), who have come to Egypt at Joseph's invitation. The author is clear. The "numerous people" (50:20) are now residents in Egypt. They have voluntarily left the land of Canaan and are now living in the fertile land of Egypt (Exod 16:3; Num 11:5). The crisis of famine reported in Gen 12 along with Abram and Sarai's move to Egypt is recapitulated when Jacob and his family migrate to Egypt during another crisis caused by the lack of food.

In sum, geographic movement is a hallmark of the book. There are movements away from, such as from the garden, from the soil (4:14), from the plain of Shinar, the Ur of the Chaldees, Haran, and finally from the land of Canaan. Humanity, and then nascent Israel, is always departing. But there are also oscillations of being in the land of Canaan, leaving, and returning—to Egypt, Gerar, and Haran. There are also, of course, uncountable movements within the land. These movements of departing, leaving, returning, and finally leaving lie at the heart of the family's experience. Yet the promise of progeny to the family, though threatened, continues to be realized; the promise of land remains only a hope. Such movement makes much sense for a book written during the Persian period, when many Yahwists lived outside the land, and some would remain so forever. Thus it is not surprising that the book holds an interest in religious behavior that could take place both inside and outside the land, practices such as circumcision, prayer, and Sabbath, practices that could stand apart from a central shrine or a temple. Moreover, it goes without saying that these rites could all have been practiced by families in their homes.

Hebrew Text

The Masoretic Text (MT) printed in the *Biblia Hebraica Stuttgartensia* (*BHS*) serves as the basis for this commentary. The MT group of texts is known for "careful copying, fine quality, and antiquity of its text in most of the biblical books" (Tov 2012, 26). Genesis is one of those books. Nevertheless, Genesis, as with all handwritten manuscripts, has been subject to human error. Such errors are not random. As Hendel comments, "All scribes at all times and places make certain predictable types of errors, most of them accidental, including such commonplaces as graphic confusion, dittography, and haplography" (Hendel 1998, 40). An example of graphic confusion, due to two Hebrew consonants that look alike, may be found in Gen 2:12, where a *waw* in the MT should be a *yod* in the word *hahê*ʾ (see Hendel 1998, 40–41 for a list of such errors in Gen 1–11). Most such instances do not provide problems for the commentator. This commentary discusses these issues, when appropriate, in the notes that follow each translation.

The text of Genesis does not present text-critical problems of the sort present in more complicated biblical books. Jeremiah offers numerous instances in which the LXX reads a shorter text than the MT, attesting to the likelihood that the LXX preserves an earlier form of the book than does the MT. Classic examples include Jer 33:14–26 and 51:44b–49a, neither of which is featured in the LXX. The commentator must routinely wrestle with these differences. In contrast, the books of Samuel in the MT contain many instances in which the MT is shorter than the LXX (e.g., 1 Sam 31:1). The DSS provide evidence that these shorter readings often derive from accidental abbreviations in the MT text, such as 1 Sam 10:27b: though present in 4QSam[a], it is missing in MT. Unlike the books of Jeremiah and Samuel, ancient texts and versions of Genesis do not offer this sort of consistently different readings from the MT.

Also unlike those two biblical books, for which there is evidence from the LXX and the DSS, another ancient text is important for the text critic: the Samaritan Pentateuch (SP). As a result, those trying to understand the ancient textual traditions must assess two complete manuscript traditions, LXX and SP, along with the fragmentary texts from Qumran (DSS). In order to do so, the interpreter must have a general understanding of how these three bodies of evidence are associated and the way they relate to the MT.

The oldest biblical manuscripts that attest to Genesis are the nineteen fragments discovered at Qumran (Crawford 2012, 353–73). They attest to a form of the biblical text that may be described as "Proto-Masoretic," that is, they offer no substantial and consistent differences from the Masoretic Text. The

Samaritan Pentateuch, which like the DSS was written in Hebrew and is thus a text and not a translated version, offers occasional readings that preserve a more original form of the Hebrew text than does the MT. In such instances, the MT's readings typically derive from scribal errors. For example, in Gen 22:13, where the MT has "a ram behind," SP reads "one ram." The copyist whose work is preserved in the MT misread a *dalet* (d, ד) for a *resh* (r, ר) (so Speiser 1964, lxxii). The SP can, therefore, be a useful resource for identifying a few readings that are not present in the MT.

The SP is also known for a variety of features, most notably the focus on Mount Gerizim as the site of legitimate Yahwistic worship. This concern is evident in Deuteronomy, though not in Genesis. Less significant elements do appear in Genesis, which Tov has characterized as "Small Harmonizing Alterations" (Tov 2012, 82–83). For example, in Gen 7:2, where the MT reads, literally, "a male and his mate," SP reads "male and female," a change that attempts to make this verse conform to the diction present in 1:27; 5:2; 6:19; 7:3, 9, 16. Such changes were, Tov maintains, designed "to remove internal contradictions or regularities from the Torah text that were considered harmful to its sanctity" (Tov 2012, 82).

The most important version for the textual critic is the LXX. Though some interpreters have suggested that the LXX represents more of an interpretation than a translation, recent scholars have consistently maintained that the book of Genesis in LXX is a "lexically and syntactically strict, quantitative representation of its source text" (R. Hiebert 2007, 1); or, as Hendel puts it, LXX is a "literalistic translation of a Hebrew *Vorlage*" (1998, 17.). Nonetheless, in some places LXX (and SP) differ from the MT. For example, in Gen 2:2 the LXX and SP read "the sixth day," which is almost certainly a change introduced in both an ancient text (SP) and version (LXX) to avoid giving the impression that the deity was working on the seventh day. Genesis 1:9 presents a different situation among the ancient manuscript evidence, one in which a reading *longer* than the MT is present in both the LXX and the DSS: "And the waters that were under the sky gathered together into their place, and the dry land appeared" follows immediately after "Let the water under the sky be gathered to one place. And so it happened." The LXX and DSS provide a report about the fulfilling of the command, a case of harmonization based on the presence of such reports on other days during which something was created, as in 1:12 (for a different assessment, see Brown 1993). Tov has concluded that the LXX's Genesis and Deuteronomy offer evidence of harmonization more so than any other feature (2012, 136).

For the commentator, the most significant text-critical issue in the book of Genesis arises in Gen 4:8, where both the LXX and the SP have Cain saying, "Let us go out into the field," a sentence absent in the MT. (Unfortunately, the DSS do not preserve this verse.) The reading in LXX and SP would lead one to think that Cain is guilty of premeditated murder; MT's reading would likely lead to a judgment of manslaughter. Most scholars think that the speech was present in the original narrative and that it was deleted due to accidental omission of a word or phrase. (Hendel deems it a case of parablepsis [1998, 128].) This text is the exception, however. There are no divergences between the MT and other witnesses (i.e., DSS, SP, LXX) of comparable importance for the interpreter of Genesis.

The genealogies in Gen 5 and 11 present a special case, since the chronologies attributed to both pre- and postdiluvian ancestors vary significantly between the ancient witnesses. The current state of research suggests that ancient scribes were concerned to address inappropriate implications and inconsistencies presented by chronologies in the MT. For example, in Gen 5, Methuselah lived 969 years according to the MT and LXX; but he lived only 720 years according to SP. The date in SP means that Methuselah died *when* the flood began; the longer lifespan means that Methuselah would have been alive during the flood, an implication that the SP tradition wanted to avoid. A similar situation occurs with Gen 11:32 MT, which lists Terah's lifespan as 205 years. Because Abram departs from Haran when he is 74, according to the Priestly author, Terah would be 145 at the time, leaving him alive well after Abram moves further into Syria-Palestine. From a narrative perspective, Terah should have passed from the scene by that time; SP solved that problem by reducing his lifespan to 145 years, having him die when Abram leaves his father's household. (For a thorough discussion of the evidence in the MT, LXX, and SP for chapters 5 and 11, see Hendel 1998, 61–80.) In sum, though there are occasional scribal errors in the MT of Genesis, instances in which textual criticism must weigh the evidence from both ancient texts and versions, the MT provides an excellent basis for the translation and comments provided here.

COMMENTARY

Genesis 1:1–31
"When God Began to Create the Heavens and the Earth . . ."

Brevity, repetition, and majesty are hallmarks of these verses, known as the Priestly account of creation. Few reports about the creation of the cosmos and of humanity have been achieved within the space of a mere thirty-four verses. The report is astonishing when one compares it to the much lengthier accounts from the ancient Near East. It is even remarkable when compared to Gen 2:4b–25, which requires twenty verses to narrate just the creation of fauna and humanity. Numerous elements are repeated throughout the account in Gen 1 (e.g., "and so it happened"), a stylistic feature that both emphasizes their place in the account and calls attention to other features that are different, such as the absence of declaring something "good" on the second and seventh days. The word "God" appears thirty-five times (a statistic that includes Gen 2:1–3, the remainder of the Priestly account of creation). There is a dominant character in Gen 1: the deity. That character persistently serves as the subject of active verbs: calling into existence, dividing, making, naming, seeing, blessing, and sanctifying. Clearly, the author has focused on the preeminent role of the deity. Nonetheless, once the created order is in place, entities that have been created will need to act. For example, both the luminaries and humanity need to govern (vv. 16, 26, 28).

This report highlights two primary structures of the cosmos: geography and time. Interpreters have typically paid more attention to the former rather than the latter. As for the geography, the author depicts the movement from the preexistent earth and watery deep to the structure in which the waters have been separated and put in their respective places, light and the heavenly objects have been called into being, the seas and earth have generated life, the earth has become habitable for land creatures, and humans have been created. As for time, the temporal building blocks of dusk and dawn, due to the presence or absence of light, delineate the notion of a day. These categories of dusk, dawn, and day, which make up a twenty-four-hour period, are used in a formula that is repeated throughout the first six days of creative activity. Their absence on the seventh day signifies that a new category is now emerging: the week; and within that week the seventh day achieves special promise when, in Gen 2:3, God makes it holy. This sanctification of the seventh day is an act that sets the stage for Israelite ritual practices on the Sabbath, religious observances involving, among other things, the cessation of work. Such practices on the Sabbath were especially important after the temple was destroyed in 587 BCE and remained significant for those Jews living in Egypt and Mesopotamia even after the Second Temple was constructed.

This account of creation includes ideas distinct from those in the earlier creation narrative, in Gen 2–3. It clearly has a broader purview: the entire cosmos rather than "the earth" of the following chapters. But the Priestly writer seems interested in doing something more than simply enlarging the canvas in which creation is depicted. This author wants to moderate or challenge some of the earlier traditions, an element that reappears throughout the book of Genesis. To this extent, Genesis includes a theological dialogue between various Israelite authors. For example, the prior author refers to humans who, soon after they were created, made decisions that would lead to their expulsion from the garden (Gen 3). In contrast, the Priestly author offers a "higher" view of humanity in Gen 1; humans are created as similar to God and charged with governing the universe that the deity has created: they have a greater responsibility than caring for a garden. Although the prior author has described the world of human habitation as "pleasant" (2:9), the Priestly author offers a stronger claim: "everything" is "very good" (1:31). Other similar distinctions abound.

1:1 When God began to create the heavens and the earth[a]—**2** the earth was
empty wilderness, the watery deep was dark, and a wind from God swept
over the water—**3** God said, "Let there be light!" And there was light.
4 God saw that the light was good. Then God separated light from darkness. **5** God named the light "Day," and the darkness he named "Night."
There was dusk and there was dawn, the first day.

6 God said, "Let there be a vault within the water; let it separate some
water from other water." **7** God made the vault and separated the water
that was under the vault from the water that was over the vault. And so it
happened. **8** God named the vault "Sky." There was dusk and there was
dawn, the second day.

9 God said, "Let the water under the sky be gathered to one place;
then let dry ground appear." And so it happened.[b] **10** God named the dry
ground "Earth" and the gathered water "Seas." God saw that it was good.
11 God said, "Let the earth yield vegetation, seed-bearing plants and fruit
trees with their own distinctive seeds." And so it happened. **12** The earth
produced vegetation, seed-bearing plants and fruit trees with their own

distinctive seeds. God saw that it was good. **13** There was dusk and there
was dawn, the third day.

14 God said, "Let there be luminaries in the vault of the sky to distinguish the day from the night. Let them be markers for significant events,[c]
for festivals, and for days and years. **15** Let them be luminaries in the vault
of the sky to provide light on the earth." And so it happened. **16** God made
the two great luminaries, the brighter light to rule the day and the dim-
mer light, as well as the stars, to rule the night. **17** God placed them in the
vault of the sky to provide light on the earth, **18** to rule over the day and
the night, and to distinguish light from darkness. And God saw that it was
good. **19** There was dusk and there was dawn, the fourth day.

20 God said, "Let the waters teem with living creatures and let the birds
fly over the earth up in the vault of the sky." **21** God created the giant sea
monsters and all the living creatures, the ones that wriggle as they swarm
in the water, of every kind, and all the winged birds, of every kind. **22** God
blessed them and said, "Be fruitful and become numerous. Fill the waters
of the seas. Let the birds be numerous on the earth." **23** There was dusk
and there was dawn, the fifth day.

24 God said, "Let the earth produce living creatures of every kind:
domestic animals, things that crawl, wild animals of every kind." And
so it happened. **25** God made the wild animals of every kind, domestic
animals of every kind, everything that crawls on the ground of every kind.
And God saw that it was good.

26 God said, "Let us make humans in our image, similar to us. Let them
govern the fish of the sea, the birds of the sky, the domestic animals, over
all the earth, and everything that crawls on the ground."

27 So God created the earth creature[d] in his image.
In the image of God he created him,
male and female he created them.

28 God blessed them and said to them, "Be fruitful, become numerous,
fill the earth, and take charge over it. Govern the fish of the sea, the birds in
the heavens, and all living things that crawl on the ground." **29** God said, "I
give to you all the seed-bearing plants that are on the earth and all the trees
that bear fruit and that have seeds: they will be your food. **30** Moreover,
to all the wild animals, to all birds in the heavens, and to everything that
crawls, to everything that breathes, all green plants will be their food."
And so it happened. **31** God looked over everything that he had made; it
was very good. There was dusk and there was dawn, the sixth day.

a. The absence of a definite article precludes the traditional translation, "In the beginning." Furthermore, comparable texts narrating creation, both biblical (Gen 2:4b–7) and extrabiblical (i.e., Enuma Elish, Atrahasis), begin with temporal clauses.

b. The LXX continues, “And the water that was under the sky was gathered together, and dry ground appeared.”

c. Cf. 2 Kgs 20:8–11; Isa 8:18; 20:3; 37:30; 38:7–8, 22; 66:19.

d. In v. 26, the noun *ʾādām* is indefinite. Here it is preceded by the definite article.

[1:1–13] The Priestly author has offered a report that commences with deep ambiguity, even though the grammar is clear (v. 1 is a temporal clause, v. 2 is a circumstantial clause, and v. 3 is the main finite clause). Although the report focuses on what is being brought into being (the temporal clause), it also reports things that exist *before* God's creative activity (the circumstantial clause). Therein lies a virtual paradox: God will create “the earth,” but “the earth” is present before God sets to work. Moreover, both “the empty wilderness” and a “wind from God” exist before God speaks. It is as if some form of matter—an empty, wild earth and dark, watery depths—were needed as the matter out of which the earth and the heavens will be made. Darkness was necessary as a counterpart for the light that soon appears. And wind-whipped waves serve as a point of contrast to the firmly fixed and tiered universe that is about to be created.

Verses 3–5 announce the creation of light and what comprises a twenty-four-hour period. God calls light into existence; cf. Ps 33:6 for the motif of creation by speaking. However, even before there is reference to the elements that comprise the day, the deity values light as “good.” What remains unclear is whether darkness is not “good,” or whether light is good only because it allows for the sequence of darkness and light, constituting a day. In any case, the deity not only speaks but also “separates,” hence the action narrated in 1:6–7. The word “day” is used in two ways in 1:5. In its first occurrence, day means “daytime,” the illumined portion of a day; in its second occurrence, day means a twenty-four-hour period of time, including daytime and nighttime. Not only that, the Priestly author includes reference to the transitional times: dusk and dawn, calling attention to the way darkness emerges and then light ensues. It goes without saying that the final phrase also serves the interest of the Priestly author, for whom the daily round of sacrifices is a constitutive part of ceremonial practice (Num 28:1–8).

Concern for the basic structure of the universe undergirds 1:6–8. If 1:3–5 depend upon the presence of darkness in the pre-creation state, verses 6–8 presuppose the presence of water in that same *time before time*. It is into those waters that the deity calls for and then makes (this is the first time in Gen 1 that the deity “makes” something) a heavenly vault, a round dome that is probably thought to be made of hammered metal. (The vault is also referred to several times in Ezekiel 1, where it is described as “shining like crystal” [v. 22], a depiction consistent with an object made of polished metal.) Here again, there is a constitutive act of separation, allowing for waters both above and below the vault. Once it is in place, the God names the vault "Sky." (This "name" can also be translated "Heavens"; the noun is plural in form but functions as a singular noun.)

The third day (vv. 9–13) is more complex than the preceding ones. There are two distinct acts: the congealing of the waters and the emergence of vegetation. It is as if the writer needs to compress earlier traditions about the creation of more than six acts into a scheme of only six days. The deity spoke, whereby the waters were amassed into a single place and dry ground appeared—two passive verbs that deemphasize the role of the deity. That role is, however, emphasized in yet a third moment, that of naming: "Earth" and "Seas." The former word has already appeared in the description of the pre-creation state. Although 1:2 refers to water twice, this is the first time that the word "Seas" is used (v. 10).

The focus in these verses is not, however, on seas but on earth. (The report will return to "seas" in v. 22.) As a compliant partner of the deity, the earth is an entity that generates vegetation. Moreover, though two different types of flora are described, plants and trees, the author states that they have a common element: the production of seeds. This emphasis on seeds is likely a subtle polemic against ancient Near Eastern religions that included rites designed to enhance agricultural fertility. The Priestly writer claims that Israel's deity created a world in which the earth would naturally yield agricultural bounty over time as plants and trees themselves provided for the next generation of such flora. In contrast to the pre-Priestly account, the Priestly author describes the trees as benign. Trees bear fruit that is available for human consumption with no prohibitions. For the Priestly author, it goes without saying that such flora are available for consumption by both animals and humans, a situation that will change with the postflood world (Gen 9:3). The two different components of the third day result in a twofold construal: both Seas and Earth are deemed "good" (vv. 10 and 12). The Seas receive the same commendation as does the Earth, even though the latter has pride of place on day three.

The first three days of creation are distinct from the next three in that the first ones involve acts of naming: Day, Night, Sky, and Earth. The first two names involve the structure of time, whereas the second two reflect the physical structure of the cosmos. Unlike the pre-Priestly account of creation in Gen 2, only the deity names things in Gen 1 (cf. 2:19).

[14–31] During these three days, God populates the structures that have just been created.

In 1:14–19, the fourth day, the deity returns to the act of separation, as was the case on the first and third days. The return to the first day focuses on the significance of illumination. Although God has already separated light from darkness and named them Day and Night (vv. 4–5), God now repeats that act of separation, underscoring it by the presence of distinct luminaries, one for the day and one for the night. They are not only to distinguish day from night but also to rule over the day and night, a motif of governance that will reappear in 1:26, 28. Since both the sun and moon were understood to be deities in ancient Near Eastern religion, this claim of the Priestly writer is striking in its proximity to such beliefs. However, the claim in 1:17 also involves a limitation on the power of both the sun and moon: each has dominion only during one portion of a twenty-four-hour period.

The sun and moon will also be a means for communicating between the deity and humans. The word translated here as "significant events" appears in texts such as 2 Kgs 20:8–11, which includes an omen that is created by the sun apparently moving backward (cf. Josh 10:12–13, where both the sun and the moon are part of the omen). In ancient Mesopotamia, eclipses were recorded as omens (cf. Isa 13:10). The word "festivals" refers to religious rites (Lev 23:2, 4, 37, 44), rituals specified for times often defined by day, week, and month. These are "festivals of the LORD" (Lev 23:2). The stars are something of an afterthought, though it is clear that biblical authors knew the identity of various astral constellations (e.g., Amos 5:8; Job 38:31). As was the case with days one and three, the report about the fourth day includes the commendation and enumeration formulas.

Verses 20–23 describe the fifth day and the creation of fauna. They belong to the two realms signified on day two, the waters and the space created by the vault. Contrary to some translations (e.g., NRSV), the sense in 1:20 is different from that in 1:11 and 24. In those two verses, the image is of a generative earth. In 1:20, however, the verb refers to the physical behavior of aquatic creatures, teeming or wriggling, not to the waters producing the aquatic creatures. The waters and the air over the earth are the places in which these forms of animal life move and have their being. However, neither the waters nor the air "bring forth" the animals. For whatever reason, perhaps because aquatic creatures and birds live at a remove from humanity, the Priestly writer intends that the faunal life created on day five be distinct from life created on day six.

The deity responds to the presence of fauna by offering a verbal blessing (v. 22). The blessing is odd, however, since it is made up of a series of imperative verbs: be fruitful, become numerous, fill, and be numerous. Genesis 1:28 and 9:1 offer a similar combination of blessing and imperative verbs. It is as if the deity has created the capacity for animals and humans to propagate, which constitutes the blessing, yet both animals and humans need to be admonished to take advantage of that capacity.

Day six involves the creation of earthbound animal life and humans. They are, however, created in vastly different ways. With 1:24–25 and the creation of animal life, the Priestly author returns to the role of the earth as generative, as was the case on day three. The fauna created on this day fall into three categories: wild animals, small life such as beetles, and domestic animals. There is no hierarchy. Since at this point in the Priestly conception of the universe, animals have not yet been granted to humans as food, domestic animals were not rated more highly than insects. Moreover, what is created on both days three and five, earthbound flora and fauna, are both deemed good, but neither are blessed. What the earth produces is good but not blessed. (The Priestly writer offers a more inclusive view of nonhuman faunal life than does the author of Gen 2, who mentions neither ocean-dwelling fauna nor insects, but only animals and birds apparently considered appropriate as companion to the earth creature.)

Things change when the Priestly writer moves to the creation of humanity. Perhaps the most striking difference from the foregoing language is the presence of first-person-plural language: "Let us." This reference to the divinity as plural reappears in the primeval history, though in pre-Priestly literature (3:22; 11:7). This language almost certainly reflects the notion of a divine council (e.g., 1 Kgs 22:19–23; Isa 6; Job 1) in which the supreme deity is surrounded by minor deities, otherwise known as "the sons of God" (e.g., Job 1:6). One might ask why, only at this point in Gen 1, does this entity appear. The answer is probably to be found in the "social" character of humanity, as symbolized by the male/female distinction, which does not allow for the notion of an originally sexually undifferentiated creature that is present in Gen 2. Hence, if humanity is to be created in some way similar to the deity, then the deity must perforce have a social quality. The Priestly writer followed the lead of the pre-Priestly literature and included reference to the divine council to suit his purposes. However, that Priestly writer uses it only once. In 1:27–31, the deity acts solely as a singular agent.

Although the Priestly writer uses the divine council as an image for divine plurality, that writer also uses the diction of an "image," a physical representation, to convey the character of the similarity between God and humanity. Just as a sculptor can model clay to make it appear like a specific human being, so in some way humanity will be similar to the deity, though again this is an analogy. The Priestly writer reuses this same language in Gen 5:3 to describe the way in which a son can be like his father, though here a real physical reality is in play. The more metaphorical usage in the ancient Near East, according to which a king is an image of God, is similar to that in Gen 1. The word translated here "similar to" pushes in this same direction, a more general notion of similarity that could be physical (e.g., Isa 40:18), but could refer to a nonphysical correspondence. The notion of humanity as being in the image of God, as would be a king, and the command to govern give this text a distinctly political cast. Humanity is to serve as a divinely appointed governor or regal figure. As noted earlier, the notion of governance appears twice in Gen 1; astral objects, the sun and moon, and humanity are both given authority over others: the former over day and night, the latter over floral and faunal life.

Much has been made of the literary style of 1:27. It appears to be poetry, as in this translation and many contemporary versions. The Masoretic Text does not construe the verse as poetry nor does the NJPS translation. However, there is a reason to think that 1:27 works as poetry, and that has to do with the issue of "number." The first two lines of the "poetry" refer to an individual, *hāʾādām*, the earth creature. (The Priestly writer uses the same word in Gen 2:7.) In the second line, the author uses a singular pronoun, "him." The final line, however, uses a plural pronoun. This refinement is typical of Hebrew poetry in which the second or third line in a parallel structure offers a more specific or developed version of what was said in the initial line. Though it may sound prosaic, 1:27 may be restated, "So God created the earth creature, . . . but God really created the earth creature as something more than an individual; they are male and female." Here the Priestly author is offering a different notion of human plurality than the one in Gen 2. Here Gen 1 claims that human plurality is the initial state, what God intended; it is not the result of an attempt to find a companion for the earth creature, a companion not part of the initial created order. According to the Priestly writer, after divine reflection, the communal deity created communal humanity.

The word "create" (*brʾ*, 1:27) often refers to something that only God can do (cf. Josh 17:15). Though elsewhere in the OT, God is described as creating the stars (Isa 40:26) or the wind (Amos 4:13), the Priestly writer here reserves God's act of creation (*bārāʾ*) for humanity, though to be sure the word appears in the very first verse of Gen 1, where God's creative activity involves everything that is created. However, although throughout the chapter God "makes" things, the deity "creates" only here during the seven-day sequence of creation.

In a chapter that can be remarkably laconic, there is striking repetition. God speaks within the divine council (v. 26), and then, much of what is said in that speech is stated directly to humanity in 1:28. There are, however, differences between these two speeches. The notion of governing is supplemented by the diction of "taking charge" (v. 28), a verb that elsewhere in the OT refers to rape (Esth 7:8) or enslavement (Neh 5:5). This diction no doubt reflects the writer's experience of the ways monarchs ruled in the ancient Near East. Apart from the relationship of these two speeches, the blessing involving fertility that appeared in verse 22 is reiterated in verse 28.

God's second speech specifies what every form of animal and human life should eat. The purview of this speech is captured by the sevenfold repetition of the Hebrew word *kol*, "all" or "every." All plants and trees are available for all animals and all humans to eat. By implication, with such a widely available vegetarian diet, no animal or human needs to be a carnivore. Furthermore, and again by implication, humans can eat from any tree, because all trees that produce fruit or nuts are available for food. This claim stands in strong contrast with the view expressed in Gen 2–3, naming two trees with fruit that was not to be eaten (2:17; 3:22). Here again, the Priestly author is providing another view of what creation involves and what its implications are for human behavior.

Verses 29–30 of Gen 1 offer an interesting revision of the role of plants yielding seeds. Earlier (vv. 11–12) seed appeared to function for propagation; now the Priestly writer makes clear that these seeds, along with the plants themselves, are specifically intended as food for animals and humans, created on the sixth day. Verse 30 also incorporates diction used by the author of Gen 2. According to this pre-Priestly account, the deity breathes the "breath of life" into the clay statue that he has molded. The Priestly writer reuses this phrase, "breath of life," but broadens its application. In the Priestly view, humans share the breath of life with animals. As a result, both humans and animals are given the same source of food.

The commendation formula at the end of Gen 1 moves beyond the one in verses 4, 10, 12, 18, 21, and 25. This formula in 1:31 refers to everything (*kol*) that God has made, not just what has been created since the preceding commendation formula in 1:25. The Priestly writer's hallmark is his judgment that the creation is "good," and at the end of the sixth day, it has become "very good." One senses that the Priestly writer is offering a claim that might cut against those Israelites who, having read Gen 2–3, might think that the created order is flawed since it so quickly leads to various forms of disarray due to what is created on the sixth day. Here the Priestly author is offering a summary judgment about all that has been created on days one through six.

The Priestly writer's presentation of creation appears to be linear, moving from the first to the sixth day. But there is another literary technique present in the chapter, that of pairing: between days one and four, days two and five, and days three and six. The first pairing focuses on light. Light or illumination takes place on the first day. Then the heavenly luminaries are created on day four. The second pair involves water. On the second day, the waters are divided and ordered into two places. Then the fifth day sees the creation of life in the waters, along with birds. The final pair highlights land, with the emergence of dry land on day three and the creation of life that dwells on the earth, both faunal and human, on the sixth day. It is as if the writer wants to avoid saying everything about one of the three topics at one time and instead prefers to circle back and readdress the topics of light, water, and dry land. This symmetry is complete at the end of the sixth day, and as such it highlights what will stand outside that symmetry of three pairs, namely, the seventh day, which appears in chapter 2.

Genesis 2:1–25
YHWH God Molds the Earth Creature

Genesis 2 comprises the conclusion to the Priestly account of creation, the first of the so-called *tôlədôt* formulae ("these are the descendants . . ."), and the beginning of the early narrative recounting the creation of humanity. As such, the chapter is utterly diverse. Even the early narrative itself (vv. 4b–25) is complex, involving a story whereby man and woman are created plus a report about a river that flows from Eden and then diverges into four major tributaries. At the outset of the chapter, the Priestly writer offers the final element in his account of creation, which stands outside the symmetrical pairs of light (days one and three), waters and sky (days two and four), and earth (days three and six) in Gen 1 and, as such, has special significance. It is the only feature in creation that is deemed holy (2:3). By including this final element to conclude the first creation account, the priest has done nothing less than create a temple of time and in time, the Sabbath, likely at a time after the First Temple has been destroyed.

The Priestly account of creation focuses on organization and structure; the primary account in Gen 2 highlights relationships, of which there are four primary ones: God and humanity, humanity and ground, male and female, and humanity with animals.

2:1 Then the heavens and the earth and all their cohorts were finished.
2 God finished the work he had been doing on the seventh day.[a] He
stopped on the seventh day from all the work he had been doing. **3** God
blessed the seventh day and made it holy because on it God stopped from
all the work of creation.[b]

4 These are the descendants of the heavens and the earth after they
had been created.

On the day that YHWH God made earth and heavens, **5** before there was
shrubbery in the field on the earth and before any of the grasses of the field
grew, since YHWH God had not yet made rain fall upon the earth and there
was no human to cultivate the ground, **6** when instead a spring bubbled up
from the earth and irrigated the entire surface of the ground, **7** then YHWH
God molded the earth creature from bits of earth. He breathed into his
nostrils the breath of life so that the earth creature came to life. **8** YHWH

God planted a garden in Eden, to the East. There he put the earth creature that he had molded. 9 YHWH God made all the trees that are beautiful to see and good for food grow up from the ground. The tree of life was in the center of the garden, as was the tree of the knowledge of good and evil.

10 A river flows out from Eden to irrigate the garden. From there it splits and becomes four branches. 11 The name of the first is Pishon; it flows throughout the land of Havilah, where there is gold. 12 The gold from that land is pure; fragrant resin and gemstones are also found there. 13 The name of the second is Gihon; it flows throughout the land of Cush. 14 The name of the third river is Tigris; it flows east of Assyria. The fourth river is the Euphrates.

15 YHWH God took the earth creature and settled him in the pleasurable garden[c] to cultivate it and to care for it. 16 YHWH God admonished the earth creature, "You may eat from any tree in the garden, 17 but from the tree of the knowledge of good and evil you may not eat. On the day that you eat from it, you will certainly die."

18 Then YHWH God said, "It's not good for the earth creature to be alone. I will make a companion appropriate for him." 19 So YHWH God molded from the earth all the wild animals and all the birds of the sky and brought them to the earth creature to see how he would name each one. And whatever the earth creature called every living creature, that was its name. 20 The earth creature gave names to all the domestic animals, to the birds of the sky, to all wild animals. However, he did not find[d] a companion for the earth creature.[e] 21 So YHWH God made the earth creature fall into a deep sleep; he was sound asleep. Then he took one of his ribs and closed up the flesh where it had been. 22 YHWH God fashioned the rib that he had removed from the earth creature into a female and brought her to the earth creature. 23 Then the earth creature said,

"This time: bone from my bone,
  flesh from my flesh.
This one shall be called 'Female,'
  since this one was taken from a 'Male.'"

24 As a result, a man leaves his father and mother and embraces his wife, such that they become one flesh. 25 The two of them were naked but the earth creature and his wife were not ashamed.

a. SP, LXX, and Syr read "sixth day," almost certainly a revision of the original "seventh day," since that text appears to violate the notion of the seventh day as a day of rest.

b. The Hebrew is difficult: lit., "because on it he stopped from all his work, which God created to do."

c. Traditionally, "garden of Eden," though the sense of Eden as a toponym is absent here. The word "Eden" can also mean "pleasure" or "bliss."

d. Or "a companion for the earth creature was nowhere to be found." The Hebrew verb "find" is not passive.

e. MT does not include the definite article, so the Hebrew word could be translated "Adam."

[2:1–3] The repetitive style so familiar in chapter 1 continues. The first two clauses (vv. 1–2a) stand in parallel formation such that they border on the poetic. Moreover, the passive verb in the first sentence is striking: it emphasizes not the agency of God as creator but the completed character of the earth, heavens, and their cohorts. The work of creation has run its course and come to an end. The term here translated "cohorts" has traditionally been rendered elsewhere by "hosts," which normally designates military forces (e.g., 1 Sam 17:45). This noun apparently refers to all that was created along with the heavens (e.g., the stars, the earth, vegetation). As a result, the next clause, which reports that the deity finished working on the seventh day, seems odd. Perhaps there was some final finish work to be done, but that would be all. But then, in an implicit play on words, God "stopped" (*šbt*) on the seventh day, a day that would become known as Sabbath (*šbt*), though that noun does not appear here. Nonetheless, the root significance of the Sabbath as a stoppage from work resides in these verses. One could say that verses 2–3 function as an etiology for the institution of the Sabbath as a ritual practice. It is built into the nature of time through which the cosmos moves. If, as many scholars think, the Priestly account of creation was formulated during the so-called exilic period, focus on the Sabbath would have been especially salient. Since the temple had been destroyed in 587 BCE, the Sabbath provided a ritual focus, equally available to those who lived outside and inside the land. Even after the Second Temple was built, the Sabbath remained important to those without immediate access to it.

Up until this point, God's creative activity has focused not only on the construction and population of the cosmos but also on the notion of time. With the appearance of light on day one, it is possible to construct the basic unit of calendrical time: the day. Subsequently, with the creation of the heavenly luminaries, other units of time emerge: festivals and years. Now the deity returns to the basic unit of time and blesses the seventh day. This is, of course, not the first act of blessing. Earlier, God has blessed marine and avian life (1:22) and humanity (1:28), though, interestingly, not the earth creatures. In those two cases, the act of blessing is followed by the admonition to "be fruitful and multiply." No such overt admonition is present in 2:3. Nevertheless, the connotation of blessing as expressed in Gen 1 may follow the same verb in 2:3: a day that has been blessed may be fruitful time. But then, the deity goes further by making that seventh day "holy." In this new cosmos, there is nothing else created holy—only the recurring seventh day. Throughout the Old Testament, strikingly, only in this verse is God the subject of this particular form of the verb: to make holy. Elsewhere, Moses, Samuel, and Solomon make people (Jesse by Samuel, 1 Sam 16:5), objects (tabernacle and its contents by Moses, Lev 8:10), or a place (the temple's middle court by Solomon, 2 Chr 7:7) holy. In Gen 2:3, the deity does something different: God makes a unit of time sacred. Interestingly, God does not deem the seventh day to be "good," a characterization that God has offered about light (1:4), earth and seas (1:10), the earth and vegetative growth (1:12), heavenly illumination (1:18), marine and avian life (1:21), animal life (1:25), and human life (1:31). The holy classification and the moral (or aesthetic) category of good do not necessarily overlap.

With the sanctification of the seventh day, the deity creates the notion of a week, though, as with the noun Sabbath, the noun "week" does not appear in these verses. In fact, the Hebrew word for week, *šābûaʿ*, rarely appears in the OT (Gen 29:27; Lev 12:5; Jer 5:24; Dan 10:2). Nonetheless, the notion of a seven-day period during which one is to work for six days and then stop on the seventh is fundamental to the notion of the Israelite Sabbath (e.g., Exod 34:21). Without the "stop" or Sabbath, there would be no week, as Israel understood that category theologically. The notion of the Sabbath as a time for rest is developed elsewhere in Priestly literature (so Lev 23:3).

[4a] This half verse was introduced as a transition between the Priestly and pre-Priestly accounts of creation and as an introduction to the latter. The so-called *tôlədôt* formulae—*tôlədôt* means "descendants" or "successors"—appears eleven times in the book of Genesis, five times in the primeval history (2:4a; 5:1; 6:9; 10:1; 11:10) and five times in the family literature (11:27; 25:12, 19; 36:1, 9) and once in the Joseph story (37:2). In all instances, the formula stands immediately before the material it introduces. For example, the descendants of Ishmael are listed immediately after the formula, "These are the descendants of Ishmael" (25:12). Hence, readers should construe 2:4a as an introduction to what follows, identifying those "descendants" as humanity. Humans are, in this editor's eyes, the progeny of the heavens and the earth, a claim that is not out of line with the pre-Priestly account of humanity's creation since humans are created out of earth.

[4b–9] The Priestly author has wisely used the diction of "day" throughout Gen 1 to complement this earlier account, which begins with the word "day." It is possible that the Priestly author created the dual divine name, YHWH God, which appears throughout Gen 2–3, as an attempt to smooth the transition from the use of Elohim in Gen 1 to the use of YHWH in Gen 4 and following. If that is the case, it is a relatively rare instance in which an earlier account has been modified by a later editor or author.

The diction and word order of "earth and heavens" (v. 4b) is consistent with this account's focus on the earth, just as the later author's phrase "heavens and earth" (1:1; 2:1) fits with that individual's concern to describe the creation of the entire cosmos.

The pre-Priestly author used a grammatical formulation—temporal clause (v. 4b), circumstantial clause (vv. 5–6), finite verb (v. 7)—that also appears in ancient Near Eastern accounts of creation: Atrahasis and Enuma Elish. The Priestly author in 1:1–3 replicates this pattern. The pre-creation state in 2:5–6, as does the Priestly account, presupposes the existence of the earth, though not in the form that ancient Israelites knew it. The word "earth" appears three times and "ground" two times in 2:5–6, indicating the stage on which the action in chapter 2 will play out. The earth in 2:5 is an earth without much: without flora of various sorts, without rain, and without humans. What does exist is water, a feature shared by the Priestly report, though it is not the cosmic or heavenly deep of Gen 1:2 but a spring that irrigates the entire earth, literally, "the face of the ground," a phrase that the Priestly writer reworked into the "face of the waters" (1:2). Of these three elements that are lacking, the pre-Priestly account narrates the beginning of plantings and the creation of humans, but not the creation of rain. The pre-Priestly author will, however, report the presence of rain in chapter 7.

The deity acts by "molding" the earth person from bits of topsoil on the ground. As is well known, this involves a wordplay in Hebrew. The earth creature, *hāʾādām*, is created from *hāʾădāmâ*. That wordplay underscores the close connection between humans and the earth out of which they are created, which they will farm and care for, and to which they will return. Again, as is well known, the verb (*yṣr*) and related noun are used elsewhere to describe the work of a potter (Isa 29:16) or worker of metal (Isa 44:10). In Gen 2, however, the statue is "inspired" by the deity with "the breath of life," a phrase that the Priestly writer will appropriate in 1:30 to describe the life force shared by humans and animals.

YHWH God then engages in agriculture by planting a garden, which is really an orchard. This writer knew the tradition of a "garden of God" (cf. Isa 51:3; Ezek 28:13; 31:8), which is also associated with the toponym "Eden." The word "Eden" can also mean pleasant or blissful (so Ps 36:9 [8]; Jer 51:34). This dual meaning of "Eden" helps explain why the writer can refer to a garden *in* Eden (Gen 2:8) and a garden *of* Eden (2:15), a phrase that could also be translated "pleasurable garden." According to Ezekiel 31, the garden of God was known for its trees, specifically cedar, fir, and plane (v. 8), as well as more generally, "the trees of Eden" (v. 18). Yet none of the trees in Ezekiel 31 bears edible fruit or nuts.

In Gen 2:9, the pre-Priestly writer builds on this tradition of trees in God's garden by commenting on all the trees in general and by identifying two trees in particular, the tree of life and the tree of the knowledge of good and evil. The trees in general are characterized by their beauty and their ability to produce edible fruit and nuts. The capacities of the two specific trees are apparently to offer immortality (3:22) and a special kind of knowledge. Although beautiful trees are part of the tradition of God's garden, these other two trees are not. Earlier creative activity is rehearsed when God makes the trees come up from the ground: both the earth creature and trees share that point of origin.

Oddly, despite the prominence of the two trees in this narrative, they receive little or no attention elsewhere in the OT. The phrase "tree of life" does appear in Prov 11:30, though it does not function there as a potential source of immortality as it does in Gen 2–3. Moreover, the phrase "tree of the knowledge of good and evil" appears only in Gen 2. Hence, one must ask what the author meant by this phrase. Knowing about good and evil is a topic that appears elsewhere in the OT. There is an age at which people do not know how to distinguish between "good and evil" and/or act on the basis of that distinction (so Deut 1:39; Isa 7:15–16). Only as they grow do they gain that ability (e.g., David in 2 Sam 14:17). In fact, this text, designed to flatter David, characterizes such an individual as a "messenger of God." Similarly, Solomon prays that he might be granted the ability to "discern between good and evil" in order to govern well (1 Kgs 3:9). Interestingly, as one ages, like Barzillai in 2 Sam 19:35 (MT, v. 36), one can lose the ability to discern between "good and bad" (so Speiser 1964, 26).

These texts suggest that a person can gain the capacity for moral judgment and ethical action by dint of maturation. Moreover, it is something that God can grant, as to David and Solomon. By way of contrast, the tree in the garden offers access to such a moral capacity in an unnatural way: by eating rather than by growing or receiving a divine grant. Isaiah 7:14–16 makes a comparable point, namely, the child Immanuel will mature at preternatural speed such that he will be able to choose the good and refuse the evil while he is still eating baby food. Normally, that would not be true for any individual. Hence, simply gaining the ability to know good and evil is probably not the reason that God prohibits eating from that tree. Rather, the deity admonishes the primal couple not to acquire improper access to such knowledge by eating from the tree of good and evil.

Both the pre-Priestly and the Priestly accounts of creation envision a place where plants grow. For the former, it is a garden; for the latter it is everywhere on the land (Gen 1:29). Clearly, the Priestly writer intended to offer a more comprehensive account of origins, one not limited to a specific place.

[10–14] This section about rivers appears intrusive. With the exception of the words "Eden" and "East," which are general in their own rights, this account names specific rivers, countries, and valuable items that would have been traded throughout the ancient Near East. It is as if reference to a river that flows out of Eden has triggered the impulse to include a report explaining what became of the waters that flowed over "the entire surface of the ground" (2:6). Only two (Tigris and Euphrates) are known. The situation of the three countries is clearer (oddly, the fourth river named, the Euphrates, is not associated with a country). Havilah is related to Ishmael and land to the east (Gen 10:7; 25:18), whereas Cush refers to Nubia and/or southern Egypt.

The initial description of the primal river is strange. It flows *from* Eden *to* the garden, a description at odds with the understanding that the garden is in Eden. This apparent confusion may result from an attempt to integrate the notion of a spring that flows out over the ground, the water necessary to irrigate the garden, with major rivers of the ancient Near East. Reference to gold and a semiprecious stone recalls the description of God's garden in Ezek 28:13. Onyx and gold are mentioned there, though fragrant resin is not (cf. Num 11:7).

[15–25] One senses that 2:15 builds on verse 8, placing the earth creature in the garden, but the garden has changed. It is now a pleasurable garden, not identified as a garden in a specific place. That pleasurable garden requires tending: hence the task of the earth creature is to work and take care of it.

Direct discourse commences in verses 16–17. (Cf. the Priestly account in which direct discourse was prominent early on, beginning in 1:3.) The deity both permits and forbids. The deity permits the consumption of arboreal food. Interestingly, the Priestly writer later expands the source of vegetarian food to plants as well as fruit/nuts/seeds (1:29–30). Neither writer, however, conceives that humans are initially carnivores. The prohibition involves one of the aforementioned trees, the one that involves knowledge of good and evil. The prohibition also includes a penalty: capital punishment (cf. Gen 20:7; Exod 19:12; 21:12; Lev 20:10; and 1 Sam 22:16 for this meaning of the infinitive absolute followed by a finite verb).

In Gen 2:18, the report becomes a narrative, one with direct discourse. The deity, in his second speech, offers the judgment that the creature is alone and needs a companion. Unlike the first speech (vv. 16–17), it is not at all clear that the deity is addressing the earth creature. Instead, the speech appears to be a soliloquy. The earth creature is apparently not privy to this speech. Yet again, the deity creates while using earth (so also vv. 7, 9). Humans are linked to both animal and plant life, since all three are created out of or from the ground. God creates birds of the sky and wild animals. (The Priestly writer will incorporate the phrase "birds of the sky" [1:30] and recast wildlife, "animals of the field," into wild animals, "animals of the earth" [1:24].)

Verses 19–20 focus on the role of the earth creature as one who gives names. The fleshing out of creation is collegial: the deity makes, and the earth creature names. In the process of naming, wildlife becomes domesticated, shown in verse 20, a fact that demonstrates the power of naming. Nevertheless, this process did not yield the appropriate companion for the human. As indicated in the above translation and note, it is not altogether clear *who* determined that there was not an appropriate companion. The preferred translation imputes that judgment to the deity. In no case does the text imply that the human makes this decision.

To fashion the needed companion, the deity departs from the prior three modes of creation out of the ground. In what appears to be an act of surgery, he uses the earth creature as the source for the companion. This act of creation elicits a new verb, to build or fashion something (*bnh*). The deity moves from being a potter to more of a woodworker. In so doing, the problem of finding no appropriate companion is resolved: a female (*ʾiššâ*) to complement the earth person, who is now described as a male (*ʾîš*), another wordplay in Hebrew that underscores the intimate connection between male and female. The world of gender distinction now exists. The Priestly writer includes similar language highlighting sexual distinction in his poem (Gen 1:27). However, he integrates that notion with the image of God rather than highlighting the importance of "flesh," as does the pre-Priestly author, who focuses on the distinction between genders.

The climax of the account occurs in the first speech given by the earth person (cf. the poem embedded in 1:26–28, although there it is voiced by the deity), a poem celebrating the successful outcome of attempts at forging a companion. Immediately following the earth creature's speech, the author provides an etiology for familial relations and the strong bond between spouses. The author introduces new categories: father, mother, wife, and, implicitly, husband. Moreover, this author reports that the man leaves his parents so that he can embrace his wife. Such does not suggest that he lives with his wife's family (matrilocality) or, necessarily, that he moves away from the physical dwelling of his parents, but rather that the spousal relationship involves the creation of a new social and emotional bond that will prove to be more powerful than the one between parent and child.

The etiology for these roles may occur here because of the presence of the word "flesh" in both 2:23 and 24. In the final verse, one is tempted to translate "embarrassed," but the Hebrew verb *bwš* has a stronger sense, that of shame (v. 25). The notions of "nakedness" and "shame" set the stage for what will follow in the next chapter.

Genesis 3:1–24
The Earth Creature and His Wife Hide Themselves

These verses are of a piece with the preceding chapter. They comprise the earliest history of humankind. In it, dialogue plays a prominent role: between an animal and a human, and between God and humans, though no dialogue between humans. In both cases, communication within the dialogues is obscure: the characters talk past each other. The deity's speeches to the snake, to the woman, and to the man are much clearer.

The chapter begins with the humans located in the garden, where they have earlier been placed (Gen 2:15, 22); it concludes with the man and woman being banished from the garden. It is therefore clear that one purpose of the chapter is to provide an explanation for why humans no longer live in a paradisal place.

Although the chapter has often been viewed as presenting a report about the first (or "original") sin, it is telling that the word "sin" does not appear in the chapter. Instead, the chapter seems intent on exploring natural human proclivities, such as the desire for good food or an appreciation of beauty, as well as the way in which humans are viewed as worrisome by the deity.

> **3:1** The snake was more cunning than any other wild animal that YHWH
> God had made. He said to the woman, "Did God really say, 'You may
> not eat from any of the trees in the garden'?"[a] **2** The woman replied to the
> snake, "We may eat from the fruit of the trees in the garden. **3** But as for
> the fruit of the tree in the center of the garden, God said, 'You may not
> eat from it. Moreover, you are not supposed to touch it; otherwise, you
> will die.'" **4** The snake responded to the woman, "You will not die, **5** since
> God knows that on the day that you eat from it, your eyes will open up.
> You will be like God, knowing good and evil." **6** When the woman saw
> that the tree was good for food, that it was beautiful to see, and that it
> was desirable to make one intelligent, she took some of its fruit, ate, and
> also gave some to her husband, who was with her. And he ate. **7** Then the
> eyes of the two of them opened up. They knew that they were naked. So
> they stitched fig leaves together and fashioned loincloths for themselves.
>
> **8** When they heard the sound of YHWH God walking in the garden
> during the breezy time of day, the earth creature and his wife hid them-

selves from YHWH God in the center of the garden. 9 YHWH God called
out to the earth creature, saying, "Where are you?" 10 He replied, "When
I heard the sound of you in the garden, I was afraid because I was naked,
so I hid myself." 11 He responded, "Who told you that you were naked?
Have you eaten from the tree from which I admonished you not to eat?"
12 The earth creature said, "The woman whom you gave to be with me,
she gave to me from [the fruit of] the tree, and I ate." 13 YHWH God said
to the woman, "What is this that you have done?" and she replied, "The
snake deceived me, so I ate." 14 YHWH God said to the snake,

"Because you have done this,
you are cursed more than any other domestic animal,
more than any other wild animal.
On your abdomen you shall crawl;
you will eat dirt
all the days that you live.
15 I will establish hostility between you and the woman,
between your progeny and her progeny."
16 To the woman he said,
"I will make your pregnancy difficult;
your bearing of children will be painful.
You will desire your husband,
but he will rule over you."
17 To the man he said,
"Because you agreed with what your wife said
and ate from the tree
from which I admonished
you not to eat,
the ground is cursed because of you.
You will eat from it with difficulty all the days that you live.
18 Thorny shrubs and thistles will grow for you;
you will eat wild plants.
19 With sweat on your face
you will eat bread
until you return to the ground
from which you were taken.
You are truly dirt
and to dirt you will return.

20 The man named his wife "Eve"[b] because she was the mother of all
(human) life. 21 YHWH God made garments of animal hide for Adam[c]
and his wife. He clothed them.

22 Then YHWH God said, "The earth creature has become like one of
us, knowing good and evil. Now, should he put out his hand and also take

from the tree of life, eat, and live forever . . . " 23 So YHWH God expelled him from the garden of Eden so that he could cultivate the ground from which he had been taken. 24 He drove out the earth creature. East of the garden of Eden, he stationed the winged creatures with blazing and rotating sword(s) to guard the way to the tree of life.

a. The interrogative particle is missing at the beginning of the snake's speech. Hence one could translate "God really said . . ."

b. Hebrew *ḥawwâ* (Eve) is a wordplay on "life," *ḥay*.

c. MT reads "Adam."

[3:1–7] Although these verses are located at the beginning of a new chapter, they are very much a continuation of the account that began in 2:4b. The elements there—the man and woman, trees, and fauna—have already been mentioned. Still, the transition between 2:25 and 3:1 is abrupt. The author does use a wordplay: *ʿārôm*, meaning "naked," in 2:25, and *ʿārûm*, meaning "cunning," in 3:1, which together bridge the two scenes. The cunning or wily character of this specific wild animal—the snake—sets the reader's expectations for the dialogue that will ensue.

The presence of a speaking animal means that the author has adopted one feature of fables, though without the overt didactic quality that is often featured in fables. That the serpent is characterized as "cunning" as opposed to "wise" helps explain this absence of a wisdom-like quality to the chapter. In the opening dialogue, there is a move away from the dual divine name. The serpent uses the generic word "God," which is characteristic of the Priestly account, though the narrator will return to that dual name in 3:8. The leading quality of the serpent's question is, indeed, a cunning revision of what the deity has actually said (2:17). Instead of the permission to eat from every tree save two, the snake converts the deity's offering of food into a prohibition of eating from *any* tree. To this the woman naturally offers a rejoinder, though she expands upon the deity's prohibition by referring not only to eating but also to touching the tree. In addition, the woman refers to the tree of the knowledge of good and evil as in the middle of the garden (v. 2), whereas Gen 2:9 states that it was the tree of life that was in the middle of the garden. It is as if the snake's recasting of the deity's words has led to the woman's doing a comparable revision of earlier information about the trees.

The woman's overstatement of God's prohibition leaves the door open for the snake to challenge and deny what the deity has promised would happen: capital punishment. The snake's reasoning is more interesting than the simple fact that he denies what God has said will be the case. First, the snake claims to know what God knows, something that the author of this account does not even claim for the humans. Second, the snake foretells what will happen if and when the woman (along with her husband) eats from the forbidden tree: their eyes will open up. In a real way, the snake "knows." Third, the snake asserts correctly that the man and woman will in some fashion have become like God (so 3:22) after they eat from the tree. What the author leaves unsaid is whether being like God is part of the rationale for the woman (and man) to eat from the tree. The author will offer three other reasons.

Perhaps the most difficult element in this text is the notion of having eyes open up. The idiom can refer to a blind person becoming sighted (so Isa 35:5). However, there is no reason to think that the woman and man are without sight. In fact, the author makes clear that the woman can see before she eats from the tree: "She saw that the tree was good for food." So, the sort of eyes opening up in Gen 3 must refer to the ability to see or experience something that is there but has not been recognized. An instructive example appears in 2 Kgs 6:8–23. An army with horses and chariots has surrounded a city. At Elisha's request, God opens the eyes of a servant so he can see the army in place. That army has been there all along; the servant just cannot "see" it and understand its implication. Similarly, the woman and man have been naked all along, but only after they gain divine knowledge from the tree are they able to "see" and perceive the significance of that knowledge.

Once the dialogue with the snake has ended, the woman "sees" the tree in three ways: that it is good for food, that it is beautiful (literally, a delight to the eyes, again emphasizing a visual aspect), and that it is desirable for providing intelligence. Of those three, two have already been mentioned in 2:9. However, that the tree is desirable as a source of intelligence is a new element. The word translated "intelligent" bears connotations of "success" or "insight," something different from gaining the "knowledge of good and evil." All three impulses are natural human inclinations. However, the tree also has the capacity to allow humans to share something that has hitherto been the exclusive possession of the deity: "the knowledge of good and evil." Pursuit of that knowledge is, however, not the explicit reason that the woman eats from the tree: she wants intelligence. What she and the man experience when they gain "the knowledge of good and evil" is not something they have sought; it is an unintended consequence. The author presents the woman as overtly desiring good food, beauty, and intelligence.

Once the man and woman eat from the tree, their eyes open up, just as the snake has said will be the case. They "see" and, as a result, "know" that they are naked. The fruit of the tree has allowed them a new kind of knowledge, yet again an unintended consequence. The first scene of Gen 3 concludes with the human's first attempt at making something, the same verb used of the deity's work in 2:18. It results in a flawed attempt to provide clothing.

[8–13] The second scene in this chapter transpires in the garden, a location that the man and woman will soon be forced to leave. The narrator sets the stage by resuming use of the dual divine name and by describing a time of the day when people could be walking about due to the presumably cool breeze. More important than the setting, however, is the wonderfully wrought dialogue between the deity and humans. God askes an initial question and does not receive a direct answer. The earth person does not tell God where he is hiding but rather reports that he is hiding and gives a reason for why he is hiding. The reason for hiding, fear due to nakedness, is oblique. The earth person might have been ashamed or embarrassed (cf. 2:25) due to his nakedness, but fear is not a natural result. Similarly, the earth person might be afraid because he and the woman have violated the deity's command and death threat, but that has little to do with the notion of nakedness. The author has created a speech that characterizes the earth person as not making much sense in response to the deity's interrogation.

The deity does respond directly to what the earth person says by asking how he knew he was naked and follows that up with a second question, asking directly whether the earth person has consumed fruit from the tree. Again, the earth person does not answer the first question and for good reason, since no one has told him that he is naked. As for the second question, he does not answer immediately but points a finger at his wife before admitting that he has eaten. With that the deity turns to the woman and asks a more general question: "What have you done?" She, like the man, points a finger but at the snake, before admitting she has eaten. The snake, however, escapes interrogation.

This scene reveals a world in which the humans hide themselves from God and in which humans do not communicate clearly with the deity. Despite the knowledge of good and evil that the humans have gained, they have lost the ability to be at ease with YHWH God.

[14–19] This poetic section continues the conversation between God and God's creatures. Now instead of questions, the deity turns to a series of sentences for misbehavior by the snake, the woman, and the man. It is difficult to know if this poetry was created by the author of the narrative or whether it was adapted from another source. (If the latter, the original narrative would have continued with banishment from the garden as the sole punishment. As it now stands, the narrative includes multiple punishments within the created order for the humans' violation of God's command.) What is clear is their etiological function. Though couched as "punishments," they really function as statements about how things that all humans experience have come to be. They explain some essential features about the world that humans inhabit: why the snake crawls and strikes, why childbirth is painful, and why people have to work hard. Several features require comment. First, diction of cursing begins (vv. 14, 17). The deity curses both the snake and the ground; the reason for the former is clear; it is less clear for the latter. Second, the sentences regarding the snake and the man both involve dirt/earth: the snake will eat dirt whereas the man (and presumably the woman) will return to dirt. Third, the punishment of the man (and presumably the woman) focuses on eating (verb "to eat" occurs five times in vv. 17–19), action that constituted the infraction for which they are being punished. Instead of picking something from trees, they will eat out of difficult circumstances and with sweaty faces. Fourth, humans will be vegetarians (vv. 17–19). This appears to be less of a punishment than a description of human life that the author knew. The negative quality in these verses has to do with the hard work that will be needed to produce the flora humans will cultivate in order to have bread to eat. The Priestly writer will incorporate the notion of an original vegetarian diet into his account of creation. Fifth, proleptically, since the humans will not have access to the tree of life, they will die and return to the earth. Now they are like God in having certain knowledge, but, since they do not have access to the tree of life, they cannot live forever, nor were they created to do so. Seen this way, 3:19 is an etiology for human mortality, not a claim about the loss of immortality. Westermann (1984, 267) puts it well, "And so death . . . is not a punishment for man's transgression, but the term of his toilsome work." Humans' arduous labor is now at an end.

[20–24] The final five verses of the chapter are heterogeneous, involving naming, clothing, and banishing. In 3:20, which offers an abrupt transition from the foregoing poetry, the man returns to the work of naming, this time offering a proper name for the woman. Both the man's and the woman's names feature wordplays. Adam's name represents his connection to the earth; Eve's symbolizes her generative role as "mother of all life."

The deity acts beneficently toward the humans by providing clothing. Instead of garments fashioned from plants, YHWH God makes garments from animal hide. (The question of whether these garments required the killing of animals or simply the harvesting of fibers was not a matter of concern for the author.) The word "make" is the same verb used in 2:18, which implies that God's act of clothing is a continuation of his creative activity. It is an act, however, that reflects the world after the poetic punishments have been uttered. The use of the word "hide" presupposes that animals have been killed to provide clothing. (And they will be killed for a sacrifice in ch. 4.) The Priestly writer offers a different perspective regarding the human-animal relationship; animals may be killed only in the postflood economy.

The final three verses cohere. The deity speaks in conciliar fashion, "Let us . . ." (cf. the earlier divine-plural language in Gen 1:26). The plural reference to the deity avoids making the claim that the earth person has become like "me," like YHWH God. Instead, YHWH God affirms that the earth person has become like a member of the divine council (cf. 1 Kgs 22; Isa 6; Job 1–2 for depictions of the divine council). Moreover, the preposition "like," introduced by the snake, remains important. The earth person is in some way similar to the deity but has not (yet) become divine. The Priestly writer will make a comparable claim when averring that humans have been created in God's image (1:26–27).

It is the "not yet" that troubles YHWH God. Verse 22 makes clear that if the earth person consumes fruit from the tree of life, he would live forever. That would make the earth person more than simply "like" the deity. To avoid that circumstance, YHWH God banishes the earth person from the garden. It seems odd that verses 22–24 refer only to the earth person and not to both man and woman. This suggests that these verses reflect an earlier story about the creation of humanity that focuses on only the androgynous earth person.

Though the task of the human is initially to cultivate the garden (2:15), now the task is to cultivate land outside the garden, which will be far more difficult. Should that harsh life prove to be too much, the earth person might try to return to the garden. To avoid that eventuality, YHWH God places half-human/half-animal winged creatures—cherubim—along with a lethal weapon to prevent the earth person from gaining access to the garden and eating fruit from the tree of life. A hallmark of the cherubim is their ability to move, due in part to the fact that they bear wings. As a result, the image created by the pre-Priestly author is of a quick-moving creature and a fiery sword, both capable of running down and killing the earth person if he tries to enter the now-forbidden garden.

In sum, by the end of pre-Priestly creation narrative, the four constitutive relationships that have been formed in Gen 2 have become problematic. The humans who were created from the ground are now alienated from it. Animals created to serve as potential partners for humans are, as symbolized by the snake, attacking them. Male and female are now in a difficult and hierarchical relationship. And humans who have worked collegially with the deity during acts of creation are now hiding from the deity and banished from the paradisal garden. Only in the last relationship is there any hint of amelioration, that due to the deity's provision of adequate garments for humans. They are now clothed as they confront life outside the garden.

Genesis 4:1–26
"Should I Be the One to Look after My Brother?"

This chapter is made up of two different styles of literature: story and genealogy. The first sixteen verses of this chapter are regularly known as the Cain-and-Abel story, a narrative that follows the one according to which humans are banished from the garden. The last ten verses of the chapter, however, are made up of diverse genealogical material, which offers a segue to the lengthy genealogy in Gen 5. The two portions of chapter 4 are, however, related. Both involve beginnings: the former features the beginning of sibling relations, formal religious practice, murder, and revenge; the latter highlights the beginnings of human culture.

The Cain-and-Abel story exists as a distinct narrative. In it, the author now uses the singular name YHWH, not YHWH Elohim, as found in Gen 2. Nonetheless, it bears a distinct structural resemblance to Gen 3. In both, humans act inappropriately; the deity interrogates them; the deity punishes them in multiple ways, including banishment; and the deity acts beneficently on their behalf. The stories make a similar point: humans have a profound proclivity to act in inappropriate ways. Further, the author continues to explore humanity's relationship to the ground. Moreover, relationships within the nuclear family, now fraternal, are in play. Despite these similarities, the Cain-and-Abel story has a much more intense mood. One hears of strong human emotions: anger and fear. Revenge is in the air. Further, there is powerful personification at work: sin is personified, as also the ground, which has a mouth, and blood, which can scream.

Verses 17–26 chart two vertical genealogies, one commencing with Cain and ending with Lamech, the other returning to Adam and ending with Seth's son, Enosh. Lamech, like his forebear Cain, is remembered primarily as someone who killed another human being. Still, that genealogy is also known for cultural developments, such as the beginning of music. Seth will, however, become the "normative" forebear. It is his genealogy that will appear in Gen 5 (and 1 Chr 1).

4:1 The earth person had sexual relations[a] with Eve, his wife. She became
pregnant and gave birth to Cain. She said, "I have created a person[b]

with [the help of] YHWH." 2 She again gave birth—to his brother, Abel.
Abel shepherded flocks, and Cain cultivated the ground. 3 After many
days,[c] Cain brought some produce from the ground as a food offering
to YHWH. 4 Abel also brought [something] from among the firstborn of
his flock, their choice parts. YHWH looked approvingly[d] at Abel and his
offering. 5 However, YHWH did not look approvingly at Cain and his
offering. Cain became very angry; his face was contorted. 6 YHWH said
to Cain, "Why are you so angry? Why has your face become contorted?
7 If you behave well, won't you be viewed well?[e] But if you don't behave
well, sin is lurking by the door. It desires you, but you must rule over it."

8 Cain spoke with his brother Abel.[f] When they were in the field, Cain
attacked[g] Abel and killed him. 9 YHWH said to Cain, "Where is Abel,
your brother?" Cain responded, "I don't know. Should I be the one to look
after my brother?" 10 [God] said, "What have you done? The sound of your
brother's blood is screaming to me from the ground. 11 Now you are cursed
from the ground, which has opened its mouth to receive your brother's
blood from your hand. 12 When you cultivate the ground, it will no longer
provide its yield[h] for you. You will be a homeless wanderer on the earth."
13 Cain said to YHWH, "My punishment is greater than I can bear. 14 You
have banished me today from the surface of the ground, and I will be hidden
from you.[i] I shall be a homeless wanderer on the earth. Whoever encounters
me might kill me." 15 YHWH responded to him, "Not so![j] Whoever might
kill Cain would be avenged seven times over." YHWH placed a mark on
Cain so that whoever encountered him would not strike him down. 16 Cain
went away from YHWH and lived in the land of Nod, east of Eden.

17 Cain had sexual relations with his wife. She became pregnant and
gave birth to Enoch, and he was a builder of a city. He [Cain] named
it after his son, Enoch. 18 Irad was born to Enoch. Irad fathered Mehujael, Mehujael fathered Methusael, and Methusael fathered Lamech.
19 Lamech married two women: the name of the first was Adah, and the
name of the second was Zillah. 20 Adah bore Jabal; he was the progenitor
of those who live in tents and have livestock. 21 His brother's name was
Yubal; he was the progenitor of all who play string and wind instruments.
22 Zillah also gave birth to Tubal-Cain, a smith skilled in working bronze
and iron. Tubal-Cain's sister was Naᶜamah.

23 Lamech said to his wives,

"Adah and Zillah, pay attention to what I say;
  wives of Lamech, listen to my words!
I have killed a person who injured me,
  a lad for wounding me.
24 If Cain has been avenged seven times over,
  Lamech has been avenged seventy-seven times over."

25 Adam had sexual relations again with his wife. She gave birth to a
son and named him Seth. "God has provided another offspring for me in
place of Abel, whom Cain had killed." 26 To Seth a son was also born.
He named him Enosh. That was when people began to use the name
"YHWH."

a. Literally, "he knew."
b. Or, "I have obtained a person. . . ."
c. Literally, "At the end of days."
d. Cf. Isa 17:7–8 for a similar use of this verb to signify approval and disapproval.
e. Literally, "a raising." The reference is to a raising of the face, though the word "face" does not appear here; cf. Job 11:15.
f. So MT; but LXX, SP, and Vulg read, "Let's go out to the field."
g. On this meaning of *qwm*, see Deut 19:11 et al.
h. Literally, "strength." For the sense of "yield," cf. Job 31:39.
i. Literally, "from the face of the ground . . . and from your face."
j. So LXX. MT reads "therefore."

[4:1–7] The number of notes associated with these verses is indicative of the philological and text-critical difficulties presented by this episode. Even the first verse is difficult. Although the author implicitly attributes the birth of Eve's son to a sexual relationship, *she* claims that the birth is due in some way to the deity. As birth mother, she has demonstrated the ability create life just as God has in the pre-Priestly creation account. The verb "create" in v. 1 (*knh*) is used elsewhere in the OT to refer to God's creative activity (e.g., Gen 14:19). It is probably for this reason that she imputes her giving birth as a cocreative act with the deity. One must also recognize the belief attested elsewhere in the OT that God is responsible for fertility (e.g., Gen 29:31; 30:22). Eve, like her husband (2:23), speaks when a new person comes into being. However, Eve and the earth person, the parents and first generation, disappear from the story after the beginning of v. 2. The names of the two sons are meaningful. "Cain" is identical to the Hebrew word for "spear" (see 2 Sam 21:16), and "Abel" is identical to the Hebrew word meaning something transitory (so Eccl 6:11–12). The names signify that Cain is like a weapon and that Abel will disappear.

For many interpreters, 4:2 provides a key to the meaning of this story, or at least an earlier or original form of this narrative: it is a narrative that reports two contrasting cultures and valorizes one over the other. Literature mediating between different, even conflicting, lifestyles is attested throughout the world, such as the ancient Near Eastern Sumerian text known as Dumuzi and Enkimdu. Were that such the case in this narrative, one would have to conclude that God has no regard for those who engage in agriculture but approves of those who keep flocks. In ancient Israel, both offerings of animals and grain were acceptable. Three things must be said about these offerings. First, the text does not use the technical vocabulary one finds in either rules about sacrifice or narratives about them. The phrase "produce from the ground" is similar to "produce from the earth" (Lev 27:30); the latter text refers to that which is to be tithed. The phrase, literally, "firstling or eldest of his flock" appears to reflect the ritual regarding the firstborn (Exod 13:11–16; Num 3:12–16). However, neither of those texts refers to multiple animals as in Gen 4, nor is there mention of their choice (or fattest) parts. (For a description of what those choice parts might have been, see Lev 8:16, 25.) Hence, though a general language of offerings is used, it does not reflect the precise diction of rituals as described in Israelite sacrificial prescriptions. Second, it is difficult to claim that Abel's sacrifice is somehow better than Cain's. In references to vegetable offerings in their raw state (cf. rules regarding processed agricultural offerings in Lev 2), there is no mention of qualitative excellence. Third, in Gen 4:4–5, the author characterizes what the brothers brought in the same way, as an "offering" (*minḥâ*). This Hebrew noun can refer to a general offering of a vegetable and/or animal (e.g., Judg 6:18–19). Hence, one may presume that both offerings, in and of themselves, are worthy of acceptance.

Genesis 4:3 begins with an odd temporal phrase; it could and perhaps should be translated with a less felicitous rendering, "at the end of many days." Such a translation would mean that a period of time has run its course. Given the emphasis on agriculture in these verses, one may infer that the crops, both agricultural and animal, have matured. Now is the time for an offering, perhaps a tithe. It is telling that when describing the quality of a tithe, whether vegetable or animal, a Priestly author writes, "Let no one inquire whether it is good or bad" (Lev 27:33). Such may be an apt comment regarding the offerings described in Gen 4.

One could imagine a dramatic report about fire consuming the offering of Cain (cf. Judg 6:21), but such is not the case. Instead, the author uses language of seeing and "face" to narrate both the response of the deity to the brothers' offerings and the response of Cain to what God does. God looks approvingly at Abel and his offering, but not so at Cain and his. Cain's face becomes contorted, or "falls," though there is the possibility of "a raised face," of "being viewed well," if he acts appropriately. The diction of "face" remains important, as also in "face" or surface of the soil and God's face (v. 14). Absent in this imagery is any reference to Abel's face, which is consistent with his absence from the second half of the narrative.

YHWH's questions to Cain in 4:6 initiate direct discourse in this episode. The questions themselves seem disingenuous. It seems clear that the deity's act of not accepting Cain's offering has elicited his response of anger. One does well to ponder the question:: Is Cain angry with God or with his brother? Based on what happens later in the narrative, one might presume the latter.

Instead of blaming Cain for an improper offering, the deity offers Cain two paths for confronting his anger: behaving well or not behaving well (an almost wisdom-like emphasis on two ways [cf. Ps 1]). The diction has moved from language of ritual practice to that of apparent morality. But, as for the descriptions of the offering, the diction is unusual. Reference to an individual doing well (*ṭwb*) in the second-person singular occurs in only a few other texts in the OT (e.g., Ps 49:19 [18]; Jer 1:12; 1 Kgs 8:18; 2 Kgs 10:30). In virtually all uses, one does well at some activity, such as building, seeing, considering. The verb normally requires another one in order to describe what someone does well. In Gen 4, however, reference to such activity is missing. The deity has admonished Cain to do well at something but does not indicate at what Cain should do well. Perhaps the aforementioned act of making an offering is in view. Perhaps doing well at managing his anger is the referent. In any case, YHWH's implicit admonition to do well at something remains obscure. (Westermann thinks that the difficulties posed by 4:6–7 reflect the fact that they are later additions to an earlier, and theologically problematic, narrative [1984, 300].)

The narrator makes clear that Cain can choose one of two options: doing well at something or not. If the former, there will be acceptance of him and perhaps his offering. If the former, he will confront a demonic figure, personified sin at his door ("sin is the demon at the door" [Speiser 1964, 31]). There is a certain asymmetry in these two outcomes. The positive one involves acceptance. The negative one does not involve lack of acceptance or rejection, but danger, the presence of a threatening figure, which YHWH admonishes Cain to master (the same verb, *mšl*, appears in Gen 3:16). Moreover, only on this occasion in the OT is sin personified. Cain confronts a dual challenge: doing well at something and mastering demonic sin. The ensuing scene demonstrates that he fails at these challenges.

As noted above, some structural points of similarity appear in Gen 3 and 4. The presence of a character apart from the deity and humans in both chapters underscores that similarity. In Gen 3 the snake's question drives the action forward. In Gen 4, demonic sin symbolizes what Cain must overcome.

[8–16] Verse 8 presents one of the most important text-critical issues in all of Genesis. The MT reads: "Cain spoke with his brother Abel. When they were in the field . . ."; but the versions cited say more: "Cain said to his brother Abel, 'Let's go out to the field.'" The former version leads one to think that Cain committed manslaughter; the latter would lead to a charge of premeditated murder. On text-critical grounds, one can argue that the MT is to be preferred since it is the more difficult reading. Further, such a view is consistent with a Cain whose anger is sparked when his offering is not accepted. (The alternative is to think of Cain as harboring a simmering anger and creating a plan to murder Abel once he lures him into the field.)

Whichever of these options is adopted, Cain kills Abel and immediately is subjected to more questions from the deity. It mirrors the question of "location" in Gen 3:9. However, here the question involves not the location of the person being addressed but a missing party, Abel. Unlike the earth person, who does not answer the deity's question in 3:9, Cain responds with a falsehood and parries with a question of his own, perhaps the most well-known sentence from this chapter, often translated, "Am I my brother's keeper?" YHWH does not dignify the killer with an answer. Rather, again like the question posed in 3:13 to the woman, YHWH offers a devastating question: "What have you done?" It is interesting that the deity focuses on the blood of the victim having drained into the ground rather than on the "simple" fact of a killing. Here again, personification is at work. Blood has a voice; it cries out from the ground rather than from within the body where it belongs. Moreover, the ground itself has "opened its mouth." Both blood and ground have human capacities, as did sin in the preceding scene.

This profanation of the ground by improperly spilled blood leads immediately to the first of several punishments. God has already cursed the ground in Gen 3:17. Now a human is cursed from the ground. In Cain's case, this means that he will no longer be able to cultivate crops, which the earth person could still do, according to Gen 3. The earth person would have needed to work quite hard to produce foodstuffs, but even if Cain tries to cultivate fields, there will be no yield from his effort. As a result, he will need to forage as he wanders from place to place, looking for food. (The Hebrew words translated "homeless wanderer" [cf. CEB, "roving nomad"; NJPS, "ceaseless wanderer"] do not include the connotation of "fugitive" [as in NRSV]. Cain is not fleeing punishment, as a fugitive would. He has already been punished.)

Though "ground" is important in 4:8–16, the word "brother" is even more frequent. By its simple presence, underscored by the memorable question in verse 9, the author highlights the fraternal relationship, just as Gen 2–3 explores the spousal relationship. This narrative foreshadows the various problematic fraternal relationships that will appear throughout the book of Genesis, most notably Isaac and Ishmael, Jacob and Esau, Joseph and his brothers. Thoughts of killing are not foreign to the latter two of these three sets.

Unlike the perpetrators in chapter 3, Cain protests the severity of his punishment. In 4:14 he repeats the punishments of becoming a forager and homeless and adds an interpretation: he will be hidden from God. Earlier, the earth person and his wife hid from the deity. Now Cain will be hidden from YHWH. He then gives voice to his fear of being killed. The word for "kill" in 4:14–15a is also present in 4:8. Though he has killed Abel, Cain does not want to be killed. His fear of being killed seems tied to his being hidden from God. While hidden, another human could do something to him. Similarly, the word for being banished (*grš*) in 4:14 is the same verb that occurs in 3:24. Being banished is a fate common to the human characters in the first two pre-Priestly stories of the primeval history.

YHWH responds by somehow marking Cain. It is impossible to know what this is. The Hebrew word is used in widely varying ways, such as the rainbow being a "mark" of God (Gen 9:12). In that case it is a visual sign. In other texts, it is more of a reminder (e.g., Josh 2:12). Whatever the case, the "mark of Cain" is one of protection, not of punishment.

The deity also offers a legal pronouncement, similar to laws formulated with a participle, as in Exod 21:12, 16, 17. In those examples, the penalty for an infraction of the prohibited act is death. That is not stated explicitly in Gen 4:15, but it is certainly implied. Exactly what is avenged seven times over remains unclear. The notion of doing something seven times may signify "full divine retribution" (cf. Pss 12:7 [6]; 79:12; Prov 6:31 [so Wenham 1987, 109]). The logic of punishment down through multiple generations (Exod 20:5) or punishment of an entire social group may also be in play.

The mood of the final verse in the narrative is odd, calmer than the prior turbulent scenes. Cain leaves YHWH; YHWH does not eject him. And Cain lives in Nod. The Hebrew verb translated "lived" can also mean "sit," "dwell" or "perch" (*yšb*). It has a clear locative sense, which stands in tension with YHWH's pronouncement that Cain will be homeless. Such tension may derive from the interest of this verse's author in claiming that Cain moves even further east than the banished earth person and his wife have gone. Still, the word Nod, used as a toponym only here in the OT, itself means "wandering." (Nod derives from the same Hebrew word "wanderer" in vv. 12, 14.) The final phrase, "east of Eden," seems to mean further east than the first human pair. Cain lives at a greater remove from the primeval garden than did his parents, suggesting that his generation has become increasingly alienated from the deity.

[17–26] The first genealogy in Genesis traces the descendants of Cain and also reports that Adam and his wife have another son, Seth, offering a second line of descent. The former line is by far the longer, covering seven generations, whereas the second only moves to the third human generation here. This two-branched genealogy is introduced before the Priestly author's work, since Gen 5, a Priestly document, takes up the genealogy Adam–Seth–Enosh and continues with it to Noah. Whether it was created by the pre-Priestly author or it existed earlier and was revised by him is difficult to determine. Given the noteworthy number of cultural etiologies, it is likely that the genealogy existed as a way of reporting how various features of ancient Near Eastern culture emerged and was redacted to fit the pre-Priestly author's purposes. That author/editor added the comment about when people began to venerate YHWH and with whom that practice was associated.

Whereas some genealogies have a quite regular way of proceeding from one generation to the next (so ch. 5), these verses show striking variation, especially regarding who is "producing" the next generation. In 4:17, 20, 22, 25, the genealogy cites women giving birth. In 4:18, 26, the genealogy refers to men as the parents. In Gen 5, by contrast, there is no reference to a woman giving birth. This variation in 4:17–26 is almost certainly evidence of diverse familial data being incorporated into a larger genealogy.

The pre-Priestly author formulated this genealogy to conform to the beginning of the Cain-and-Abel story. Both begin with a report that a male has sexual relations with his wife, whereupon she becomes pregnant and gives birth to a son. Instead of a story, that report in 4:17 leads into a report about what the son accomplished. Verse 17 does, however, present ambiguity. It is possible to translate: "He [Enoch] built a city, and he [Cain] named it after his son Enoch." Alternatively, one could offer: "He [Cain] built a city and named it after his son Enoch" (so NIV, CEB explicitly). The reader wonders, Who did the author think was a city builder? The proper name occurring just before the verb "he built" is Enoch, suggesting that Enoch built the city. However, if Enoch is the subject of the verb "he built," then the subject of the ensuing verb "he named" must be Cain, if that person is naming the city after his son, Enoch. A further complication arises: if Cain is the city builder, there is distinct tension between the foregoing episode, calling him a homeless wanderer—and the putative claim here that he is an urban figure. That tension can be handled on redaction-critical grounds, explaining that the two portions of Gen 4 come from different sources. The above translation construes Enoch as the builder and Cain as the namer. In the context of this chapter, it seems counterintuitive to view Cain as the first city-builder. (Cf. Westermann [1984, 322, 327], who deletes the noun "his son" and translates, "He called it Enoch, after his own name." He counts Enoch as the builder and the namer.)

The genealogy moves quickly from Enoch to Lamech and his two wives, a new form of marriage, polycoity, which will appear again in the family literature. With Lamech, the vertical genealogy branches out into a horizontal one, listing three brothers. Their names involve assonance: Jabal, Jubal, and Tubal-Cain. Each son is identified as the progenitor of an important feature of human culture: nomadism, music, and metalworking. One purpose of this genealogy, apparently, is to document the emergence of culture, including urbanism. The view is one in which humanity, over time, develops new abilities or ways of being in the world. Urbanism and nomadism, two contrasting lifestyles, are included in the list. One is not viewed as more appropriate than another. The inclusion of this list in Gen 4 stands as another way of viewing cultural difference: the Cain-and-Abel story, in its prebiblical version, may have been a narrative highlighting the superiority of pastoralism.

Lamech's speech to his wives interrupts the genealogy. There is a backstory to the poem: someone has wounded Lamech. Lamech wants his wives to know that he has killed this person and, in so doing, has exacted a kind of revenge even greater than that which God has promised will take place if Cain is killed. Lamech's poetic speech presupposes the story of Cain and Abel in its present form. One may, therefore, infer that this speech was created for its current literary context; it is connected to the Cain-and-Abel story by the motifs and diction of killing and vengeance. The author of the genealogy and speech was intent on claiming that these features of human life continued, even as humans developed a more sophisticated culture. Killing and revenge would play as important a role in people's lives as would music and bronze ornaments. According to the move of revenge from seven times (4:15) to seventy-seven times, the pre-Priestly writer thought there had been a marked increase in violence even as human culture evolved.

This genealogy concludes with a return to Adam and his wife. The formulation is similar though not identical to 4:1. Reference to conception is omitted. In both cases, however, *Eve* (though not mentioned by name in 4:25) names her son. And in both cases, she offers a wordplay to explain the name. "Seth" sounds like the Hebrew word translated as "provided." The Sethite genealogy continues into the next generation with the birth of Enosh (cf. 5:6–32).

Chapter 4 concludes with a striking claim: at the third human generation, humans started invoking the name of YHWH. The author does not, of course, mean that the divine name had not been used earlier in the narratives. Rather, he thinks that as early as the time of Enosh, people were worshiping YHWH by name. This statement should be viewed as yet another instance of development in human culture: the inception of religion and, more particularly, Yahwistic religion. (Such a judgment contradicts what the Priestly writer believed, that the revelation of YHWH's name took place at Sinai. Nonetheless, the Priestly editor did not delete this verse.) It is doubtful that the author of this verse associated this practice with the Sethite line. The claim is a temporal one: "at that time," not "with these people." In sum, the author/redactor has created a chapter that charts the beginnings of human reproduction, murder, revenge, nomadism, urbanism, music, metalworking, and religion. For the pre-Priestly writer, human life was, even at this early time, irreducibly complex.

Genesis 5:1–32
The Descendants of Adam

Readers often avoid this lengthy genealogy. After all, some of the names have already appeared in the much briefer genealogy in 4:17–22. Moreover, the ages associated with the ten individuals in Gen 5 are outlandishly long. Nonetheless, these thirty-two verses provide evidence of the creative ways in which the Priestly authors took the tradition of an antediluvian list of kings and deployed it to suit their interests, one of which was to maintain that the humans could pass their nature, created in the likeness of God, from one generation to the next. This continuing presence of likeness passes from Adam to Seth; Cain is no longer a part of the genealogy.

When reading 5:1–2, even the casual reader will be struck by the similarities between those verses and 1:27–28. Clearly the author of Gen 5 was referring to that prior text. Whether Gen 5 is of a piece with Gen 1 is quite another matter since there are some significant differences between the two chapters. For example, Adam as a proper name is absent in Gen 1 but present in Gen 5. One may assume that the creator of Gen 5 has introduced the name of Adam from the pre-Priestly material in Gen 2–3. Similarly, in 5:29 the author alludes to God's cursing the ground, a motif also taken from Gen 2–3. One senses, therefore, that Gen 5 is a Priestly text that depends upon earlier pre-Priestly and earlier Priestly traditions.

5:1 This is the scroll of Adam's descendants.
On the day that God created Adam,[a]
he created him in the likeness of God.
2 Male and female he created them,
he blessed them,
and named them "Adam,"[a]
on the day that they were created.

3 When Adam had lived 130 years, he sired a child in his likeness,
according to his image,[b] and named him "Seth." 4 After he sired Seth,
he lived eight hundred years; he sired other sons and daughters. 5 In all,
Adam lived 930 years; then he died.

6 When Seth had lived 105 years, he sired Enosh. 7 After he sired
Enosh, Seth lived 807 years; he sired other sons and daughters. 8 In all,
Seth lived 912 years; then he died.

9 When Enosh had lived ninety years, he sired Kenan. 10 After he sired
Kenan, Enosh lived 815 years; he sired other sons and daughters. 11 In all,
Enosh lived 905 years; then he died.

12 When Kenan had lived seventy years, he sired Mahalalel. 13 After
he sired Mahalalel, Kenan lived 840 years; he sired other sons and daughters. 14 In all, Kenan lived 910 years; then he died.

15 When Mahalalel had lived sixty-five years, he sired Jared. 16 After
he sired Jared, Mahalalel lived 830 years; he sired other sons and daughters. 17 In all, Mahalalel lived 895 years; then he died.

18 When Jared had lived 162 years, he sired Enoch. 19 After he sired
Enoch, Jared lived eight hundred years; he sired other sons and daughters.
20 In all, Jared lived 962 years.

21 When Enoch had lived sixty-five years, he sired Methuselah. 22 After
he sired Methuselah, Enoch walked with God for three hundred years;
he sired other sons and daughters. 23 In all, Enoch lived 365 years.
24 Enoch walked with God; and then he was no more, because God took
him.

25 When Methuselah had lived 187 years, he sired Lamech. 26 After
he sired Lamech, Methuselah lived 782 years; he sired other sons and
daughters. 27 In all, Methuselah lived 969 years; then he died.

28 When Lamech had lived 182 years, he sired a son. 29 He named him
Noah, saying,

> "From out of the ground that God has cursed,[c]
> this one will provide relief[d]
> from our work and from the pain of our hands."

30 After he sired Noah, Lamech lived 595 years; he sired other sons
and daughters. 31 In all, Lamech lived 777 years; then he died.

32 When Noah was five hundred years old, he sired Shem, Ham and
Yaphet.

a. One could translate "humanity" (so Gen 1:26), though it is clear that in two of the four cases in which the Hebrew word *ʾādām* appears in the first two verses, it is used as a proper name.

b. In Gen 1:26, the prepositions are reversed: "in our image, according to our likeness."

c. This clause is the final part of v. 29 MT, but the threefold repetition of the preposition *min* in which the final one has a different sense requires this transposition.

d. This verb, *nḥm*, replicates the two consonants that make up the name of Noah in Hebrew.

[5:1–2] The first words of Gen 5 could have been written in a different way. They are similar to a number of other texts in Genesis, all of which use the Hebrew word *tôlədôt*, meaning "descendants," and introduce what follows the formula (Gen 2:4a; 6:9; 10:1; 11:10, 27; 25:12; 36:1, 9; 37:2). Following the pattern of this text, Gen 5:1 could have read, "These are the descendants of Adam." In its current form, however, Gen 5:1 offers a much stronger claim. It insists that what follows is a document, fixed and unchangeable, not simply a malleable oral tradition. Ancient Israelites, no doubt, knew about the flexible character of genealogies. They could change to suit new social, political, and religious realities. Further, the author of Gen 5 was almost certainly aware of the close connections between his genealogy and the one in Gen 4, which includes so many of the same names. Though not free to change that genealogy because Gen 4 bore the authority of tradition, the author of Gen 5 could asseverate that "This" one (*zeh*) is the real and authoritative version of the earliest human genealogy. One may infer that Gen 5 depends upon those other *tôlədôt* formulae and was, therefore, written after them. From this perspective, Gen 5 is an apologetic text, advocating a view of early humanity different from the one promulgated in Gen 4. If Gen 4 is an etiological genealogy and concludes with a song of vengeance, then, as will become clear, Gen 5 is a theologized genealogy, offering a contrasting and more positive picture of humanity. This theological stance about humanity is consistent with what is present in Gen 1.

After the powerful prosaic title, the author turns to poetry, as has an earlier author in Gen 1:27. The poetic formulation begins with the phrase "on the day of the creating" (lit.) and concludes with the phrase "on the day that they were created." Clearly, the poet wanted to signal the beginning and the end of the poem by this inclusio, which uses the words "day" and "creation."

This poem is striking in at least four ways. First, it highlights the notion of "day." There is no comparable statement in Gen 1:26–30, which reports the creation of humanity. Only in the formulaic Gen 1:31 does the word "day" appear. Put another way, from the perspective of Gen 1, humanity was created on the sixth day, as were the land animals. However, from the perspective of Gen 5, that day was not the sixth day; it was the day on which humanity was created. It was not the sixth of seven days; it was not the day on which both land animals and humans were created. Genesis 5, therefore, lifts up *that* day as of special importance in a way that Gen 1 does not. Thus Gen 5 builds on Gen 1 but moves beyond it, focusing on God's creation of "Adam," and not on a sixth day when both animals and humans are created.

Second, Gen 5 formulates as poetry more than what was cast as poetry in Gen 1. In Gen 1:28, the act of "blessing" is set in prose, whereas the act of blessing in Gen 5 appears in one of the poetic lines. The author of Gen 5 recasts some of the earlier prose material into poetry.

Third, although the order of activity in Gen 5 follows that of Gen 1:27–28—creation in image/likeness, creation of male/female, blessing—there is something new in Gen 5:2. God names the new creatures "Adam." This act is both similar to and different from what has transpired in Gen 1. On the first three days in that chapter, God calls light "Day," darkness "Night," dome "Sky," dry land "Earth," and waters "Seas." One could say that God was providing names for those features of the cosmos, but the word "name" itself is not used in Gen 1:4–9. In Gen 5:2, however, the author uses the idiom of "calling a name = naming" (which is also present in Gen 2:20, a pre-Priestly text, when humanity names the animals). One has the sense that the author of Gen 5 viewed the creation of humanity as not having truly been completed until it was provided with a name. And that provision occurs early in Gen 5. Again, Gen 5 seems to be integrating both pre-Priestly and Priestly traditions.

Fourth, in the second line, the author uses the less frequent word to characterize the similarity between humans and deity, "likeness" rather than "image." This word is more abstract; it offers a more physical and less royal connotation than does "image" (though, to be sure, the word "image" reappears in 5:3).

Verse 3 is, perhaps, the most important verse in Gen 5: here the author makes a theological refinement of Gen 1 and a response to the pre-Priestly material with which the author is in vigorous dialogue. Genesis 3–4 offers a picture of humanity that suggests a movement away from the initial state of creation. Humanity is now outside the garden, away from the place where God has walked and talked with humans, who are now wandering the earth and becoming increasingly violent. One might wonder how the notion of humanity presented in Gen 1 relates to this "history."

The author of Gen 5 avers that humanity still exists in some mysterious way in the deity's likeness. To make this case, the Priestly writer formulates a new lineage, one that begins with Adam and then moves to his son Seth. Further, and even more important, Adam has the capacity to pass on the likeness of the deity to his own son. According to this perspective, humanity has not lost the critical closeness to the deity, as has been suggested by the pre-Priestly tradition.

[3–31] The names in Gen 5 overlap with some of those that appear in Gen 4, as shown below.

It is possible that both genealogies stem from a common source since they share at least six names. In both chapters, the genealogies are linear, focusing on the movement from one generation to the next through a single heir. The genealogy in Gen 5 recognizes the presence of Adam's other offspring: "He sired other sons and daughters"; they are of no interest to this author, who nevertheless is concerned to list the lifespans of those in the genealogy. Though there is a general move toward shorter lifespans, Kenan, Jared, Methuselah, and Noah interrupt that sequence. One therefore must be careful not to think that the

Genesis 4	Genesis 5	
Adam	Adam	930 years
Cain	Seth	912 years
Enoch	Enosh	905 years
Irad	Kenan	910 years
Mehujael	Mahalalel	895 years
Methushael	Jared	962 years
Lamech	Enoch	365 years
	Methuselah	969 years
	Lamech	777 years
	Noah	950 years (Gen 9:29)

author thinks humanity is becoming diminished over time. Rather, the imagery is of a humanity living far longer lives *before* the flood than after that deluge. This same claim is made by the Sumerian king list, which attests to stunningly long reigns of the kings on the list. The first two kings on the list reigned for 28,800 and 36,000 years, respectively.

Two individuals receive special mention: Enoch and Lamech. The former is unusual both because he did not live as long as his compatriots in the genealogy and because he "walked with God" and God "took him" (5:24). His lifespan of 365 years may be related to the number of days in a complete year. One might assume that the brevity of his life in this genealogy requires an explanation, and the ambiguous language about walking with God provides the answer. The diction of walking with God is also used by the Priestly writer in a genealogical notice about Noah (Gen 6:9). There it is conjoined to claims about Noah's preternatural righteousness. In these two cases, the verb *hālak* occurs in the hithpael form. Elsewhere the closest parallel occurs in Mal 2:6, where the verb is in qal form. Interestingly, this prophetic text refers to the requirement that Levitical priests should "walk with me in integrity and rightness." Here, as was with Noah, walking with God involves an ethical form of life. That Enoch does not die can be interpreted as a reward for such a style of life, even though it is abbreviated. That he is "taken by God" probably means that he does not die but is translated to heaven. The same language of being taken by the deity is used of Elijah's ascent into heaven (2 Kgs 2:1–12).

Lamech figures prominently at the end of the Cainite genealogy in Gen 4. There he utters poetry about vengeance. In Gen 5, he also gives voice to poetic speech, but it does not bear such negative freight. Instead, he offers an augury based on the birth of his son, Noah. His prediction is based on a wordplay. The name Noah sounds like a Hebrew word meaning to be consoled or comforted (*nḥm*). Noah will provide "relief," a claim that almost certainly refers to

Noah's postdiluvian role as a vintner (Gen 9:20). The relief will be from work that humans must do. That same word for work (*ʿṣh*) appears in Gen 3:17, as does the diction about God cursing the ground. This poetic piece, therefore, offers further evidence of Gen 5's dependence on both pre-Priestly and Priestly traditions.

Lamech's speech within the context of the primeval history is somewhat ironic. Noah is to be, as his father thought, a preeminent figure, but as the flood survivor, not as the first to plant a vineyard. Moreover, his role in creating wine may have provided some with relief from their toil, but it also resulted in various forms of errant behavior, so Gen 9:20–27.

[32] The genealogical formula present in Gen 5 is different in this verse. The verb shifts from "lived" to "was." And Noah is identified as a "son" of five hundred years, not simply "five hundred years old." All the other patriarchs were simply listed along with the cardinal number. This variation suggests that the genealogy is changing and, perhaps, that this formulation does not belong with the preceding verses. The change that is taking place involves the presence of multiple named children in one generation. The genealogy is branching out rather than simply descending. Though other fathers in Gen 5 have multiple children, Noah's children are the first that are all known by name.

Genesis 6:1–8:22
YHWH Regrets Creating Humanity

The two biblical versions of the flood story differ not only in important details but also in their assessment of the flood's significance. The pre-Priestly version downplays the importance of the flood since, in essence, the deluge did not take into account the proclivity of humans to act in evil ways even after the flood has taken place (see Petersen 1976, 438–46; Clines 2012, 74–84). The Priestly version, in contrast, enhances the nature and scale of the flood, such as its source and duration, and understands it to be the occasion for the first covenant that God makes with humans. The Priestly author/editor preserved the earlier version but edited his own version into the earlier "text" so as to lessen the conflict between them. So that readers can appreciate the sophisticated editorial work of the Priestly writer and editor, I have first offered the translation as it left his hand, the so-called canonical version, the admixture of the two versions. However, to make clear the striking differences between the versions, I have printed them up separately (following von Rad 1972).

The biblical flood stories provide one of the most convincing examples of Israel's adaptation of ancient Near Eastern literature for their own purposes. The most important exemplars are the Atrahasis myth and the Gilgamesh epic, both of which are readily available in excellent and widely available translations (e.g., Dalley 1989). Though these texts differ in completeness and in some details, the narrative in these two literatures is more similar than are the two biblical versions to each other. In essence, the ancient Near East tradition involves a decision by Enlil to destroy humanity because they have become numerous and their noise has disturbed his sleep. Enlil first tries to starve them and then afflicts them with disease. Each time humans are told about a ritual that will help them survive. Enlil then decides to send a flood. Another god, Enki, surreptitiously reveals this fact to the flood survivor, variously known in the texts as Atrahasis or Utnapishtim. Enki tells Atrahasis to build an ark, which he seals with tar, and to load it with animals, birds, and his family. The boat that the survivor constructs includes "the seed of all living things," "all that there was," "all my kith and kin," domestic and wild animals, and "all kinds of craftsmen" (Dalley 1989, 110–12). The flood wrought by Enlil comes as a result of a severe thunderstorm, so tremendous that it frightens the gods.

After the flood has raged for seven days, the ship lands on a mountain, where after seven days the survivor sends out three different birds in sequence. After the last one fails to return, the survivor provides a sacrifice and offering. The gods "smelt the pleasant fragrance, the gods gathered like flies around the sacrifice." The gods then decide to make the flood survivor immortal (a status potentially available to Gilgamesh in the epic). At the end of the Atrahasis myth, the text stipulates some rituals that will result in population control, a way to address the problem that the flood was supposed to solve. Since the Atrahasis myth dates to the eighteenth century BCE and since the Gilgamesh epic was known in Syria-Palestine (a Late Bronze Age Akkadian text was found at Megiddo, though this text of the epic did not include the flood episode), there can be little doubt that Israelite authors knew it and also knew that it was part of what would be expected in a credible version of any primeval history. What remains fascinating are the utterly different ways two Israelite authors appropriated this ancient Near Eastern story, as the comments seek to make clear.

Israelite authors confronted a major challenge when retelling the story of the flood. A hallmark of the ancient Near Eastern versions is the conflict between Enlil and Enki, the god who wants to destroy humanity and the god willing to save them. The Israelite authors did not have this luxury. Instead, they needed to tell the story with YHWH in the roles of both Enlil and Enki, a constraint that created a certain tension within the character of the deity.

We begin with Gen 6, which includes two distinct pieces of literature. On the one hand, verses 1–4 report intercourse between minor deities and human women, with an additional note about the Nephilim. On the other hand, 6:5–22 comprises the beginning of the flood narrative. This narrative is made up of two distinct strands: the primary pre-Priestly account and the Priestly version. Verses 5–8 belong to the pre-Priestly version; verses 9–22 belong to the Priestly version. Each of the two biblical versions provides its own rationale for the flood. Moreover, from a redaction-critical perspective, 6:1–4, since it occurs immediately before the Priestly rationale for the flood, functions as an additional warrant for God's decision to send a flood.

> **6:1** When the number of humans began to increase throughout the world,
> daughters were born to them. **2** The sons of God recognized that the
> human daughters were beautiful, and they took whomever they wanted
> as wives for themselves. **3** Then YHWH said, "My spirit will not inhere in
> humanity forever since they are flesh. Their lifespan shall be 120 years."
> **4** (The Nephilim were on the earth in those days, and also afterward.)
> When the sons of God had intercourse with the human daughters, they
> bore children to them. These were the ancient heroes, famous men.
>
> **5** When YHWH recognized the great human evil on the earth, that
> all intentions and plans in their hearts were evil all the time, **6** YHWH

regretted that he had made humanity on the earth. He was terribly sad.[a] 7 YHWH said, "I will wipe out humanity that I have created from the earth—from humanity to the animals to the crawling things to the birds of the sky—because I regret that I made them." 8 Noah, however, found favor in the sight of YHWH.

9 These are the descendants of Noah. Noah was a righteous man, devout in his generation. Noah walked with God. 10 Noah sired three sons: Shem, Ham, and Yapheth.

11 God deemed the earth to be ruined; the earth was filled with violence. 12 God looked at the earth; it was ruined. All flesh had taken a ruinous path on the earth. 13 God said to Noah, "An end is coming to all flesh because the earth is filled with violence because of them. I am about to destroy the earth. 14 Make for yourself an ark out of wood; make compartments in the ark; coat the interior and exterior with tar. 15 This is how you shall make it: 450 feet in length overall, with a beam of 75 feet, and 45 feet high. 16 Make a hatch for the ark; you shall set it one foot from the top deck. You shall place a door in the hull of the ark, and you shall make a second and a third deck below the top deck. 17 I am about to bring floodwaters on the earth to destroy all flesh that has the breath of life from under heaven. Everything on the earth will die. 18 However, I will establish my covenant with you. You shall come into the ark, you, your sons, your wife, and your sons' wives along with you. 19 From everything that lives, from all flesh, you shall bring two of each species into the ark to preserve faunal life along with you. They shall be male and female. 20 From each species of bird, from each species of animal, from each species of that which crawls on the ground, two from all of them will come with you to preserve faunal life. 21 You shall also take provisions from everything that is edible. You shall collect it. It will provide food for you and for them." 22 Noah accomplished everything that God had ordered him to do.

a. Literally, "It was sad to his heart."

7:1 YHWH said to Noah, "You and your entire household shall go into the ark because I have seen that you are righteous before me within this generation. 2 From all the clean animals you shall take seven pairs, the male and its mate; and from the animals that are not clean, one pair, the male and its mate; 3 also from the birds of the heavens, seven pairs, male and female, to keep their progeny alive throughout all the earth. 4 For in seven days I will make it rain upon the earth, forty days and forty nights. I will wipe out all life that I have made from the surface of the earth." 5 Noah did everything that YHWH had ordered him.

6 Noah was six hundred years old when the floodwaters covered the earth. **7** Noah, his sons, his wife, and the wives of his sons went into the ark with him because of the floodwaters. **8** From among the clean animals, from among the animals that are now clean, from among the birds, and from among all that crawl on the ground, **9** they came two by two to Noah and the ark—male and female, just as God had ordered Noah. **10** At the end of seven days, the floodwaters covered the earth.

11 In the six hundredth year of Noah's life, on the seventeenth day of the second month, on that very day, all the springs of the deep burst out and the windows in the heavens broke open. **12** The rain fell on the earth for forty days and forty nights. **13** On that very day, Noah along with Shem, Ham, Yapheth (Noah's sons), Noah's wife, and the three wives of Noah's sons went into the ark, **14** they and all species of wild animals, all species of domestic animals, all species of life that crawls on the ground, and all species of birds.[a] **15** They came to Noah and the ark, two by two, from among all flesh that has the breath of life. **16** Those that went in from among all flesh were male and female, just as God had ordered him. Then YHWH shut him inside.

17 The flood covering the earth persisted for forty days and forty nights. The waters kept getting deeper; they raised the ark. It rose above the earth. **18** The waters rose and grew very deep over the earth. The ark floated on the surface of the waters. **19** The waters rose even more over the earth. They covered all the tall mountains that touched the sky.[b] **20** The waters rose to a depth of twenty-three feet and covered the mountains. **21** All flesh that had moved across the earth died: birds, domestic animals, wild animals, everything that had swarmed across the earth, and all humans as well. **22** All on dry land that had the breath of life in them died. **23** He wiped out everything that had subsisted all across the earth—humanity, animals, swarming things, and birds of the sky. They were wiped off the earth. Only Noah and those with him in the ark remained. **24** The water rose over the earth for 150 days.

a. So LXX; MT adds, "all birds, all with wings."
b. Literally, "that were under the heavens."

8:1 Then God remembered Noah, all the wild animals, and all the domestic animals that were with him in the ark. God made wind blow over the earth, whereupon the waters receded. **2** The springs of the deep and the windows of the heavens were dammed up. And the rain was prevented from falling from the heavens. **3** The water slowly went down off the land. The waters had dropped by the 150th day. **4** On the seventeenth day of the seventh month, the ark landed on top of the Ararat mountain range.

5 The waters slowly continued to go down until the tenth month. On the
first day of the tenth month, the mountaintops began to appear.
6 At the end of forty days, Noah opened the hatch in the ark that he
had made. 7 He released the raven; it flew around until the waters on the
earth had dried up. 8 Then he released the dove[a] to determine whether
the waters had subsided from the surface of the land. 9 The dove could
not find a place to alight, so it returned to the ark, since the waters still
covered all the land. 10 He waited seven more days and again released
the dove from the ark. 11 The dove returned to him in the evening. It had
an olive twig in its beak. Then Noah knew that the waters had subsided
from the land. 12 He waited another seven days and released the dove;
this time it did not return.
13 On the first day of the first month during his 601st year, the waters
dried up from the land. Noah removed the cover of the ark and looked out.
The surface of the ground had dried out. 14 On the twenty-seventh day
of the second month, the earth was dry. 15 God said to Noah, 16 "Leave
the ark, you, your wife, your sons, and the wives of your sons, who are
with you. 17 Bring out with you all that is alive with you, all flesh, birds,
animals, everything that crawls on the ground. They shall move about,
be fertile, and become numerous throughout the earth." 18 Noah, his sons,
his wife, and the wives of his sons who were with him left. 19 All the wild
animals, all the domestic animals, all the birds, everything that crawls on
the ground[b] left the ark.
20 Then Noah built an altar to YHWH. He selected from among all
the clean animals and from among all the clean birds and offered burnt
offerings on the altar. 21 YHWH inhaled the fragrant odor, and YHWH
thought to himself, "I will never again curse the ground on account of
humanity because the inclination of the human heart is evil from its
youth. I will never again strike dead all life as I have just done.

22 "As long as the earth exists,
planting and harvest, cold and warmth,
summer and winter, day and night
will not cease."

a. MT "the dove from him," which may mean "his dove," a trained bird.

b. So LXX. MT reads, "All the animals, all the crawling things, all the birds, everything that crawls on the ground."

[6:1–4] These four verses offer a brief narrative about the origins of human mortality. To this extent, it may be characterized as a myth of organization. Its basic plot does not depend upon a narrative known elsewhere in the ancient Near East. Yet the biblical narrative does share one important feature with the Atrahasis myth: its reference to an increase in the population of humanity (v. 1). In the Atrahasis myth, this is viewed as a problem, with the ensuing flood as an attempt to decrease the number of people who are disturbing the gods. In Gen 6, by contrast, the increased population is, in and of itself, not a problem. Nonetheless, the deity takes action as soon as the marriage between human women and minor male deities has taken place. The deity knows that the boundary between the world of the gods and the world of humans has been crossed, an issue already raised in Gen 3:22, and that soon progeny, as partially divine, might live "forever."

In Gen 3, the threat of humanity living forever depends upon action by humans: their possibly returning to the garden and eating from the tree of life. In Gen 6, however, the threat comes from minor deities who cohabited with beautiful women.[1] These women would likely give birth to a generation of creatures who were, in theory, part divine and part human. To address this situation, the deity, in a brief and abrupt monologue, announces that human beings will live no longer than 120 years. To this extent and from a redaction-critical point of view, this limitation puts an end to the longevity reported in Gen 5.

The diction present in the narrative is significant. By choosing the word "daughters" instead of "women," the author focuses on the notion of family, progeny, and generational descent, all of which are important in the primeval history. Moreover, the notion of "daughters" corresponds to the way in which the minor deities are described as "sons." The significance of word choice continues in 6:3. The Hebrew word for "spirit" in 6:3 is different from the Hebrew phrase "breath of life" in 2:7. And the word "flesh" in 6:3 does not appear in Gen 2–3. Instead, the author of this compact narrative has chosen to define humanity in terms different from the primary story of creation, which focuses on humanity as taken from earth (cf. Isa 40:5 for another instance in which humanity is characterized as "flesh").

As the parentheses in the translation suggest, 6:4a is intrusive. A later editor wanted to offer an explanatory gloss, identifying the heroes mentioned at the end of the 6:4 with the giants attested in Num 13:33. There, Israelites claim to have seen Nephilim, the progenitors of the Anakites, a people famous for their size (so, e.g., Deut 2:10). That this would mean the Nephilim have survived the flood did not apparently bother this editor.

Genesis 6:1–4 now stands immediately before the flood narrative. Hence, from a redaction-critical perspective, one may read it as evidence of the "ruin" (6:12) that has pervaded the cosmos. The presence of the term "flesh" in the Priestly version of the flood suggests that 6:1–4 was written by someone familiar

1. The "sons of God" (RSV: Deut 32:8 [Q, LXX]; Job 1:6; 2:1; and Ps 29:1 MT) make up the divine plurality reflected in Gen 1:26 and 3:22. In addition, they belong to the divine council, evidence of which is also found in 1 Kgs 22; Isa 6; and Ps 82:1.

with the Priestly account. From the perspective of the author of 6:1–4, "all flesh" (6:12) includes the generation born to human women mating with divine fathers. In sum, Gen 6:1–4 bears multiple meanings. The story functions as a mythic etiology for humanity's limited lifespan and as one of the rationales for the flood.

Pre-Priestly Version of the Flood
(Gen 6:5–8; 7:1–5, 7, 16b, 8–10, 12, 17, 22–23;
8:6a, 2b, 3a, 6b, 8–12, 13b, 20–22)

6:5 When YHWH recognized the great human evil on the earth, that all
intentions and plans in their hearts were evil all the time, **6** YHWH regretted that he had made humanity on the earth. He was terribly sad. **7** YHWH
said, "I will wipe out humanity that I have created from the earth—from
humanity to the animals to the crawling things to the birds of the sky—
because I regret that I made them." 8 Noah, however, found favor in the
sight of YHWH.

7:1 YHWH said to Noah, "You and your entire household shall go into
the ark because I have seen that you are righteous before me within this
generation. **2** From all the clean animals you shall take seven pairs, the
male and its mate; and from the animals that are not clean, one pair, the
male and its mate; **3** also, from the birds of the heavens, seven pairs, male
and female, to keep their progeny alive throughout all the earth. **4** For in
seven days I will make it rain upon the earth, forty days and forty nights.
I will wipe out all life that I have made from the surface of the earth."
5 Noah did everything that YHWH had ordered him.

7 Noah, his sons, his wife, and the wives of his sons went into the ark
with him because of the floodwaters.

16b Then YHWH shut him inside.

8 From among the clean animals, from among the animals that are
now clean, from among the birds, and from among all that crawl on the
ground, **9** they came two by two to Noah and the ark—male and female,
just as God had ordered Noah. **10** At the end of seven days, floodwaters
covered the earth.

12 The rain fell on the earth for forty days and forty nights.

17 The flood covering the earth persisted for forty days and forty
nights. The waters kept getting deeper; they raised the ark. It rose above
the earth. **22** All on dry land that had the breath of life in them died. **23** He
wiped out everything that had subsisted all across the earth—humanity,
animals, swarming things, and birds of the sky. They were wiped off the
earth. Only Noah and those with him in the ark remained.

8:6a At the end of forty days, **2b** the rain was prevented from falling
from the heavens. **3a** The water slowly went down off the land.

6b Noah opened the hatch in the ark that he had made. **8** Then he
released the dove to determine whether the waters had subsided from
the surface of the land. **9** The dove could not find a place to alight, so it
returned to the ark, since the water still covered all the land. **10** He waited
seven more days and again released the dove from the ark. **11** The dove
returned to him in the evening. It had an olive twig in its beak. Then Noah
knew that the water had subsided from the land. **12** He waited another
seven days and released the dove; this time it did not return.

13b Noah removed the cover of the ark and looked out. The surface of
the ground had dried out.

20 Then Noah built an altar to YHWH. He selected from among all
the clean animals and from among all the clean birds and offered burnt
offerings on the altar. **21** YHWH inhaled the fragrant odor, and YHWH
thought to himself, "I will never again curse the ground on account of
humanity because the inclination of the human heart is evil from its
youth. I will never again strike dead all life as I have just done.

22 "As long as the earth exists,
  planting and harvest, cold and warmth,
summer and winter, day and night
  will not cease."

[6:5–8] Genesis 6 reflects the interest of the gods in the world of human affairs. Genesis 6:2 reports that the minor deities have recognized that human women are beautiful. In Gen 6:5, YHWH recognizes that humans are acting innately and all the time with moral abandon. Both verses attest to the fact that the deities that comprise the divine council are cognizant of the created world, of both its beauty and its sin. The author repeats the word "all" in 6:5, emphasizing the totality of human evil.

YHWH regrets having made humanity, a response that leads to a decision to wipe out not only humanity, but also all other living creatures. YHWH's assessment of humanity leads to his decision to wipe out all life. The verb "wipe out" (*mḥh*) bears the meaning of total destruction, so Judg 21:17 in referring to the possibility of the annihilation of the tribe of Benjamin. Unlike the later Priestly writer (6:12), this author presents a picture of human sin that results also in the punishment of life that is innocent. Human evil results in an ecological disaster.

The notion of the deity regretting something or changing his mind is not infrequent in the OT (cf. Jonah 3:10; Jer 26:13). However, in these cases, the regretting or changing takes place before the action that would be regretted.

The only other instance in which the deity regrets action already taken is 1 Sam 15:11, a text in which YHWH regrets having made Saul king. (This highly anthropomorphic view of the deity's feelings and the changing of the deity's mind obviously stands in contrast with most other ancient Israelite views: see 1 Sam 15:29; Num 23:19; cf. Exod 32:14.)

In Gen 6:7, the presence of the verb "to create" (*br*ʾ), which appears in P (Gen 1:1, 27; 2:3–4; 5:1–2), strongly suggests that the Priestly author introduces this language into the pre-Priestly material. He would do so to highlight his claim that the flood involves the destruction of the entire created order, not just the destruction of humanity, which is the punishment envisioned by the pre-Priestly author. The text in its original form emphasizes just the destruction of humanity, but the redacted form of the text highlights the impact of human sin on all animal life. Human sin has led to an ecological catastrophe, especially in the eyes of the Priestly editor.

Noah is chosen to survive the flood because "he found favor in the eyes of YHWH." The visual diction continues: God has earlier "seen" that humans are evil. The idiom of finding favor in someone's eyes is common in the OT. Perhaps the text most similar to Gen 6:7 is Exod 33:17, in which the deity reports to Moses that he has found favor in God's eyes. There, like the case in Gen 6:8, the approbation does not involve a claim about either person's moral quality. Such was also the case with the survivor of the flood in the ancient Near Eastern tradition. The situation is different in the Priestly version, a tradition in which an individual and others survive due to Noah's righteousness.

[7:1–8:13b] The pre-Priestly view of the flood itself is both similar to and different from its ancient Near Eastern predecessors. To understand this relationship, as well as to enable a comparison with the later Priestly view of the flood, it is important to identify the source of the flood, the duration of the flood, and what survives the flood. For this version of the flood, the punishment by flood results from a heavy rain. As for the calendar, the rain falls for forty days. Next is the sending out of three birds over a period of twenty-one days. The flood therefore lasts sixty-one days. Noah and his family, along with seven pairs of clean animals and one pair of unclean animals, survive the flood. It is clear, based on the postflood sacrifice, that the clean animals are needed for proper sacrificial rituals. (The phrase "two by two" and the divine name "God" in 6:9 likely stem from an editor who tried to integrate the pre-Priestly with the Priestly accounts; so Speiser 1964, 52–53.)

The pre-Priestly flood lasts longer than the one in other ancient Near Eastern traditions. However, it is far less dramatic. The author narrates the flood itself in less than four full verses. Far more attention is devoted to the drying up of the earth and the threefold sending out of the dove. On the assumption that the pre-Priestly version of the flood has been well preserved, this version downplays the flood. The reason for that diminished narration occurs in the postflood scene.

[8:20–22] As with the flood, the pre-Priestly version of the narrative is both similar to and different from other ancient Near Eastern traditions. It is similar because Noah, like Utnapishtim/Atrahasis, offers a sacrifice; and in both traditions, the deity senses the fragrance of the offering. However, the differences are quite significant. In the ancient Near Eastern story, the survivor is granted immortality. Not so with Noah. Instead, the pre-Priestly version emphasizes the enduring quality of the natural order. Time, the seasons, and the agricultural year will endure. The poetry occurs in the form of binary opposites. Of the four, only one involves humanity: planting and harvest. The other three will transpire even if humanity is not present. It is as if the pre-Priestly author wants to emphasize that the earth can continue in a proper manner even if a sinful humanity does not live on it. This view of the earth is, of course, very different from that of the Priestly author (so 6:11).

Even more important, the issue of human immorality reappears. YHWH recognizes, as he has before the flood, that humans are innately evil, a claim that implicitly applies to the survivor of the flood and his family. As a result, YHWH will never again curse the ground or strike dead all life. (If 8:21 implies that the flood was a cursing of the ground, the pre-Priestly writer understands God to have cursed the ground on two different occasions, here and in Gen 3:17.) Such action does not achieve the implicit goal of providing a human being who would behave properly. The deity will need to accommodate humans as they are, sinful from their very beginnings as "youth." This claim by the pre-Priestly writer raises questions about what the flood accomplishes. It does yield a divine guarantee about the natural order, but only as long as the earth exists. As for humanity, many have been struck dead, presumably due to humanity's errant ways. But the survivor will essentially be no better than those who have died.

Priestly Version of the Flood

(Gen 6:9–22; 7:6, 11, 13–16a, 18–21, 24;
8:1–2a, 3b, 4–5, 7, 13a, 14, 15–19; 9:1–17)

6:9 These are the descendants of Noah. Noah was a righteous man, devout
in his generation. Noah walked with God. 10 Noah sired three sons: Shem,
Ham, and Yapheth.

11 God deemed the earth to be ruined; the earth was filled with violence. 12 God looked at the earth; it was ruined. All flesh had taken a
ruinous path on the earth. 13 God said to Noah, "An end is coming for all
flesh because the earth is filled with violence because of them. I am about
to destroy the earth. 14 Make for yourself an ark out of wood; make compartments in the ark; coat the interior and exterior with tar. 15 This is how
you shall make it: 450 feet in length overall, with a beam of 75 feet, and

45 feet high. **16** Make a hatch for the ark; you shall set it one foot from the top deck. You shall place a door in the hull of the ark. And you shall make a second and a third deck below the top deck. **17** I am about to bring floodwaters on the earth in order to destroy all flesh that has the breath of life from under heaven. Everything on the earth will die. **18** However, I will establish my covenant with you. You shall come into the ark, you, your sons, your wife, and your sons' wives along with you. **19** From everything that lives, from all flesh, you shall bring two of each species into the ark to preserve faunal life along with you. They shall be male and female. **20** From each species of bird, from each species of animal, from each species of what crawls on the ground, two from each for all of them shall come with you in order to preserve faunal life. **21** You shall also take provisions from everything that is edible. You shall collect it. It will provide food for you and for them." **22** Noah accomplished everything that God had ordered him to do.

7:6 Noah was six hundred years old when the floodwaters covered the earth.

11 In the six hundredth year of Noah's life, on the seventeenth day of the second month, on that very day, all the springs of the deep burst out and the windows in the heavens broke open. **13** On that very day, Noah along with Shem, Ham, Yapheth—Noah's sons—Noah's wife, and the three wives of Noah's sons went into the ark, **14** they and all species of wild animals, all species of domestic animals, all species of life that crawls on the ground, all species of birds. **15** They came to Noah and the ark, two by two, from among all flesh that has the breath of life. **16a** Those that went in from among all flesh were male and female, just as God had ordered him.

18 The waters rose and grew very deep over the earth. The ark floated on the surface of the waters. **19** The waters rose even more over the earth. They covered all the tall mountains that touched the sky. **20** The waters rose to a depth of twenty-three feet and covered the mountains. **21** All flesh that had moved across the earth died: birds, domestic animals, wild animals, everything that had swarmed across the earth—and all humans as well. **24** The water rose over the earth for 150 days.

8:1 Then God remembered Noah, all the wild animals, and all the domestic animals that were with him in the ark. God made wind blow over the earth, whereupon the water receded. **2a** The springs of the deep and the windows of the heavens were dammed up. **3b** The waters had dropped by the 150th day. **4** On the seventeenth day of the seventh month, the ark landed on top of the Ararat mountain range. **5** The waters slowly continued to go down until the tenth month. On the first day of the tenth month, the mountaintops began to appear.

7 He released the raven; it flew around until the waters on the earth had
dried up. 13a On the first day of the first month during his 601st year, the
waters dried up from the land. 14 On the twenty-seventh day of the second
month, the earth was dry. 15 God said to Noah, 16 "Leave the ark, you, your
wife, your sons, and the wives of your sons, who are with you. 17 Bring out
with you all that is alive, all flesh, birds, animals, everything that crawls
on the ground. They shall move about, be fertile, and become numerous
throughout the earth." 18 Noah, his sons, his wife, and the wives of his sons
who were with him left. 19 All the wild animals, all the domestic animals,
all the birds, everything that crawls on the ground left the ark.

At the outset, it is helpful to identify some of the primary differences between the Priestly and other flood accounts. As with the pre-Priestly version, the deity offers a moral rationale for the flood. But the Priestly author provides a far broader indictment: the earth has been ruined and is full of violence. Rather than mention just humanity, the Priestly author condemns "all flesh," a phrase that includes fauna as well as humanity. Moreover, the source of the flood is different from both the ancient Near Eastern and the pre-Priestly accounts. The floodwaters do not come from rain but from the waters named in Gen 1:2 that, on the second day of creation, had been located both below and above the realm of the earth. As for chronology, the Priestly author dates various moments of the flood according to Noah's age. The flood breaks out on the seventeenth day of the second month of Noah's six hundredth year. The waters dry up on the twenty-seventh day of the second month of Noah's 601st year. The flood therefore lasts a little longer than one year. This stands in marked contrast to the weeklong flood in ancient Near Eastern texts and to the two-month flood in the pre-Priestly text. Finally, those who survive the flood are Noah's family and one pair of all animals. The Priestly source cannot not allow for the distinction between clean and unclean animals until the Priestly torah has been revealed to Moses. Unlike both the ancient Near Eastern and the pre-Priestly account, there can therefore be no sacrifice in the postflood scene. Instead, the Priestly version offers a grander conclusion: the creation of a covenant between God and humanity with the fauna. All these features of the flood in the Priestly tradition allow one to conclude that the flood is a cosmic and theologically significant moment for the Priestly writer, more so than for either the ancient Near Eastern or the pre-Priestly accounts.

[6:9–22] The Priestly flood narrative is introduced by one of the *tôlədōt* formulae, identifying Noah's progeny. (The prior formula names the descendants of Adam [Gen 5:1], and the next one names the descendants of Noah's sons [10:1].) The genealogical note is enhanced by comments about Noah's righteousness. Noah, like Job, was known for his righteous and devout behavior (Job 1:1). Both of them belong on the list of moral heroes cited by Ezekiel (14:14). These biblical characters are so righteous that they can save others by their righteousness. In the cases of Noah and Job, this claim refers to their ability to save members of their families; Noah does so by having them with him on the ark during the flood. Not only that, Noah also "walked with God," a quality that he shares with Enoch (Gen 5:22). That phrase, too, is related to an ethical style of life (see comments on Gen 5).

The Priestly rationale for the flood offers a far broader indictment than that of his predecessor. The entire earth and all flesh are ruined. The verb "ruined" (*šḥt*, 6:11–13, 17; 9:11, 15) is used elsewhere to describe a clay vessel that is ruined while it is being made (Jer 18:4) and to characterize a garment that has been ruined by water and dirt (13:7). The latter text comments, "It was good for nothing." So was the earth, according to the Priestly theologian. The earth had been ruined because of rampant violence. It is, perhaps, no surprise that another member of the Priestly tradition, Ezekiel, also indicts Israel for violence. He characterizes violence as "bloody crimes" (7:23) and "oppression" (45:9), the sorts of activity that lie behind the more general diction in Gen 6:11. Moreover, the Priestly writer deems all flesh to have acted in ruinous ways, a judgment not shared by the pre-Priestly author. It is as if the Priestly thinker finds it necessary to argue that since all fauna perishes, their punishment must be deserved.

The Genesis description of the ark and its construction share features with the boat described in the Gilgamesh epic. Both are sealed with tar and have multiple decks, a hatch, dimensions described, a door, and a porthole or hatch. Clearly, the Priestly author knew the ancient Near Eastern story of the flood in many of its particulars.

Immediately after the bleak judgment that all flesh will die, God makes provision for life to continue. The provision is via a covenant (6:18) with Noah. Only in Gen 9 does the Priestly author explain that the covenant will exist not only between God and Noah, but also between God and Noah's descendants and all fauna. This foreshadowing of the covenant in 6:18 establishes the basis for the deity's directive that not only Noah's family shall be present in the ark, but also a male and female of "everything that lives." There is, of course, an implicit tension between the Priestly author's judgment that all flesh has acted ruinously and deserves to die and that representatives of all flesh shall survive the flood. By dint of God's order that Noah take on board food for both humans and animals ("them" in 6:21), it is clear that the deity intends for both humans and animals to survive the flood.

[7:6, 11, 13–16a, 18–21, 24] The verses from the Priestly hand in Gen 7 are noteworthy in the way they describe the source for the floodwaters. They do not stem from storm clouds. Rather, they comprise water breaking into the space around the earth from both above and below the earth. These are the primordial waters described by the Priestly writer in Gen 1:2, the waters that, when separated on the second day of creation, were located both above the heavens and below the earth. The notion that the deity controls and establishes limits or boundaries for these cosmic waters is attested elsewhere in the OT. Job 38:8 refers to waters having been limited by bounds, bars, and doors. Proverbs 8:29 speaks of limits for the sea, and 8:28 even speaks of "the springs of the deep," the same phrase that appears in Gen 7:11.

The noun translated "flood" appears in Ps 29:10, where God is enthroned above the floodwaters, those waters that the deity has ordered into place in creation. According to Gen 7:11, the waters that have been separated and restrained now break through their boundaries and wash into the space where humans and animals live. It is nothing less than a reversion to the state of the universe before God's acts of creation.

There is a tension between the abrupt breaking out of water from both above and below the earth and the narration of the floodwaters in 7:18–20, 24. Instead of envisioning a tidal wave, the Priestly writer depicts the waters as slowly rising until the ship floats well above the earth. Still, the inexorably rising water leads to a truly apocalyptic destruction of all human and animal life.

[8:1–2a, 3b, 4–5, 7, 13a, 15–19] "God remembered Noah" is a striking anthropomorphism from the hand of the Priestly author. The claim is part of the theology embedded in the Noachian covenant. That God remembers Noah offers a warrant for thinking that God will honor the promise made in Gen 9, that the deity will remember the covenant made between God and all flesh.

As a result of that remembrance, God slowly makes the flood subside, a process that mirrors the waters that earlier rose slowly. To stop the flood, the deity must close the apertures in the heavens and the deep from which the floodwaters stem. The Priestly writer is far more interested in the gradual diminution of the flood than he is in narrating the traditional account involving the release of multiple birds. In 8:15, direct communication between God and Noah resumes, having stopped in 6:21 with the orders on what is to be taken onto the ark. Now God orders those on the ark to leave. More important than the report about the birds is the command to leave the ark and, even more, the recapitulation of language found in Gen 1 to be fertile and become numerous. In Gen 1, such diction is presented in imperative language and directed to fish and fowl (1:22) and humans (1:28). In 8:17 it appears in the indicative and is directed to the animals. One may wonder about the reason for this concern about faunal fertility. The answer comes in Gen 9: now humans may kill animals for food. Hence, since their numbers will fall due to human predation, the animals must become numerous for their species to survive. Humans are to be fertile and numerous to take charge of the earth; animals are to become numerous to be food for humans.

Due to the length of this section, the translation and comments on Gen 9, which provides the Priestly postflood scene, occur in the next chapter.

Genesis 9:1–17
God Makes a Covenant with Noah, His Progeny, and All Creatures

After the brief conclusion of the primary, pre-Priestly author's flood account (Gen 8:20–22), the Priestly author weighs in with a much fuller and more theologically creative alternative. This author takes the postflood moment as the occasion to introduce the first covenant promulgated by God in the book of Genesis. This strategy is consistent with the elevated significance with which the Priestly writer portrays the flood story as a whole. His version is longer and of greater scope than is the version of the primary author. The primary author's conclusion recapitulates the notion of humans' propensity to err; the Priestly author links his conclusion to hallmarks of Gen 1: the notion of blessing and the admonition to propagate and fill the earth.

The Priestly postflood account is more complex than that of the non-Priestly writer. The act is made up of two scenes. The first one (9:1–7) involves a reordering of the world as created in Gen 1. God now enlarges the human diet by permitting them to eat animal flesh. The second (vv. 8–17) reports that God makes a covenant with all "flesh." "Flesh" is, therefore, a motif that integrates these two scenes. Still, the first scene focuses on permissible (and, by implication, impermissible) death, whereas the second scene highlights God's preservation of all life. Direct discourse is prominent in these verses. "God spoke" appears four times: 9:1, 8, 12, and 17.

The first scene is made up of one speech; the second scene includes three speeches. In every instance, the speaker is God. The first scene is related directly to Gen 1 since it commends a change from the dietary practice stipulated in Gen 1:29. Humans are now permitted to eat the flesh of animals. Yet 1:30 does not extend that permission to animals, and neither does Gen 9. In the first scene, God addresses both Noah and his sons. The second scene does not involve Gen 1 and presents, instead, reflection about the recent flood and the promise that no more such floods will occur. This promise is expressed in the first covenant reported by the Priestly writer (there will be another in Gen 17). The first two speeches in the second scene are addressed to Noah and his sons; the last speech is apparently offered only to Noah.

The speeches in these two scenes address multiple topics: diet, killing, and covenant. The topics are diverse enough to suggest that these verses are an amalgam from various hands, each using the moment immediately after the flood to authorize an important practice or concept.

The issues of life and death inhere in the postflood accounts preserved in ancient Near Eastern texts, though in ways quite different from that of the Priestly writer. In the flood account as preserved in the Gilgamesh epic, Enlil, whose plans to kill off humanity have been frustrated by Enki, grants eternal life to the survivor of the flood. By way of contrast, the rituals and personnel listed at the end of the second tablet of the Atrahasis epic report the existence of women who will bear children and several classes of women who will apparently kill children. The biblical postflood accounts stand in stark contrast. Instead of offering eternal life, God makes an "eternal" covenant with Noah and his progeny. Instead of death to certain children, God advocates death for those who kill a human. Death and life resound in both the ancient Near Eastern and the Priestly postflood accounts, though in strikingly different ways.

> **9:1** God blessed Noah and his sons. He said to them, "Be fecund and
> become numerous; fill the earth! **2** Fear and terror of you will fall upon
> all earthly animal life—from the birds of the air to everything that moves
> upon the ground to all the fish of the sea. They have been given into your
> control. **3** Everything that moves, that which is still alive, will become a
> source of food. Just as I gave you green plants, now [I give you] every-
> thing. **4** However, you shall not consume flesh with its lifeblood in it.
> **5** Moreover, I will demand [something] for your own lifeblood. I will
> demand it from any animal, and I will demand it from any human: one
> person for another human life.
>
> **6** "Whoever pours out human blood,
> that person's blood will be poured out by another person;
> because in the image of God,
> he made humanity.
> **7** As for you, be fecund and become numerous.
> Move throughout the earth and rule over it."[a]
>
> **8** God said to Noah and his sons who were with him, **9** "I am making
> my covenant with you and with your progeny after you, **10** and with every
> living creature that is with you—birds, domesticated animals, all wild
> animals, every animal that came out of the ark with you.[b] **11** I will keep
> my covenant with you. Never again will all flesh be destroyed[c] by flood-
> waters. Never again will there be a flood to destroy the earth." **12** God
> said, "This is the sign of the covenant that I am drawing up between
> me and you and all living creatures with you for enduring generations.
> **13** I have placed my bow in the clouds; it will be a sign of the covenant
> between me and the earth. **14** When I make clouds appear over the earth,
> and the bow appears in the clouds, **15** then I will remember my covenant

that is between you, me, and every living fleshly creature;[d] there will never again be floodwaters to destroy all flesh. 16 When the bow is in the heavens, I will see it and remember the enduring covenant between God and every living fleshly creature that is on the earth." 17 God said to Noah, "This is the sign of the covenant that I have made between me and all flesh that is on the earth."

a. MT *ûrəbû*, "multiply," is almost certainly a scribal error for *ûrədû*, which appears in Gen 1:28.

b. Omitting the final three words of the verse in the MT, "to all wild animals," a dittographic expansion of that same phrase from earlier in the verse. Those three words do not appear in the LXX.

c. Literally, "cut off."

d. Integrating *bĕkol bāśār* into the translation is difficult, as it is in v. 16.

[9:1–7] The Priestly account of the flood involves a virtual reversion to the pre-creation state. As a result, one should expect that some of what has occurred at the time of creation will need recapitulation. Humans do not need to be created, but something else is needed to enable the created order to function properly again. As a result, God rehearses the action attested in Gen 1:28. First, there is an act of blessing (see Gen 1:22, 28; 2:3; 5:2).

The report of an act of blessing raises the same question prompted by Gen 1:22, 28; 2:3. Does the blessing happen in the speech that reports blessing? Or does the blessing happen independently of the deity's speech? In the first two of the aforementioned texts, the announcement of blessing is followed immediately by a divine speech. In both cases, the speech offers a command: "Be fruitful and multiply!" It is difficult to construe that command as an act of blessing, though the capacity for fertility may be construed as a blessing, as in Gen 17:16, "I will bless her, and moreover I will give you a son by her" (NRSV). Then, in Gen 2:3, another Priestly text, God blesses the Sabbath, but the author offers no divine discourse. One may, therefore, infer that the blessing is an independent act of the deity; it happens before God speaks. Blessing in Gen 9 is God's beneficent action, which continues from the time of creation. God has earlier blessed the birds, fish, humans, and the Sabbath. Now God reaffirms the blessing of humans by blessing the flood survivor and his sons.

The set of imperatives in 9:1 is not as long as that in Gen 1:28: the command to "subdue" has been omitted, though presumably not abrogated. It has been replaced here, however, with the notion of "fear and terror." Humans are not ordered to terrorize animals. Instead, what is allowed in 9:3, the consumption of animal flesh, naturally means that animals will fear humans. Though the Priestly writer knows that humans are permitted to kill and consume only certain animals (see Lev 11:2–23 for the list of permissible animals, whose basic categories are land animals, fish, fowl, and insects), the writer also knows that animals will fear that such may be their fate. Hence, Gen 9:2 refers to all animal life, not simply those that humans will eat. Further, one senses that in this scene the Priestly writer is describing a time before the ritual Torah has been provided. As 9:3 puts it, "every moving creature" may be consumed. Here the Priestly writer may also be thinking that other humans may properly eat foods that Israelites do not eat.

In this first speech, the deity announces a new state of affairs within the created order. The relationship between humans and the animal kingdom will change. Now the animals will dread their human overlords. The careful reader of 9:2 will, however, recognize that the dictions, "fear and terror" and "authority," have been used elsewhere in the OT. "Fear and terror" describe the dread that the "the nations" will experience when Israel enters the land (so Deut 11:25). Moreover, the literal phrase "into your hand," translated "authority" above, appears in texts that describe YHWH giving control of the local population to the conquering Israelites (e.g., Josh 10:19; Judg 3:28). From the perspective of the animals, humans are now enemy troops. From the perspective of the Israelites, animals are there to be killed, just as were their human enemies.[1] The reason for this changed relationship appears in Gen 9:3. Humans may now kill animals as a source for food. No animal is forbidden, yet. That will come with the Priestly torah (Lev 11; cf. Deut 14:3–21). But there is a hint of that torah in the phrase, "that which is still alive." Leviticus 11:39 and Deut 14:21 recognize that humans might eat the flesh of an animal that they did not kill. Those who do such will become unclean and must undergo a rite of purification. However, at least in Deut 14, such flesh can be consumed by an alien or a foreigner without such a penalty. Here again, the postflood period is not the same primeval history as before the flood. Israelite particularities are beginning to appear.

As soon as animal flesh is offered as a source of food, there is a corresponding prohibition: humans may not eat the blood found in a freshly killed animal. So 9:3 hints at a Priestly torah; 9:4, in which imperative discourse resumes, derives from it. The Priestly writer stipulates that humans may not eat flesh with blood still in it. According to Lev 17:10, 13–14 and Deut 12:23, this stricture was laid only on Israelites and those living with them. In Gen 9, it has been universalized. One might imagine that Gen 9:4 was inserted by a Priestly scribe, someone interested in placing that mandate in an early and prominent place. The rationale for this prohibition hinges on the close association between blood and life, so Lev 17:14 and the proper use of the blood in the altar ritual (17:11). The verse solves a problem created by the new condition in which humans can now eat the flesh of animals. God solves that problem with a new command.

1. Lohfink understood this new situation well: "The peace between human and animal that was characteristic of Paradise is replaced by a new order of war: note, a war between human and animal, not between human beings" (1984, 124).

Despite the differences between the primary authors and the Priestly writers' conclusion to the flood story, in both instances the animals, creatures that have been on the ark with humans, die. In one case, they are sacrificed, becoming food for the deity; in the other case, they are killed, becoming food for humans.

Verses 5–6 of Gen 9 seem, at first glance, unrelated to the prior verses in the postflood account. However, there are two connections. The first link is provided by two words in 9:4 that are repeated in 9:5: "blood" and "life." It is as if the writer says, since those words are under discussion, here are some related issues that need to be addressed now. Second, both verses 4 and 5 commence with the same particle (*ʾak*). This particle never appears in such a repeated fashion elsewhere in the OT. One has the sense that a scribe repeated it here to introduce information that he deemed appropriate. That scribe introduced a new issue, the killing of a human. However, this topic is linked to the foregoing verse by the notion of lifeblood. The expansion highlights the inestimable value of a person's life. If someone is killed, whether by another human or an animal (see Exod 21:28–32 and other ANE texts) and presumably apart from war, the deity seeks recompense.

Genesis 9:5 is repetitive; it is possible to imagine a poetic structure of three parallel lines, with each one including the verb "demand" (*drš*). The repetition of that verb presses the interpreter to ask: What is the deity demanding? The law regarding an ox that gores a human makes clear that the animal is to be killed (Exod 21:28–32). Moreover, if the animal has behaved that way in the past, the owner will also be put to death. Does that mean a human who kills another human should routinely be executed? Genesis 9:5 does not answer that question; verse 6, however, does.

If 9:5 is poem-like, 9:6 is clearly poetry. It is printed so in most English translations as well as in the critical edition of the Hebrew Bible (*BHS*). If 9:5 is an addition to 9:4, then 9:6 is probably an addendum to 9:5. Hence, verses 5–6 are editorial expansions devoted to the topic of the spilling of human blood. Verse 7 functions as the second page of an envelope, rehearsing the language found in the first line of this speech. The diction in 9:7 is odd, since *šrṣ* is most often used of animals. Still, the same basic mandate is given at both the beginning and the end of this scene: become numerous. This is especially apt coming at a time when the human race has been radically depleted by the flood.

There is a certain logic to these additions concerning the killing of humans. If people kill each other, they will have a difficult time propagating and filling the earth. That same issue, human propagation, is addressed at the end of the flood account in the Atrahasis myth. (The texts could not be more different, however. Atrahasis seems interested in *limiting* the growth of the human race.)

That someone who spills human blood should have his blood spilled by a human exemplifies the principle of talion (punishment in kind, e.g., "an eye for an eye"). The two cola of 9:6a really require no warrant. However, the biblical author provides one anyway (v. 6b). It is not a legal principle; rather, it is a theological norm. A spiller of blood, which apparently is not limited to murder, has defamed humans, who are created in the divine image. As a result, the deity permits, even requires, humans to avenge that death. To cause the death of a human constitutes an offense against the deity who has created that person (on blood in Gen 9, see Petersen 2012, 242–50).

[8–17] The second scene is made up of three speeches rather than the solitary speech of the first scene. Just as the first scene was enclosed by similar diction, so too is the second one, the making of a covenant. The speeches seem highly repetitive. Further, Noah and his sons continue to be addressed (the "you" in vv. 9, 11, 12 is plural), though that situation changes in the final speech (v. 17).

The first speech of the second scene (vv. 8–11) initiates a new topic: covenant. Here the Priestly author is doing significant conceptual work. He introduces a topos (topic): a covenant with its "sign"; this topos will appear also in Gen 17. By means of this topos, the Priestly author is able to integrate the primeval period with that of the early family stories. In so doing, the theologian affirms that God works in similar ways throughout various periods and with various entities, both human and nonhuman. In both Gen 9 and 17, a covenant works differently from the Sinaitic covenant (Exodus) and its reflexes (Deuteronomy). There, the primary obligation rests upon humans. In Gen 9, God takes on the obligation of preserving life for both humans and animals. Covenant here really means a divine oath.

Both the non-Priestly and Priestly postflood scenes focus on a stable future. The non-Priestly source talks about "the ground" and "the earth." God will never curse the ground; the earth will continue in its natural order. Humans here are something of an afterthought. The Priestly author, in contrast, highlights "life," both animal life and human life, as what God has created. God makes a covenant with such life. Hence, to call this covenant Noachian is a misnomer; it is a covenant with all life.

In 9:11, the "you" is plural, referring presumably to Noah and his sons and their wives, but possibly to the animals and birds as well. Verse 11 is also repetitive. Some scholars have suggested that the two negative asseverations preserve two alternative accounts (so Westermann 1984, 471). It is, however, better to construe these two sentences as parallel constructions, similar to structures attested in Hebrew poetry. In so doing, the lines demonstrate that both "all flesh" and "the earth" are the object of God's concern. One does wonder why the author emphasizes that God will never destroy by using a flood. Does the author mean to leave open the option that God can still use drought, earthquake, or fire to destroy human life or the earth (cf. Zeph 1:2–3)?

Genesis 9:12–16 comprise the third speech, which highlights the "sign" of the covenant. God continues to address a plural "you." God's activity still involves humans, animals (all living creatures), and "the earth." The sign is the rainbow. Again, the lines of this speech are repetitive, reflecting the parallelistic discourse of Hebrew poetry. This stylistic feature focuses on the various parties to the covenant: God, you, future generations, every living creature, and the earth. Instead of such a list, repeated lines do the work of underscoring how vast a network of relationships are created by this covenant.

The imagery of the bow in the heavens remains open to interpretation. Many scholars have observed that the iconography of a god or king with a bow is well-known throughout the ancient Near East (on YHWH using a bow as a weapon, see Ps 7:12–13; Hab 3:9; Zech 9:13). To place that bow in the heavens after the flood may well introduce a motif of demilitarization. Other scholars think the bow simply refers to the rainbow, which would often appear "in the clouds" after the storm (cf. Ezek 1:28). One should hold open the option of seeing both meanings in the text, though the overt reference to "my bow" makes it difficult to think that a military weapon is not in view. It is certainly possible that the motif of the bow presents the same physical form of something curved, as does the lapis lazuli necklace Mami wears in the Atrahasis epic after the flood, a necklace "by which I remember it (?) daily (?) forever (?)" (Dalley 1989, 34). For the Priestly author, something more transcendent than a necklace that the deity might wear is necessary. Here, too, the Priestly theologian is at work, creating a new, though similar in physical shape, cosmic symbol as the sign of this first covenant.

The fourth speech (Gen 9:17) in the postflood is directed only to Noah. It, unlike the others, is crisp, without parallel lines. Further, it is the first time that the diction of making a covenant is set in the past tense. The act has been accomplished, as this summation reports. Moreover, this summation underscores the breadth of the covenant. It does not refer just to Noah or his sons, but instead, expansively, to "all flesh that is on the earth."

Genesis 9:18–29
Noah Plants a Vineyard and Becomes Inebriated

This episode marks a major transition in the book of Genesis. The flood story is now over. New realities emerge. No earlier genealogies, reports, or narratives have referred to the world of peoples or places experienced directly by those who lived in ancient Israel. Now such entities, both in Mesopotamia and in Syria-Palestine, begin to appear. The story about Noah and his sons introduces that world when it identifies Ham's son as Canaan. As a result, the postflood era depicted here becomes a quite different narrative world from that conveyed in Gen 1–5. With the exception of Gen 11:1–9 (see below), cultural particularity looms large from Gen 9:18 onward.

9:18 The sons of Noah who emerged from the ark were Shem, Ham, and
Yapheth. Ham was the father of Canaan. **19** These three were the sons
of Noah. And from these three the entire earth was strewn[a] with people.
20 Noah, a man of the earth, took the initiative[b] and planted a vineyard.
21 When he drank some of the wine, he became drunk and lay naked[c]
inside the tent. **22** When Ham, the father of Canaan, saw the nakedness
of his father,[d] he told his two brothers, who were outside. **23** Then Shem
and Yapheth took a blanket and placed it on their shoulders. They walked
backward and covered the nakedness of their father. Their faces were
turned aside, so they did not see the nakedness of their father. **24** When
Noah awoke from his wine, he knew what his youngest son had done.

25 He said,

"Cursed be Canaan
A servile slave[e] he shall be to his brothers!"

26 He also said,

"Blessed be YHWH,[f] God of Shem;
May Canaan be his slave!
27 May God enhance[g] Yapheth!
May he live in the tents of Shem,
and may Canaan be his slave!"

28 After the flood, Noah lived 350 years. **29** Noah lived 950 years, after
which he died.

a. This verb is often thought to derive from *npṣ*, which is typically translated "to disperse or scatter." If one repoints the form as a niphal of *pwṣ*, one may translate "strewn," as above. It is no accident that in Gen 11:9 the deity scatters (*pwṣ*) people.

b. The verb *ḥll* (hiphil), which means to begin something, elsewhere in the primeval history is followed by an infinitive (4:26; 6:1; 10:8; 11:6). Here the ensuing verb is finite, creating an instance of verbal hendiadys: he began / he planted.

c. The hithpael permits either a passive or reflexive translation. Either is possible here.

d. The phrase "the nakedness of his father" probably refers to Noah having intercourse with his wife, mother of the three sons: so Lev 18:7 (see comments).

e. Literally, "a slave of slaves," an expression that signifies extreme inferior status.

f. Cf. NRSV, "Blessed by the LORD my God be Shem."

g. The verb in Hebrew is *yapt*, which creates a pun with the name Yapheth.

[9:18–19] Genesis 9:18 offers information similar to that found in Gen 6:10. Readers already know the names of Noah's sons. The writer responsible for Gen 9:18–19 is, however, interested in doing more than simply providing names. Instead, he makes clear that all those who lived after the flood stemmed from these three individuals, precluding the possibility that Gen 6:4, "and also afterward," might refer to another surviving lineage. Prior references to fathers who sired multiple children simply reported that a father bore a named son as well as "other sons and daughters." That imprecision does not occur here. All of the sons are named and specified to be three in number. Further, the author anticipates, by using the verb *pwṣ/npṣ*, the scattering and filling of the earth reported in Gen 11:9.

The symmetry of the sons' names is interrupted by a note about the progeny of Ham. There is obviously no interest in identifying the children of either Yapheth or Shem, though such information was no doubt available to the author (so Gen 10). An author or editor has explained that Ham was the father of Canaan, a note repeated in 9:22. These two notes set the stage for Noah's cursing of Canaan in 9:25–27.

[20–27] The first verse of this report about Noah, wine, and its impact on his family begins with allusive language. In the genealogy in which Noah initially appears (Gen 5), the author provides a popular etymology of his name. Noah will provide "comfort" (*nḥm*)—part of the Hebrew word sounds like Noah—from the ground that YHWH has cursed (5:29). So 9:20 alludes to this cursed ground and identifies wine as providing such "comfort." In so doing, the author hints that whatever the ground provides will be complex, since it has become the object of God's curse. That "complexity" quickly manifests itself in Noah's becoming drunk from some of the wine he has produced.

At this point in the report, the narrator offers a guarded version of what transpires. Translators typically envision lying Noah naked on the floor of the tent. There is no reference to floor, however. Further, if the verb is reflexive, then Noah is engaged in some activity. Leviticus 18:6–8 reveals the nature of that activity. There, the verb *glh*, to uncover or reveal, means to engage in sexual intercourse. Moreover, the nakedness of a father is defined as one's mother (Lev 18:7). This same verb and phrase are used in Gen 9. Noah is described as engaged in the act of "uncovering," and Ham sees the nakedness of his father: thus Ham sees his mother naked. This is an oblique way of saying that Ham sees Noah having intercourse with Ham's mother. That activity is, of course, not forbidden. (Leviticus 18, of course, forbids Ham from having intercourse with his mother, though it is possible to construe Gen 9 as referring to such incestuous behavior.) But, presumably, it would have been considered inappropriate for any of the sons to watch their parents engage in sexual intercourse. Since the author depicts Noah as inebriated, one might infer that Noah has become oblivious to the presence of one of his sons in the tent. (Only in 9:24 is the reader informed that Ham is the youngest son, information that may explain why Ham is in the tent.) Thus it is Ham's misfortune to see just such activity, since he is apparently inside the tent.

Once Ham has seen his parents, he tells his brothers, who are "outside." (The fact that Ham tells his brothers anything makes it clear that *Ham* was not engaged in sexual activity, either with his father or mother, as some have suggested. Further, it is unlikely that the author intends us to think that Ham shouted such information, as has been posited.) Shem and Yapheth, taking care not to see what Ham has experienced, walk backward with a blanket and cover, probably, both their father and Ham's mother.

Verses 25–27 provide the only place in which Noah is given speech. He adopts a pattern of speaking attested elsewhere in the OT. These verses may be compared to other "testamentary blessings" (i.e., Gen 27:27–29, 39–40; Gen 49; Deut 33), texts in which a father (Isaac, Jacob) or father figure (Moses) pronounces the future that lies ahead for their children. In Gen 27 and 49, the father speaks directly to the sons, using second-person pronouns. In Gen 9, however, the language is impersonal. Noah speaks *about* his sons, not to them. The absence of direct speech, especially between the father and those about whom he predicts a positive fate, suggests a certain distance between the generations. If the narrative about Adam and Eve involves alienation between husband and wife, and the story of Cain and Abel reflects alienation between siblings, this episode speaks of alienation between parents and children.

These curses and blessings are distinctive in other ways. (1) A person is cursed, God is blessed. In no other testamentary blessings are individuals cursed by the father, though the rhetoric of cursing does appear in Gen 27:29; 49:7 (in which the anger of Simeon and Levi is cursed). (Cf. Deut 33:11, 13, 16, 20, 23, 24 for the language of blessing, though in different phrases; in no case does *bārûk YHWH* [Blessed be YHWH] appear in testamentary blessings.) (2) The language of enslavement rules the rhetoric (cf. Gen 27:29, 40; 49:8). (3) The futures of the three sons are intertwined: one will be enslaved to the other two. And the two sons who flourish are envisioned as living in the same tents (a somewhat ironic proposition, given what just happened in Noah's tent). In sum, the three sons do not achieve success or failure apart from what happens to their siblings.

There can be no doubt that Ham suffers radical critique. Just as earlier, the deity has cursed the ground and the snake, now Noah curses one of his sons. Why? And why is *Canaan* and not Ham cursed? One is initially reminded of the proverb against which Ezekiel inveighs, "The fathers have eaten sour grapes, and the children's teeth are set on edge" (Ezek 18:2 RSV). So it is not unusual for a descendant to suffer for the "sins" of an earlier generation. However, why just Canaan? According to the Table of Nations, Ham has four sons: Cush, Egypt, Put, and Canaan. But only Canaan is singled out for curse in Gen 9.

The answer lies in the complex function of Canaan in the book of Genesis. According to the Table of Nations, Canaan was made up of multiple ethnic identities (10:15–18); it could be identified with certain boundaries, which were associated with cities on the coast (from Sidon south to Gaza) and cities near the Dead Sea. Elsewhere in Genesis, "Canaan" appears primarily in the phrase "land of Canaan" (e.g., 36:6; 37:1; 42:5; it is especially prominent in the Joseph narrative) but can also appear in formulations such as "daughters of Canaan" (28:8). In 9:26–27, Canaan is a person, not a place, which makes the later formulations especially important. Canaanites are proscribed as potential marital choices for Isaac (24:3) and Jacob (28:1). Moreover, Judah marries a Canaanite (38:2). And, according to the Table of Nations, Het (the progenitor of the "Hittites") is a son of Canaan; these "Hittites," according to Genesis, also represent problematic marital choices (so Gen 26:34–35).

Canaan symbolizes those peoples who, by dint of the threat posed by intermarriage, threaten the identity of Israel. Hence, the author responsible for the story in Gen 9 describes the rationale for a sociopolitical norm: Canaan is to be subordinated to all other peoples. For Israelites, it is inappropriate to marry from among an entity that symbolizes lower social class, those subject to enslavement.

Verse 27 suggests that Yapheth and Shem do not receive identical blessings. One poetic line reads, "He [Yapheth] will dwell in the tents of Shem." (Gunkel [1997, 82] thought it was "an intentionally secretive expression.") Many interpreters have understood this claim to mean that these two brothers would live amicably together (cf. Ps 133:1), presuming that Shem would remain in what were originally his tents. However, the notion of living in someone else's tents more literally means that one party dispossesses another (so 1 Chr 5:10; Ps 78:55). This meaning comports well with the first poetic line in Gen 9:27, which has Yapheth expanding his territory.

The poetry, therefore, appears to offer a different perspective than does the narrative. The story denigrates Ham (as Canaan) and elevates his brothers, whereas the poetry not only denigrates Ham but also elevates Yapheth over Shem. The latter element is surprising, since Israel traces its descent from Shem, who would, according to this poetry, have suffered at the hands of Yapheth. This poetic tradition has been incorporated in a prose context that has a narrower interest: denigrating Ham (Canaan).

[28–29] These verses, along with 9:18–19, offer genealogical details that surround the report about Noah's drunkenness and its impact on his sons. Hence, the episode is bracketed by an inclusio (9:18–19, 28–29) made up of typical Priestly material.

Genesis 10:1–32
The Descendants of Noah

The fourth *tôlədôt* formula introduces a genealogy built around Noah's sons. This genealogy offers almost numbing detail about the world's population "after the flood" (10:1). Since Noah has fathered three sons, the world is tripartite, at least in theory. However, those who created this genealogy have struggled to make diverse groupings fit this scheme, such as having the population of the Arabian Peninsula located in two places, known as Seba (10:7), in the line of Ham; and Sheba (10:28), in the line of Shem. Asshur appears twice (vv. 11, 22). This genealogy offers an early anthropological vocabulary. People can be distinguished by several variables: where they live, to whom they are related, and what language they speak. The author is interested in this kind of variety and does not offer value judgments about them.

Genesis 1–11 includes a number of genealogies. Those in Gen 5 and 11:10–26 are vertical or linear, listing one person per generation. By contrast, Gen 10 is horizontal or branching out. Though Gen 5 proceeds through ten generations, Gen 10 never reports more than two generations. Breadth rather than depth is a hallmark of the genealogy in Gen 10.

Genesis 10, however, offers more than a cultural, ethnic, and linguistic taxonomy. The map is not static: people are moving around. According to 10:5, "coastal peoples" have branched out from all those just named. Thus verse 18 reports that Canaanites spread abroad.

This genealogy stands in tension with Gen 11:1–9. The story about the tower of Babel concludes with YHWH creating different languages. However, Gen 10 presupposes linguistic diversity. Each of the three primary groupings is known to have its own language (v. 5) or languages (vv. 20, 31). There is also tension concerning the location of humanity. According to Gen 11:2, all humanity is located in one locale; they settle in Shinar (southern Mesopotamia). According to Gen 10, humanity has already been dispersing. This dissonance between the two chapters demonstrates diverse traditions about the origins of linguistic diversity alongside different understandings of who descended from whom (so Asshur; 10:11, 22).

Genesis 10 is a crucial and creative chapter. It is crucial because it sutures the generation of those who survived the flood to later human history. That is a link absent in the extant corpus of ancient Near Eastern literature. According to the flood narrative as included in the Gilgamesh epic, Utnapishtim and his wife survive the flood, but there is no reference to their progeny. In fact, they are deified and removed from the normal realm of human affairs. Moreover, the Atrahasis myth, the other major text that includes a recounting of the flood, does not refer to the survivors of the flood once the waters have abated, save the phrase "A man survived the catastrophe." Genesis 10 fills this gap by integrating the generation of those who were on the ark with those who came later.

One may compare this chapter to 1 Chr 1:4–23, a text that includes much of what appears in Gen 10. But 1 Chr 1 omits Gen 10:1, 5, 9–12, 18b–21, 30–32. There can be no doubt that the genealogy in Chronicles depends upon the one in Gen 10.

10:1 These are the descendants of Noah's sons: Shem, Ham, and Yapheth.
Children were born to them after the flood.

2 Yapheth's sons were Gomer, Magog, Madai, Javan, Tubal, Meshech,
and Tiras. **3** The sons of Gomer were Ashkenaz, Riphath, and Togarmah.
4 The sons of Javan: Elishah, Tarshish, Kittim, and Dodanim.[a] **5** From
them, the coastal peoples branched out, in their territories, each with its
own language, made up of their families and their states.

6 Ham's sons were Cush, Egypt, Put, and Canaan. **7** The sons of Cush
were Seba, Havilah, Sabtah, Raamah, and Sabteca. The sons of Raamah were Sheba and Dedan. **8** Cush [also] sired Nimrod; he was the first
mighty person on earth. **9** He was a mighty hunter, empowered by YHWH.
People therefore say, "[He is] like Nimrod, a mighty hunter empowered by YHWH." **10** His kingdom began with Babel, Erech, Accad, and
Calneh,[b] in the land of Shinar. **11** From that territory, he went to Asshur
and built Nineveh—that vast city,[c] Calah, **12** and Resen, which is a great
city, between Nineveh and Calah. **13** Egypt sired Ludim, Anamim, Lehabim, Naphtuhim, **14** Pathrusim, Casluhim—the Philistines came from
there—and Caphtorim.

15 Canaan sired Sidon, his firstborn, and Heth, **16** and the Jebusites, the
Amorites, the Girgashites, **17** the Hivites, the Arkites, the Sinites, **18** the
Arvadites, the Zemarites, and the Hamathites. The Canaanite families
then spread out. **19** The border of the Canaanites stretched from Sidon,
in the direction of Gerar, as far as Gaza, and in the direction of Sodom,
Gomorrah, Admah, and Zeboiim, as far as Lasha.[d] **20** These are the sons
of Ham, according to their families, their languages, their territories, and
their states.

21 To Shem children were also born; he was the father of all the sons
of Eber, the older brother of Yaphet. **22** The descendants of Shem were
Elam, Asshur, Arpachshad, Lud, and Aram. **23** The descendants of Aram

were Uz, Hul, Gether, and Mash. 24 Arpachshad sired Shelah and Shelah
sired Eber. 25 Two sons were born to Eber: the name of one was Peleg
because during his lifetime the earth was divided; the name of his brother
was Joktan. 26 Joktan sired Almodad, Sheleph, Hazarmaveth, Jerah,
27 Hadoram, Uzal, Diklah, 28 Obal, Abimael, Sheba, 29 Ophir, Havilah,
and Jobab; all these were sons of Joktan. 30 The land in which they lived
extended from Mesha in the direction of Sephar, the hill country in the
east. 31 These are the sons of Shem, according to their families, their
languages, their territories, and their nations.

32 These are the families of Noah's sons, according to their lines of
descent and their nations. From them the nations of the earth branched
out after the flood.

a. MT *dōdānîm* is probably a scribal error for *rōdānîm*, which appears in 1 Chr 1:7 and refers to those who lived on the island of Rhodes, a population consistent with people living near water (see Gen 10:5, "coastal peoples").

b. The Hebrew consonants can be revocalized and translated as "and all of them. . . ."

c. Reading *rĕḥōbōt ʿîr* as an abstract plural, not as a place name.

d. SP offers a more expansive definition: "from the river of Egypt to the great river Euphrates and to the Mediterranean Sea."

This cultural map purports to describe the state of affairs immediately after the flood and before the period associated with Abraham. Many commentators have asked: What cultures does the author know and introduce into this genealogy? The answer to this question might help identify the time when this specific text was written or, at least, the historical/cultural context that it reflects. If the map were homogeneous, such a question might be relatively easy to answer. However, it seems clear that there are at least two different maps present in Gen 10. Those working from a source-critical perspective identify a primary form of the genealogy, typically attributed to P. That genealogy is typically identified in 10:1a, 2–7, 20, 22, 31–32. This genealogy focuses on the branching-out genealogy of Noah's sons. Each is identified with heirs, and each receives the summary statement present in 10:5, 20, and 31. However, this primary genealogy has been supplemented, but not symmetrically. One feature characteristic of the supplementary material is the verb *yalad*, "to sire" (e.g., vv. 8, 15, 24). However, the genealogy of Yapheth has received no additional material. Three of Ham's four sons receive further notice. Cush, whose sons are initially named in 10:7 of the primary genealogy, receives another son in 10:8, Nimrod. Verses 7–11 describe his significance. Egypt and Canaan, whose sons are not named in the primary genealogy, have heirs named in 10:13 and 10:15–17, respectively; in both cases the genealogies are branching out. Finally, Shem also has additional heirs, but in his case, the additional material

(vv. 24–28) is more linear than branching out. The supplementary material is, therefore, heterogeneous. It does not all stem from the same hand.

Though many of the names can be identified with ancient places and populations attested in the second millennium BCE (e.g., v. 10, Erek [or Uruk]), in the supplementary material are also names associated with the late second/early first millennium, such as the Philistines (v. 13). There is no clear evidence of names specific to the Persian period, suggesting that this genealogy, or at least the traditions embedded in it, dates to no later than the sixth century BCE.

[10:1] The first verse shares the *tôlədôt* formula, "these are the 'descendants,'" with nine other texts in Genesis. Unlike Gen 5:1, beginning the list of Adam's descendants; 6:9–10, listing the sons of Noah; and 11:10, starting the list of Shem's descendants; Gen 10:1, like 2:4a, identifies descendants of plural entities. In Gen 2, "the heavens and the earth" are the progenitors; in Gen 10, the sons of Noah are the generative generation. One might read this verse as a report that the sons are fulfilling the mandate they have received in 9:1. There, Noah and his sons are ordered to "be fruitful, multiply, and fill the earth." Noah has already sired children, so the command is really made to his sons, and Gen 10:1 reports, in summary fashion, that they have accomplished it. The rest of the chapter narrates precisely who has been born. But it does more. It takes seriously the third verb of the command, "Fill the earth," especially since 10:5 and 10:18 explicitly refer to people spreading out. Parts of this chapter no doubt existed as an independent genealogy; verse 1 helps make it cohere with the large Priestly narrative.

[2–5] The genealogy starts on a surprising note, with Noah's youngest son, Yapheth, and works back to his oldest son, Shem. That order permits Shem's lineage to stand near the listing of its descendants, Terah and Abram, in Gen 11:10–26.

Just as Isaac is less than fully fleshed out among the three patriarchs, so too Yapheth is less important to the story in Gen 9 and the genealogy in Gen 10 than are his two brothers. It is, therefore, not surprising that Yapheth's genealogy is less extensive than those of his brothers. Yapheth and his sons belong to the northern Mediterranean environ and territory to the east of it. Commonly accepted identifications include Gomer, north of the Black Sea; Madai = Media; Javan = Ionia; Kittim = Cyprus. If one accepts the reading proffered in textual note a, then this genealogy includes specific reference to the island of Rhodes. These identifications are interesting, but the task of interpreting the names associated with Yapheth requires more than placing them on a map, especially if the authors who created this chapter did not create this list.

One must begin with several observations. First, the name Yaphet appears only in Gen 1–11 and in 1 Chr 1:4–5, which depends on Genesis. In no case is there any elaboration of that figure. The name is a cipher, occupying a place in a genealogy, but without innate significance. Second, according to Gen 10:2–4, Yaphet bears seven sons, one of whom has three sons, another of whom bears four sons, totaling fourteen progeny. Most of these fourteen names are infrequent in the OT (Tarshish is the most widely attested). It is, therefore, striking that eleven of the fourteen names appear in the book of Ezekiel (cf. Westermann 1984, 509). Ezekiel 27 and 38 are the two lodes. In these chapters, the names appear in proximity: Ezek 38:2, for example, includes Magog, Meshech, and Tubal; 38:6 refers to Gomer and Beth-Togarmah. Put another way, these names belong together as a suite of foreign peoples. They were not assembled by the author of Gen 10. When needing to flesh out the genealogy of Yapheth, that author appropriated these listings from an unknown source, which is elsewhere attested in Ezekiel. In Ezek 27, these nations are listed by dint of their mercantile activity with Tyre. (Ezekiel 27 is a lamentation over the destruction of Tyre.) Third, in Ezekiel these names bear negative connotations. They belong to the enemies that will be decimated in the cosmic war foreseen in Ezek 38–39, the great destruction of Gog.

The names associated with Yapheth betray knowledge of traditions attested elsewhere in biblical literature, lists such as those found in Ezekiel 27 and 38. However, they are unlike the lists found in Ezekiel in two important ways. First, unlike some of Ezekiel's lists, they do not reflect knowledge of Persian-period names (e.g., Ezek 27:10, "Paras"; 38:5, "Persia"). Second, the author of Gen 10 has "pacified" these names. They are no longer enemies or agents of trade but simply symbols of humanity who live to the north of Israel and on the coasts. Verse 5 reports that humanity is spreading out. A strict construal of the grammar suggests that the descendants of Javan (10:2, 4), not all the sons of Yaphet, are responsible for this dispersal (so Westermann 1984, 508).

The genealogy in Gen 10:2–5 is integral to Gen 10: it is not part of the supplemental material. Still, this basic portion of the genealogy is itself a creative redeployment of a separate tradition. This fact suggests that the basic genealogy of Gen 10 is an artifice, created to make a rhetorical point about the character of postflood humanity emerging from Noah's three sons; it is growing and moving.

[6–20] Oddly, there are fewer verses attributable to the basic genealogy of Ham than for that of Yapheth. Some names may have been replaced by supplemental material: the progeny of Egypt and Canaan are depicted only with the supplementary formula, "x sired y." In the primary genealogy, only the progeny of Cush is identified.

Ham had four sons, and with them the needle of the compass swings to the south. Cush lay to the south of Pharaonic Egypt. Put may refer to the land west of Egypt (i.e., present-day Libya). Canaan may appear odd. Ambiguous though its precise location might be, at least in 10:6, Canaan refers to territory in the Levant, likely the coast and coastal plain. The primary genealogy focuses on

Cush and then his son Raamah. Those names highlight areas to the south (e.g., Sheba, south of Egypt; and Sabtah, on the Arabian Peninsula). Yet there is overlap with other portions of supplementary material in Gen 10, since Sheba (v. 7) also appears in 10:28. These verses present a genealogical sketch that creates impressionistic geography rather than a definitive map.

Verses 8–19 are typically attributed to a different hand. They contain the hallmark "x sired y" formula, which reappears in 10:13, 15. This supplement focuses initially on Nimrod, in a distinctive body of material (10:8–12). It is distinctive not only because of its interest in one cultural founder but also because of its vocabulary. Only here in Gen 10 does the phrase "kingdom" appear (v. 10).

Nimrod functions as an eponymous ancestor for Mesopotamian cultures (e.g., Babel first, the older portion of Mesopotamia; then Assyria) even though he is born to someone from the southern region of Mesopotamia. Though this genealogy relates Nimrod initially to the breadth of Mesopotamia, the cities listed in 10:11–12 all lay in Assyria, the land in northern Mesopotamia with which he is associated in Mic 5:6: "They shall rule the land of Assyria with the sword, // and the land of Nimrod with the drawn sword." He is noteworthy since the biblical author knows an epigram about him, "[He is] like Nimrod, a mighty hunter empowered by YHWH." This is the sort of thing that can be said about a powerful hunter, someone like Samson (Judg 14:5–6) or David (1 Sam 17:36). Such a saying emphasizes, among other things, that empowerment by YHWH is available to various peoples, not just to Israel. This great Mesopotamian hero is, like other populations, on the move—from southern Mesopotamia to the region of Assyria. There he is remembered as builder of a city, Nineveh. Yet Calah, rather than Nineveh ("that great city" [Jonah 1:2]), is remembered as "the great city." Kalah (about 25 miles SW of Nineveh) is also known now by the name Nimrud, after its "founder" Nimrod.

The Nimrod material stands in some tension with other texts in Gen 1–11. Nimrod is identified as the first mighty person. However, Gen 6:4 states that mighty persons were born to the human women after being impregnated by minor deities. In addition, though Nimrod is not called the first city builder, his role seems to be in tension with that of Enoch, who "built a city" (Gen 4:17).

Two more sons of Ham receive attention, first Egypt, then Canaan. In the case of Egypt, odd geography, as was true for Cush fathering Nimrod, continues. Verses 13–14 list sons and one "derivative," the Philistines. Scholars have been unable to decipher many of these names. Still, Lehabim probably refers to Libya; Caphtorim definitely refers to Crete, and it was probably intended as the "source" for the Philistines rather than Casluhim (see Amos 9:7; Jer 47:4). Here one has the clear sense of a genealogist trying to make ethnicity fit a structure: Egypt as the progenitor of the Philistines.

The Canaanites seem to be odd members of the Hamite family, even though strong "historical" connections existed between Egypt and the Levantine coast during the Amarna period (1353–1322 BCE). Canaan sired many peoples: eleven names appear, two of which (Sidon and Heth) are in the singular. All of those "families" were perceived as mobile (v. 18). The verb in 10:18, "to spread out" (*pwṣ*), is also in Gen 11:4; thus, two proximate texts speak of humanity spreading out, the first by dint of human initiative, the second as the source of human worry. However, the families are not of a piece. Five Phoenician cities are embedded in the list (Arkites, Sinites, Arvadites, Zemarites, and Hamathites). This grouping emphasizes the coastal character of the Levantine population. Again, an author has likely appropriated an independent tradition when fleshing out the genealogical frame of Noah's three sons.

Distinctive here is the delimitation of borders (to a lesser extent in v. 30). Verse 19 describes the territory of these Canaanites. One would be hard pressed to draw a map based on this information. The author was, at a minimum, staking out a claim for much of the territory that belonged to "larger Israel," with Sidon and Gaza signifying the Mediterranean border, and Sodom and neighbors its southeastern extent. Nothing lay in the heights east of the Jordan. Like the "geography" present elsewhere in Gen 10, the description is impressionistic.

[21–31] Verse 21 stands out for a variety of reasons: it does not include Ham, even though it mentions Yapheth as a brother; it has no analogue in the sections dealing with Ham and Yapheth; and it highlights Eber, a name that is cognate with the term "Hebrew." If Eber is to the Hebrews as Nimrod is to the Mesopotamians, it is interesting that the former cuts a far less significant figure in the genealogy than does the latter. The primary form of the genealogy exists only in 10:22: Shem has five sons. One, Asshur, has already appeared in verse 11, demonstrating again the fluidity present in this genealogy. Only one son, Aram, a population that lives to the northeast of Israel, is traced into the second generation. (Elam and Asshur also can be located to the northeast of Israel.) Another hand traced the lineage of another son, Arpachshad, a line that will reappear in Gen 11:10, though there only in a purely linear genealogy.

In 10:25, a scribe added the phrase, "because during his lifetime the earth was divided." The verb translated "divided" derives from the same trilateral stem, *plg*, as does Peleg. That scribe offered a pun built from Peleg's name to identify the generation during which "division" occurred. But what division did the scribe have in mind? The answer is almost certainly to be found in Ps 55:10 [9]. Here, an Israelite poet calls on the deity to confuse some group and to "divide their speech," the same verb as in Gen 10:25. This invocation no doubt alludes to the primal "dividing" of speech, the subject of Gen 10–11. So, one may rightly infer that the dividing referred to in Gen 10:25 is linguistic. In the view of this scribe, linguistic diversity dates to the time of Peleg.

Verses 26–30 are obscure. They probably refer to an area to the southeast of Israel. Since so many of the names are unknown and since these verses focus on Joktan, there must have been a distinct tradition about this figure. Again, the author has included a separate body of tradition, adding to the impression that this so-called Table of Nations is truly comprehensive and complete.

The most surprising feature of 19:21–31 is what these verses do *not* contain. This lineage is, after all, the one from which Israel will trace its heritage: Shem to Arpachshad, Shelah, Eber, and on down to Abram. And yet, nothing is special or noteworthy about this lineage. Another heritage includes a memorable figure, Nimrod. Shem's line includes no such heroes. The genealogy seems to be reporting that Israel's progenitors are part of a common humanity. There is nothing innately distinctive about their heritage during this postflood period. The emergence of a hero from the line of Eber will need to wait until the period narrated in the family literature.

[32] In reading or hearing the just-created map, Israelites would be presented with an ideology concerning Israel's origins. Israel could trace its lineage back through Shem, the oldest of Noah's sons. Here the status of the elder remains intact, as with Terah's sons. Further, Israel, like its neighbors in Syria-Palestine, is related to great cultures: in Israel's case, Asshur; for the Canaanites, Babylon. Moreover, both the primary and the supplemental materials emphasize the "dynamic" quality of life. People move or "spread out": coastal peoples migrate (v. 5); Nimrod "went to Assyria" (v. 11); the Canaanite families branched out (v. 18). However, there is no migration of the peoples who descend from Shem. Only later will Terah and then Abram follow this pattern. But the precedent has already been set by those associated with Noah's other sons. In sum, this genealogy offers a warrant for Israel's forebears to move into and claim a new land.

Still, the formula that appears in verses 5 (partial there), 20, and 31 underscores the commonality of the peoples that stem from Noah's sons. They can all be known by their families, languages, territories, and states. Everyone presumably has a right to such identifying marks.

Genesis 11:1–9
"Come, Let Us Build for Ourselves a City and a Tower"

The so-called tower of Babel episode has often been viewed as the final narrative portion of the primeval history. However, as has become clear, the post-flood chapters present a move away from the truly primeval period and, instead, address specific peoples and places.[1] The context for these nine verses has been established in the preceding chapter, the Table of Nations. There, in the genealogy of Ham, one line of descent moves from Ham to Cush, who is associated with Mesopotamia. More specifically, "the beginning of his kingdom was Babel, Erech, and Accad, all of them in the land of Shinar" (10:10 NRSV). That genealogy establishes the expectation that some people inhabit the land of Shinar and that others dwell elsewhere.

Genesis 11:1–9 attests to this specific place and the city of Babylon, but not as one among a number of other places of habitation. From a narrative perspective, Gen 11 belongs either before or parallel to the Table of Nations. Genesis 10 and 11:1–9 accomplish, in effect, the same end: they explain how humanity became linguistically and geographically differentiated. The word "language" appears in 10:5, 20, and 31. Genesis 10 achieves that goal by creating an elaborate genealogy; Gen 11 offers a report about the deity's dissatisfaction with the behavior of a uniform humanity. So Gen 10 attests to a "natural" evolution; Gen 11 speaks of an incursion by the deity.

Allusion to a time when all people speak the same language is attested elsewhere in the ancient Near East. A text known as Enmerkar and the Lord of Aratta refers to a primeval period when "the whole universe, the people in unison" spoke "to Enlil in one tongue." The text goes on to report that Enki:

> Changed the speech in their mouths,
> [brought(?)] contention into it,

1. Westermann (1984, 535) recognizes this quality when he writes, "Gen 11:1–9 hovers between primeval and historical event." T. Hiebert more recently maintains that the story is an apology on behalf of cultural diversity (2007, 29–58). But see Strong's critical response (2008, 625–34).

Into the speech of man that
[until then] had been one.[2]

This Sumerian text shares one essential feature with Gen 11. Linguistic diversity is understood to be the result of an act by a deity. It does not just happen, so to speak, as one might assume from reading Gen 10. Further, if Jacobsen's interpretation is apt, Enki's act, though not one of punishment, was designed to thwart humans from inappropriately exercising their full human potential (1992). And this issue, too, is at work in Gen 11. An inability to understand one another results from linguistic diversity. In this story about humans living in one place and undertaking a building project, Israel has included an ancient etiology for linguistic diversity, one also attested in Sumerian literature.

11:1 Now, when all the earth had one language and identical vocabulary,
2 and as people migrated[a] from the east, they found a broad valley in the
land of Shinar and settled *there.* 3 They said to each other, "Come, let
us make bricks and burn them."[b] (They used brick instead of stone and
bitumen instead of mortar.)[c] 4 Then they said, "Come, let us build for
ourselves a city and a tower with its top in the sky so that we might make
a name for ourselves. Otherwise, we will be scattered over the face of the
entire earth." 5 YHWH came down to examine the city and the tower that
the humans had built. 6 Then YHWH said, "They are, indeed, a unified
people and with one language. This is just the beginning of what they
might do. Now nothing that they intend to do will be impossible for them.
7 Come, let us go down and mix up their language *there* so that one person
may not understand the speech of his compatriot." 8 Then YHWH scattered them from *there* over the face of the entire earth, whereupon they
stopped building the city. 9 Therefore, it was called Babel, because *there*[d]
YHWH mixed up the [primal] language of the entire earth, and from *there*
YHWH scattered them over the face of the entire earth.

a. Literally, "as they migrated."
b. Thus the bricks were fired, not dried in the sun; so T. Hiebert 2007, 35 n. 18.
c. See comments for explanation of the two wordplays in this verse.
d. *Šam* (there) may be a wordplay (italicized above) on the phrase "it was called," which in Hebrew includes the word "name" (*šem*).

2. Kramer 1968, 111. Jacobsen translated lines 154–55 in a different fashion:
did . . . the Lord of Eridu
alienate the tongues in their mouths as many as he had put there,
the tongues of man that were as one.
Jacobsen denies that "contention" per se is present in the speech (1992, 403–16).

This narrative involves two quite different issues: the notions of place and linguistic diversity. One is tempted to suggest that Gen 11:1–9 is made up of two originally separate traditions that have been joined in the current story. Verses 1, 6, 7, and 9 deal primarily with language; verses 2–5 and 8 focus on what humanity is doing at a specific place.[3] The fact that an ancient Near Eastern tradition about the origins of linguistic diversity does not involve a city or a tower would support this contention. Nonetheless, it is possible to read these nine verses as a brief but complex story in which both these issues have been artfully intertwined. The story occurs in two basic parts: the first (11:1–4) deals with humanity; the second (11:5–9) focuses on the deity's response.

[11:1–2] The first two verses begin abruptly and sit loosely in their larger literary context. The Table of Nations has just finished reporting the vast cultural, linguistic, and geographic diversity that stems from Noah's sons, children born (past tense) after the flood. Here Gen 11:1 alludes to a time *before* such diversity emerged, a time when only one language existed.

Not only is the temporal sequence disturbed, so is the syntax. It is unusual to find two unrelated circumstantial clauses before the finite verb, "they found." And the grammar itself is odd, since there is no clear referent for either the pronominal suffixes or the finite verbs in 11:2 ("as they migrated," "they found," "they dwelled"). Not since before the deluge has the text given explicit reference to people or humankind as a collective entity. Only in 11:5 is that missing subject provided: "the humans."

In verse 2, the narrator has introduced a tantalizing allusion to a prior biblical text: the phrase *miqqedem*, which has been translated "from the east." This same phrase is present in Gen 3:24, where it is regularly translated "east of." (Gen 4:16 also links Eden with the east.) According to Gen 3, once out of the garden, humanity moves east of it. Hence, the eastern side of the garden apparently needs protection, which the deity provides by means of the cherubim with the flaming sword. The cherubim guard the path to the tree of life. Now, in Gen 11:2, humanity is pictured as coming *from* the east. The biblical author may be suggesting that a much-expanded humanity is now on its way back to the area where the garden lies, a situation that, due to their numbers, poses an even greater threat than when the primal pair is originally ejected.

The author leaves vague the precise place where the unnamed actors stop. They are in the plain of Shinar and at a place "there," a word that reappears in verses 7, 8, and 9. Though the popular etymology in 11:9 associates their location as Babel, it is up until that final verse just "a place."

3. Gunkel (1997, 94–95) maintains that Gen 11:1–9 is made up of two distinct stories: one involving a city and the confusion of languages, and the other involving a tower and the dispersion of humanity.

[3–4] Verse 3 also commences in odd fashion. The narrator describes people preparing building materials but without any stated goal. Perhaps as important as the activity itself is the fact that what they do is reported in direct speech. The narrator could have conveyed a report about humans making and curing bricks. But direct speech is of especial importance here since it presents humans as linguistic beings and symbolizes their ability to communicate easily among themselves: they use their "one language" (11:1).

The narrator does deem it necessary to offer a culture sidebar, an aside explaining that what might have appeared to be strange building materials to Syro-Palestinian readers, people who were used to constructions of stone and mortar. Moreover, this sidebar is nicely wrought. In both cases the building materials that function similarly also sound alike. They use "brick" (*lĕbēnâ*) for "stone" (*lə*ʾ*āben*) and "bitumen" (*ḥēmār*) instead of "mortar" (*ḥōmer*). To make the first pun work, the author affixed the preposition *lə* to the noun ʾ*eben* (stone). Further, the author used a non-Semitic word for bitumen (*ḥmr* is apparently cognate with Egyptian *mrh*) instead of biblical Hebrew *kōper*, which is cognate with Akkadian *kupru*. In sum, verse 3b is an artful and learned construction, not a quickly jotted footnote.

The as-yet unidentified builders now explain the rationale for their activity. (It is almost as if they come up with the idea for a city and a tower only after they have a pile of bricks ready to use.) For the narrator to introduce the motive at this point in the report underscores the happenstance character of this human activity. They stop at a place "there" (v. 2) without having any specific purpose in mind. They make bricks without any stated goal. Once "there" and with bricks, three goals emerge: (1) to build a city, (2) to build a tower, and (3) to make a name. All three ploys are designed to prevent them from being scattered, removed from that unnamed "place."

All three ploys require comment. (1) The "perpetrators" are not the first to build a city. That behavior is first associated with Enoch (Gen 4:17), who later "walked with God" (5:22, 24). So it is difficult to condemn the intent to build a city. (2) The tower is more complicated, especially the phrase "with its top in the sky." Speiser maintains, contra the notion that construction of this tower implies an assault on the heavens, that the Hebrew expression reflects the description of Esagila (a temple compound in Babylon), as depicted in Enuma Elish (1964, 75–76). However, such appeals to Mesopotamian analogues, whether sacral or very tall structures, may be unnecessary. Reference to very tall structures made by humans appears elsewhere in the OT, as in Deut 1:28, a text in which the pre-Israelite cities and their fortifications are described as "in the heavens," the same phrase that occurs in Gen 11:4. In sum, the phrase simply refers to an ancient "skyscraper." Here again, the tower itself need not be understood pejoratively.

In addition, the Hebrew word *migdāl*, translated as "tower," does not typically refer to a sacral structure (e.g., the tower in Isa 5:2). Hence, even if Speiser is correct in maintaining that the biblical author alludes to ancient Near Eastern descriptions of the construction of a major shrine, which includes specific reference to making bricks, the biblical version has become "secularized." According to Enuma Elish, the minor gods proposed the creation of a city and a shrine for Marduk, but humans have no such explicit theological intent for their construction project in Gen 11.

Finally, (3) the humans' interest in making a name for themselves raises a question: is this an inappropriate thing to do? At least three things must be said in response. *First*, with one exception, the deity is the one who makes a name for himself in the OT. Such action is typically associated with founding events, such as signs and wonders enacted in Egypt (Neh 9:10) or the splitting of the waters (Isa 63:12). *Second*, according to 2 Sam 8:13, David made a name for himself. This claim appears immediately after the narrator has chronicled some of David's wars and his dedication of certain valuable objects to the deity. *Third*, according to 2 Sam 7:9, YHWH will make David a great name "like the great ones who are in the earth." Here an author clearly recognizes that others have had prominent reputations (and since they are "in" the earth, the reader is probably to understand that their names outlive them). It is this notion that undergirds other texts, such as Gen 12:2 and 1 Kgs 1:47, which understands the deity as having the capacity to make someone's name great. In sum, having such a great name is appropriate for deities, kings, or heroes (e.g., the "men of name" or renown in Gen 6:4). Here, however, a biblical author reports that all humans want to build a city and tower, thereby to achieve a name; all humanity is attempting to do what only a few can achieve.

Verse 4 concludes with what is probably best described as a purpose clause. The acts of building and making are designed to prevent humanity from being scattered "across the face of the whole earth." This clause seems related to 11:2, which reports the settling down of humanity. The grammar of verse 4 is noteworthy. Humanity fears that it will be scattered. That passive verb leaves ambiguous the means by which humans might be scattered. The biblical author describes it less as an overt fear than as a general level of anxiety. Further, the primary biblical author, in typical laconic fashion, does not explain why humans are uneasy about being scattered.

[5–8] Only now is the subject of the prior verbs clarified. "The humans" are those who have undertaken the just-described building projects. The phrase *bənê hāʾādām* is used here for the first and only time in the primeval history. Earlier, Gen 6:1–4 has recounted the deeds of the *bĕnê hāʾĕlōhîm*, the minor deities. Now the perspective shifts to humanity, while the plural world of the deity still lurks in the phrase "let us."

It is impossible to read 11:5 without detecting a sardonic tone. The deity must "go down" to see what the humans have made.[4] What the humans have built is apparently not visible from the heavenly heights. What they have built is not visually impressive, yet what the humans have done disturbs the deity. YHWH is moved to speak, apparently here in a soliloquy. The deity notices that all humans speak one language and explicitly links that to their ability to accomplish everything that they intend to do. Clearly, such an outcome is not acceptable.

Verse 7 continues the deity's direct discourse, miming the discourse of the humans. Just as they have said, "Let us . . . ," so does the deity. The "us" almost certainly refers to the minor deities who make up the divine council. They have already been addressed in a similar situation. Genesis 3:22 reports, in direct discourse, the deity referring to "us," those who possess the knowledge of good and evil and live forever. There, as in Gen 11, certain prerogatives are clearly to be preserved for the world of the divine. Doing anything one might conjure, such as living forever, belongs to the world of the divine.

The notion of being "there," at a place (*šām*), remains prominent in this story (11:2, 4, 7–9). In principle, the inception of linguistic diversity could occur anywhere; yet it happened at that "place," which the narrator locates somewhere in the land of Shinar. The notion of an inability to "understand" becomes linked to this place.

As the reader leaves verse 7, one expects a report that such confusion takes place. That report does occur, but in 11:9. Verse 8 intrudes; it concerns human building and divine scattering. One expects the deity to undertake an act of confusion. Instead, the text records an act of scattering. Though 11:8 appears intrusive, it includes the now-frequent reference to "place" (*šām*). If verses 7 and 8 do stem from originally separate traditions, the compositor has integrated them by repeating this locative particle, *šām*. (If v. 7 is not an original portion of the narrative, then v. 8 follows naturally after v. 6.)

The deity does to humanity precisely what people have feared, being scattered across the entire earth. Neither work on a city or tower (it is significant that the tower is not mentioned in v. 8 MT, though it is present in SP and LXX) nor the attempt to make a name has the hoped-for effect. YHWH undertakes the work of scattering precisely because the humans engage in such activity. The means by which they seek to achieve their end became the reasons why their goal is not achieved.

The narrator concludes verse 8 on an ambiguous note. The city is apparently unfinished, there is no reference to the tower, humans apparently do not have

4. It does seem odd that the deity needs to "go down" again; the repetition of the verb has convinced some interpreters that vv. 5 and 7 derive from originally separate narratives.

a name, and it is not clear that anyone remains in the "place" since the humans are scattered "from there." The place has become decidedly unimportant.

[9] The final verse of the tower episode sounds more like an etiological appendage than it does the denouement of a narrative. People have been already scattered (v. 8), a fact repeated in the final part of this verse. The act of confusion is now reported, but less as a part of the earlier narrative than a warrant for a popular etiology of the name Babel. The author of this verse has focused on the final word of verse 8, "the city." (The absence of the tower at the end of v. 8 may represent a conscious attempt to focus the end of the narrative on the city.)

As befits the literature attesting to the postflood condition, 11:9 refers to a specific place, *bābel*, Babylon, and offers a popular etymology for it. (Cf. the use of "therefore" in Gen 32:32 to introduce another etiology.) The author creates a wordplay, linking the Hebrew word *bālal* (to mix) with the toponym *bābel*. That wordplay, which derives from Biblical Hebrew, differs from the meaning of Babylon in Akkadian. There it means "Gate of the Gods." In this etiological addendum, the Hebrew construal represents an assault on the self-proclaimed importance of Babylon. The popular etymology confirms the end of the story, which presents Babylon as unfinished and depopulated. (Babylon was defeated, though not destroyed, by Cyrus of Persia in 539 BCE.)

In sum, Gen 11:1–9 conveys no human assault on the heavens. Instead, humanity is depicted as wanting to dwell in a particular place. In attempting to establish this presence, humans undertake certain actions—trying to build a city and a tower and intending to make a name for themselves, all of which, especially their grasping for fame, symbolize inappropriate action. Even more of a problem is that humanity, though being fruitful and multiplying, is not filling the earth. So God scatters them.

11:10–26
The Descendants of Shem

Immediately after the tower of Babel episode, the compositors provide two genealogies, one that traces the descent from Shem and another that follows the line of Terah. The first, Gen 11:10–26, appears to be consistent with the genealogies in Gen 5 and 10, though it is unlike Gen 5 in not reporting deaths. Genesis 11:10–26 offers no branching out in the genealogy until the final generation. In fact, the genealogy in 11:10–26 recapitulates a portion of the Shemite genealogy found in Gen 10; the first five names of the genealogy in Gen 11:10–26 also appear in Gen 10.

It is appropriate that this genealogy appears immediately after the narrative about the tower. The humans had intended to make a name (*šēm*) for themselves. The genealogies that surround this story make clear that a name, personified by Shem (*šēm* in 10:21–31; 11:10), already exists. Israel will trace its lineage through this nameful man.

> **11:10** These are the descendants of Shem. When Shem was one hundred
> years old, he sired Arpachshad two years after the flood.[a] **11** Shem lived
> five hundred years after he sired Arpachshad; he sired other sons and
> daughters.
>
> **12** When Arpachshad was thirty-five years old, he sired Shelah.
> **13** Arpachshad lived 403 years after he sired Shelah; he sired other sons
> and daughters.[b]
>
> **14** When Shelah was thirty years old, he sired Eber. **15** Shelah lived 403
> years after he sired Eber; he sired other sons and daughters.
>
> **16** When Eber was thirty-four years old, he sired Peleg. **17** Eber lived
> 430 years after he sired Peleg; he sired other sons and daughters.
>
> **18** When Peleg was thirty years old, he sired Reu. **19** Peleg lived 209
> years after he sired Reu; he sired other sons and daughters.
>
> **20** When Reu was thirty-two years old, he sired Serug. **21** Reu lived 207
> years after he sired Serug; he sired other sons and daughters.
>
> **22** When Serug was thirty years old, he sired Nahor. **23** Serug lived two
> hundred years after he sired Nahor; he sired other sons and daughters.

24 When Nahor was twenty-nine years old, he sired Terah. 25 Nahor lived 119 years after he sired Terah; he sired other sons and daughters.
26 When Terah was seventy years old, he sired Abram, Nahor, and Haran.

a. The MT's ages of the individuals in the genealogy are different from the ages in the Septuagint, which themselves are different from those in the SP. The latter version and text present larger numbers than those in the LXX. For discussion, see McEvenue 1971, 55–59; Westermann 1984, 560–62.

b. The LXX includes a name and generation, Kainan, between Arpachshad and Shelah. One might surmise that the LXX represents an attempt to create a list of ten names, to parallel the ten names in the genealogy of Gen 5. Yet 1 Chr 1:24–25 attests the list of names as found in Gen 11.

[11:10] Genesis 11:10 commences with the fifth exemplar of the *tôlədôt* formula present in Genesis. Heretofore, each formula introduced the totality of human life (2:4a; 5:1; 6:9; 10:1). In contrast, 11:10 follows only one of Noah's three sons: Shem. The progeny of Ham and Yapheth are no longer in view. This genealogy therefore represents a narrowing, a move beyond a "universal" primeval history, a shift that began as early as the postflood scene in Noah's household with its Syro-Palestinian entities.

[10–26] The names and the numbers each deserve comment. Whether one follows the larger numbers of the SP or the smaller numbers of the MT, during the course of nine generations, the lifespans become decidedly shorter. The basic purport of the genealogy in 11:10–26 involves the shortening lifespan of these nine postdiluvian Israelite ancestors. They are much shorter than those individuals named in Gen 5, and they become shorter within the genealogy itself—from six hundred years (Shem, vv. 10–11) to 148 years (Nahor, vv. 24–25). (Terah lives longer than his father, reports Gen 11:32; the report about *his* age does not belong to the genealogy of vv. 10–26.) The list begins with Shem, who was born before the flood, and ends with Abram's father. Therefore the list covers more than just nine generations; it marks the transition from the primeval period to Israel's immediate ancestors. The transition is not, however, absolute. People remain the same; they bear children and live for an allotted period. They simply do not live as long as did those of the hoary past, nor are they "the ancient heroes, famous men" (Gen 6:4 [CEB]).

The names of those included in the genealogy are diverse. Shem, Arpachshad, Shelah, Eber, and Peleg also appear in Gen 10:21–25, and in that order. Serug, Nahor, and Terah can be localized in northeastern Syria, in the vicinity of Haran, a toponym associated with Abram (Gen 11:31), so Westermann (1984, 563–64). These toponyms, cities named Sarugi (cf. 11:21–23) and Til-Nahiri (cf. 11:22–25), serve a strategic purpose in the genealogy. Strikingly, the place names have been personified; they have become people—Serug and Nahor! (This same duality will occur with Haran in Gen 11:27–32.) The genealogy leading to Terah and Abram can be identified with a specific region. The primeval history associated humanity with Mesopotamia, and the tower-of-Babel episode resulted in the scattering of humanity. Now this genealogy, focusing just on the Shemite line, identifies them with one among the many places to which humanity has moved, the area of Haran.

The data concerning Terah offer a big surprise (v. 26). When he becomes a father, he is seventy years old, much older on entering fatherhood than any of the other members of the genealogy except Shem. Most of the others are in their thirties when they become parents. This note about Terah probably reflects a concern not to make Abraham appear too unusual, since he too becomes a parent in his old age. The Priestly author has inherited a tradition according to which Abraham is eighty-six years old when he becomes a father (Gen 16:16). This stands in stark contrast to the ages of parenthood in Gen 11. As a result, it is likely that a Priestly editor attributes a greater age for Terah so that Abraham's age at the births of Ishmael (and Isaac, 21:5) will fit at least one of his forebears.

As with Gen 5:32, which reports that Noah sired three sons, this genealogy concludes with a similar result. Terah sires a triumvirate: Abram, Nahor, and Haran. Of these three names, two are associated with one place: Haran and Nahor (so "the city of Nahor" [Gen 24:10]). But the other one is not: Abram. As a result, Abram is distinguished from his siblings in not being "localized." He and his family are free to move about in the land that God will show them (Gen 12:1).

Genesis 11:27–32
The Descendants of Terah

The sixth *tôlədōt* formula in Genesis introduces what appears to be another genealogy. It is, perhaps, better to think about these verses as a merged report and genealogy. Moreover, the genealogical materials themselves are more "complicated" than are those that have preceded it. There is new vocabulary, "daughter-in-law," and new relations, uncle-nephew. Two elements hold this data together: relationships between generations and relationships beyond those of the primal family (i.e., husband-wife, parent-child, sibling). The biblical authors have now begun to focus on one lineage and, as a result, are exploring different kinds of relationships.

The report also includes toponyms and movement; it is anchored to three places: Ur of the Chaldeans, Haran, and Canaan. Only one of these three names has appeared earlier in the book: Canaan. Oddly, neither "Ur" nor "Haran" appears in the broad sweep of Gen 10. This genealogy report is also colored by death, barrenness, and delay. Haran's death is untimely since he predeceases his father. The genealogy concludes with a report about Terah's death (though the genealogy in Gen 5 also includes reports of individuals' deaths, its last verse does not end on that note). Readers also learn that Abram's wife, one of two women identified in the genealogy, is barren. Finally, though Terah has apparently intended to take his family to Canaan, they do not reach that land, stopping instead at Haran, where Terah dies. Like Moses, he does not reach the land that he seeks.

11:27 These are the descendants of Terah. Terah sired Abram, Nahor, and
Haran; and Haran sired Lot. **28** Haran died before Terah, his father, while
he was still in the land of his birth, in Ur of the Chaldeans. **29** Abram
and Nahor took wives for themselves. The name of Abram's wife was
Sarai and the name of Nahor's wife was Milcah, who was the daughter
of Haran, who himself was the father of Milcah and Iscah. **30** Sarai was
barren; she had no child.[a]

31 Terah took Abram his son and Lot, the son of Haran, his grandson,
and Sarai, his daughter-in-law, the wife of Abram his son. They left Ur of
the Chaldeans for the land of Canaan. When they arrived at Haran, they

took up residence there. 32 When Terah was two hundred fifty years old,
Terah died in Haran.

a. MT has *wālād* instead of the more usual *yeled. Wālād* is also found in some MSS of 2 Sam 6:23, which likewise refers to a woman (Michal) who has "no child."

[11:27–30] The genealogical formula that has most recently appeared in Gen 11:10, "These are the descendants of Shem," reappears, though now introducing the lineage of Terah. (Similar formulae reappear for Ishmael [25:12], Isaac [25:19], Esau [36:1, 9], and Jacob [37:2].) Oddly, Genesis does not include the expected line "These are the descendants of Abram." He and his sons are apparently subsumed under the heading "these are the descendants of Terah."

This genealogy offers sparse information about Terah's three sons and their families. It identifies the wives of Abram and Nahor, but not of Haran. Since Haran has a son, Lot, one may presume that he was married. Moreover, the origins of Nahor's wife are made clear, whereas those of Sarai are not. Nahor's wife, Milcah, was his niece, the daughter of Haran. Haran has three children: Lot, Milcah, and Iscah, whereas Abram and Sarai have none because "Sarai was barren." The future of Terah's lineage might well be expected to lie with either Lot or the progeny that might be born to Nahor and Milcah. As it so happens, Nahor and Milcah's granddaughter, Rebekah, will become Isaac's wife (24:15). In contrast, Abram has married a person of unidentified genealogy (cf. 20:12, where a different author deems Sarah to be Terah's daughter) and someone who is unlikely to bear an heir to him since she is "barren."

[31–32] These verses are filled with action, most of it unexplained. Why does Terah decide to go to "the land of Canaan"? Though later biblical texts highlight the fertility of that area, nothing to this point in Genesis has been said about the land of Canaan. Why does Terah take Abram, Sarai, and Lot and not Nahor and his wife? Why does Terah leave Nahor and Milcah in Ur? And why do Terah and his family decide to take up residence in Haran? The author of the report offers no hints of answers to these questions. It may be best to read this movement from Ur to Haran as of a piece with the action most recently reported in Gen 11, the divinely enacted scattering of humanity (11:8–9). Terah's journey from Ur to Haran belongs to the movement engendered earlier in the chapter. His departure is not random but inheres in the movement of humanity that will fill the earth. But it is one that will occur in stages. He will lead his family from Ur to Haran. It will be left to Abram to take the family from Haran to "the land that I will show you" (12:1).

Genesis 11:27–32 are somber verses and filled with mystery. They include two deaths, one in Ur (Haran) and one in Haran (Terah). And the only woman among those who go to Haran is barren. Genesis 11 features death, infertility, and a delayed move. The final verses are a fitting coda to the ending of the tower-of-Babel episode: people are still on the move. But now that movement is quietly leading to a future that involves "the land of Canaan," mentioned specifically in Gen 12:5, and eventually children. To that extent, these verses function rather like a prologue to the narratives involving Abram/Abraham and Sarai/Sarah.

Genesis 12:1–9
YHWH Commands Abram, "Go to the Land I Will Show You"

Genesis 12:1–9 gives a report with two speeches and several itineraries. As befits a report, there is minimal narrative tension. As soon as YHWH commands Abram to go, he leaves Haran.

The first speech, which takes place in Haran, is inextricably connected to what follows it. The deity commands Abram to go (v. 1, *hlk*), and he goes (v. 4, *hlk*). The deity commands Abram to leave his native land (v. 1), whereupon Abram leaves Haran (v. 4). The deity commands Abram to go to the "land" (v. 1, *ʾereṣ*), and he arrives at "land" (v. 7, *ʾereṣ*), which is then promised to him (v. 7). The composer has begun to develop Abram's character as someone who is dutiful.

The vocabulary in these nine verses is oriented around geography. The word "land" (*ʾereṣ*) appears seven times, "place" (*māqôm*) once (v. 6), "hill country" (*har*) once (v. 8). And toponyms are prominent: Haran appears four times, Canaan two times, Bethel two times, Shechem, Ai, and Negeb once each. This diction emphasizes the issue of place, which will occupy Gen 13 as well. This first portion of the Abrahamic narrative addresses the land where Abram will dwell before it turns, in ensuing chapters and with greater length, to the matter of his progeny, though, of course, the latter issue is mentioned in verse 7. The diction of blessing is also important; the word appears five times, whether as noun or verb. Though Abram will be blessed (v. 2), others will as well (v. 3). This promise of "international" blessing seems appropriate as one delivered when Abram is living in Haran.

Oddly, even though place looms large in these verses, there is no explicit promise of land in the deity's first speech. Nor is there explicit reference to Abram's having an heir in that speech. Those two issues are finally addressed in the deity's brief second speech (v. 7), a speech directed to Abram once he is in the land. It is as if Abram's movement within the land and his subsequent presence at Shechem elicit YHWH's direct promise to him.

12:1 YHWH told Abram, "Go from your native land[a] and from your father's
household to the land that I will show you. **2** I will make of you a great
nation. I will bless you and make your name great so that you will be a

blessing. **3** I will bless those who bless you, and I will imprecate the one[b] who curses you. All the peoples[c] of the earth will be blessed through you."[d]

4 Abram went, just as YHWH had told him. Lot went with him. Abram was seventy-five years old when he left Haran. **5** Abram took Sarai, his wife, and Lot, his nephew, and all the possessions that they owned as well as the people they had acquired in Haran. They set out to travel to the land of Canaan. When they arrived in the land of Canaan, **6** Abram crossed into the land as far as the place Shechem, the terebinth of Moreh. The Canaanites were in the land then. **7** YHWH appeared to Abram and said, "To your progeny I will give this land." There Abram built an altar to YHWH, the one who had appeared to him. **8** From there he moved on to the hill country, east of Bethel. He pitched his tent with Bethel to the west and Ai to the east. He built an altar to YHWH and invoked the name of YHWH. **9** Abram then traveled slowly[e] toward the Negeb.

a. Literally, "your land and your birth/parentage."

b. SP, LXX, Syr, and Vulg read, "Those who curse you."

c. Or "families." The noun *mišpəḥōt* often refers to social units that imply a blood relationship.

d. Or one could translate with a reflexive sense: "All the peoples of the earth will bless themselves through you." See Grüneberg 2003.

e. Literally, "by stages."

[12:1–3] YHWH's speech to Abram possesses signal importance. Though it is not the starting point for the ancestral section, which begins in 11:27 (P), 12:1 does represent the first appearance of the deity since YHWH has scattered humanity at the end of the tower-of-Babel episode (11:9).

The speech is directly related to what follows it in 12:4–9 (see above). Moreover, the speech also builds on that which has preceded it in the primeval history. In contrast to the disarray at the end of the tower-of-Babel episode, von Rad (1972, 154) finds the deity acting in a new way, selecting and blessing Abram. Following von Rad, it is possible to identify several elements in the pre-Priestly primeval history that do shift in Gen 12:1–3. The deity would take the initiative rather than responding to the errant behavior of humans. The deity was providing direction rather than leaving humanity scattered "over the face of all the earth" (11:9). The deity would take responsibility for providing someone with a name, in contrast to the humanity's attempt to make a name for themselves (11:4). The deity would be responsible for the world of cursing and blessing, rather than leaving that in human hands (9:24–27). These are fundamental changes from the way things were narrated in the basic form of the primeval history.

However, Gen 12:1–9 is related to the primeval history in its "final form," that is, the form that includes both Priestly and non-Priestly material. Only P refers to the world of nations (10:32), and Gen 12:2 offers a promise that

Abram will become part of that world ("a great nation" [v. 2]). Moreover, the genealogy and report with which the P family literature begins (Gen 11:27–32) refer explicitly to Terah's destination as "the land of Canaan." And Abram enters that "land of Canaan" (12:6). And, most importantly, the language of "blessing" is pervasive in P's primeval history (e.g., 1:22, 28; 2:3; 5:2; 9:1). Such language surely leads into the formulation present in 12:2–3, where the word "bless/ing" (*brk*) appears no less than five times. In sum, Gen 12:1–3 is a pivotal, transitional text between the complete primeval history and the family literature. As such, it was likely written by someone who was aware of the Priestly material and hence can be construed as post-Priestly literature.

Much of the linkage between the primeval history and Gen 12:1–3 occurs in the first two verses. Verse 3 stands apart. It offers two responses to the question, How might Abram become a blessing? The first part of 12:3 transforms a standard cursing/blessing formulation attested in Gen 27:29, "Cursed be everyone who curses you, and blessed be everyone who blesses you" (// Num 24:9). This form of "automatic" cursing and blessing, which lacks an identifiable agent as the author of either cursing or blessing in Gen 27, is recast in Gen 12 with active verbs. Accordingly, some other person will bless Abram. At that point, YHWH will then bless that party. Only then does Abram become a blessing—through the deity's response to his having been blessed by someone else. Abram's becoming a blessing is inherently relational. It depends upon him receiving blessings from others. The obverse case is only implied, that Abram becomes a curse to others when the deity curses those who have cursed Abram. Still, the singular verb, "the one who curses you," stands in significant contrast to the plural number of those who will bless Abram (see Miller 1984, 472–76).

The notion of Abram being a blessing for others is reformulated in the final portion of the verse. It differs from the first part of verse 3 because the deity is not mentioned. The author has reverted to a passive (or reflexive) verb. Further, the ambiguity of how the blessing will be achieved reappears. But this final clause highlights the vast extent of his blessing. The circle of blessing broadens such that "all the families of the earth" will receive it. An individual may be cursed, but all the collectivities, the peoples, stand to benefit from whatever Abram signifies. In sum, verse 3 emphasizes blessing over curse. From a literary perspective, the one who curses is surrounded by those who bless and those who will be blessed.

The final portion of 12:3 is part of a discourse about the extent of Abram's blessing. The claim is reiterated for Abraham (18:18; 22:18), Isaac (26:4), and Jacob (28:14; of these texts, all but 28:14 refer to "nations" rather than "peoples" being blessed; also, the verb *brk* in 12:3; 18:18; 28:14 is niphal; and hithpael in 22:18; 26:4). Most, if not all, of these texts, stem from a late theological stratum in the literature, one concerned with the way in which Israel can relate positively to other folk.

The notion of Abram/Abraham being blessed by others is embedded in the family literature. In Gen 14, after Abram is victorious in battle and has rescued Lot, Melchizedek of Salem, a priest of El Elyon (God Most High), "blesses" Abram. The text does not report that the deity directly blesses Melchizedek but does imply that he receives bounty since Abram "gave him one-tenth of everything," presumably booty from the war. This episode may offer a paradigm for what such mutual blessing might have meant for the author of Gen 12:3.

[4–9] Verses 1–3 are often set off from verses 4–9. The first three verses, after all, comprise a speech; then verses 4–9 (except for part of v. 7) report Abram's journey. Nonetheless, both on source and literary-critical grounds, it is licit to understand 12:4 as the result of YHWH's command in the first speech.

It is telling that Lot's presence with Abram is mentioned before that of Sarai. Is this indicative of kinship obligation? And why is Lot mentioned yet again in 12:5? The answer lies in the importance of the Abraham-Lot subplot in the Abrahamic saga. Family literature is, almost by definition, interested in ways that families come to exist as well as in the ways that they separate.

Verse 5 reports that Abram leaves for Canaan. This, of course, was the goal of his father. Terah departed from Ur with his family, intended to settle in the land of Canaan, but stopped at Haran and died there (11:31–32). However, there is no explicit reason to think that Abram thought Canaan would, itself, be the land that God would "show" him." Rather, he is depicted as continuing the journey his father had begun and, in obedience to YHWH, expecting some further indication of where he was to stop and dwell.

The text leaves unstated the precise way YHWH "shows" (v. 1) Abram which land should be the goal for his journey. But the fact that the verb "to see" is used in both 12:1 and 7 suggests that YHWH's appearing to Abram as soon as he has arrived in Canaan is an indication that Abram has arrived at the promised place. Before YHWH's appearance (v. 7), Abram is not reported to have built any altars. However, once YHWH has identified the area as "this land," Abram soon builds two altars (vv. 7–8).

This biblical narrator reports that only after Abram pitches his tent between Bethel and Ai does he "invoke the name of YHWH" (v. 8). The literal expression "call on the name of YHWH" appears elsewhere in Genesis (4:26; 13:4; 21:33; 26:25). It is striking that Abram does not "worship" in this way at any of the three cities (Shechen, Bethel, and Ai) that have just been mentioned. One has the sense of the author suggesting that Abram is open to ritual sites that already exist (e.g., the terebinth at Moreh; 12:6), but that he is also doing something distinct, such as building new altars and also worshiping in places that are altogether new, such as the dwelling site between Bethel and Ai. Once Abram builds an altar there, he invokes the name of YHWH.

The picture created in 12:4–9 portrays a trek from north (Shechem) to south (Bethel and Ai), accompanied by the creation of ritual sites. Ultimately, Jacob will be associated more prominently with Bethel than was Abram/Abraham, but for the author of 12:1–9, Abram is the one who lays initial claim to "this land" (v. 7), which is roughly the tribal territory of Ephraim (Shechem lies just north of the northern border of Ephraim). After remaining near Bethel and Ai for an unspecified amount of time, Abram moves slowly even farther south on a major journey toward the Negeb.

Genesis 12:10–20
Abram Tells Sarai in Egypt, "Say That You Are My Sister"

This is the first of the so-called "wife-sister" stories (cf. Gen 20; 26:1–26), the first two of which present Abraham as the protagonist; Isaac is featured in the third one. This narrative serves multiple purposes. It demonstrates the tenuous hold that the lineage of Terah has on the land to which they have migrated. It establishes a motif of leaving the land during a time of famine, a motif that will, with Egypt as the land of plenty, recur late in the book. It foreshadows the plagues that YHWH will use against Egypt when the people are enslaved there and the wealth that Israel will accumulate when it leaves Egypt (Exod 12:35). Moreover, the narrative begins to flesh out the character of Abram, who now speaks for the first time. That so much can be accomplished in eleven relatively brief verses testifies to the skill of the person who has composed this narrative.

For many interpreters, study of the wife-sister stories has involved an attempt to determine which is the earliest version and to which so-called source each may be attributed. More recently, the focus has turned to literary approaches, which involve an attempt to discern what is distinctive about each use of the wife-sister motif. This is the approach taken in these pages, though I contend that these verses can be attributed to the primary author of the Abrahamic saga.

> 12:10 There was a famine in the land, so Abram went down to Egypt to
> live as an immigrant[a] because the famine was very severe in the land.
> 11 When he was about to enter Egypt, he said to Sarai, his wife, "Look,
> I know that you are a very beautiful woman. 12 So, when the Egyptians
> see you, they will say, 'This is his wife.' They will kill me but let you
> live. 13 Say that you are my sister so that it may go well for me because of
> you, and so that I might remain alive on account of you." 14 When Abram
> entered Egypt, the Egyptians observed that the woman was, indeed, very
> beautiful. 15 When the officials of Pharaoh saw her, they praised her to
> Pharaoh so that the woman was taken into Pharaoh's household. 16 On
> account of her, things went very well[b] for Abram. He had sheep, oxen,
> male donkeys, male and female slaves, female donkeys, and camels.
>
> 17 But YHWH afflicted Pharaoh and his household with terrible[c]
> plagues because of Sarai, the wife of Abram. 18 Pharaoh summoned

Abram and said, "What is this that you have done to me? Why did you
not tell me that she was your wife? 19 Why did you say, 'She is my sister,'
with the result that I took her as my wife? Now, here is your wife. Take
her and begone!" 20 Pharaoh gave his men orders concerning him. They
sent him away, along with his wife and all he had.

a. So CEB.
b. Literally, "It went very well." Cf. v. 13.
c. LXX adds "and painful."

[12:10–16] The first sentence of the story presents a serious problem confronting Abram and those with him. The land to which they have just moved is suffering from a famine. Since they have already journeyed to the southern portion of the land of Canaan (the Negeb), it makes narrative sense for them to continue onward to Egypt, which the omniscient narrator presumes is not suffering that same plight. (The situation in Gen 41:53–57 appears different, since Egypt, too, experiences a famine.) The details of 12:10 stand in contrast to the journey described earlier in the chapter, since there is no reference to Lot going with him into Egypt. However, Gen 13:1 clearly assumes that Lot is with Abram and Sarai the entire time.

If famine is now the first threat to Abram, danger to his life because of Sarai's beauty is the second. The first threat is shared by all those with him; the second is a threat only to Abram. Just as he has acted to solve the first threat, now he creates a plan to address the second one: asking Sarai to report that she is his sister, not his wife. The plan works, though not in ways that Abram has apparently anticipated. Not only is Abram's life saved, but Sarai, since she is not married in the eyes of the Egyptians, becomes available as a potential spouse. Then she is taken not by just any Egyptian male, but by Pharaoh. The clear presumption is that she now is lost to Abram as a spouse and functioning as a spouse of Pharaoh. At this point the narrator refers to her as "the woman" (vv. 14–15), hinting that she has lost her identity as an Israelite and as Abram's wife. She is an object, someone "taken into Pharaoh's household."

In such a terse story, it is telling that Abram offers two reasons for his plan: (1) that "it may go well with me" and (2) "I might remain alive." The first goal seems to move beyond Abram's initial concern about the threat to his life. Prosperity, not just survival, are this character's two concerns. The narrator need not report that Abram's life is spared; the story itself testifies to that fact. However, 12:16 goes to some length in reporting the ways in which "it went well" for Abram because of Sarai, the same vocabulary used in verse 13. "Going well" means the acquisition of much domestic livestock and enslaved persons. The list stands out due to its length in this short narrative. Things have, indeed, gone very well for Abram. He is alive and wealthy; and he has lost his wife.

[17–20] The woman who lost her name now regains it. Sarai moves from being "the woman" to resuming as "Sarai, Abram's wife," since she retained that status in the eyes of the deity. She becomes the rationale for YHWH to enter the narrative. YHWH afflicts Pharaoh and his household "*because of Sarai, Abram's wife*." (One might even assume that Sarai suffers as a result of such punitive action since she is, from the perspective of the narrative, still in Pharaoh's household.)

The narrator is uninterested in explaining how Pharaoh learns about the cause of the plagues (cf. Gen 20:3, where God reveals the identity of Sarai to the king in a dream). Instead, the narrator presents Pharaoh as an interrogator, slashing at Abram with three questions. The first is general: "What have you done?" One might suppose that is rhetorical, the answer being clear to both Pharaoh and Abram. The second and third questions probe for Abram's rationale. Interestingly, the third question, a positive version of the second question, hints that *Abram* was the one who has said Sarai was his sister rather than the planned speech by Sarai, in which she was supposed to say that he was her brother. (Here, again, Sarai has lost agency.) Receiving no answer to his questions, Pharaoh, through his deputies, dismisses "him": here Abram also loses his name. The Hebrew words *qaḥ wālēk*—short and harsh-sounding imperatives, "Take her and begone"—underscore the abrupt tone of Pharaoh's dismissal.

In sum, this telling of the wife-sister story focuses on the dissonance between Abram's plan and that of the deity. Abram's plan is designed to save his life and to gain wealth. YHWH, on the other hand, is concerned to restore Sarai to her status as "Abram's wife." The character of Abram is fuller than at the beginning of the story, though the narrator offers no overt negative assessment of this individual who was so palpably concerned with his own survival and "well-being." His plan has threatened his ability to have the promised children (so 12:7); that is surely not lost on the ancient writers and editors. The presence of such children is clearly inherent in God's plan.

Genesis 13:1–18
Abram Says to Lot, "Is Not the Entire Land before You? Leave Me"

Genesis 13, often viewed as a relatively unimportant portion of the Abrahamic saga, is significant due to (1) the conflict that emerges between Abram and Lot and (2) the implications of the resolution for both of them. Important features of the two primary characters emerge, with Abram appearing as the more hospitable person. The frequent reference to "tents" (vv. 3, 5, 12, 18) underscores the lifestyle of these two individuals, even as they live near cities. In the epilogue to the story, the deity, who has not been mentioned until verse 14, addresses Abram, promising that he, not just his progeny (12:7), will receive the land in which he now lives. Most, if not all, of the chapter has been composed by the primary author.

13:1 Abram went up from Egypt toward the Negeb, he, his wife, and all
that he had; Lot was with him.

2 Now Abram was very wealthy—having livestock, silver, and gold.
3 He proceeded slowly[a] from the Negeb as far as Bethel, the site where he
had first pitched his tent, between Bethel and Ai, **4** to the site of the altar
that he had previously constructed. There Abram called on the name of
YHWH. **5** Lot, who was going with Abram, also possessed flocks, herds,
and tents. **6** The land was not able to support them both living together in
the same place since they had so many possessions; they were not able
to live together. **7** There was conflict between the shepherds of Abram's
livestock and between the shepherds of Lot's livestock. At that time, the
Canaanites and Perizzites lived in the land.

8 Abram then said to Lot, "Let there be no conflict between me and
you, and between my shepherds and your shepherds, since we are kinsmen. **9** Is not the entire land before you? Leave me. If you go to the
left, I will go to the right. If you go to the right, I will go to the left."
10 Lot looked around and saw the territory of the Jordan, that all of it was
well supplied with water—all the way to Zoar (this was before YHWH
destroyed Sodom and Gomorrah); it was like the garden of YHWH or
like the land of Egypt. **11** So Lot chose for himself the entire Jordan plain.
He traveled eastward. The two kinsmen were separated from each other.

12 Abram lived in the land of Canaan, and Lot lived among the cities of
the plain. He pitched his tent near Sodom. 13 Now the people of Sodom
were evil, sinners against YHWH.

14 YHWH said to Abram, after Lot had separated himself from him,
"Look around and see from this place where you currently are—to the
north, to the south, to the east, and to the west. 15 For all this land that
you can see I will give to you and to your offspring in perpetuity. 16 I
will make your offspring like the dust of the earth, such that if someone
could count the dust of the earth, your offspring could also be counted.
17 Get up and walk throughout the land, in its width and breadth, since I
will give it to you." 18 So Abram struck camp, went, and lived near the
oaks of Mamre, which are at Hebron. He built there an altar to YHWH.

a. Literally, "by stages" or "by departures."

[13:1] Verse 1, a report, is transitional, lying between the first wife-sister story and the narrative concerning conflict between Lot and Abram. The verse functions in at least two ways. First, it moves Abram from Egypt back to the land of Canaan, a journey mandated by Pharaoh (12:19). Second, verse 1 reintegrates Lot into the story. Though Gen 12:10–20 does not refer to Lot as going down to Egypt with Abram, the clear sense of 13:1 has Lot accompanying Abram into the Negeb from Egypt. The story about their conflict can only begin when Lot and Abram are in the same place.

[2–7] The disjunctive clause at the beginning of 13:2 signals the beginning of a new story. In the first scene (vv. 2–7), the narrator sets the stage for the conflict between Lot and Abram, though he gives neither of them voice in these verses. (In fact, Lot never speaks in Gen 13.) The first portion of the scene focuses on Abram (Lot is not mentioned until v. 5). Verses 2–4 characterize Abram as wealthy, though his wealth is more "diversified" than is Lot's (cf. v. 5). Moreover, this wealth links Abram to his life before the journey to Egypt, with possessions and enslaved persons as mentioned in 12:5. In Gen 13 his wealth is described in a different way, involving "livestock, silver, and gold." Interestingly, none of these words appear in the list of property that Pharaoh gives to Abram (12:16), though domestic livestock appear in both lists. Reference to silver and gold belongs more to the world of royal wealth than it does to the finances of the family literature. To be sure, Abram pays for a burial ground with silver, and he sends gold jewelry as gifts (Gen 24). One may suppose that the claim for Abram possessing both silver and gold is based on traditions that lie behind Gen 23 and 24. However, it is more likely that the phrase "livestock, silver, and gold" is simply formulaic, a way of characterizing the nature of his wealth, consisting of livestock and precious metals.

With 13:3–4, the author makes clear that Abram is returning to a place where he had earlier settled. This is not a new entry into the land; it is a place at which religious practice was of fundamental importance. An altar has been built earlier, and Abram has invoked the name of YHWH. This return underscores that the land is now to be associated with Abram and not with someone else, even though Canaanites and Perizzites also live in that land (v. 7).

Verse 5 brings Lot into the scene. He, too, is wealthy, but the wealth is different from that of Abram. He owns flocks and herds, the same words used for what Pharaoh gave Abram (12:16). Some scholars have suggested that Lot was not as wealthy as Abram, though the text does not seem interested in making this distinction. Their wealth was different in kind, but not necessarily in total value. For substantial conflict to arise, Lot and his property would need to balance that of Abram's. The strife would not be consequential if Lot does not have the same high level of wealth as Abram.

The syntax is verse 6 is difficult, allowing some interpreters to think that crowding is the only reason for Lot and Abram to part ways (Westermann 1985, 177). Yet the reasons are several. First, the land itself cannot support them: the number of their livestock is too large for the territory where they are located. Second, the number of animals and shepherds make it impossible for them to exist peaceably together (v. 7). Both ecological problems and those of human interaction make conflict inevitable.

[8–13] Before the conflict becomes worse, Abram takes action. Here the narrative highlights the importance of this action by letting Abram speak. First, Abram appeals to the fact that both he and Lot belong to the same lineage. (The resolution of conflict within the lineage of Terah is a hallmark in the book of Genesis.) Abram's rhetorical question is interesting, since the narrator has, in 13:7, reported that the land is not empty. The verb "leave" (v. 9) is in the imperative. Abram is really ordering Lot to do something. However, he takes the edge off the command by offering Lot his choice of land.

Lot's decision is grounded in what has already transpired in the book of Genesis. The land that he sees, part of the Great Rift Valley channeling the Jordan River, elicits two similes: it is like the garden depicted in Gen 3, and it is like Egypt, to which Abram (and Lot?) traveled during a time of drought. Both places, the garden and Egypt, are watered by rivers, which is also the case with the land that Lot now sees. Only by hindsight, which the author offers in verse 10, does one know that this choice is fraught with danger.

The conflict is resolved when Lot and Abram separate. The author narrates this conclusion quickly and without extraneous description. Yet their respective final destinations do elicit comment. Abram resides in "the land of Canaan," which is where he has originally settled. Lot pitches his camp among the cities of the Jordan territory, at/near Sodom, a place known to the author, if not to Lot, as not only wicked, but populated by people who sin against YHWH (v. 13). Lot lives near or with the inhabitants of Sodom, and Abram with the Canaanites and Perizzites. The former are likened to the wicked people who lived before the flood (6:5); the latter elicit no overt comment.

[14–18] At this point in the narrative, the conflict has been resolved. Lot and Abram now live in separate places. As a result, one may characterize the final five verses as an epilogue. The implications of the preceding narrative are explored, though only for Abram. Lot is no longer in view here. The deity, though not "appearing," now addresses Abram. Lot has earlier looked out over the territory where he and Abram have lived (v. 10). Now the deity invites Abram to do the same (the verbs in Hebrew are identical), to "look around" (lit., "lift his eyes") and "see" the land, though now from the vantage of where he had settled in "the land of Canaan." The deity then makes a dual promise of giving Abram land and progeny, a duality that reverberates through the family literature. In fact, the image of progeny as numerous as the dust of the earth reappears in the repeated promise to Jacob (Gen 28:14). After this speech there is more action. The deity has commanded Abram to move about the land, to explore it. And so he does, finally settling in Hebron, far to the south of where the deity has been speaking with him. Just as Abram orders Lot to move, God commands Abram to move.

In sum, one of the ways in which conflict is resolved in this story is physical separation, which is presented to the reader as a strategy promulgated by Abram. (In Gen 12, Abram's strategy of having Sarai identify herself as his sister is less astute and is not affirmed by the deity as is his decision in this chapter.) The conflict is of two sorts: ecological burden and human disagreement. The removal of one group from the territory solves both problems. The presence of Abram at first near Bethel and Ai and then later, without Lot, near Hebron and Mamre underscores the legitimacy of his claim to the land; he is now related to more places than has earlier been the case. In addition, the story has implications for "national identity," since Lot is the eponymous ancestor of two nations: Moab and Ammon (19:37–38). Genesis 13 ensures that Abram's progeny, here understood as inheriting the territory of what will become Judah and Israel, have laid claim to the land west of the Jordan and the Dead Sea. In addition, the story highlights Abram as a strategic thinker, one who can even be understood as gracious to his nephew. And the narrative presents him as a wealthy individual, someone able to move throughout the land—from Bethel and Ai to Hebron without difficulty. The number of toponyms throughout the chapter (Negeb, Bethel, Ai, land of Canaan, cities of the plain, Sodom, oaks of Mamre, Hebron) underscores the importance of place and who belongs where as it evolves in these verses.

This narrative does far more than portray Lot as a foil for Abram. He is that, indeed, but he is also a potential heir in the lineage of Terah. This story removes him geographically from the land that was the object of Terah's original migration. As a result he becomes less likely to share in the promise made to Abram, a fact made even more clear in the chapters that ensue.

Genesis 14:1–24
Abram Marshals His Troops to Rescue His Kinsman

It has become a commonplace to characterize Gen 14 as "odd man out" in the family literature. The canvas presents a much larger field of vision, including kings from distant empires, than do the surrounding chapters. The verses offer royal and international perspectives. The chapter is populated by strange names associated with diverse political entities. The events described and the characterization of Abram stand at odds with what one finds in Gen 12–36. Further, the form of the literature and certain linguistic features distinguish it from those other chapters. The challenge for an interpreter is to characterize Gen 14 adequately in its own right and to determine what role it plays within the larger Abrahamic saga. Fortunately, 14:1–11 bears affinities to a genre of literature attested in Mesopotamia, the so-called *naru* texts. They testify to a great king who defeats a military coalition. The coalitions are imaginary alliances, including real opponents from different historical contexts as well as fictional enemies. These verses also share features with other biblical and extrabiblical texts, including a chronology based on a specific king's reign.

The chapter introduces two royal alliances, one of empires (14:1) and another of city-states (v. 2). The empires defeat the city-states. Another alliance, one based on kinship and led by Abram, defeats "their enemies" (v. 15), an entity that almost certainly refers to the victorious alliance of kings. Though Abram consistently fights with or interacts with kings, he is different in kind from them. The author highlights his virtue and his role as kin to Lot.

14:1 In the days of Amraphel, king of Shinar; Arioch, king of Ellasar;
Chedorlaomer, king of Elam; and Tidal, king of Goiim;[a] **2** they waged
war against Bera, king of Sodom; Birsha, king of Gomorrah; Shinab, king
of Admah; Shemeber, king of Zeboiim; and the king of Bela, which is
Zoar. **3** All these fought in an alliance at the valley of Siddim, that is, the
Salt [Dead] Sea. **4** They had served Chedorlaomer twelve years, but in
the thirteenth year they rebelled. **5** In the fourteenth year, Chedorlaomer
and the kings who were with him defeated the Rephaim who were in
Ashteroth-karnaim, the Zuzim in Ham, the Emim in Shaveh-kiriathaim,

6 and the Horites in the hill country of Seir as far as Ail-Paran, which
is near the edge of the wilderness. 7 Then they came back and went to
En-mishpat, which is Kadesh, and destroyed all the territory of the Amalekites, and also that of the Amorites, who lived in Hazazon-tamar. 8 The
king of Sodom, the king of Gomorrah, the king of Admah, the king of
Zeboiim, and the king of Bela, which is Zoar, all went out and joined
forces for battle at the valley of Siddim against 9 King Chedorlaomer of
Elam, King Tidal of Goiim, King Amraphel of Shinar, and King Arioch
of Ellasar—four kings against five. 10 Now the valley of Siddim contained many tar pits such that when the kings of Sodom and Gomorrah
fled, they fell into them there. The rest fled into the hill country. 11 They
then plundered Sodom and Gomorrah, including all their foodstuffs, and
left. 12 As well, they took Lot, Abram's nephew, who had been living in
Sodom, and his possessions, and left.

13 Someone who survived came and told Abram the Hebrew, who was
living near the terebinths of Mamre, the Amorite, the kinsman of Eshcol
and Aner; they were covenantal allies of Abram. 14 When Abram heard
that his kinsman had been captured, he loosed[b] his vassals, the ones born
in his household, 318 in number, and went in pursuit as far as Dan. 15 He
and his troops[c] marshaled themselves against their enemies at night. He
defeated them and then pursued them as far as Hobah, which is north
of Damascus. 16 Then he brought back all the possessions, and he also
brought back Lot, his kinsman, along with his possessions, and along
with the women and other people.

17 The king of Sodom came out to meet him at the Valley of Shaveh,
which is the King's valley, upon his return from defeating Chedorlaomer
and the kings who had been with him. 18 Melchizedek king of Salem
brought out bread and wine; he was a priest of El Elyon. 19 He blessed
him, saying,

"Blessed is Abram by El Elyon,
Creator of heaven and earth;
20 and blessed is El Elyon,
who delivered your enemies into your hand!"

He [Abram] gave him [Melchizedek] one-tenth of everything. 21 Then
the king of Sodom said to Abram, "Give me the people, but you take
the property!" 22 Abram responded to the king of Sodom, "I have sworn
to YHWH[d] El Elyon, creator of heaven and earth, 23 that I would take
neither thread, nor sandal thong, nor anything else that belongs to you
so that you could not claim, 'I made Abram rich.' 24 Nothing except for
what the young men have eaten and a portion for the men who were with
me: Aner, Eshcol, and Mamre. Let them take their share."

a. The syntax of the first two sentences is awkward: the kings' names in v. 1, which appears to be a temporal clause, are not easy to link with the subject of the verb in v. 2.

b. MT *wayyāreq* is difficult to translate. The verb can mean "to unsheath a sword." See Speiser 1964, 103–4, for a concise discussion of the philological issues.

c. Literally, "his servants."

d. LXX, Syr, and the Genesis Apocryphon (of the DSS) do not include "YHWH." The divine name may have been inserted to accommodate concern about the presence of the Canaanite formulation, El Elyon.

[14:1–12] Many comments on these verses have involved an attempt to identify the names of kings, especially, and nations with entities known from the ancient Near East.[1] In some cases, Gen 14 alludes to a well-known toponym, including Elam, an empire that flourished to the east of ancient Mesopotamia and just north of the Persian Gulf; or to a likely royal name, such as Tidal, generally understood to reflect the Hittite royal name Tudhaliyah (there were at least five Hittite rulers so named).[2] Other names such as Bela, and toponyms such as Goiim, have not been successfully associated with any nation. Put another way, some names may well be literary creations, with others deriving from one or another country.

Since many such attempts have foundered, it seems appropriate to focus on other issues, the most fundamental of which is the literary genre(s) present in Gen 14. To address this issue, it is appropriate to make the following observations, especially about the first portion of the chapter. First, the text includes a description of military alliances. Second, the group described in 14:1, especially if Shinar refers to Babylon (so Gen 10:10; 11:2), involves kings and major empires; the one described in verse 2 refers to small, Syro-Palestinian cities, all of which were probably located near the Dead Sea. Third, the alliances are of unequal strength: four kings of major empires versus five kings of small city-states. The reader would likely predict that the major empires will defeat the smaller ones, which is what happened in the first battle.

Several of these features may be found in a certain form of cuneiform texts, the so-called *naru* literature. Yochanan Muffs, following H. Güterbock, offers the following definition: the *naru* is "an historical romance whose original purpose was the glorification of monarchs such as Sargon I and Naram-Sin and evidently [the exaltation] of other later kings of equal fame" (Muffs 1982, 82). Salient features of the *naru* literature include the presence of artificially constructed names, other "real" names drawn from a wide range of historical contexts, military coalitions, the adulation of a heroic figure, and the syntactic sequence of "when . . . then." All these features appear in Gen 14:1–16,

1. For example, Astour 1966, 65–122; Margalith 2000, 501–8. Emerton (1971, 24–47) has challenged many identifications advocated in the two aforementioned studies.

2. Speiser 1964, 107; Margalith 2000, 501–2.

suggesting that searching for a "real" battle would be ignoring the character of the literature present in these verses.[3] Rather than a chronicle, it is more like a royal legend, highlighting Abram's surprising and remarkable military might and moral virtue. Abram, like other subjects of the *naru* literature, is presented as similar in kind but ultimately different from the rulers listed in Gen 14. His alliance is based on family and covenant, not on his role as king of a vast territorial empire.

Verses 1–2 sketch the military alliances, whose battle sets the stage for Abram's exploits. Amraphel, Arioch, Chedorlaomer, and Tidal, all apparently located in or near Mesopotamia, are reported to have fought with Bera, Birsha, Shinab, Shemeber, and the king of Bela. Before this battle, Chedorlaomer's alliance had fought with and conquered other Syro-Palestinian entities: Rephaim, Zuzim, Emim, Horites, Amalekites, and Amorites. After this battle, Bera's alliance comes out to fight with Chedorlaomer's league and is defeated. Focus then narrows to two of the cities, Sodom and Gomorrah—not on their kings, Bera and Birsha, respectively—and their despoliation. As something of an afterthought, the author adds that Lot, Abram's nephew, and his property are also captured.

[13–16] The ensuing verses report Abram's response to the capture of his nephew and his property. The author is intent on portraying Abram as part of an alliance, though not a royal one. Abram is living near an Amorite named Mamre, a person with two brothers: Eshcol and Aner. The narrator identifies all three as having a covenantal relationship with Abram. However, the raison d'être for Abram's departure is the capture of his relative. When Abram leaves to fight those who had attacked Sodom, no mention is made of his allies going with him. (Only in v. 24 does the author report that Aner, Eshcol, and Mamre have accompanied him in his campaign.) Instead, he marshals a private army at night and defeats "his enemies." This report stands in stark contrast with the battles described in 14:1–12. The enemies are not named. Few details of the battle are provided (cf. vv. 6–7, 10). Instead, the author highlights Abram fighting with his private retainers and deploying them strategically, dividing them into thirds and fighting at night.

The very brief statement about Lot in 14:12 refers to his being taken captive and the plunder of his property. Things change in verse 16. Abram returns from battle with "all the property," "Lot," "his possessions," and "women and other people." Abram is clearly bringing back much more than Lot and what belongs to him. It is as if Abram is returning with what had been captured from Sodom (and Gomorrah, v. 11). His apparent motive, rescuing Lot (v. 14), has resulted in

3. Margalith's description of the text as a "*para-mythe*" and its "pseudo-historical background" is consistent with Muff's approach, though Margalith does not refer to the *naru* literature (2000, 504–5).

a restoration of people and property far beyond the confines of his extended family. The scale of his plunder may have raised questions about his real motives, an issue that is explicitly addressed in the final scene of the chapter.

[17–24] These verses describe one scene in which Abram interacts with two local kings: Bera of Sodom (his name is not present in vv. 17 and 22; see v. 2) and Melchizedek of Salem. Bera would have been part of the alliance defeated by Chedorlaomer, whom, as 14:17 makes clear, Abram has just defeated. Yet again, the text makes no attempt to construe Abram as a typical royal figure. Rather, the author focuses on his character as "blessed" and as virtuous. The report therefore bears the features of a legend.

After ranging from northern Israel (Dan) to Syria (Hobah, north of Damascus), Abram returns to a valley near Jerusalem. Royal language, so prominent in the chapter, is used to describe it as "the King's valley." This location would help explain the appearance of Melchizedek of Salem, assuming Salem to be an abbreviated word for Jerusalem. Less clear is why the king of Sodom is at hand if Sodom is at the southern end of the Dead Sea.

Verses 18–20 appear to be intrusive; they interrupt the appearance of Bera (king of Sodom, v. 17; cf. v. 2) and the interaction between Bera and Abram (vv. 21–24). Reference to Melchizedek, a name that means "My king is righteous," also appears in Ps 110:4. There YHWH swears, concerning a king in Zion, "You are a priest forever according to the order of Melchizedek." In this regard, two things are important. First, this psalm attests, as part of royal ideology throughout the ancient Near East and in Israel, that the king holds priestly prerogatives. For example, David exercises priestly roles (e.g., 2 Sam 6:18–19; 24:25). Second, such a role is hereditary, in an "order" or "lineage" of Melchizedek. So, too, David's sons are known to be priests (2 Sam 8:18).

In his priestly role, Melchizedek presents bread and wine and offers a dual blessing. The former presents something of a puzzle. Both bread (e.g., Exod 25:30; Lev 23:17, 20) and wine (e.g., Num 15:1–10) are used in Israelite rituals. However, there is no ceremony that specifies the two in combination. Hence, it is not clear whether the bread and wine are to be consumed by Abram or presented as an offering to YHWH. Fortunately, the blessing is less problematic. Though the prose introduction reports that Melchizedek "blessed him," the poetic speech allows for the above translation "blessed is . . ." rather than the traditional "blessed be . . ." That Melchizedek uses the idiom of "El Elyon" (as in Ps 78:35) is telling since the pre-Israelite population of Jerusalem is using this idiom about the Canaanite high God, El, the god thought to have created the universe (so Cross 1973, 50–52). In response, Abram gives Melchizedek one-tenth of what he has retrieved from Chedorlaomer. (Later in Genesis, Jacob promises to give God a tenth of his property: 28:20–22. Then Deut 12:6, 11 attests to the general practice of tithing; also, Deut 14:28–29 and Num 18:21–24 specify that the practice of tithing is designed to provide help to widows, orphans, resident aliens, and Levites.) Whether Abram's gift to Melchizedek is for maintaining the cult or to help those in need is difficult to determine. More important is the fact that Abram responds to Melchizedek's actions and speech with a gift, a gift to Melchizedek, not to God. Abram leaves without being in Melchizedek's debt.

Surrounding this episode (vv. 18–20) is the interaction between Abram and the king of Sodom, which involves the disposition of what Abram has rescued from Chedorlaomer. Bera initiates the dialogue by using imperative verbs ("give . . . take") directed at Abram. People and goods are under discussion. Strikingly, nothing is said about Lot or what has belonged to him. The king wants slaves, and he assumes Abram is interested in other spoils of war. Abram demurs in a flashback, citing an oath he has made not to take anything that has come from the king's city. Here, too, Abram is concerned not to be in someone else's debt. He agrees that his allies, Mamre, Aner, and Eshcol, can receive their share of the spoils. But as for Abram, the king of Sodom is not the one who has or will make Abram wealthy. Abram, already a wealthy man with his own private army, has fulfilled the obligations of kinship and does not need a reward from Bera.

Genesis 15:1–21
YHWH Makes a Covenant with Abram

Genesis 15 reports the making of a covenant between the deity and Abram. But much more than that is at work in this chapter. The first six verses present a dialogue cloaked in prophetic language, addressing the issue of inheritance and progeny, and then concluding with the narrator's theological interpretation of what has transpired in the dialogue. The next portion includes yet another dialogue, but this one focuses on the issue of land. The making of the covenant is a response to Abram's question about how he might know that he will actually possess the land. The notion of "inheritance" (from *yrš*) holds together these two portions of the chapter. Direct discourse, especially that spoken by the deity, is prominent in this chapter. Many scholars view Gen 15, especially the first six verses, as a source-critical hodgepodge from diverse authors (see von Rad 1972, 182–83). Verses 12–16 are probably later additions to the text. They temporally qualify the promise of the land made through the covenant.

15:1 After these things, the word of YHWH came to Abram in a vision,
"Do not fear, Abram, I am your shield. Your recompense will be very
great." **2** Abram said, "O my Lord YHWH, what might you give me? I
continue to be childless. The son of Mesheq is in my house, Eliezer."[a]
3 Abram continued, "You have not given me an heir. Hence a member of
my household will inherit from me." **4** Then the word of YHWH came to
him, "This individual will not receive your inheritance. Instead, someone to whom you are a father will receive your inheritance." **5** Then he
brought him outside and said, "Look at the heavens and count the stars, if
you are able to count them." Then he said to him, "Your progeny shall be
like that." **6** He then trusted YHWH, who, because of that trust, deemed
him to be righteous.[b]

7 He said to him, "I am YHWH, who brought you from Ur of the Chaldees, to give to you this land to possess." **8** He said, "My Lord, YHWH,
how might I know that I will possess it?" **9** He responded, "Bring me a
three-year-old heifer, a three-year-old female goat, a three-year-old ram,
a turtle dove, and a pigeon." **10** He brought to him all these animals and cut
them in half. He placed each half over opposite the other, though he did

not cut the birds in half. 11 When birds of prey flew down to the carcasses,
Abram drove them away.

12 As the sun set, a deep sleep fell on Abram; a massive and murky
sense of terror fell over him. 13 He said to Abram, "You should know
that your progeny will be resident aliens in a land that is not their own.
The natives will enslave them and oppress them for four hundred years.
14 Then I will judge the nation that they served. Thereafter, they will come
out with great possessions. 15 As for you, you will go peacefully to your
ancestors. You will be buried at a good old age. 16 But they will return
here in the fourth generation, because the sins of the Amorites are not yet
sufficient [to warrant their expulsion]."

17 When the sun had set and it was dark, a smoking firepot and a flaming torch passed between the cut-up carcasses. 18 On that day, YHWH
made[c] a covenant with Abram, saying, "To your progeny I give this
land—from the river of Egypt to the Great River, the Euphrates River;
19 the [territory of the] Qenites, the Qenizzites, the Qadmonites, 20 the
Hittites, the Perizzites, the Rephaim, 21 the Amorites, the Canaanites, the
Girgashites, and the Jebusites."

a. The MT reads, "the son of Mesheq is in my house—he is (of/from) Damascus, Eliezer." See comments.

b. It is possible to read either Abram or the deity as the subject of the second verb in this sentence. The notion of the deity viewing someone as righteous is the more compelling option (so Westermann 1985, 223). See Deut 24:13 for a similar use of "righteousness" as well as Ps 106:31 for almost exactly the same phrase, used of God's view of Phinehas after he interceded on behalf of Israel.

c. Literally, "cut a covenant," the phrase typically used in the pre-Priestly material for making a covenant.

[15:1–6] Chapter 15 sits loosely in its narrative context. "After these things," a phrase that reappears later in the book (22:1, 20; 39:7; 40:1; 48:1), creates only the vaguest connection between this chapter and what has come before it. Such a tenuous connection between various episodes in the Abrahamic saga has traditionally been attributed to the originally independent character of portions of the material. Such is almost certainly the case here. Nonetheless, Gen 15:1 does build upon the most recent of "these things" since it adduces a martial image, the battle shield, which is consistent with the picture of Abram in Gen 14 as a warrior/general. This allusion to martial activity is underscored by the presence of the phrase "Do not fear!" which was routinely uttered before the inception of a holy war. Finally, in this first verse is explicit reference to "recompense." At the end of the preceding chapter, Abram has forsworn taking any property (Gen 14:21–23) from the kings who were defeated. Now, it seems that Abram will receive his due for having participated in the alliance against Chedorlaomer.

In sum, Gen 15:1 has been composed in such a way that it is related to Gen 14 and the world of war.

The metaphor of the deity as a battle shield is well-known in the Psalter (e.g., Pss 3:3; 18:3 [2], 31 [30], 36 [35]; 115:9–11). In Gen 15, it may bear an even more powerful meaning. It appears that each of the patriarchs was associated with a specific metaphor for the deity with whom he was associated: Abram with "Shield" (Gen 15:1), Isaac with "Fear" (31:42), and Jacob with "Bull" (49:24 MT, lit.; "Mighty One," NRSVue). Hence, Gen 15:1 functions as an announcement of this special metaphor by means of which Abram's God will be known.

That same first verse reflects other Israelite traditions, namely that of prophetic rhetoric. YHWH did not simply speak to Abram (as, e.g., in Gen 12:1). Instead, "the word of YHWH came to Abram in a vision." The formula "the word of YHWH came to . . ." appears prominently in the book of Jeremiah and in Kings as the standard way to express the conveyance of the deity's word to a prophet (e.g., Jer 7:1; 11:1; 18:1; 1 Kgs 16:1; 17:2). It is licit to characterize the phrase as Deuteronomistic, which is indicative of the date during which this text was probably written: no earlier than 587 BCE. The phrase "in a vision" refers to one typical way in which a prophet encounters the deity, in a vision (here an auditory vision, since there is no report of Abram seeing something, unless one is to assume that the viewing of the stars counts as the visual component). (This motif of Abram as prophet continues in v. 4, "the word of YHWH came to him" and appears again in Gen 20:7.) One may therefore conclude that the presentation of Abram in Gen 15:1 is something of an amalgam, incorporating language and traditions associated with both holy war and prophecy. The ancient Israelite authors are deploying various images as they try to express the significance of their progenitor.

With verse 2, the reader enters a world of dialogue. After YHWH's initial admonition and promise, Abram demurs, asking a question. He appears not to doubt that the deity might offer him some recompense. The issue is, rather, what will happen to all that when Abram dies. Abram recognizes that an heir does exist in his house. Yet it is not someone for whom he is a father. The son's name is Eliezer, and he is the offspring of Mesheq. (Mesheq as a name appears only here; it is impossible to know if this is the father's or mother's name. Due to this ambiguity, a later redactor tried to clarify the identity of this individual by defining him as a male and by associating him with Damascus, which was more of a "known" than the name Mesheq.) Since he was a member of the household, Eliezer was, apparently, in a position to inherit from Abram. (See Speiser 1964, 112, for a brief discussion of the different types of heirs according to Hurrian family law. He maintains that the individual known here as Eliezer would have been an "indirect heir," not born to either Abram or Sarai.) In 15:3, Abram restates the issue with greater clarity and vehemence. He accuses YHWH of not providing him with an heir, which he has promised to do. Eliezer, now explicitly identified as a member of the household, stands to inherit whatever YHWH will provide for Abram. Inheritance is a key issue in these verses. The verb *yrš* (to inherit) appears five times in 15:3–8. Abram is challenging the deity to make good on his prior promise that Abram will have offspring to inherit the land and, presumably, other goods as well (Gen 13:15). (Whether the Eliezer in ch. 15 is the same servant who appears throughout Gen 24 remains to be seen.)

The narrator presents the deity responding to Abram by, again, using prophetic rhetoric. YHWH does not speak directly to him; rather, "the word of YHWH" comes to Abram. In this "word," the deity engages Abram's challenge directly and denies it. There will be an heir for whom Abram will be the biological father. To underline this promise, the deity takes Abram outside and emphasizes the innumerable progeny that will make up his family. This motif underscores YHWH's promise, whether one counts the dust of the earth (13:16), the grains of sand on seashore (22:17), or the stars in the heavens (15:5; 22:17).

YHWH's appeal to the stars appears to have swayed Abram since the narrator reports that he now trusts what the deity has promised. Such trust in the promise of the deity is at work in another biblical text, Isa 7. There Isaiah admonishes Ahaz to trust in YHWH's ability to protect Jerusalem. Ahaz, however, does not trust (v. 9). The issue is not just believing in the deity but also trusting that the deity will do something. Abram's trust apparently involves not only a willingness to think that Abram's progeny would, indeed, be vast, but that he would be able to pass on an inheritance to the next generation. Inheritance was, after all, the key issue early on in the dialogue.

The conclusion to this dialogue (v. 6) has occasioned much reflection. Early Christian writers understood this text to exemplify what it was to believe in God and, thereby, to be "justified by faith" (Gal 3:6–9). As Ps 106:31 makes clear, the deity can deem someone to be righteous because of an action. It is noteworthy that the issue of Abram's righteousness is at stake here; and it comes up again in Gen 18:19, which involves "doing," not simply "trusting." Here, as elsewhere in the Abrahamic saga, including Gen 18, the narrators seem to be raising explicit theological issues. Von Rad (1972, 185) was on the mark when he claimed that 15:6 "has almost the quality of a general theological tenet." Westermann (1985, 222), characterizes it as a "theological reflection."

[7–21] The deity again offers a self-identification, one using the first-person independent personal pronoun followed by a qualifier. In verse 1, YHWH self-identifies as a shield. In verse 7, YHWH refers to the deity's past behavior, appealing to a specific moment in Abram's life, his leaving Ur of the Chaldeans. That Abram's family left Mesopotamia is part of the standard tradition about Abram. However, the version attested in Gen 11–12 is different from the one here. Earlier, the biblical narrators reported that Terah moved his family from Ur to Haran. Then the deity commanded Abram to go to "a land that I will show to you" (12:1). The version in 15:7 offers a theological interpretation of that earlier event, using the vocabulary "brought up," normally associated with the exodus (e.g., 46:4; 50:24). What is earlier described as a migration by Terah is here construed as an exodus from Mesopotamia.

This theological construal of Terah's and Abram's journey is linked to 15:1–6 by the presence of the verb *yrš*. But the meaning of the verb has changed, from "inherit" to "possess." Since the phrase "give to possess" appears so frequently in the book of Deuteronomy (e.g., 3:18; 12:1), one should infer that the author of this dialogue depends upon that linguistic usage (so Westermann 1985, 224). That change in meaning is consistent with the new topic at work in the final fifteen verses of the chapter, foretelling the acquisition of land.

For the second time in this chapter, Abram responds to the deity's self-identification by raising a question. As a result, one may characterize 15:7–21 as the second dialogue of this chapter. Abram challenges the deity to offer tangible evidence that he will, indeed, possess the land. This challenge seems different from the one posed in verse 2. There Abram wonders how the deity can do anything to give him what he is being promised. Here in verse 8, Abram's question has the tone of "Prove it." One is reminded of the episode in which Gideon challenges the deity to verify that God will, indeed, save Israel through using Gideon. By having the fleece become wet with dew and the ground around it dry, Gideon will "know" that what God has proclaimed will indeed transpire (Judg 6:36–40). In Gen 15, Abram likewise wants to "know" that he will possess the land. In this case, however, the deity rather than Abram unveils actions to verify the deity's announcement concerning possession of the land.

The deity responds to Abram in two ways: by making a covenant and by offering an oracle while Abram sleeps. The report about the making of a covenant occurs in 15:9–11, 17–21 (see Petersen 1977, 7–18). Abram is commanded to slaughter the three animals bilaterally and then to lay the carcass halves in rows. The sacrifice appears similar to that described in both biblical and extrabiblical texts: Jer 34:18 and Sefire Stela I.A.40, both of which describe a calf that has been cut in two (see below).

The compositor who inserted verses 12–16 did so in an exceedingly artful fashion. Just as the vultures "came down" in verse 11, so now the sun goes down and a deep sleep falls on Abram (v. 12; cf. Gen 2:21). The motif of forces heading downward is common to verses 11 and 12, but the forces in verse 12 are no longer avoidable. Unavoidable darkness and deep sleep convey an ominous tone. The author depicts a situation in which Abram is more than just asleep: he has been overpowered. This ominous note foreshadows the people's difficult fate, which the deity is about to proclaim. Since, according to verse 12, Abram is asleep, what happens in 15:13–16 occurs as a dream. The reader is presented with another visionary audition in this chapter, this time in a sleeping vision.

At first blush, verse 13 appears to offer a direct response to Abram's question in verse 8. Abram has asked how he might know that he will possess the land;

the deity now says, "Know . . ." Moreover, these verses pick up the language of exodus used in verse 7, suggesting that the compositor was clearly interested in integrating this dream audition into the surrounding text. Nonetheless, this audition does not help Abram know that he will possess the land: that "proof" occurs in 15:17–21. Verses 12–16 testify that there will be a delay in Israel's possession of the land. These verses allude to Israel's four hundred years of enslavement in Egypt. Though they do not occupy the land during that time, they will leave Egypt with "possessions," movable property rather than the promised real estate. Verse 16 seems to be yet another explanation for the delay, one declaring that the sins of the prior occupants of the land have not become great enough to warrant driving them from the land. This notion is also found in the Deuteronomistic history (e.g., Deut 9:4; 1 Kgs 14:24; 2 Kgs 17:8; 21:2). Further, this same verse offers a quite different chronology: four generations rather than four hundred years (see Exod 12:40). These five verses, then, reflect the work of multiple hands, all interested in explaining the delay in the fulfillment of God's promise of land to Abram.

Verse 17 returns to the scene of the carcasses, probably the original continuation of verse 11. Here the visual features (cf. v. 1) are striking. In a spectral and nocturnal scene, Abram sees two fiery objects moving between the cut-up corpses. Some scholars have suggested that this rite reflects a tradition of self-cursing: Whoever does not live up to the obligations of a pact will be like one of the slain animals. Such rites are attested both in the ancient Near East and in biblical literature (Jer 34:18–20) during the first millennium. In Jer 34:18, the deity states, "I will make the men who broke my covenant by not carrying out the stipulations of my covenant which they made before me like the calf that they cut in two and then passed between its parts." Similarly, Sefire Stela I.A.40 reads, "Just as this calf is cut in two, so may Matiʿel be cut in two and may his nobles be cut in two" (Fitzmyer 1967, 14–15). If Gen 15 bears this significance, then the deity, as symbolized by the smoking firepot and flaming torch, would be the one taking such an oath of self-curse, which would be an otherwise unattested rhetorical ploy by a deity, either in Israel or the ancient Near East.

However, bilateral slaughter did not necessarily involve the notion of self-curse. An ancient Anatolian text reports the following ritual: "If the troops have been beaten by the enemy[,] they perform a ritual 'behind' the river, as follows: they 'cut through' a man, a goat, a puppy, a little pig: they place half on this side and half on that side, and in front of a gate of . . . wood and stretch a . . . over it, and in front of the gate they light fires on this side and on that, and the troops walk right through, and when they come to the river they sprinkle water over them[,] and in front of the gate they shall place half on this side, and they place half on that side" (Goetze 1938, 90). This bilateral rite involves purification. Hence, one may infer that bilateral slaughter rites, even those in which some person moves between the pieces of carcass, need not involve a self-curse.

Another act of bilateral slaughter helps paves the way for a new understanding of Gen 15. It occurs in the Babylonian myth of creation. In Enuma Elish (IV, 135–140; VII, 83, 135), the author recounts the means by which the cosmos is created. Marduk, after killing Tiamat, splits her corpse "like a bivalve into two parts." With one half, he creates the heavenly vault, and with the other he fashions a base for the earth. Here bilateral slaughter serves as the basis for the creation of something new: the cosmos.

That something new can also be a covenant. Some texts in the ANE attest the taking of a vow and the making of a covenant by means of sacrifice. The so-called Alalakh treaty involved the slaughter of a sheep: "Abba-AN is under oath to Yarimlim and also he cut the neck of a lamb. (He swore): I shall never take back what I gave you" (McCarthy 1963, 57). Similarly, Ps 50:5 and Exod 24:3–8 attest the notion that blood sacrifice seals the covenant between YHWH and Israel. In sum, the sacrifice and nighttime ritual presented in Gen 15:9–11, 17 probably has multiple meanings: almost certainly a rite of enacting a covenant and, possibly, a self-curse taken by the deity. In the current context, the rite is designed to answer the question Abram poses in verse 8. Abram is supposed to know that he will possess the land because God makes a covenant guarantying that promise.

Verses 17–21 offer the original response to Abram's question, though in a form designed to answer other questions as well. Verse 18 makes clear that what has just transpired is the making of a covenant, in this case the ratification of a promise rather than a covenant involving mutual obligations. So the real answer to the question Abram poses in verse 8 is the covenant offered by the deity.

Verses 18b–21 do more than answer the question. In verses 7–8, both the deity and Abram seem to know the nature of the land that has been promised. Now, however, the land is defined in two ways: geographically and ethnically. Both definitions are expansive. The rivers that define the extent of the land are the Euphrates and the River of Egypt. The latter is almost certainly not the Nile but instead the Wadi el-Arish, which lies in the Negeb and runs, on a seasonal basis, into the Mediterranean. This river/wadi serves elsewhere as a way to describe the boundaries of Israel (e.g., Num 34:5, where it is known as the "stream of Egypt"). The same word, *naḥal* (stream), appears in Gen 32:24 (32:23).

Complementing the riverine boundaries is a fulsome list of peoples whose land Israel will possess. Ten entities are named. The author obviously has drawn on a traditional listing. Verses 19–21 are another way of defining what was already outlined in verse 18. And 15:19–21 offer an alternative list of peoples to those identified in 15:16.

The listing in 15:19–21 is the longest of all such tabulations. Four of the names do not appear in any comparable lists: Qenites, Qenizzites, Qadmonites, and Rephaim. Other comparable lists of the early inhabitants of the land include Exod 23:23; 34:11; Deut 7:1; Josh 3:10. The list in Gen 15:19–21 attests peoples thought to have inhabited the land before the Israel possesses it. So, even though the Rephaim are not present in the typical lists of six or seven names, they were known to have lived in the land (e.g., Gen 14:5; Deut 2:20; 3:11; Josh 12:4). This hyperbolic listing of people serves well the purpose of the author, to emphasize the vast extent of the territory that has been promised to Abram.

The depiction of Abram in Gen 15 complements that of Gen 14. In the prior chapter, he functions as general. In the latter chapter, he has become a vigorous conversation partner with the deity. This feature of Abram's character needs to be juxtaposed with the traditional one of him as "the father of faith." Such dialogues help flesh out what Abram's "faith" involves. On two occasions Abram challenges what the deity has said. At the end of the first dialogue, the deity adjudges Abram as "righteous" (15:6). Moreover, Abram's second dialogue has eventuated in the creation of a covenant between the deity and Abram, one in which the deity has taken on an obligation of granting land to Abram and his posterity.

Genesis 16:1–16
Hagar and the Birth of Ishmael

This story about the birth of Ishmael might appear to be self-standing, unrelated to what has gone before. Such is not the case. These verses build on several brief notices that have occurred earlier in the family literature. They reiterate the status of Sarai as someone who has been unable to bear children (Gen 11:30). They allude to Sarai and Abram's sojourn in Egypt, when the family acquired, among other things, maidservants (the same word is in 12:16 and 16:1). Finally, they are directly related to the promise that the deity made to Abram, that he would have offspring (13:15; 15:5). A biblical author has knit these elements into a story that grows out of the interactions within the household of Abram and Sarai and that involves Abram's secondary wife, Hagar. These interactions will continue in Gen 21, thereby enabling these two chapters to function as a subplot in the larger Abraham-and-Sarah narrative. Much in the story is disturbing to the contemporary reader: Sarai's harsh treatment of Hagar, Abram's removal of her from the household, the divine command for Hagar to return to suffer more abuse from Sarai. The absence of any overt moral judgment by the author is characteristic of much family literature, whether within or outside biblical literature.

16:1 Sarai, Abram's wife, had not borne children for him, but she had an
Egyptian maidservant, whose name was Hagar. 2 Sarai said to Abram,
"YHWH has prevented me from bearing children. Have intercourse with
my maidservant.[a] Perhaps I may gain status[b] by means of her." Abram
did what Sarai said. 3 Sarai, Abram's wife, took Hagar, her Egyptian
maidservant, after Abram had lived ten years in the land of Canaan, and
gave her to Abram her husband, to be his wife. 4 He had intercourse with
Hagar, whereupon she became pregnant. When she discovered that she
was pregnant, she looked down on her mistress.[c] 5 Sarai then said to
Abram, "May the wrong done to me be on you! I gave you my maidservant for sexual intimacy. When she discovered that she was pregnant, she
looked down on me. May YHWH judge between me and you!" 6 Abram
responded to Sarai, "Your maidservant is under your control. Do to her
whatever you think is appropriate." Sarai then made her life so miserable
that she ran away from her.

7 The messenger of YHWH found her near a spring in the desert, the
spring on the way to Shur. 8 He said to Hagar, "O maidservant of Sarai,
where have you come from and where are you going?" She responded,
"I am fleeing from Sarai, my mistress." 9 The messenger of YHWH said
to her, "Return to your mistress. Continue to suffer abuse at her hand."
10 The messenger of YHWH said to her, "YHWH will make your progeny
so numerous that they cannot be counted." 11 The messenger of YHWH
said to her:

"You are indeed pregnant. You will bear a son.
You will name him Ishmael.
YHWH has truly responded to your affliction!
12 He will be a mustang[d] of a man.
His hand will be against everyone,
everyone's hand against him.
He will live in conflict with all his kin."

13 She then gave YHWH, the one who had spoken to her, a name,
"El Roi,"[e] because she said, "Have I truly seen the Deity after having
been seen?"[f] 14 Therefore, the well was called "Be'er-lahai-roi."[g] It lies
between Qadesh and Bered.

15 Hagar bore a son for Abram. Abram named the son whom Hagar
bore to him Ishmael. 16 Abram was eighty-six years old when Hagar bore
Ishmael to Abram.

a. Literally, "Go to my maidservant."

b. Literally, "be built up"; the verb is passive in form.

c. The vocabulary is visual, lit., "Her mistress became insignificant in her eyes."

d. Literally, "wild ass," but the noun "mustang" connotes better the notion of an unbridled and wild member of the horse family.

e. Which could be translated, "El who sees" or "God of sight."

f. The Hebrew is difficult. My translation presumes that the word *hălōm* (hither) in the MT was originally *hāʾĕlōhīm*. Cf. Speiser 1964, 119, following Wellhausen, who offers another option, "Did I really see God, yet remained alive?" That proposal is rejected by Gunkel (1997, 189), who proposes, "Here I have seen the end of my distress."

g. Literally, "Well of the Living One who sees me."

[16:1–6] The primary author begins by setting the stage. At the outset, it offers no new information. The ancient audience needs to be told neither that Sarai was Abram's wife nor that she could not bear children. Both have been stated in earlier episodes. Further, it would have come as no surprise that Sarai owns an Egyptian maidservant, since Pharaoh has given maidservants to Abram when he and Sarai were in that country (Gen 12:16). By repeating the known, the author sets the stage for Sarai's surprising proposal.

Rather than simply report what Sarai intends, the author allows readers to hear Sarai's voice, though, interestingly, not Abram's. Sarai's voice is the dominant one; readers hear her direct words, and the narrator reports that Abram responds to her "voice" (16:2). Sarai offers a "theological" explanation of her plight, "YHWH has prevented me from bearing children." Nothing in the biblical text to this point has prepared readers for such a claim. Nonetheless, the opening and closing of wombs, the ability to bear children, was regularly imputed to the deity in ancient Israel. Later in the family literature, an author writes that YHWH "opened the womb" of Leah (29:31) and later "opened the womb" of Rachel (30:22). The plight of Hannah is comparable: "though YHWH had closed her womb" (1 Sam 1:5). Of these four women, Sarai is the only one who claims that the deity has prevented her from becoming pregnant. In the other three cases, the narrators offer this theological perspective, but not the women themselves. The author of Gen 16 has, therefore, created a powerful Sarai, one who can interpret her situation for herself.

The second portion of Sarai's speech is equally compelling. Her statement, "Perhaps I may gain status by means of her," clearly shows that Sarai is concerned about her place and status within the family. Sarai is acting in her own self-interest, and not inappropriately. One of her primary roles as wife in a patrilineal culture is to bear a male heir. Without fulfilling that role, she would lose face and power.

If she can present a child to her husband through the instrument of a surrogate spouse—she does give Hagar to him "as a wife" (v. 3)—then Sarai can achieve the power that belongs to her role as primary wife or matriarch.

According to the narrator, Abram hears and, presumably, ponders this proposal. In verse 2, the Hebrew phrase, literally, "heard the voice of," can regularly be translated, "obeyed." However, the delay imputed at the beginning of verse 3—the note about Abram having lived ten years in the land of Canaan—and the report of Sarai's giving Hagar to Abram thereafter hints that the narrator intended readers to think that Abram heard and pondered Sarai's proposal but did not act on it immediately.

As is typical of Hebrew narrative, much remains left unsaid. The narrator does not suggest that Sarai should have interceded with the deity to open her womb. And there is only the slightest of suggestions that Abram demurred from accepting Sarai's proposal. It, like Abram's plan in Gen 12, receives no overt condemnation. Moreover, neither plan ultimately succeeds.

The narrator offers a chronological note at the beginning of 16:3 that is difficult to understand. It is part of the same chronology that appears in 12:4, which reports that Abram was seventy-five years old when he leaves Haran and, presumably, enters Canaan for the first time. Since there are no times stated between 12:4 and 16:3, probably the author of 16:3 refers to the initial entry into Canaan, and not Abram's return to Canaan from Egypt. That understanding of the chronology has Abram at eighty-five when he has intercourse with Hagar and then eighty-six (Gen 16:16) when she gives birth to Ishmael.

Sarai quickly reappears as the dominant force in this report: she "took" and "gave." Moreover, the author emphasizes that in this act she has created a new familial structure since she gives Hagar to Abram "as a wife." Abram now has two wives. Just as Sarai has been part of Pharaoh's family, now another Egyptian becomes a wife to Abram, an example of polycoity, which has become necessary because Sarai is unable to bear children.

Abram complies with Sarai's plan, and Hagar becomes pregnant, which immediately leads to complications, probably unforeseen, in the household. The first problem occurs in the relationship between the two "wives." The secondary wife looks down on the primary wife because she is able to do something that has been impossible for Sarai. The status of Sarai has fallen, at least in the eyes of the woman who will be bearing a son to Abram. This view of Sarai by Hagar naturally leads to a response from the matriarch. Though readers do not know how Hagar expresses her new view of Sarai and how Sarai initially responds to Hagar, the author presents readers with Sarai's verbal response to Abram. Sarai is given voice at this point in the story; Hagar is not.

Some commentators have suggested that this portion of the report exemplifies Prov 30:23:

> Under three things the earth trembles;
>   under four it cannot bear up:
> a slave when he becomes king,
>   and a fool when glutted with food;
> a contemptible woman when she gets a husband
>   and a maid when she supplants her mistress. (Prov 30:21–23 NRSVue)

The vocabulary for "mistress" and "maid" is identical to that in Gen 16. Nonetheless, Hagar has not really "supplanted" Sarai, as Abram's response to Sarai makes clear. Hagar remains a maidservant even after she has become pregnant. Sarai has intended to achieve higher status by the birth of the child. And Hagar's belittling of Sarai has not changed that. The friction is interpersonal, not legal. But it is presented as the natural outcome of a household in which there are two wives.

Sarai again addresses Abram, and does so in very forceful language. Sarai presents her case and then calls for a legal resolution: "May YHWH judge between me and you." The phraseology is virtually identical to the language in 1 Sam 24:12, 15, where David makes the same plea, that YHWH should judge between Saul and David. In that text, the author makes clear that such "judging" will involve the deity's pleading David's case and vindicating him. The same sentiment is implied in Gen 16.

Sarai's invective directed at Abram might seem surprising. After all, she is the one who has proposed that he impregnate Hagar. She perceives herself to have been wronged, but first she becomes angry with Abram, not with the person whom she thinks has wronged her. Further, her speech seeks remedial redress at his hand. Sarai appears to be appealing to the truly powerful parties—YHWH and Abram; in so doing, her speech to Abram suggests that she thought she did not have sufficient power to deal with Hagar herself. To use the language of her own plan, she has not achieved sufficient status to do that. Rather than "being built up," Sarai seems to have lost power, due to Hagar's having become pregnant and despising Sarai.

Abram's first speech in this episode appears at this point. It is a speech that clearly places the problem back in Sarai's hands. He does this literally by saying that Hagar is "in your hand," the idiom for control or power in Biblical Hebrew. Abram empowers Sarai and reemphasizes Hagar's lower status. He does not refer to her by name but characterizes her as "your maidservant." This construal also prevents the reader from continuing to think about Hagar as Abram's wife (so v. 3). Further, Abram uses imperative verbs, just as Sarai has done with him (v. 2). It is as if Abram is saying to Sarai, "This was your plan; Hagar is your maidservant; you deal with her." Finally, Abram admonishes Sarai to do what is appropriate (Hebrew, "good") in her "eyes." The author has nicely used the notion of eyes. Sarai has become insignificant in Hagar's eyes. Now Abram tells Sarai to do what is good/appropriate in her own eyes. (For an informative use of the idiom, "good in someone's eyes," see 2 Sam 15:26. David says to Zadok, "Let him [the deity] do to me whatever seems good to him." In this case, the "good" can mean either that David is permitted to return to Jerusalem or that he must flee.) The use of the phrase "good in someone's eyes," along with Abram's empowering speech, results in Sarai's turning back to her maidservant. She makes life hard for Hagar, though in ways the author does not describe. As a result, Hagar flees "from her." Sarai is the cause for Hagar's flight, just as Hagar has been the cause for Sarai's belittling.

[7–16] The first scene focuses on Sarai; the second one is primarily concerned with Hagar. But she is not the first character to appear in the second scene. Instead, rather abruptly, "the messenger of YHWH" finds her. One almost has the sense that the messenger has been looking for her and only now discovers where she is.

The Hebrew phrase "messenger of YHWH" is often translated "angel of the Lord" (so NRSV). That rendering, however, creates too great a distinction between the messenger and the deity. The "messenger," on occasion, appears to be the way YHWH appears.

It is worth noting that the deity or the world of the deity appears in diverse ways in the family narratives. YHWH can appear directly to an individual (Gen 35:9). On other occasions, the deity appears as a "man" (32:25), as one messenger (21:17; 22:11, 15; 31:11), as two messengers (19:1, 15), as one of three men (ch. 18), or as multiple messengers (28:12; 32:1). Some texts virtually equate the presence of the deity with the presence of the messenger (so Gen 22).

The messenger finds Hagar at a specific spring. Though the location of Shur is unknown, Westermann (1985, 244) has contended that since Shur means wall, one may infer that Hagar is heading toward the forts that guard the Egyptian border. Put another way, Hagar is trying to reach her native land.

The messenger interrogates her, continuing the legal tone invoked earlier by Sarai. In his speech, the messenger puts Hagar in her place. His first words are "Hagar, maidservant of Sarai." Her identity is known to this stranger. The questions that the messenger poses are not designed to seek information; rather, they are designed to interrogate the runaway slave girl. Of the two questions he poses, Hagar addresses only one, and her response may not really be an answer to the messenger's question. The messenger poses questions that could be answered using geographic language. Hagar responds with the reason for her journey, not the location from which she is coming or the location toward which she is walking. Moreover, just as the messenger labels her as maidservant, Hagar speaks of Sarai as her mistress. The statuses of the two female protagonists remain intact, even though Hagar has fled the household of Abram and Sarai. In so doing, the presence of these nouns foreshadows Hagar's return to the household that she has just left.

Verses 9–12 are filled with speeches by the messenger, though oddly the narrator creates three separate speeches by using the phrases "and he said" (v. 8), "said to her" (v. 9), and "also said to her" (v. 11). The first of the three speeches is anguishing and fraught with mystery. Why would the deity intend that Hagar return to the household where she has suffered such abuse? Genesis 21, of course, requires her presence there so that, somewhat ironically, she and her son can be thrown out of Abram's household rather than simply escaping, as she has done in Gen 16. It is difficult to say more.

The second and third speeches focus not on Hagar but on her progeny, though in different ways. The first speech refers to all of Hagar's descendants, not just Ishmael. Just as the deity has promised that Abram will have innumerable progeny (Gen 13:16; 15:5), the messenger makes the same promise to Hagar. If Abram is a patriarch because of such a vast heritage, Hagar becomes a matriarch in a similar manner. The third speech is a poem that focuses on the child with whom Hagar is pregnant. The lines identify his gender, what he will be named (and the rationale for the name), and his character, as well as the way that character manifests itself in relation to his relatives. The name Ishmael (lit., "God hears") introduces a new form of sensory perception, earlier (v. 4, the verb "to look") and then again (in v. 13, "to see"), visual imagery is prominent. Now hearing appears. In addition, the metaphor, "mustang of a man," signifies strength, the lack of domestication, and one who dwells in the wilds (cf. Gen 21:20–21; Jer 2:24; Job 39:5–8).

Ishmael, of course, is an eponymous ancestor of the Ishmaelites, a group of tribes living in the northern part of the Arabian Peninsula. Though some Arabian tribes are judged negatively in prophetic oracles against the nations (e.g., Isa 21:11–16; Jer 49:28–30; but cf. Ps 83:5–7 [4–6]), there is minimal reference to Ishmaelites having negative interactions with Israel. The Ishmaelite genealogy (Gen 25:12–18) contains names of groups listed in the oracles against the nations, such as Dumah (Gen 25:14; Isa 21:11). Hence, the reference to strife with kin probably refers to relations with other tribes living in the Arabian Peninsula. The relation of Israel to the Ishmaelites is more distant than to other members of the Terahite lineage, such as Esau and the Edomites.

Hagar responds, not by naming her son (v. 15 reports Abram as doing that), as she has been commanded to do, but by naming YHWH as "El-Roi," literally, "God who sees." Hagar reintroduces the imagery of seeing and characterizes her treatment by the deity as someone who has been seen. What the messenger characterizes via auditory diction, Hagar interprets via visual language. The location of the well, Beer-lahai-roi, literally, "Well of the Living One who sees me," is unknown. What matters is the name, which again highlights the fact that the deity has seen and responded to Hagar's plight.

The final verse of this episode is almost certainly to be attributed to the hand of the Priestly writer. As such, it ignores Hagar's return to the household of Abram and Sarai and simply reports that Hagar gives birth to a son. Abram, not Hagar (cf. v. 11), names him. It is as if once Hagar is back in Abram's household, she has lost the power given to her by the messenger of the deity. Hagar is now a maidservant to Sarai and not able to name her own son. She bears the son "for Abram"; hence he is the one who will name his son. Moreover, nothing is said about Sarai having gained status by the birth of this child (cf. v. 2). Instead, the author highlights the fact that Abram now has a son, one who can bear the promises that have been made to Abram.

Genesis 17:1–27
God Makes an "Everlasting Covenant" with Abraham and His Progeny

Genesis 17 presents the second covenant attested by the Priestly tradition, the first having emerged in Gen 9. In both covenants there is a "sign": the rainbow in 9:12–17 and circumcision in 17:11. The exposition of the sign is important in both texts. This author inherited a tradition about a covenant between the deity and Abraham, unlike the situation in Gen 9, in which the Priestly author created the notion of a covenant between the deity and all humanity. The covenant attested in Gen 15, in the pre-Priestly material, occurs as a response to Abram's question to the deity, "How am I to know that I shall possess it?" (15:8). The covenant was designed to assure Abram that he would, indeed, possess the land. To that end the deity apparently takes an oath, assuring Abram that the deity will ensure his ownership of the land. Nothing is required of Abram. The situation in Gen 17 is decidedly different. Here Abraham, the males in his household, and his male descendants must all be circumcised. If that does not happen, the uncircumcised person will be banished from the community. However, there is no sense that the community itself could break the covenant; only one member of it could do that. Further, the covenant in Gen 17 involves both the promise of progeny (v. 4) and the granting of land (e.g., v. 8), with the former having far greater prominence. This time, the deity specifies that Sarai/Sarah will be the mother of that line (v. 19), whereas in Gen 15 God has only promised that Abram/Abraham would be the father of his heir.

Genesis 17 is a complex Priestly composition, including material from diverse sources, such as the torah regarding circumcision. The deity speaks a great deal: in a statement of self-identification (vv. 1–2) and in three distinct speeches apart from God's initial proclamation in verses 1–2 (vv. 4–8, 9–14, 15–16, 19–22), which lay out the purport of the covenant and its entailments. Genesis 17 belongs to a small though important group of long Priestly compositions in Genesis, only two of which appear in the family literature. They comprise 1:1–2:4a; 6:9–22; 9:1–17; 17:1–27; and 23. These passages focus on God, Noah, and Abraham, highlighting creation and the making of the two primary covenants in the Priestly tradition.

17:1 When Abram was ninety-nine years old, YHWH appeared to Abram.
He said to him, "I am El Shaddai. Walk before me and be blameless 2 so
that I may establish[a] my covenant between me and you and make you
exceedingly numerous." 3 Then Abram bowed down deeply, whereupon
God said to him, 4 "As for me, my covenant is with you. You will become
an ancestor of many nations. 5 You will no longer be named Abram; rather,
your name will be Abraham. I have made you the ancestor of many nations.
6 I will make you exceedingly fruitful; I will establish nations from you;
kings will come forth from you. 7 I will set my covenant between me, you,
and your progeny after you for generations to come—as an everlasting
covenant—to be God for you and for your progeny after you. 8 I will give
to you and your progeny after you the land in which you are sojourning,
the land of Canaan, as an everlasting possession. I will be God for them."

9 Then God said to Abraham, "As for you, you must keep my covenant,
you and your progeny after you, for generations to come. 10 This is my
covenant between me and all of you, your progeny after you: you must
circumcise every male. 11 You shall circumcise the flesh of your foreskin.
This shall be a sign of the covenant between me and all of you. 12 Every
male who is eight days old shall be circumcised, for each ensuing generation, including a slave born into the household and one purchased with
your money—a foreigner who is not of your line. 13 Indeed, you must
circumcise the slave born into your household and one purchased with
your money. Thus will my covenant—an everlasting covenant—be in
your flesh. 14 An uncircumcised male, one who has not been circumcised
in the flesh of his foreskin, this person shall be cut off from his people.
He has broken my covenant."

15 God said to Abraham, "As for Sarai your wife, she will no longer
be named Sarai, but her name will be Sarah. 16 I will bless her; indeed,
I will give to you a son from her; him I shall bless.[b] She will engender
nations. Kings of peoples will come from her." 17 Abraham bowed down
deeply and chuckled, saying to himself, "Can a son be born to a man
who is one hundred years old? Or can Sarah, who is ninety years old,
bear a child?" 18 Abraham then said to God, "If only you would be with
Ishmael!"[c] 19 God responded, "No, Sarah your wife is going to bear a son
for you, and you will name him Isaac. I will set my covenant with him as
an everlasting covenant for his progeny after him. 20 And as for Ishmael,
I have heard your plea. I will bless him. I will make him fruitful and will
make him exceedingly great. He will sire twelve princes. I will make him
a great nation. 21 However, my covenant I will establish with Isaac, whom
Sarah will bear to you at this time next year." 22 When he had finished
speaking with him, God ascended from Abraham.

23 Abraham took Ishmael, his son, and all the male slaves born in his
household, and all who were purchased with his money—every male
among the men of Abraham's household—and he circumcised the flesh
of their foreskin on that same day, just as God had commanded him.
24 Abraham was ninety-nine years old when he was circumcised in the
flesh of his foreskin. 25 Ishmael, his son, was thirteen years old when he
was circumcised in the flesh of his foreskin. 26 Abraham and Ishmael
his son were circumcised on the very same day, 27 and all the men of his
house, house-born slaves as well as those purchased with money from a
foreigner, were circumcised with him.

a. On the syntactic sequence of imperative followed by a cohortative, see *IBHS* 34.6. Many of the examples cited there are translated as purpose clauses.

b. MT reads "bless her." LXX, Syr, and Vulg read "bless him."

c. Literally, "If only Ishmael might be for you."

[17:1–14] Scholars have regularly observed that this chapter presents another version of a covenant between God and Abraham, first reported in Gen 15. Interestingly, Gen 17 begins in a fashion similar to the two dialogues in Gen 15. (The Priestly writer in Gen 17, who typically uses the world Elohim for God, does incorporate the name YHWH here. The change from El Shaddai to YHWH [so Exod 6:3], which lies behind the usage in Gen 17, may be relevant to this text in the change from the name Abram to Abraham.) The deity offers a statement of self-identification via the independent personal pronoun followed by some qualifying description. In Gen 15, those qualifiers were "your shield" (v. 1) and "who brought you from Ur of the Chaldees" (v. 7). In Gen 17, the new qualifier is "El Shaddai," God Almighty. But after that self-identification, dialogue does not immediately follow. Instead, the deity makes two speeches, the last one of which is relatively long (vv. 3–8, 9–14). It is as if the deity wants to have a significant say before allowing Abraham into the conversation. And the deity's "say" involves announcing the covenant and its implications. The covenant is far more than a response to what Abraham might say, as was the case in Gen 15. To this extent, one has the sense that the Priestly author of Gen 17 is offering an alternative view of that covenant between God and Abraham, one that places greater emphasis on covenant per se. In Gen 15, the making of the covenant is a response to Abraham's challenge to the deity. The establishment of the covenant and the articulation of its "sign" by the deity are the raison d'être for Gen 17.

The deity self-identifies as El Shaddai, the meaning of which is obscure. The traditional translation, "God Almighty," stems from early rabbinic times.[1]

1. So Speiser 1964, 124.

The most widely accepted, though not universally so, etymological explanation derives Shaddai from a Northwest Semitic word for "mountain." And since the Canaanite high god El was known to dwell on a mountain, this derivation makes considerable sense. The phrase El Shaddai appears five times in Gen (17:1; 28:3; 35:11; 43:14; 48:3) and Shaddai alone in 49:25.[2] It is by far the most frequent of the divine names formulated with El. Hence, for good reason, the Priestly writer in Exodus characterizes El Shaddai as the name by which Abraham, Isaac, and Jacob know the deity (see Exod 6:3). In Gen 17, it is not altogether clear whether El Shaddai bears special meaning and why that name should elicit a response of the sort commanded in verse 1. It is more likely that the reference to El Shaddai here is simply indicative of the Priestly writer's claim that this divine name typifies the period of the matriarchs and patriarchs, a time before the revelation of God's name as YHWH.

The initial statement by the deity announces a requirement: Abraham must be *tāmmîm* (blameless) so that God can make a covenant with him. This should not be surprising, since, according to the Priestly source, the human with whom God has earlier made a covenant, Noah, was "righteous and blameless" (*tāmmîm*, 6:9). In Gen 17, however, the individual is ordered to be blameless. To that extent, one may infer that Abraham's obedience to God's covenant is the way in which that blameless life should be lived.

The noun "covenant" appears repeatedly (13×) in Gen 17. It is so prominent that Westermann terms it a classic example of a catchword (1985, 256). Perhaps even more significant than its frequency is the way in which it is modified. It is not Abraham's covenant; rather, it is *God's* covenant. The noun appears with the first-person pronominal suffix eight times: "my covenant" (vv. 2, 4, 7, 9, 10, 13, 14, 21; see also 9:9, 11, 15). And in the initial statement of self-identification and pronouncement (17:1–2), the deity identifies the heart of the covenant: the promise to Abraham of numerous progeny. Abraham responds not by speaking, as in Gen 15, but by prostrating himself (v. 3), an act of worshipful obeisance. This response is followed by the first of several speeches by the deity (vv. 4–8). These speeches are related to the three key individuals identified in the chapter: "as for me" (v. 4), "as for you" (v. 9), and "as for Sarai/Sarah" (v. 15).[3]

Verses 4–8 adumbrate "my covenant" and do so by exploring what it means for the deity, "as for me" (v. 4), to make this covenant. The promise of progeny, even numerous progeny, has appeared in prior texts (13:16; 15:5). Distinctive here is the language about nations and royalty. It is one thing to promise that

2. El Shaddai is associated more often with Jacob than with Abraham. Westermann (1985, 258) maintains that El Shaddai appears only in P texts, with the exception of Ezek 10:5.

3. There is an "as for Ishmael" (v. 20), but that phrase does not initiate a new speech. The fact that it does not initiate such a speech is appropriate since Ishmael is less important to this chapter about God's covenant than are the other three parties.

Abram/Abraham will sire "a great nation" (so 12:2). It is quite another to think that he will generate a "multitude of nations" (the term "nations" appears in vv. 4, 5, 6; and kings in v. 6). If one focuses on the Syro-Palestinian political universe, Moab and Ammon will stem from the patrilineage of Terah, but not from Abraham. However, Ishmaelites and Edomites will ultimately stem from Abraham, though Gen 17 makes a point of saying that the Ishmaelites will have princes (but not kings). And, of course, the two Yahwistic nations, Israel and Judah, will be able to trace their heritage to Abraham. However, there is little reason to think that the Priestly author was focusing just on Israel and Judah as the "multitude of nations," so one may identify at least four nations that might be viewed as fulfilling this promise: Ishmaelites, Edom, Israel, and Judah. Moreover, this text surely reflects a time when the fulfillment of this promise was understood as having been best accomplished when these peoples were known to have been independent political entities.

The covenant is to be "everlasting" or "enduring" (v. 7). This same adjective was used to characterize the first Priestly covenant (9:16). But one does well to ask what, precisely, will endure. Genesis 17:7 emphasizes that the deity's promise to be "God for you and your progeny after you" is the long-term commitment. This Priestly formulation stands in some contrast with the way in which the Sinaitic covenant is expressed: "I will be your God, and you shall be my people" (Lev 26:12). That tone of mutuality is not as prominent in Gen 17, which emphasizes the divine character of the covenant, "my covenant."

This covenant has multiple ramifications, one of which involves the renaming of both Abram and Sarai.[4] In both cases, the changes are minor. A new penultimate syllable appears to create "Abraham," and the final syllable of "Sarai" is replaced with a new one to create "Sarah." In both cases, these changes were understood to bear meaning: Abram (great father) to Abraham (father of many); Sarai (?) to Sarah (royal woman). There is an absence of symmetry since it is not clear what "Sarai" might have meant, unlike the situation with "Abram." Nonetheless, Sarai's new name, meaning something like princess or courtier, certainly signifies a person of high standing. The new relationship created by God's covenant offers new names, which reflect higher status in both cases.

The notion of an enduring covenant is not peculiar to these two major covenants in the Priestly corpus (cf. Ps 105:10–11; and 1 Chr 16:14–17, where YHWH begins the "patriarchal" covenant with Abraham, Isaac, and Jacob). The notion of "enduring" is associated with the Davidic covenant (2 Sam 23:5, cf. Isa 55:3) as well as with various rituals or ritual personnel: Exod 31:16 (Sabbath); Lev 24:8 (Sabbath bread); Num 18:19 (covenant of salt); Num 25:13 (covenant of peace and priesthood). In addition, various relatively late

4. These changes of name are not nearly as profound as will be the case with Jacob/Israel (Gen 32:28; 35:10).

prophetic texts anticipate the creation of an enduring covenant in the future (Isa 61:8; Jer 32:40; 50:5; Ezek 16:60; 37:26). Hence, one should not view the enduring character of the covenant between Abraham and the deity as distinctive for this covenant alone. It perhaps is better to think that covenants are by their very nature intended to endure. This is especially so with a covenant that involves a promise by the deity that a family will become numerous over time.

As a coda, verse 8 concludes the deity's first long speech, but with an integral tone of its own. The deity promises that "the land in which you are sojourning, the land of Canaan" will belong to Abraham and his descendants. And the deity qualifies that grant with the same adjective used of the covenant itself: it shall be an "everlasting possession." This way of construing the grant of land as a part of the Abrahamic covenant differs from that in Gen 15. In 15:18, the deity promises to give the land to Abraham's descendants, whereas in 17:8 God grants the land to Abraham and, subsequently, to those who follow him. The notion of Abraham actually possessing land may not have been part of the earliest traditions. The fact that the Priestly version of the covenant includes it may explain why this same author is so interested in describing the way in which Abraham actually acquires land—the purchase of the Machpelah cave (Gen 23). The final moment of the coda includes a reprise of the essential theological claim, already implied in 17:2, "I will be their God."

The deity's second major speech commences with an expression that focuses on Abraham: "as for you" (v. 9). These six verses spell out the implication of God's covenant for Abraham and his progeny. They begin with the general notion of "keeping the covenant," but quickly move to focus on a single rite: circumcision. What follows is less a ritual text that simply describes the way in which circumcision should take place and more a reflection about circumcision, involving both Abraham's male progeny and the males in his household. These verses stipulate how circumcision is related to the notion of covenant: it is the "sign" of the covenant. They stipulate when the rite should be performed: on an eight-day-old infant; and report those who should be circumcised: any who belong to the household. This passage prescribes a penalty for the individual who is uncircumcised: banishment. No comparable guide to circumcision is found elsewhere in the Old Testament.

Circumcision involves the cutting of the tissue at the end of a male penis. This necessarily involves the spilling of blood. It is surely no accident that blood is overtly present in Gen 9 and in Gen 15, two prior texts that involve the creation of covenants. And blood from sacrificial animals will be constitutive for the covenant made at Sinai (Exod 24:5–8, "the blood of the covenant"). The presence of blood seems to be essential for the making of a covenant.

However, it would be inappropriate to think that blood works the same way in all these texts. Blood in Gen 9 is multivalent, involving animal blood that is not to be consumed, human blood that is not to be spilled, and a legal principle involving what happens when human blood is shed. In Gen 15, animal sacrifice symbolizes the taking of an oath by the deity. In Exod 24, animal blood is scattered on the altar and on the people. If the altar symbolizes the presence of the deity, this act may highlight the bond between YHWH and the people, which has been created through both parties having been scattered with blood. Genesis 17 is unique: it features human blood without involving death. Instead, the human male sexual organ is inscribed with a knife, spilling minimal blood. Since that organ is essential to procreation, such a ritual act highlights an essential feature of the covenant made in Gen 17, signifying that the lineage of Abraham will become "exceedingly numerous."

The Priestly writer establishes the household as the context in which circumcision takes place. Every male of the household is to be circumcised. The report that both slaves born within the household and those purchased "with money from a foreigner" (v. 27) makes clear that circumcision is prescribed for those who would not have been considered part of Terah's lineage. And though females are not circumcised, they can be present for the rite; this is even true for the mother, who, according to priestly ritual, would just be concluding her postpartum rites of purification (Lev 12). Clearly, the household is the primary place where the ritual affirmation of the Abrahamic covenant takes place. It is a ritual that allows each new generation to be incorporated into the "people" (v. 14) and can be practiced both in the land or elsewhere. Circumcision is not unique to ancient Israel, a claim made in the book of Jeremiah (9:25–26) and attested in extrabiblical evidence (see "Circumcision" in *NIDB* 1:667–69). Though the Philistines are described as "uncircumcised" (2 Sam 1:20) and certain Canaanites are uncircumcised (Gen 34:15), other cultures clearly engage in the practice.

The notion of circumcision as a "sign" of the covenant is extremely important. The covenantal sign functions as a theological interpretation of circumcision within the Israelite context. And this is the second time the Priestly author has accomplished such an interpretive task. In Gen 9:12, virtually the same phrase occurs: "the sign of the covenant [that I make] between me and you." The rainbow is given an Israelite interpretation. So too circumcision, which, like the rainbow, was known and no doubt understood in different ways by other cultures. For Israel, it now symbolizes and helps reify the covenant between the deity and Abraham. Such an interpretation no doubt replaces earlier understandings of the rite (cf. Exod 4:24–26).

Though the speech begins referring to "you" in the singular, "You must keep my covenant" (v. 9), all verbs and pronouns in 17:10–12 and 13b are plural. This variance suggests that the formulations in verses 10–12, 13b are appropriated by the Priestly author from a source that included such instructions. Further, these plural words stress the ultimately corporate character of keeping the covenant. All males residing in the community are required to be circumcised.

The final portion of the deity's speech regarding the sign of the covenant reprises the notion of an enduring covenant. The sign/rite of the covenant is what will enable the covenant to endure over time. Only those males who are circumcised are permitted to remain in the community and, hence, serve as fathers in the Abrahamic lineage. Not only will the deity be Israel's God; the males will also be specially marked from one generation to the next.

One might have expected the mandate for circumcision to be limited to Abraham and his male progeny. Not so! It is to be a household rite, including not only the males whom Abraham sires, but also all other males who belong to the household. Verses 12–13 belabor the point that two different kinds of slaves, those born in the household and those acquired via mercantile transaction, must be circumcised. One might have thought that, based on the eight-day stipulation, only those males who have been children in the household would need to be circumcised. Verses 12–13 (as well as Gen 34) make clear that all males must or could undergo this ritual.

Here as with other biblical texts, Israelite rituals are open to non-Israelites, at least as defined genealogically. Passover, too, can be celebrated by those who are not Israelites. In fact, there is a certain "resonance" between the torah for Passover and Gen 17. According to Exod 12:43–50, a resident alien could celebrate Passover, but only if he and his male relatives are circumcised. Both rites are open to resident aliens and those enslaved who are part of the household. (According to Exod 12:44, any enslaved person "who has been purchased may eat of it [the Passover] after he has been circumcised.") Here, as with Gen 17, authors are concerned about the way in which an enslaved person comes into the household. Both the rites of circumcision and Passover, though boundary rituals (i.e., rituals that establish the perimeter of the Yahwistic community), are open to those born outside the lineage of Terah.

The final verse stipulates a penalty for the male who is not circumcised. William P. Brown notes the irony of an "uncut male" being "cut off" from his community (private communication). The notion of cutting off from one's people or banishment from the household or community is attested elsewhere in the Hebrew Bible. The penalty is at home in texts that describe violations in the ritual sphere. Infractions that culminate in this fate include any of these: eating leavened bread during Passover (Exod 12:15); misuse of holy anointing oil (30:33); misuse of incense (30:38); working on the sabbath (31:14); eating food from a sacrifice while in an unclean state (Lev 7:20–21); eating inappropriate food from a sacrifice (7:22–27); not presenting an offering to the Lord (17:4). The author of Gen 17 understood the requirement for circumcision to belong to this world of ritual activity, along with punishments for nonadherence. Clearly, circumcision, as a rite practiced by many cultures, has been reinterpreted here and placed within the world of ritual specific to Israel.

Although Gen 17 highlights the importance of circumcision for the lineage of Abraham, the remainder of the book remains silent about the practice. There is no reference to Isaac having circumcised Jacob or Esau, no reference to Jacob having circumcised his twelve sons, and no reference to Joseph having circumcised Ephraim or Manasseh. This narrative oddity suggests that Gen 17 serves as the etiology for the rite, but that it was actually practiced in a different cultural/ritual context, likely the exilic or early postexilic period, rather than the era portrayed in the family narratives.

[15–22] The deity's final speeches, though addressed to Abraham, concern Sarah, the third major character in this chapter. Here is real dialogue. Abraham interacts with the first speech of the deity, who in turn responds to him. Sarai's name is changed (see above) at the outset. Though her two names are probably variant forms with the same meaning, the new name clearly means something positive for the ancient author. Sarai would become a noble woman (cf. Judg 5:29; 1 Kgs 11:3; Esth 1:18). Further, she will be "blessed" (cf. the blessing promised to Abraham in Gen 12:2). But the utterly new promise involves that of her becoming a mother to Abraham's son. She will be the source for the nations and kings promised in the deity's first speech.

The author describes Abraham's response artfully. On the one hand, he falls prostrate, as he has earlier (17:3). On the other hand, he chuckles to himself, asking if these two old people can give birth to a son. This interior speech is no doubt part of a tradition concerning the birth of Isaac. In Gen 18:11–12, another author reports that Sarah laughs to herself when she hears someone say that she will give birth. And she also asks a question. Both texts offer a wordplay on the name of the son who will be born. The verb "he laughs" is *yiṣḥaq*; the name Isaac is *yiṣḥāq*. However, the wordplay is an integral part of the narrative in Gen 18, whereas it is an aside in Gen 17. Here it provokes no comment, either by the deity or by the author. Still, the two rhetorical questions that Abraham speaks to himself lead to the obvious answer, "No." That negative answer explains what Abraham says next, asking the deity to consider Ishmael, who already exists, who lives in the household, and who will soon be circumcised (v. 25).

The dialogue continues when the deity denies that request. Still, God invests time in responding to Abraham's concern about Ishmael's future. The deity's response (vv. 19–21) builds on the rhetoric used earlier in the chapter. Ishmael, like Abraham and Sarah before him, will be blessed (12:2; 17:20). He too will be fruitful (17:6, 20). Ishmael too will become exceedingly great/numerous (vv. 2, 20). But there will be differences. "Princes," not kings, will stem from Ishmael, and he will be the source of only one nation (vv. 6, 20). Moreover, God will not make a covenant with him as he will with Isaac (vv. 2, 21). In sum, Ishmael will share in some but not all the weal promised to Abraham and Sarah. Thus Ishmael bears special status among those members of the family who are not part of the main line of descent (i.e., Moab, Ammon, Edom).

Verse 22 concludes the encounter between Abraham and the deity. The reference to "finished talking" is unusual. It calls attention to the fact that a great deal of speaking has just taken place (the deity has spoken five times and Abraham twice, once to himself and once to God). The author has presented a report involving speeches and a dialogue, not a story. Moreover, the deity "ascends," another unusual motif, attesting to this author's conviction that the deity must descend to interact with humans (cf. 11:7 for the deity descending and 35:13 for the deity ascending) and then return to the heavenly sphere.

[23–27] These verses accomplish at least three purposes: to demonstrate that Abraham will keep the covenant, that he acts to accomplish it quickly, and that Abraham's concern for Ishmael continues. The report builds on the instructions regarding circumcision and is replete with the details offered there (vv. 10–13). The attention to such detail confirms that Abraham is indeed "keeping the covenant." The author states twice that Ishmael is circumcised. This epilogue highlights only one element of the covenant, the sign of the covenant. What did not need to be reported was that God Almighty was now Abraham's God.

Genesis 18:1–15
God Promises Abraham That Sarah Will Have a Son

Genesis 18–19 includes three kinds of literature (report, narrative, and dialogue), held together by means of a journey by the deity and by the presence of two scenes in which hospitality is offered to visitors. As such, these chapters appear to be a distinct body of literature. On that journey, the deity visits Abraham and Sarah, engages Abraham in dialogue, visits Sodom through his messengers, and then destroys Sodom, saving Abraham's relatives. The deity appears as one of three individuals; the other two appear explicitly again in 18:16 and 19:1 (by implication). The divine plurality integrates 18:1–15 with the rest of chapters 18 and 19.

Genesis 18:1–15 is unusual. At heart, it is a report that a child will be born to someone. To this extent, it is similar to other announcements that a child will be born, so Gen 15:4–5 and Isa 7. However, a smaller set of such passages features an announcement given to a "barren" woman (Judg 13:2–3; 1 Sam 1:1–17; 2 Kgs 4:14–16). In Judg 13 and 1 Sam 1, the report includes a raison d'être for the child's existence. Similar statements about the child's existence are absent from Gen 18. It is as if the reason for the child's existence has been laid out in Gen 17. To this extent, Gen 18 depends upon the preceding chapter. (From a narrative perspective, Gen 18 is unnecessary because a son has been promised to Sarah already in 17:16, 21, a promise that could lead directly to 21:1–2, which reports the birth of that son.) Further, Gen 18 reduplicates the promise of a son, comments about an older couple giving birth, and features the motif of laughter, elements all present in Gen 17. In sum, Gen 18 offers an alternate understanding of the announcement of Sarah's pregnancy, one that explores the human issues involved in that development. Unlike Gen 17, the announcement is made so that Sarah can actually hear it, albeit indirectly. The scenes in Gen 18 are also unusual, since all the characters achieve some depth: emotions (Sarah's fear), a perceived challenge to YHWH's abilities ("Is anything too difficult for YHWH?"), interior speech (Sarah's), Abraham's hospitality. Also uncharacteristic of typical Hebrew prose is the rather full description of the stage on which the action takes place: at Abraham's tent "during the heat of the day."

18:1 YHWH appeared to him [Abraham] at the terebinths[a] of Mamre,
while he was sitting at the entrance to the tent during the heat of the day.
2 He looked up and saw three individuals standing near him. Upon seeing them, he ran from the entrance to the tent to greet them, and then he
bowed down. **3** He said, "My lord, if I have found favor with you, do not
pass by your servant. **4** Let a little water be brought so that you may wash
your feet and then rest under the tree. **5** Let me bring a bit of bread so that
you may regain some strength. After that you can travel on—since you
have come so near to your servant." They responded, "Fine, do as you
have said." **6** Abraham hurried back to the tent, to Sarah. He said, "Quick!
Three large measures[b] of special flour.[c] Knead [it] and prepare some
loaves." **7** Abraham ran to the herd, took a choice, tender calf, and gave
it to the servant, who hurried to prepare it. **8** He then took some curds and
milk along with the calf that he had prepared and set it all before them.
He stood near them, under the tree, while they ate.

9 Then they said to him, "Where is Sarah, your wife?" He answered,
"There, in the tent." **10** Then one said, "I will return to you at the time of
calving,[d] Sarah your wife will then have a son." Sarah had been listening
at the entrance to the tent, which was behind him.[e] **11** Now Abraham and
Sarah were getting on in years. Sarah had stopped menstruating. **12** As
a result, Sarah laughed to herself, thinking, "After having no children,
shall I have such joy,[f] especially since my husband is so old?" **13** YHWH
said to Abraham, "Why did Sarah laugh, thinking 'Will I really bear a
child when I am so old?' **14** Is anything too difficult for YHWH? At the
appointed time, the time of calving, I will return; Sarah will have a son!"
15 Sarah objected, "I did not laugh," because she was afraid. Then he said,
"No, you did laugh."

a. The Hebrew word *ʾēlôn*, or its plural construct *ʾēlônê*, appears elsewhere in Genesis (12:6). In each case, the noun is associated with a place: Moreh and Mamre. Other Hebrew nouns—*ʾallôn* (Gen 35:8), *ʾēlâ* (Gen 35:4), and *ʾallâ* (Josh 24:26)—appear to be semantically related. All may refer to a tree, whether oak or terebinth, at a shrine, under which burials (of objects or corpses) could take place.

b. Hebrew *səâ*, which may involve ca. seven quarts each or ca. one-third of a bushel.

c. MT offers two words for flour: *qemaḥ* and *sōlet*. The former is "ordinary flour" (Westermann 1985, 279); the latter is "a kind of semoliṇa" (Speiser 1964, 134), a special grain.

d. Literally, "at the time of life."

e. SP reads a feminine-singular pronoun, in which case the text would be translated, "she was behind him."

f. The feminine noun *ʿednâ* appears only here in the OT. The masculine form of the noun, *ʿēden*, means "joy, delight" (Ps 36:9 [8]; Jer 51:34). There is no overt sexual connotation.

[18:1–8] The first eight verses, though they report the arrival of the deity, focus on Abraham. They present him as hurriedly active, a deferential and consummate host. They also present YHWH as one of multiple persons, who are in no hurry. The first part of the first verse functions rather as both a title and a summary: "YHWH appeared to Abraham at the terebinths of Mamre." This "appearance" of YHWH reiterates language found in Gen 17:1, according to which God appears to Abraham in order to make the covenant as described by the Priestly author. Unlike Gen 17, however, the appearance of the deity is conveyed in a way quite different from how God is depicted in either of the covenantal reports (Gen 15 and 17). In Gen 15, Abraham experiences the deity in a vision; in Gen 17, the deity "appears" to Abraham. In Gen 18, the deity literally walks into the scene. YHWH is one of several individuals, all of whom belong to the divine realm (cf. 19:1, which presumably identifies the other two individuals as "messengers").

The scene is set, both temporally and physically. It is a time of shimmering heat and a time when one takes shelter from that heat, hence Abraham's location at the opening of the tent. When he meets the strangers, he apparently greets only one, likely the first one he encounters. Abraham is at his most loquacious in his first speech to them. Though the vocabulary involves diminutives—a little water, a little bread—the speech extends over three verses, which hints at how the author wants to characterize Abraham—someone who provides immediate and significant hospitality.

It is difficult to know what to make of the references to trees in this first scene. On the one hand, terebinths (see n. a) were associated with places at which shrines existed. On the other hand, "the tree" (vv. 4, 8) appears to have no sacral significance. In both verses, it is a place to find respite from the sun. Interestingly, though Abraham suggests that the three individuals rest under the tree, it is he who enjoys the shade of the tree.

The meal itself is munificent. Abraham apparently calls for a bushel of flour to be prepared. That plus a calf and dairy products would have produced far more than what three "normal" people could eat. The meal is hyperbolically grand, a counterpoint to the marked understatement in verses 4–5. (It is not clear to what extent this meal would violate the ban on "cooking a kid in its mother's milk" [Exod 23:19; 34:26; Deut 14:21].)

This first scene ends in ambiguity. In Gen 18:7, Abraham hands over the calf to a servant, who prepares it. Verse 8 offers no overt change in subject from the final verb in verse 7; the servant could well be the subject of all the verbs in verse 8. Similarly, the three individuals never abandon their collective identity. Even though Abraham addresses only one of them, they speak jointly (v. 5). Further, just as the identity of the three individuals blur, so do the identities of Abraham and his servant. What remains unambiguous is the great size of the meal that is set before the three individuals. Perhaps readers should not be surprised that the author never reports that they finish eating!

[9–15] In this second scene, the passivity of the individuals gives way to interrogative discourse and dialogue. The threesome, still speaking as one, ask the whereabouts of Sarah, who is the focal point of the scene. Just as Abraham is near the entrance of the tent at the beginning of the first scene, now Sarah is just inside the tent at the beginning of the second one.

One might think that verse 10 follows naturally upon Abraham's response to the individuals. Such, however, is not the case. In verse 10, a visiting speaker neither addresses Sarah nor responds to her physical location. (After v. 9, there is no more corporate speech.) Rather, one of the three visitors speaks directly to Abraham, predicting both his "return" and that Sarah will give birth to "a son." The connection between return and birth seems simply to be chronological: this visitor makes a point that not more than one year from now, Sarah will have a son. The time will be when animals give birth, in the spring. This way of identifying the moment when Isaac will be born makes that birth seem somewhat less "miraculous," since Sarah will be giving birth at the time of regular fecundity in the faunal world.

Still, the narrator notes that for Abraham and Sarah to engender a child would be highly unusual, given their respective ages. That Sarah no longer menstruates emphasizes this point. Sarah, not Abraham, responds—and in two ways: externally and internally. (Abraham's response to this proclamation has occurred in 17:17–18: he spoke out loud.) What everyone could hear was her laughter, another play on Isaac's name (laugh, *yiṣḥaq*; Isaac, *Yiṣḥāq*). However, the narrator does not permit her to speak out loud. Rather, she talks to herself. She, like Abraham, asks a rhetorical question. But her question has less to do with whether or not such a child might be born and far more to do with her own situation: "Shall I have such joy?" Some commentators view this joy as sexual pleasure. That does not seem to be at issue. The joy of being a mother and of receiving the status that bearing a son within a patrilineal kinship structure would give lies at the heart of her question. Her laughter provides no real clue about her internal response to what the individual has said about her to Abraham.

Verse 13 makes clear to the reader that YHWH is the individual who is conversing with Abraham. However, nowhere in the two scenes that comprise 18:1–15 does the author suggest that either Abraham or Sarah perceive that the deity has appeared to them, though verse 14 does refer to YHWH as the provider of the child. The reader learns this at the outset (v. 1), and that knowledge is reinforced in verse 13, but the two human characters (Abraham and Sarah) never recognize the true identity of the individuals who have dined and spoken with them.

The deity responds to Sarah's laughter, not to her interior speech, and he talks to Abraham *about* her, not directly *to* her. This lack of direct dialogue reinforces the apparent misconstrual of Sarah's interior speech. The deity's question about "why" focuses on a speech such as that made by Abraham in the preceding chapter (17:17–18). Sarah's speech, however, focuses on the possibility of joy. The deity focuses on what the deity can do, provide a child, not upon the impact that the birth of that child will have upon Sarah, providing joy. It is almost as if the deity and Sarah are talking past each other.

The deity then responds to Sarah's internal rhetorical question with a voiced rhetorical question: "Is anything too difficult for YHWH?" The answer, of course, is "No." The deity turns Sarah's question regarding her own happiness into a theological question involving the capability of the deity. This question is built on standard affirmations found elsewhere in the OT about the incomparable power of the deity (e.g., Exod 15:11; Num 11:23 [though with different vocabulary]; Job 37:14).

The end of the scene ends in a quibble between the deity and Sarah. The narrator provides the reason for this confrontation: Sarah is "afraid." The object of her fear remains unclear. One might assume that it is the new theological weight created by the rhetorical question. But the author does not clarify the point. Only now are the deity and Sarah in direct dialogue, and about a far less important issue than the birth of a son or the possibility that she might enjoy true pleasure. Their argument about whether or not she laughed is almost laughable, a comic touch to this alternative presentation of the announcement that Sarah will give birth. Isaac, "laughter," will truly be an appropriate name for her son.

Genesis 18:16–33
Sodom and Gomorrah:
"Should Not YHWH Act Justly?"

The mood of the chapter changes even though the multiform deity remains present. "The individuals," presumably all three, depart from Mamre, with Abraham helping them on their way. Speech, not action, characterizes the rest of the chapter. In 18:16–21, only the deity is heard, and Abraham hears him less than readers do, since the first of the deity's two speeches (vv. 17–19) is either an internal speech or one directed at the other two "individuals." The deity's speeches (vv. 17–19, 20–21) then give way to dialogue between Abraham and YHWH, which is the highlight of this section. The many speeches address critical issues about justice: as a quality expected of Abraham and his lineage and as a quality to which the deity can be held accountable.

18:16 The individuals left and surveyed Sodom. Abraham was still with
them, to help them on their way. **17** YHWH said, "Shall I hide from Abraham what I am about to do? **18** Abraham is to become a very powerful nation, and all the nations of the earth will be blessed through him.
19 Truly, I have entered into a relationship[a] with him[b] so that he may
charge his sons and his household after him to observe the way of YHWH,
to do righteousness and justice, and so that YHWH might bring to fruition
concerning Abraham all that he has promised him." **20** Then YHWH said,
"The outcry from Sodom and Gomorrah[c]—it has become great. Their sin
has become gravely serious. **21** I will descend and discover whether their
outcry, which has reached me, accords with all that they have done. And
if not, then I will know it."

22 The individuals then turned and proceeded toward Sodom. Now
Abraham was still with them, standing before YHWH.[d] **23** Abraham
approached [him] and said, "Will you indeed sweep away the innocent
with the guilty? **24** Perhaps there are fifty innocent people within the city.
Will you indeed sweep them[e] away and not spare that place on account
of the fifty innocent who are in it? **25** Far be it from you to do such a
thing—to kill the innocent with the guilty such that what happens to the
guilty also happens to the innocent. Far be it from you. Should not the
Judge of the entire earth act justly?" **26** YHWH said, "If I find at Sodom

fifty people within the city, then I will forgive the whole place on account
of them." **27** Abraham responded, saying, "I am now prepared to speak
with my Lord, even though I am dust and ashes. **28** What if five of the fifty
righteous are missing? Will you destroy the entire city because of five
who are not there?" He responded, "I would not wreak destruction if I
found forty-five there." **29** Again, he spoke to him, saying, "Perhaps forty
might be found there." He said, "I would not do it on account of the forty."
30 Then he said, "Do not let my Lord be angry, even though I continue
to speak. Perhaps thirty may be found there." He said, "I would not do it
if I find thirty there." **31** He said, "I am again prepared to speak with my
Lord. Perhaps thirty will be found there." He said, "I would not destroy it
on account of the thirty." **32** He said, "Do not let my Lord be angry, even
though I speak one last time. Perhaps ten will be found there." He said,
"I would not destroy it on account of the ten." **33** Then YHWH left after
he had finished speaking with Abraham. Abraham returned to his place.

a. Literally, "known" (*ydʿ*), a verb used to characterize a covenantal relationship.

b. SP and LXX do not include the pronominal suffix on the verb.

c. A literal translation of the Hebrew text requires the outcry to come from these cities rather than there to be an outcry concerning them. Gomorrah appears only here in Gen 18. It probably entered the narrative, based on the report of destruction in Gen 19:24.

d. The Masoretic apparatus (*tiqqune sopherim*) reports that the text originally read, "but YHWH remained standing before Abraham," a text that would have been deemed impious by early scribes.

e. LXX supplies "them."

[18:16–21] The deity begins his speech (vv. 17–21) with a question. It is not clear whether the speech is a soliloquy or is directed to the deity's companions, though the latter seems more likely. But how far does the question extend? Many modern translations put the question mark at the end of verse 18 (e.g., NRSVue, NJPS). That construal makes it difficult to translate verse 18, which does not seem to belong as part of the question. Instead, 18:18, along with 18:19–20, offer reasons why the deity should, in fact, explain to Abraham what he is about to do. As a result, it seems preferable to understand verse 17 as the question, which is answered implicitly in the affirmative and with the rationale for the affirmative response given in verses 18–20.

The way in which the question is posed, "Shall I conceal?" as opposed to "Shall I reveal?" suggests that the deity has intended to inform Abraham of his actions all along. The impetus is for communication, not for concealment. Further, when reading this question, readers are like Abraham, not yet privy to what the deity is intending "to do." Hence, the question focuses on the issue of "concealment" since the nature of what YHWH intends has not yet been built into the narrative.

Verses 18–19 clearly belong to the same world as other "blessing" speeches, speeches in which Abraham is thought to provide a blessing to others (Gen 12:3; 22:18; 26:4; 28:14). The theologic of these two verses is not self-evident. Verses 18–19 are designed to offer a rationale for the deity's decision to let Abraham know what will happen. Abraham will be a great nation, and through him others will be blessed. One might assume that those in Sodom and Gomorrah could be eligible for such blessing. Indeed, Abraham does argue on their behalf, that if the deity can find, finally, ten righteous persons in Sodom, the city might receive a reprieve. Further, since YHWH and Abraham already stand in a covenant relationship (it is no accident that ch. 18 follows on the heels of ch. 17), it is appropriate for YHWH to let Abraham "know" what YHWH plans to do. Less clear is the final portion of 18:19. Here the grammar changes to third-person references about the deity, suggesting that a later hand may have fleshed out the end of the speech. In any case, the author was obviously interested in exploring how Abraham's family and household would become one means by which the blessing is provided to others. They will accomplish justice and righteousness. Also, this verse first introduces the language of "righteousness and justice," which lies at the core of what follows in the next scene (vv. 22–33). Both Abraham's household and lineage and the deity are involved in a world in which righteousness and justice are of paramount importance.

The language and theological perspectives present in the deity's first speech are distinctive. The notion of benefit to other peoples belongs to the "blessing" tradition, which is relatively late.[1] The language about justice and righteousness is more at home in the prophetic and wisdom literature than it is in the family literature. Moreover, "the way" reflects a form of piety that is at home in the Psalter (e.g., 119:1, 32). The final portion of this first speech, then, has provided the author an opportunity to link this chapter to the following one with the keyword "righteous" and to develop a more abstract form of theological reflection than one typically reads in the family literature.

The deity's second speech reveals what the deity intends to do: investigate the situation in Sodom. Though the speech in 18:20–21 is not explicitly directed at Abraham, he must have heard it. That would explain the deity's earlier question to himself and Abraham's questioning of the deity that begins in verse 23. There are really two ways to understand the "outcry." This translation opts for a collective sense of outcries, perhaps outlandish noise, possibly laments or complaints coming *from* the two cities. Another option is to think that others have uttered outcries *against* these cities. In either case, the deity has heard something. Moreover, there is evidence of "their sin." Hence, the deity wants to "see" what is truly the case. No plan has yet been formed. "The Judge of the entire earth" (v. 25) is still taking evidence. This image of the deity as one

1. So Westermann 1985, 288.

interested in investigating an allegation or a problem resonates strongly with Gen 11, the tower-of-Babel story. There, too, the deity goes to investigate a problem before making a decision about what will happen.

Once the second speech has concluded in 18:21, the individuals separate. Two are presumably going down (cf. 19:28) to see what is happening at Sodom. These two appear next in 19:1, there identified as "messengers" (though later, in 19:12, 16, they are "men" again). One of the three visitors, YHWH, remains with Abraham.

[22–33] The narrative could continue without verses 23–33. The messengers are on their way, and they could arrive at Sodom without benefit of what Abraham and YHWH discuss. The dialogue between Abraham and YHWH could be viewed as intrusive, retarding the movement toward Sodom.[2] Hence, one must determine the meaning of this dialogue and the way it works within the larger narrative.

The dialogue between Abraham and YHWH has often been viewed as a dialogue about justice, using moral categories. Such a view has been based on a relatively wooden translation of key terms in the dialogue. The words *ṣaddîq* and *rāšāʿ* are regularly translated as meaning "righteous" and "wicked," respectively. Of course, these words *can* have those meanings. However, texts such as Deut 25:1 clearly show that these same words can mean "innocent" and "guilty," conveying judicial rather than moral nuance. Such is the meaning they bear in Gen 18. The deity is trying to determine whether the evidence presented sustains a verdict of guilty, thereby deserving of punishment. The primary difference between a case as in Deut 25 and the case in Gen 18 involves the number of people involved. The question at stake is stark: in a corporate entity, such as a city or nation, how many innocent people will keep all the guilty from being punished, "swept away"?

The dialogue between Abraham and YHWH presumes that Abraham has heard YHWH's plans, as announced in 18:20–21, plans that involve an investigation. Abraham's query takes seriously the legal context of such an investigation. His initial question presupposes that the investigation will take place and that the evidence will be conflicted. Both guilty and innocent people will be found in the city.

Even though the dialogue may have been written by a postexilic author, the vocabulary present in the dialogue links it to the scenes that both precede and follow it. The language of "righteousness and justice" appears in verse 19, where the terms function as moral norms, as they do, for example, in prophetic rhetoric. In 18:23–27, however, the word *ṣaddîq* has the meaning of *innocent*

2. The dialogue may stem from a hand later than the rest of Gen 18–19. Blenkinsopp writes, "Genesis 18:23–32 is a midrash on the destruction of Sodom occasioned by the destruction of Jerusalem in 586 BCE and the theological problems to which this event gave rise" (1982, 129).

rather than righteous. And the word "justice" (v. 25) is now used of the deity as judge. Moreover, the language of "sweeping away" appears in 18:23–24 and again in 19:15, 17. Hence, though the dialogue might appear as quite different from the surrounding literature, it has been linked to it lexically.

Abraham raises the legal issue in the very first sentence of the speech. The remainder of the dialogue is simply a way of working out a set of answers to the basic question: "Will you indeed sweep away the innocent with the guilty?" The dialogue that follows ultimately does not offer a final answer since the reader/hearer does not know whether ten innocent people can be found in the city. If not, will YHWH punish the entire city? Instead, the dialogue demonstrates that the deity is willing, as "Judge" (v. 25), to hear a variety of cases and to make decisions about them. In each case, one might presume that Abraham is satisfied and might conclude, "No, you obviously will not sweep away the innocent with the guilty." But that is never said. Instead, the author focuses on the verbal interplay between the two characters. Abraham's first speech is by far the longest of either character. It poses two interrogative challenges, an interrogative envelope around the speech. The first is couched in the second person (you), and the second in the third person, "the Judge." Third-person speech predominates throughout the rest of the dialogue, a tactic for creating a more formal and impersonal tone. With such artifice, the author has developed the character of Abraham as an astute interlocutor.

This speech is not the only place in the OT where the deity is addressed as a "judge" (cf. Jer 11:20; Pss 7:11; 94:2 especially). The deity was clearly understood to function in a judicial role (Gen 16:5; Ps 7:9), even asked to do such (Pss 26:1; 35:24; 43:1). In that role, the deity is understood to act righteously (Jer 11:20; Pss 7:12 [11]; 9:5 [4]). By using this image, Abraham helps to create a rhetorical world for the dialogue. It is one in which Abraham can present a case and then pose it to the deity as a judicial official. Earlier in the chapter, the deity has expected "justice" from Abraham's lineage (v. 19); now Abraham expects it from the deity.

YHWH does not respond directly to Abraham's florid rhetoric (vv. 23–25) and responds only to the question Abraham posed about the fifty innocent individuals. As judge, he will spare the "place," vocabulary that continues the rhetoric of abstraction. (Sodom is not mentioned again after v. 26.) The speeches begin to intertwine, with the two characters even saying the same things but in differing ways. For example, when Abraham speaks about the second case, he talks of fifty lacking five (vv. 27–28); the deity is more abrupt, identifying forty-five (v. 28). After that exchange, the dialogue becomes briefer. Abraham starts mentioning only numbers. That they refer to innocent individuals is presumed. And the deity's responses (in Hebrew) become shorter—six words in 18:29, and four words in verses 30, 31, 32. Moreover, repetition mounts; in

18:31 Abraham repeats what he said in 18:27, and 18:32 repeats his speech in 18:30. The deity's speeches are even more formulaic, especially the last four.

Why this dialogue stops with ten individuals is not clear. One may surmise that the deity has demonstrated the ability to serve as a just judge. In any case, it is the deity, not Abraham, who breaks off the conversation. The deity heads on "his way," presumably to join the other two visitors, and Abraham returns "to his place."

Genesis 19:1–38
The Destruction of Sodom and Gomorrah

Genesis 19 clearly continues the narrative begun in 18. Moreover, Gen 19 offers the final elements of what might be characterized as the Abraham-Lot tradition, which appears earlier in the book (chs. 11–14). Chapters 18–19 function together in numerous ways. Both commence with scenes in which the world of the divine appears at someone's dwelling. However, Gen 18 begins with three individuals near Abraham in the middle of the day; Gen 19 commences with two persons (cf. 18:22; 19:1) approaching Sodom in the evening. Daytime offers a setting for hospitality and analytical dialogue; nighttime permits criminal assault, cosmic destruction, and drunken sexual transactions. Together, day and night, suggest that the author has offered one day in the life of Abraham. (Ancient readers, knowing the distance from Mamre to the area around the Dead Sea, would not have presumed that all the action is taking place on one day.) That day begins in midday and concludes on the next day with Abraham looking over the desolate landscape (19:27–28).

Since Gen 18 belongs integrally with Gen 19, one of the issues that readers confront is the relation of the dialogue in Gen 18 to the action in Gen 19. It seems likely that the author is interested in depicting Lot as "innocent," when compared with the "guilty" men of the city. Still, contemporary readers will certainly find Lot's offer of presenting his two virgin daughters to the crowd as reprehensible. If his offer had been accepted, he would have been guilty as an accessory to gang rape. The author saves Lot from that judgment by having the "messengers/men" intervene, blinding the men of the city. As a result, Lot remains innocent of the sort of crimes for which the city will be destroyed, though he is subject to unstated critique for offering his daughters to be sexually assaulted.

In the Abraham-Lot tradition, Lot is associated with Sodom as early as Gen 13. And Sodom exemplifies a "wicked" city even at that point (13:13). Lot, however, never receives overt criticism. In fact, the dialogue in Gen 18 might be read as an apology on behalf of a "righteous" Lot, whom Abraham does not think should suffer punishment. Though Lot is never described as righteous, Abraham argues on behalf of a small number of righteous people in the city, and one might think that Lot was one of them. Still, by the end of

Gen 19, Lot, fearful of living in the hill country and, for some unknown reason, unwilling to live in a small city, ends up dwelling in a cave with his two daughters. Drunk on two consecutive nights, he impregnates both of them. At this point, the narrative functions as a statement about the origins of Moabites and the Ammonites, whom Israel traces to Lot's sons: Moab (lit., "from father") and Ben-ammi (lit., "son of my people").

19:1 The two messengers reached Sodom in the evening. Lot was sitting at the city gate of Sodom. When Lot saw them, he arose to meet them and then bowed down. **2** He said, "Please, my lords, turn aside to the house of your servant. Spend the night. Wash your feet. Then you may get up early in the morning and go on your way." They replied, "No, we will spend the night in the town square." **3** Lot urged them vigorously such that they turned aside to him. They came to his house. He then prepared a feast for them, even baking flat bread, whereupon they dined. **4** Before they went to bed, the men of the city, the men of Sodom, young to old, the entire male population, surrounded the house. **5** They yelled at Lot, saying to him, "Where are the men who have come to you this evening? Bring them out so that we can have sex with them." **6** Lot came out to them and closed the door behind him. **7** He said to them, "Do not behave in such an evil way, my fellow citizens. **8** Look, I have two daughters who are virgins. Let me bring them out to you so that you may do with them as seems appropriate to you. But as for these men, do nothing since they have come under the protection of my roof." **9** They said, "Out of the way![a] This person has come to live as a resident alien, and now he would judge us! Now we will deal worse with you than with them." Then they struggled vigorously with Lot and were about to break down the door, **10** when the men extended their hands, brought Lot to them inside the house, and closed the door. **11** Then they struck the men, young to old, who were at the doorway with a blinding light,[b] so that they were unable to find the door.

12 The men then said to Lot, "Who, besides your sons-in-law, sons, and daughters, belong to you here? Bring everyone with you out of the place[c] **13** because we are about to destroy this place due to the vast outcry against this place, which has reached YHWH. YHWH has sent us to destroy it." **14** Hence, Lot went out and said to his sons-in-law, those who had married his daughters, "Get up and flee from this place because YHWH is about to destroy this place." His sons-in-law, however, thought he was joking.

15 When morning dawned, the messengers exhorted Lot, "Get up! Take your wife and your two daughters who are with you lest they be swept away on account of the guilt[d] of the city." **16** Lot delayed, so the men seized him, his wife, and his two daughters by the hand, because

of YHWH's compassion for them, and brought them[e] out and left them[e]
outside the city. 17 After they had brought them out of the city, they[f] said,
"Save yourselves! Do not look behind you! Do not remain anywhere in
the plain! Head to the hills lest you be swept away!" 18 Lot responded to
them, "No, my lords. 19 Your servant has found favor in your eyes. You
have acted with great kindness with me, to save my life. I am, however,
unable to save myself in the hills since something terrible might follow
me such that I would die. 20 Rather, there is this nearby small town to
which I might flee: it is insignificant. Let me save myself there. Isn't it
insignificant? And my life would be saved." 21 He said to him, "I grant
you a favor in this matter as well. I have decided not to destroy this city
about which you have spoken. 22 Hurry! Flee there, since I am unable to
do anything until you reach that place." (Therefore, it is known as Zoar.)
23 The sun rose over the land when Lot reached Zoar.

24 Then YHWH rained sulfur upon Sodom and Gomorrah, and fire
[came] from YHWH, from the heavens. 25 He destroyed these cities, the
entire plain, and all the inhabitants of the cities, even the plants growing
on the ground. 26 Lot's wife[g] looked back and became a pillar of salt.

27 Abraham arose early in the morning [and went] to the place where
he had stood before YHWH. 28 He looked down over Sodom and Gomorrah, over all the land of the plain. He saw a smoke-filled land, like the
smoke from a kiln.

29 When God destroyed the cities of the plain, God remembered Abraham. He removed Lot from the disaster when he destroyed the cities
where Lot had lived.

30 Lot left Zoar. He and his two daughters lived together in the hill
country, since he was afraid to live in Zoar. He and his two daughters
lived in a cave. 31 The older daughter said to the younger one, "Our father
is getting old, and there is no man on earth who might approach us according to the manner of all the earth. 32 Come, let's get our father drunk with
wine so that we might lie with him and gain offspring from our father."
33 So, they got their father drunk with wine that night. Then the older one
lay with her father. He did not know when she lay down or when she got
up. 34 On the next morning, the older one said to the younger one, "Last
night I lay with my father. Let's get him drunk with wine again tonight.
You go and lie with him so that we might both gain offspring from our
father." 35 So, they got their father drunk with wine again that night. Then
the younger one lay with him. He did not know when she lay down or
when she got up. 36 Both the daughters thus became pregnant from their
father. 37 The older one bore a son and named him Moab[h] (he is the ancestor of contemporary Moabites). 38 The younger one also bore a son. She
named him Ben-ammi[i] (he is the ancestor of contemporary Ammonites).

a. MT reads *wayyōmərû*; LXX does not include it, though probably originally part of the text. The translation reads more smoothly without that repetition.

b. So Speiser 1964, 139, who identifies the Akkadian cognate *šunwurum*.

c. MT *hammāqôm* could refer either to the city or the house. The former had been characterized as a "place" (18:26), whereas Abraham's dwelling was known as a "place" (18:33). SP, LXX, and Syr read "this place," which takes the former option, "this place" as the city, no doubt influenced by the phrase *hammāqôm hazzeh* in v. 13.

d. The word *ʿāwôn* can mean either guilt or punishment due to the guilt.

e. The pronouns are third-masculine singular in Hebrew, no doubt construing Lot, his wife, and two daughters as a collective referent.

f. The subject of the verb is third-person masculine singular. LXX, Syr, Vulg read the plural.

g. MT simply reads "his wife."

h. Moab might be understood to mean "from father."

i. Literally, "son of my people."

[19:1–11] Chapter 19 commences as did chapter 18. Strange "men/messengers" encounter the male head of a household. The venues are quite different, however. Abraham resides near a shrine; Lot lives in a city known for its wickedness (Gen 13:13). Moreover, the initial encounters occur in different places. Abraham is at home; Lot is at the city gate. The temporal settings are also different. Abraham is visited at midday, Lot at dusk. These differences lead the reader to expect different outcomes from the story in Gen 19, which is now being set in motion.

The narrators attest that both Abraham and Lot act in a hospitable fashion. However, when comparing 18:2–8 with 19:1–3, it becomes clear that Abraham outdoes Lot. Lot functions like a foil to Abraham. Abraham hurries before bowing down; Lot simply bows down. Abraham offers a place to rest, water for washing feet, and food. The author goes on to describe the preparations for the feast that will ensue. Lot, in contrast, invites them to his house so that they can wash their feet and spend the night inside. (Though food is forthcoming, Lot does not mention that when inviting the messengers.) The simple length of the description of Abraham's hospitality when compared with that of Lot underscores that Abraham has done much more.

The initial verses do not, however, impugn Lot. He offers hospitality appropriate to the time of day when the messengers appear. Lot invites them to his house. One may infer that Lot's insistence that they stay with him (v. 3) depends upon his knowing the risks of spending a night on the streets and his concern about what might happen to them. The two "messengers" who visit Sodom must be the two "men" who departed in 18:22 and who reappear retitled as "men" in 19:12. Their encounter with Lot is, presumably, both chance and providential. He happens to be at the city gate. Moreover, he and his daughters survive the catastrophe because the messengers "happen" to lodge at his house. Verse 4 creates the transition from Lot's hospitality to the assault at evening. The verb in the very first clause foreshadows what is to come. The verb "to go to bed" or "to lay down" can also mean to have sexual relations (see Gen 34:2), which is the intent of those who appear at Lot's house.

The episode narrated in 19:4–11 bears remarkable similarity to Judg 19:16–26. There, too, visitors, a Levite and his concubine, come to a city and intend to spend the night in the square. They are "urged" not to do that and are invited into someone's house. Then males of the city assemble outside the house and demand that the male visitor be handed over to them so that they can rape him. The host refuses and then offers both his virgin daughter and the visitor's concubine to them. The males do not agree to this proposal. Soon thereafter the Levite shoves his concubine out the door. She is then raped and dies due to the assault. Common to both stories are the presence of a male visitor, the potential overnight in a city square, hospitality offered by a city dweller, males of the city intent on homosexual rape, the counteroffer of females for sexual satisfaction, and the survival of the male visitor(s).

Many scholars think that the tale in Judg 19 is the earlier version of the story. Less important than this judgment is attending to what is distinctive about the version in Gen 19. Several features stand out in this text. First, the assault is not realized, due to the blindness wrought by the visitors. Second, Lot, who offers hospitality, is really not a native of the city (19:9). He shares, with Abraham, the status of "resident alien." Third, the description of the number involved in the assault is larger than that in Judg 19. In Gen 19, the author uses hyperbole, "the entire male population." Fourth, in Gen 19, the males want to rape more than one individual. Fifth, the males of the city in Gen 19 do not accept the offer of heterosexual rape, as did the males in Judg 19. One may conclude that the episode in Genesis emphasizes the otherness and depravity of a non-Israelite city, which deserves to be destroyed.

In Gen 19:4–5, the author has created a surreal scene. The entire male population of the city congregates at Lot's house. This hyperbolic depiction is the virtual obverse of the way in which the population of Nineveh, a city also known for its wickedness (Jonah 1:2), is described: at the behest of Jonah's speech, they all repent (3:8). That foreign population is wildly righteous. The population of Sodom, by contrast, is utterly wicked. This description of total depravity is important since it not only warrants the destruction to come, but also makes clear that the conditions for possible reprieve, established in Gen 18, have *not* been met. Once Lot and his family have been removed, the entire male population of the city deserves to be obliterated.

The author of Gen 19 then offers a dialogue similar to the one in Judg 19:22–24. The dialogue in Genesis is, however, longer. It presents three speeches as opposed to the two speeches in Judges. The first speeches in both texts (Gen 19:5; Judg 19:22) include the demand from "the men of the city" to "know" the male guest(s). The responses are similar as well, including the admonition not to "act wickedly" (*r*ʿʿ, Gen 19:7; Judg 19:23), the offer of two women to the men of the town, and the appeal not to harm the visitors (Gen 19:8; Judg 19:24). In Judges (19:25), after the second speech, the townspeople "would not listen," whereupon the Levite hands over his concubine. In Genesis, the townspeople offer another speech (Gen 19:9), in which the object of their violence shifts from the messengers to Lot. Only then, when the city's males are about to attack Lot and his house, do the messengers act to protect him.

Noteworthy in the speech of the Sodomites is their comment about Lot's status. In verse 7, Lot tries to establish common ground with those who are at his door by calling them "fellow citizens." However, in an aside directed to other Sodomites (v. 9), the author makes clear that they view him as a foreigner, a perception that helps justify the reader's view that Lot might deserve to be spared (even though he has offered his daughters to be raped!). It is ironic that the Sodomites complain about Lot appearing to judge them, since they are about to suffer judgment from "the Judge of all the earth" (18:25). Lot, like the rest of the patrilineage of Terah, remained resident aliens in the land and subject to the animosity of the native population. As a result, Lot needs divine protection as well as the sort of aid that Abraham has earlier provided for him (Gen 14).

[12–29] The report about the destruction of Sodom is surprisingly lively and vivid, including both details about the various human responses to the deity and details about the catastrophe. At several points, there is resonance with the story about the flood. Lot, like Noah before him, has the capacity to save others. In addition, God "remembers" Abraham (19:29), just as God has remembered Noah (8:1).

Once the townspeople's attack against Lot's household has been foiled, the two visiting "men" take action. They admonish Lot to move his extended family from the city, since the deity has decided to destroy it. The contents of this speech do not square easily with the preceding chapter's depiction of YHWH coming down to investigate the outcry against the city (18:20–21). Neither an investigation nor a pronouncement of judgment is overtly reported. One may infer that the scene of assault, which has just occurred (19:1–11), has persuaded the deity that the city is indeed gravely sinful (18:21).

In the men's speech to Lot, a new element appears. What is to be destroyed is now described as "this place." Language about a city does continue, but "place" appears three times as well (19:12, 13, 14). Such a development is consistent with the character of the destruction, which involves far more than that of the cities, Sodom (and Gomorrah; so v. 25).

Only now does it seem likely that those who belong to Lot (v. 12) might be about ten, the number set for innocents in 18:32 (Lot and his wife, at least two virgin daughters, at least two sons, at least two daughters with their husbands, sons-in-law), and that the city might escape destruction. Still, Abraham's earlier speech (ch. 18) was not so much an intercession for Sodom as it was a plea on behalf of his extended family, Lot's household. The earlier dialogue established the possibility that Sodom might not be destroyed due to the presence of a small number of "righteous" people, but events that take place after that dialogue make clear that the city deserves to be annihilated and that Lot and his family are eligible to be saved.

Lot initially complies with the mandate from the men (v. 12). He goes to his sons-in-law, who presumably are living with Lot's daughters in their parents' household, the patrilocal residence. Though he warns his sons-in-law, they think he is joking, thus dooming them and their wives. Just as Sarah laughs to herself in 18:12, now part of Lot's extended family laughs, a laughter that results in their deaths.

A narrative gap occurs after 19:14. Now it is morning. The men order Lot to leave, along with those in his family who are willing to be saved. They now number only four. Lot himself apparently dallies, such that the men forcibly remove Lot, his wife, and his two daughters. Once outside the city, one might assume that Lot and his family are safe. Such is not the case. "They" command Lot to flee to the hills and not to look back. Lot still does not move and instead offers a plea that he not be compelled to live in the hill country but rather in Zoar. As is the case in many traditional cultures, the mountains are viewed as an alien and dangerous environment.

The area from which Lot is commanded to flee is described as the "plain" (v. 17). The word *kikkār* can mean something round. The "*kikkār* of the Jordan" (Gen 13:10) is the oval area Lot selects as a place of residence. Moreover, its area includes cities, "the cities of the plain" (Gen 13:12; 14:2), one of which is Sodom and another of which is Zoar (13:10). Only the word *kikkār* appears in 19:17, though it no doubt refers to the same area described in Gen 13.

Sodom has often been associated with one of the tells on the southeastern shore of the Dead Sea. Here a broad flat area has several tells (notably Numeira and Bab edh-Dhra). The cities were occupied during the third and early second millennia BCE. If ancient Israelites made this association, then the geographic implications have Lot being commanded to ascend from the southeastern coast of the Dead Sea to the Moabite highlands. However, some scholars have argued that Zoar was located at the southern end of the Dead Sea, in which case Lot would not have been required to make that steep ascent to about a mile higher. At present, there is no consensus about the actual site of Zoar.

Lot's request to live in Zoar occupies a surprising amount of space. A careful reading of his speech (19:18–22) demonstrates that several issues are at stake. First, he is afraid of the hill country and some unknown disaster. Second, he presents Zoar as a less significant city than the other cities of the plain. (Whether this is simply a play on the meaning of Zoar, which means "small," or reflects demographic reality is impossible to know.) Third, Lot is concerned to save his life, which is clearly a severe challege. In verse 19, he apparently thinks his life has been saved; in verse 20, it is yet to happen. Fourth, based on the messenger's response in 19:21–22, Lot is, in effect, asking that Zoar be spared from destruction, in which case it is one of the cities of the plain to be destroyed.

When the messenger responds to Lot (v. 22), he makes a truly remarkable statement. God cannot destroy the cities of the plain until Lot is in Zoar. This could simply be an etiology for some city in the plain of the Jordan that has escaped destruction. However, more seems to be at work. If Lot and his family enter Zoar, then there are, in theory, a small number of "righteous people" in the city. Though numbering less than ten, they might offer the deity grounds for not destroying this town. Lot becomes the reason why Zoar survives the conflagration. Then the narrator takes over and reports what happens until the destruction has been completed. Once the decision to destroy Sodom has been made and once Lot's status has been resolved, there is no more room for conversation or negotiation. Verse 23 continues the overt use of temporality—the language of day and night, which helps make chapters 18–19 cohere.

Verses 24–29 describe the destruction of the plain and its cities. (Sodom is often associated with Gomorrah and also with Admah, Zeboiim, and Zoar [14:8]). Various biblical authors have apparently drawn on the narrative of Gen 19. The diction of the city's destruction as being "overthrown" (*hpk*) is a hallmark of such references (19:29; so Deut 29:23; Isa 13:19; Jer 50:40; Lam 4:6). So too is the language of sulfur and fire along with the verb "to rain," which, when linked with the language of fire, becomes ironic. Westermann (1985, 306) has observed that fire and sulfur are a stock image in the OT to describe the destruction of a city or nation (Deut 29:23; Ps 11:6; Ezek 38:22; Isa 30:33; 34:9). Since sulfurous deposits and large salt formations occur in the Dead Sea basin, reference to these minerals may have an etiological function. And the latter etiology was important to the flow of the story since it removed Lot's wife from the scene and allowed him to become sexually available to his daughters.

Verses 27–28 are separated from verses 24–26 by another narrative gap, which is again created by reference to day-night language. On the morning after Sodom has been destroyed, Abraham goes out early, only to see the smoking ruin. He has returned to the place where his conversation with the deity ended in an open-ended fashion (18:32). Now Abraham learns by implication that fewer than ten righteous people were found in Sodom.

Though the Masoretes construed 19:29 to introduce the final scene involving Lot and his daughters, the verse is probably attributable to P since the divine name shifts to Elohim. It really concludes the report about Sodom's destruction. Moreover, this verse offers a theological interpretation about what has just transpired. Without it, one might think that Lot and his daughters survive because YHWH had acted compassionately toward them (19:16). The author of verse 29 wants to offer a corrective, a move typical of the Priestly hand. God has remembered Abraham and, because of that, let Lot live. The notion is similar to that of the deity's remembering Noah and all the animals (Gen 8:1). The Priestly writer does not want readers to think that Lot has a status comparable to Noah. Hence that individual has Abraham function as an object of God's remembering. Lot is saved because of Abraham. Since Lot, through his sons, will signify Moab and Ammon, one might understand Abraham here, as in Gen 14, to have wrought a blessing to some of the earth's families (so Gen 12:3).

[30–38] The conclusion to the Lot saga explains how it is, after the death of Lot's wife, that the lineage will continue. These verses highlight the ingenuity of Lot's daughters (cf. Tamar's comparable trickery; Gen 38). This episode, moreover, continues to flesh out the character of Lot. The final piece of the saga about Lot plays out in significant contrast to the geographic setting established in Gen 13:9–13. Instead of continuing to live in an Edenic plain, Lot dwells in a cave, and not with his wife but instead with his two daughters. He has come to this sorry state not due to any act of the deity but for fear of remaining in Zoar. The reason for that fear is unspecified, as is the reason for his terror at the prospect of living in the hill country. In verses 30–38, Lot is the subject of only one verb, "to leave" (v. 30; with the exception of "he did not know," vv. 33, 35). Thereafter, Lot's two nameless daughters are the primary actors. Once the narrator establishes the geographic setting of the report, all attention focuses on Lot's daughters, especially the older one (though the Hebrew translated "younger," *ṣĕʿîrâ*, is a virtual wordplay on the city name Zoar, *ṣōʿar*). The author does not present their plan as one having overtly to do with preserving their father's lineage, though the plan of making their father drunk and then having sex with him achieves that result. The temporal language of day and night continues: verse 33, "night"; verse 34, "the next day."

This scene has often been read as denigratory both to Lot and his daughters. It certainly does portray Lot in an unfavorable light; he is afraid without reason, guilty of being drunk, and engaging unknowingly in incestuous sexual activity. Such sexual unions were probably proscribed according to the principles that lie behind Lev 18. (One may compare this episode with that of Noah lying drunk in his tent and being observed by a son. See the comments on Gen 9 for a discussion of Ham's sexual behavior.) As for the daughters, they claim certain knowledge, but it is flawed. There are other men with whom they might have had sexual relations. (The narrator takes care not to refer explicitly to sexual activity. Interestingly, the word "earth" appears twice in this verse: "not a man on earth," "the way of the earth." That repetition underscores the cosmic tone of what happened at Sodom.) Nonetheless, they necessarily have a limited vision of the world from the cave to which their father has led them. And they take initiative, as does Tamar, when she is unable to secure an heir in a more traditional manner. It is, therefore, appropriate to describe the daughters' behavior as that of "tricksters," being unable to achieve power through "normal" or public channels and, like Tamar, needing to resort to hidden sexual subterfuge. There is a distinct irony in the Lot saga; Lot offers up his daughters to heterosexual gang rape and then later, when drunk, has intercourse with them.

Some scholars question whether 19:37–38 was originally part of the Lot saga. They have viewed this account, like 25:30, as a late etiology, linking the family stories to Syro-Palestinian political realities. (Gen 19:37–38 and 25:30, along with 16:11–12 and 21:19, depict origins of nations that lived to the south and east of Israel: Ammonites, Moabites, Edomites, and Ishmaelites.) Both the names Moab, "From Father," and Ben-ammi, "One of My People," can be understood to derive from the sexual union between Lot and his daughters. It is not clear whether these popular etymologies are intended as a slur upon those two peoples. Neither the name Edomite nor Ishmaelite bears such negative connotations.

Those narratives and reports associated with Lot comprise a discrete minor saga. Both Abraham and Lot are legitimate heirs within the patrilineage of Terah (Gen 11:27), though Abraham belongs to an older generation. Abraham's brother, Haran, is Lot's father. The third brother, Nahor, remains important to the family, though he and his male descendants do not move into the so-called promised land. Seen from this vantage point, one issue that the presence of Lot and Abraham together raises is how they will live together as part of the same family. Much of the saga involves the ways in which they move apart (chs. 13; 19), with Lot ultimately becoming the progenitor of two nations different from Israel.

The character Lot functions as a foil to Abraham. Lot chooses fertile land, though apparently beyond the purview of what was promised to Abraham. That choice ultimately dooms Lot's hold on any land in Palestine. Lot's heirs reside to the east of the promised land. Both characters are depicted as gracious hosts, though Abraham offers greater hospitality than Lot, who even offers his daughters to be raped. Both characters have intercourse with someone other than the primary wife. By virtually any standard, Abraham's relationship with Hagar is more acceptable than is Lot's with his daughters. Finally, Abraham acts on behalf of his nephew in ways that the nephew cannot reciprocate. In Gen 14, Abraham rescues Lot from his status of prisoner. In Gen 18, Abraham establishes the theological groundwork that lets Lot and some of his family escape from Sodom. Lot is saved because "God remembered Abraham" (19:29).

Lot's daughters symbolize a future in which Lot's lineage will continue to be important for Israel. The accession of their sons, Moab and Ammon, to their respective territories was, according to the book of Deuteronomy, not the result of accidental escape or migration but due to the act of the deity. As a result, Israel is proscribed from attacking them: "Do not harass Moab or engage them in battle, for I will not give you any of its land as a possession, since I have given

Ar as a possession to the descendants of Lot" (Deut 2:9; see the comparable probation for Ammon in Deut 2:19). Moreover, from one of these nations, Moab, will come one of David's ancestors, Ruth (1:4; 4:13, 17). The relationship of Ammon and Moab to Israel is of a different sort than is the relationship of other groups that spin off from the family, such as the Edomites.

Genesis 20:1–18
Abraham Calls Sarah His Sister When in Gerar

Genesis 20 is a classic "doublet," a text that provides a different version of the same basic narrative, in this case about the patriarch passing off his wife as his sister, which also appears in Gen 12:10–20. The situation, moreover, appears similar to scenes in the two texts reporting the making of a covenant between the deity and Abraham (Gen 15; 17). This analogy breaks down, however, since Gen 20 is really one of three versions of the wife-sister story; Gen 26 offers that third example. Each version takes a basic motif, the construal of the matriarch as the patriarch's sister, and deploys it in different ways. In Gen 20, the patriarch is characterized very differently from the figure who appears in both Gen 12 and 26. Abraham is cast in a more favorable light in Gen 20. Moreover, Gen 20 is much longer than the other two versions. The expansion occurs in speeches, primarily in the dialogues between Abimelek and God and between Abimelek and Abraham. Further, each of the three versions has a separate theme. In Gen 20, an overt theological issue is at work: how one should think about "the fear of God" when living in a foreign land. This theme is complemented by several theological elements unusual in the family literature: the notion of God's providential control (v. 6), a prophet as intercessor, the diction of prayer (vv. 7, 17), and the aforementioned "fear of God." These elements likely reflect the hand of a post-Priestly author.

This version clearly depends on the version in Gen 12: no reason is offered when Abraham calls his wife his sister. Readers must import the reason from Gen 12. Similarly, only in verse 17 do readers learn explicitly about a plague of sterility that has afflicted Abimelek's household. The reader familiar with Gen 12 infers that such has happened at an earlier point in the narrative. As a result, one may conclude that this version has been written by an author who knows that readers will be familiar with the basic motif from its prior occurrence in Gen 12.

20:1 Abraham traveled from there to the land of the Negeb. There he lived
between Qadesh and Shur. He then spent time as an immigrant in Gerar.
2 Abraham said this about Sarah, his wife, "She is my sister." Abimelek,
king of Gerar, then sent for and took Sarah. **3** God came to Abimelek in

a nocturnal dream. He said to him, "You are as good as dead because of
this woman whom you have taken. She is the wife of another man." **4** Now
Abimelek had not approached her. Hence, he responded, "My Lord, would
you kill an innocent person?[a] **5** Did not he himself say to me, 'She is my
sister'? Moreover, she herself also said, 'He is my brother.' I have acted
in this instance with a blameless heart and innocent hands." **6** The deity[b]
answered him in that same dream, "I know you have acted in this instance
with a blameless heart. I myself prevented you from sinning against me.
That is why I did not allow you to touch her. **7** Now restore the man's wife.
He is a prophet. He will pray for you so that you will live. But if you do
not restore her, know that you and all who are with you will die."

8 So Abimelek got up early the next morning, summoned all his
servants, and reported all these things to them. The people were terrified. **9** Abimelek then summoned Abraham and said to him, "What have
you done to us? How have I sinned against you such that you brought
against me and my kingdom such great blame? You have behaved to
me in ways that should not be done." **10** Abimelek continued to speak to
Abraham, "What did you think you were doing in this affair?" **11** Abraham responded, "I simply thought that there was no fear of God in this
place, that they would kill me because of my wife. **12** Moreover, in fact,
she *is* my sister: She is the daughter of my male ancestor but not of my
mother. And she has become my wife. **13** When God made me wander
away from my father's house, I said to her, 'This is what you must do[c] for
me: in every place that we go, say about me, 'He is my brother.'" **14** So
Abimelek took sheep, cattle, male slaves, and female slaves and gave
them to Abraham. He also restored Sarah, his wife, to him. **15** Abimelek
then said, "Look, my land is before you. Dwell wherever it looks good
to you!" **16** And to Sarah he said, "I have given one thousand pieces to
your brother. It is a restitution[d] for you and for all who are with you.
You are now totally vindicated."[e] **17** Then Abraham prayed to the deity[b]
whereupon God healed Abimelek, his wife, and his female slaves so that
they were able to bear children, **18** since YHWH had closed every womb
in the household of Abimelek because of Sarah, the wife of Abraham.

a. MT is problematic. Speiser (1964,149), among others, has offered the best explanation: "an old textual corruption" from dittography has resulted in the secondary creation of *hgyhgm* out of an early *hgm*.

b. Literally, "the *ʾĕlōhîm*," not simply *ʾĕlōhîm*, as in v. 3.

c. Literally, "This is the obligation."

d. Literally, "a covering of the eyes."

e. The last three words in the MT are ungrammatical. I follow Gunkel (1997, 222) in restoring *wʾt klw nkht*, which involves placing the waw with the penultimate word.

[20:1–7] This second of the wife-sister stories not only depends upon the initial version (Gen 12:10–20) but was also written with an eye to its immediate literary context. The initial words in 20:1, "from there," presuppose a geographic location, vague though it is. This phrase points the reader back to Abraham's previous travels, which most recently have placed him looking down over the destroyed landscape of the Dead Sea plain (19:27–28). Before that, he has been living near Mamre. (Both "the plain" and Mamre locate Abraham far to the south of the sites Shechem and Bethel, which he has left to travel through the Negeb to Egypt [12:6–7].) Whatever the "from there" might designate, the toponyms in 20:1 (Negeb, Qadesh, and Shur) indicate that the writer understands Abraham to be moving further south. No reason is offered for travel in this direction. Moreover, the final clause in 20:1 reports that Abraham has moved from that far-southern area to the west, to Gerar, a city located between Beersheba and Gaza (and nearer to the latter). Again, the author offers no explanation for this movement, unlike in the first wife-sister story, in which famine in the land explains Abraham's journey to Egypt. What is important is Abraham's status as an "immigrant," the same status he is accorded in the first wife-sister story (12:10).

Abraham's first speech (v. 2) is as abrupt and without rationale as is his move to Gerar, again suggesting that the author of Gen 20 presumes that readers already know the inner workings of the story. Thus 20:2 summarizes action that requires more than twice that amount of text in an already terse Gen 12.

The appearance of the deity to Abimelek at night is of a piece with other epiphanies as described in the family literature (e.g., Gen 28:10–17; 32:24; cf. 22:1–3, which implies that God has spoken to Abraham at night). However, within the family literature, overt reference to dreams appears only here, in Gen 28:12, and Gen 31:10–24. Moreover, the diction in Gen 20 differs from that in the description of Jacob's dream: 28:12 states "he dreamed" while 20:3 describes the deity as coming to Abimelek in a dream, as is also the case with Laban (Gen 31:24). This formulation emphasizes that the deity is intervening, preventing Abimelek from having intercourse with Sarah. Since Gen 20 appears after the deity has stated that Sarah will bear a son to Abraham (17:16), it is important that Abimelek not have sexual access to her. (The situation in Gen 12 is different since at this point in the story, there has been no promise that Sarah would bear a son to Abraham.)

God initiates his dialogue with Abimelek by reporting that he is as good as dead, in effect passing a death sentence on him. Abimelek challenges this verdict by reporting that he is blameless (*tām*) and innocent (*niqyōn*). Moreover, he reports that both Abraham and Sarah have claimed to be brother and sister, respectively (v. 5 is the only moment in the text where Sarah's voice is heard, and here it is quoted by Abimelek).

Here, too, the narrative is related to an issue that has been before Abraham earlier, in Gen 18: whether or not any "righteous" people are in a city, a foreign one. Here the deity affirms that Abimelek is indeed blameless (v. 6). In addition, the deity emphatically claims control of these events: "I prevented you from sinning against me." (The notion of God who is in such control resonates with the theology present in the Joseph novella: Gen 45:5–7.) The phrase "against me" is striking. The offense that Abimelek might have committed would not have been simply against Abraham but first of all against God. This claim is consistent with how Abraham later construes his prior concern, that there was no "fear of God in this place" (20:11). The issue of a foreign king having sexual access to Sarah here is overtly theological in a way not claimed in Gen 12.

Abimelek's innocence aside, the deity requires that he return "the man's wife," not because he is a prophet, as some translations suggest (e.g., NRSV, "for he is a prophet"), but to avoid a "sin against the deity." The restoration of Sarah to her husband will then enable Abraham to intercede on behalf of Abimelek so that he, and all who are with him, will not die. Abraham, in this role as intercessor, is characterized as a prophet. Construing Abraham as an intercessor might derive from his dialogue with the deity (Gen 18), in which he argues on behalf of a city in which a certain number of righteous or innocent people might be living. That he would be characterized in this role as a prophet is, however, somewhat surprising since few prophets depicted in preexilic texts acted as intercessors. Amos's intercessory oracles (Amos 7:1–6) are the exception rather than the rule. Nonetheless, the post-Priestly author of Gen 20 thought that intercession was a hallmark of prophetic activity, thereby permitting Abraham to be labeled a prophet. The initial dialogue in Gen 20 concludes on the note with which it begins: the threat of death. But to underscore the severity of the threat at the end of the dialogue, the author enlarges the threat of death to include not only Abimelek but also "all who are with you."

[8–18] The narrative moves from evening to early the next day, from the world of dreams to the realm of royal initiatives. Abimelek summons various parties, beginning with his royal retinue. Thereafter he calls for Abraham, charging him with inappropriate behavior, things that "should not be done." Unlike the first wife-sister story, Abraham defends himself when confronted by the ruler, doing so in two ways. The first may be understood to reflect Abraham's recent experiences regarding Sodom, a foreign city known for its sin (18:20). Genesis 20 presents Abraham as worried that such a condition might also obtain in Gerar, a city in which he is a foreigner. The phrase "fear of God" is one way that ancient Israelite writers conceived of proper piety. The phrase is especially prominent in wisdom literature (e.g., Prov 1:7; 2:5; 8:13; 9:10; 10:27; 14:27; 15:33; 19:23; 22:4; 31:30). This is the only place the phrase appears in the book of Genesis, suggesting that the author is someone who is influenced by the wisdom tradition. More to the point, Abraham has thought no one in Gerar fears God. Yet he has been wrong, as the narrative demonstrates to this point. Hence, Abraham moves to his second defense, that Sarah is indeed his sister. His argument here is, at first reading, less clear. However, since the Hebrew noun normally translated "father" can also mean "male ancestor" (e.g., Gen 10:21), Abraham seems to be claiming that Sarah is a female relative (cf. Gen 24:60), one who belongs to the patrilineage of Terah. That Abraham returns to the use of a ruse in 20:13 suggests that the author is portraying the second defense as a tour de force rather than as a compelling defense.

In the final portion of Abraham's response to Abimelek, one again finds the author omitting information that is presumed from the version in Gen 12. Abraham reports that he has asked Sarah to call him "brother," but he does not explain why. The reason, the woman's beauty, mentioned in 12:11 for Sarah and 26:7 for Rebekah, remains unstated here. What is mentioned here is Abraham's claim about the deity controlling his movement. The deity has "made Abraham wander" (20:13), a verb in the hiphil conjugation that often bears negative connotations. This claim, no doubt based on Gen 12:1, underscores the theology present in Gen 20: a deity is in control of human destiny.

After the dialogue has concluded, Abimelek enriches Abraham with livestock and enslaved persons (v. 14). The gain of material wealth in Gen 12 comes at a different place in the story. Here Abraham receives livestock and enslaved persons as payment for the temporary loss of his wife, which could be viewed as an unseemly transaction by this post-Priestly author. In Gen 20, Abraham gains such property only when Abimelek returns Sarah to him "as his wife." Moreover, Abimelek offers Abraham land on which to live, an element absent from Gen 12 but present, though in a different way, in Gen 26. Just as Abraham has offered Lot a choice of where to live (Gen 13:9), so now Abimelek does something similar for Abraham. Though Gen 20 does not report that Abraham accepts his offer, Gen 21:22–34 makes clear that he continues to live as an immigrant in Gerar.

Overt concern for Sarah's status as untouched and unsullied continues in 20:16, though the author does include a sardonic touch, having Abimelek refer to Abraham as "your brother." That concern is echoed in verse 18, when the author refers to the cause of the plague as having to do with Sarah. (In v. 18, the presence of "YHWH," and not "Elohim," suggests that this verse may have come from a later hand, making more definite the character of this plague.) The plague of infertility is especially apt, since it would have been terrible if Sarah were impregnated by Abimelek. The plague of infertility has kept that from happening. That the final words of the narrative are "the wife of Abraham" is important as a corrective to other ways Sarah has been construed in the narrative ("my sister," "daughter of my male ancestor"; v. 12).

In sum, this version of the wife-sister narrative presents the four characters in a positive light. God is in control; Abimelek is innocent; Abraham is a prophet; and Sarah has not been "touched" by the foreign king. Yet it is a world in which sin is potentially present. Abimelek asks Abraham how he, Abimelek, might have sinned against Abraham (v. 9); God warns Abimelek about sinning against God (v. 6). Nevertheless, by the end of the narrative no human character is deemed culpable.

Genesis 21:1–34
Isaac Is Born; Hagar and Ishmael Are Banished

Genesis 21 is made up of diverse material: two reports and one narrative. The first report, 21:1–7, and the narrative, 21:8–21, are related. That first report describes the birth of Isaac; the narrative relates the implications of his birth for the larger household. The second report, 21:22–34, depicts Abimelek and Abraham making a covenant at Beersheba. All three of these texts are connected to prior episodes in the familial literature. Verses 1–7 include a report that Abraham circumcises his son, the requirement for which is laid down in Gen 17. Verses 8–21 comprise the second of two narratives about Hagar and Ishmael (the first occurs in Gen 16), one of the important subplots in the Abraham-and-Sarah saga. Then, 21:22–34 alludes to Gen 20, in which Abraham interacts with Abimelek. One has the sense that, especially with the two reports, the compositors are creating a denouement, which includes various final comments about one and another element in the Abrahamic saga.

21:1 Now YHWH cared for Sarah as he had promised. He did for Sarah
what he had said he would. **2** She became pregnant and then bore a son to
Abraham in his old age, at the time that God had promised him. **3** Abraham named his son, the one whom Sarah had born to him, Isaac. **4** Abraham circumcised his son Isaac when he was eight days old, just as God
had commanded him. **5** Abraham was one hundred years old when his
son Isaac was born to him. **6** Sarah said, "God has created laughter for
me. Anyone who hears of it will laugh with me." **7** And she said, "Who
would have said concerning Abraham, 'Sarah has nursed children.' But
I have borne a son during his old age!"

8 The child grew and was weaned. On the day that Isaac was weaned,
Abraham made a great feast. **9** Sarah saw the son of Hagar the Egyptian,
whom she had born to Abraham, laughing at her son, Isaac.[a] **10** She then
said to Abraham, "Get rid of this female slave and her son. The son of this
female slave shall not receive an inheritance along with my son, Isaac."
11 This was an anguishing moment for Abraham, on account of his son.
12 God said to Abraham, "Don't be so upset about the boy and about your
female slave. Do whatever Sarah tells you because your progeny will be

known through Isaac. **13** And as for the son of the female slave, I will
make him a great[b] nation because he is your offspring." **14** So Abraham
got up early the next morning, took some bread and a skin of water, and
gave it to Hagar. He set the child on her shoulders[c] and sent her away. She
left and wandered about in the wilderness near Beersheba.

15 After they had finished the water that was in the skin, she placed
the boy under one of the shrubs. **16** She then went and sat down at some
distance from him, about the distance of an arrow shot by bow, and said,
"Don't let me see the death of the child!" Then she cried aloud, weeping.[d]
17 Then God heard the sound of the youth;[e] whereupon a messenger of
God called to Hagar from the heavens and said to her, "What is happening
to you? Do not be afraid, because God has heard the sound of the youth
where he is. **18** Get up, pick up the boy, and hug him,[f] for I will make him a
great nation." **19** Then God opened her eyes, whereupon she saw a well of
water. She went and filled the skin with water and gave the youth a drink.

20 God was with the youth. He grew, lived in the desert, and became
a great archer.[g] **21** He lived in the desert of Paran. His mother acquired a
wife for him from the land of Egypt.

22 About that time, Abimelek and Phicol, his general, said to Abraham, "God is with you in all that you are doing. **23** Now take an oath
with God as witness that you will not deceive me, my progeny, or my
descendants. Just as I have acted kindly with you, you should act kindly
with me and with the land in which you are residing." **24** Abraham said,
"I take that oath."

25 Abraham then reproached Abimelek concerning the water wells
that the servants of Abimelek had seized. **26** Abimelek responded, "I was
unaware who had done this thing. Further, you did not report it to me.
Finally, I had not heard about it until this very day." **27** Abraham took
sheep and cattle and gave them to Abimelek. The two of them made a
covenant. **28** Abraham set aside seven young ewes from the flock. **29** Abimelek said to Abraham, "Why have you set aside these seven young
lambs?" **30** He responded, "The seven young lambs that you are about to
receive from me are a testimony that I dug this well." **31** Therefore, that
place was called Beersheba because the two of them swore an oath there.
32 They made a covenant at Beersheba. Abimelek and Phicol then arose
and returned to the land of the Philistines. **33** Also, Abraham[h] planted
a tamarisk tree at Beersheba. He worshiped YHWH, El Olam, there.
34 Abraham resided in the land of the Philistines for many years.

a. LXX reads "with Isaac, her son." Some such phrase must have been omitted from the MT. Many interpreters have suggested that the word *məṣaḥēq*, yet another play on the name of Isaac, means "playing" or even "fondling" (cf. Gen 26:8, which uses the word this way). I prefer to preserve the notion of laughter here, though perhaps derisively. Just as Hagar has looked with contempt at Sarah, now Ishmael laughs at Isaac.

b. SP, LXX, and Syr read "great," which is not in MT.

c. The word order of the MT is confused. It suggests that Abraham put the bread and water on her shoulder, whereas LXX understood the text to mean that Abraham put the boy on her shoulder. This act fits the story, one in which she puts the child under a shrub (v. 15). The story in itself does not easily accommodate the age of the boy according to the Priestly document's chronology. Abraham is 86 years old when Ishmael is born, says 16:16. Now, in 21:5, he is 100. This chronology, however, is secondary to the narrative about Hagar in Gen 21, one that understands Ishmael still to be a small child when he and his mother are ejected from Abraham's household.

d. LXX reads, "Then he cried aloud and wept," no doubt a harmonization designed to accommodate v. 17.

e. Literally, "God heard the voice/sound of . . ."

f. Literally, "strengthen your hand on him." There is a related idiom (so Ezek 16:49; Job 8:20 CEB, NIV), meaning to aid or comfort.

g. The phrase *rōbeh qaššāt* is difficult. The first word may derive from a verb (*rbb* II) meaning to shoot arrows, as in Gen 49:23. If so, the phrase could be translated lit., "shooter of arrows (with) bow." Or the first word may stem from the word (*rbb* I) meaning "to be great/many."

h. SP, LXX include "Abraham"; the name is missing in MT.

[21:1–7] These seven verses focus on the birth of Isaac, but they do not present an integrated report. It is best to think of them as offering linkages with other relevant texts in the family literature, mostly to previous texts, and in one case foreshadowing what is to come.

Verse 1 appears redundant, though it reflects an almost poetic parallelism, highlighting the reliability of God. If the deity says he will do something, it will happen. This verse moves beyond God's speech to Abraham in 18:10, a text that focuses in the first instance on "you," Abraham. Genesis 21:2 alludes directly to 18:10, referring to the claim that YHWH will act at a specific moment. Evident is God's concern for Sarah, at both the beginning and the end of this section. God has acted on her behalf (21:1), and she will enjoy the sound of joyous laughter along with the delight of nursing her child (vv. 6–7). As something of a counterpoint, the verses also iterate the fact that Isaac is born to an old man (vv. 2, 5, 7). There is similar repetition underscoring Isaac as "his son" (vv. 3, 4, 5).

These verses also highlight Abraham's obedience to the Priestly version of the covenant, Gen 17:12, which stipulates circumcision on the eighth day after a child is born. Verse 4 belongs to the same world as does 17:1, 12, which dates the Priestly version of the covenant and the institution of the rite of circumcision to Abraham's ninety-ninth year. Genesis 17–21 is therefore, for the compositor, happening in a brief temporal compass. In constructing this chronology, the authors make it clear that the deity does not wait long to act as he "had promised" (21:1).

Verse 6 seems oddly located. One might expect it to have followed immediately upon the birth of her son. Verses 6–7, however, seem directly related to the tradition attested in 18:12–15: Sarah's laughter. Equally odd is the text's lack of interest in exploring the wordplay with the name Isaac, which derives from the same Hebrew word, "laughter."

[8–21] Verse 8 sets the chronological stage for the ensuing narrative. Sarah's nursing of Isaac comes to an end when Isaac is weaned. The first three verses set in motion forces that result in the expulsion of Hagar and Ishmael from Abraham and Sarah's household. Though the narrative is ambiguous about the precise character of Ishmael's behavior or inner state, it is clear about the circumstance driving the story: Abraham has fathered two sons with two different women.

Sarah is the protagonist. She takes umbrage at the inappropriate interaction between Isaac and Ishmael. Sarah also argues that Ishmael should receive no inheritance. She is presumably claiming that Hagar does not have the status of a wife. If she did, Ishmael might be construed as a firstborn son and thereby be eligible for a "double portion" of his father's estate (so Deut 21:15–17). The narrator makes clear that Hagar is to be viewed not as a wife but rather as a "female slave," a noun that appears four times in 21:10–13.

The narrator is equally clear about Ishmael, who is not named in the narrative. Instead, he is "the son of Hagar" (v. 9), "her son" (v. 10), "his son" (v. 11), "the boy" (v. 12), "the son of the female slave" (v. 13), and "the child" (v. 14). This set of nouns and phrases anonymizes Ishmael, a narrative technique that eases his removal from the household. He is no longer a named person and, hence, can be a person more easily deleted from the narrative. The same cannot be said for Hagar; her name continues to appear.

The narrative, in this initial scene and thereafter, is both implicitly and explicitly full of emotion. Sarah is clearly angry when she orders Abraham to get rid of Hagar and Ishmael. Moreover, the narrator describes Abraham as one who is in deep distress. He, however, does not respond directly to Sarah. Instead, God seconds Sarah's orders, affirming that Isaac will be Abraham's heir and that "the son of the slave woman" will become a "great nation." Sarah's influence continues since God even uses Sarah's diction (v. 10) about Ishmael. Abraham obeys both Sarah and God. He gets up early the next morning (cf. this same idiom when Abraham sets out to sacrifice Isaac; Gen 22:3) and expels her from the household with meager rations.

The second scene of the narrative is deeply poignant. Time has elapsed since Abraham sent her away. She and the boy have wandered east from Gerar and are now in the wilderness near Beersheba. (Hagar is now doing what Abraham has done after leaving his ancestral home, "wandering"; the same verb is used with this sense earlier: 20:13.) The water is gone. Hagar finds some shade for her son under a shrub and then moves away to weep, hoping that she will not see him die. Her imperative soliloquy, "Don't let me see the death of the child!" does not use the more expected "my child" or "my son." She has accepted the depersonalized language of Sarah, Abraham, God, and the narrator.

God intervenes, just as in 21:12, though the reason for the intervention is ambiguous. The narrator reports that the deity has heard the sound or voice of the youth. However, the narrative suggests that the deity may be responding to what Hagar has said. In either case, God admonishes Hagar to pick up the boy and hug him because he will become the progenitor of a great nation (so also v. 13). The revelation of a well (cf. Num 22:31 and 2 Kgs 6:17 for the motif of God's opening someone's eyes to see what is already there) and her providing water to the "boy" conclude the scene. The notion of Hagar's "seeing" resonates with her having seen the Lord (Gen 16:13).

In the epilogue, the narrator offers details about "the boy." That he lived apart in the wilderness is significant (cf. the Ishmaelite genealogy in 25:13–16 and the references to "encampments"). Also important is the fact that his mother, who was an Egyptian, secures an Egyptian wife for him. That marital choice means that Ishmael has married outside the patrilineage of Terah, another way of underscoring that he is no longer an heir of Abraham.

[22–34] The loose connective tissue "about that time" suggests that this report does not have an integral relationship with either what comes before it or after it. That Abimelek and Phicol just start talking to Abraham strongly suggests that this report once followed immediately after Gen 20. The *Stichwort* (catchword) "well" in verses 19 and 25 may help explain why the account is now placed here. Further, much is paralleled in Gen 26:27–33: both involve a well at Beersheba and legal discourse. Language of "residing in the land" (vv. 23, 34) functions as an envelope for the report. The envelope underscores Abraham's tenuous foothold in that territory. So, too, does Abimelek's insistence that Abraham swear the ensuing oath.

The lengthy oath that Abimelek proposes is grounded in his theological affirmation that God is with Abraham, a judgment that, presumably, grows out of what transpired in Gen 20. That same affirmation appears in Gen 26:28 for Isaac, though there it may derive from the Philistines' judgment about the reason for Isaac's wealth. The rationale in Gen 21 emphasizes that God has been with Abraham in all that he does rather than simply what he owns. The actions of the two contracting parties continue to be important. Abimelek refers to his past loyal behavior with Abraham and insists that Abraham reciprocate, not only with him but also with the land in which he is residing. The oath reaches far beyond Abimelek—to his posterity and to the land over which he rules. In 21:23, the prolixity of language concerning later generations is puzzling. The terms "progeny" and "descendants" seem to be synonyms.

One might think that the oath would serve as the basis for resolving the dispute reported in 21:25–26. However, the oath, though taken between the two parties, is really one that obligates Abraham, not Abimelek. Still, the oath, which Abraham makes in good faith, apparently permits him to appeal to the king concerning the well that his underlings have taken over. Abimelek responds with a crisp and reasonable defense, even though he does not deny that some of his servants have seized the well.

Abimelek and Abraham make a covenant to resolve this dispute. Nonetheless, the character of the covenant does not permit the reader to know who is in the right. If Abraham were correct in thinking that Abimelek's men had taken control of his well, then it would not have been necessary for him to offer Abimelek a gift or payment for the well. If Abimelek's claim of innocence is correct, he could have simply commanded his men to retreat from the well. The report and dialogue in 21:27–30 are designed to verify that Abraham has dug the well, not that he is purchasing the well from Abimelek. Abraham maneuvers Abimelek into accepting his gift of sheep and oxen and, in so doing, obligates Abimelek to him. The legal diction—"witness," "oath," "swear," and "covenant"—underscores the binding character of the interaction. The seven female sheep presumably function as an etiology for Beersheba, which can be construed to mean "well of seven." The ambiguity of the toponym Beersheba, which can also be interpreted as "well of oath," explains the reference to an oath (v. 31) as a part of the transaction, though the word "oath" (*šebaʿ*, 21:31) that appears in the word Beersheba is different from another word translated "oath" (*ʾālâ*, 26:28).

The final three verses offer ambiguity. On the one hand, Gen 20 has depicted Abraham living in Philistine territory, where he presumably still lives during the events recounted in Gen 21. On the other hand, 21:32 pictures Abimelek *returning* to Philistine territory. This dissonance may reflect diverse traditions lying behind these verses. Or it may attest to the claim that Abraham has staked out his own land by digging a well in the area; what was Philistine land has now become, in part, land owned by Abraham. (Beersheba is not normally reckoned as belonging to the Philistines.) Reference to a sacred tree and veneration of YHWH via El diction underscore the claim that Abraham and his family have made on this territory.

Genesis 22:1–24
God Commands Abraham to Sacrifice Isaac

Genesis 22 continues to attract, challenge, and repel readers. The idea that YHWH would ask a father to kill his son is repelling, and the notion that Abraham would be willing to sacrifice his son challenges notions of parental responsibility. Moreover, the chapter has been heard in diverse ways. In Jewish tradition, it is known as the Aqedah, literally, the "binding," whereas in Christian tradition the emphasis is on sacrifice, often as a prefigurement for the sacrifice of Christ by the heavenly father. The focus of this commentary is different, since it builds on the way in which the Hebrew Bible itself understands this moment, namely, as God's testing of Abraham. The story of the test itself was sufficiently troubling in antiquity such that a later author added a second ending (vv. 15–18) in an attempt to understand this test.

It is appropriate to characterize Gen 22 as a legend. The text portrays Abraham as a religious hero, obeying the deity without any qualms. To this extent, the chapter is similar in genre to the prose prologue of Job and the stories associated with Daniel. All three individuals obey the deity in almost automatic fashion. Of the three texts, the literature presenting Abraham is more finely wrought.[1]

This episode is loosely related to the foregoing events. Genesis 22:1 and 20 both begin with temporal phrases that introduce what were originally separate forms of literature into the flow of the saga about Abraham (so too Gen 15:1). However, one does well to remember that in the foregoing chapter Abraham has expelled Ishmael from his household. Isaac really is, for all intents and purposes, his sole heir.[2]

As the comments will make clear, this chapter was likely written by a post-Priestly author, one with profound theological interests, whose work is related to that found in other post-Priestly texts such as Gen 20. The bibliography devoted to Gen 22 is immense. In my judgment, significant interpreters of this

1. Westermann describes the text as one made up of the three elements of a test (1985, 354–55). That is more a comment about the structure of the narrative than it is about the genre of the literature.

2. Islamic tradition, however, identifies *Ishmael* as the individual whom Abraham almost kills. See, e.g., Leemhuis 2002, 125–39.

chapter include an artist (Rembrandt), a philosopher/theologian (Kierkegaard), a biblical scholar (von Rad), and scholars in the field of comparative literature (Auerbach and Alter). I am indebted to all of them.

22:1 After these events, the deity[a] tested Abraham. He said to him, "Abraham," whereupon he responded, "Yes."[b] **2** He said, "Take your son, your
only son, Isaac, whom you love, and go to the land of Moriah. Offer him
there as a burnt offering upon one of the mountains that I will identify for
you." **3** Abraham got up early in the morning. He saddled his donkey and
took his two servants with him as well as Isaac, his son. He split the wood
for the burnt offering, set out, and went off toward the place that the deity
was going to identify for him. **4** On the third day, Abraham looked up and
saw the place off in the distance. **5** Abraham said to his servants, "Remain
here with the donkey. The lad and I will go on ahead. We will worship and
then return to you." **6** Abraham took the wood for the burnt offering and set
it upon Isaac, his son. Then he took in his hand the fire-starting implement
and the knife. The two of them went on together. **7** Isaac said to Abraham,
his father, "Father." He responded, "Yes, my son." He replied, "We have
the fire-starting implement and the wood, but where is the animal[c] for the
burnt offering?" **8** Abraham responded, "God will see to it that there is the
lamb for the burnt offering, my son." The two of them went on together.

9 They came to the place about which the deity had spoken to him.
Abraham built an altar there, arranged the wood, bound Isaac, his son,
and laid him on the altar, on top of the wood. **10** Then Abraham raised
his hand and took the knife to slaughter[d] his son. **11** The messenger of
YHWH called from the heavens: "Abraham! Abraham!" whereupon he
responded, "Yes." **12** He said, "Do not raise your hand against the lad!
Don't do anything to him. Now I know that you are a God-fearing person.
You have not withheld your son, your only son, from me." **13** Abraham
then looked up and saw a[e] ram with its horns caught in the shrubs. Abraham went over, took the ram, and offered it as a burnt offering instead of
his son. **14** Abraham named that place "YHWH sees to it." (Even today,
it is called "On the mountain of YHWH it is provided.")[f]

15 The messenger of YHWH called to Abraham from the heavens
a second time **16** and said, "I swear by myself, saying of YHWH, that
because you have done this—you have not withheld your son, your only
son— **17** I will bless you and make your progeny as numerous as the stars
in the sky or the grains of sand on the seashore. Your progeny will possess
the gates of their enemies. **18** All the nations of the earth will bless themselves through your progeny because you obeyed me." **19** Then Abraham
returned to his servants. They arose and went together to Beersheba.
Abraham resided in Beersheba.

20 After these events, someone said to Abraham,[g] "Milcah has given
birth to sons for your brother Nahor. 21 Uz, his firstborn; Buz, his
brother; Kemuel (the father of Aram), 22 Kesed, Hazo, Pildash, Yidlap,
and Betuel." 23 Betuel became the father of Rebekah. These eight Milcah
bore for Nahor, Abraham's brother. 24 Also, his concubine, Reumah,
bore children: Tebah, Gaham, Tahas, and Maakah.

a. The Hebrew texts reads *hā'ĕlōhîm*, lit., "the God."

b. MT *hinnēnî*, lit., "here I am," but without any locative significance.

c. *Śeh* can mean lamb but can also refer to a goat or other animal, typically a small one. The noun is not frequently used of sacrifices, though see Deut 17:1; 18:3.

d. This verb is used elsewhere to describe the killing of children for a sacrifice (Isa 57:5; Ezek 16:21; 23:39), always condemning such activity. More typically, it refers to the slaughtering of animals for a sacrifice.

e. MT reads "behind," which makes little sense. SP, LXX, and Targum Jonathan reflect the correct reading, "one." It would have been easy for a copyist to mistake the *resh* for the original *dalet.*

f. The repetition of the phrase YHWH *yir'eh* in v. 14 and the difficulties in translation suggest that the text is disturbed. The second half of the verse is probably an addition. The translation here is intended to convey the ambiguity in the Hebrew. See similarly Westermann 1985, 363.

g. Literally, "It was said to Abraham."

[22:1–2] The notion of the deity testing either the people as a whole, a group, or separate individuals is attested elsewhere in the Hebrew Bible.[3] Furthermore, the people can test God, a motif that occurs with striking frequency in reference to the wilderness traditions (Exod 17:2, 7; Num 14:22; Deut 6:16; Pss 78:18, 41, 56; 106:14). In the latter texts, to "test" has the sense of trying God's patience or angering the deity (so, e.g., Ps 78:17–18). When God tests humans, the idea of testing is very different. Testing by the deity is structured so that the deity will know or verify something (e.g., "test to know" in Deut 8:2). God tests people to discover something: if they will follow the torah regarding manna (Exod 16:4), if they will keep the commandments (Deut 8:2), if they will love YHWH (Deut 13:4 [13:3]), to find out what is in Hezekiah's heart (2 Chr 32:31). These goals for testing are typically found in the same sentence with the verb "to test." That is not the case in Gen 22. Only in verse 12 does the reader learn what the purpose is for the test: for the deity to be able to say, "Because now I know that you are a God-fearing person." Based on the biblical texts listed above, one should assume that the ancient reader would

3. Westermann (1985, 356) rightly notes that the deity only tests Israel or Israelites. Ruppert (1972, 55–63) maintains that the "testing" tradition has its roots in Deut 33:8. Then the Elohistic tradition (Gen 22; Exod 20:20) developed this tradition by linking it to the fear of God.

find it odd for the purpose of the test not to be communicated when the test is announced.

The "test" of Gen 22:1 does share one element with another biblical text. In Exod 20:20, an author describes Moses's response to the people's fright in the following way: "Do not be afraid; for God has come only to test you and to put the fear of him upon you so that you do not sin." Thus Exod 20 and Gen 22 share the vocabulary of testing and the fear of God. In Exod 20, the deity, through the theophany, intends to *put* the fear of God "upon" the people. In Gen 22, the goal is different: the deity wants to *verify* that Abraham does, indeed, fear the deity, though the reader—and Abraham—only discover this goal in verse 12.

Other biblical "tests" are far less severe than this one.[4] Elsewhere God provides manna to see how the people will respond, or God appears in a theophany to engender proper reverence. The difference between the test in Gen 22 and all other tests reported in the OT may help explain why the deity is introduced in such an abstract and impersonal way as "the God."

The test involves an edict from the deity that Abraham immolate his son on some not yet identified mountain. The *ʿōlâ* (22:2, 13) is a sacrifice in which the entire animal is burned upon the altar (so Lev 1, describing a burnt-offering sacrifice at the temple, with the participation of priests). The animal sacrificed was to be a male, one without blemish.

The biblical author is far less interested in making the burnt offering conform to other such sacrifices than in evoking the deep difficulties that confront Abraham. The author does this by repeating the obvious, even when it doesn't need to be stated: Abraham loves Isaac (v. 2), Isaac now is his only son (v. 2), "son" is repeated (vv. 6, 7, 8, 12), the "father" is present (v. 7). This piling up of filial and paternal vocabulary emphasizes the familial feature of this narrative. It is not simply a matter of a child being sacrificed; it is also the slaughter of a child by his father that lies at the root of the test.

The location of the sacrifice is tantalizingly specific and, yet, finally vague. A much later author apparently identified the goal of Abraham's journey to be the Temple Mount in Jerusalem. More specifically, that author related "the mount of Moriah" (2 Chr 3:1) with the land of Moriah, in which there were mountains (Gen 22:2). This conflation of the details in 2 Chronicles strongly suggests that the description is a late adaptation of Gen 22, and even the possibility that Gen 22 itself is a post-Priestly text.[5] Further, the text in Chronicles adopts the spelling *hammōrîyâ*, literally, "the Moriah," as it is found in Gen 22. In sum, the details of 2 Chr 3 do not help identify where Abraham went. Abraham was commanded to go to an unknown land in which stood an unnamed peak. The narrative simply attests that the deity would let Abraham know where to go. This

4. Some have compared the deity's treatment of Job with that of Abraham.

5. For a discussion of Moriah as an allusion to Jerusalem, see Levenson (1993, 114–23).

first scene ends with the deity's speech. One might have expected Abraham to engage the deity in dialogue (cf. Gen 18), but the father is curiously silent.

The first of several "gaps" in the narrative appears after verse 2 (others appear after vv. 3, 6, 8). The deity apparently appears to Abraham at night. However, he does not get up until the morning. Such gaps, no doubt conscious literary constructions, tease the reader into contemplating what might have occurred during the time that is not narrated, especially Abraham's response to what he has been commanded to do.

[3–4] Verse 3 is noteworthy due to the prominence of verbs (so also vv. 6 and 9). The author has carefully structured the narrative such that the pace varies significantly. Much action takes place in verse 3. By deploying six verbs, the author is, by the end of the verse, able to depict Abraham setting off on his journey. The only surprising detail is the presence of two servants, who neither speak nor are, by themselves, the subject of any verbs in the story. Still, they remain with Abraham until the story's end (v. 19).

The second and longest narrative gap appears after verse 3. The narrator picks up the story when the four males have been on the road for over two days. Again, the reader can only imagine what sort of conversation and interactions were taking place. The author focuses overtly on the length of the journey and the fact that Abraham discerns the place of the sacrifice. According to verse 2, the deity would let Abraham know where it would be. That happens (v. 4), but readers are not privy to the way in which Abraham comes to know its identity.

Abraham sees[6] "the place" (vv. 3–4). This way of describing the site for the sacrifice is ominous in its ambiguity: the place will be a place of death and immolation. In addition, the Hebrew word *māqôm* (place) can bear the special connotation of a "holy place." This meaning is clearest in Gen 12:6, "Abram passed through the land to the place at Shechem, to the terebinth of Moreh." "The place at Shechem" is, in the author's eyes, a shrine of some sort, here associated with a sacred tree. So too Jacob, when on the initial leg of his journey, encounters a sacred *māqôm* (28:11, 19), though he does not know at first that it is holy. Abraham, in both Gen 12 and 22, apparently has the capacity to discern the presence of a holy site, a natural place for a sacrifice.

[5–6] Once Abraham has discerned "the place," he decides it is time to part company with the two servants. His speech to them has posed difficulties for interpreters. When Abraham reports, "We will return to you," with "we" referring to Isaac and himself, one might think that Abraham does not presume that he will actually need to slaughter his son. But such a construal makes a mockery of the deity's test. It is no test if Abraham thinks he will not need to make the sacrifice. As a result, one must read this speech as a ruse—to prevent the servants from interfering with what he intends to do. Interestingly, Abraham

6. The verb "to see," *rʾh*, appears in vv. 4, 8, 13, and 14.

speaks about Isaac as a *naʿar*, "youth" or "servant," the same word the narrator has been using to describe Abraham's servants. This way of characterizing Isaac may be a subtle way to begin viewing him as something other than Abraham's own son and, hence, easier to kill.

The narrator offers greater detail in verse 6, both fleshing out what has happened earlier and foreshadowing what is to come. The reader learns more about what Abraham has brought on this journey: not just wood, mentioned in verse 3, but also the knife and implement for making a fire, such as a striking stone and scraps of tinder. As von Rad has pointed out (1972, 240), Abraham takes the more dangerous elements, those he will use to ignite the burnt offering. He lays the wood on Isaac, wood onto which Isaac will later be tied as the offering.

The phrase with which verse 6 concludes, "The two of them went on together," is poignantly repeated at the end of verse 8, a repetition atypical of the spare character of Hebrew prose written by the primary author. The repeated phrase subtly alludes to the return from the mountain that Abraham anticipates, a trip that he will need to make by himself.

[7–8] Verses 7–8 offer the only dialogue in this narrative. The initial two speeches echo the first direct discourse in Gen 22: one party identifying another, the second then responding with *hinnenî*, "Here I am." Next Isaac queries his father about the absence of an animal for the sacrifice. There is some irony in Abraham's response since the "animal" that Abraham says the deity is providing is Isaac, whom the deity has provided to Abraham and Sarah (Gen 17:16).[7] Though the author spends minimal time developing the character of Isaac, he is presented here as aware of the purpose for the trip, to make a burnt offering.

[9–14] The narrative now moves to its climax. Father and son have arrived at "the place." With their many verbs, verses 9–10 function as 22:6 does; Abraham hurriedly does many things (he is the subject of seven verbs in these two verses). The bustle of activity sets the stage for Isaac's death. He is bound on the pile of wood placed on the altar that Abraham has just constructed. Then, in classic deus ex machina fashion, the deity intervenes. Isaac is saved from death, and Abraham is saved from having to kill him.

Verse 11 reiterates the sequence of direct address, followed by *hinnēnî/hinnenî* (cf. vv. 1, 7). The deity summons Abraham again, this time repeating his name, and Abraham responds exactly as he has the first time. The deity commands him not to do anything to harm the boy since "now I know that you are a God-fearing person." Finally, both Abraham and the reader (and presumably

7. The noun *śeh* is used metaphorically of humans in Jer 50:17; Ezek 34:17, 20, 22.

Isaac) are privy to the reason for the test, though, even at this point, neither Abraham nor Isaac knows overtly that it has been a "test."

The construct form of the participle of the verb "to fear" followed by the deity—"God-fearing" person—occurs eight times in the Old Testament (HB sequence: Gen 22:12; Isa 50:10; Pss 25:12; 128:1, 4; Prov 14:2; Job 1:8; 2:3; Eccl 7:18). Based on these texts, how does one who fears the deity behave? As one might expect, the language is often general (e.g., Ps 128:1); the one who fears God walks in his ways, or someone who is "blameless, upright, turning away from evil" (Job 1:8; 2:3). The notion of obeying the deity is voiced in only one text and is further defined by "obeying the voice of his servant," presumably the so-called suffering servant (Isa 50:10). In sum, the notion of a radical obedience such as what Abraham confronts in Gen 22 falls outside the normal discourse about the one who fears the deity. As a result, it is inappropriate to view Abraham as an "everyman," offering a paradigm of faith that is to be emulated. Walking with the deity is one thing (Ps 128:1); climbing a mountain and being willing to kill one's child is another. Something strange, beyond the pale of "normal" religious behavior, is at work in this chapter.

Another chapter in the Abraham saga may help, though not fully, explain the theological dynamics of Gen 22. In Gen 20 (another a post-Priestly text), when Abraham attempts to explain why he has depicted his wife as his sister, he states, "I thought there is no fear of God at all in this place" (Gen 20:11).[8] However, even before this sentiment has been reported, the reader knows that Abraham has been wrong in this judgment. Abimelek and his countrymen *do* fear God. Genesis 22 may be another radical case (Gen 20 is also radical, since Abraham has permitted his wife to become part of another man's household), one in which an author, perhaps even the same author, explores what it would mean for the character of Abraham to work out, in "fear and trembling,"[9] the notion of fearing God.

Verses 13–14 offer the denouement, the working out of the narrative after the climactic scene in which Abraham's hand is stayed. Familiar vocabulary reappears (e.g., Abraham "looks up" [so v. 4]). This time he espies a ram. The Hebrew word *ʾayil* is more specific than the "animal" mentioned earlier (vv. 7–8); it is a mature, male sheep. Further the noun regularly occurs in ritual texts (e.g., Exod 29:15; Lev 8–9; Num 6:17). This typical noun symbolizes the story's return to the normal world of sacrifice and worship. Sheep, not children, are to be offered up as burnt offerings. And that now happens.

Verse 14 focuses on the place and, especially, the way this place will now be known. The text is difficult to translate, suggesting that it may represent the

8. Cf. Westermann 1985, 361–62.

9. To follow S. Kierkegaard's lead in redeploying this phrase; Ps 55:5.

work of multiple hands (see note f). In the first part of the verse, the phrase "YHWH sees to it" builds on Abraham's response to Isaac's question about the animal.[10] Abraham has said, "YHWH will see to it that there is a lamb." Though such a response is ambiguous at that point in the narrative—the animal probably refers to Isaac—by the end of the narrative, the saying has gained a new meaning. YHWH has seen to it that there is an animal for the burnt offering. And it is a ram, not Isaac.

A later hand has tried to develop the notion of "seeing," but in the sense of "revelation": YHWH revealed himself on that mountain. The last portion of the verse probably reflects an attempt to link Moriah to the temple in Jerusalem (so 2 Chr 3:1 and the comments on Gen 22:2).

[15–19] With the exception of 22:19, these four verses are almost certainly a later reflection devoted to exploring the implications of the test reported earlier in the chapter.[11] Genesis 22 must have puzzled ancient readers, just as it vexes contemporary interpreters. This speech makes the case for the significance of the test, and it does so by drawing on other material.

Verses 15–19 are a pastiche of quotations and allusions to phrases that appear elsewhere in the book:

- I will bless you—Gen 12:3
- Offspring as numerous as the stars—15:5; 26:4
- Offspring as numerous as the sand—32:13 (12)
- Offspring occupy gates of their enemies—24:60
- Nations bless themselves through your offspring—18:18; 26:4 (cf. 12:3; 28:14)

A later compositor has borrowed phrases and sentiments, with special focus on progeny (the word appears three times in these two verses), since the issue of the survival of progeny has been at stake in the test. For this author, Abraham's obedience solidifies the promises regarding both the number and status of Abraham's descendants.

This addition also interprets the character of the test. What was left by the original author as a test regarding the mysterious character of "fearing God" has become a more straightforward one: "obeying the voice of the Lord." Of course, Abraham does obey God, but, as has become clear, the one who fears God is involved in a richer "walk with God" than simply obeying commands. This inner biblical interpretation has tried to move beyond the notion

10. Gunkel (1997, 236) and Westermann (1985, 362) rightly recognize that the phrase is not a toponym but more of a theological affirmation, though epigrammatic to be sure.

11. Westermann's judgment is representative: "There are only a few texts in Gen 12–50 which are so easily recognizable as an addition" (1985, 363).

of fearing God, which is more elusive elsewhere in the OT, as a rationale for the test.

Verse 19 is the natural conclusion to the original story. Unnatural, however, is the way in which the narrative identifies those who return from the mountain. The text explicitly identifies only Abraham and then reports that he and his servants return to Beersheba (one would have expected them to return to "the land of the Philistines" [Gen 21:34]). One might read this verse and think that Isaac does not return with his father. The implications are obvious. It is, no doubt, better to view the omission as a conscious literary strategy of the author, one that continues to deemphasize the importance of Isaac as a character in the story.

One final theological note: The deity is named in diverse ways in these nineteen verses: the God (vv. 1, 3, 9), God (8, 12), messenger of YHWH (v. 11, 15), and YHWH (v. 14). Rather than bespeaking different sources or traditions, such ambiguity about the name and, hence, identity of the deity may reflect a genuine question that this chapter raises: What sort of deity would ask a father to kill his son?

[20–24] The final five verses of this chapter are loosely appended to the tale of the test. They begin almost exactly as did the first verse of Gen 22, with the loose connective tissue, "after these events," which is clearly a formula used to integrate originally disparate material (cf. 15:1). The genealogy so introduced could have appeared at any number of places in the Abraham saga, such as before Gen 21, after the chapter, or even in its middle, after verse 8. In its current location, the report about the children of Nahor emphasizes the asymmetry between the fertility of the brothers. At this point in the saga, Abraham has fathered just two children, one of whom, Ishmael, has been lost to him; and another of whom has just escaped death; meanwhile his brother Nahor has fathered twelve. Abraham will have more sons (so 25:2, which, along with Ishmael and Isaac, total eight sons), but never as many as Nahor. Further, the genealogy looks ahead to the future of the boy who has just survived since it makes explicit mention of the woman whom Isaac will marry, Rebekah. She is the only grandchild mentioned in the genealogy. Startling in its omission is the name of her brother, Laban. Such focus on Rebekah indicates that the author's intention is now shifting toward the next generation in the patrilineage of Terah. Sarah will die soon, and immediately thereafter Rebekah and Isaac will marry.

Apart from its role at this place in the saga, the genealogy by itself reports that Nahor had twelve sons, as will both Ishmael (Gen 25:12–18) and Jacob (Gen 48). Obviously, popular tradition held an expectation that a patriarchal figure would father this number of sons. The genealogy identifies one people with whom Israel will regularly interact, the Aramaeans. Kemuel (the name also appears in Num 34:24 and 1 Chr 27:17, but referring to two different individuals), is listed as their ancestor. Elsewhere, Aram appears in Gen 10:22,

23 as a descendant of Shem, but the name Kemuel is not present there. As a group, these twelve names appear to represent peoples dwelling to the east or south of Israel.

This genealogy has almost certainly been created using impersonal rhetoric (i.e., third-person language). However, the redactors have revised the beginning of the genealogy such that it is reported to Abraham in direct discourse. Hence, there is reference to Nahor, "your brother." The more original rhetoric, Nahor as "his brother" (v. 23), is preserved within the genealogy.

Genesis 23:1–20
Abraham Buries Sarah

In this chapter, a Priestly author has written a lengthy report about Abraham's purchase of land, the overt purpose for which is burial of Sarah's body. The report focuses on the dialogue between Abraham and the "Hittites," especially Ephron. By the end of the chapter, readers learn that Abraham, and presumably his heirs, have acquired not only a burial plot, but also land with trees, perhaps an orchard, thereby giving him new status as he lives among the "people of the land."

23:1 Sarah lived one hundred twenty-seven years; such was the length of
Sarah's life. 2 Sarah died at Kiriath-arba (that is, Hebron) in the land of
Canaan. Abraham went to mourn for Sarah and to weep over her. 3 Abraham got up from beside his dead spouse and spoke to the Hittites: 4 "I am
a resident alien in your midst. Sell[a] me property for burial so that I may
bury my dead near me." 5 The Hittites responded to Abraham: 6 "Pray,[b]
listen to us, my lord. You are a mighty prince in our midst. Bury your
dead in the best of our graves. Not one of us would keep you from using
his grave to bury your dead." 7 Then Abraham arose and bowed down
before the people of the land, the Hittites. 8 He said to them, "If you are
willing to let me bury my dead, please listen and intercede on my behalf
with Ephron, son of Sohar, 9 so that he might sell the cave of Machpelah,
which he owns—the one at the edge of his property. May he sell it to
me as a burial ground in your presence for its full value—property for
burial." 10 Now Ephron was sitting among the Hittites. Ephron the Hittite
answered Abraham within earshot of the Hittites, even those who were
going into the gate of the city, 11 "Pray,[c] my lord, listen to me. I grant you
the property and the cave that is in it. I grant it to you in the eyes of my
compatriots. I grant it to you so that you may bury your dead." 12 Abraham [again] bowed down before the people of the land. 13 He spoke to
Ephron within earshot of the people of the land, "If you would only listen
to me! I am presenting you with silver for the property. Take it so that I
might bury my dead there." 14 Ephron responded to Abraham: 15 "Pray,
my lord, listen to me. Land worth four hundred shekels of silver; what

is that between you and me? Bury your dead." 16 When Abraham heard Ephron, he weighed out for Ephron the silver that he had promised when he was within earshot of the Hittites—four hundred shekels of silver at merchant's rate of exchange.

17 Hence, the field of Ephron, which was at Machpelah, east near Mamre, the land, the cave in it, and all the trees that were on the property, everything within its borders was deeded[d] 18 to Abraham in a real estate transaction, witnessed by the Hittites, all those who were entering the gate of their[e] city. 19 Then Abraham buried Sarah, his wife, in the cave in the field of Machpelah, near Mamre (that is, Hebron) in the land of Canaan. 20 The property and the cave in it were deeded from the Hittites to Abraham as property for burial.

a. The verb *nātan* can mean giving in exchange for something else, not just give away (so Gen 30:4 and Petschow 1965, 117).

b. So Speiser, who reads MT *lōʾ* at the end of verse 5 as *lû* and as the beginning of v. 6 (1964, 170). This same particle appears in vv. 11, 12–13, 14–15.

c. Reading *lû*, with Speiser and the reconstructed end of verse v. 5.

d. For this sense of *qwm*; cf. Lev 25:30; 27:19; Ruth 4:7.

e. MT reads "his" city, which cannot mean Abraham's city. The antecedent to the pronominal suffix is *Ḥēt*, as in the sons of *Ḥēt*, or Hittites.

[23:1–2] The report commences with information about Sarah's lifespan. This in itself is unusual, since she is the only one of the matriarchs for whom the authors offer this detail. Still, in these introductory verses, Abraham is the subject of as many verbs as is Sarah: he "mourned" and "wept," a formulaic description of lamentation. This fact suggests that the authors are concerned primarily about Abraham's response to her death and its consequences and not about Sarah herself.

Verse 2 raises some tantalizing questions. A literal construal of the Hebrew has Abraham going "in." Where did he go? Into a city? Into a temple? The authors offer no answer. As a result, a less literal translation, "Abraham proceeded to mourn . . ." may be preferable.

Equally challenging is the question of place. Genesis 23 deploys four toponyms: Kiriath-Arba, Hebron, Mamre, and Machpelah.[1] The authors used the first three to help define the location of both the place of Sarah's death and the cave that Abraham purchased. In verse 2, Kiriath-Arba is equated with Hebron. But in verse 19, Mamre is equated with Hebron. It would appear that those for whom this text was written did not know the location of either Kiriath-Arba or Mamre but did know where Hebron was (cf. Gen 35:27; Josh 15:13; 21:11;

1. Two of these place names involve numbers. Kiriath-Arba might be translated "city-four," and Machpelah is built on the Hebrew stem *kpl*, meaning "double."

Judg 1:10 for a similar equation). (Machpelah, too, is defined by reference to Mamre/Hebron in v. 19.) The only biblical text that does not define Kiriath-Arba as Hebron is postexilic (Neh 11:25), which may suggest a similar date of composition for Gen 23.

[3–9] These verses narrate Abraham's encounter with those among whom he dwells. The chapter describes them as Hittites and as "the people of the land," probably referring to the same group to avoid repetition. The "Hittites" in Genesis are, as Westermann and others have argued (1985, 373), not a reference to the ancient culture of Anatolia, but a late way to describe the pre-Israelite inhabitants of the land used especially by the Priestly writers.[2] Here too, the linguistic evidence attests to a postexilic composition.

Abraham speaks first in what will be a dialogue of three speeches. He identifies himself as a *gēr tōšāb*, literally, a residing alien (these words appear first in the MT of v. 4, further emphasizing their importance). As a *gēr* or *gēr-tôšāb*, Abraham would have been able to acquire property. (The non-Israelite *gēr tôšāb* in Lev 25:47 could purchase an enslaved person.) Neither expression is common in Genesis (*gēr* appears elsewhere in Genesis only in 15:13, a reference to Israel's alien status in Egypt). Further the phrase *gēr tôšāb* appears elsewhere in the Hebrew Bible only in the Holiness Code, a late Priestly composition (Lev 25:35, 47).

The "Hittites" underscore Abraham's solitary status: he is "in our midst." (This emphasis on being within or among them continues [so vv. 5–6].) Nonetheless, he follows their initial response with an imperative verb "give," here meaning "sell." Though an alien and outnumbered, Abraham can still use forceful rhetoric.

The goal is acquisition of land appropriate for interring a corpse. (Interestingly, Abraham refers to "my dead," not to Sarah. Clearly the author continues to focus on Abraham.) Abraham seeks an *ʾaḥuzzat qeber*, a phrase that reappears in Gen 49:30; 50:13, both of which allude to Gen 23. The phrase is similar in construction to *ʾaḥūzzat ʿôlām*, "an everlasting property" (Gen 17:8; 48:4). (Lev 25:34 also contains the phrase for open land around Levitical cities that will belong to the Levites "forever.") The two phrases may be conceptually related. Land acquired as a burial ground will presumably function as such in perpetuity. Abraham's acquisition of this property therefore presages YHWH's perpetual grant of land to Israel.

The "Hittites" respond with language also attested in economic transactions. The Hebrew word *šmʿ* (listen) can mean to reach an agreement concerning the

2. So Van Seters (1975, 45): "There seems to be no distinction in Genesis among the terms Canaanite, Hittite, and Amorite, though a preference may be seen in the use of any one term by a particular literary source, and in this respect the term Hittite is usually assigned to the Priestly source."

sale of property (Tucker 1966, 82 n. 17; so also Petschow 1965, 118 n. 125). One could translate, "Pray, agree with us, my lord." Their speech continues by lauding Abraham as a "mighty prince." The word *nāśîʾ* occurs two other times in Genesis (25:16; 34:2). In both cases, the individual is a regional or tribal leader. One may, therefore, infer that Abraham has been deemed by the "Hittites" to be a leader of some regional group. (He appears to have a similar status in Gen 14.)

After this florid introduction, the "Hittites" offer a subtle rejoinder. They affirm that they will permit Abraham to bury his dead in a grave that belongs to one of the people of the land. By appending pronominal suffixes to the word for "our graves," "his grave," the Hebrew text emphasizes that the "Hittites" will retain ownership of the graves. At least in this initial response, then, they do not appear willing to sell Abraham land. For this reason, Abraham must rise again and make his case, this time involving a far more specific request.

In verse 9, Abraham makes a concrete proposal; this time he bows down before the "Hittites." He builds on the word *šmʿ*, which has been uttered by the "Hittites" in the preceding verse. (In both places, it means "hear/agree.") Abraham reports that he wants to buy a particular burial site, "the cave of Machpelah," for its full value from Ephron.

The toponym Machpelah is used with some ambiguity in this chapter. In 23:9, it refers to a cave. In 23:17, it seems to refer to a general area; in 23:19, it refers to the field in which the cave is located. Unlike Kiriath-arba, however, the authors must have thought that their readers know the general location of Machpelah, though in 23:17 and 19 it is identified as near Mamre.

Abraham's proposal appears to involve not only purchasing a cave, but also designating it as a burial place. There is no reason to think that the cave has been a burial site. As a result, Abraham's request involves not only sale but the limitation of the use to which that site might be put. In any case the purpose for the purchase has become an overt part of the negotiation.

Caves occurring naturally in chalk or limestone were an important place for burial in Late Bronze and Iron Age Judah. Such mortuary practice was "the practice of the indigenous Bronze Age highland population" (Bloch-Smith 1992, 39). As a result, one may assume that Abraham's proposal does not surprise the "Hittites." Excavated cave tombs contain roughly equal percentages of males and females, which is not the case with other forms of burial, such as bench tombs or jar burials (70). As a result, it is reasonable to think that "the cave or bench tomb was the dwelling for individuals who were thought to continue a form of existence and so were provided with the basic necessities of life and some amenities: vessels with food and liquid, lamps for light, jewelry and amulets for protection, models to invoke sympathetic magic, personal items, and tools" (148). None of these were, however, of interest to the author of Gen 23. That individual focused on the acquisition of the cave, not the burial.

[10–16] The flow of the report is interrupted by a nonverbal clause, with which 23:10 begins. "It so happened" that Ephron is there and hears Abraham's request. There is no need for intercession, as Abraham has proposed.[3] The author now offers information about the setting for these dialogues; it is occurring in the city gate, which includes small rooms for the legal proceedings (so Ruth 4) and economic transactions. As a result, reference to the "Hittites" attests to proper protocol. These individuals who hear what is being said function as witnesses to the business that is taking place.

As with 23:3–9, these verses contain a dialogue of three speeches, but this time Ephron initiates the conversation, using language ("hear/agree") that has been part of the earlier dialogue. Here, Abraham is rhetorically surrounded as well as physically "in the midst" of the Hittites. But Abraham is more than surrounded, since Ephron ups the ante. Instead of agreeing to sell the cave by itself, Ephron proposes, in three parallel clauses, that Abraham buy the field as well as the cave. Moreover, he agrees to the purpose for which the land and cave will be put: a burial ground. Ephron emphasizes his willingness to complete the transaction by repeating the verb *nātan*, "give/sell," three times (v. 11) and by referring explicitly to those who witness his offer.

Abraham quickly accedes to this proposal (vv. 12–13) by explicitly mentioning the property, not the cave. The author highlights Abraham's deference (he bows down again) and the fact that his speech has been witnessed. Abraham then stipulates the form of payment: it will be in silver.

Once Abraham has suggested the vehicle for payment, Ephron then stipulates the cost: four hundred shekels.[4] That appears to have been a very high price. When Jeremiah purchased a field, he invested only seventeen shekels of silver (Jer 32:9–10). But a high price makes sense here. Abraham is under severe pressure to find a place to bury Sarah. Moreover, if Abraham is a "mighty prince," he can afford to invest in this significant way. Further, the biblical writers have developed the character of Abraham as a person with great wealth (cf. Gen 13:2). Finally, this field is a toehold in the land that has been promised to Abraham and his progeny (so Gen 17:8). For all these reasons, the land is invaluable and, hence, worth a high price.

Hence, Abraham "has heard" (this verb has now appeared six times with this sense in the chapter), that is, agreed, and so he pays the requisite sum to Ephron. In all likelihood, the silver is weighed out in the form of jewelry or small bars. The author makes clear that the transaction is undertaken according to the typical weights and measures used by merchants of the time, further enhancing the verisimilitude of the scene.

3. The author continues to emphasize that Abraham is "in the midst" of the Hittites. Now Ephron, too, is "in the midst" of the Hittites.

4. The shekel was both a weight (8.25 grams) and, beginning in the Persian period, a coin.

[17–20] With the dialogue and transaction now concluded, the report moves toward resolution. The property is "transferred" to Abraham. Verse 17 follows the format of real estate transactions by describing the location and what is in or on the land. In this case, Abraham receives not only the cave and field, but also the trees in the field. One might speculate that Abraham has purchased an orchard, but the text offers no explicit warrant for such a claim. In any case, now in possession of the cave, Abraham proceeds to bury Sarah. The chapter concludes with verse 20, reiterating the formula of property transfer present in verse 17.

Numerous commentators have recognized that this chapter appears to reflect real-life business dealings. As a result, they have searched through ancient Near Eastern texts that attest real estate transactions. The documents that bear the strongest similarities are the so-called "written dialogue documents," cuneiform texts that date to the Neo-Babylonian period. These tablets offer a written record of real estate agreements that include seven basic elements: Title, Dialogue (offer and acceptance), Payment formula, Transfer or purchase clause, Seals and Witnesses, and Date.[5] The second element is distinctive, since it reports the speeches of the seller and purchaser. It is just such dialogue that is present in 23:11–15. Moreover, other features of this pattern also appear in Gen 23: description of the payment, report of the transfer of property, and allusion to the witnesses. However, not all elements are present, demonstrating that Gen 23 is a report about a real estate transaction rather than the legal document attesting the contract.

The author of Gen 23 has developed one element in the written dialogue document: the dialogue itself. Instead of a brief speech outlining the offer followed by the speech of acceptance, Gen 23 includes two dialogues of three speeches each, one set between Abraham and the "Hittites," another between Ephron and Abraham. The speeches as well as the prose that introduces them highlight the tone of formality and protocol that set the tone for the negotiation.

What then is the function of this chapter within the book of Genesis and, especially, for the Priestly writer who composed it? This question is best answered by observing that Gen 23 is one of only two texts in which the family acquires land. (The other is Gen 33:19, when Jacob purchases a portion of a field. Here too, the purchase price is given. Moreover, the land is not purchased for use as a burial ground, though it is later used for that purpose: Josh 24:32.)

When one reads Gen 12–36 and focuses only on the pre-Priestly material, one finds no instance in which the family gains a toehold in the land. They

5. So Tucker 1966, 81. See the description of the form by Petschow 1965, 119. Cf. Westbrook (1971, 29–38), who maintains that a second-millennium practice, a "double transfer" of land, lies behind Gen 23. However, this background seems unlikely since Petschow's example involves a king. The "Hittites" in Gen 23 appear more as witnesses than as those who receive title and then hand it on to Abraham.

are always on the move. They themselves explain their movements in various ways, as due to famine, a result of conflict, a command from the deity, a migration. Sometimes no reason is given. But there is no other clear acquisition of land. This is what these Priestly authors want to challenge. They do this to insist that the deity's promise is being realized, but only in a limited way.

Genesis 23 establishes the legitimacy of the family's claim to own land in "the land of Canaan" (23:19). Moreover, it foreshadows Israel's acquisition in the land. To be sure, YHWH promises/gives the land (e.g., Gen 15:7; 17:8; 35:12). However, to have a place to live (33:19), to worship El (33:20), and to honor their dead (Gen 23), Abraham and Jacob act to bring that promise to partial fruition. YHWH's giving is enhanced by their purchasing.

Further, these authors identify this place in Judah as *the* place in which the family buries its dead. Priestly tradition reports that Abraham, Sarah, Isaac, Rebekah, Jacob, and Leah are all interred there (Gen 49:31; 50:13). (Only Rachel is buried elsewhere, near Bethlehem; Gen 35:19.) This cave associated with the name Machpelah is, however, a burial place important only for the lineage of Terah up through Jacob's generation. (Even though tradition has it that "the bones of Joseph" are brought from Egypt to Israel, they are buried at Shechem [Josh 24:32; cf. Gen 50:25], not Machpelah.) When Israel is a family, Machpelah is their burial ground, but not afterward.

This chapter involves more than just a report about the creation of a family cemetery. The acquisition of these specific sites, those mentioned in Gen 23 and 33, is no doubt symbolically significant. Hebron and Shechem are both major shrines. It will be appropriate for Israel to think that they have received part of their heritage from an early time. In sum, Gen 23 involves multiple issues, including the characterization of Abraham, family burial, legal acquisition of land, and holy sites.

Genesis 24:1–67
Abraham's Servant Finds an Appropriate Wife for Isaac

Genesis 24 presents the longest story in the ancestral literature. Unlike some ancestral narratives, the author has included considerable dialogue, with one especially lengthy speech (vv. 34–49). Direct speech occurs in approximately two-thirds of the sixty-seven verses. The chapter is unusual not only for its length but also in its dramatis personae. Neither a matriarch nor a patriarch is prominent. Abraham quickly fades from the scene. The same may be said for the other patriarch, Betuel, who is Laban's and Rebekah's father. Instead, the unnamed servant achieves pride of place. Unlike comparable stories, narratives in which a male encounters either his wife-to-be or her family at a well (Gen 29:1–14; Exod 2:15–21), the male suitor has been replaced by a surrogate, his father's old and senior servant.[1] Members of the younger generation—Laban, Rebekah, and Isaac—have been placed on center stage by the end of the story, with Rebekah as more dynamic than her spouse Isaac.

These unusual features have led many interpreters to attribute the chapter to a post-Priestly hand and to date it to the postexilic period.[2] Numerous scholars have noted one or another element in the chapter that bespeaks the Persian period. For example, the phrase "YHWH, God of the heavens and God of the earth" is strikingly similar to other late texts (e.g., Jonah 1:9; Ezra 1:2; Neh 1:4). For such reasons, one may think about Gen 24 as a latecomer to the ancestral narratives. A Persian-period author may have fleshed out an earlier brief report about the marriage of Rebekah to Isaac and turned it into a major narrative focusing on Abraham's servant and expressing convictions about the ways of YHWH as providential deity. This narrative was placed between the report of Sarah's death (Gen 23) and the account of Abraham's subsequent marriage and demise (Gen 25). The reference to Isaac being comforted after his mother's death (24:67) may be an overt attempt to integrate this story with the foregoing chapter.

1. Alter (1981, 51–57) characterizes these as "betrothal type scenes."

2. See Rofé 1990, 27–39. Among other things, Rofé examines vocabulary, syntax, legal institutions, theology, and literary style in dating this narrative to the Persian period.

24:1 Abraham had become old, advanced in years.[a] Moreover, YHWH
had blessed Abraham in all manner of ways. **2** Abraham said to his aged
servant, the one who had authority over everything Abraham possessed,
"Place your hand under my thigh. **3** I will make you swear by YHWH,
God of the heavens and God of the earth, that you will not secure a wife
for my son from among the daughters of the Canaanites, in whose midst
I currently dwell. **4** Rather, to the land of my origins and to my kin you
shall go to secure a wife for my son Isaac." **5** The servant then responded
to him, "Perhaps the woman will be unwilling to return to this land. Shall
I bring your son back to the land from which you have come?" **6** Abraham answered him, "Make sure that you do not take my son back there!
7 YHWH, God of the heavens, who brought me from the house of my
father and from the land of my kin, who spoke with me, and who swore
to me, 'To your progeny I will give this land,' he will send his messenger
before you so that you will be able to secure a woman for my son from
there. **8** If, however, the woman is unwilling to accompany you, you
would be free from this, my oath. Nonetheless, never take my son back
there." **9** Then the servant placed his hand under his master Abraham's
thigh and swore to him about this matter.

10 The servant took ten of his master's camels, along with some of
the finest of his master's goods, and went to the city of Nahor in Aram
Naharaim. **11** He made the camels kneel down outside the city beside the
well—at evening, the time when women came out to draw water. **12** He
said, "YHWH, God of my master Abraham, please decide[b] something
today; act graciously toward my master Abraham! **13** I am standing here
near this spring of water. Daughters from the people of the city are coming out to draw water. **14** May the young woman to whom I say, 'Please
lift your vessel so that I may have a drink!' and then who responds, 'Have
a drink! I will even water your camels'—may she be the one whom you
have appointed for your servant Isaac. By means of this, I will know that
you have acted graciously with my master."

15 Before he had finished speaking, there was Rebekah—who had been
born to Betuel, son of Milcah, wife of Nahor, brother of Abraham—coming out [of the city]. Her water vessel was on her shoulder. **16** The young
woman was very pretty, a virgin; no man had known her. She went down
toward the spring, filled her vessel, and then came back up. **17** The servant
ran to meet her. He said, "Would you please let me sip a little water from
your vessel?" **18** She responded, "Drink, my lord." Then she quickly lowered the vessel into her hands and let him drink. **19** When he had finished
drinking, she said, "I will also draw water for your camels, so that they
will have enough to drink." **20** Then she quickly poured out the vessel into
the trough and ran back to the well to draw more water; she drew enough

for all the camels. 21 Now the man had been looking[c] at her quietly, to
determine whether or not YHWH had made his trip successful.

22 Once the camels had finished drinking, the man took a gold
nose ring, weighing a half shekel, and two arm bracelets, weighing ten
shekels.[d] 23 He said, "Would you please tell me whose daughter you are?
Is there space for us to spend the night at the home of your father?"
24 She responded to him, "I am the daughter of Betuel, son of Milcah,
whom she bore to Nahor." 25 She continued saying to him, "We have
both plenty of straw and fodder and space to spend the night." 26 Then
the man bowed his head and worshiped YHWH. 27 He said, "Blessed be
YHWH, God of my master Abraham, who has not abandoned his love
and loyalty toward my master. As for me, YHWH has led me on the way
to the home of my master's kin."

28 The young woman then ran and told her mother's household about
all these things. 29 Rebekah had a brother whose name was Laban. Laban
ran out to the man, who was near the spring.[e] 30 When he had seen the
nose ring as well as the bracelets on his sister's wrists, and when he heard
what Rebekah, his sister, reported, "This is what the man said to me . . . ,"
he went to the man, who was still standing near his camels at the spring.
31 He said, "Come in, O blessed of YHWH![f] Why are you standing outside when I have prepared the house and also a place for the camels?"
32 So the man went into the house, where he unloaded the camels. He
[Laban] gave straw and fodder to the camels along with water with which
to wash not only his feet, but also the feet of the men who were with him.[g]
33 Then something to eat was set before him, but he said, "I will not eat
until I have had my say." So they said, "Speak on."

34 He said, "I am the servant of Abraham. 35 YHWH has truly blessed my
master such that he has become wealthy. He has given him flocks, herds,
silver, gold, male and female servants, camels, and donkeys. 36 Sarah, the
wife of my master, bore a son for my master after she became old. And
he has granted to him all that he has. 37 My master made me swear, 'You
shall not take a wife for my son from among the Canaanite women, in
whose land I live. 38 Instead, you shall go to my ancestral house, to my
kin,[h] to find a wife for my son.' 39 I said to my lord, 'Perhaps the woman
will not come with me.' 40 He responded to me, 'YHWH, before whom I
have walked, will send his messenger with you. He will make your journey
successful. You will surely find a woman for my son from my kin, from
my ancestral house. 41 Then you will be free from my oath, since you
have gone to my kindred. Even if they do not give [her] to you, you will
be free from my oath.'

42 "Today, I came to the spring and said, 'O YHWH, God of my master
Abraham, if only you would make my journey, which I have been on,

successful. 43 I am standing by this spring of water. Let the young woman
who is coming to draw water and to whom I say, 'Please give me a sip to
drink,' 44 and who says to me, 'Go ahead and drink, and moreover I will
draw water for your camels,' be the woman[i] whom YHWH had chosen
for the son of my master."

45 "Before I had finished saying this to myself, Rebekah was coming
out, her water vessel on her shoulder. She went down to the spring and
drew water. Then I said to her, 'Please give me something to drink.'
46 She quickly let the vessel down and said, 'Drink, and I will also water
the camels.' So I drank, and she also watered the camels. 47 Then I asked
her, 'Whose daughter are you?' And she replied, 'The daughter of Betuel,
son of Nahor, whom Milcah bore to him.' At that point I placed a ring
on her nose and bracelets on her arms. 48 Thereafter, I bowed down and
worshiped YHWH. I blessed YHWH, the God of my master Abraham,
who faithfully led me on the way to acquire the daughter of my master's
relative for his son. 49 Now, tell me if you will deal loyalty and faithfully
with my master. If not, tell me that as well, so that I may turn either to
the right or to the left."[j]

50 Laban and Betuel responded: "This matter comes from YHWH.
We are not in a position to say that it is either good or bad.[k] 51 Here is
Rebekah. Take her and go! Let her be the wife for the son of your master
according to what YHWH has spoken."

52 When the servant of Abraham heard their words, he bowed down
to YHWH. 53 Thereafter the servant brought out ornaments of silver and
gold as well as precious fabrics and gave them to Rebekah. In addition,
he gave precious things to her brother and her mother. 54 Then they all
ate and drank—he as well as the men with him. They spent the night.
When they arose in the morning, he said, "Send me to my master!" 55 Her
brother and her mother said, "Let the young woman remain with us several days—maybe even ten. After that you can go." 56 He replied to them,
"Do not detain me since YHWH has made my journey successful. Send
me so that I may come to my master!" 57 They said, "Let us summon the
young woman. We shall ask her." 58 So they summoned Rebekah and said
to her, "Will you go now with this man?" She said, "I will go." 59 Hence
they sent Rebekah, their sister, and her maid,[l] the servant of Abraham,
and his men. 60 They blessed Rebekah, saying to her:

"Our sister, may you become
  prodigiously numerous.
May your offspring possess
  the gates of their enemies."

61 Then Rebekah and her maids got up, mounted the camels, and followed the man. So the servant took Rebekah and left.

62 Now Isaac had moved from Beer-lahai-roi;[m] he now resided in the
Negeb. 63 At dusk one evening, Isaac went out to the field in order to
think.[n] When he looked up, he saw camels approaching. 64 And when
Rebekah looked up, she saw Isaac, whereupon she dismounted quickly
from the camel. 65 She said to the servant, "Who is that man, walking
through[o] the field to meet us?" The servant replied, "He is my master." So
she took her veil and covered herself. 66 The servant recounted for Isaac all
the things that had happened. 67 Isaac brought her to the tent of his mother
Sarah. He took Rebekah, and she became his wife. He loved her. Isaac was
thus consoled after the death of his mother.

a. The connotation is not one of senility (cf. Gen 18:11, but note also 1 Kgs 1:1). Josh 13:1 and 23:1 offer instructive and similar usage. Apart from Genesis, all other instances of the phrase *bāʾ bayāmmîm* occur in the Dtr history.

b. Cf. Num 35:11 for a similar use of *qrh* in the hiphil.

c. The root is *šāʾâ.*

d. The so-called "light" shekel weighed almost two-thirds of an ounce. Hence, the nose ring specified here would have weighed ca. one-third of an ounce, and both bracelets would have weighed well under one pound.

e. This clause is almost certainly a variant of what is reported at the end of v. 30. It does not belong here, since, in v. 30, Laban is still receiving Rebekah's report.

f. The phrase *brwk YHWH* also appears in v. 27, though with a different meaning.

g. With the exception of the first verb, the identity of the subject of the verbs in this sentence is ambiguous. Laban must be the subject of the verb "gave," since "the man" is the recipient of the water.

h. Literally, "to my father's house, to my clan."

i. The servant uses two different words for young woman: *ʿalmâ* in v. 43 and *ʾiššâ* in v. 44.

j. Presumably, the servant, by using the binary opposition of right/left, is saying that he wants to know if he needs to go somewhere else, whether to the right or to the left. Gen 13:9 does not offer comparable usage.

k. Here one may take "good/bad" more literally than in Gen 31:24; 2 Sam 13:22. Neither of those texts speaks of "good or evil."

l. On etymological grounds, one could translate "wet nurse," which would, however, not fit the context. The individual was probably Rebekah's servant/nurse from the time she was a small child. The maid's death and burial are reported in Gen 35:8.

m. On the location of Beer-lahai-roi, see Gen 16:14.

n. The phrase *lāśûaḥ* is perplexing. See Vall 1994, 513–23; Rendsburg 1995, 558–60. Rendsburg's proposal that the verb means "to urinate," though possible, does not seem to fit the context. I opt for reading the verb as derived from the same root as the noun *śîḥâ*, "thought or meditation" (Job 15:4; Pss 119:97, 99).

o. On this use of the preposition *bĕ*, see *IBHS* 11.2.5.b.

[24:1–9] The author opens and closes this scene by using the word "thigh." The OT attests a custom according to which someone who took an oath placed his hand under the upper thigh of the person who has required him to swear the oath (see Gen 47:29). (The claim that the upper thigh refers to the genitals is possible but not certain. It is interesting that the "thigh" appears in a narrative about Jacob [32:32], but there it does not set the tone as it does in Gen 24.) The presence of this word, then, emphasizes the seriousness of the episode. It involves serious legal obligation.

Within the scene itself, the author sets the stage for much of what will follow, so much so that we may construe these first nine verses as a prologue. Both Abraham and his unnamed servant are construed as *zāqēn* (old). The author underlines Abraham's senior status by describing him as advanced in years. Elsewhere in the OT, that phrase can refer to a character who is about to vanish from the story, such as Joshua (Josh 23) and David (1 Kgs 1). Joshua 23 is of special importance since Joshua is not only described in the same way as Abraham (Josh 13:1), but soon thereafter Joshua himself reports, "And now I am about to go the way of all the earth" (23:14). Hence, when ancient readers heard Abraham characterized as advanced in years, they expected to soon learn about Abraham's death, reported in the next chapter (Gen 25:7–11).

The author also swiftly construes Abraham as "blessed." That feature, along with his age and obvious wealth, "all that he had" (24:2), makes clear that the blessed quality of Abraham's life is not contingent upon the success or failure of his servant's mission. According to the biblical narrator, Abraham never hears about nor sees Rebekah. Since Abraham is about to pass from the scene, this is a story that points fundamentally to the future, not to the past or present.

Verses 1–9 also introduce us to the major character of this story, the anonymous servant. The role that this individual performs is far more than that of a powerless member of the household. Rather, he functions as an emissary of Abraham, someone enfranchised to disburse Abraham's resources and to contract the formal marital arrangements, which were normally conducted by members of the family (as is the case with Rebekah's family). This "high view" of the servant resonates with the role of the servant as portrayed in Isa 40–55. There, too, a servant, who is sometimes anonymous (Isa 52:13) and sometimes identified as Israel (44:21), has a truly prominent role.

These first five verses overtly involve the quest to find a wife for Isaac. Covertly, the "real" issues are those of kin and geography. The wife must come from Abraham's kin, who live in the land of his origins. However, Abraham's son cannot go to that "land." The word "land" (*ʾereṣ*) appears six times in verses 1–9 and is referred to another three times by "there." Such repetition signals the importance of land and residence in this narrative. Abraham's strongest rhetoric appears in his command to the servant, "Do not take Isaac **there**!" Why is it so important that Isaac not travel to Mesopotamia? After all, Abraham has left the land, going to Egypt and Gerar, and Jacob will leave the land and go precisely to the place that Abraham forbids Isaac from visiting. The text offers no clear answer.

Since this text probably has its origins in the Persian period, the issue regarding presence in the land of Israel is especially important. That was a time soon after many Israelites have returned from exile. Hence, Abraham's insistence in not having Isaac leave the land functions as an admonition to those living in the land during the Persian period. Just as Abraham and Sarah have recently returned to this land (most recently having lived in Gerar: Gen 20), so later Israelites are to remain there as well. Mesopotamia, the land to which many Judahites have been exiled, was, for some of them, an attractive place. Not all those banished returned to the Levant. Genesis 24 takes pains to distinguish between the appropriate genealogy for the matriarch: she must come from the patrilineage of Terah; and the appropriate place for residence: the promised land. That may be why Abraham speaks so strongly about the need for Isaac to remain in Syria-Palestine.

Echoes of the Persian period appear most prominently in the overt theology of this scene. The deity is described as God of the heavens and the earth. This phrase appears elsewhere only in the books of Jonah (1:9), Ezra (e.g., 1:2), and Nehemiah (e.g., 1:4), texts written in the Persian period. Less overt is the way in which the deity becomes present in this story. Abraham assures his servant that God's messenger will go "before" him (vv. 7, 40). Verse 40 associates the presence of the messenger with the success of the servant's mission, but the story never reports anything about the appearance or activity of the messenger (cf. the role of the messenger in Gen 16; 19; 21; 22; 31). This mysterious individual clearly belongs to the world of deities. The motif of God's messenger going "before" someone is at home in the narratives involving Moses and the Israelites in the wilderness. There, too, God assures an individual, Moses, that God's messenger will go "before" him. And there too, it is clear that the messenger and God are essentially one. (In Exod 13:21, "YHWH went in front of them," whereas according to Exod 14:19, "the messenger of God who was going before the Israelite army.") In sum, the prologue in Gen 24 attests that the mighty God of heaven and earth will prepare the way for Abraham's servant's journey.

[10–27] In one verse, the author narrates both the preparations for the journey and its completion. The only information we receive is the number of camels: ten. That large number is presumably necessary both to carry gifts along and to bring back the woman and her retinue. Still, the author generally avoids specificity. Just as readers do not know the name of the servant, here they know only the general area to which he travels, Aram Naharaim (e.g., NRSV translates these two words as "Mesopotamia" in Deut 23:5 [4] and 1 Chr 19:6). The name of the city, which one might infer to be Haran (so Gen 11:31), is not given. What is important is the family connection. It is "the city of Nahor," Abraham's brother and father of the bride-to-be.

The servant's decision to stop by the well outside the city receives no explanation. The reader does not know if the servant has a long-established plan that depends upon the presence of a well. What the author does report is a brief description of the scene at eventide while quoting a prayer uttered by the servant. At least two things stand out in this prayer. First, in its opening and closing moments, it uses the word *ḥesed*, which may be translated "deep loyalty" or "loving-kindness." Elsewhere in the story, the servant refers again to God having exercised that quality toward Abraham (v. 27), and he also asks that same loyalty from Rebekah's family (v. 49). Second, the servant expects God to decide who the bride should be. He assumes that God will "decide" (v. 12) or "appoint" (v. 14). The servant's job is to create a process that will permit the deity's decision to become clear. The theological perspective here is unusual. Nowhere else in Gen 12–36 does the deity make decrees or plans that must then be discovered by humans. This world is far more similar to that present in the Joseph short story, where the notion of God ordaining certain human activities is clear.

The process does more than simply identify the woman. What she will offer to do, provide water for both the servant and his camels, is behavior that hints at the sort of character the author thinks appropriate for a potential matriarch. She is a person who will offer gracious hospitality to someone whom she does not know. When the servant finds this sort of person, then he will know that God has dealt with deep kindness toward Abraham.

The author wants readers to know that this plan begins to work before it has even been announced. What the servant has asked for has already been decided and implemented by the deity. Rebekah is on her way out of the city even as he finishes speaking (to himself, so v. 45). The reader is provided with information that the servant will only learn later. For example, readers know that she belongs to Abraham's family (v. 15) long before the servant does (vv. 24, 27). She possesses admirable qualities of beauty and virginity. And again, readers know this before the servant learns about them.

In this scene, the author structures a faster pace, as signaled by the vocabulary: the servant runs (v. 17); Rebekah acts quickly and runs (v. 20). Yet, despite this speed, there is a counterpoise of conversation and quiet. The servant observes her, trying to learn whether she is the one whom YHWH has chosen. Moreover, they engage in a substantial dialogue, sparked by two questions—one indirect, one direct—posed by the servant (v. 23). In those conversations, the author continues to develop the character of Rebekah as hospitable. The servant asks for room to spend the night; she offers bedding and fodder, as well as a place to stay.

One might have thought that, by the end of verse 19, the servant would know that she is the one. She has fulfilled the conditions he has set out that will enable him to know whom YHWH has selected. And, to be sure, he rewards her with jewelry, which suggests that he knows she has passed the test. However, the servant only recognizes that he has truly succeeded when he learns that she belongs to the patrilineage of Terah. The woman whom YHWH has selected is a member of the correct family, a condition that fulfills Abraham's command to go to "my kin" (v. 4). Only then does he bless and thank YHWH for having led him to his master's kin. The servant gradually, rather than suddenly, realizes she is the one.

Commentators have noted the similarity between this scene at the well and two other narratives: Gen 29:1–4 (Jacob meets Rachel) and Exod 2:15–22 (Moses meets Reuel's seven daughters). Robert Alter has identified common elements to all three: "travel to a foreign land, encounter there with a future bride . . . at a well, drawing of water, 'hurrying' or 'running' to bring the news of the stranger's arrival, a feast at which a betrothal agreement is concluded" (Alter 1996, 115). Within this common form, Gen 24 offers some unique features. Someone other than the bridegroom makes the journey. Further, Rebekah, and not the male, draws water. Moreover, hurrying occurs within the scene itself, not simply as the characters move from the well to the homestead. In addition, Gen 24 defines the well as near a city. Such is not the case with the other two stories. Finally, whereas Jacob and Moses appear as strong characters at the well, here Rebekah comes to the fore, especially in comparison to the character who would normally be here, Isaac as suitor. The biblical author has apparently taken a stock scene and recast it, emphasizing the role of the bride or heroine over against that of the groom. In so doing, the author has been able to highlight the suitability of Rebekah as a potential matriarch. This scene concludes with the servant speaking to the deity. Whereas earlier the servant has prayed for help, appealing for God to act based on "loving-kindness" (*ḥesed*, vv. 12–14), now the servant thanks the deity, affirming the basis of God's action in that same love (*ḥesed*, v. 27). Prayer surrounds this encounter between the servant and Rebekah.

[28–49] The scene at Rebekah's home involves some dissonance in the larger narrative. Earlier the servant has asked about the household of her father (v. 23); now the narrator speaks about the household of Rebekah's mother (v. 28). How might one explain this distinction? It is unlikely that the text attests a matrilineal family, given the predominance of the patrilineage of Terah. Further, though Rebekah's father, Betuel, is identified by name four times in this chapter, her mother is identified only once and by role, not by name (v. 55; cf. vv. 57, 59). Though the text offers no explicit information, it is reasonable to assume that Betuel is no longer alive. The author compensates for his absence as a character by repeating his name. (In addition, the larger story offers a certain symmetry: both Isaac and Rebekah have lost a parent of the opposite gender.) Rebekah's brother Laban is the surrogate parent, just as the servant is the surrogate suitor. The author seems to be making a point: even though a parent may be dead, the other members of the household, family or not, will help the lineage survive.

Oddness and ambiguity follow upon the dissonance. Due to a confused text (see note e), one hears about Laban leaving his house on two different occasions (vv. 29 and 30). In verse 31, Laban asks the man why he is still standing outside, even though there has been no explicit invitation to invite the servant inside. In verse 32, one hears about "men who were with him," people who have not been mentioned before but about whom one hears later (v. 59). Finally, the subject of the verbs in verse 32 is unclear. Who unloads the camels? Is it the servant or Laban? The Hebrew text remains ambiguous.

Amid these oddities, the servant's speech is piercingly clear. It begins with "I am Abraham's servant." (The narrator has been describing this individual as "the man" since v. 21.) This is one of the longest utterances in the entire book of Genesis (vv. 34–49). It, of course, rehearses much of what has happened up to this point in the chapter. However, one must say at least six other things about this speech. First, it has a frame of reference that extends beyond this chapter. The servant reports that God has blessed Abraham by making him wealthy. This claim is not only one of fact, that Abraham has gotten wealth; it also entails a theological explanation of that wealth. Other texts in Genesis attest to Abraham's wealth (e.g., 13:2), but no other text attributes Abraham's wealth to the deity or an act of blessing (cf. 26:12–13, where such a claim is made about Isaac's wealth). Second, the servant reports that such wealth is now in Isaac's control. This is the first time such a claim is made in Genesis (cf. Gen 25:5). This public statement about the disposition of Abraham's property is clearly offered here as grounds for having Rebekah accept the servant's proposal of marriage to Isaac. He is now the wealthy and hence potentially attractive spouse. Third, the servant's report in 24:40–41 reinterprets earlier events. Abraham has assured the servant before the trek by promising that YHWH's messenger would accompany him (v. 7). However, Abraham did not talk about the "success" of the trip. That verb (*ṣlḥ*) is used only of or by the servant (vv. 21, 40, 42, 56).

Fourth, the servant's comments about how he might be freed from the oath if the woman refuses to come with him (v. 8) do not square easily with what the servant says in verse 41, at which point he is concerned that her family may not give her in marriage. Fifth, the servant changes the order of events that have transpired at the well. Whereas earlier we were told that the servant gives her jewelry after she has watered the camels but before he has asked her questions about her lineage, now readers are told that he has given her the jewelry only after he has learned that she belongs to the patrilineage of Terah. Sixth, and of great import, the servant uses language he has used in his concluding prayer, but in an entirely new way. Earlier (v. 27), the servant has spoken about YHWH's love of and loyalty toward Abraham. In verse 48, he omits such language from the report of his prayer. Instead, he introduces it into his overture to Rebekah's family. The servant wants to know if they will exercise those same qualities toward Abraham: loyalty and faithfulness. The unspoken assumption is that if God acts this way toward Abraham, they should as well. Moreover, that assumption is undergirded by the belief of the author that humans may be challenged to act in ways that conform to the way God acts with humans, in loyal and faithful ways. In sum, this long speech by the servant is anything but a slavish recital of earlier verses. Instead, it is an inventive discourse, reconstructing the past and presenting a powerfully persuasive case before Rebekah and her family.

The servant's speech offers magisterial rhetoric. He has known from the outset of the chapter that finding the right woman is one thing; convincing her and her family to let her go with him is quite another. This speech is designed not simply to let Rebekah, Betuel, his wife, and Laban know what has happened. It is created to convince them that she should become Isaac's husband. The servant ends up challenging them to act in a godlike way. By the end of the speech, one might expect the servant's tone to be celebratory. However, the "success" of which the servant has spoken (vv. 40, 42) has not really been achieved. He must hear from them before he knows whether he must seek elsewhere to find a wife for Isaac.

[50–61] The family responds. Many scholars delete Betuel's name, since this is the only place that he appears as a live character in the narrative and because his name should occur before that of his son (e.g., Westermann 1985, 389). Further, in verses 55 and 57, Laban and Rebekah's mother are the family spokespersons.

The family speaks in a theological fashion and by using binary language that the servant has just introduced. They follow his plea of a need to know, "Tell me yes or no, to the right or to the left" (v. 49), with saying neither "bad nor good" (v. 50). Prefacing that binary statement—which surely means what it does in Gen 31:24, that they can say nothing—comes their response to the servant's claim. They agree that this happenstance is God's doing, and they tell the servant to take Rebekah to become Isaac's wife. (Interestingly, the servant never once mentions Isaac's name throughout this chapter.) The servant has won them over.

This scene is beset by considerable ambiguity. One might normally expect the servant to be giving gifts to the family, the so-called bride-price (i.e., something in payment for exchange of the woman). Such is not the case here. Rather, the servant continues his ploy of trying to gain the family's acquiescence by giving gifts, which, when accepted, obligate the recipients to him. In addition, it might seem odd that Rebekah is twice called "sister" (vv. 59, 60; LXX uses the term 2× in v. 60). This may reflect the significant role of Laban, who, as her brother, could most naturally use this term. Or the term may be used as a term of endearment (e.g., Prov 7:4; Song 4:9; 5:1). In either case, Rebekah leaves with riches and blessing. The contrast with another departure from Laban's house is palpable (Gen 31).

Rebekah achieves pride of place in this scene. She receives truly expensive gifts from the servant, including those of gold and silver, and her family's blessing. Her family gives her the option of delaying, but she gives the final word, "I will go." Thus she is the one who actually initiates the departure (v. 61). Verse 61b offers a summary of this action, though emphasizing the role of the servant.

[62–67] This final scene is remarkable, more economically sketched than earlier moments. Isaac has moved (from Beersheba to the Negeb), though he still possesses his mother's tent. He has gone out at evening for a quiet walk but is disturbed by a herd of camels. In quick compass and with pleasant symmetry, we hear about two individuals who "look up": Isaac sees camels, and Rebekah sees Isaac, though she does not yet know his identity. Just as the author has earlier reported her mounting the camel at the outset of the journey, here he describes her as quickly dismounting. When Rebekah asks about the man's identity, the servant does not repeat what the author has already reported, that the man is Isaac. Instead, he offers "new" information: Isaac is (now) "my master," a phrase that has, up until this point in the story, been reserved for Abraham. The aged Abraham of the prologue has now been succeeded by his son, as reported in the epilogue. The dialogue ends with the phrase, "He is my master."

The author spares the reader from having the servant recount, yet again, all that has happened. Instead, we learn about the new relationship between Isaac and Rebekah. They become husband and wife, and he loves her. The prior generation, however, casts a powerful shadow on this concluding scene. Even though Abraham has, more or less, disappeared, Sarah, though unnamed, is twice present. Isaac brings Rebekah into his mother's tent, and Isaac is, in this new relationship, consoled concerning his mother's death. (This emphasis on "mother" harks back to Rebekah's own powerful mother and relatively quiet father.) Further, the passive verb, "was consoled," befits Isaac's character.

Summary

Genesis 24 provides a narrative in which an anonymous servant successfully discharges his duties. The author twice introduces us to the character of God's "messenger." Abraham tells the servant, and then the servant tells Rebekah's family about this messenger who will accompany him on the trip. Even though readers hear little about this messenger, there can be little doubt that the author deems him to be providentially present and responsible for the success of the servant's trip (so especially v. 40). The messenger is an agent of providence. Genesis 24 underscores this notion of the deity's providential guidance by referring to a deity who decides what will happen (v. 12) and who Isaac's wife will be (v. 44). Such language and conviction are not common elsewhere in the ancestral narratives.

Complementing the almost-absent messenger is the anonymous servant. This servant has a primary role in the creation of the next generation that will bear the divinely granted promise of progeny. The story is not didactic; it is not designed to offer the servant as a paradigm for human behavior (though the author does present the servant as a skilled rhetor). Rather, this narrative underscores the powerful role that a servant can have. When juxtaposed with Isaianic poetry, "Israel, you are my servant" (Isa 44:21), this chapter takes on new meaning. Israelite readers could think about the ways in which their community might function as a powerful servant people. By the Persian period, Israel would recognize itself in that role, as is made clear in Lev 25:55, "for to me the people of Israel are servants."

Genesis 25:1–11
Abraham Dies

This section recounts the remainder of Abraham's life (vv. 1–6) as well as the report of his death and burial (vv. 7–11). The hands of both the composer and the Priestly tradition are in evidence. The latter offers genealogies (vv. 1–4, 7–11), and the former a report (vv. 5–6), which addresses the disposition of Abraham's property.

25:1 Abraham remarried; her name was Qeturah. **2** She bore Zimran,
Yoqshan, Medan, Midian, Yishbaq, and Shuach. **3** Yoqshan bore Sheba
and Dedan. The sons of Dedan were Asshurim, Letushim, and Leummim.
4 The sons of Midian were Ephah, Eper, Chanok, Abida, and Eldaʿah. The
aforementioned were all the sons of Qeturah. **5** Abraham gave all that he
had to Isaac. **6** But to the sons of the secondary wives[a] that he had, Abraham gave gifts. Then, during his lifetime, he sent them away from Isaac,
eastward, to territory in the east.

7 Abraham had lived 175 years. **8** Abraham breathed his last and died
at a good old age, old and fulfilled.[b] He was gathered to his kin. **9** His
sons Isaac and Ishmael buried him in the cave of Machpelah, in the field
of Ephron, son of Sochar, the Hittite, which was near Mamre, **10** the field
that Abraham had purchased from the Hittites. Abraham and his wife
Sarah were buried there. **11** After Abraham's death, God blessed his son
Isaac. He settled at[c] Beer-lahai-Roi.

a. The noun *pîlegeš* has been translated regularly by the English noun "concubine," which designates a woman with whom a man has a sexual relationship of long term, but to whom he is not married. In the Hebrew Bible, the noun may not bear all these meanings. Judges 19, which narrates the fate of an unnamed concubine, construes "a certain Levite" as her husband and refers to her father as the Levite's father-in-law.

b. Another burial formula, Gen 35:29, includes the phrase *śəbaʿ yāmîm* (full of days). In 25:8, the adjective "full" occurs without the noun "days" (though the noun is present in SP, LXX, Syr, and some tg MSS—probably to harmonize 25:8 with 35:29), but it is coupled with the phrase "good old age," which also appears in 15:15.

c. The preposition *ʿim*, when used in a locative sense, signifies "the end point of an action" (*IBHS* 219).

[25:1–6] This genealogy and report, filled with genealogical data, strives to present a fulsome portrayal of Abraham's family after Sarah's death. (The Chronicler also includes this genealogy [1 Chr 1:32–33].) Abraham does not remain a widower. Moreover, his wife, Qeturah, bears six sons, far more heirs than has Sarah. Of those six, the genealogist reports about the progeny of Yoqshan and Midian. Yoqshan's two sons, Sheba and Dedan, also appear in Gen 10:7 as brothers, but as sons of Raamah. Of these two sons, the text provides information about the children of Dedan. (Dedan's sons do not appear in the Chronicler's version.)

The most prominent of Abraham's sons with Qeturah, Midian, is associated with a land and people to the east of the Gulf of Aqabah, an area far to the southeast of ancient Israel. Here again, one of Israel's neighbors, the Midianites, are understood to derive from the lineage of Terah. Furthermore, this genealogy continues to encircle the land of Israel with those relatives. The Priestly author in Genesis, however, is interested in more than simply listing progeny and associating them with Israel's neighbors. These verses not only report about Abraham's relationship with Qeturah, but also assess its implications for the children whom Abraham has fathered with Hagar and Sarah.

After presenting the genealogy of those who derive from Qeturah, the author reports that the familial property has been handed on to Isaac. This statement disallows any claim on Abraham's estate by someone other than an heir of Isaac. Immediately following that clarification, the reader learns that Abraham honors his paternity by presenting "gifts" to "the sons of his secondary wives." The use of the noun *pîlegeš* obscures this report (see note a). Before this verse, no woman with whom Abraham has sexual relations is characterized as a *pîlegeš*. Further, besides Sarah, who is certainly the primary or senior wife, the other two women who bear children to Abraham, Hagar and Qeturah, occupy different statuses. Hagar is the servant of Sarah, whereas Abraham marries Qeturah. Neither has the status of a wife secondary to Sarah. Their roles as secondary derive from the statuses of the sons that they bear. Both Ishmael, born to Hagar, and Midian, born to Qeturah, are secondary to the primary heir, Isaac, born to Sarah. Thus, verse 6 probably alludes to unnamed women with whom Abraham has sexual relations and who bear children to him, women other than Qeturah.

The issue of property remains important. The narrator reports that Abraham gives "gifts" to all his sons. One might imagine that such gifts are material tokens, but the term *mattānâ* (gift) can, according to Ezek 46:16–18, be a grant of land, one made to sons. However, the distribution of Jehoshaphat's estate offers a more direct analogy to that of Abraham and his sons. Jehoshaphat's primary heir, Jehoram, is his eldest son and receives the dynastic crown. To his other sons, Jehoshaphat gives "many gifts, of silver, gold, and valuable possessions" (2 Chr 21:3). This gifting exemplifies what the biblical author attributes to Abraham's treatment of his many sons.

Once so gifted, Abraham does to Qeturah's sons what he has done to Hagar and Ishmael: he "sent them away" (cf. Gen 21:10). In both cases, the secondary heirs go to the east/southeast, banished from the land of their birth.

[7–11] As with Sarah, a Priestly tradent reports Abraham's death, using standard formulae. Unlike Sarah (as well as Rebekah, Jacob, Rachel, and Leah), his life is judged to be complete and good. Only Isaac's lifespan (180 years when compared to Abraham's 175 years) is described in similar ways (cf. Gen 35:29).

Verse 11 has seemed odd to many interpreters. Some (e.g., Van Seters 1975, 248) think it belongs better at the end of Gen 24. In its current placement, however, the verse attests to the movement from one generation to the next. Both the patriarch and the deity can bless the next generation. YHWH "blesses" Isaac just as YHWH has earlier promised to "bless" Ishmael" (Gen 17:20). The verb here, though it could refer to a onetime event, probably reflects continual activity by the deity (cf. Gen 12:3).

Genesis 25:12–18
The Descendants of Ishmael

These verses, which at first appear to be solely a genealogy, do more than trace descent. They report the death of the eponymous ancestor and offer information about the places in which the Ishmaelites dwelled. Also, they trace the fate of Ishmael, as foreseen in Gen 16:12.

25:12 These are the descendants of Ishmael, son of Abraham, whom Hagar,
Sarah's Egyptian servant, bore to Abraham. **13** These are the names of the
sons of Ishmael, named according to their birth order. The firstborn of
Ishmael was Nebaioth, then Kedar, Adbeel, Mibsam, **14** Mishma, Dumah,
Massa, **15** Hadad, Tema, Jetur, Naphish, and Kedemah. **16** These are the
sons of Ishmael. These are their names, according to their settlements
and their encampments, twelve leaders according to their tribes. **17** Now
Ishmael lived 137 years. He died[a] and was gathered to his people. **18** The
aforementioned people dwelled from Havilah to Shur, which is close to
Egypt, on the route to Assyria. He had lived[b] in conflict with all his kin.

a. Literally, "he expired and died."
b. Literally, "he fell." Cf. Judg 7:12, where the verb *npl* has the sense of "dwell."

[25:12–18] A genealogy associated with Ishmael has been preserved in two places: Gen 25 and 1 Chr 1:29–31. In the latter chapter, the genealogy of Abraham with Qeturah occurs after that of Ishmael; in Genesis, the genealogy of Qeturah appears first. The two lists of names associated with Ishmael are identical, both the names and their order.

Most of these names are attested elsewhere in the Hebrew Bible, only Adbeel, Mibsam, Mishma, Hadad, and Kedemah appear just in Gen 25 and 1 Chronicles 1. Most appear elsewhere in prophetic books. Both Dumah (Isa 21:11–12) and Kedar (Jer 49:28–29) are the subject of punitive oracles, but only the latter might be associated with the Ishmaelites, a name that does not appear in the text. One has the sense that the creator of Gen 25:13–15 was interested in fleshing out a list of twelve names—to make the Ishmaelite family/polity similar to that of the Israelites as the twelve sons of Jacob.

The genealogy in Gen 25 functions in several ways. The authors wanted readers to know something about the birth order of these sons (cf. Gen 36:15, which also identifies the "firstborn") as well as the places that they lived (cf. a similar attempt to classify names by places of dwelling in Gen 36:40, 43). Not only does the author refer to distinct places of dwelling but also describes a general area: from Havilah to Shur. If Westermann (1984, 217–18; 1985, 399) is correct in thinking that Shur is on the Egyptian border with Syria-Palestine and that Havilah refers to somewhere in the Arabian Peninsula, then the area is to the south of Israel. It may be that Gen 25:16 alerts readers to the fact that these names are both people's names and toponyms (i.e., Tema was a son, but also a place where he lived and of the same name).

The material in 25:17–18 is disturbed: all of 17 and the end of 18 focus on the figure of Ishmael, but 18a treats the progeny of Ishmael, as have verses 12–16. It appears that a redactor added verses 17–18a since there was a tradition about how long Ishmael lived (cf. Gen 36, in which there is more genealogical material about Esau, but no report about the length of his life, his death, or "quality" of life). By adding 25:18a, the compositor has separated material dealing with Ishmael in verse 17 from that in 18b.

Oddly, these verses that highlight the status of the Ishmaelites do not follow up on the promise that God made to Abraham, that he would "bless" Ishmael. They do, however, draw on Gen 16:12, in which the same words appear, "he will . . . with all his kin." The verb used in Gen 16:12, to dwell (*škn*), appears in 25:18. This overlap provides good reason to think that whoever composed this genealogical summary of the Ishmaelites wanted it to conform to other texts in Genesis about that group. However, in so doing, the author focuses on an unfortunate feature of Ishmael's existence rather than on the promised blessing. The absence of such language about blessing may reflect the presence of such language in 25:11. The real bearer of God's blessing will be Isaac, not Ishmael.

Genesis 25:19–34
Esau Sells His Birthright to Jacob

Though brief, this genealogy and report about the birth of Jacob and Esau offers playful and profound insight. The verses function like a prologue, more than once emphasizing the motif of tension that will permeate the literature associated with Jacob. That tension is not, however, laid at his feet exclusively since the author portrays the parents engaging in preferential treatment of their sons. A later editor has observed that the intrafamilial tension will play itself out in national terms, with Esau signifying Edom, a nation and people with which Judah often stood in conflict.

25:19 These are the descendants of Isaac, the son of Abraham. Abraham had fathered Isaac. **20** Isaac was forty years old when he married Rebekah, the daughter of Betuel, the Aramaean from Paddan-Aram, who was the sister of Laban, the Aramaean. **21** Isaac pleaded to YHWH on behalf of his wife because she was barren. YHWH responded to his prayer such that Rebekah his wife became pregnant. **22** The sons fought together[a] inside her. As a result, she said, "Why must it be this way for me?" She then went to seek YHWH.[b] **23** YHWH responded to her,

Two nations are in your womb;
  two different peoples will emerge[c] from your abdomen.
One people will be stronger than the other people;
  the older will serve younger one.

24 When she was due to give birth, there were twins[d] in her womb. **25** The first emerged ruddy all over, like a hairy garment. They called him Esau.[e] **26** After that, his brother emerged, grasping the heel of Esau. He named him Jacob. Isaac was sixty years old when they were born.

27 When the boys grew up, Esau had become a person who knew how to hunt, an outdoorsman,[f] whereas Jacob was a quiet man, a homebody.[g] **28** Isaac loved Esau because he liked to eat game, but Rebekah loved Jacob.

29 Once, when Jacob was preparing stew, Esau returned from a hunt.[h] He was exhausted. **30** Esau said to Jacob, "Let me eat some of that red stew! I'm about ready to faint." (Therefore, he was known as Edom.)

31 Jacob responded, "First sell me your birthright!" 32 Esau replied, "Look, I'm about to die [from hunger]. Of what use is my birthright?" 33 Jacob said, "First swear an oath!" So he swore to him and sold his birthright to Jacob. 34 Then Jacob gave Esau bread and lentil stew, whereupon he ate, drank, got up, and went out. In this fashion Esau despised his birthright.

a. The root meaning of the verb *rṣṣ* is to smash something or treat someone improperly. This reflexive use bears negative connotations: the activity is more than just that of two active infants in one womb.

b. The phrase "seek YHWH" appears in Ezra 4:2, although with *ʾĕlōhîm* as the object. There it clearly means "worship." The usage here is probably closer to Ps 34:5 (4), "I sought YHWH, and he answered me, and delivered me from all my fears"; or Ps 77:2, "In the day of my trouble I seek YHWH."

c. Literally, "will be divided." The niphal form of *prd* appears in a genealogy (Gen 10:5) and refers to a group of peoples emerging from an earlier generation.

d. MT *tômim* should be *tôʾămīm*, but the *aleph* (ʾ) has quiesced. Cf. Gen 38:27.

e. The etymology of "Esau" is not clear. It could derive from *ʿśh*, which might mean "doer," and would be consistent with this character, who acts more than he thinks.

f. Literally, "a man of the field."

g. Literally, "a dweller (in) tents."

h. Literally, "from the field."

[25:19–20] In the genealogical preface to the literature associated with Jacob (vv. 19–20), the authors report that Isaac married Rebekah. That marriage has already been reported in Gen 24:67 (though the writing of Gen 24 may postdate this genealogy). Genesis 25:19–20 provide information typical of a Priestly hand, such as the age of Isaac when he married Rebekah. Less typical is the emphasis on Rebekah as a woman belonging to an Aramaean family. Both her father and brother are characterized as "the Aramaean." Genesis 24, which refers to both Betuel and Laban, never depicts them in this way. Instead, they are, implicitly, part of Abraham's family (so Gen 24:4, 27, 38, 41, 48). Verses 19–20 breathe the air of national distinction rather than family relation, an atmosphere that will continue in the ensuing verses.

[21–26] This portion of the prologue has regularly been attributed to a hand different from that responsible for verses 19–20. Here the author builds on a detail that could have been part of a genealogy.[1] In 25:21–26, the author offers a report about the way in which the patriarch Isaac addresses the childless situation differently than did Abraham and Sarah. But that is not the only difference. The role of the deity is different in this chapter as well.

1. The report about Sarah's barrenness (Gen 11:30) is part of a genealogy (11:27–32). That genealogical detail, repeated in Gen 16:1, then becomes part of a narrative. Obviously, the boundaries between genealogy, report, and narrative are permeable.

In Gen 16, Sarah's initial speech sets a tone quite different from that which operates in Gen 25. Sarah reports that the deity has prevented her from bearing children. One might suppose that such a claim would preclude her from petitioning the deity for children, since it is the deity's decision that she does not bear children. Hence, she takes things into her own hand and offers Hagar to Abraham. Things could not be more different in Gen 25. The patriarch rather than the matriarch takes the initiative. Further, Isaac pleads for her, not for himself (the word translated "plead" may have once referred to pleading accompanied by animal sacrifice). And the end result is different. Although Sarah remains barren at the end of Gen 16, Rebekah becomes pregnant.

The tone of the report shifts significantly in 25:22; this is the first place at which the note of conflict appears. Readers not only learn of multiple births coming, but also that the unborn children are fighting inside her. At the outset is conflict, even before the boys are born.

Just as her husband sought the help of the deity in a difficult time, now she "seeks" YHWH. The language of "seeking YHWH" or God is prevalent in the OT, especially in Psalms and Chronicles. It normally involves petitioning on behalf of oneself (e.g., Ps 34:5 [4]) rather than someone else, which was the case with Isaac's earlier prayer. Further, "seeking YHWH" may have involved going to a shrine. Rebekah goes somewhere (v. 22), and that is the case in other texts that involve seeking the Lord (e.g., 1 Chr 21:30).

If seeking YHWH involves an attempt to have a negative condition ameliorated, as one might expect (so Ps 77:3), then Rebekah's search goes for naught. The text offers no evidence that the unborn children stop fighting. What she does receive is an oracle, the brief poem in verse 23. Rebekah's discomfort is, at least, explained. One may look back at verses 21–22 and observe a remarkable emphasis on both parents acting to communicate with the deity (an implicit contrast with the story of Abraham and Sarah).

The deity's response to Rebekah has often been viewed as a poetic fragment used by the author of this report. Such a judgment seems unlikely. It is natural for an author to construct a speech of the deity in poetry. Such is the case in Gen 16:11–12. Thus 25:23 makes up a poem, not just a fragment of poetry. And it is a good poem, moving from a brief explanation of Rebekah's discomfort to the surprising conclusion that the expected status based on birth order will be reversed (so Jeansonne 1990, 146–47). The details of the poetry fit integrally with the situation; since the four lines neither begin nor end abruptly, it is reasonable to think that the lines were penned by the author of the prologue to the Jacob story.

The purport of the deity's address to Rebekah is this, cast in direct discourse: "The struggle you are experiencing is not surprising since the 'natural' order, the older dominating the younger, will be reversed. That reversal is being proleptically played out in your womb." Such a declaration is similar in kind to the poetry in Gen 49 and Deut 33. Both of these poems address the respective fates of future generations and, on occasion, the relative status of siblings (Gen 49:8; Deut 33:24). Whereas the rhetoric of Gen 49 and Deut 33 is that of the eponymous ancestors of tribes, the poet speaks in Gen 25 of the eponymous ancestors of nations (Israel and Edom).

Ancient readers of this text knew both the principle of primogeniture and the many occasions in which it did not dominate. Genesis 38 offers one such case, one in which the second-born son is more prominent than the first among twins, where the second-born child immediately usurps the role of the firstborn, who is marked by a crimson thread on his arm (38:28–30). The very act of marking the arm suggests how important it is to identify the firstborn. Verse 24 seems reduplicative since the narrator has already alerted the reader to the presence of a multiple birth. The presence of another report about the birth of twins (Gen 38:27) may have influenced the composition of Gen 25. (The last three words of 38:27 are virtually identical to those of 25:24.)

The author takes pains at this point to describe not only the birth order but also to offer a thumbnail description of each baby. Esau, the firstborn, is clearly ruddy or covered with blood and matted with hair. This description includes two puns. The word translated "ruddy" is in Hebrew *ʾadmônî*, which sounds like Edom, the country associated with Esau. The word for "hair" is *śēʿār*, similar to Seir, the hilly topography of Edom. Oddly, no etymology is offered for "Esau."

The narrator characterizes Jacob by his action, not by his physical appearance. This focus on action rather than appearance suggests that Jacob will truly be the more powerful person. Jacob is born, grasping Esau's *ʿāqēb*. This act becomes the warrant for his name, *Yaʿăqōb*. Esau's heel becomes the basis for Jacob's name!

[27–28] The prologue offers a temporal gap between verses 26 and 27. The author leaves Esau and Jacob as infants and joins them again as young adults. The prenatal strugglers have now become different sorts of person (cf. the fraternal diversity attested in Gen 4), representing polar opposites.[2] They live in different places: Esau outdoors, Jacob inside. Esau's earlier ruddiness is consistent with this characterization, Jacob as "grasper" is less so. Esau is the more fully formed and consistent character; Jacob's identity is still being formed. He will neither stay at home nor stay inside during the course of his life.

The motif of the powerful hunter and/or outdoorsman is known in both biblical and extrabiblical literature. Genesis 10:9 attests Nimrod as a "mighty one of the field," a great hunter. And the Gilgamesh epic portrays Enkidu as the quintessential outdoorsman. His physical appearance is strikingly similar to Esau's:

2. Some interpreters think the text reflects the distinction between hunting (Esau) and herding (Jacob) cultures. Such a view fails to take account of the familial context and loyalties at work in the story (cf. Golka 1999, 134–35).

"His whole body was shaggy with hair" (so Speiser 1964, 196). This, however, is a description of the animalian Enkidu when he is grown; that of Esau stems from the time immediately after he is born. Further, if the contrast between Esau and Jacob is between the outdoor man and the indoor person, that between Enkidu and Gilgamesh is between the uncultured and the cultured man.

Isaac loves Esau, but Rebekah loves Jacob. In so writing, the author continues to set the boys apart. There is asymmetry here as well. Isaac loves Esau because of the game that he brings for him to eat. However, the narrative includes no rationale for Rebekah's love for Jacob. One might hypothesize that she loves him because he stays at home with her and is cooking, but the text offers no explicit warrant for such a judgment. The author is content to report, though not assess negatively, the different loyalties at work in the family.

It may never be possible to discern the most original element of conflict in these verses. Nonetheless, the author has introduced four forms of conflict: fraternal sibling strife, parental favoritism, difference in lifestyle, and the possibility of national conflict, hence setting the stage for intense friction throughout the story involving these two brothers.

[29–34] These six brief verses comprise a report that further develops the characters of Jacob and Esau. The episode is linked to verse 28 by the phonetic similarity of *ṣyd* (game) and *zyd* (stew). Esau provides game (v. 28); Jacob cooks stew (v. 29), but not using Esau's game. (Only at the end of the episode does the author make clear that Jacob's stew is of the vegetarian variety, thus further charting a difference between Jacob and Esau, since Esau is one who brings home game that would be used in a meaty concoction.)

Dialogue between Jacob and Esau predominates in this report. Each brother speaks twice, with Esau initiating the conversation. What he says is utterly in character. He has been out hunting and comes home exhausted (and perhaps empty-handed). He asks his brother for something to eat from the pot in which he has been preparing a stew. (It is unclear whether one should think that Jacob is, as cook, doing work typically performed by women or servants. Genesis 18:6–7 suggests such, but Gideon does prepare food: Judg 6:19.) That first speech includes the word *ʾādōm*, "reddish" stew, which is the second time that this chapter has associated Esau with the color red (see v. 25). A later editor has made sure that readers associate that reddish stew with Esau and Edom. This second instance of a popular etymology for Edom, along with the two ways in which Esau loses property, suggests that verses 29–34 were not always part of the Jacob-Esau narrative.

Jacob's response offers a classic non sequitur. He commands his brother to sell him his birthright. Many interpreters have assumed that the sale price was the dollop of stew, but that is left unsaid. What is a birthright (*bĕkōrâ*), and how might it be sold? The first question is relatively easy to answer. Deuteronomy 21:15–17 preserves a case law involving a man with two wives. It stipulates that the father must give the birthright to the older son, even if that son has been born to the unfavored wife. Further, the *bĕkōrâ* comprises two-thirds of property available for inheritance. Following this logic, Jacob is attempting to double his inheritance and at the same time reduce his brother's by half. There are, however, texts in the OT suggesting that the *bĕkōrâ* was more a general status than a specific inheritance (e.g., Gen 43:33; 1 Chr 5:1), though the two could obviously be related. As for the second question, there is no other example in ancient Israel of a child "selling" a birthright to a sibling. Once Jacob has Esau's word, which in the biblical author's eyes is equivalent to the sale of the birthright (v. 33), Jacob gives Esau what he has initially requested. In sum, though the reader may not be sure about what actually constitutes the "birthright" in this episode, by the end Jacob, not Esau, possesses it.

The pace of the narrative picks up at this point. Verse 34 concludes with five verbs: eat, drink, arise, go, despise. The last verb provides the author's judgment about the character of Esau. He has despised something that should not be despised. The author provides no comparable judgment about Jacob. Esau starts the dialogue, but Jacob uses it, along with Esau's physical condition and character, to gain a long-term advantage over his sibling. Esau will lose status with Jacob again (Gen 27), but on that occasion he does not despise that status; he is tricked out of it.

Genesis 26:1–35
Isaac Calls Rebekah His Sister When in Gerar

Genesis 26 is the "Isaac" chapter in Genesis. Here, and only here, does the reader find material devoted primarily to the least well-known patriarch. Even here, the material is not exclusive to him. Verses 1–11 provide another example of the wife-sister tale, a story that has already been told twice about Abraham and Sarah. Moreover, 26:12–33 finds a parallel in 21:22–34, which also involves a well, an oath with Abimelek, and the naming of Beersheba. Nonetheless, Isaac is a distinctive figure. He has a higher status when dwelling in a foreign land than does Abraham, especially in Gen 12. Both episodes in Gen 26 emphasize the Philistine context in which Isaac dwells. That is not the case in Gen 20, where Abraham sojourns in Gerar, not characterized as Philistine. And the term "Philistine" appears only late in the Beersheba episode in Gen 21 (vv. 32, 34). In Gen 26, Isaac routinely finds himself in contentious situations. In no case, however, does he appear responsible for this strife. Further, he and his servants seem almost single-minded in their pursuit of wells! Abraham and his servants dig one well; Isaac and his men work with many wells (v. 18), four of which he names (vv. 20, 21, 22, 33).

Genesis 26 creates an interlude in the story of Jacob and Esau. In chapter 25, Jacob has acquired Esau's birthright; in chapter 27 Jacob will secure the blessing intended for Esau. Moreover, Gen 26 provides the composer with an occasion to take language of promise originally given to Abraham and associate it with Isaac. The chapter appears to include material from a hand or hands different from that of the composer, namely, portions of verses 3–5, 15, 33.

> **26:1** There was a famine in the land, different from the earlier famine,
> which occurred when Abraham was alive. So Isaac went to Abimelek,
> king of the Philistines, who was in Gerar. **2** YHWH appeared to Isaac[a]
> and said, "Do not go down to Egypt! Dwell in the land that I will identify
> for you! **3** Sojourn in this land![b] I will be with you and bless you. Truly, I
> will give to you and your progeny all these countries. I will carry out the
> oath that I swore to Abraham, your father. **4** I will make your progeny as
> numerous as the stars in the sky, and I will give your progeny all these
> lands, such that all the nations of the earth will be blessed through your

progeny, 5 because Abraham obeyed me, keeping my charge, commandments, statutes, and instructions."

6 Hence Isaac dwelled in Gerar. 7 The men of the place asked him about
his wife. He responded, "She is my sister," since he was afraid to say,
"She is my wife," lest the men of the place kill him because of Rebekah,
because she was very good looking. 8 Once, after Isaac had lived there for
a while, Abimelek, king of the Philistines, looked down from the window.
He saw Isaac fondling[c] Rebekah, his wife. 9 Abimelek summoned Isaac
and said to him, "Look, she is your wife! How could you say, 'She is my
sister'?" Isaac responded, "Because I thought that I might die because of
her." 10 Abimelek said, "See what you could have done to us! It would
have been easy for one of us[d] to lie with your wife, in which case you
would have brought guilt upon us." 11 As a result, Abimelek issued an
edict to all the people: "Anyone who hurts this man or his wife will die."

12 Isaac planted a crop in that land. In that same year, he received a
hundredfold;[e] YHWH had blessed him. 13 The man [Isaac] was increasingly rich such that he became truly wealthy. 14 He possessed flocks,
herds, and a great many servants. Hence the Philistines envied him.
15 (Therefore the Philistines had filled with rubble all the wells that the
servants of his father Abraham had dug while he was still alive.) 16 So
Abimelek said to Isaac, "Leave us! You have become too powerful us!"

17 Hence Isaac went from there and encamped in the valley of Gerar.
He continued to live there. 18 Isaac dug again the wells for water that
the servants[f] of his father Abraham had dug while he was still alive.
(The Philistines had filled them after the death of Abraham.) He used the
same names for them that his father had given them. 19 The servants of
Isaac dug in the valley and found there a well with flowing water. 20 The
shepherds of Gerar argued with the shepherds of Isaac, contending, "The
water belongs to us." As a result, he named the well, "Quarrel [*ʿēśeq*],"
because they quarreled with him there. 21 They [Abraham's servants]
dug another well, whereupon they [the shepherds of Gerar] argued also
over it. So he named that well "Accusation [*śiṭnâ*]." 22 He moved on from
there and dug yet another well. They did not argue over it, so he named
it "Breadth [*Rehoboth*]."

23 He then went up from there to Beersheba. 24 On that very night,
YHWH appeared to him and said, "I am the God of Abraham your father.
Do not be afraid, for I am with you; I will bless you and make your
progeny numerous because of my servant Abraham." 25 He built an altar
and invoked YHWH there. He pitched his tent there. Also there, Isaac's
servants dug a well.

26 Abimelek traveled to him [Isaac] from Gerar, along with Ahuzat,
his adviser, and Phicol, the commander of his army. 27 Isaac said to him,

"Why have to you come to me? You have disdained me and expelled me
from being with you." 28 They responded, "We have seen that YHWH is
with you. Hence, we propose that there be a sworn agreement between
you and us. Let us make a covenant 29 so that you will not act malevo-
lently with us, just as we have not harmed you and have acted only beneficently with you and have sent you away peaceably. You now are truly
blessed by YHWH." 30 He prepared a feast so that they could eat and
drink. 31 In the morning, they arose and swore mutual oaths. Then Isaac
sent them on their way. They left him on peaceable terms. 32 On that same
day, the servants of Isaac came and told him about the well that they had
dug. They said to him, "We have found water!" 33 He named it "Oath"
[*šibʿâ*]."[g] Hence the name of the city is Beersheba even today.

34 When Esau was forty years old, he married Judith, daughter of
Beʾeri, the Hittite, and Basemath, daughter of ʾElon, the Hittite. They
created a contentious atmosphere for Isaac and Rebekah.

a. MT reads "him."

b. LXX does not include "that I will identify for you! Sojourn in this land!" These words may not belong to the earliest form of the text. The final words of v. 2 may have been drawn from the end of Gen 22:2.

c. MT includes a pun, *yiṣḥāq məṣaḥēq* (lit., "Isaac causing to laugh, jesting").

d. Literally, "one of the people."

e. Literally, "one hundred *šəʿārîm*." The noun is a hapax legomenon. It could mean one hundred measures, though the quantity is unknown, or 100 percent.

f. MT accidentally omitted "servants," but it is present in SP, LXX, and Vulg. Other verses (15, 19, 25) in this chapter strongly suggest that the word belongs here.

g. This Hebrew word can be understood in several ways. Speiser (1964, 202) offers three possibilities: "seven," "satedness," and "oath," arguing for the final option, a position I find convincing (cf. Gen 21:30–32).

[26:1–11] Readers have heard the bare bones of this narrative earlier. A patriarch declares that his wife is his sister because he is afraid that the foreigners among whom he dwells would take his beautiful wife and kill him. Each version of this tale is, however, distinctive. In this version, the patriarch does not simply go to a foreign land, he goes "to King Abimelek." This narrative offers a higher view of the patriarch's status than the foregoing ones. He initiates contact with the king, whereas in Gen 12:18 and 20:9, Abraham is summoned by a foreign ruler.

The initial phrase in this version of the wife-sister story—"There was a famine in the land, different from the earlier famine, which occurred when Abraham was alive"—represents the composer's attempt to distinguish this telling from at least one other version, probably the one preserved in Gen 12:10–20.

Since 26:1 refers to only one famine, probably Gen 26 became part of the family literature before the time when Gen 20 was introduced into the Abraham saga. (See the comments on Gen 20 for other reasons to think that chapter entered the family literature at a relatively late date.)

Verses 2–5 find no parallel in the other two wife-sister stories. In Gen 12 and 20, the deity appears to or addresses the foreign king. Here, in four verses that interrupt the "standard" story, the deity appears to Isaac. The speech is unusual, both in the context of the wife-sister story and in comparison to speeches addressing other patriarchs. Genesis 26:2 includes an admonition that Isaac not go down to Egypt, an admonition that would have made optimal sense if it had occurred in Gen 20. However, in Gen 20, Abraham and Sarah travel to Gerar, as Isaac does in Gen 26, not to Egypt. One does not, therefore, expect that he would have gone down to Egypt. Isaac is commanded, in effect, to stay where he is, since, according to 26:1, he has already gone to Gerar. In verse 3, he is then told, "I will give your offspring all these lands," which must include Gerar, in Philistine territory. This promise of the land in which the patriarch is residing when the wife-sister episode takes place is part of neither Gen 12 (located in Egypt) nor Gen 20 (located in Gerar). There is no scholarly consensus about the location of Gerar, though it must have been in Philistine territory. Many interpreters have situated it on the eastern border of that territory in the Shephelah, west-northwest of Beersheba. As a result, any notion of an Israel whose borders would extend to the "river of Egypt" (Gen 15:18) probably includes Gerar.

Land, as such, is important in this version of the wife-sister story. The word "land" (*ʾereṣ*) appears six times in the first four verses, four times in the singular, twice in the plural. Isaac is commanded to live in "this land," presumably Gerar. If he does, God will give him and his descendants "all these lands," presumably lands defined by the presence of other stereotypic pre-Israelite inhabitants (e.g., Hittites, Canaanites, Philistines). The ideas and language seem to reflect that of Gen 17:8 (a Priestly text), in which God promises Abraham that he will give him and his descendants the land in which they reside as aliens. Genesis 26 offers a variant of this tradition, since it places Isaac outside the heart of the "promised land" when God makes this promise to him. (In Gen 17, Abraham might be dwelling at Mamre; so 18:1). One senses a certain tension between 26:2 and 26:3. On the one hand, verse 2 sets the expectation that YHWH will at some future point reveal where Isaac is supposed to go (cf. the very similar language in 22:2). On the other hand, the very first words of verse 3 command Isaac to remain where he is. This tension may be due to a hand different from the composer in parts of verses 3–5.

The things promised to Isaac—divine presence (e.g., Gen 28:15 [clause with no verb]; 31:3 [clause with verb]), blessing (Gen 12:2), land (17:8), progeny as stars of heaven (22:17), and the blessing to the nations/families of the earth

(22:18)—all appear elsewhere in the family literature. This speech of the deity (26:2–5), however, seems closely related to the one in 22:15–18 (a text almost certainly a later addition to the original version of Gen 22). Genesis 22:16 is *the* place at which God takes an oath, "By myself I have sworn. . . ." This is almost certainly the oath to which Gen 26:3 refers (the language of covenant is used in other texts, as in Gen 15 and 17). It is no accident, therefore, that 26:5 refers to Abraham obeying God's voice (v. 5a), which is the same language used in Gen 22:18 to characterize Abraham's action in that chapter. In Gen 26, a traditional language of promise and blessing has been recast in dependence on Gen 22. Yet both texts (22:15–18 and 26:3–5) are secondary to their contexts. The least common element in the promissory language of 26:3–5 involves the notion of divine presence: "I will be with you." It appears elsewhere with reference to Jacob (Gen 31:3) and Moses (Exod 3:12), but not with Abraham.

This speech offers a new (theo)logic. God will act bountifully toward Isaac and his progeny not only because of what has been promised to Abraham but also because of what Abraham has done. Abraham has obeyed God. As a result, God will make the offspring of Isaac numerous (26:4). Isaac, too, must obey God; he must remain in "this land." This condition, if Isaac accedes to God's command, will result in God's presence and in God's giving him and his progeny "these lands." It is as if each generation must comply with a new set of conditions in order to ensure the fulfillment of what has been announced in 12:1–3.

The final verse of the deity's speech concludes with vocabulary that appears prominently elsewhere in the Hebrew Bible. "To keep a charge" is a phrase found in Leviticus and Ezekiel; both texts feature ritual discourse (Lev 18:30; 22:9; Ezek 44:16; 48:11). And "commandments, statutes, and instructions" is the sort of language one finds frequently in the book of Deuteronomy (cf. 6:1; 8:11; 11:1, though the word "my instructions" does not appear in that book). Such language is also in Exod 16:28; 18:16; and Ezek 44:24. In sum, the formulation of what Isaac is to obey draws on other texts in the Hebrew Bible, a number of which date to the Persian period.

After this weighty speech by the deity, the narrator continues. Isaac's settling in Gerar is no longer an act of expediency, as might be the case if the text did not include 26:2–5. Now it is an act of obedience: Isaac stays in Gerar and does not go down to Egypt, which is what the deity has commanded. The story continues in a fashion similar to the other versions, with the claim that the matriarch is the patriarch's sister. Overt reference to the beauty of the matriarch is not present in Gen 20, such that Gen 26:7 seems more closely related to the version in Gen 12:11.

Verse 8 follows a gap in the narrative. Isaac and Rebekah have been in Gerar "for a while." Isaac has remained "close" to the king, such that the king can see him from his window. Here again, the story subtly emphasizes Isaac's high status and presents the king as something of a voyeur. At verse 8 this version takes a pronounced turn away from the other two versions. Abimelek observes Isaac and Rebekah behaving in a way showing that they are husband and wife. Put another way, the foreign king discovers the ruse on his own. Such is not the case in either Gen 12 or 20. In the first account, "YHWH afflicted Pharaoh" (12:17). In the latter one, "God came to Abimelek in a dream by night" (20:3). In Gen 26, the deity does not communicate with the foreign potentate. The absence of such communication is consistent with the interest in emphasizing the high status of Isaac, indicated here by having the foreign king deal not with Israel's God but instead with the patriarch.

The dialogue that ensues is similar to Gen 12. Isaac is summoned, as was Abraham (12:18; 20:9), and interrogated. Isaac's defense is more in line with Gen 12 than with Gen 20. He appeals to his fear of being killed (26:9) rather than to the legitimacy of characterizing his wife as his sister (cf. 20:12). For Abimelek, the issue is also apparently one of life or death, since he offers an edict, "Anyone who hurts this man or his wife will die."

In Gen 12, the ancestral couple leaves the foreign land after the wife-sister story. Not so in either chapter 20 or 26. In Gen 26, they remain in the land, which is consistent with the theme of land struck early in the chapter. Only after further residence will they become wealthy (and this in contrast to Gen 12 and 20, where Abraham is given riches by the king). Abimelek's edict, with which the narrative concludes, is the vehicle by means of which Isaac and Rebekah are able to remain in Gerar. They are now protected by royal decree.

[12–33] The reports about Isaac's wealth could have been part of the wife-sister story since Abraham becomes wealthy at the ends of each of the earlier tales. In Gen 26, however, the motif of the patriarch's wealth occurs outside the wife-sister story. The author of Gen 26 is interested in writing a narrative showing the ancestral couple staying outside what came to be Israelite territory "as aliens" for a protracted period of time. One has the sense that the author of this chapter is reflecting on what it means to live outside the land. This may suggest a perspective similar to that of Israel's experience in exile.

The picture of life in 26:12–33 is decidedly different from that in verses 1–11. Whereas the first part of the chapter takes place in a time of drought and, presumably, of low crop yield, verses 12–33 refer to excellent agricultural productivity and many wells. The author of this report does not intend for readers to think that these circumstances are simply a function of the natural cycle of drought and plenty. Instead, the author observes, "YHWH had blessed him" (v. 12). Isaac has, as commanded, resided in that foreign land. Hence the deity is obliged to bless him. For this author, such blessing means wealth, as in the sequence of clauses in 26:12–13. Isaac is not only a successful planter of crops; he is also a successful pastoralist. Moreover, he has many servants (vv. 14, 16, 19).

Such material well-being of an extraordinary sort is not, in the eyes of the author, an unmitigated blessing by the deity. The Philistines become jealous. Further, because Isaac has become so powerful, they admonish him to leave them (v. 16). Within the context of this chapter, that order to leave Gerar raises a problem since the deity has earlier commanded Isaac to dwell "in this land." The narrator portrays Isaac as attempting to honor both mandates, by moving from the city of Gerar to the valley of Gerar. He leaves Abimelek but remains in the land. (Verse 15 is clearly intrusive, because v. 16 follows immediately upon v. 14. Verse 15 might naturally fit just before v. 18, or it may be a variant of what currently appears in v. 18.)

The valley of Gerar provides the setting for 26:17–22, which report the digging of many wells. Biblical Hebrew distinguishes cisterns (*gēb*, Jer 14:3; *bôr*, Jer 38:6) and springs (*ʿayin*, Gen 16:7) from wells (*bəʾēr*). Wells are dug and then lined with stones or other suitable objects. Any but the shallowest wells require a significant labor force (so "Water Works," *ABD* 6:886), which is consistent with the depiction in Gen 26. Of the wells listed in this chapter, "Quarrel" is listed as having an observable flow of water (v. 19). Most wells apparently filled far more slowly.

Verses 17–22 function in multiple ways. They explain why Isaac's servants need to clear wells that have been created by Abraham's servants, but that later, for no clear reason, have been filled up by the "Philistines." They report that Isaac initially talks about these redug wells, using names that Abraham has given them (v. 18), but they dwell on the naming of the wells that Isaac's servants themselves have created (vv. 19–22): "Quarrel," "Accusation," "Breadth." Finally, they depict Isaac slowly on the move. After digging "Quarrel" and "Accusation," he "moved on from there" to a place otherwise unnamed, where a well without contention is excavated. Isaac is slowly leaving the land in which he has been commanded to stay. He has been expelled from Gerar by Abimelek and has endured enmity with the herders of Gerar in their valley. Accordingly, it is time for him to leave.

The slow journey on which Isaac has embarked takes him to Beersheba, where he remains through the remainder of the chapter. The word *bəʾēr* means "well," so even though Isaac has left the land of Gerar, he is still occupied with wells, as the digging of the well reported at the end of 26:25 demonstrates.

The narrator emphasizes that as soon as Isaac reaches Beersheba, the deity appears to him "on that very night" (26:24). The deity's speech is multifaceted. YHWH self-identifies as "the God of your father Abraham," the first time in Genesis that the motif of the "god of the father" appears. Further, what was promised in verse 3, "I will be with you," has now been realized, "for I am with you." Still in the future remain the issue of blessing (cf. v. 3, though v. 12 reports that YHWH has already blessed him) and numerous progeny (cf. v. 4). Finally, consistent with 26:5, the deity reports that the fulfillment of these promises is for Abraham's sake (i.e., not for Isaac or what Isaac has just done).

By way of response, Isaac builds an altar (in 12:8 Abraham builds an altar at Bethel; in 35:7 Jacob builds an altar at Bethel), though there is no reference to sacrifices being offered on the altar. Instead, he worships, literally, "call[s] on the name of YHWH," activity in which Abraham also engages when he builds an altar (12:8). At this point in the chapter, the speech of the deity emphasizes that even though Isaac has left "this land" (cf. v. 3), he is still in acceptable territory and remains an heir to the promises originally made to Abraham.

This report about the digging of a well at Beersheba (vv. 25, 32–33) is interrupted by verses 26–31. It is as if the composer wants to retell portions of 21:22–34, though now about Isaac. Both Gen 21 and Gen 26 use language about an oath and a covenant between Abraham and Abimelek, and later between Isaac and Abimelek. The reasons, however, are different. In Gen 21, the covenant is made to resolve conflict concerning a well, which is then named Beersheba. In Gen 26, the motivation has to do with the potential for future conflict, "so that you will not do us harm" (v. 29). It is literally a "peace" (*šālôm*, vv. 29, 31) treaty, which is clearly based on language used earlier in the chapter, in Abimelek's edict (v. 11). Abimelek appeals to a time when Isaac was less powerful, a time when the "Philistines" did him no harm. Now that Isaac is powerful, the Philistines want Isaac to reciprocate. Further, Abimelek casts Isaac's status in theological terms: "You are truly now blessed by YHWH." Isaac is both blessed now (vv. 12, 29) and can anticipate blessing in the future (v. 24).

"On the same day" that Isaac sends Abimelek and his legation on their way, his servants report that water has been discovered in the well that they have dug. This author is interested in "immediacy," things happening in close proximity because of the way either the deity (v. 24) or people (v. 32) have behaved. Because Isaac has successfully negotiated an oath with Abimelek, an oath that is Abimelek's idea, it is appropriate that the well be successful and be known as "well of oath," or Beersheba.

The text does not report that Isaac and Abimelek make a covenant, only that they exchange mutual oaths. In Gen 21 Abraham and Abimelek swear an oath and make a covenant. It may be, however, that mutual oaths function similarly to a covenant. A later hand has annotated the narrative by observing that the name of Beersheba for this city was in play during the composition of Genesis.

[34–35] A note of contentiousness runs through this chapter. Earlier the strife was between the inhabitants of Gerar and Isaac's servants. Now conflict occurs inside the patrilineage of Terah. One member of that patrilineage is "marrying out." The composer returns to Esau (last mentioned in Gen 25:34), who has married two women (an instance of polgyny). He marries two "Hittite" women, marital choices that further disenfranchise him. ("Correct" wives would have come from the patrilineage of Terah.)

As a function of those marriages, one might have expected Esau to leave the scene. As we know from Gen 27, however, he continues to live with his family of origin—along with his two wives. Though the author does not explain the reasons for the "contentious atmosphere" that Esau, Judith, and Basemath have created, one may speculate that it is due to the competition between these two wives as well as Esau's resentment due to the loss of his birthright. That contentious atmosphere foreshadows the more serious conflict that will emerge in the next chapter.

Genesis 27:1–28:9
Jacob Acquires Isaac's Blessing

Genesis 27 builds upon the relationships and characterizations established in Gen 25, though Esau is far less the impetuous youth of that earlier chapter, and Rebekah, rather than Jacob, is the astute trickster. Though the fates of the children are in play, here their parents have even more important roles. In the first two scenes, both parents order their sons into action. Of the two parents, Rebekah is the far more powerful. Genesis 26, "the Isaac chapter," seemingly interrupts the larger narrative devoted to Jacob and Esau. It does, however, establish a contrast to the character of Isaac as portrayed in Gen 27. In Gen 26, Isaac bests a king and generals. But in Gen 27, he is less potent, in part due to his advanced age. By the end of Gen 27, the relative statuses of Esau and Jacob have been underscored, and Jacob has fled the land to Haran. Such plot elements are of fundamental importance to the family story. That the younger brother, Jacob, will ascend over his older brother is no accident. It develops both from their own interactions (Gen 25) and those of their parents (Gen 27). Although the deity is invoked to confirm the boys' relationship (27:28), the family members create the sons' respective statuses. Jacob's flight allows him not only to interact with the deity in signal fashion (28:10–20; 32:22–32), but also to gain wealth and experience as one who must interact with another member of the family: Laban.

The word "bless/blessing" occurs twenty-three times in Gen 27 and therefore highlights what is at stake as the action takes place. In Gen 25, Jacob garners the status of the firstborn from Esau. Now, due to Rebekah's machinations, he can capture his father's blessing, which includes God's sanction. The Priestly version of the blessing granted to Jacob (27:46–28:9) offers a much less fractious depiction of the episode. The blessing is not the result of trickery, and a greater emphasis is placed on the blessing as given by the deity (28:3–4) rather than as something granted by the father. Jacob's departure is less a hurried escape from the threat presented by his brother, which is communicated to him by his mother, and more a trip mandated by his father so he may find an appropriate spouse.

27:1 When Isaac had grown old and was unable to see, he summoned
Esau, his older son, and said to him, "My son," and he responded to

him, “I’m here.” 2 He said, “I’ve grown old, and I don’t know when I
will die. 3 Take your weapons, your quiver and your bow; go out into
the open country and hunt game for me. 4 Then prepare some delicious
food for me, the kind that I love. Bring it to me to eat so that I can bless
you before I die.”

5 Rebekah happened to be listening when Isaac talked to his son Esau.
Esau then went out into the open country to hunt and bring back game.[a]
6 Rebekah said to her son Jacob, “I heard your father say to Esau your
brother, 7 ‘Bring me some game and prepare some delicious food for me
to eat so that I can bless you before YHWH before I die.’ 8 Now, my son,
do as I say, just as I’m telling you. 9 Go to the flock and get me two fine,
young goats so I can prepare them as delicious food for your father, the
kind of food he loves. 10 You will then bring it to your father so that he
will eat and bless you before he dies.” 11 Jacob responded to his mother
Rebekah, “But Esau my brother is a hairy man, and I have smooth skin.
12 Perhaps my father will touch me and think that I am mocking him. In
so doing, I could bring a curse upon myself instead of a blessing.” 13 His
mother said to him, “Your curse would be upon me, my son. Now, do
as I say. Go, get [them] for me.” 14 So he went and brought [them] to
his mother. His mother then prepared delicious food, the kind his father
loved. 15 Then Rebekah took the best clothes of Esau, her older son,
which were with her in the house, and put them on Jacob, her younger
son. 16 She also put the pelts of the young goats on his hands and around
his smooth neck. 17 Then she handed the delicious food and the bread that
she had prepared to Jacob her son.

18 He went to his father and said, “My father,” who responded,
“Indeed, who are you, my son?” 19 Jacob said to his father, “I am Esau,
your firstborn son. I have done as you instructed me. Get up and eat some
of my game so that you can bless me.” 20 But Isaac said to his son, “How
were you able to find it so quickly, my son?” Jacob responded, “Because
YHWH your God made it happen.” 21 Isaac said to Jacob, “Come here so
that I may touch you, to see whether or not you are my son Esau.” 22 So
Jacob approached Isaac his father, who touched him and said, “The voice
is the voice of Jacob, but the hands are the hands of Esau.” 23 He did not
recognize him because his hands were like the hairy hands of Esau. As a
result, he blessed him.[b] 24 Then he said, “Are you really my son Esau?”
to which Jacob said, “I am.” 25 He said, “Bring it to me so that I can eat
some of my son’s game and then bless you.” So he brought it to him and
he ate. He also brought him wine, and he drank. 26 Isaac his father said to
him, “Come here and kiss me, my son.” 27 So he approached and kissed
him, whereupon Isaac smelled the scent of his clothes and blessed him.
He said,

"See, the scent of my son
is like the scent of the open country that YHWH has blessed.
28 May God grant you rain showers from the sky,
olive oil from the earth,
and an abundance of grain and wine.
29 May peoples serve you,
nations bow down before you.
Act as a lord over your brothers,
so that your mother's sons will bow down before you.
Anyone who curses you will be cursed,
and anyone who blesses you will be blessed."

30 Immediately after Isaac had finished blessing Jacob, and just as soon
as Jacob had left his father Isaac, Esau his brother came in from the open
country. 31 He had also prepared some delicious food and brought it to
his father. He said to his father, "My father, please sit up and eat some
of his son's game so that you can bless me." 32 His father Isaac said to
him, "Who are you?" And he responded, "I am your firstborn son, Esau."
33 Then Isaac shuddered violently and said, "Who then is the one who has
hunted game and brought it to me so that I ate all of it before you arrived
and have blessed him? And, indeed, he shall be blessed!" 34 When Esau
heard what his father said, he screamed violently, with great bitterness.
Then he said to his father, "Bless me as well, my father." 35 He responded,
"Your brother came deceitfully and has stolen your blessing." 36 Esau
said, "Isn't he well named as Jacob? He has replaced[c] me twice now. He
stole my birthright and now he has stolen my blessing."[d] He then said,
"Don't you have some other blessing for me?" 37 Isaac answered Esau,
"I've already placed him as a lord over you. What could I do for you,
my son?" 38 Esau said to his father, "Do you have only one blessing, my
father? Bless me as well, my father!" Then Esau cried out and wept.

39 Isaac his father responded,
"You will dwell far from the olive groves of the earth,
far from the rain showers from the sky.
40 You will live by your sword,
and you will serve your brother.
But when you tear yourself loose,
you will tear his rope from your neck."

41 Esau was furious at Jacob because of the blessing that his father
had conferred. Esau thought to himself, "The time when my father will
be mourned is approaching. Then I will kill my brother Jacob." 42 When
Rebekah was told what her son Esau was saying, she summoned her
younger son, Jacob, and said to him, "Your brother Esau is plotting to kill
you. 43 Now, my son, do as I say! Flee immediately to Laban, my brother,

in Haran! 44 Live with him for a while, until your brother's rage dissi-
pates, 45 until your brother's anger toward you subsides and he forgets
what you have done to him. Then I will send for you and bring you back
from there. Why should I be deprived of both of you on the same day?"
46 Then Rebekah said to Isaac, "My life has become unbearable
because of the Hittite women. If Jacob were to marry one of these Hittite
women, these women who live here,[e] why should I remain alive?"
28:1 As a result, Isaac summoned Jacob, blessed him, and decreed,
"You shall not marry a Canaanite woman! 2 Go to Paddan-Aram, to the
house of Betuel, your maternal grandfather. Marry one of your uncle
Laban's daughters. 3 El Shaddai will bless you, make you prosperous, and
give you many children so that you will become a grouping of nations.
4 He will give to you the blessing of Abraham, not only to you but also
to your descendants, so that you can take possession of the land in which
you have been living, the land that God gave to Abraham." 5 Then Isaac
sent Jacob off. He went to Paddan-Aram, to Laban the son of Betuel, the
Aramaean, the brother of Rebekah, Jacob and Esau's mother.
6 When Esau realized that when Isaac had blessed Jacob and sent him
off to Paddan-Aram so that he would marry a woman from that region,
saying to him, "You shall not marry a Canaanite woman!" 7 and that
Jacob had obeyed his father and mother and had gone to Paddan-Aram,
8 Esau knew how reprehensible Canaanite women were to his father. 9 So
Esau went to Ishmael and married Mahalath, the daughter of Abraham's
son Ishmael and the sister of Nebaioth, in addition to his other wives.

a. LXX reads "for his father" instead of "and bring."
b. This "blessing" may be an accidental dittographic expansion from v. 27.
c. The verb ʿ*qb* (replaced) sounds like the name Jacob.
d. The word for "birthright," *bəkōrâ*, sounds like the word for "blessing," *bərākâ*.
e. Literally, "such as these women of the land."

[27:1–4] The chapter commences with a scene involving the father and his older son, drawing upon vocabulary introduced in Gen 25:27. Esau is a person who knows how to hunt game, and he is at home in the open country, away from his family's tents. The reader knows all that by the end of chapter 25. What is new is the role of Esau as one who prepares food. Esau as cook presents him as similar to Jacob, who is preparing food when Esau loses his birthright (25:29). In neither instance, however, does Esau fare well. Both Jacob and Rebekah, in their role as cooks, fare better.

This initial scene leaves out explicit reference to the parents' affections for their respective sons as the narrative has announced them earlier: Isaac loves Esau, Rebekah loves Jacob. Nor are those affections referred to explicitly elsewhere in the chapter: they are presumed. However, the diction of love is present: Isaac loves delicious food (27:4, 14). Isaac's newly introduced love of good food opens the door for working out the complicated loves that the parents have for their respective sons. One might have thought that Isaac loved game simply for its taste or because it is typically roasted over a fire (cf. Prov 12:27). However, since Rebekah is able to prepare two young domestic animals that are pleasing to Isaac, it appears that the preparation rather than the meat itself is crucial.

The notion of a father blessing his sons is, of course, attested elsewhere in Genesis. The scenes of Noah in Gen 9:25–27 and of Jacob in Gen 48–49 offer interesting points for comparison. In both texts, the father offers blessings (and curses) that create and/or reflect the different statuses and fates of various sons. In Gen 27, however, Isaac has intended to give only one blessing, the one for the elder son.

It is striking that, in two of the paternal blessing texts in Genesis, the father is described as having limited, if any, vision. In both Gen 27 and 48, the final outcome depends upon the absence of sight; Isaac cannot see that he is blessing Jacob, and Jacob cannot "see" that he is elevating Ephraim over Manasseh, even though he knows whom he is blessing. The absence of "sightedness" does not preclude the granting of blessings that will enable the family to flourish.

Perhaps most striking to the reader is Isaac's condition for blessing. The grammar leaves no doubt that Isaac's blessing should depend upon Esau's bringing him some game to eat. There is no similar condition in the other texts concerning paternal blessing. Jacob is depicted as ill, whereupon Joseph brings his two sons, Ephraim and Manasseh, to receive a blessing. However, Joseph must do nothing other than present his sons. Esau, in contrast, is supposed to demonstrate his prowess as a successful hunter and cook in order to receive his blessing. This, of course, did not happen.

[5–17] The author underscores, though in a new way, the diverse parental affections. In verse 5, Esau is described as Isaac's son, and in verse 6, Jacob is similarly noted as Rebekah's son. The dynamics initially described in chapter 25 remain in play. And the author continues to overstate the obvious: that Jacob is Rebekah's son (27:8), that Esau is Jacob's brother (v. 6), and that Rebekah is Jacob's mother (v. 11). In so doing, the author highlights this narrative as family literature.

This scene, which focuses on Rebekah and Jacob, commences with Rebekah "listening." Such behavior recalls Sarah's posture at the entrance to the tent, "listening." There too, the couple in question is advanced in years. And there too, the matriarch is keeping track of the household's activities. Here, however, Rebekah does more than observe. What she hears drives her into action: the perpetration of a ruse that will enable her younger son to receive the blessing that Isaac is intending Esau to receive. The plan is self-evident, though two elements require comment. First, when Rebekah reports Isaac's speech to her younger son, she elaborates upon what Isaac has said, inserting the phrase, "before YHWH" (v. 7). In so doing, she interjects a theological dimension, which underscores the significance of the blessing that Jacob might receive. ("Before YHWH" often appears in ritual contexts, as in Lev 1:3, 5, 11; Pss 68:3 [2]; 95:6, but cf. Speiser [1964, 205], who argues that here it means "with the LORD's approval.") Second, the pelts or skins from the freshly killed young goats will certainly give the impression of recently killed game. Isaac would perceive the bloody pelts to be the bloody hair of Esau after he has just killed and cleaned a wild animal. Third, Jacob is a willing, though worried, participant. He knows that his father might discover the deception and take it out on him. Rebekah responds in two ways: by asserting that whatever curse might ensue would fall upon her and by creating yet another plan of deception by using animal pelts to cover Jacob's arms and neck. In so doing, her role as trickster continues.

[18–29] This third moment in the story begins in ironic fashion. Though the two characters use the intimate diction of "my father" and "my son," Isaac does not know which son he is addressing. Based on the first scene, he assumes, with some uncertainty, that the recipient is Esau. And Jacob builds on that supposition when he states explicitly that he is Esau. The narrator continues in this fashion (e.g., in v. 20): Isaac refers to Jacob as "my son," which, though accurate, reflects the success of Rebekah's plan.

Verses 18–26 comprise a tight dialogue of eleven speeches, most very brief, in which Isaac challenges the identity of "his son." Is he really Esau, as he claims to be? Jacob is now on his own as he plays out his mother's plan. Neither he nor she have counted on Isaac's wonderment at Jacob's prompt arrival. However, Jacob, truly his mother's son (cf. v. 6), offers a theological explanation, claiming that "YHWH **your** God," meaning YHWH, Isaac's God, has made it happen. Nor has mother or son considered Jacob's voice. Fortunately for Jacob, the narrator embeds Isaac's observation about Jacob's voice in a sentence with the apparently weightier evidence of his pelt-covered hands. The scene is replete with verbs about coming near and touching, even kissing. This motif of nearness may strike the reader as ironic since father and son are now becoming separated by the ruse of mistaken identity.

If Jacob appears here as a competent interlocutor, Isaac comes across as somewhat skeptical; nevertheless, Isaac lets three of his senses overpower his doubt. (A fourth sense, hearing, created the doubt.) He touches the pelts and is misled by them. He tastes the food and is misled by Rebekah's successful preparation of food that he supposes to have been prepared by Esau. And when kissing Jacob, he is misled by the odor of the pelts. He imputes that odor to the open country, though it is really that of the domestic herd near his dwelling. Touch, taste, and smell prevail over hearing. Sight, of course, cannot play its typical role due to Isaac's lack of sight.

The poetic blessing (vv. 27–29) is introduced with a segue based on the motif of the scent that has convinced Isaac of Jacob's identity as Esau. Moreover, the introductory verse construes the open country as "blessed," which itself is a link into the formal blessing in 27:28–29. This blessing involves several components: fertility, international power, fraternal power, and reciprocal blessing/cursing. The notion of blessing pervades these verses, though there is a certain tension between the first two lines of the poetry and what follows. Isaac makes clear that the open country has already been blessed. Uncultivated land, the earth in its natural state, has yielded food from game. However, at least in Isaac's eyes, God still needs to provide for the fertility of cultivated land, which will provide grain, wine, and olive oil. This is the land that Jacob will inhabit.

Blessings of fertility for the land appear prominently in Genesis, both here and in Gen 49. In particular, Jacob's blessing of Joseph (49:25–26) refers to the heavens and the mountains, though there is no reference to specific agricultural bounty as there is in Gen 27. Specific reference to rain resonates with texts such as Deut 7:13; 28:12; and even more in the poetic Gen 27:28, which specifies not only rain showers but also grain and wine. It is surely no accident that Deut 33:28 refers to "Jacob's abode," since Jacob's blessing in Genesis involves exactly the elements mentioned in Deut 33:28.

Verse 29 moves to human interactions involving Jacob both as nation and as sibling. In both instances, others will "bow down" before him. Reference to "peoples // nations" may seem odd, given the primacy of familial relationships in this story. However, the narrative concerning Jacob and Esau is always, at some level, a narrative about Israel and Edom (Gen 25:23; ch. 36). It is not a far step to move from rhetoric about one nation bowing down to Israel, to envisioning many nations doing so. Genesis 49 provides a point of similarity to 27:29b, since there Judah's brothers will "bow down" before him (49:8; cf. 37:9–11). (Reference to brothers in 27:29 almost certainly reflects the familiar situation of Jacob's many sons; so Gen 49 and Deut 33.) The royal connotation of bowing down is clear, since Judah can refer to the Southern Kingdom and Jacob to the Northern Kingdom.

The final element of reflexive cursing and blessing stands in the tradition of YHWH's blessing of Abraham (Gen 12:3). (Cf. Num 24:9, where this same formula appears. In Balaam's oracles, Israel is routinely referred to as Jacob [Num 23:7, 21, 23; 24:5, 17, 19], which demonstrates the significance of the tradition of his blessing as attested in Gen 27. It is the only contested blessing in Genesis!) In both cases, the blessing of an individual by the deity can move beyond that person. Any human who blesses Abraham or Jacob will himself or herself be blessed.

[30–40] Though a rapid reading of these verses suggests that this dialogue is similar to the one that has just preceded it, the emotional register is quite different. Verse 30 implies that the two brothers have almost run into each other. Moreover, the first speech of Esau is more deferential than that of Jacob. Such formality stands in contrast to the overt emotions of Isaac as he shudders and Esau as he screams. This level of emotional and physical expression is unusual, not only in the family stories but also elsewhere throughout the book of Genesis (cf. Gen 22 for a quite different world). The familial relationships that undergird this story receive unusual repetitive attention: "his brother" (v. 30), "his father" (vv. 30, 31 [2×], 32, 34 [2×], 38, 39), "my father" (31), "his son" (31), "your brother" (35, 40). In ironic fashion, such repetition underscores the fractures occurring within this family. As this scene progresses, Isaac's initial shock and physical distress subside; those of Esau do not (so v. 38).

The three questions in 27:36–38 and the responses to them attest to a family that is coming apart. Esau asks Isaac whether he has a blessing for him. Isaac responds indirectly, reporting that he has already blessed Jacob. Esau then asks pointedly if Isaac has only one blessing. And again, Isaac does not answer directly yet offers not a blessing but a reversal of the blessing that has been granted to Jacob. The fertility that Isaac has granted to Jacob (v. 28) is now unavailable to Esau. The familial power that Isaac has given to Jacob (v. 29) means that Esau will be subservient to Jacob (v. 40). Different, however, is the first part of 27:40: Esau will live "by [his] sword." Though some commentators think this means that Esau has been condemned to live in a violent way, the phrase may be a provision of empowerment. Although Esau is not granted the reflexive protection of a divinely provided curse on his enemies as Jacob has received, he is not powerless. He will have a sword to protect himself, and he will ultimately escape his servile status, just as Edom successfully revolts against Judah (2 Kgs 8:20–22). As was the case with Cain and Ishmael before him, though he is lost to the lineage, he is not without protection and status.

[41–45] These verses comprise the denouement to this lengthy episode. Jacob has won his father's blessing. Now Jacob learns that though he need not have feared a curse from his father, he does need to worry about his brother's anger. Again, the primary mover is Rebekah; Jacob does not speak in this scene. She discerns what Esau is thinking, that he is planning to kill Jacob after Isaac dies. The narrator signals Esau's emotional state in verse 41, when he reports that Esau is furious at Jacob. His fury, however, does not work itself out immediately but in a plan. Rebekah, however, counters his plan with one of her own. Yet another "brother" comes into view: Rebekah's brother Laban. She commands Jacob to flee from his brother and to take refuge with her brother in Haran.

The pre-Priestly author's final contribution to this narrative (v. 45) may strike some readers as odd. Esau's anger might dissipate, but it is difficult to imagine that he would forget having been cheated out of both his birthright and his blessing. Rebekah, who throughout the narrative seems astute, appears here to be disingenuous, offering a judgment about Esau to Jacob that she is unlikely to think is the case. Her chief goal is to remove Jacob from the scene. Moreover, as her final question demonstrates (v. 45), her speech to Jacob is prudent. (Rebekah will also pose a question to Isaac in verse 46, a question introduced again by the word *lāmmâ* [why], which receives no direct response.) According to her plan, both of her sons will remain alive.

[27:46–28:9] Most scholars agree that these verses may be attributed to the hand of the Priestly writer (the same may be said for the similar formulations in Gen 48:3). They offer a different reason for Jacob's departure from the household of Isaac and a different (and "better") characterization of Jacob. As a result, the tension between Jacob and Esau is removed. First, the pre-Priestly writer pictures Jacob fleeing from his home at Rebekah's request due to Esau's plan to kill him. Not so here. The Priestly writer places Jacob in dialogue not with Rebekah but with Isaac, who is concerned not about the threat from Esau but instead about the choice of a proper spouse for Jacob. Rebekah, who remains powerful in the Priestly material, has triggered Isaac's concern with the question posed in 27:46. It is an apt question due to the report of Esau's prior marriage to two Hittite women (26:34–35). Jacob does not flee in fear but leaves obediently in search of a proper mate. Second, Jacob receives blessings: they are rooted in the past (28:4), conferred in the present (28:6), and promised for the future (28:3–4). Moreover, the blessings are not the result of trickery. Neither Jacob nor Rebekah is instrumental in their conveyance. Third, since there is no trickery, Esau is not an angry character. He is simply aware that Isaac blessed Jacob (28:6–7). In sum, the Priestly narrator has depicted a more acceptable Jacob than was present in the preceding chapter. And the family itself is less riven by subterfuge than was the case in Gen 27: all members of the family appear in a better light than in 27.

One may also discern a difference in the blessing present in the Priestly material. Though there is reference to the deity in Gen 27:28, the earlier blessing by Isaac is fundamentally a pronouncement by the patriarch. In 28:3–4, the blessing is overtly theological. The deity is mentioned explicitly as the source of the blessing. This blessing stems from the blessing that God has given to Abraham, whose name appears two times (vv. 3–4). Moreover, the divine name, El Shaddai (v. 3) has appeared earlier in the Priestly text recounting the Abrahamic covenant (Gen 17:1).

Familial relationships continue to be important, though now the relationships have moved beyond those of a so-called nuclear family. Betuel is a maternal grandfather; Laban is an uncle of Jacob, a son of Betuel, and a brother of Rebekah; Rebekah is the mother of Jacob and Esau. The author even invests time in outlining the relationships of the family into which Esau marries (28:9).

There is striking diversity in the way that the women whom Jacob might have married are described: Hittite (27:46), Canaanite (28:6). These labels are typical descriptions for those who are in the land before its acquisition by the

Israelites (cf. Gen 23, a Priestly text, which describes Abraham buying land from the Hittites). Esau has already married two such Hittite women (26:34–35, another Priestly text). Now he marries a third wife, Mahalath, the sister of Ishmael's firstborn son, Nebaioth (Gen 25:13). In so doing, Esau remains within the lineage of Terah. As a result, Esau and Ishmael may be viewed as in an alliance though outside the primary line of inheritance, which will now move through Jacob.

The emphasis on the search for an appropriate spouse in this Priestly material appears rooted at least as much in a negative perception of possible spouses in the local population as it does in marriage to someone in the patrilineage of Terah. The diction is strong: Rebekah claims that her life has become unbearable; Esau learns that the local women are reprehensible to Isaac. It is difficult to read such assessments and not recall equally strong rhetoric concerning the marriage of Israelite males with non-Israelite women (Ezra 9–10; Neh 13:23–27). It is surely no accident that the list of the non-Israelite women is headed by "the Canaanites, the Hittites" (Ezra 9:1), the same names present in Gen 27:46–28:9. Such similarity probably reflects the provenance that lies behind these Priestly verses.

Genesis 28:10–22
Jacob Dreams at an Awe-Inspiring Place

The narrative about Jacob (Gen 25:19–36:43) includes two episodes (28:10–22 and chs. 32–33), the first a report and the second a story, that narrate his movement away from and back to the promised land. The report is briefer, focusing on the nocturnal dream epiphany at Bethel. The latter is longer since it involves not only the nocturnal epiphany at Peniel, but also the preparations for and encounter with Esau. Together, they offer transitional moments of liminal import: Jacob encountering the world of the divine.

From the hand of the pre-Priestly source, Gen 28:10–22 focuses on a place that is only named Bethel at the end of the episode. What has earlier been known as Luz and then becomes Bethel is referred to six times (v. 11 [3x], 16, 17, 19) as, literally, "the place." Such focus on geography is especially appropriate as Jacob is in the process of leaving the land of his immediate family and moving to ancestral territory associated with the patrilineage of Terah.

28:10 Jacob left Beersheba and traveled toward Haran. **11** He happened
upon a special place[a] and spent the night there since the sun had already
set. He took one of the stones from that place, put it under his head, and
slept at that place. **12** When he dreamed, there was a ramp placed on the
ground with its top touching the sky. God's messengers were going up
and down on it. **13** YHWH stood over it[b] and said, "I am YHWH, the God
of Abraham your father and the God of Isaac. The ground on which you
are lying I will give to you and your descendants. **14** Your descendants
will become like the dust of the ground. You will spread out to the west,
east, north, and south. All the peoples of the earth will be blessed through
you and your descendants. **15** Moreover, I am with you now. I will take
care of you wherever you go, and I will bring you back to this land. I will
not leave you until I do everything that I have promised you." **16** Then
Jacob woke from his sound sleep and said, "YHWH is certainly here in
this place, and I didn't know it!" **17** He was awestruck and said, "What
an awe-inspiring place this is. It is none other than the dwelling place of
God, the gateway of the heavens."

18 When Jacob got up in the morning, he took the stone that he had put
under his head, erected it as a stela, and anointed the top of it with oil. **19** He
named that place Bethel, even though the name of the place had already
been Luz. **20** Jacob made a vow and said, "If YHWH God is with me and
takes charge of this journey that I am now making, providing me with bread
to eat and clothes to wear, **21** and brings me back safely to the household
of my father, then YHWH will become my God. **22** Moreover, this stone
that I have erected as a stela will function as the dwelling place of God.
From everything that you give to me, I will definitely give a tenth to you."

a. Literally, "the place."
b. Or "by it," "by him."

The report commences with an aura of mystery. Verse 10 begins with two toponyms, but verse 11 anchors Jacob in an unnamed place. That vagueness and the word "the place" recall Abraham's journey to the otherwise unattested land of Moriah, which in Gen 22:3–4, 9 is also called "the place." However, "the place" in Gen 28 is holy, nothing less than a point of contact between the divine habitation and the world of humans.

The revelatory dream is striking, portraying a rare instance in which there is physical access between the earthly and heavenly worlds. Though it is a commonplace to think that 28:12 depicts a "ladder," the Hebrew word *sullām*, which occurs only once in the OT, could signify a ramp, a ramp with steps, or a staircase. Regardless of the nuance, it provides a means by which divine messengers can move between heaven and earth (cf. Gen 11:4). This imagery stands in contrast with that present in Gen 22, in which such a messenger communicates with Abraham from heaven. The Jacob story seems more comfortable with messengers or an incognito deity (Gen 32:22–32) on the human plane.

This imagery from the world of dreams is, however, less important than the speech of the deity who is positioned at the top of the ramp. That speech, especially 28:14, includes elements similar to the speeches to Abraham in chapters 12 and 13: the promise of progeny and land. The specific similarities are striking: "like the dust of the earth" (13:16; 28:14), peoples of the earth will be blessed through you (12:3; 28:14); west, east, north, and south (13:14; 28:14); your descendants (13:15; 28:14). The speech in Gen 28 especially emphasizes the importance of progeny. The deity invites Abram to look in the cardinal directions, to survey the extent of the land that he and his progeny will possess (13:14); God promises in 28:14 that Jacob's progeny will spread to the four cardinal directions. The promise becomes more than a claim about the land they will possess; it foresees movement beyond the boundaries of the land, including the places to which Israel will be taken in exile. This spread of Jacob's progeny will be a "blessing" to those among whom they dwell.

The deity then moves from this version of the ancestral promise to a promise just for Jacob: "I will be with you." God has directed those same words to Isaac (26:3, 24), but now they carry a different significance since Isaac is living in the land. In contrast, Jacob is now leaving the land. Such divine assurance is therefore a promissory note of the deity's protection as Jacob goes to "the land of the people of the east" (29:1). Direct discourse plays a prominent role in the episode. Jacob offers two soliloquies during the night (vv. 16, 17) and then another speech after he arises in the morning. The reader is privy to distinct moments during the night and another in the morning even though this compressed report reads as if things are happening quickly.

Jacob responds in diverse ways to his dream. First, he recognizes that he is at a holy place. Though the imagery of a ramp leading to the heaven suggests that the deity dwells there, Jacob thinks that the deity "is in this place," that it is the dwelling place of the deity as well as "the gateway of the heavens." In this scene Jacob is verbally overwhelmed by the power of the sacred as he uses diction about the places where the deity might dwell.

Second, Jacob takes the stone that has served as his pillow and places it vertically as a stela. Such stelae, or standing stones, are attested elsewhere in Genesis. Jacob erects a stela at Rachel's grave (35:20). Both he and Laban set up stelae when they made a covenant (31:45, 51). In all three cases, when Jacob erects a stela, it has a commemorative function. In addition, when Jacob erects the stela in Gen 28, he enacts a ritual, an anointing with oil. That ritual does not make the place sanctified: it was already special, holy. Rather, it is a ritual of recognition, coincident with the renaming of this place where the deity dwells and/or is available to humans.

Third, Jacob's naming of Bethel establishes an inextricable connection between him and that place. In Gen 35:14–15, the Priestly writer reiterates the actions of Jacob that are present in 28:18–19: the erection of a stela, the pouring of oil on it (though the Priestly writer also includes a drink offering), and the naming of the site as Bethel. Jacob encounters Bethel on his way out of the land *and* when he returns. However, he does not remain there.

Fourth, Jacob makes a remarkable conditional vow (vv. 20–22a). The deity has already promised he will bring Jacob back to the land (v. 15). Nonetheless, in his vow Jacob in effect negotiates a deal with the deity. Only if God *does* bring him back, as well as feed and clothe him, will YHWH be Jacob's God. Jacob is bargaining to have YHWH be his God, just as YHWH has been Abraham and Isaac's God (vv. 13, 20). In 28:13, the deity does not claim to be the God of Jacob. Instead, the deity promises to care for Jacob on his journey. The process by which YHWH becomes Jacob's God is different from the way in which YHWH establishes a relationship with Abraham. The covenant between YHWH and Abram/Abraham (Gen 15; 17) is the means by which YHWH becomes the God of Abraham. With YHWH and Jacob, here no new "covenant" is said to be enacted. Rather, the deity providentially promises and ensures that Jacob will return from his journey, and Jacob promises to claim YHWH as his God.

Fifth, Jacob commits to a tithe in a striking move within direct discourse to God (Gen 28:22b). Earlier, the deity has spoken directly to Jacob (vv. 13–15). However, when Jacob responds, he does not speak *to* God but *about* God (vv. 16, 17, 20–22a). Things change in 28:22b. There, the direct address suggests that Jacob is well on the way to affirming YHWH as his God.

Tithing is associated with two of the patriarchs: Abraham (14:20b) and Jacob. Abraham gives one-tenth of the spoils captured in war to Melchizedek (14:16, 20), who has just exercised his royal priestly role by blessing Abraham (14:19–20). Jacob, however, commits to tithing to God, not to a human; he will give to God one-tenth of what the deity will provide for him. The narrative about Jacob never makes explicit what property the deity does provide for him, though one might infer that the flocks and herds he brings back to the land might count (33:11). There is, however, no reference in the later narrative to Jacob making a tithe of any of his property. He gives gifts from his flocks and herds to Esau, not to God (33:10–11).

In sum, these thirteen verses, known primarily for the imagery of contact between the earth and the heavens in a dream, are especially significant due to the manifold ways in which Jacob responds to both the dream and what the deity says to him.

Genesis 29:1–35
Jacob Works for Laban and Marries Leah and Rachel

Genesis 29–31 comprises a three-chapter narrative about the interactions between Jacob and the household of Laban. The narrative is bookended by two liminal moments: Jacob's dream at Bethel (ch. 28) and Jacob's nighttime struggle at the Jabboq River (ch. 32). The Jacob-Laban narrative is also set within the even larger context of Jacob's flight and, thereafter, preparation to meet his brother Esau. Thus one purpose of the narrative is the search for a safe place to weather his brother's plans to kill him. Also important is his parents' goal of finding an acceptable wife (27:46–28:5).

The narrative early on is replete with kinship language: "my brothers" (29:4), "his daughter" (v. 6), "the daughter of his uncle" (v. 10), "his uncle" (v. 10), "relative of her father" (v. 12), "Rebekah's son" (v. 12), "her father" (v. 12), "his nephew" (v. 13), "my flesh and blood" (v. 14). Jacob is clearly introduced as a member of the family. And it is a lineage into which he marries. By the end of the Jacob-Laban narrative, however, the author has made clear that Jacob and Laban, though related, belong to groups that have different customs, speak different languages, live in different places, and worship different deities. The familial ties have become less important than the differences between the groups associated with Jacob and Laban. The sons of Jacob will, by the end of the book of Genesis, have become the Israelites. The Jacob-Laban narrative is instrumental in the process of Jacob's descendants moving from family to nation.

The motif of deceit plays out prominently throughout the narrative. Laban deceives Jacob by giving him Leah instead of Rachel on his wedding night. Jacob deceives Laban during the breeding of lambs and goats. Rachel deceives Laban by both stealing and then hiding his teraphim. Within this network of deceit, the author confers a measure of respectability on all three characters. Rachel's trickery is, in her eyes, justified because her father has more or less disowned her and Leah. Jacob's trickery is, in his eyes, justified because Laban tricked him first. Laban is apparently justified because he, ultimately, creates a strategy, a covenant, that will permit him and Jacob to separate peacefully from each other.

From a literary perspective, the narrative first presents Jacob as a titan, able to move a rock that has hitherto required a group of shepherds to roll it away from the well. In Gen 30, Jacob displays sexual prowess as he fathers eleven sons and one daughter. In that same chapter, he displays specialized knowledge about how to breed livestock to his advantage. And in the final chapter, he has become a skilled speaker. He makes two long orations (31:5–13, 36–42), the first to his wives, the second to Laban. These speeches, some of which may betray the hand of a post-Priestly author, introduce a theological perspective ("God has been with me"; 31:5, 42) and provide new information about the injustice and difficulties Jacob has suffered. These capacities that Jacob now possesses help set the stage for his upcoming encounters with a "man" at the Jabboq and, then, with Esau.

29:1 Jacob got to his feet and went toward the land of the Easterners. **2** He
looked up and saw a well in the field and three flocks of sheep resting by
it. The flocks were watered from that well, but a large stone was on the
mouth of the well. **3** When all the shepherds[a] gathered there, they would
roll the stone away from the mouth of the well and water the sheep.
Thereafter, they put the stone back to its place on the mouth of the well.

4 Jacob said to them, "My brothers, where are you from?" They
responded, "We are from Haran." **5** He said, "Do you know Laban, son
of Nahor?" They responded, "We know him." **6** He said, "Is he well?"
They responded, "He is well. And here is his daughter Rachel, arriving
with the sheep." **7** He said, "It is still the hot time of the day, not the time
to gather the animals. Water the sheep; then go and pasture them." **8** They
said, "We can't until all the flocks are gathered and the stone is rolled
from the mouth of the well. Then we water the sheep."

9 While he was still talking with them, Rachel arrived with the flock
that belonged to her father; she was a shepherdess. **10** When Jacob saw
Rachel, the daughter of his uncle Laban, along with the sheep that
belonged to his uncle Laban, he approached and rolled away the stone
from the mouth of the well and watered the flock of his uncle Laban.
11 Then he kissed Rachel and wept loudly. **12** Jacob told Rachel that he
was a relative of her father and that he was Rebekah's son, whereupon
she ran and told her father.

13 When Laban heard the report about Jacob, his nephew, he ran to
meet him. He hugged him, kissed him, and brought him to his home,
whereupon he recounted to Laban everything that had happened. **14** Laban
said to him, "You are certainly my flesh and blood."[b] Jacob stayed with
him for one month.

15 Then Laban said to Jacob, "Since you are my relative, should you
work for me for nothing? Tell me what your wages should be." **16** Now
Laban had two daughters. The name of the older was Leah, and the name
of the younger was Rachel. **17** Leah's eyes were delicate,[c] and Rachel had

a beautiful figure and was very pretty. 18 Jacob loved Rachel and said,
"I will work seven years for Rachel, your younger daughter." 19 Laban
responded, "It is better for me to give her to you than to give her to any
other man. Remain with me." 20 So Jacob worked seven years for Rachel.
It seemed like only a few days because of his love for her.

21 Jacob said to Laban, "Give me my wife so that I may go in to her
since I have fulfilled the designated time." 22 Then Laban gathered all the
people of that place and held a feast. 23 At night, he took his daughter Leah
and brought her to Jacob such that he went in to her. 24 (Laban gave his
maidservant Zilpah to her, to Leah his daughter, to be her maidservant.)
25 In the morning, it was Leah! Jacob said to Laban, "What have you done
to me? Didn't I work with you for Rachel? Why have you deceived me?"
26 Laban answered, "In our place, we don't give the younger before the
older one. 27 Complete the week for this one, and we will also give to you
the other one, when you have worked with me for another seven years."
28 Jacob did just that. He completed her week, whereupon Laban gave
Rachel his daughter to him as his wife. 29 (Laban gave his maidservant
Bilhah to Rachel, his daughter, to be her maidservant.) 30 Then Jacob also
went in to Rachel. He loved Rachel more than Leah. He worked with him
seven more years.

31 When YHWH recognized that Leah had been demeaned, he opened
her womb, but Rachel was barren. 32 Leah conceived and gave birth to
a son. She named him Reuben; for she said, "YHWH saw my suffering.
Surely now my husband will love me." 33 She conceived again and gave
birth to a son. She said, "Because YHWH heard about my being hated,
he has also given this one to me." She named him Simeon. 34 Then she
conceived yet again and gave birth to a son. She said, "Now, this time,
my husband will relate to me as his wife because I have given birth to his
three sons." Therefore, he was named Levi.[d] 35 She conceived again and
gave birth to a son. She said, "This time I will praise YHWH." Therefore,
she named him Judah. Then she stopped giving birth.

a. So SP, LXX; MT has "all of the flocks."
b. The idiom in English. MT: "my bone and flesh."
c. Or "weak."
d. SP and LXX read, "she named him."

[29:1–14] This portion of Jacob's journey commences, presumably, at Bethel, although that toponym does not appear in chapter 29. Instead, the narrator identifies the place to which he is going, "the land of the Easterners." One expects the author to refer to "Paddan-Aram," since that is the toponym present in Isaac's directions to Jacob (28:2). That phrase also appears in reports about his journey (33:18; 35:9) as well as about the place where his sons are born (35:26). It is also listed as the dwelling place of "Betuel, the Aramaean" (25:20). Despite the prominence of this place-name (Aramaea) in the traditions about Jacob's sojourn with Laban, the author uses a vaguer phrase, one introducing not the connotations of family but those of geography. The phrase "land of the East" appears in Genesis as the place to which Abraham exiles the children born to his wife Keturah (25:6). The phrase appears elsewhere in the OT as a place where enemies of Israel live (e.g., Judg 6:3, 33). The phrase "Easterners" functions similarly as a description of those whom God will destroy (Jer 49:28). In sum, "the land of the Easterners" does not lead an ancient reader to think that Jacob is heading toward a welcoming place.

The negative connotations of that toponym are, however, soon reversed. In a classic "well scene" (cf. Gen 24; Exod 2), Jacob encounters people whom he immediately—and for no overt reason—construes using kinship language, "my brothers." The well scene is similar to the one in Exod 2 to the extent that a large stone can be moved only by multiple shepherds. However, the hero (Jacob, Moses) can move the stone by himself and, after doing so, water the flock of an owner whose female relative the hero will marry.

Exodus 2 offers no dialogue between the parties when they are at the well. Genesis 29, however, provides dialogue that not only is suffused with kinship terms but also introduces Jacob as someone who does not hesitate to tell the local population how to do their work (v. 7). The dialogue between Jacob and "the brothers" retards the report about Rachel's arrival. The brothers have reported to Jacob that she is "here" (v. 6), but the narrator does not report her arrival until verse 9. Whatever differences between what the "brothers" normally do and what Jacob tells them to do quickly vanish when Rachel arrives with Laban's flock. Jacob performs the expected heroic feat at the well and then kisses her and weeps, actions that quickly result in Jacob being taken into Laban's household. The "brothers" are no longer in play; it is not even clear that they are the same collectivity as Laban's sons (31:1).

Also important in this dialogue is the presence of the toponym Haran. The brothers cite this city as their home. This toponym occurs in the preceding chapter as the place toward which Jacob is traveling (28:10). Even more important, Rebekah has told Jacob that he is supposed to go to "my relative Laban in Haran" (27:43). So, once the brothers mention Haran, Jacob knows that the threat implied by his having reached "the land of the Easterners" has been alleviated.

The almost redundant use of kinship diction (e.g., 29:10) drives home the familial bond between Laban and Jacob. The corporal vocabulary of "bone" and "flesh" does the same. Less clear is the character of the final "telling." Jacob tells Rachel that he is her father's relative and Rebekah's son. Rachel relates this same information to Laban. Once in Laban's house, Jacob tells him "everything that had happened." One can only wonder what Jacob reports. The only information the author provides is Laban's response, which leads one to conclude that Jacob must have reported about his family, its place in the lineage of Terah, and his search for an acceptable spouse. Less likely would have been reports about his flight from Esau or his dream at Bethel.

[15–30] Although kinship language continues, there is a new dynamic: Jacob as an employee of Laban. Verse 15 presumes that Jacob has already begun working for Laban. On the basis of such work, Laban invites Jacob to specify what he should be paid, as Laban will do again in 30:28. Jacob's response is somewhat surprising. The Hebrew noun typically refers to some form of monetary payment (e.g., Deut 24:15; 1 Kgs 5:20 [6]; Ezek 29:18). This, however, is not the case here. Jacob prefers to receive a wife rather than wealth, a decision consonant with one of the reasons that he has come to Paddan-Aram.

Before allowing Jacob to respond, the narrator offers new information: Laban has two daughters, and Rachel is more attractive than Leah. (It is as if Rachel has not been introduced in the opening scene at the well.) Verse 17 presents a difficult problem for the translator. Is the narrator describing Leah's eyes as attractive or unattractive? The Hebrew word used to describe Leah's eyes can bear both positive and negative meanings. Furthermore, though the implication of Jacob's choice is that he chooses Rachel because of her beauty, that is not said explicitly. His choice is overtly based on his love for her. Verse 20 underscores the depth of his love. As a result, it is likely that the author is in effect saying, "While Leah's eyes were delicate, Rachel, who had a beautiful figure and was very pretty, was even more attractive." Such a claim would comport with the view that the ancestral mothers were especially attractive, so Sarah (Gen 12:11, 14) and Rebekah (Gen 24:15–16).

Laban's response is shrewd. He says that he prefers to "give" her to Jacob rather than to any other man. He does not, however, overtly agree to Jacob's proposed term of service. Nonetheless, the dialogue results in seven years of labor, with Jacob thinking that he will receive Rachel after those seven years. When the seven years are completed, Laban sponsors a wedding celebration. After the banqueting, Laban sends *Leah* to sleep with Jacob. In the morning, when Jacob recognizes what has happened, he interrogates Laban with three probing questions. Again, Laban's response is shrewd (v. 26). He doesn't answer Jacob's questions directly but instead offers a rationale for his behavior: it would violate their cultural norms to permit the younger daughter to marry before her older sister. The use of first-person-plural grammar ("our place," "we") emphasizes that Laban claims to act on behalf of a shared ethos; he does not want to be viewed as a sole deceiver. Whether or not there is such an ethos, Laban demands that Jacob finish the week of festivities for his marriage to Leah. (The motif of Jacob "completing" a period of time, whether seven years or one week, is important in the narrative.) Laban's diction about his daughters in 29:27 ("this one," "the other") is oddly impersonal. In any event, Laban wants Jacob to finish the week of wedding festivities. Laban will eventually give Rachel to Jacob, though on the condition that Jacob work another seven years for Rachel. Once Jacob completes the "week" of years, Laban does give Rachel to Jacob, though apparently no festivities are associated with that marriage. Embedded in this narrative are two parenthetical reports (vv. 24, 29) that Laban presents each daughter with a handmaid, two women whose fertility will prove to be of critical importance to the story of this family.

Such is the contractual situation. The human dimension, however, intrudes. Although the omniscient narrator has earlier reported Jacob's deep love for Rachel, he now conveys new information about Jacob's affection: he loves Rachel *more than* he loves Leah. This asymmetry of affection drives the story forward in verse 31.

[29:31–35 (+ 30:1–13)] The deity becomes prominent for the first time in the Jacob-Laban narrative. The report is striking since YHWH is acting on behalf of Leah, not Jacob. The motif of the barren matriarch is in play. Just as God has acted on behalf of Sarah and Rebekah, when they have been unable to bear children, so here too the deity responds to the plight of the lesser loved woman, Leah. Both Rachel and Leah appear to have been infertile, though the deity now makes it possible for Leah to conceive a child.

Genesis 29:21–30:24 offers a report about the children birthed by Leah, along with her handmaid Zilpah, and Rachel, along with her handmaid Bilhah. With the exception of Levi, Leah and Rachel name the children. (Both Rachel and Jacob will provide names for Benjamin: 35:18.) In the case of all the sons, the name is provided with an interpretation of its significance, though this is not the case for Leah's daughter, Dinah. Leah gives birth to Reuben, Simeon, Levi, Judah, Issachar, and Zebulun. Her handmaid, Zilpah, gives birth to Gad and Asher, sired by Jacob. Rachel gives birth to Joseph. Her handmaid, Bilhah, gives birth to Dan and Naphtali, sired by Jacob. The mothers' speeches explaining the names of seven sons (Reuben, Simeon, Judah, Dan, Issachar, Zebulun, and Joseph) refer to the deity. Most of the speeches attest to the theological conviction that God has acted on the mothers' behalf by providing children for them. The social world of the mothers is also prominent, given the women's speeches mentioning the husband (29:32, 34; 30:1, 18, 20), children (30:1, 3, 24), son (30:6), sister (30:8), women (30:13).

Though the acts of intercourse are rarely reported (only in 30:4, 16), the numerous moments of conception clearly imply that Jacob is having sex with all four women. Here too, he is presented in a heroic role as progenitor. It bears saying again that Jacob's sons are eponymous ancestors for the tribes of Israel. However, unlike Gen 49, where the sons are clearly construed as tribes and, in the cases of Judah and probably Joseph, as nations, the sons' names in these two chapters are understood to reflect their significance for their mothers and not that of a later polity.

These verses, however, offer more than a skeletal genealogy. The author has continued to elucidate the intrafamilial dynamics between the two wives and between each of them and Jacob. In fact, 29:31–30:24 could be told as a story without any reference to named children, as in my following paraphrase:

> After God opened Leah's womb, she gave birth to four sons. When Rachel saw that Leah had given birth, she criticized Jacob, who then got angry with her. She responded by giving Bilhah to Jacob, and Bilhah gave birth to two sons. Then, when Leah learned that she had become infertile, she gave Zilpah to Jacob, whereupon Zilpah gave birth to two sons. As time went on, Reuben, Leah's first son, found in the field some plants that were thought to induce fertility. Though Rachel tried to secure the plants, Leah refused and made Jacob have sex with herself. Leah then had two more sons and one daughter. Finally, God remembered Rachel, and she gave birth to a son.

In this narrative emotions come to the surface: Leah's feelings of being unloved, Rachel's jealousy of her sister's fertility, Jacob's anger at Rachel, and Leah's feeling that Rachel has stolen her husband. So, the narrative *even without the names* offers evidence of the interpersonal difficulties of a marriage based on sororal polygyny (on which see Steinberg 1993). Genesis 30:8 expresses well the tension between the two sisters in such a marriage.

Genesis 29:31–35 offers an important perspective about God's response to Leah's plight as an unloved wife and to the fact of Rachel's infertility. The author does not impute Rachel's infertility to God but does affirm that the deity is responsible for Leah's fertility. (And the author will attribute Rachel's later fertility to God, 30:22.) As a result, Leah gives birth to four sons: Reuben, whose name means "Look, a son"; Simeon, whose name plays on the Hebrew word "to hear"; Levi, whose name plays on the Hebrew word meaning "to join oneself"; and Judah, whose name plays on the Hebrew word for "praise." Leah's declarations about the births of Reuben, Simeon, and Judah affirm her belief that God has responded to her plight as an unloved wife.

Genesis 30:1–43
Bilhah, Zilpah, Leah, and Rachel Bear Children

This chapter is a direct continuation of the birth reports that began in 29:31. Genesis 30:1–25 reports that all four women give birth, Jacob's two wives and their maidservants. The reports are infused with tension between Rachel and Jacob and between Leah and Rachel. Only in 30:25, after eleven of Jacob's sons and his daughter have been born, does the narrative of his sojourn with Laban resume. The motif of fertility is present in both sections of this chapter. One or another of the women was fertile due to the action of the deity. Then Leah uses mandrakes that Reuben has provided to enhance her fertility (vv. 14–21). Later, in 30:25–43, the fertility of livestock is in play. Yet Jacob, not the deity, is thought to control the fertility of the flocks (though 31:12, in a dream report, has the deity seeming to claim responsibility for the striped, speckled, and spotted male goats that breed with the female animals).

30:1 When Rachel saw that she had not given birth to any children for
Jacob, she was jealous of her sister. She said to Jacob, "Give me children
or I will die." 2 Jacob got very angry with Rachel and said, "Am I like
God, one who has prevented you from having the fruit of the womb?"
3 She responded, "Here is my maidservant Bilhah. Have sex with her so
that she may give birth on my knees such that I might also gain children
through her." 4 So she gave him her maidservant Bilhah as a wife, and
Jacob had sex with her. 5 Bilhah conceived and gave birth to a son for
Jacob. 6 Rachel said, "God has acted justly for me. He listened to me
and has given me a son." Therefore, she named him Dan. 7 Bilhah, the
maidservant of Rachel, conceived again and gave birth to a second son
for Jacob. 8 Rachel said, "I have had a fierce struggle with my sister, and
I have won." She named him Naphtali.

9 When Leah saw that she had stopped giving birth, she took Zilpah,
her maidservant, and gave her to Jacob as a wife. 10 Zilpah, the maidservant of Leah, gave birth to a son for Jacob. 11 Leah exclaimed, "Good
Fortune!" So she named him Gad. 12 Zilpah, Leah's maidservant, gave
birth to a second son for Jacob. 13 Leah said, "I am so happy, especially
because women see that I am happy." She named him Asher.

14 At the time of the wheat harvest, Reuben went out and found mandrakes in the field. He brought them to his mother, Leah. Then Rachel said
to Leah, "Give me some of your son's mandrakes." 15 Leah responded to
her, "Isn't it enough that you have taken my husband? And now would
you take my son's mandrakes?" Rachel said, "He may lie with you tonight
because of your son's mandrakes." 16 When Jacob arrived from the field
in the evening, Leah went out to meet him. She said to him, "You must
come to me because I have secured you due to my son's mandrakes." So
he lay with her that night. 17 God responded to Leah. She conceived and
gave birth to a fifth son for Jacob. 18 Leah said, "God has given me my
security because I gave my maidservant to my husband." So she named
him Issachar. 19 Leah conceived again and gave birth to a sixth son for
Jacob. 20 Leah said, "God has provided me with a wonderful gift. Now
my husband will honor me because I have given birth to six sons for him."
So she named him Zebulun. 21 After that, she gave birth to a daughter.
She named her Dinah.

22 Then God remembered Rachel and responded to her by opening
her womb. 23 She conceived and gave birth to a son. She said, "God has
removed my shame." 24 So she named him Joseph, saying, "May YHWH
give me another son."

25 After Rachel had given birth to Joseph, Jacob said to Laban, "Let me
go so that I may travel to my place and my country. 26 Grant me my wives
and my children for which I have served you so that I can leave. You know
the work that I have done for you." 27 Laban said to him, "If I may say so, I
have divined that YHWH has blessed me because of you." 28 He continued,
"Specify your wages, and I will give them to you." 29 Jacob responded,
"You know how I have worked for you and how the cattle have done with
me. 30 You had little before I arrived. Now it has grown incredibly. God
has blessed you based on whatever I did. But now how can I make do for
my household?" 31 Laban said, "What can I give you?" Jacob responded,
"Don't give me anything. Just do this one thing, and I will return and shepherd your flock and watch over it. 32 Let me pass through the entire flock
today and remove from it all the speckled and spotted sheep and all the
black lambs, and the spotted and speckled goats. Those shall be my wages.
33 This is how my innocence will be verified, when, in the future, you come
to examine my wages. If any nonspeckled or nonspotted goats or any non-
black lambs are found with me, they will count as stolen." 34 Laban said,
"Good! Let it happen just as you have said." 35 On that same day, Laban
removed the striped and spotted male goats and the speckled and spotted
female goats, all that had some white coloring and all the black lambs. He
put his sons in charge of them. 36 He moved them a three-day journey away
from Jacob while Jacob took care of the rest of his flock.

37 So, Jacob took freshly cut branches of poplar, almond, and plane
trees and peeled white strips in them, exposing white wood under the
bark. 38 Then he put the branches that he had peeled in front of the flocks
at the watering troughs, where the flocks came to drink and where they
mated when they came to drink. 39 When the flocks bred in front of the
branches, they gave birth to striped, speckled, and spotted young. 40 Jacob
then set apart the lambs, making the flock face the striped and the black
animals in the flock of Laban. He kept his flock separate; he did not put
them near Laban's flock. 41 When the fittest animals of the flock mated,
he put the branches in front of them by the watering troughs. They mated
near the branches. 42 However, he did not put them out for the weakest
animals of the flock. The weakest became Laban's, the fittest Jacob's.
43 So, the man [Jacob] became very wealthy. He owned many flocks,
female and male slaves, camels, and donkeys.

[30:1–24] (See comments on 30:1–13 in the preceding chapter.) This continued report about the birth of Jacob's sons is organized according to the birth mothers: Bilhah, Zilpah, Leah, and Rachel. In the first two cases, it is clear that the maidservants function as surrogate mothers for their mistresses. In 30:1–8, the author highlights the tension between Rachel and Jacob: she is jealous; he is angry. Rachel responds, as did Sarah before her (Gen 16:2), by offering her maid to Jacob. In so doing, Rachel will gain children through this surrogate mother. Bilhah bears two sons: Dan, whose name plays on the Hebrew word for "judge" or act justly; and Naphtali, whose name plays on the Hebrew word for "wrestle." Rachel underscores the preternatural character of the struggle with her sister by characterizing it as *divinely* fierce (*ʾĕlōhîm*, v. 8).

Leah then gives Jacob *her* maid (vv. 9–13) to gain even more sons than the four she has birthed earlier (29:31–35). Zilpah gives birth to Gad, whose name plays on the Hebrew word for "fortune." ("Gad" in Isa 65:11 MT appears to be the name of a deity known as "Good Fortune"; so CEB.) She also bears Asher, whose names plays on the Hebrew word meaning to be "happy."

Verse 14 marks a shift in the report. One of the sons, Reuben, has now grown and has found some plants for his mother Leah, some of which Rachel wants. These verses require special comment since the use of mandrakes for fertility is ambiguous. The mandrake root, thought to be effective in enhancing sexuality and fertility, can be consumed by humans, though it can be poisonous. The reference to mandrakes in Song 7:13 implies that it was hung up, rather like mistletoe in Western cultures. Genesis 30 offers no evidence about how the mandrakes were used. The author does make clear that, once the mandrakes are in Leah's possession, they allow her to claim Jacob as her sexual partner for the night, though only after a fraught dialogue with Rachel. Rachel pleads with Leah to give her some mandrakes. Leah defends her position by accusing

Rachel of stealing her husband. Rachel clearly feels the bite of that charge, since she acquiesces and affirms Leah's right to have sex with Jacob that evening. The author offers a theological perspective on these interactions by reporting, "God responded to Leah," even though there is no reference to Leah having pleaded with the deity in the surrounding verses. Leah gives birth to Issachar, whose name plays on the Hebrew word for wages or security; and Zebulun, whose name plays on the Hebrew word for honor or exaltation. She also bears Dinah. Though there is no overt etymology here, her name reflects the same Hebrew root as Dan, signifying justice or judgment.

The final three verses of the birth reports focus on Rachel, who has not yet given birth. God "remembered" her (cf. the Priestly writer's report about God remembering Noah and the animals on the ark: Gen 8:1; and God remembering Abraham: Gen 19:29), making her fertile so that she gives birth to Joseph. She offers two naming speeches: the first focuses on the event that has just transpired; the second points toward the future. In the first, Rachel offers a play on the Hebrew word meaning "to remove" (*ʾāsap*). In the second, his name plays on the Hebrew word meaning "add" or "do again" (*yāsap*). Unlike the names of his brothers, Joseph's name has less to do with him than it does with Rachel's desire for another son, according to the second wordplay, one who will be Joseph's brother. As such, the name foreshadows the birth of Benjamin, which does not occur until Gen 35:16–20.

Genesis 29:31–30:24 is enclosed (29:31; 30:22–23) by references to the deity's role in creating this family. God "saw" Leah's plight and "remembered" Rachel. In both cases, this divine response results in conception for the women. God is not overtly involved with the fertility of Zilpah and Bilhah. Moreover, Gen 30:24 leaves the birthing report incomplete. Rachel asks for another child, whose birth will not be reported until Gen 35:16–18.

[25–43] Even though 30:24, when reporting the birth of Joseph, implies that Rachel will give birth to more sons, verse 25 signals that the birth of Joseph marks the conclusion of the birthing that will take place in Paddan-Aram. Jacob wants to return to "my place" (v. 25), and this is in contrast to staying in Laban's "place" (29:26), a place where the customs are different from Jacob's homeland. Jacob's initial proposal involves his desire to return to that homeland with his wives and children. Nothing more. His wives, are, after all, what he and Laban have agreed would be his wages (29:15–18). Laban responds in an oblique fashion, reporting to Jacob that Laban has discovered through some form of divinatory practice that "YHWH has blessed me because of you," a version of the blessing that the patriarchs can provide (so Gen 12:3 and, especially, the blessing as conferred on Jacob: 28:14). This, in something of a non sequitur, leads Laban to ask Jacob what his wages should be (30:28). His response could be read as a refusal to let Jacob leave. Is Laban asking Jacob to stay and work for him? Or could it mean that Laban is prepared to let Jacob leave and to send him on his way with a share of the "blessing" that Laban has enjoyed due to his work in Paddan-Aram?

Jacob agrees with Laban, recognizing that Laban has indeed been blessed by Jacob's presence and that such a blessing is manifest in the increased size of Laban's herd. But Jacob then poses a question about his ability to provide for his own household. And here again (v. 30) is ambiguity. Is Jacob suggesting that he can only provide for his household if he returns to his homeland? That was his original request. Or is he now building on Laban's offer of wages to make a claim on part of the herd, for the growth of which he has been largely responsible? Laban ignores Jacob's questions and repeats his invitation that Jacob name what Laban should provide to him.

Jacob rejects the notion of being "given" anything but, as the serious negotiation moves forward, proposes that he take care of the flock and then remove from that flock sheep and goats of a certain coloration. What is now a serious negotiation moves to Jacob's specific proposal, that sheep and goats with certain coloration become his property. The proposal even includes a means by which it can be verified since if, in the future, there are any animals in Jacob's flock without such coloration, they should belong to Laban. Laban immediately agrees.

Some interpreters think that the striped, speckled, spotted, or black animals are of lesser value, which would make Jacob's proposal especially attractive to Laban, who presumably is to keep the white animals. That seems appropriate since Laban's name means "white." However, Laban goes to great pains to remove the animals with the distinctive coloration (vv. 35–36); hence, the mere fact that the animals can be readily distinguished seems more important for the narrative than indicating a potential difference in value.

There is no specific reference about Jacob's discovery of Laban's deceit in removing the distinctively colored animals (though cf. 31:41), only a detailed report about how Jacob re-creates the herd of such animals by breeding them as they face peeled branches, which, once peeled, would have appeared similar to the coloration of the animals that Laban has removed from the flock. Moreover, Jacob puts the branches in front of only the fittest and presumably distinctively colored animals, thus enhancing the quality of his flock. He does not put them in front of the weaker and presumably white animals, which means that Laban's flock includes less vigorous animals. (The meaning of 30:40a is unclear.) The chapter concludes with a reprise about Jacob's wealth. It clearly reflects similar claims about those of his forebears (cf. 12:16), since up to this point in the Jacob-Laban narrative, there is no reference to male slaves, camels, and donkeys. This listing of Jacob's property sets the stage for a complaint made about Jacob's wealth by Laban's sons (31:1).

Genesis 31:1–55
Jacob and Laban Resolve Their Conflict

This chapter, along with the two preceding ones, belongs to the three-chapter-long narrative of Jacob's sojourn with Laban. According to Gen 29, Jacob arrives in the land of the Easterners alone and without property, marries two women, and begins to have children. In Gen 30, the narrator reports the growth of his household and wealth. Then Gen 31 provides an extended narrative about his departure from Laban and the complications that it involves. A preponderance of dialogues and long speeches dominate this chapter. By the end of the chapter, Jacob has successfully disengaged from Laban.

Genesis 31 is a remarkable tale of duplicity: Laban deceives Jacob, Rachel deceives Laban, and Jacob deceives Laban. There is potential for violence, but the story ends with an accommodation, the creation of a covenant that separates and protects the two parties. The chapter also provides a narrative that attests to the differences between the worlds of Laban and Jacob: different territories, different deities, different languages—differences that manifest themselves in the distinction between Israelites and Aramaeans.

> 31:1 He [Jacob] heard what Laban's sons had been saying, "Jacob has
> taken everything that belonged to our father. He has gained all of this
> wealth from what belonged to our father." 2 Moreover, Jacob understood
> that Laban no longer liked him, in contrast to what had formerly been the
> case. 3 YHWH said to Jacob, "Return to the land of your forebears and of
> your relatives! I will be with you." 4 So Jacob summoned Rachel and Leah
> to the field where he had his flock. 5 He said to them, "I understand that
> your father no longer likes me, in contrast to what was formerly the case.
> Nonetheless, the God of my father has been with me. 6 You know that I
> worked for your father as hard as I could. 7 Though your father cheated me
> and changed my wages ten times, God did not allow him to hurt me. 8 If
> he said, 'The speckled will be your wages,' then all the flock gave birth to
> speckled animals. And if he said, 'The striped will be your wages,' all the
> flock bore striped animals. 9 In this way, God has taken the flock of your
> father and given it to me.

10 "Once, during the mating season, I had a dream and saw that the male goats mounting [females of] the flock were striped, speckled, and spotted. 11 The messenger of God said to me, 'Jacob.' I said 'Yes.' 12 He said, 'Look up and see that all the male goats that are mounting the flock are striped, speckled, and mottled. I have seen everything that Laban has been doing to you. 13 I am the God of Bethel, the place at which you anointed a stela and made a vow to me. Now get up and leave this land and go to the land where you were born.'" 14 Rachel and Leah responded and said to him, "Do we still have any property or an inheritance in our father's household? 15 Haven't we been treated as foreigners? He has wasted the money given for us. 16 All the riches that God has taken from our father now belong to us and to our children. So do whatever God has told you to do."

17 So Jacob got up and put his children and wives on the camels. 18 He drove all his livestock and all the property[a] that he had acquired in Paddan-Aram in order to go to Isaac, his father, in the land of Canaan.

19 Now when Laban had gone to shear his flock, Rachel stole the teraphim that belonged to her father. 20 Jacob deceived Laban,[b] the Aramaean, because he did not tell him he was going to leave so quickly. 21 So, he left quickly with all that belonged to him. He started out, crossed the Euphrates,[c] and set out for the mountainous terrain of Gilead.

22 When, after three days, Laban learned that Jacob had left quickly, 23 he took his relatives with him and pursued him for seven days until he caught up with him in the mountainous terrain of Gilead. 24 (God had appeared to Laban, the Aramaean, in a dream at night and said to him, "Be careful about what you say to Jacob, whether favorable or unfavorable.")

25 Laban caught up with Jacob. Now Jacob had pitched his tent in mountainous terrain. So Laban and his kinsmen camped in the mountainous terrain of Gilead. 26 Laban said to Jacob, "What have you done? You have deceived me by driving away my daughters like captives of war.[d] 27 Why did you leave quickly in secret? You deceived me and didn't let me know. I would have given you a joyful send-off with the music of tambourine and lyre. 28 I was denied the chance to kiss my sons and daughters goodbye. You have acted foolishly. 29 I have the power to harm you severely, but the God of your father said to me last night, 'Be careful what you say to Jacob, whether favorable or unfavorable.' 30 You have gone because you really longed for your father's household, but why did you steal my gods?" 31 Jacob answered Laban, "Because I was afraid, since I thought you would take your daughters away from me. 32 Whomever you find with your gods will not remain alive. With your kinsmen, investigate for yourself to see what is here with me. Take what might be yours." Jacob did not know that Rachel had stolen them.

33 Laban went into Jacob's tent and into Leah's tent and into the tent of the two maidservants, but he did not find anything. So he left Leah's tent and went into Rachel's tent. 34 Now Rachel had taken the teraphim and put them in the camel's saddlebag and was sitting on them. Laban rummaged through the tent but could not find anything. 35 Rachel said to her father, "My lord, don't be angry with me, because I'm unable to get up. I'm having my period." So, he searched thoroughly but could not find the teraphim.

36 Jacob got angry and quarreled with Laban. He said to Laban, "What is my offense? What is my sin for which you are pursuing me so intently? 37 You have searched everything, and what have you found that belongs to your household? Put it here in front of my family and your family so they may decide between the two of us. 38 For twenty long years I was with you. Your ewes[e] and female goats didn't miscarry. And I didn't eat any rams from the flock. 39 I didn't bring to you any killed by wild animals. I took the loss myself. You required compensation from me for any stolen during the day or at night. 40 This is how it was for me: during the day, the heat devoured me; during the night, cold did the same: I was unable to sleep. 41 These twenty years I have been in your household. I worked fourteen years for your two daughters and six years for your livestock. Moreover, you changed my wages ten times. 42 Had not the God of my father, the Fear of Isaac, been with me, you would have sent me with nothing. But God knew about my plight and everything that I had done and vindicated me last night."

43 Then Laban answered Jacob, "The daughters belong to me; the children belong to me; and the flocks belong to me. Everything you see is mine. But what I can do now about my daughters or the children they have borne? 44 Come now, let's you and I create a covenant. It will be a witness between you and me." 45 So Jacob took a stone and erected it as a stela. 46 Jacob said to his relatives, "Gather some stones!" So they gathered stones and made a pile. They ate a meal there at the pile. 47 Laban named it "Yegar-sahadutha,"[f] whereas Jacob named it "Galeed."[g] 48 Laban said, "This pile is a witness today between me and you." Therefore, he named it both "Galeed" 49 and "the Mizpah"[h] because he said, "May YHWH be a lookout between me and you when we are distant from each other. 50 If you oppress my daughters or if you marry women other than my daughters, even though no one is with either of us, know that God is a witness between me and you."

51 Laban continued speaking to Jacob, "Look at this pile and this stela, which I have set up between me and you. 52 This pile is a witness, and the stela is a witness, attesting that I should not cross beyond the pile to you, and you should not cross beyond the pile—or the stela—to cause

harm. 53 May the God of Abraham and the God of Nahor—the God of
their father—execute justice between us." Jacob swore by the Fear of his
father Isaac. 54 Jacob offered a sacrifice on the mountain. He invited his
relatives to have a meal, so they ate a meal together and spent the night
on the mountain.

55 Laban got up early in the morning, kissed his children and daughters, and blessed them. Then he left to return to his own place.[i]

a. In MT, "livestock, his possession" is a dittography.
b. Literally, "stole the heart of Laban."
c. MT, "the river."
d. Literally, "captives of sword."
e. The Hebrew word for "ewe" (*rāḥēl*) is identical to "Rachel."
f. Aramaic for "the heap of witness."
g. Hebrew for "pile of witness."
h. Hebrew for "lookout post."
i. Gen 32:1 in the MT.

[31:1–18] The first portion of the chapter develops a complex rationale for Jacob and his family to leave Paddan-Aram. Jacob learns that Laban's sons think he has acquired wealth that has earlier been Laban's. He also intuits that Laban no longer likes him. Moreover, in an abrupt report, the deity commands Jacob to return to his own country and family. In sum, the author wants to make clear that Jacob has multiple reasons for leaving Laban's land.

Jacob initiates his departure by summoning Rachel and Leah away from their home and into a field. His speech (vv. 5–13) to them develops this rationale by reiterating Jacob's perception that Laban no longer likes him and by adducing a report about Laban's having cheated him, yet another reason to leave. In 31:7–9, the narrator provides more information about Laban's deceitful behavior toward Jacob: changing wages in the form of different livestock. Interestingly, the statement in verse 9, "God has taken the flock of your father and given it to me," confirms the claim of Laban's sons (v. 1). Verses 10–12 revert to the report and refer to the events before the deity's speech in verse 9. Reference to the deity's protection of Jacob (v. 7) foreshadows Jacob's claim about help from the deity in verse 42. In verse 12, the narrator uses the word "see" in two senses: Jacob "sees" the flock in a dream, and God "sees" Jacob's plight. Within the dream, Jacob hears the deity speak self-referentially, though in an awkward formulation: "the God of Bethel" (v. 13). Reference to this toponym underscores that the deity is "at home" at Bethel, a city toward which Jacob should now travel. The mention of Bethel offers yet another reason for Jacob to leave Paddan-Aram. Jacob's speech appeals to his own hard work, to God's protection of him, to the divinely influenced breeding behavior of Laban's flock, and to the definitive presence of God at Bethel.

Rachel and Leah respond by offering their perspective as Laban's daughters, which complements the perspective of Laban's sons (v. 1). They pose two rhetorical questions, an asseveration and an imperative admonition, the latter complementing the deity's command to Jacob. The argument that undergirds the questions presupposes customs and financial transactions that have not been an overt part of the narrative. Their only inheritance has been Laban's "gift" of Zilpah to Leah and Bilhah to Rachel. The agreement between Laban and Jacob refers to Jacob's servitude, not to payment. One might infer that the wives complain that the property created by Jacob through animal husbandry came to Laban, whereas a portion should have been given to them as a dowry. Also, they seem to agree with their brothers that Jacob has secured some of their father's property; unlike their brothers, they do not blame Jacob but instead attribute that transfer of property to divine initiative (v. 16). In fact, they claim that, insofar as Jacob has acquired the property, it now belongs to them and their children, a claim that serves as a corrective to Jacob's statement that the property belongs to him (v. 9). From this perspective, God has righted the wrong done to them by their father. As a result, they are willing to leave as Jacob does what God has commanded him to do. In fact, they *order* him to do so. The narrator then reports that Jacob takes his wives, his children, his livestock, and other property and leaves Paddan-Aram.

[19–42] The next portion of the narrative begins with a startling flashback, to a time before Jacob's departure. The flashback helps explain why he is able to leave: Laban is away from his home. His absence makes it possible not only for Jacob to make preparations to leave but also for Rachel to steal her father's teraphim. Moreover, the narrator characterizes Jacob's hasty departure as deceitful. The departure therefore involves both deceit and theft. The description of Laban as an Aramaean enhances the notion of his emerging "difference" from Jacob and his daughters, who are now being treated as foreigners.

Teraphim are referred to elsewhere in the OT, most notably in Judg 17–18 and 1 Sam 19:13–16, where they clearly are physical objects. In 1 Samuel, they can approximate the presence of a human figure. Both Jacob (Gen 31:32) and Laban (v. 30) refer to them as "gods." And in the prophetic corpus, teraphim appear as media for divination (Ezek 21:21; Zech 10:2). They clearly are ritual objects of great value. However, it remains unclear why Rachel wants them. These teraphim play no role beyond the confines of Gen 31. They do, however, play a very important literary role in Gen 31. The search for them prompts Jacob to make an unknowing threat to Rachel when he says that whoever has taken the teraphim will die. They allow Rachel to "trick" her father by falsely claiming that she is having her period so that he cannot search the saddlebag on which she is sitting and into which she has put the teraphim. When Laban is unable to find them, Jacob becomes angry and throws down a challenge to Laban (vv. 36–42), to which Laban can offer no vigorous rhetorical response.

Jacob's strategic departure, which has given him a good head start, enables him to reach the mountainous terrain in an area known as Gilead, which lies east of the Jordan River. He has come close to reaching the "land of Canaan" but is not quite there when Laban and his relatives reach him. Their encounter is prefaced by a dream reported by the omniscient narrator. God intervenes with Laban, warning him to speak carefully with Jacob, an admonition that Laban reports to Jacob when they meet (v. 29) and to which Jacob refers (v. 42).

Instead of a physical fight, Laban and Jacob joust verbally. Laban begins with a long speech (vv. 26–30), which is replete with interrogative rhetoric. He asks three questions, two of which pose the essential question, "Why?" as in "Why did you leave in haste?" and "Why did steal my gods?" Whether or not Laban would have created a going-away celebration, as he claims, remains ambiguous. Laban even appears to sanction Jacob's departure (v. 30), when he admits that Jacob longs to be with his family of origin. Jacob defends himself by saying that he has feared Laban would take his daughters away from him. Then he goes on the attack with an oath condemning anyone who might have taken Laban's gods, an oath that really functions as an asseveration that no one in Jacob's retinue has taken those gods. The narrator then reports Laban's search for the teraphim. In these verses, the narrative slows down, creating tension as Laban moves from one tent to the next while trying to locate the stolen property. He fails to find them due to Rachel's false report that she is menstruating. Verse 35 provides an interesting perspective on Rachel's relationship with her father, as she calls him "my lord." This is the person whom she and Leah have earlier said was treating them as foreigners (v. 15).

After Laban fails to find the teraphim, Jacob launches into the longest speech in the chapter (vv. 36–42). His response is of two parts. In the first (vv. 36–37), he asks Laban to identify what he has done wrong and challenges Laban to present anything that Laban can identify as his own. Jacob therefore moves beyond the search for teraphim to claim that no one of his retinue has taken anything that belongs to Laban. In the second part, he appeals to the time that he spent with Laban, a time during which he labored heroically and with great hardships on behalf of Laban's flocks. He even adduces a new chronology, adding six years of service to gain the flocks to the fourteen years he worked for Leah and Rachel. He even accuses Laban of cheating on Jacob's wages (v. 41), a charge he has reported earlier to Leah and Rachel (v. 7). (This charge may reflect Laban's behavior in 30:35–36.) He concludes by making a theological claim that if God had not responded to his mistreatment, he would have nothing and, further, he affirms that God has continued to act by warning Laban during the preceding night's dream (vv. 29, 42).

[43–55] Since the verbal jousting has produced something of a draw, with no clear way forward, Laban moves the confrontation to a solution. In a striking hyperbolic claim, Laban responds by denying Jacob and his daughters' claims about who is the rightful owner of the flocks and of Laban's daughters. He is no longer negotiating about receiving his property but rather proposes a solution that will avoid violence and create a legal standoff. He proposes the creation of a covenant between himself and Jacob. The word "between" is key. Elsewhere in the non-Priestly literature in Genesis, a covenant is "with" another party (Gen 15:18). This covenant is "between" Laban and Jacob. As the scene develops, there is ambiguity about what counts as the witness. Initially, it is the covenant. But in 31:50, God is the witness. And in verse 48, the heap of stones, perhaps an altar (cf. Josh 22:26–27), functions as a witness. (Cf. Josh 24:27, a text that describes one stone as a witness to the covenant between God and Israel.) The covenant between Laban and Jacob is something of an amalgam of covenant traditions: deity, stones, stelae, and oath.

In verses 44–50, Laban is the speaker, the one who proposes the creation of a covenant and the one who formulates an oath, one that expressly forbids Jacob from harming Laban's daughters or from taking additional wives. Jacob, in contrast, is the doer. He takes a stone and erects it as a stela (v. 45), as he has done earlier at Bethel (28:18). He also orders his family to collect stones and make a pile of them (v. 46).

During the creation of the covenant, the narrator emphasizes that Jacob and Laban belong to two worlds of increasing difference. Laban names the heap using Aramaic words, whereas Jacob uses Hebrew vocabulary (v. 47). Though the phrases have the same meaning, this difference in language, not just dialect, signifies an emerging cultural gulf between these two families. They now belong to distinct linguistic realms. The author does, however, show Laban to be "multilingual" since he uses Hebrew words to label the heap of stones and the stela (vv. 48–49). That phrasing continues to emphasize the notion of the covenant as something "between" them.

In the final portion of the chapter (vv. 51–55), Laban continues to be the primary speaker while the narrator no longer gives voice to Jacob. Laban's final speech (vv. 51–53) concludes the creation of the covenant that he has proposed. Interestingly, he now claims to have erected the stela and the pile of stones, a statement consistent with his earlier assertion that everything really belongs to him (v. 43). He construes them as boundaries, territorial markers, between the two protagonists. Neither should cross "to cause harm." This boundary reinforces the notion of difference expressed in the different names for the heaps of stones.

Verse 53 presents the oath sworn by both parties. The literary context presents Laban as the speaker, though the speech includes a later author's note, explaining the identity of the God of Nahor as the tutelary deity of Laban's lineage. The narrator also supplements the original speech by reporting that Jacob (also) swears by "the Fear of his father Isaac," the word "fear" referring specifically to the deity associated with Isaac and not with Abraham. (Cf. Gen 15:1 for the possible name of the god of the father associated with Abraham, "the Shield," as well as the formulation in 32:9, which appears to distinguish these two tutelary deities.) References to the God of Abraham and to the God of Nahor, as well as the name of Isaac's God, complement the earlier differences of language and territory, helping forge the cultural identities of these two groups.

The following verse (v. 54) is ambiguous in two ways. It may or may not refer to a meal associated with the making of a covenant (cf. Exod 24:11). Much depends upon whether or not one construes "his relatives" to include Laban and his kinsmen, the second ambiguity. When in verse 46 the narrator refers to Jacob's relatives, that group almost certainly does not include Laban and his kin. The same may well be the case in verse 54. The next verse (31:55 NRSVue = 32:1 MT) makes clear that, regardless of the aforementioned ambiguities, in the morning Laban is able to kiss his daughters and grandchildren, as he has hoped to do (so v. 28). He then blesses them and returns to his home.

Genesis 32:1–32
Jacob Wrestles with a "Man"

This chapter includes two "moments" during Jacob's return from his sojourn with Laban. The first involves Jacob's preparations for his encounter with Esau, prefaced by Jacob's encounter with "messengers from God." (Reference to two camps [vv. 2, 7] may explain why verses 1–2 are prefixed to the rest of the chapter.) After that encounter, Jacob decides to use the strategies of a gift, prayer, and flattery to appease Esau. The second moment is tied to the first by reference to nighttime (vv. 13, 21); the connotation of darkness heightens the expectation of drama as the two brothers approach each other. The second moment features Jacob's physical engagement with "a man." The chapter is, therefore, bracketed by two mysterious encounters between the world of the divine and Jacob: the deity's encampment and the preternaturally powerful adversary.

The MT of Gen 31 contains fifty-four verses. The first verse of Gen 32 in the MT is cited as 31:55 in most English translations (as cited here).

32:1 While Jacob went on his way, messengers from God confronted him.
2 When Jacob saw them, he said, "This is the encampment of God." So
he named that place, "Two Camps."

3 Jacob sent messengers ahead of him to Esau his brother—to the
country of Seir, the land Edom. 4 He ordered them, "You must say this
to my lord, to Esau: This is what your servant Jacob has to say, 'I have
stayed with Laban up until now. 5 I now own oxen, donkeys, flocks, male
and female slaves. I'm telling you so that you will view me favorably.'"[a]

6 When the messengers returned to Jacob, they said, "We met your
brother Esau. He's coming to meet you, and he has four hundred men
with him." 7 Jacob was frightened and became anxious. So he divided
the people who were with him, along with the flocks, herds, and camels,
into two camps. 8 He thought to himself, "If Esau comes to one camp
and decimates it, then those who are left in the other camp will survive."

9 Jacob said, "O God of my father Abraham and God of my father
Isaac, YHWH who spoke to me, 'Return to your land and to your relatives; I will deal well with you.' 10 I am so unimportant when compared
to all the good and faithful things that you have done for your servant. I

had only a walking stick when I crossed the Jordan. And now I own two camps. 11 Please save me from the power[b] of my brother Esau because I fear him; he might come and kill the mothers and children. 12 You have said, 'I will certainly deal well with you and make your progeny like the grains of sand on the seashore, which are impossible to count since they are so numerous.'"

13 Jacob spent that night there. [In the morning] he took a gift for his brother Esau from what he had there: 14 two hundred female goats, twenty male goats, two hundred ewes, twenty rams, 15 thirty camels giving milk and their calves, forty cows, ten bulls, twenty female donkeys, and ten male donkeys. 16 He handed them over to his servants, each herd by itself, and he said to his servants, "Go ahead of me. Leave room between each of the herds." 17 He ordered the first one, "If when Esau my brother meets you and asks you 'To whom do you belong? Where are you going? To whom do these ahead of you belong?' 18 then you should say, 'They belong to your servant Jacob. It is a gift sent to my lord. He [Jacob] is right behind us.'" 19 He also ordered the second one, the third one, and those coming after the flocks, "This is how you should address Esau when you have found him. 20 And you should also say, 'Your servant Jacob is right behind us.'" He thought to himself, "I can appease him with the gift that is going ahead of me. Maybe he will deal favorably with me." 21 So though the gift went on ahead of him, he spent that night in the camp.

22 He got up during that night and took his two wives, his two maids, and his eleven sons and crossed the ford of the Jabboq. 23 He took them and sent them across the stream along with everything that he had. 24 Jacob was left alone. A man wrestled with him until dawn. 25 When he saw that he could not overpower him, he jabbed his hip and dislocated Jacob's hip while he wrestled with him. 26 He said, "Let me go since day is breaking." He [Jacob] replied, "I won't let you go until you bless me." 27 So he said to him, "What is your name?" He replied, "Jacob." 28 Then he said to him, "You won't be called Jacob anymore. You will be Israel since you have contended with God and with humans and won." 29 Then Jacob asked him, "Tell me your name." He replied, "Why do you want to know my name?" Then he blessed him there. 30 Jacob named the place Peniel, thinking "I have seen God face-to-face and escaped alive." 31 The sun shone on him as he left Peniel; he was limping because of his hip. 32 Therefore, Israelites even now do not eat the tendon that is attached to the hip because he jabbed his hip at the tendon.

a. Literally, "in order to find favor in your eyes."
b. Literally, "hand."

[32:1–21] The first moment during which Jacob prepares to meet Esau begins with a mysterious, two-verse confrontation between Jacob and "messengers from God." This is not the normal "messenger of YHWH" (e.g., Gen 16:7; 24:7, 40; 31:11). The Hebrew phrase translated "confronted" can refer to an attack (e.g., Amos 5:19), though that is probably not the case here. The author pays less attention to the character of the encounter and focuses instead on providing an etiology for the toponym "Two Camps."

The reference to messengers of God belongs to the same world as that attested in Gen 28. (These two chapters are the only instances in which the phrase "messengers of God" appears in the OT, though the notion of a divine plurality, as in "the sons of the gods" [Gen 6:1–4] or the divine council [1 Kgs 22], clearly reflects a similar mindset.) In both Gen 28 and 32, the author identifies the place where Jacob encounters this collective deity. This similarity may suggest that one function of the reports is to memorialize a site at which an unusual epiphany took place. In neither case does the presence of the messengers appear threatening or disturb the natural order, as would be the case with a theophany (e.g., Judg 5:4–5; Ps 18:7–15; Hab 3:3–15). Since there is reference to a plurality of human messengers (32:3), an editor may have prefixed Gen 32:1 due to this plural use of "messengers."

The author identifies numerous strategies that Jacob will use in order to survive: flattery of Esau, tactical division of those with him, strategic prayer, and gifting. Jacob's opening gambit is a speech attesting to his wealth. It remains unclear why Esau would view Jacob favorably due to his holdings in domestic animals and slaves. Perhaps the very fact of his providing this information to Esau will redound to his favor, as opposed to Esau finding it out on his own. The narrator does not report the encounter between Jacob's messengers and Esau. Instead, after this narrative gap between verses 5 and 6, they tell him that Esau is on his way with four hundred men. If Jacob has a large household, Esau has a personal army. This communication between the brothers at a distance foreshadows their personal encounter and dialogue. Here, the threat of a forcible encounter, unlike verse 1, is palpable. As a result, Jacob devises a strategy of dividing his herds and those who are with him (no longer just slaves, so v. 5), into two camps (the same word that appeared in v. 1, suggesting again a rationale for the juxtaposition of these two scenes). Here the narrator reveals Jacob's interior life: he "thinks to himself": in both verses 8 and 20, the narrator depicts a person plotting carefully his strategy for dealing with Esau.

Verse 5 introduces a phrase, "view favorably," which will reappear three times in the next chapter (33:8, 10, 15). By the end of that sequence, Jacob has made Esau feel that he (Esau) is being viewed favorably by Jacob, a surprising turnabout from Jacob's stated feelings of threat and fear. Verses 9–12 comprise an unusually long prayer, one that includes a number of rhetorical strategies: quoting the deity (v. 9) and, in so doing, holding God to account to "deal well with him"; attesting to Jacob's humility (v. 10); the plea that he and his family be saved from Esau; and a second quotation in which Jacob again holds the deity to his word. In both quotations, Jacob refers to his family. In verse 9 he alludes to his relatives, those who live in the land to which he is returning; in verse 12 he cites his progeny, whom God has promised will be as numerous as sand on the seashore, the first time this metaphor occurs in the narratives about Jacob (cf. Gen 22:17, where it is applied to Abraham's progeny; and 28:14, where Jacob's children are likened to the innumerable grains of dirt on the earth). This promise clearly cannot be fulfilled if Jacob's children (v. 11) are killed. The imperative plea for rescue in verse 11 appears in numerous psalms of petition (in NRSVue, e.g., Pss 31:2; 51:14; 59:2; 109:21). The prayer sits loosely in the narrative. It could have been placed after verse 8 or after verse 21, suggesting that it may be a later addition to the story.

Jacob's final ploy is that of a gift: a multitude of animals from his flocks (vv. 14–15). The use of a gift is inspired because it creates an obligation if it is not reciprocated. Jacob divides the animals into five groups (goats, sheep, camels, cattle, and donkeys), sending one after another with an explicit explanation: "They belong to your servant Jacob. It is a gift sent to my lord. He [Jacob] is right behind us." Jacob carefully uses the diction of "lord" and "servant" to elevate Esau, diction that inheres in Jacob's first speech to Esau (vv. 4–5). Absent, however, is the vocabulary used by the narrator in this scene: "brother" (vv. 13, 17). That familial vocabulary would have been counterproductive, reminding Esau of the fraught sibling relationship between them. The narrator underscores Jacob's sagacity when he describes the questions that Jacob predicts Esau will pose when he sees these animals.

Jacob's use of his servants, sent out to accompany the five flocks, delays the direct encounter between the two brothers and heightens the tension about what will happen. (The significance of his servants saying "he is behind" is obscure.) In verses 13–21, Jacob instructs his servants about how to address Esau, as in verses 3–5. In the former text, the narrator does not report what Esau said by way of response. In verse 17, Jacob himself imagines what Esau will say: "To whom do you belong? Where are you going? To whom do these ahead of you belong?" The questions are subtle. The narrator provides an answer only to the third one. The answer to the first one is surely "Jacob." Less clear is the answer to the second. According to the narrative, one might imagine "To meet you, Esau." The narrator offers a twofold answer to the third question: "They belonged to our master Jacob, but they are a gift to you, Esau." This answer emphasizes the importance of the gifting strategy (the word "gift" appears four times, in vv. 13, 18, 20, and 21). The final sentence of this moment highlights the role of gift qua gift, not the fact of its comprising multiple droves of livestock. That same sentence, along with verse 13, creates an envelope around the scene by means of the clause "He spent that night."

The action has slowed: all that happens in these verses takes place during one evening.

[22–32] The author/editor has created a brilliant literary setting for this remarkable episode. This scene both delays and sets the stage for Jacob's encounter with Esau. Moreover, the action is happening under cover of darkness: nighttime is the overt link between verses 21 and 22.

Verses 22–23 make clear that this episode, at least in its present form, has been composed with its current placement in mind. Jacob has already divided the herds and "the people" into two groups (v. 7). Now he attends to his immediate family, though Dinah, who will appear prominently in chapter 34, is not mentioned as a daughter. Although there is some ambiguity in the action—did Jacob accompany them across the river (v. 22) and then go back to the other side, or did he simply send them across the Jabboq (v. 23)?—the author makes clear that Jacob remains alone on the bank after his family has reached the other side.

As is typical of some biblical narratives, an initial sentence summarizes the action that follows: "A man wrestled with him until dawn." That is the capsule description of this episode. It is a physical encounter between two apparent humans. The Hebrew word for wrestle (*ʾabaq*) sounds like the word Jabboq. The Jabboq is a tributary that flows west into the Jordan River circa twenty-five miles north of where the Jordan empties into the Dead Sea. The actual location of this encounter may be less important than the assonance between the verb "wrestle" and the name of the river.

Verses 25–31 comprise the elaborated report, with a dietary etiology as a suffix (v. 32). Two elements intertwine in the report: physical engagement and dialogue. Why they wrestle in the first place is unclear. The word order, "the man wrestled with him [Jacob] until dawn," suggests that the man is the aggressor. In any case, the wrestling match sets up the conditions for the dialogue. When the man is unable to overpower Jacob, he injures him. Even after that, however, Jacob has not been defeated, so the man asks Jacob to let him go, the first instance of direct speech in these verses. (The notion of a character who must vanish at dawn appears in the text at this point.) Jacob demurs, saying he will only let the man go if the man blesses him. The imagery is almost comic: two individuals grappling with each other while discussing a blessing and names.

At this point, the dialogue pivots away from the language of blessing to that of names. Each character asks the other for his name. In the first instance, Jacob reveals his own name as Jacob, whereupon the man renames him "Israel," offering a popular etymology, deriving the name Israel from the Hebrew word *śrh*, to contend or to strive. This word occurs at only two places in the OT: Gen 32 and Hos 12:3–4. In both instances, it refers to Jacob's encounter with a person who represents the world of the divine.

The man defines "Israel" as meaning Jacob "contended with God." The name Israel, by itself and derived from that same word, could also mean "El contends." Moreover, the name Israel may derive from a different word, *śrh* II, in which case it would mean "El rules." A search for etymological origins is less important for understanding this text than is the recognition that Jacob is commended for his struggle, and that struggle is here defined as involving more than just the wrestling narrated in these verses. The man commends Jacob for struggling "with God and with humans." The humans are not identified, but one can imagine that the man refers at least to Esau and Laban. Jacob's life, involving many conflicts, is viewed positively by the man. (Hosea 12:2–4 also refers to Jacob's struggling with God/messenger. However, there the struggle is part of an indictment of Jacob for his misdeeds. That version of Jacob's biography probably predates the version in Genesis. The author of Gen 32 recasts the figure of Jacob into far more positive terms as his story seeks to portray Jacob as *the* progenitor of Israel. Jacob is not named Israel in Hosea 12. Instead, he is associated there with the name Ephraim.) Once he is renamed, Jacob says, using an imperative verb, "Tell me *your* name!" The man asks why he wants to know and avoids giving him a direct answer. Instead, he blesses Jacob, acceding to what Jacob has requested in verse 26. And with that, the encounter ends.

The denouement begins with an etiology for the toponym Peniel, which means "the face of God" (cf. the spelling "Peniel" in v. 31). Oddly, the notion of seeing God per se is not an issue in the story. Exodus 33:20 (and Isa 6:5) attests to the notion that seeing the deity means risking death, a conviction that lies behind Jacob's remark that he has seen God face-to-face and remained alive. This comment about seeing the face of God derives more from the name and etiology of Peniel than it does from the narrative itself. Only in verse 30, in a secondary etiology, does explicit reference to the deity appear. Read without this verse, the narrative is inherently ambiguous about the identity of "the man." The narrative admits that he is strong, though not strong enough to defeat Jacob; devious (the dislocation of Jacob's hip); and able to change a person's name as well as to offer a blessing. That conjunction of features may well explain why Hosea 12 characterizes his struggles as with God // messenger. Also present in the denouement is a dietary etiology (v. 32). New vocabulary occurs here: *gîd*, tendon, of the *nāšeh*, muscle. This dietary prohibition occurs nowhere else in the OT.

The denouement also includes a final comment about the just-concluded conflict. Jacob limps away from Peniel with the sun shining on him. Whether the man needs to vanish as the sun comes up, as one might expect, is left unsaid. The narrator focuses on the illumined and injured Jacob as he goes to face Esau. He has proved that he can surmount a godlike threat and is now ready to confront the threat posed by Esau.

It is impossible to read and reflect about 32:22–32 without recognizing that the author/editor who created the Jacob story has placed two nocturnal encounters with the deity at critical and parallel junctures. In Gen 28 Jacob envisions the world of the divine, receives a promissory note from God, and then negotiates by means of a vow that YHWH will, indeed, be his God. With such affirmations, Jacob proceeds to leave his family and country and to encounter Laban. In Gen 32, on his way back to the land and before he encounters Esau, he encounters a sole member of the divine world, whether the deity or a representative of the deity remains ambiguous, as it is in Hosea 12. He requests a blessing and receives one. In addition, he is given a new name, one that symbolizes his identity as the forerunner for Israel, its true eponymous ancestor.

Genesis 33:1–20
Jacob Encounters Esau

After seeing Esau, Jacob prepares for the encounter with his brother. In so doing, he adopts numerous strategies that may enable him to survive. He creates a staged presentation of his family. Thereafter, the two brothers engage in three spirited dialogues, with Esau initiating each one. Jacob manages Esau into accepting his gift and avoids allowing Esau either to accompany him or to station Esau's men with him. Jacob tries to deceive Esau by telling him that Jacob will meet him in Seir (south of the Dead Sea), a place that Jacob clearly has no intention of visiting. Gunkel (1997, 355) captures well the sense of the scene: "Jacob's sole concern is how he can quit his [Esau's] dangerous company." By the end of this chapter, the two brothers have reached an accommodation, resulting in their separation. Calling it a reconciliation (a position for which Westermann [1985, 530] advocates) overstates what has transpired between them. With the exception of 33:18–20, these verses stem from the pre-Priestly hand, although the divine name Elohim "God" has been introduced throughout.

> **33:1** Jacob looked up and saw that Esau was coming, and four hundred men were indeed with him. So he divided the children between Leah, Rachel, and the two maidservants. **2** He placed the maidservants with their children at the front, then Leah with her children, and finally Rachel and Joseph. **3** But he went on ahead of them and bowed down seven times as he approached his brother.
>
> **4** Esau hurried to meet him, embraced him—putting his arms around his neck—and kissed him, whereupon they wept. **5** Then he looked up and saw the women and the children and said, "Who are these with you?" He responded, "God has been gracious to me with these children of your servant." **6** The maidservants and their children approached and bowed down. **7** Then Leah and her children approached and bowed down, and then Joseph and Rachel approached and bowed down. **8** He said, "What do you mean with these flocks[a] that I have encountered?" He responded, "To find favor with you, my lord." **9** Esau said, "I have plenty, my brother. Keep it for yourself." **10** Jacob said, "No. If I have found favor with you,

accept my gift from me. I have seen your face, and it is like seeing the
face of God because you are pleased with me. 11 Take my gift[b] that was
sent to you because God has been gracious to me and because I have all
that I want." He urged him so that he took it.
12 Then he said, "Let's break camp and travel together. I'll accompany
you." 13 He responded to him, "My lord knows that the children are weak
and that the flocks and herds, which are nursing, are a worry for me. If
they are driven too hard, even for one day, all of the flocks will perish.
14 Let my lord go on ahead of your servant. I will lead ahead slowly,
based on the pace of the cattle that are ahead of me and on the pace of
the children, until I reach my lord in Seir."
15 Esau said to him, "Let me leave with you some of the people who
are with me," to which he responded, "Why do this if I have found favor
with you, my lord?" 16 So Esau returned that day on his way back to Seir.
17 But Jacob traveled toward Succoth. He built a house for himself and
constructed booths for his cattle. Therefore, the place is named Succoth.
18 Jacob came safely to the city of Shechem, which is in the land of
Canaan, on his way from Paddan-Aram. He camped outside the city.
19 From the sons of Hamor, the father of Shechem, he acquired a parcel
of land for one hundred qesitahs, where he had pitched his tent. 20 He built
an altar there and named it El Elohe Israel.[c]

a. Literally, "this company."

b. Literally, "my blessing." Cf. 1 Sam 25:27 for another case in which this noun is properly translated as "gift."

c. "God, the God of Israel."

[33:1–17] The narrative builds on details introduced in Gen 32, including the reference to four hundred men accompanying Esau (32:6). However, Jacob's division of those with him seems different from that reported in 32:7. There he divides the people into two groups, presumably half in one group, and half in another. But Gen 33:1 offers a different picture: four groups, one with each of the four women. Verse 2 suggests that each woman has charge of the children to whom she has given birth. That means six with Leah, two with Zilpah, two with Bilhah, and one with Rachel. The fact that Joseph is named—as opposed to mentioning him simply as "her son" or "her child"—betrays an interest in the status of Rachel as mother of the son whom Jacob will love more than any other of his siblings (so Gen 37:3) and foreshadows her role as mother of Benjamin.

This strategy mirrors that of Jacob's dividing up the herds into four groups: goats, sheep, cattle, and donkeys (ch. 32). In both cases, Jacob emphasizes the numbers and diversity of those involved, humans and animals. The obvious difference is that the humans are not offered as a present to Esau in Gen 33. As the chapter wears on, the prominence of children offers both evidence of God's grace (v. 5) and the basis for Esau's sympathy (v. 13).

Verses 3–7 comprise the account of not only the encounter between Jacob and Esau but also the place of the women and children in the proceedings. Jacob meets Esau and bows down seven times, action clearly symbolizing the putative difference in their respective statuses. The sevenfold repetition is probably both hyperbole and stereotypic. Reference to someone bowing down to their superior seven times appears as "a gesture of submission in the Amarna letters" (Speiser 1964, 259). The narrator reports a physical encounter: an embrace and weeping. The emotional world that lies behind the physical actions remains inchoate. Instead, Esau's gaze turns to the women and children. The fourfold presentation of those accompanying Jacob and of their bowing down reinforce Jacob's initial prostrations.

Verses 8–15 present the heart of the chapter: verbal combat between the brothers. There are three exchanges, each of which is introduced by Esau: verses 8–11, 12–14, 15. Esau is the initiator, both in their physical encounter and in their dialogues. In these verses, the subject shifts away from Jacob's wives and their children to Esau's earlier encounter with the flocks that Jacob has sent ahead. "This company" (v. 8) almost certainly refers to the herds that Jacob has intended as a gift. Jacob's response is oblique: he avoids mention of a gift at this point, though he continues addressing Esau as his "lord." Esau rejoins by refusing to accept the gift and by using kinship language, "my brother." As a result, Jacob's strategy of gifting is threatened. Jacob, therefore, demurs with a direct "No." He continues to use the motif of "finding favor" and now introduces the diction of a gift. Moreover, he introduces a metaphor, "seeing the face of God." To see the face of God regularly involves life-threatening danger (so 32:30!), and that notion surely lies behind Jacob's statement, even while Jacob suggests that Esau is pleased, or has shown favor, to Jacob. Jacob's well-crafted speech (vv. 10–11) results in Esau accepting the gift, a strategy that works to help secure Jacob's well-being. It is unclear whether the narrative presents Jacob giving Esau a gift/blessing as recompense for his having stolen Esau's blessing in Gen 27. In any case, the ploy of gifting appears to predominate. The narrator underscores the intensity of Jacob's rhetoric: "Jacob urged Esau."

In the second exchange (vv. 12–14), Esau presents an immediate threat. Jacob has hoped for disengagement, but Esau proposes to accompany Jacob. So Jacob must formulate yet another rhetorically compelling response, one that depends upon the presence of his children and herds (vv. 13–14). He aptly points out that they must travel slowly, more so than Esau was apparently willing to do. Esau has no retort. One should note the indirect imperative at the beginning of verse 14; Jacob is still speaking deferentially to Esau. However, Jacob also presents Esau with a false lead (v. 14), since Jacob surely does not plan on going to Seir (far to the south) even though he told Esau he would meet him there. This feature of the narrative, more than any other, suggests the remaining tension and conflict between two brothers.

Esau presents his final challenge to Jacob in verse 15. If Esau cannot accompany Jacob (v. 12), then Esau parries by suggesting that he leave some of his four hundred men with Jacob. Jacob answers with a question by reintroducing the diction of "finding favor," to which Esau can provide no answer. Jacob's posing the question "Why?" reveals the absence of a credible motive for Esau. With this silence, Esau departs, never to see his brother again until they bury their father (35:29).

This series of three verbal joustings concludes with Jacob having won the battle. A display of family and possessions, a gift, wit, and separation achieve Jacob's purposes. He survives the encounter with his brother and is therefore able to continue his journey, first to Succoth and then westward across the Jordan into the land of Canaan. The episode concludes with a popular etymology for the town of Succoth.

[18–20] These verses probably comprise a Priestly notice, reporting on Jacob's journey and his establishing a claim on the land. The Priestly author emphasizes that though Jacob is in the land of Canaan, he, like Abraham (Gen 23), acquires a legal foothold in the land. Reference to the sons of Hamor acknowledges the generational continuity of both the Canaanite and the Israelite groups. Both Shechem and Jacob can point to their fathers, Hamor and Isaac, respectively. Shechem bears two meanings here: urban entity and a forebear of Hamor. The names Shechem and Hamor appear in 34:2, which may explain the placement of 33:19 and chapter 34. Yet another of the El names, "El Elohe Israel," appears only here in Genesis. Altar construction will take place again at Bethel (35:1, 3). Abraham has purchased land for a tomb (Gen 23); now Jacob buys this plot to build an altar, which he names.

Genesis 34:1–31
Shechem Rapes Dinah, and Her Brothers Exact Revenge

Although the episode seems extraneous to the larger story of Jacob, it foreshadows his parental response to the familial crisis presented in the first chapter of the Joseph story. And it is the first instance in which the sons of Jacob, who are now grown, act. Hitherto, they have been only children. The episode is the first occasion in which a portion of Jacob's sons are singled out by name, a feature that will recur in Gen 37–50.

Two different groups are in play, the urban Shechemites and the pastoral Israelites. Both involve two generations: one of Hamor and Jacob, and the next involving their sons and daughters. The chapter's hallmark is violence. It commences with rape,[1] continues with self-mutilation by the males living in and around Shechem, and concludes with Simeon and Levi killing all the males who have circumcised themselves. The verb "take" (*lqḥ*), though it needs to be translated with different verbs in English, appears with striking frequency in the chapter (vv. 2, 4, 9, 16, 17, 21, 25, 26, 28). With only two exceptions, the object of the verb is a human being. Thus we may infer that one issue important to the author is the exercise of authority of one individual over another or one group over another.

This episode probably stems from the hand of an author otherwise unrepresented in Genesis (as with Gen 14). The chapter makes no reference to the deity, either as YHWH or God. In both chapters, 14 and 34, separate ethnic or tribal entities predominate. The level of internecine violence seems more at home in the book of Judges than in Genesis. Both texts refer to slaughter by the sword, though the word "sword" rarely appears in Genesis. The attack on a peaceable people is similar to the Danite attack on a peaceable city (Judg 18). One may theorize that the episode is tailored and introduced into Genesis to provide a warrant for the negative judgments about Simeon and Levi in Gen 49:5–7. There they are known to have used swords and to have acted violently.

1. There is some controversy over whether the biblical author is describing a rape in v. 2. Thus van Wolde (2002, 528–44), e.g., argues that the text does not; Scholz (2000) argues that it does. I agree with the latter position. Here versification for Gen 34 follows English versions.

Marriage outside the lineages of Israel is a central issue in the text. Deuteronomy 7, which also refers to the Canaanites and Perizzites, proscribes intermarriage with the native population. However, Gen 34 does not polemicize the Shechemites for having proposed intermarriage. Rather, the brothers act because their sister's honor has been violated. Family honor rather than intermarriage per se is at stake.

34:1 Dinah, the daughter of Leah whom she bore for Jacob, went out to see
the daughters of the land. **2** When Shechem, son of Hamor the Hivite, the
prince of the land, saw her, he grabbed and raped her.[a] **3** He subsequently
felt close to Dinah,[b] the daughter of Jacob. He loved the young woman
and spoke affectionately with her. **4** Shechem said to Hamor his father,
"Get this young woman to be my wife."

5 Now Jacob heard that he had violated Dinah, his daughter. Since his
sons were out in the field with his livestock, Jacob remained silent until
they came back. **6** Hamor, the father of Shechem, went out to talk with
Jacob. **7** Jacob's sons came back from the field. When they heard, the men
were outraged, violently angry. It is a sacrilege against Israel for someone
to have sex with the daughter of Jacob. Such simply is not done.

8 Hamor said to them, "My son Shechem loves your daughter. Please
give her to him as a wife. **9** Intermarry with us. Give us your daughters
and take our daughters for yourselves. **10** Live among us. The land will
be available for you. Live and roam through it. Acquire property in it."
11 Shechem said to her father and to her brothers, "If I have found favor
with you, whatever you ask of me I will give. **12** Set a very high bride-
price and gift, and I will provide whatever you ask of me. Just give the
young woman to me as my wife."

13 The sons of Jacob responded deceitfully to Shechem and to Hamor
his father because he had violated Dinah their sister. **14** They said to them,
"We are unable to do this thing, to give our sister to someone who is
uncircumcised. It would be a disgrace for us. **15** We could only agree
to this if you become like we are, if you circumcise every one of your
males. **16** Then we will give our daughters to you, take your daughters for
ourselves, live among you, and become one people. **17** But if you don't
respond to us and become circumcised, then we will take our daughter
and leave."

18 Their proposal seemed good to Hamor and to Shechem, the son
of Hamor. **19** The young man didn't hesitate to do it because he desired
the daughter of Jacob. He was more important than all the others in his
father's household. **20** Hamor and Shechem his son went to the gate of
their city and said to the men of their city, **21** "These men desire peace
with us. Let them live in the land and roam through it. The land is large

enough for them. Let us marry their daughters, and let us give them
our daughters. 22 The men will only agree to live among us, to be one
people, if all of our males are circumcised just as they are circumcised.
23 Won't we then own their livestock, their property, and all their [other]
animals? We only need to agree with them, and they will live among us."
24 Everyone who heard Hamor and Shechem his son responded favorably. All of them were circumcised, everyone who went out through the
gate of the city.

25 On the third day, when they were still in pain, two of Jacob's sons—
Simeon and Levi, Dinah's [full] brothers—took their swords and attacked
the peaceable city. They killed all the males. 26 They killed Hamor and
Shechem his son with the sword and took Dinah from Shechem's house
and left. 27 Jacob's [other] sons came upon those who had been slain and
plundered the city because they had violated their sister. 28 They took
their flocks, their herds, their donkeys, and whatever was in both the city
and the country. 29 They took their property and took captive all of the
little ones and their wives. They plundered all that was in their homes.
30 Then Jacob said to Simeon and Levi, "You have alienated me from
them, making me odious to those who live in the land, the Canaanites,
the Perizzites. I am outnumbered. If they conspire against me and attack
me, I and my household will be destroyed." 31 They responded, "Didn't
he treat our sister like a whore?"

a. Literally, "he grabbed her and lay with her and raped her."
b. Literally, "his soul was drawn to Dinah."

[34:1–4] Verse 1 sets the tone for this narrative that primarily narrates the action of men. Leah has given birth to a girl, Dinah, born "for" (or "to") Jacob. Verse 1 is the only moment in the chapter when women act as agents: Leah giving birth and Dinah going out to see other women. After verse 1, Leah disappears from the text, and Dinah is either the subject of conversation or taken from the home of Shechem. Her whereabouts thereafter do not concern the narrator. Dinah's excursion appears to be neighborly. The phrase "daughters of the land" picks up on 33:18, "the land of Canaan." As such, the text emphasizes that Jacob's family remains in a foreign land, despite the property that Jacob has just purchased (33:19). To that extent, the family is vulnerable.

Verses 1–4 exemplify classic, laconic Hebrew prose narrative. The critical action that creates the crisis takes place in just four verses. Moreover, these verses contain a jarring juxtaposition of moods, rape, and then apparent affection. After Shechem rapes Dinah, he speaks lovingly to her (cf. Hos 2:16 [14] for the same instance of a male speaking affectionately to a female, a scene in which YHWH comforts Israel after having uttered words of punishment to her). Shechem's feelings of affection result in his desire to marry Dinah. In Gen 34:4, the word "get" is the same Hebrew word translated "grabbed" in verse 2.

[5–12] Verses 5–7 explore the implications of the rape in the eyes of Jacob's household. The responses are strikingly different. Although Jacob learns about the rape, he says nothing until his sons return from the field. It is difficult to know if the narrator is faulting Jacob for his initial inaction. Beginning at this point, there appears to be an undertone of ritual diction in the chapter. In verse 5, *tm'* could be translated "make ritually impure," followed by reference to the blood rite of circumcision (v. 14). Verse 5 surely, though in an understated way, holds Jacob accountable for his silence (cf. Jacob's implied silence in Gen 35:22).

The narration seems disjointed in verse 6. Shechem's father Hamor appears (the phrase "went out" is the same phrase that appears in v. 1; it is clearly not as dangerous for Hamor to traverse his country as it has been for Dinah), apparently in response to his son's order (v. 4), but there is no reference to his interaction with Jacob. Instead, once Jacob's sons appear, *they* engage Hamor (v. 8). Jacob does not reappear until verse 30. Verse 7 offers an interesting choice of words. Jacob's sons are now "men," a fact that foreshadows the violence to come. The narrator offers a report about the angry response of the brothers rather than letting them speak directly. Interestingly, the word "Israel" is here used as a collective noun (v. 7), not a reference to Jacob. This usage reflects the move from family to nation that is occurring near the end of the book of Genesis. The brothers' anger apparently has more to do with Israel's honor being violated rather than the rape itself. The phrase "such simply is not done" is an appeal to propriety, to custom, again focusing the issue on a violation of communal norms rather than on the assault suffered by Dinah. As such, the phrase also appears in the scene in which Amnon rapes Tamar (2 Sam 13:12). Since the latter scene does not involve sex between an Israelite and a non-Israelite, the violation of customary behavior must involve sex that has not been legitimated by social norms, in the latter case a violation of norms against incest.

Verses 8–12 offer two speeches directed to the brothers, one by Hamor (vv. 8–10) and the other by Shechem (vv.11–12). The former restates the affection that Shechem feels for "your daughter," an odd circumlocution since Hamor is addressing her brothers. But the rhetoric makes sense given what follows: Hamor proposes the exchange of daughters in intermarriage. The verb "take" in verse 9 is the same as the one translated "grabbed" in verse 2. That proposal is enhanced with the inducements that the family of Jacob may live in the land and acquire property there. Shechem takes a different tack by offering to provide whatever bride-price the brothers suggest. (The practice of a bride-price is attested in the book of the covenant [Exod 22:16–17]; the law there regulates the behavior of a male who has "seduced" a virgin to whom he is not engaged. First Samuel 18:25 presents the case of a hyperbolic bride-price, 100 Philistine foreskins.)

[13–24] In verse 13, the narrator intrudes with an introductory summary of the brothers' speech that follows. That they speak "deceitfully" is less of a moral judgment and more of a signal that they are creating a plan to avenge the disgrace Dinah and they have suffered. The brothers offer a tactic for universal male circumcision so that the Shechemites may become eligible for intermarriage. (Yet such a plan would violate the norms articulated in Deut 7:3.) According to Gen 17:12–13, circumcision is expected of slaves and foreigners who are part of an Israelite household. It goes without saying that the author of Gen 34 knows the ritual of circumcision.) In 34:16 the notion of being "one people" is hyperbole; it is an idea neither suggested nor accepted by the Shechemites. The brothers' threat of "taking our daughter" (v. 17) rehearses the verb used of Shechem's "taking" of Dinah (v. 2).

Hamor and Shechem lead the negotiations with their countrymen. But even before they propose the plan to them, the narrator reports that Shechem is immediately circumcised (v. 19). Reference to Shechem's importance (v. 19) at this point in the narrative probably means that if he circumcises himself, one can expect others to follow suit. (The narrative sequence is odd: given the later report about the Shechemites being incapacitated after being circumcised, one does not expect Shechem to be going to the gate with his father in v. 20.) His rationale is affection for "Jacob's daughter." In verse 23, it is clear that another rationale emerges for the Shechemites: the ability to gain the property of Jacob's household. Shechem's rationale is, by contrast, "untainted." That the city gate is the place for the intra-Shechemite conversation underscores the seriousness, even legality, of the deliberations (cf. the negotiations in the city gate in Ruth 4). Hamor and Shechem literally speak with one voice to the effect that the citizenry agrees, and all males are circumcised. In sum, by the end of verse 24 both sides have acted with duplicity: the Israelites have proposed comity but have managed to have the Shechemites injure themselves, an act that will lead to their slaughter; and the Shechemites have agreed in the hopes of plundering the Israelites.

[25–31] With the brothers' plan in place, two of them (Dinah's full brothers) kill the incapacitated Shechemite males. To attack a "peaceable city" is similar to the violence narrated in the Danite attack with swords against Laish (Judg 18:27). Simeon and Levi are the perpetrators since they, like Dinah, were born to Leah. But Leah also bore Reuben, Judah, Issachar, and Zebulun. One might have expected Reuben to take the lead since he was the firstborn of Dinah's brothers. Once the Canaanite males are dead, the rest of Jacob's sons, not just those born to Leah, ravage the city, taking plunder of animals, property, and people (children and the widows of those who have just been killed). The participation of all the sons is appropriate since "the sons of Jacob" collectively have been speaking deceitfully to Hamor and Shechem. What the Shechemites have been planning to do to the Israelites, take their flocks and their property, the Israelites now do to the Shechemites. Jacob's response jumps back to the action of Simeon and Levi (v. 30). (He does not mention the plundering by his other sons.) He does not critique them for acting deceitfully or for the brutal slaughter, but rather for endangering him and his household. Now that the Shechemites are no longer a threat, Jacob worries about the larger groups of Canaanites and Perizzites, who have not been previously cited in this narrative.

The concluding portion of the chapter's focus on Simeon and Levi is surely related to the poem in 49:5–6. There, too, Leah's sons head the list of Jacob's sons (vv. 3–15). Each son receives a comment except for Simeon and Levi, who are cited together. They are known for violence with their swords. Verse 6 refers to their killing men and hamstringing oxen. Only the former is attested in Gen 34, which suggests that the poem knows another and likely older tradition about their violent ways. The author of Gen 34 likely includes reference to Simeon and Levi to help the chapter fit within other portions of Genesis (ch. 49). This suggests that chapter 34 was a relatively late addition to Genesis.

Genesis 35:1–29
Jacob Buries Rachel, after Which Isaac Dies

Genesis 35 is a miscellany, offering reports about the creation/naming of ritual sites, the naming of people, notes about death and burial, references to diverse places, and a genealogy. There is a striking number of toponyms, the presence of which lay claim to the breadth of the land that Israel will claim as its own. Bethel receives pride of place; Jacob both names it and then leaves it. The first fifteen verses offer much of what the Priestly author has to say about Jacob. In this author's eyes, Jacob is a righteous and obedient character, not the hard-bargaining and vigorous person in the pre-Priestly narrative.

35:1 God said to Jacob, "Get up and go to Bethel. Reside there and make
an altar to the God who appeared to you when you fled from your brother
Esau." 2 So Jacob said to his household and all who were with him, "Get
rid of the foreign gods that you have. Purify yourselves and change your
clothes. 3 Let's get up and go to Bethel. I will make an altar there to the
God who responded to me when I was having a difficult time, the one
who was with me on my journey." 4 They gave to Jacob all the foreign
gods that they had along with their earrings, whereupon he buried them
under the oak that was at Shechem.

5 As they traveled, a divine terror struck the surrounding cities so
that they didn't pursue the sons of Jacob. 6 Jacob and all who were with
him came to Luz, that is Bethel, which was in the land of Canaan. 7 He
built an altar there and called the place El Bethel because God had been
revealed to him there when he fled from his brother. 8 Rebekah's nurse
Deborah died and was buried under an oak, just down from Bethel. He
named it Allon-Baccuth.[a]

9 God appeared again to Jacob when he left Paddan-Aram, and he
blessed him. 10 God said to him, "Your name will no longer be Jacob;
your name will be Israel." So he was renamed Israel. 11 God said to him,
"I am El Shaddai.[b] Be fertile and become numerous. A nation, even a
group of nations, will come from you. Kings will descend directly from
you.[c] 12 The land that I gave to Abraham and to Isaac I will also give to
you; and I will give it to your progeny after you." 13 God then went up

from the place where he had spoken with Jacob.[d] **14** Jacob erected a stela
at the place where God[e] had spoken with him, a stone stela, and he poured
a drink offering on it and anointed it with oil. **15** Jacob named the place
where God had spoken with him Bethel.

16 Then they traveled from Bethel. When they were still far from Ephrath, Rachel went into labor as she was about to give birth. **17** When her
labor was especially difficult, the midwife said to her, "Don't worry;
you will have another son." **18** As she was losing consciousness—she
was dying—she named him Ben-oni,[f] whereas his father called him
Benjamin.[g] **19** Then Rachel died and was buried on the way to Ephrath,
that is, Bethlehem. **20** Jacob erected a stela at her tomb; it has been a stela
for Rachel's tomb up until today. **21** Israel traveled on and pitched his tent
near the tower of Eder.

22 While Israel lived in that land, Reuben went and slept with Bilhah,
the secondary wife of his father. Israel heard about it.

Jacob had twelve sons: **23** The sons of Leah: Reuben (Jacob's firstborn), Simeon, Levi, Judah, Issachar, and Zebulun. **24** The sons of Rachel:
Joseph and Benjamin. **25** The sons of Bilhah, Rachel's maid: Dan and
Naphtali. **26** The sons of Zilpah, Leah's maid: Gad and Asher. These are
the sons of Jacob who were born to him in Paddan-Aram.

27 Jacob came to Isaac his father at Mamre, that is, Kiriat-Arba or
Hebron, where Abraham and Isaac had lived as resident aliens. **28** Isaac
lived 180 years. **29** Isaac took his last breath and died. Old and after a full
life, he was gathered to his people. His sons Esau and Jacob buried him.

a. "Oak of Weeping."
b. Traditionally, "God Almighty." Literally, "Mountainous El."
c. Literally, "will descend from your lower abdomen."
d. Literally, "him."
e. Literally, "he."
f. "Son of my mourning."
g. "Son of the right."

[35:1–8] According to the report featured in 33:18–20, Jacob has purchased land and established a temporary residence at Shechem. In Gen 35, however, the Priestly writer offers a rationale for his departure from that place. God commands Isaac to travel to Bethel and live there, not just "camp" as earlier at Shechem. The Priestly author clearly knows the earlier account (Gen 28), according to which Jacob stays at Bethel after he leaves his home, fleeing from Esau. There is, however, no reference to Jacob's conditional vow (28:20–22). That report about Jacob stands in contrast to the idealized Priestly image of Jacob present in chapter 33. Instead, the Priestly writer describes Jacob constructing a new ritual installation, an altar.

Jacob responds to the command to go to Bethel by calling for a rite of purification. He mandates the disposal of "foreign gods," purification, and the changing of clothes. The Priestly writer almost certainly is familiar with the Deuteronomistic rhetoric present in Josh 24. There Joshua demands that the people "put away the foreign gods that are among you" (v. 23). Notably, this also takes place at Shechem. Moreover, earlier in that chapter, the Deuteronomistic author refers to a tradition that the veneration of foreign gods has been part of the religious practice of the patriarchs and matriarchs. The Priestly author is able to build on this tradition and, in so doing, explain how it is that one form of foreign gods, the teraphim that Laban characterizes as "my gods" (Gen 31:30) and that Rachel has stolen from Laban, are removed from Israelite possession. It is likely that the earrings (35:4) incorporated symbols of foreign deities.

The diction of purification (*ṭhr* in the hithpael, v. 2) is not limited to Priestly literature, though it is present there (Lev 14:4–31). Typically the discourse involves purifying the people from something, such as from the sin at Baal Peor, which has involved the veneration of foreign gods in Josh 22:17. In the consecration of the Levites, purification involves a change of clothing (Num 8:7). The author of Gen 35 is, therefore, more likely interested in describing the removal of the people's impurity than in describing eligibility for the move to Bethel. It is an overstatement to characterize that move as a pilgrimage since there is no indication that people will return to Shechem (or any other place). A pilgrimage, as understood by historians of religion, does not involve a permanent change of residence.

It is important to note that Jacob does not behave as Moses does when confronted with idolatrous behavior. Instead of destroying the objects, Jacob buries them at a ritual site, the oak at/near Shechem, a ritual site initially associated with Abraham (12:6). They are objects holy to a part of the Terah lineage and, therefore, require appropriate disposition. That they are buried fits well with the theme of burial elsewhere in this chapter (so vv. 8, 19, 29). Such disposition does not degrade the significance of Shechem as a shrine (so Josh 24).

Jacob is the only "patriarch" who erects stelae (Gen 28:18; 31:45; 35:14, 20), an act that is viewed as idolatrous in the book of Deuteronomy (16:22). Jacob's stelae are installed at places of diverse importance. They can identify the site of an epiphany or covenant making; they can mark a tomb. Both Abraham and Jacob built altars; only Jacob erects stelae.

The Priestly author's travel report emphasizes that God enables Jacob and his family to move safely from Shechem to Bethel. Genesis 35:6 fulfills the promise of the deity in 28:15 to bring Jacob back to the land. A "divine terror" prevents anyone from attacking them. The report culminates with Jacob's construction of an altar, as commanded by the deity at the outset of the chapter. Here again, the Priestly author construes Jacob to be an obedient hero, one who not only goes to Bethel and builds an altar there but also purifies the people before the trip, something the deity has not overtly commanded. He does more than he is required to do. What Jacob has called "the house of Elohim" in 28:17 now becomes "El Bethel" or "God of Bethel." Verse 7 works, as do verses 1, "when you fled from your brother Esau"; 9, "again"; and 13, "where he had spoken with him," to underscore the significance of this place as part of Jacob's prior history. These verses emphasize that Jacob has previously been at Bethel.

As befits the chapter as a miscellany, the Priestly author reports the death and burial of Rebekah's nurse Deborah; though known earlier (24:59), she has not been identified by name till now. For the author, this report is warranted due to the place of her burial—at Bethel, the significance of which has been reported in the prior verses. Again, burial is an important motif in the chapter.

[9–15] These verses from the Priestly author appear as a sequel to Jacob's having fulfilled the deity's command. Now at Bethel and with the altar built, God appears to Jacob "again," though this time not in a night vision. God blesses Jacob, gives him a new name (Israel), and reveals a new (to Jacob) divine name. Much of the deity's speech echoes the diction present elsewhere in the Priestly corpus: "Be fruitful and multiply." Jacob inherits the promises made to Abraham in Gen 17. In fact, these verses echo much from Gen 17. Abram receives a new name, Abraham. The deity appears as "God Almighty." Jacob is promised land and progeny. He is told that he will sire nations and that kings will stem from him. And the deity goes "up" from Abraham when God has finished speaking with him (17:22; 35:13). All these elements appear in both chapters 17 and 35. There are some subtle differences, however. In 17:6, the deity promises to make Abraham fruitful; in 35:11, God commands Jacob to "be fruitful and multiply," a clear citation of the Priestly version of creation (Gen 1:28). In Gen 17, God makes a covenant with Abraham and promises to bless Sarah and Ishmael, whereas in Gen 35, God blesses Jacob (v. 9). In sum, the Priestly author has taken pains to make clear that Jacob stands in the tradition of the covenant that God has made with Abraham. In the priests' eyes, Jacob is a character like the preternaturally obedient and righteous Abraham. However, the Priestly author does not explicitly identify Jacob as a covenant partner.

As if to create symmetry with Jacob's first visit to Bethel, the author reports that he erects a stela and pours oil on it, just as he does in 28:18. Bethel remains a place where God speaks with Jacob, but not a place known as "the house of God." Still, Jacob names the place Bethel (28:19). Thus concludes Jacob's residence at Bethel.

[16–21] The author's focus shifts from Jacob to Rachel and to the birth of Jacob's twelfth son. The family has moved southward from Bethel and encamped near Ephrath, a site identified with Bethlehem in 35:19 (so also in Gen 48:7). The midwife's response to Rachel's difficult labor, "Don't worry; you will have another son," seems like a non sequitur, as if fear of death can be assuaged by the birth of a male child. Following the birth of her son and her death, the Priestly author reports that the child has received two different names, which sound similar, but the name Jacob offers is the one that wins out: "Benjamin." It is appropriate to note that Ephrath probably lies on the border between Benjamin and Judah, likely in Judah. For the author, the birth of this child there establishes a Benjaminite claim on that tribal territory. The presence of Jacob's name "Israel" allows for a key word connection between verses 21 and 22.

[22–29] These verses comprise a report of sexual misconduct, a list of Jacob's (here called "Israel") sons organized according to their birth mother, and a report of Isaac's death. Verse 22a offers a laconic statement about Reuben's having had sex with Bilhah, one of his father's wives. Jacob's hearing about it and then doing nothing foreshadows Jacob's quietude in Gen 37:4—and perhaps echoes his apparent inaction in 34:5. Only with his testamentary words does Jacob respond to Reuben's behavior (49:4).

With 35:22b, the name "Jacob" reappears, demonstrating that verses 22–29 stem from different sources. The list of sons has probably been placed here due to a link through the firstborn Reuben with 35:22a. Oddly, Benjamin is listed along with his eleven brothers as having been born in Paddan-Aram. Verses 16–21 testify otherwise, again demonstrating that these final portions of Gen 35 come from different hands.

Mamre, Kiriath-Arba, and Hebron are the final toponyms in the chapter. They link Isaac's residence with that of his father and locate him in Judah. There has been a consistent movement from north to south (Shechem to Mamre). The death and burial notice for Isaac has been slightly elaborated, as was the case with Rachel's death: Rachel dies slowly; Isaac takes a last breath. Given the identification of the grave sites for Deborah (v. 8) and Rachel (v. 19), it seems odd that the site of Isaac's burial is not identified. There is no suggestion that he was buried in the cave of Machpelah, which was east of Mamre.

Reference to Esau and Jacob demonstrates that Jacob's strategy has worked; there is a degree of comity between the brothers. The presence of Esau's name here allows for the connection between this death-and-burial report and the genealogies of Esau that follow in Gen 36.

Genesis 36:1–43
The Descendants of Esau

As befits the eldest sons of two patriarchs who do not receive the familial inheritance, Ishmael and Esau receive their respective genealogies in Genesis. Ishmael's is briefer (25:12–18) probably because his mother does not have the same status as did Esau's mother, Rebekah. Esau, by contrast, is the principal character of the much longer Gen 36. The material in this chapter is diverse, including a list of Esau's descendants through three wives, two lists of tribal leaders, a list of Horites, and a king list. And there is a minimum of nonformulaic reporting (e.g., v. 24).

The Priestly source in this chapter presents a benign version of the separation between Jacob and Esau. The longest report in the chapter appears in verses 6–8, which provide the Priestly rationale for the separation between the two brothers: the two of them held so much livestock that the land could not support both living in the same place. One may compare this text to Gen 13:5–7, which offers the same basic rationale for the separation of Abram from Lot. This latter text, however, stems from the primary source, not the Priestly hand, and it refers to conflict between the servants of Abram and Lot. The Priestly writer apparently borrows this motif from Gen 13 but chooses to avoid referring to any conflict between Jacob and Esau.

36:1 These are the descendants of Esau, that is Edom. 2 Esau married
Canaanite wives: Adah, daughter of Elon the Hittitie; Oholibamah, daughter of Anah, son[a] of Zibeon the Hivite; 3 and Basemath, Ishmael's daughter, who was the sister of Nebaioth. 4 Adah gave birth to Eliphaz for Esau;
Basemath gave birth to Reuel; 5 Oholibamah gave birth to Jeush, Jalam,
and Korah. These are the children of Esau, who were born to him in the
land of Canaan.

6 Esau took his wives, his sons, his daughters, all those who lived in
his household, his cattle, all his livestock, and all the property he had
acquired in the land of Canaan and went to a land far away from his
brother Jacob. 7 Since they had so many possessions, they were not able
to live together. The land where they had been dwelling could not sustain

both of their holdings of livestock. 8 So Esau, that is, Edom, lived in the
mountainous terrain of Seir.

9 These are the descendants of Esau, ancestor of Edom, in the mountainous terrain of Seir. 10 These are the names of Esau's sons: Eliphaz,
son of Adah, the wife of Esau; Reuel, son of Esau's wife Basemath.
11 The sons of Eliphaz were Teman, Omar, Zepho, Gatam, and Kenaz.
12 Timna was the mistress of Eliphaz, Esau's son. She birthed Amalek
to Eliphaz. These were the sons of Adah, Esau's wife. 13 These were the
sons of Reuel: Nahath, Zerah, Shammah, and Mizzah. These were the
sons of Esau's wife, Basemath. 14 These were the sons of Esau's wife
Oholibamah, daughter of Anah, son[a] of Zibeon. She gave birth to Jeush,
Jalam, and Korah for Esau.

15 These are the tribal chiefs[b] of the sons of Esau. The sons of Eliphaz,
Esau's firstborn: Chief Teman, Chief Omar, Chief Zepho, Chief Kenaz,
16 Chief Korah, Chief Gatam, Chief Amalek; these are the tribal chiefs
of Eliphaz in the land of Edom. These are the sons of Adah. 17 These are
the sons of Esau's son Reuel: Chief Nahath, Chief Zerah, Chief Shammah, and Chief Mizzah. These are the tribal chiefs of Reuel in the land
of Edom. These are the sons of Basemath, Esau's wife. 18 These are the
sons of Esau's wife Oholibamah: Chief Jeush, Chief Jalam, and Chief
Korah. These are the tribal chiefs whom Oholibamah, daughter of Anah,
gave birth for Esau. 19 These are Esau's, that is, Edom's, sons. These are
their tribal chiefs.

20 These are the sons of Seir the Horite, who live in the land: Lotan,
Shobal, Zibeon, Anah, 21 Dishon, Ezer, and Dishan. These are the tribal
chiefs of the Horites, the sons of Seir in the land of Edom. 22 The sons
of Lotan were Hori and Heman. Lotan's sister was Timna. 23 These are
the sons of Shobal: Alvan, Manahath, Ebal, Shepho, and Onam. 24 These
are the sons of Zibeon: Aiah and Anah; he is the Anah who found water
in the wilderness when he was shepherding the donkeys of his father
Zibeon. 25 These are the children of Anah: Dishon and Oholibamah,
daughter of Anah. 26 These are the sons of Dishon: Hemdan, Eshban,
Ithran, and Cheran. 27 These are the sons of Ezek: Bilhan, Zaavan, and
Akan. 28 These are the sons of Dishan: Uz and Aran. 29 These are the
tribal chiefs of the Horites: Chief Lotan, Chief Shobal, Chief Zibeon,
Chief Anah, 30 Chief Dishon, Chief Ezer, and Chief Dishan. These are the
tribal chiefs of the Horites, chief by chief in the land of Seir.

31 These are the kings who reigned in the land of Edom before a king
reigned over the Israelites. 32 Bela, king of Beor, reigned in Edom. The
name of his city was Dinhabah. 33 Bela died, whereupon Jobab, son
of Zerah of Bozrah, succeeded him as king. 34 Jobab died, whereupon
Husham of the land of the Temanites succeeded him as king. 35 Husham

died, whereupon Hadad son of Bedad, who defeated Midian in the territory
of Moab, succeeded him as king. The name of his city was Avith. 36 Hadad
died, whereupon Samlah of Masrekah succeeded him as king. 37 Samlah
died, whereupon Shaul of Rehoboth on the Euphrates succeeded him as
king. 38 Shaul died, whereupon Baal-hanan son of Achbor succeeded him
as king. 39 Baal-hanan son of Achbor died, whereupon Hadar succeeded
him as king. The name of his city was Pau; his wife's name was Meheta-
bel; she was the daughter of Matred, daughter of Mezahab.

40 These are the names of the tribal chiefs of Esau, according to their
clans, where they are located, and by their names: Chief Timna, Chief
Alvah, Chief Jetheth, 41 Chief Oholibamah, Chief Elah, Chief Pinon,
42 Chief Kenaz, Chief Teman, Chief Mibazar, 43 Chief Magdiel, and
Chief Iram. These are the tribal chiefs of Edom, that is Esau, according
to where they live in the land they possess.

a. LXX, Syr have "son"; MT has "daughter."

b. The noun, often translated "clan" in this chapter, can refer to persons, so Exod 15:15.

[36:1–14] Verses 1 and 8 stress the eponymous character of Esau. To speak of Esau is, at one and the same time, to think about the people and territory of Edom. The first genealogy (vv. 2–5) focuses on Esau's three wives—Adah, Basemath, and Oholibamah. The first two had only one son each, Eliphaz and Reuel, respectively; Oholibamah gave birth to three sons: Jeush, Jalam, and Korah. This family of Esau stands in contrast to the one described in 28:6–9. In that version, Esau marries Mahalath, a daughter of Ishmael, "in addition to the wives he had." This phrase may be a gloss to take account of the wives named in Gen 36. In any case, no genealogy in Gen 36 attests to a link between Esau and the Ishmaelites.

Once that family of two generations has been announced, the Priestly writer offers his version of the separation between Esau and Jacob. Esau has become wealthy. Unlike the episode narrated in Gen 27:41–45, in which Rebekah tells Jacob to flee to Haran because Esau wants to kill him, Gen 36 offers a benign picture, one in which both brothers have acquired so much livestock that the land cannot support them. The same quasi-ecological tone struck in Gen 13:6, in which the land cannot support both Abram's and Lot's herds, appears here in 36:7, using the same vocabulary. In both cases, one of the parties moves away: Lot to the "plain of Jordan" (13:10–13), Esau to mountainous terrain of Seir/Edom, south of the Dead Sea.

The second genealogy (vv. 9–14) focuses on Esau's sons and their progeny. Eliphaz has five sons and Reuel four sons. The text reports no sons born to the three sons of Oholibamah. It is of interest that Timna, a mistress of Eliphaz, gives birth to Amalek, who is also listed in verse 16 without reference to his mother. This genealogy therefore places Amalek/Amalekites, who often fought against Israel (e.g., 1 Sam 15:2–3), in the lineage of Esau.

[15–43] The genealogy in Gen 36:15–19 introduces new diction, that of a tribal chief. Each of Esau's grandsons is listed as such. The names of these grandsons are, with one exception, the same as those identified in verses 9–14. The only difference is the addition of Korah to the sons of Eliphaz. The names of two of Eliphaz's sons appear in Israelite genealogies as well. (Korah belongs to the Levitical lineage [e.g., Exod 6:21], and Kenaz belongs to Caleb's lineage and was an eponymous ancestor of the Kenizzites [cf. Gen 15:19; Josh 14:6].)

Verses 20–30 cover different ground. They begin with reference to Seir the Horite. He appears to be the earliest and eponymous ancestor associated with Edom (or Seir), the land to which Esau has moved. His sons are those who "lived in the land," meaning the indigenous population. Of Seir's seven sons, one has a daughter, Oholibamah, who, according to the three previous genealogies in this chapter, is a wife of Esau. This genealogy therefore attests to intermarriage between the native people of Edom and those who moved there, those associated with Esau.

These verses raise a question about the relationship between the Horites and Edom. According to some scholars, the Horites are related to the people who live in Seir, the mountainous area of Edom, and who are distinct from those who trace their lineage from Esau and live in the nonmountainous terrain of Edom (*ABD* 3:288). This theory differs from the picture presented in Deut 2:12, 22, according to which the Horites have been displaced by those related to Esau. In either case, Gen 36:20–30 presents a genealogy that would be of antiquarian interest for the Priestly writer composing Gen 36. The genealogies' important function in this chapter is to articulate the relationship between the Seirites and the Edomites by dint of Esau's marriage to Oholibamah, a Seirite woman.

Verses 31–39 describe Edom as having a monarchic polity. The list identifies eight kings, one succeeding another after the preceding king's death. In several cases, the list includes detailed notes, such as the name and lineage of a king's wife. In three cases, a king is associated with a city, Dinhabah (v. 32), Avith (v. 35), and Pau (v. 39). Apart from the use of this list in 1 Chr 1:43–51, the names of the cities appear nowhere else in the OT, and their locations are uncertain. Again, the Priestly author is including data of primarily antiquarian interest.

The final four verses of the chapter rehearse the names of Edomite tribal chiefs, now eleven, unlike the fourteen listed in 36:15–19. Moreover, the names differ from that prior listing. By the end of the list (v. 43), the formula regarding Esau/Edom has been reversed to Edom/Esau, making the move from family to nation. This same move is taking place for the sons of Jacob becoming Israelites as the book of Genesis moves to its conclusion.

Genesis 36 offers evidence of the Priestly author/editor's interest in characterizing diverse polities. The various elements of this chapter construe Esau/Edom/Seir as a family, as a set of tribes, and as a monarchy. The Chronicler's appropriation of the list in 36:31–39 begins with the note, "These are the kings who reigned in the land of Edom before any king reigned over the Israelites" (1 Chr 1:43). Such a report no doubt lies implicitly behind the inclusion of the list in Genesis.

Genesis 37:1–36
Israel Loves Joseph More than His Other Sons

This chapter inaugurates the Joseph short story, the protagonist of which is Jacob's son Joseph, one of the two sons born to Rachel. Chapter 37 functions as a prologue to the entire short story, while also including a prologue for just this chapter (vv. 1–4). As a whole, the chapter introduces characters who will be prominent until the last chapters of the story and the book: Jacob, Joseph, and Joseph's brothers. Moreover, motifs important later in the short story (i.e., dreams and their significance, clothing) appear. Finally, the chapter foreshadows the superior status that Joseph will have once he has become prominent in Pharaoh's court. Genesis 37, moreover, has a literary integrity of its own. In the first four verses, the narrator quickly sketches the intrafamilial dynamics that will result in Joseph's descent into slavery and his move to Egypt. In addition, the brothers are revealed to be something other than a monolithic entity. There are "factions": the sons of Bilhah and the sons of Zilpah. And two brothers, Reuben and Judah, create plans of their own. By the end of the chapter, Joseph is as good as dead to his family, especially to his brothers, but alive to his owner, Potiphar.

37:1 Jacob had settled in the land where his father had dwelled as an
immigrant, in the land of Canaan. 2 These are the descendants of Jacob.

Joseph, when seventeen years old, was shepherding the flock with
his brothers. He was an assistant to the sons of Bilhah and the sons of
Zilpah, the wives of his father. Joseph made negative comments about
them to their father. 3 Israel loved Joseph more than all of his other sons
because he was a son of his old age. He made a long-sleeved coat[a] for him.
4 When his brothers discerned that their father loved him more than he
loved them, they hated him and were unable to talk peaceably with him.

5 When Joseph had a dream and reported it to his brothers, they hated
him all the more.[b] 6 He said to them, "Hear about this dream that I have
had. 7 We were making bundles of grain stalks in the middle of the field
when my bundle grew and became upright. Then your bundles encircled
and bowed down to my bundle." 8 Then his brothers said to him, "Are you
going to reign over us? Are you going to rule us?" And again, they hated
him all the more because of his dream and what he had said.

9 He had another dream and recounted it to his brothers. He said,
"I have had another dream. The sun, the moon, and eleven stars were
bowing down to me." 10 After he had recounted it to his father and to
his brothers, his father challenged him and said, "What is [the meaning]
of this dream that you have had? Will I, your mother, and your brothers
come to bow down toward the ground before you?" 11 Then his brothers
got angry with him, but his father pondered the matter.

12 When his brothers left to shepherd the flock of their father in
Shechem, 13 Israel said to Joseph, "Aren't your brothers working as shepherds in Shechem? Come now: I'm going to send you to them." And he
said, "OK." 14 He said to him, "Go and see if things are going well with
your brothers and with the flock. Then let me know how things stand."
So he sent him from the valley of Hebron.

And he arrived at Shechem. 15 Someone encountered him while he
was wandering in the countryside and asked, "What are you looking
for?"16 He responded, "I'm looking for my brothers. Please tell me
where they are working as shepherds." 17 The man said to him, "They've
left here, but I heard them say, 'Let's head toward Dothan.'" So Joseph
went after his brothers and found them in Dothan. 18 When they saw
him in the distance, before he had reached them, they plotted to kill him.
19 One of them said to the others, "Look, the dream expert[c] is arriving.
20 Come on, let's slay him and toss him into one of the pits. We can say
that a wild animal has devoured him. Then we'll see what becomes of
his dreams." 21 When Reuben heard [their plan], he saved him [Joseph]
from them. He said, "We shouldn't attempt to take a life." 22 Reuben
continued, "Don't shed any blood. Toss him into one of the pits in the
wilderness, but don't injure him"—[he said this] so he could save him
from them and return him to his father. 23 So when Joseph came to his
brothers, they stripped off his coat, the coat with long sleeves that he was
wearing, 24 grabbed him, and tossed him into a pit. The pit was empty:
there was no water in it.

25 Then they sat down to eat. When they looked up, they saw a caravan
of Ishmaelites coming down from Gilead. Their camels were carrying
fragrant rose oil, balsam, and mastic, which they were taking down to
Egypt. 26 Judah said to his brothers, "What do we gain if we slay our
brother and cover up his murder?[d] 27 Let's sell him to the Ishmaelites.
That way we won't do him violence—he is our brother, our very flesh."
His brothers agreed. 28 Then, when some Midianite merchants were passing by, they dragged Joseph up out of the pit and sold Joseph to the
Ishmaelites for twenty pieces of silver. They then took Joseph to Egypt.

29 When Reuben returned to the pit, [he discovered that] Joseph was no
longer there and tore his clothing. 30 He returned to his brothers and said,

"The boy isn't there. What am I going to do?" 31 So they took Joseph's
robe, slaughtered a goat, and dipped the coat into its blood. 32 They then
sent the long-sleeved coat to their father, reporting, "We found it. See
whether or not the coat belongs to your son." 33 He recognized it and said,
"It is my son's coat. A wild animal must have devoured him; Joseph must
have been ripped apart." 34 Jacob tore his cloak, put ashes on his abdomen, and mourned interminably for his son. 35 All his sons and daughters
came to comfort him, but he refused to be comforted, saying, "I will
certainly go down to Sheol while still mourning my son." His father wept
over him. 36 The Midianites sold him to the Egyptians, to Potiphar, an
official of Pharaoh, commander of the bodyguards.

a. Cf. LXX, "a multicolored coat."

b. LXX does not contain this clause, which seems to make more sense if it appears initially in v. 8.

c. Literally, "this master or lord of dreams."

d. Literally, "hide his blood."

[37:1–11] The short story opens with a rather vague geographic reference, at least compared to the specificity featured in previous narratives and reports. The narrator in Gen 35 states that Jacob lives "on the other side of the tower of Eder." Now in Gen 37, he is located more broadly "in the land of Canaan," a phrase present in the prior family literature (e.g., Gen 12:5, 6; 13:12; 16:3). This broader brushstroke is consistent with the larger geographic canvas of the short story, since its characters—Israelites, Midianites, and Ishmaelites—are on the move from Syria-Palestine down to Egypt. Toponyms do appear soon (i.e., Shechem in vv. 12–14, valley of Hebron in v. 14). Nonetheless, the "land of Canaan" is present at both the beginning and ending (49:30; 50:5, 13) as the place of Jacob's residence and burial, the land that a "family" left and to which, many generations later, a "people" will enter. The author of 37:1 underscores the increasing settledness of the family's presence in the land. In contrast to his father's status as an immigrant, Jacob has now settled in the land. This landedness of Jacob at the outset of the short story offers a foil to the presence of Joseph in Egypt at the end of this chapter, and to the presence of the people of Israel in Egypt at the end of the short story (and the end of the book of Genesis).

The presence of the *tôlədôt* formula, "these are the descendants of Jacob," offers yet another context, a genealogical one. Just as the literature concerning Abraham was introduced by the phrase "these are the descendants of Terah" (Gen 11:27) and that concerning Jacob was introduced by the phrase "these are the descendants of Isaac" (Gen 25:19), so the *tôlədôt* formula here introduces literature concerning Joseph with reference to his father, Jacob. In all three places in which this formula occurs, the family includes more than a sole protagonist. Lot appears alongside Abraham, Esau alongside Jacob, and here, eleven brothers alongside Joseph. As befits a story that concludes with the family becoming a people, this is the final time that the *tôlədôt* formula will occur with reference to the entire family (cf. Num 3:1, where it refers only to a priestly lineage). In sum, the first two verses of Gen 37 are of a piece with the family literature and with the prior *tôlədôt* formulae.

Things change in 37:2b–4, the prologue to the Joseph short story. In this prologue, the narrator not only offers information about Joseph, his age and role as shepherd, but also describes relationships between the characters, forces that will drive the story. The diction is strong: negative comments, love, hate, unable to talk peaceably. Moreover, this is not the first time that parental favoritism appears in the family literature, most notably Isaac's love of Esau and Rebekah's love of Jacob (25:28). In that family, "Esau hated Jacob" (27:41) and planned to kill him. However, due to Rebekah's love for Jacob, she protected him from Esau's plot to kill him. The situation is different for Joseph: his father, the one who loves him, appears unaware of his other sons' hatred of Joseph. Moreover, instead of helping him escape from them, later in the story he sends Joseph to them, jeopardizing the life of this son whom he loves. Interestingly, Joseph stands apart from the intense emotional language; though his father loves him and his brothers hate him, the narrator reports nothing about Joseph's own emotions. They will be revealed only much later in the larger story.

Joseph's status is clearly reported at the outset of the prologue. He is a *naʿar*, an assistant or helper, to certain of his brothers (37:2; cf. 22:3 and Num 22:22, in which a *naʿar* is servant of a person with higher status). Joseph is an assistant to the sons of his father's secondary wives, Bilhah (mother of Dan and Naphtali) and Zilpah (mother of Gad and Asher). That these sons are not named in the Joseph short story suggests that they are of less importance than the sons who are named, Reuben and Judah, sons of Leah, one of Jacob's two primary wives; Joseph was, of course, a son of Jacob's other primary wife, the now deceased Rachel. So, though Joseph was Jacob's favorite child, he was young and held lower status among his older brothers.

The prologue is replete with the diction of familial relationships, as it should be: brothers, sons, father's wives, their father, his sons, son, his brothers. Such a surfeit of words to describe familial relations stands in almost ironic tension with the disarray that is building within the family, sponsored as it is by the tensions created by love and hate among the various parties.

The most well-known feature of the prologue is surely the coat that Jacob gives to Joseph. Though the precise appearance of the coat remains uncertain, it clearly symbolizes Jacob's preference for Joseph (cf. 2 Sam 13:18–19, the only other place mentioning such a garment, worn by David's daughter Tamar; one may infer that the garment is appropriate wear for a princess). The rationale offered for the presentation of the coat is Joseph's having been a child of Jacob's old age. That same rationale would permit Benjamin to receive such a coat; Benjamin was born to Rachel. However, since Benjamin's birth has coincided with the death of his (and Joseph's) mother, Jacob's feelings about the two boys would likely be quite different. The coat will function importantly throughout the narrative. His brothers strip it off and, later, use it as a ruse. Moreover, the coat introduces the motif of garments, more generally, which will appear importantly not only in this chapter (cf. Gen 37:34) but also later in the short story (39:13; 41:42). At the outset of the story, Joseph is clothed in a special coat. He is later stripped not only of that coat, but also of a lesser garment (so 39:13). And then, when he has achieved power, he is clothed in "fine linen."

Once the stage has been set, the narrator describes two dreams by Joseph and their reception (37:5–11). This episode is introduced by a verse that summarizes what happens. The reader knows in advance what is coming. Moreover, this episode is important for at least two reasons. First, it motivates the brothers to take action against Joseph once they are together (vv. 19–20). Second, it introduces the motif of dreams, which will become prominent later in the story (chs. 40–41).

Joseph reports his first dream to his brothers (vv. 5–8). Its effect is incendiary, leading the author to report at both beginning and end of the episode that the brothers "hated him all the more." The dream requires no overt interpretation. The brothers know immediately what it means, though their two questions suggest that they do not think the dream foretells what will happen. Three verbs place the supremacy of Joseph over his brothers in a distinct world, that of royal rule. Joseph uses the language of "bowing down." That verb is used when someone appears before a king in the world of royal protocol (e.g., Mephibosheth before David: 2 Sam 9:8; Nathan before David: 1 Kgs 1:23]). The brothers refer to "reign" (*mālak*), the same root used in the noun "king" (*melek*) and "rule" (*mšl*), which also alludes to the dominion of a king (e.g., 2 Sam 23:3; Zech 6:13). The same root found in "rule" appears later in the short story in reference to Joseph's rule over Egypt (Gen 45:8, 26). This diction helps readers construe Joseph's later exercise of authority in Egypt as one of royal character, not simply political power. Several chapters later, Joseph's brothers bow down before him (42:6).

The second dream is broader in scale and drawn from a different world. The day and nighttime skies replace that of grain cultivation. Joseph reports it not only to his brothers but also to his father. Such an audience befits a dream that, in almost allegorical fashion, refers to Joseph's father, mother, and brothers. Here, again, a verb with royal connotations (bow down) appears. The presence of the moon, which symbolizes his mother, seems odd, since Rachel's death and burial have already been reported before the inception of the Joseph short story (Gen 35:16–21). One senses that the astral imagery has been created to complete a full roster of heavenly objects rather than a report about who is alive at a specific time. In this second dream report, Jacob, not the brothers, responds. He does so in interrogative fashion, as did his sons before him. Here, though, Jacob's first question is different from his second one and from his sons' prior questions. Those three queries are all meant to elicit a negative response. However, Jacob's first question asks Joseph to explain the nature of the dream. Jacob challenges Joseph to justify his use of the dream idiom. Joseph offers no response. In both cases, then, the family members challenge the future portrayed in the dreams. The presence of the verb "come" (v. 10) foreshadows that future as one in which Jacob and his sons will not only bow down to Joseph, but they will also need to go somewhere to do so, down to Egypt.

One might think that the two dreams are of a type described in Gen 41. There, Joseph reports to Pharaoh that the double dreams mean that what has been envisioned will happen (41:32). That seems less the case in Gen 37 since the second dream moves beyond the first one, including Joseph's parents, leading to ambiguity and a new emotion, jealousy. In the final clause of verse 11, the narrator reports that Jacob "pondered the matter," though without specifying "the matter." If it refers to Joseph's second dream, it means one thing. If it refers to the jealousy and hate of Joseph's brothers, it means something else. Jacob's behavior in the next scene suggests the former option may be in play. In any case, the members of the family are portrayed at the end of the prologue as emotional (the brothers' jealousy) and reflective (Jacob's pondering the matter).

[12–36] Verses 12–14 portray Joseph's interaction with his father, who wants to send him to see how his brothers are faring, to learn about their *šālôm*. This reference to *šālôm* stands in contrast to what is said in verse 4, where the brothers were unable to speak *šālôm* to Joseph. That sending Joseph to check on his brothers might place Joseph in danger, a danger to Joseph's *šālôm*, seems not to have crossed Jacob's mind. Joseph appears equally unworried.

The prologue is vague on geography; the narrative of Joseph's capture and enslavement is not. He is sent from the valley of Hebron northward to the area around Shechem and from there down (NW) to Dothan. This is over 100 miles, no minor trip. Hebron is in central Judah, 3,000 feet above sea level. Shechem is in mountainous highlands, 1,800 feet; Dothan is 12 miles northwest of Shechem in the valley of Dothan, 1,150 feet. On that trip, Joseph is unable to find them without help from an unnamed individual who, like Jacob, pushes Joseph toward his brothers.

Verse 18–36 depict the ad hoc response of the brothers to Joseph's unanticipated appearance. Verse 18, like verse 5, introduces and summarizes what is about to happen: a plot to kill Joseph. The brothers act as a whole; no individual is identified as responsible for the plan. As a group, they want to put an end to "this dreamer." His dreams of rule rather than Jacob's favoritism appear to be the primary reason for their antagonism. Once the plot has been hatched, the oldest of Leah's sons, Reuben, intercedes, offering an alternative plan that will keep Joseph alive, so that Reuben can bring Joseph back to Jacob. He appeals that no blood be shed and apparently convinces his brothers. So they tear off Joseph's infamous garment, symbolizing his father's favoritism, and throw him into a pit, all part of the original plan. The word "pit" bears connotations of death and the netherworld (e.g., Pss 16:10; 28:1). So, though Joseph is still alive when dispatched to a pit, he is thrown into a place that symbolizes the power and place of death.

While eating a meal, the brothers espy Ishmaelite spice traders on their way to Egypt. (Dothan was on a major east-west trading route, from Gilead to the seacoast and thence to Egypt.) This eventuality leads to yet another ad hoc plan: selling Joseph. Judah, another son of Leah, proposes that he be sold rather than killed. His brothers agree to this plan. (Some scholars have argued that vv. 25–27 derive from a different author's hand, likely someone concerned with developing the character of Judah, a figure who dominates the next chapter. The ambiguity of who sells Joseph to whom—Midianites to an Egyptian [v. 36], or Midianites to Ishmaelites to an Egyptian [v. 28]—may also reflect such diverse authorial hands.) Neither Reuben's nor Judah's plan works. Before the brothers can act, Midianite traders remove Joseph from the pit and sell him for twenty pieces of silver. (Lev 27:5 lists the value of a male who is five to twenty years old as twenty shekels.) Though Judah's plan is for the brothers to receive that sum, Gen 37:28 makes clear that foreign traders are the ones who profit. Reuben has hoped to retrieve Joseph from the pit, but the Midianites take Joseph before Reuben returns.

So Joseph's fate is sealed, at least from the brothers' perspective: he is on his way to Egypt (v. 28). But that is not the end of this portion of the narrative, the denouement. The primary version of the tale resumes when Reuben discovers that his attempt to protect Joseph has failed. After ripping his clothing, which presages Jacob's later action (v. 34), Reuben returns to his brothers, distraught, asking them what can be done. Though there is no verbal answer, the ensuing action provides the answer to Reuben's question. The brothers create yet another ad hoc plan, making it appear that Joseph has been killed by a wild animal. Oddly, the narrator does not describe the brothers as taking the coat to Jacob, viz., "they sent the coat" (v. 32).

Throughout 37:21–30, there has been an inchoate characterization of the named brothers: Reuben wants to return Joseph to Jacob; he is emotional. Judah, in contrast, does not want Joseph to be killed, but he is willing to sell him into slavery. And the brothers as a group, in their final speech, disassociate themselves from Joseph, referring to him as "your son" rather than as "our brother" (v. 32). Moreover, when they are last mentioned (v. 35), the brothers and sisters (cf. 46:7; though elsewhere only one sister is named, Dinah: 30:21) are trying to comfort Jacob, comfort for the suffering that the brothers themselves caused. The episode concludes on a poignant note: Jacob refuses to be comforted, recognizing that he will only see Joseph again when he dies, a sentiment strikingly similar to the one expressed by David when his first son with Bathsheba dies (2 Sam 12:23).

Genesis 38:1–30
Judah Proclaims, "Tamar Is More Righteous Than I Am"

With only the thinnest of temporal, narrative tissue connecting it to the foregoing chapter, Gen 38 focuses on two characters: Judah, who plays a crucial role later in the Joseph narrative (ch. 44); and Tamar, giving birth to a son who belongs to the lineage of David. Its location (ch. 38) within the Joseph short story helps develop the character of Judah, who, near the end of Genesis, will receive praise from his brothers (49:8) and have royal prerogative (49:10). That being said, many scholars question whether chapter 38 was originally part of the Joseph short story or whether it was a later addition. One may certainly read the Joseph story without including Gen 38, and little would be lost. Though there is no end in sight to this controversy, it does suggest a good reason to attend to this chapter as a story in its own right.

Genesis 38 functions beyond its borders in several ways: by showing how an Israelite male responds to solicitation of a foreign woman, by developing the character of Judah within the Joseph short story, and by providing a link between Judah and King David through Judah's son Perez. The picture of Judah in Gen 38 is complex; he is both a dupe and yet able to recognize someone who is better than he is. He is a foil for Joseph in the next chapter, a character who does *not* fall for a foreign woman. Tamar, in contrast, is well labeled by Judah himself: "righteous" (v. 26). She must, however, achieve her goals by subterfuge, which is consistent with the role of a trickster (cf. Rebekah in Gen 27).

This is a chapter in which impregnation, or the lack thereof, is a vital issue. It is a story in which one character prevents impregnation by not allowing Tamar to have sexual access to Shelah. It is a story in which the person who is supposed to impregnate Tamar does not and the one who is not supposed to do so does. One might even say that Judah as progenitor is a subtext: he fathers Er, Onan, Shelah, Perez, and Zerah. It is a chapter in which the deity executes Jacob's two older sons earlier, one without explanation. Ultimately, this chapter is a story about death and birth.

> **38:1** Something happened at that time: Judah went down from his brothers
> and encamped near an Adullamite man, whose name was Hirah. **2** While

there, Judah saw the daughter of a Canaanite man, whose name was Shua.
He married her, whereupon he had sexual relations with her. 3 She became
pregnant and consequently gave birth to a son, whom he called Er. 4 She
became pregnant again and gave birth to a son whom she named Onan.
5 Then she again gave birth to a son and named him Shelah. She[a] was in
Chezib when she gave birth to him. 6 Judah took a wife for Er, his firstborn;
her name was Tamar. 7 But Er, his firstborn, was wicked in God's view; so
God executed him. 8 Judah then said to Onan, "Go to your brother's wife
and fulfill your responsibility. Provide progeny for your brother." 9 Since
Onan knew that the progeny would not belong to him, when he had sexual
relations with her, he ejaculated onto the ground, refusing to provide progeny for his brother. 10 This was wicked in God's view, so he executed him
as well. 11 Judah then said to his daughter-in-law Tamar, "Stay in your
father's house as a widow until my son Shelah grows up," worrying that
he too, like his brothers, would die. So she returned to her father's house.

12 After a long time, the daughter of Shua, Judah's wife, died. Then,
after working through his grief, Judah and his friend Hirah went up to his
sheepshearers at Timnah. 13 When Tamar was informed, "Your father-
in-law is going up to Timnah for the shearing of his flock," 14 she took
off her widow's clothing, wrapped herself in a shawl, and sat down at
the entrance to Enaim, which was on the way to Timnah, since she knew
that although Shelah had grown up, she had not been given to him as a
wife. 15 When Judah saw her, he thought she was a prostitute because she
had covered her face. 16 So he left the road and went over to her and said,
"Let me have sex with you." He didn't know that she was his daughter-
in-law. She replied, "What will you pay me to have sex with you?" 17 He
responded, "I'll send you a kid goat from the flock," to which she said,
"Not unless you give me something valuable until you send it." 18 He
replied, "What sort of valuable thing should I give you?" She said, "Your
seal, its cord, and the staff that you are holding." He then gave them to
her and had sex with her, whereupon she became pregnant from him.
19 She got up, left, took off her shawl, and put on her widow's clothing.

20 Judah sent a kid goat from his flock with his friend the Adullamite,
to recover the valuable things from the woman, but he could not find her.
21 He asked the men from that place, "Where is the consecrated worker[b]
who was along the road near Enaim?" They responded, "There wasn't
any consecrated worker at that place." 22 So he returned to Judah and said,
"I couldn't find her. Moreover, the men from that place said there wasn't
any consecrated worker there." 23 Judah said, "She can have the valuable
things. Otherwise, we will be a laughingstock. In any case, I did send the
goat, but you couldn't find her."

24 About three months later, Judah was informed, "Your daughter-in-
law Tamar has had illicit sex and has become pregnant from her prostitution." Judah responded, "Bring her out so that she can be burned."
25 As she was being brought out, she sent a message to her father-in-law,
"By the man who owns these things, I have become pregnant." She said,
"Examine the seal, the cord, and the staff." **26** Judah recognized them and
said, "She is more righteous than I am since I did not give Shelah to her."
He did not have sex with her again.

27 When it was time for her to give birth, there were twins in her womb.
28 While she was giving birth, one child stuck out his hand. The midwife
took it and tied a red string around his hand and said, "This one came out
first." **29** But then he withdrew his hand and his brother emerged, whereupon she said, "You have certainly burst out on your own." He was named
Perez. **30** Then his brother, who had the red string on his hand, emerged.
He was named Zerah.

a. So LXX; MT reads "he."

b. The noun *qədēšâ* has often been translated as "cult prostitute." However, since there is minimal evidence for so-called "cultic prostitution," it is better to use a neutral phrase such as "consecrated worker."

[38:1–11] As the initial phrase makes clear, the temporal relationship between chapters 37 and 38 is vague. This loose connection may be evidence that Gen 38 was added to the Joseph short story after it was completed. Judah, mentioned in Gen 37:26, comes to the fore in this brief narrative. Despite the temporal ambiguity, there is geographic specificity. Judah's friend Hirah is associated with Adullam. Adullam is located in the tribal territory of Judah, lying west of Bethlehem. It is an area mentioned in the story of David's rise (1 Sam 22), so it is probably no accident that the end of Gen 38 also bears a connection to David (see below). Chezib (v. 5, more typically known as Achzib) is in the same general area. Oddly, Judah's wife is not named here, though his daughter-in-law is.

Judah's choice for his spouse is unusual. To this point in the family literature, males who elect a spouse not belonging to the patrilineage of Terah are no longer an integral part of the family associated with the patriarchs and matriarchs, as with Ishmael and Esau. Within the literary boundaries of the Joseph narrative, however, three of Jacob's sons marry outside the family: Judah (Gen 38), Simeon (Gen 46), and Joseph (Gen 41). Judah and Simeon marry Canaanites, and Joseph an Egyptian. The family, which is on its way to being a people/nation, has entered a phase in which the genealogy is far more inclusive than has hitherto been known to be the case.

The situation created by the death of Er—married and without children, yet with a surviving brother—called for the custom known as the Levirate marriage. Deuteronomy 25:5–10 offers a case similar to that of Gen 38. If a man dies, his widow shall not marry outside the family. Instead, the dead man's brother shall marry the widow and provide her with offspring so that this person will stand in the dead brother's line of inheritance. Deuteronomy 25 makes clear that the surviving brother must marry the widow, not simply impregnate her. Judah's order to Onan does not overtly include this stipulation. Moreover, Deut 25:7–10 provides a mechanism by which the surviving brother can legally avoid marrying the widow. In Gen 38, Onan does not follow this legal procedure but instead simply fails to impregnate Tamar. In sum, Deut 25 provides a general background for understanding why Judah orders Onan to provide Tamar with a child, but the absence of a marriage between Onan and Tamar, plus Onan's avoidance of the accustomed manner and thus refusing the responsibility of a brother, mean that this particular series of events do not follow the usual pattern of the Levirate procedure.

The narrator has crafted his report of these goings-on carefully. Readers are told that Onan repeatedly has intercourse but never ejaculates inside Tamar (v. 9). In addition, when Judah tells Tamar to return to her father's house, the narrator labels her as Judah's daughter-in-law, an ironic turn of phrase, emphasizing his relationship to her just as he is sending her away.

The status of a widow such as Tamar is surely difficult, especially since she is not part of the patrilineage of Terah. Within the Israelite community, a widow without children can return to the household of her father (so the case reported in Lev 22:13). The situation in the book of Ruth—an Israelite family moves to Moab, where two Israelite sons marry Moabite women and then die—is somewhat different. There Naomi admonishes her widowed daughters-in-law to return to "your mother's house" (Ruth 1:8). These two texts suggest that if Shelah were not alive, Judah would be following standard practice in telling Tamar to return to the household of her parents. However, Shelah does exist, and Judah's overt language to Tamar, that she should wait for him to grow up (Gen 38:11), apparently covers up his covert strategy to keep her away from him since Judah fears that Shelah, too, may die. In sum, both son (Onan) and father fail in their responsibility to Tamar.

Death pervades these early verses, as will the threat of death to Tamar later. The deity kills Er, Judah's firstborn son, because he is wicked. The narrator offers no evidence of his wickedness. Onan also is put to death when he does not fulfill his responsibility toward Tamar. Moreover, Judah's unnamed wife is also about to die.

[12–23] Yet another vague clause, "after a long time," introduces the next portion of the narrative. The narrator focuses on Judah, the death of his wife, his grief, and the life he lives as a widower. Unlike the widow Tamar living at her father's house, Judah is a public figure, traveling to Timnah and Enaim (Timnah is in the territory of Judah, and Enaim is likely so as well) as he manages his livestock. One senses that the narrator reports Judah's status as a widower to set the narrative context in which he seeks the services of a prostitute.

Just as providence pervades the story of Joseph as a whole, so too in this chapter: Tamar happens to be told (v. 13) that her father-in-law is taking a trip. The same irony present in verse 11, where the narrator refers to Tamar as Judah's daughter-in-law, occurs here when the narrator describes Judah as Tamar's father-in-law. In spite of that relationship, he does not recognize her, even in the most intimate of behaviors.

Tamar's strategy of pretending to be a prostitute works perfectly. She knows how Judah will respond to her presence. What, presumably, she does not know is what form of payment Judah will offer. If he offers silver or some other form of generic payment, her strategy will not work. She wants not just to become pregnant but to get pregnant by a member of her late husband's family. One of her goals, to use the diction of Deut 25:6, is to keep her late husband's name from being "blotted out from Israel." Since Shelah has not been given to her, Judah is an obvious, though unusual, choice. But she also needs to protect herself from the charge of illicit sexual activity, which will in fact be made. Tamar desperately needs not to be paid with a kid, since that would mean relinquishing the object enabling her to identify Judah as the one who has impregnated her. The kid will presumably have been slaughtered, which would disallow Tamar from proving any connection to Judah. Hence, she needs to garner some property that belongs to Judah and Judah alone. Judah himself opens that door when he invites Tamar to stipulate what sort of valuable thing he might leave with her until he provides her with a kid goat. Of the three items she identifies, the seal, whether stamp or cylinder, is distinctive. The narrator does not report whether it has an imprinted scene or some letters. In either case, however, the imprint on clay is idiosyncratic to Judah. The cord, presumably, allows the owner to wear the hollowed-out cylinder seal or stamp seal with a hole in it around the neck.

It does seem odd that the narrator reports the fact of her having become pregnant even before she has departed from the scene. In any case, after leaving the scene of her encounter with Judah, she removes the shawl that she has used to disguise herself and puts on the garments that signify her status as a widow. What the narrator does not report is whether she returns to her father's house.

The narrator makes clear that Judah intends to honor his original offer of payment, which will also allow him to retrieve the property he has given Tamar. However, rather than going himself to find the "prostitute," he sends his friend Hirah with the kid goat. Hirah makes inquiries about a "consecrated worker," but to no avail. Apparently at the time of the encounter, no one other than Judah saw Tamar near Enaim in disguise. As a result and in the interest of not losing face, Judah stops the search for the "consecrated worker." This choice of diction is somewhat puzzling since it was not used in verse 15, where the general Hebrew noun for "prostitute" occurs. Hirah is the person who first uses the noun "consecrated worker," which may give the appearance of his search a more respectable cast. Judah does not use the term, nor does the narrator.

[24–30] The climax in the narration occurs when Tamar's pregnancy becomes public knowledge. Judah "is told" about it (v. 24) just as Tamar "was told" (v. 13) about his trip. Judah is presumably told because Tamar is his daughter-in-law, though it is not clear why her father, to whom presumably she has returned and with whom she is living, does not have greater responsibility for her at this point than Judah does. In any case, the anonymous speech underscores the public relationship between Judah and Tamar, which stands in contrast to their private sexual relationship, one that only Tamar, Judah, and Hirah know. Judah quickly sentences her to death, apparently following the strictures of Deut 22:22. However, the focus in Deut 22 is initially on the man in the adulterous relationship: "If a man is caught lying with the wife of another man. . . ." Judah says nothing about the publicly unknown male by whom Tamar has become pregnant, though implicitly he has sentenced that person to death, a self-sentence of death. Moreover, Lev 20:12 offers an even more direct prescription relevant to this case, "If a man lies with his daughter-in-law, both of them shall be put to death." Even when Judah learns Tamar's identity, he does not invoke this sort of statute, which would mean the death penalty for both of them. Instead, he pronounces Tamar to be more righteous than he, the implication of which is that both of them are righteous and that neither should be put to death. It is as if Judah's unwillingness to provide Shelah to Tamar has created a situation in which it is permissible for Tamar to take the initiative to provide an heir for her husband, even if it involves a violation of the statute in Lev 20:12.

Judah's order that Tamar be burned to death is consistent with the punishment for certain illicit sexual behaviors (e.g., Lev 20:14, a case in which one man has sexual relations with his wife and mother-in-law. In this instance, all three parties are to be executed by fire). Elsewhere, stoning is the stipulated punishment for a woman who has sexual relations with one man before her marriage to another (Deut 22:21).

The birth of Tamar and Judah's children comprises the denouement. The presence of twins, who appear to be in conflict, recalls Rebekah's pregnancy with Jacob and Esau. The significance of the boys lies both in the order of their birth and in their names. Perez achieves firstborn status by "bursting" out of Tamar's womb. The name Perez means "bursting" or "spreading out," whereas Zerah bears the denotation of something that shines. Judah's relation to his two sons is unclear. The narrator reports that he never again has sexual relations with Tamar, but nothing is said about him and these sons. They are included in the genealogy of the tribe of Judah, and Perez stands in a direct line from Judah to David (1 Chr 2:1–15, cf. Ruth 4:18–22). This genealogy will ultimately include three non-Israelite women: the daughter of Shua (Bath-Shua in 1 Chr 2:3), Tamar, and Ruth. In this regard, Gen 38 foreshadows Joseph's marriage to the Egyptian woman, Asenath (41:45).

Genesis 39:1–23
Joseph Flourishes in Potiphar's House but Is Falsely Accused

Perhaps the best-known episode in the Joseph short story, Gen 39 stands out from Gen 37 primarily because of its overtly theological character. Chapter 37 never refers to Israel's deity; in Gen 39 the word "YHWH" appears eight times, and the word "God" once. Both at the beginning and end of this chapter, the narrator emphasizes that "YHWH was with" Joseph" (vv. 2, 21, 23). In Gen 37, Joseph was subject to the machinations of his brothers; in Gen 39, he is supported by the deity and becomes a legendary hero due to both his work ethic and his high moral character. Still, the narrator does not think that Joseph's success is due to his "wise" behavior. Rather, it is because God has acted on his behalf. Though Gen 39 is decidedly different from Gen 37, it sets the stage for later developments in the short story by foreshadowing the role Joseph will have as second-in-command to Pharaoh. That Joseph has been sold to an "official of Pharaoh" and is later put in a prison reserved for royal prisoners proves to be providential; such connection to the court will help pave the way for Joseph's ultimate place there.

Still, Gen 39 bears its own literary integrity, comprising a report (vv. 1–6a) and a narrative, replete with dialogue. As in Gen 37, Joseph has power and status early on and then suffers the loss of both due to the plans of an antagonist. He is then rescued from the status of a foreign prisoner, which consequently begins his ascent. The narrator takes considerable interest in depicting Joseph's interactions in "the house." Ambiguity and surprise prevent the narrative from being simply a retelling of a person falsely accused of sexual assault, a widespread motif. Though the episode is often labeled "Potiphar's Wife," it could equally well be titled, "The LORD with Joseph in Potiphar's Household."

> **39:1** When Joseph had been brought down to Egypt, Potiphar, who was an
> official of Pharaoh, the chief officer of the palace guards, and an Egyp-
> tian, purchased him from the Ishmaelites, who had brought him down
> there. **2** YHWH was with Joseph. He became successful while he was in
> the house of his Egyptian master. **3** His master perceived that YHWH was
> with him. In everything that he did, YHWH made him successful. **4** So
> Joseph found favor in his sight and served him. He [Potiphar] appointed

him over his house; everything that he owned he put under his control. 5 After he had appointed him over his house and over all that he owned, YHWH blessed the house of the Egyptian because of Joseph. YHWH's blessing was present in both the house and the fields. 6 He [Potiphar] relinquished control of his property and put it under Joseph's control. Potiphar didn't care about anything except the food that he ate.

Now Joseph had a great build and was very handsome. 7 After a while, his master's wife noticed Joseph and said, "Lie with me." 8 But he refused and said to his master's wife, "What! With me here, my master doesn't care about what goes on about the house. He has placed everything he owns under my control. 9 No one is more powerful in this house than I am. He has withheld nothing from me except you because you are his wife. How could I do such a terribly evil thing and sin against God?" 10 Even though she kept saying this to Joseph every day, he would not agree to lie with her—or even to be near her. 11 However, one day when he entered the house to do his work and when no one else was there in the house, 12 she grabbed his garment and said, "Lie with me." He ran outside, leaving his garment in her hand. 13 When she saw that he had left his garment in her hand and had run outside, 14 she shouted to the others in her house and said to them, "He brought this Hebrew man to amuse us, but he approached me to lie with me. Then I screamed. 15 When he heard me raise my voice and shout, he left his garment with me and ran outside the house." 16 She kept his garment with her until his master came to his house. 17 When she told him this same story, "The Hebrew slave whom you brought to amuse us approached me, 18 but when I raised my voice and screamed, he ran outside, leaving his garment with me."

19 When his master heard what his wife said to him, "This is what your servant has done to me," he became angry. 20 Joseph's master took him and put him into the prison where the royal prisoners were incarcerated. While he was in prison, 21 YHWH was with Joseph, acting benevolently toward him. He [YHWH] made him appear favorably in the view of the prison's administrator. 22 The prison's administrator entrusted all the prisoners who were incarcerated into Joseph's care. He was responsible for everything that happened there. 23 The prison's administrator exercised no oversight over Joseph's responsibilities because YHWH was with him. YHWH made everything that he did succeed.

[39:1–6a] These verses comprise a report that functions as a prologue, providing essential background information for the narrative that follows. The first verse is somewhat rough, repeating the "bringing down" of Joseph (the verb *yrd* has been used previously by Jacob when he refers to his own "going down" to Sheol: 37:35). This narrative note is linked to the "Ishmaelite" tradition

(37:27–28) rather than the "Midianite" one (37:36), which mentions Potiphar in 37:36. The narrator is especially interested in identifying the national identities of those with whom Joseph is associated: the Ishmaelites take him to Egypt, and Potiphar is an Egyptian (39:1, 2, 5). In 38:5, Joseph's master is called "the Egyptian," not Potiphar. These labels emphasize that Joseph is now living outside the land of Canaan (37:1), where the short story began. Joseph is a foreigner.

Joseph's fall in Gen 37 is due to multiple causes: his arrogance, his father's favoritism, and his brothers' malevolence. His ascent is an entirely different matter. Unlike Gen 37, the deity plays an overt role. The theological claim that "YHWH was *with* Joseph" is central. The omniscient narrator knows this and so does Potiphar (39:3), but Joseph is apparently unaware of the source of his success. Moreover, the deity is more than someone "accompanying" Joseph. The deity is active, blessing Potiphar's house and holdings (v. 5) and enabling Joseph to succeed (vv. 2–9). One might say that these are the manifestations of YHWH's presence with Joseph, yet it remains an unknown to Joseph, an invisible presence. Only the reader is aware.

The notion of God being "with" someone occurs with Abraham (Gen 21:22), Isaac (Gen 26:3), and Jacob (Gen 31:3). In these three cases, each person is told that such is or will be the case. In contrast, Joseph is never informed that YHWH is with him. This situation is similar to the claims made about YHWH's presence with David (1 Sam 16:18; 17:37; 18:12, 14, 28; 2 Sam 5:10). As is the case with Joseph, David's successes are attributed to YHWH's presence with him (1 Sam 18:14, 28; 2 Sam 5:10). People other than David recognize that YHWH is with him (1 Sam 16:18; 18:12). And though Saul offers a felicitation that YHWH be with David (1 Sam 17:37), no one tells David that has happened. In the cases of both Joseph and David, someone other than the individual in question, whether a character in the narrative or the omniscient narrator, reports that YHWH is with a person, which constitutes the key to their "success." One may speak of a "YHWH with *x*" tradition, which probably originated with David and has been reused about Joseph. It is not a notion that inheres in the wisdom tradition, according to which human behavior is the key to success. Nor is it a key feature of the basic narrative in Gen 39, which depends upon Joseph's exemplary behavior when he is propositioned by Potiphar's wife.

One might ask why this theological motif is so prominent in Gen 39. Why is it absent in Gen 37 or in the ensuing acts in the short story? One possible answer: the narrator intends to demonstrate that YHWH will be an active agent even outside the borders of ancient Israel as soon as Joseph reaches Egypt. This notion would bear special relevance to those Yahwists who, like Joseph, are forced to live outside the land of Canaan/Israel. Another possible answer: the chapter was written by someone other than the one who wrote most of the Joseph short story.

Almost as soon as the narrator reports that YHWH is with Joseph, readers learn that Joseph has been taken into a "house," a word repeated in both the prologue and the narrative. It is *the* keyword in the text, appearing in verses 2, 4, 5 [3×], 8, 9, 11 (2×), 14, 16 for Potiphar's house and in vv. 20 (2×), 21, 22 (2×), 23 in reference to the prison, literally "house of bondage." And when Joseph runs "outside," it is the "house" of Potiphar that he is leaving (vv. 12, 13, 15, 18). When he is outside, he is outside of the "house." To be sure, Joseph's success in these two Egyptian houses presages his success in Pharaoh's house (41:40). However, the notion of house in Gen 39 appears as an ambiguous place. In both houses, Joseph is able to flourish, to gain the approval of his masters. However, the first house is also a place where, despite his successes, he can be misjudged and lose the power and status he has achieved. The two houses in Gen 39 are circumscribed spaces in which Joseph lives, initially as a slave and then as a prisoner.

Finally, the deity who is present with Joseph acts benevolently toward Joseph's master. YHWH blesses not only the house of Potiphar but also all his possessions, even his field, all "because of Joseph." The promissory note given to Abram, "Through you all the families of the earth will be blessed" (Gen 12:3), is working itself out in Egypt while Joseph is enslaved.

[6b–23] What has throughout the prologue been a report about Joseph and Potiphar now becomes a story in which Potiphar's wife appears. She is an unnamed antagonist. Though readers become aware of Joseph's physical appearance, they know nothing comparable about either Potiphar or his wife. (Joseph, like King David, is "handsome" [cf. 1 Sam 16:12].) Potiphar's wife propositions Joseph, who responds to her twice-spoken order with a lengthy speech, the last component of which provides a theological construal. To accede to her demand would be more than morally repugnant: it would be a "sin against God." The diction of sin is infrequent in the family literature. The most striking case occurs in the late theological narrative in Gen 20 (see v. 9), a text in which the foreign king Abimelek challenges Abraham's perceptions about whether people in foreign lands act appropriately. And in both Gen 20 and 39, an infraction against "God" (*ʾĕlōhîm*), not YHWH, is in play. (The verb *ḥṭʾ* [sin] does appear twice more in the first-person perfect form in Gen 43:9 and 44:32.) To lie with another man's wife would violate wisdom norms (e.g., Prov 7:4–27), but the downfall of the male is construed in the wisdom literature not as a sin against God, but as fatal folly. In contrast, the author of Gen 39 theologizes the misdeed, which makes the chapter something more than a rehearsal of wisdom norms.

The demonstrative pronoun in the phrase "this house" emphasizes the singularity of the house in which the action takes place. It is more than "a" house. It is the house in which the foreigner Joseph has flourished. Yet it is an ambiguous place, known already as "the Egyptian's house" (v. 5). Yet in verse 14 it is known as "her house," and in verse 16 it becomes "his house." Whether Potiphar's or his wife's "house," it is clearly not Joseph's house: he runs "outside" to escape Potiphar's wife, a location that symbolizes his outsider status as a Hebrew (v. 17).

The narrator underscores the house's ambiguity by the way in which the two Egyptian characters are described. In verse 16, when referring to the wife awaiting her husband's return, the author describes Potiphar as "his master" as opposed to the expected "her husband." In so doing, the narrator includes Joseph in the description of Potiphar, who is less important as her husband than he is as Joseph's master. The same locution occurs again in verse 19, "his master"; and in verse 20, "Joseph's master." Potiphar has lost his name by the end of the story; in fact, the name appears only in the first verse of Gen 39, in contrast to the presence of Joseph's name, which occurs four times in verses 19–23.

Potiphar remands Joseph to prison, which may seem a milder fate than one would expect. According to wisdom norms, dalliance with another man's wife could lead to fatal consequences, and the same is likely the case in ancient Egyptian law (Eyre 1984, 92–105).

Comments on the story would be incomplete without attention to the singular garment that Joseph was wearing, no doubt some sort of loincloth. Just as a glorious coat in Gen 37 has been used to prove that Joseph is dead, so too the garment in Gen 39 is used to prove that Joseph has committed a sexual assault. In both cases the garment is used to reach false conclusions: Joseph is neither dead nor a sexual predator. Still, they symbolize his status in the two stories. The coat attests to Jacob's favoritism, and the loincloth signifies that he is a menial worker. However, the presence of garments in the Joseph short story does not end here. He changes from prison to clean garments when he appears before Pharaoh (41:14). He then receives "garments of fine linen" (41:42) when he becomes viceroy. At the end of the story, Joseph's garments no longer convey a false message: they reflect his real power in Egypt.

Verses 21 reads as almost a reprise of what has happened earlier in the chapter. He is put into another house, this time a prison. While there, YHWH is "with him" as when he has entered Potiphar's house. He is viewed favorably by the prison's administrator, as earlier by Potiphar. Neither character needs to worry when Joseph is at work (vv. 6, 23). He takes charge of everything there, as was the case in 39:4. In all this, YHWH makes him successful (so v. 2). Even in the role of prisoner, Joseph is able to flourish much as when enslaved. Twice he was confined in a house; twice YHWH helped him succeed.

In sum, Gen 39 depicts Joseph as someone who has prospered in two different houses early during his sojourn in Egypt. His success is ultimately attributable not simply to his hard work but especially to the fact that "YHWH was with him," a highly theological interpretation of Joseph's flourishing early in his Egyptian sojourn.

Genesis 40:1–23
Joseph Interprets the Dreams of Pharaoh's Wine Steward and Baker

The stage for Gen 40 has been set in 39:20–23. Joseph is in prison, exercising oversight of everyone and everything that happens there. Chapter 40 offers a vignette of one event in his work in the prison. However, Joseph's role vis-à-vis the incarcerated wine steward and the head baker is more that of a servant than that of an overseer: "He served them" (v. 4). There is, thus, some tension between Joseph as an "elevated" inmate in 39:21–23 and that of Joseph as servant of other prisoners in Gen 40. Moreover, Gen 40 is far less overtly theological than Gen 39. "YHWH" is not mentioned in Gen 40, and Joseph refers to "God" only once, in a highly ambiguous formulation (v. 8). In sum, the worlds of chapters 39 and 40 are not the same, even though Joseph is imprisoned in both chapters. The chapter is, however, integrally related to the larger Joseph short story due to the presence of dreams and their significance in chapters 37 and 41.

40:1 After some time, the wine steward of the king of Egypt and the baker
offended their lord, the king of Egypt. **2** Pharaoh was angry with his two
officials, the chief wine steward and the head baker. **3** So he placed them
in the custody of the house of the chief officer of the palace guards, the
prison where Joseph was incarcerated. **4** The chief officer of the palace
guards assigned Joseph to them; he served them for some time while they
were in custody. **5** On the same night, the two men—the wine steward
and the baker for the king of Egypt who had been incarcerated in the
prison—each had a dream, each with its own meaning. **6** When Joseph
came to them in the morning, he could see that they were disturbed. **7** So
he asked the officials who were with him in the custody of his master's
house, "Why do you appear so sullen today?" **8** The responded to him,
"We had dreams, but there is no interpreter for them." Joseph said to
them, "Don't interpretations come from God? Tell them to me."

9 So the chief wine steward told his dream to Joseph. He said to him,
"In my dream there was a vine in front of me. **10** And on the vine were
three shoots. And while it grew, blossoms emerged and turned into
bunches of grapes. **11** Pharaoh's cup was in my hand, so I took the grapes

and squeezed them into Pharaoh's cup and then put the cup in Pharaoh's
hand." 12 Joseph then said, "This is what it means: the three shoots are
three days. 13 On the third day, Pharaoh will elevate you[a] and restore you
to your position. You will [again] put Pharaoh's goblet into his hand as
was formerly the case when you were his wine steward. 14 Please remember me after you have achieved success. Act with compassion toward me.
Let Pharaoh know about me so that you can get me out of this place.[b] 15 I
was kidnapped out of the land of the Hebrews! I have done nothing since
being here to justify their having put me into this pit."

16 When the head baker saw that the interpretation was favorable, he
said to Joseph, "I, too, had a dream. There were three baskets of baked
goods[c] on my head. 17 In the highest basket were all sorts of food for
Pharaoh to eat, but birds were eating them out of that basket on my head."
18 Joseph responded, saying, "This is what it means: the three baskets are
three days. 19 On the third day, Pharaoh will decapitate you[d] and impale
your body on a wooden stake. Birds will eat the flesh from your corpse."

20 On the third day after this happened—Pharaoh's birthday—he held
a banquet for all his servants and released[e] the chief wine steward and
the head baker to be among his servants. 21 He restored the chief wine
steward to his duties regarding wine, whereupon he put the goblet in
Pharaoh's hand, 22 but he impaled the head baker just as Joseph had interpreted [their dreams] for them. 23 Nonetheless, the chief wine steward did
not remember Joseph; he forgot about him.

a. Literally, "raise your head."

b. Literally, "this house."

c. Or "white flour."

d. Literally, "raise your head from you." On decapitation in ancient Egypt, see Picardo 2007, 221–52.

e. Literally, "raised up the head of." Cf. 2 Kgs 25:27, which uses the same phrase in the sense of releasing someone from prison, in this instance a king of Judah by a foreign king.

[40:1–4] The first four verses comprise the prologue of this scene in the Joseph short story. The piling up of titles—chief officer of the palace guards, chief wine steward, head baker—show that Joseph is moving ever closer to the Pharaonic court, even though he remains in prison. The scene has moved from the private house of Potiphar to an official prison (though with some ambiguity about that place since it is initially described as "the house of the chief officer of the palace guards," which would be Potiphar's house, the setting for ch. 39). However, the next clause, perhaps redactional, corrects that impression, making clear that Joseph is, indeed, in "the prison." Though in the preceding chapter the narrator makes clear that Joseph has achieved considerable status in the prison, he clearly has the role of a servant to the two Pharaonic officials in chapter 40. This suggests that chapters 39 and 40 may stem from different hands, a hypothesis consistent with the theological differences between the two chapters.

Readers already know why Joseph has been put in prison. Potiphar has imprisoned him due to his wife's false accusation against Joseph. In contrast, both Pharaonic officials have "offended" (or "sinned against") their overlord. The justice of their imprisonment highlights the injustice of Joseph's incarceration.

[5–19] Dreams by the two officials interrupt the state of affairs that has continued "for some time." Those responsible for the Joseph short story are intent on showing that Joseph remains in prison for a long time. His ascent from that fate happens only gradually.

This episode develops the character of Joseph in at least two ways. Most obviously, the narrator presents Joseph as a gifted interpreter of Egyptian dreams. Moreover, and unlike the way in which the younger Joseph is presented in Gen 37, he is an astute analyst of people. Even in his status as a servant, he is able not only to see that the two officials are distraught but also to engage them in productive dialogue. This attention to the inner world of humanity, which is uncommon in the family literature, will recur in the Joseph short story (e.g., 45:1–3).

The report about the two dreams introduces readers to the world of dreams and interpretation not only in the Hebrew Bible but also in the ancient Near East. What is important about that world for the Joseph short story is the notion that dreams provide omens about the future. That is the case with Joseph's earlier dreams and will also be true with Pharaoh's dreams (ch. 41). There is, however, a major difference between Joseph's dreams and those of the Egyptians. The former do not require an interpreter, but the latter do. Joseph's dreams are readily understood by both the person who dreams and the persons who hear a dream report. The dreams of the two Egyptians are understood to have a meaning that requires an interpreter. (Interestingly, the Hebrew word *ptr* [to interpret] appears only in Gen 40–41, though it is cognate with the Aramaic word *pšr*, which appears in Dan 2:4, a text involving a foreign court in which an Israelite must interpret a king's dream [cf. Gen 41].) The role of dream interpreters is well attested in ancient Mesopotamia, less so in ancient Egypt.

In any case, Joseph, without any formal training, which would normally have been required for someone to undertake that role, takes on the task of dream interpretation. He does so, however, by posing an ambiguous rhetorical question: "Don't interpretations come from God?" Many interpreters have thought that the implied answer is "Yes, they do come from God." (So von Rad, who states, "Joseph's answer . . . is completely polemic" [1972, 371].) Angelic interpreters provide interpretations of Zechariah's visions; dreams in the ancient world were sometimes characterized as "sleeping visions." This is, after all, the position of Daniel. When confronted with Nebuchadnezzar's dream (Dan 2), Daniel recognizes that the deity has revealed to the king what will happen. He is able to report and interpret it because "the mystery was revealed to Daniel in a vision of the night" (2:19). The situation with Joseph is somewhat different. Joseph does not appeal or refer to the deity. He simply requests that the officials tell him their dreams. Joseph's actions are those of a dream interpreter who does not need the deity helping him to exegete the dreams of Pharaoh's officials. The interpretations are something that he can offer. If the dream interpretations in this chapter ultimately "come from God," they are mediated directly through Joseph.

The dream of the chief wine steward, as well as that of the head baker, derive from their worlds of employment, the preparation of beverages and the provision of baked goods. The first vision depicts the preternaturally fast growth of a grapevine—from shoots to buds to blossoms to grapes to juice in Pharaoh's goblet. The work of the vintner has proceeded with alacrity and has achieved its goal of providing wine. One should assume that, consistent with the emphasis on fast growth, the juice quickly becomes wine for Pharaoh's cup. Joseph's interpretation focuses on only one element of the dream, the last, the wine. There is no clear connection between the shoots and a measure of time, days. Nonetheless, it appears that since the dream depicts the head wine steward doing his duty successfully, the dream can be understood to depict a positive outcome, which Joseph offers. The chapter uses the Hebrew phrase "to raise one's head" with diverse nuances (vv. 13, 19, 20–22). Here it means to elevate or lift someone up from a lower status.

Since the dream will likely result in a good outcome for the chief wine steward, Joseph makes a plea for his help. Three things are important here. First, Joseph refers to his plight as a person who has been "kidnapped out of the land of the Hebrews" (40:15; cf. 39:14 for use of the term "Hebrew"). This view of his past focuses more on his removal from his native land than it does on his capture by his brothers. It relates to Joseph having been taken from the pit (37:28) by Midianites, who sold him to some Ishmaelites, who took him to Egypt. Foreigners are more culpable for Joseph being taken from the land than are his brothers. Second, Joseph construes his treatment by Potiphar, having him imprisoned or "put in this pit," as unjust (40:15). He has been doubly wronged, kidnapped out of his native land, and then in a foreign land being mistreated. Third, Joseph's plea is made to an Egyptian official; the text reports no comparable plea to God for help.

Joseph's interpretive strategy with the dream of the head baker is similar, though it takes account of more details in the dream. The three baskets become three days, the same kind of claim made about the number 3 in the prior dream. However, other details in the second dream are important. Reference to his head leads to a comment about decapitation. And the birds eating baked goods become carrion-devouring vultures. The second dream receives more of an allegorical interpretation.

[20–23] In these verses, the denouement of the narrative, Joseph's interpretation works itself out. With Pharaoh's birthday feast as the catalyst, the baker and wine steward are released from prison, subject to the fate of their dreams as interpreted by Joseph. Unfortunately for Joseph, even though he is a successful analyst of those dreams, the one person to whom he has appealed for help, the chief wine steward, forgets about him. As a result, Joseph is no better off at the end of the chapter than he was at the beginning. Yet this time he has not suffered due to a malevolent plan or to a false accusation of sexual assault. Simple human forgetfulness keeps him in prison. Nonetheless, the seeds for his ascent from "the pit" (v. 15) have been planted. Two of the prisoners have their "heads raised up," one by being restored to his former role, the other by decapitation. Of the three, only Joseph remains in prison, awaiting restoration—the raising up of *his* head.

Genesis 41:1–57
Pharaoh Appoints Joseph over All Egypt

This long chapter constitutes the turning point in the Joseph short story. At the beginning, Joseph is still incarcerated; by the end he is Pharaoh's second-in-command. Such change in status is due to multiple factors: the chief wine steward's remembering him, Joseph's ability to interpret Pharaoh's dreams, and the fortuity of a crisis depicted in the dreams, for which Joseph proposes a solution. Joseph achieves greatness well before the crisis occurs and before the solution that he proposes has worked successfully. His success is achieved as both a dream interpreter and a strategic planner, rather than as a proved administrator. Joseph's plan does work. In so doing, Joseph—and Egypt—become the source of food not only for the starving Egyptians, but also for those who are hungry from "the entire world."

The chapter also includes important details that link this chapter not only with the Joseph short story but also with the family literature. First, the motif of clothing reappears: when Joseph is summoned to appear before Pharaoh, he changes his clothes (41:14), an act symbolizing the transition from prisoner to freed person. Then, after he has interpreted Pharaoh's dream and made his proposal, Pharaoh outfits him in "garments of linen," symbolizing his elevated role at the Pharaonic court. Clothes may not make the man, but they certainly signify his changing status. Second, the issue of ethnic identity emerges. Pharaoh gives Joseph an Egyptian name. Moreover, Pharaoh gives Joseph someone for a wife, Asenath. Joseph is becoming an Egyptian. However, when he and Asenath have children, Joseph gives them Hebrew names (Ephraim and Manasseh), names that will permit them to be eponymous ancestors for two of the twelve Israelite tribes. Thus Joseph is like Moses after him, a figure with both Israelite and Egyptian heritage and married to a non-Israelite. Third, this chapter includes subtle language about forgetting and remembering. The stage for this was set in the final verse of the preceding chapter. There we are told that the chief wine steward "did not remember Joseph but forgot him." In 41:9, the chief wine steward, after learning that Pharaoh's courtiers could not interpret his dreams, remembers "a young Hebrew" being able to interpret *his* dream. Here, forgetting and remembering are things that humans do: the chief wine steward recognizes that his forgetting Joseph was wrong. But later in this chapter, when naming Manasseh, Joseph makes an astonishing claim, "God has helped me to forget all my misery and everything about my father's household" (see 41:51–52). Here, forgetting is a boon, a God-given one. Joseph reports that his current condition in Egypt has allowed him to "forget" his misery and his fractious family of origin. For this writer, memory is a complex phenomenon.

41:1 At the end of two entire years, Pharaoh dreamed that he was standing
by the Nile. 2 Seven well-fed, healthy-looking cows were coming up
out of the Nile and were grazing on marshy plants, 3 when seven ugly,
emaciated cows were coming up behind them. And they stood near the
other cows on the bank of the Nile. 4 The ugly and emaciated cows
consumed the seven well-fed, healthy-looking cows, whereupon Pharaoh
woke up. 5 Then he fell asleep and dreamed a second time. Seven heads of
grain were growing on one stalk, good and healthy. 6 Then seven skinny
heads of grain, shriveled from the east wind, sprouted behind them. 7 The
skinny heads of grain swallowed up the seven healthy and mature heads
of grain. Then Pharaoh woke up. What a dream! 8 In the morning, he was
so deeply upset[a] that he summoned all the omen priests and scholars of
Egypt. Pharaoh recounted his dream for them, but none could offer him
an interpretation.

9 The chief wine steward then said to Pharaoh, "Today I remember
what I have done wrong. 10 When Pharaoh was angry with his servants, he
incarcerated me and the head baker in the house of the chief officer of the
palace guards. 11 One night we both dreamed, each having a dream with
its own meaning. 12 A young Hebrew was there, a servant of the chief
officer of the palace guard. We recounted [them] to him, whereupon he
interpreted our dreams, each with its own meaning. 13 His interpretations
for us came to pass. I was restored to my position, but the head baker
was impaled."

14 So Pharaoh summoned Joseph. He was quickly brought from the
dungeon. After he had shaved and changed his clothes, he came to Pharaoh. 15 Pharaoh said to Joseph, "I dreamed, but there is no one to interpret it. I have heard that when you hear a dream, you can interpret it."
16 Joseph responded to Pharaoh, "No one other than God will provide
a response favorable to Pharaoh."[b] 17 Pharaoh said to Joseph, "In my
dream, I was standing on the bank of the Nile. 18 Seven well-fed, healthy-
looking cows were coming up out of the Nile and were grazing on marshy
plants 19 when seven thin, very ugly, emaciated cows were coming up
behind them. I have never seen such ugly cows like these anywhere in
Egypt. 20 The emaciated, ugly cows consumed the earlier mentioned
seven well-fed cows. 21 However, after they ingested them, one would
not have known that they had ingested them; they were just as ugly as

before. Then I woke up. 22 I fell asleep again[c] and saw in my dream seven
healthy and mature heads of grain growing on one stalk. 23 Then seven
sterile, skinny heads of grain, shriveled from the east wind, sprouted
behind them. 24 The seven skinny heads of grain swallowed up the seven
good heads of grain. I recounted it to the scholars, but no explanation was
forthcoming for me."

25 Joseph then said to Pharaoh, "Pharaoh's dreams are the same. God
has explained to Pharaoh what he is doing. 26 The seven good cows are
seven years just as the seven good heads of grain are seven years: it is the
same dream. 27 The seven ugly and emaciated cows who were coming
up behind them are seven years just as the seven skinny heads of grain,
shriveled from the east wind, are seven years of famine. 28 As I've just
told Pharaoh, God has shown to Pharaoh what he is doing. 29 Seven years
of great abundance throughout the land of Egypt are coming. 30 But then
seven years of famine will follow them. All the abundance in the land of
Egypt will be forgotten; famine will destroy the land. 31 The abundance
in the land will be known no more because of the famine, which will
be terribly severe. 32 In this instance the twofold character of Pharaoh's
dream means that the matter is, according to God, inevitable; God will
make it happen soon. 33 Pharaoh should immediately find someone who
is savvy and wise and appoint him over the land of Egypt. 34 Pharaoh
should proceed to designate administrators throughout the land in order to
collect one-fifth [of the produce] from the land of Egypt during the seven
abundant years. 35 They should gather all the produce during these good
years that are coming. They should store threshed grain under Pharaoh's
authority; they should protect the food in the cities. 36 That food will be
a reserve for the land during the seven years of famine that will transpire
in the land of Egypt so that the land will not be wiped out."

37 The proposal seemed good to Pharaoh and his servants. 38 Pharaoh
said to his servants, "Who could we find other than this person who
embodies the spirit of God?" 39 Pharaoh said to Joseph, "Because God
has informed you about all this, there is no one as savvy and wise as you
are. 40 You shall be over my house, and all my people will follow your
lead. Only with regard to the throne will I be more powerful than you."
41 Then Pharaoh said to Joseph, "Look, I have appointed you over the
entire land of Egypt." 42 Pharaoh took off the signet ring from his hand
and put it on Joseph's hand. Then he had him outfitted in garments of
linen, and he placed a gold ornament around his neck. 43 He had him ride
as second-in-command in his chariot. The people[d] called out, "*Abrek!*"[e]
In this way he was appointed over all the land of Egypt. 44 Pharaoh said
to Joseph, "I am Pharaoh, but without your approval no one throughout
the entire land of Egypt will raise his hand or take a step." 45 Pharaoh

named Joseph "Zaphenath-paneah" and gave him Asenath, daughter of
Potiphera, priest of ʾOn, for his wife. Joseph traveled throughout the land
of Egypt.

46 Joseph was thirty years old when he began to work for Pharaoh,
king of Egypt. Joseph left Pharaoh and went on his way throughout all
the land of Egypt. **47** The earth produced abundantly during the seven
fertile years. **48** He collected all the produce of those seven years, when
there was abundance throughout the land of Egypt,[f] and stored food in the
cities; he stored food in the cities from the fields nearby. **49** Joseph piled
up grain like the sand of the seashore. He accumulated so much that it
couldn't be counted; one could not count it.

50 Before the years of famine, Joseph had two sons, whom Asenath,
daughter of Potiphera, priest of ʾOn, bore for him. **51** Joseph named the
firstborn Manasseh because "God has helped me to forget all of my
misery and everything about my father's household." **52** He named the
second Ephraim because "God has helped me to flourish in the land of
my misfortunes."

53 When the seven abundant years in the land of Egypt were over, **54** the
seven years of famine began, just as Joseph said they would. There was
famine in every country, but in the land of Egypt there was food. **55** When
everyone in the land of Egypt began to starve, they cried out to Pharaoh
for food. Pharaoh responded to all the Egyptians, "Go to Joseph, do what
he tells you to do." **56** When the famine had extended throughout the entire
country, Joseph released the grain that was in them—the cities[g]—and sold
it to the Egyptians. The famine became severe throughout the land of
Egypt. **57** In addition, [people from] the entire world came to Egypt to
buy [grain] because the famine was severe throughout the entire world.

a. Literally, "his spirit was troubled."

b. Or, "No one other than God can respond concerning the welfare of Pharaoh."

c. LXX, Syr, and Vulg. MT does not include this clause.

d. Literally, "they," which could be either the people or Pharaonic officials.

e. An Egyptian word that sounds like the Hebrew word *berek* (knee), which in this context would mean "genuflect."

f. SP, LXX. MT does not include the word "abundance."

g. Literally, "Joseph released all that was in them." LXX reads, "Joseph opened all the storehouses."

[41:1–36] Though, at the beginning of this chapter, a temporal phrase indicates a precise passage of time (cf. the beginning of ch. 40, which makes a nonspecific reference to the passage of time), there is no prologue to this chapter, which extends over a much longer period of time than did any of the previous chapters in the short story. In fact, the reference to two years in 41:1 is followed by more temporal specificity, seven years followed by another seven years, when Joseph interprets Pharaoh's dreams as well as the report that Joseph was thirty years old when Pharaoh gave him supreme authority over Egypt. (This is thirteen years since readers met the seventeen-year-old Joseph: 37:2.) It is as if things need to move ahead with precision after Joseph's indeterminate years in Potiphar's household.

Chapter 40 introduced the Pharaonic court, and it is that setting in which the opening scene of Gen 41 takes place. In this scene, the narrator describes two dreams of Pharaoh. In doing so, the narrator often uses participles rather than finite verbs to convey the action (e.g., vv. 1–2), a narrative tactic to make the action seem present to the reader.

The dreams are set in the Egyptian agricultural world: animal husbandry and the production of grain. And the visual images in the dreams—well-fed versus emaciated livestock, healthy versus shriveled plants—would not have been viewed as unusual. What is unusual is the action. The first dream is, perhaps, less strange, although it does turn herbivorous animals into carnivores. The dream concerning grain is even stranger. One part of the plant, the head of grain, develops the ability to devour the head of grain on another stalk. (On the assumption that the grain is either emmer, an ancient type of wheat, or barley, there is one head per stalk.) The image of one "head" devouring another has essentially personified the stalk of grain, turning it into a ravenous person. In any case, both dreams conclude with negative images: that which is healthy is negated. They are nightmares, which is exactly the sense of "what a dream!" (v. 7). That phrase could refer just to the second dream, but it more likely reflects the judgment, later confirmed by Joseph (v. 25), that the two dreams really function together as one dream.

When Pharaoh's courtiers are unable to interpret his dream(s), the chief wine steward recalls Joseph, "a young Hebrew." With his relatively lengthy report, the steward inaugurates direct discourse in this chapter (vv. 9b–13). His speech offers a flashback to the events narrated in Gen 40, attesting to Joseph's prior ability as a dream interpreter. Once Pharaoh hears this report, he has Joseph promptly brought from the dungeon. Joseph observes standard court protocol by shaving and donning new clothes before appearing before Pharaoh. First, Pharaoh does not command Joseph to interpret his dream but tells Joseph he has heard that Joseph is able to interpret dreams. This statement gives Joseph (and the narrator) an opening to make a theological point: God is the one who can clarify dreams. Unfortunately, the precise claim that Joseph makes is ambiguous. According to the above translation, Joseph seems to say that only God can ensure that the interpretation will be favorable to Pharaoh. However, the option in note b allows for Joseph to say that only God can respond regarding Pharaoh's welfare, that is, Joseph does not imply that the response will be favorable to Pharaoh. In either case, Joseph apparently means that a response can be forthcoming, that he is the agent of the deity, and that the response will address Pharaoh's well-being. In fact, the interpretation of the dreams concerns the welfare of the land of Egypt—and the entire world—not just the welfare of Pharaoh.

Pharaoh's report to Joseph occurs as direct discourse, not in the voice of the narrator, as in 41:2–7. And Pharaoh's speech offers a longer, more detailed account of the dreams than did that of the narrator, eight verses instead of six. For example, the bad cows are "ugly, emaciated" in verse 3; but in verse 19 they become "thin, very ugly, emaciated." In the earlier version, Pharaoh offers no comment; in the second, he comments, "I have never seen such ugly cows like these anywhere in Egypt." The earlier version makes no comment about the impact of the ugly cows eating the good ones; in the second, Pharaoh observes that even after the ugly cows ate the good ones, they were as emaciated as before. The recounting of the second dream has not been expanded as much as for the first one, but the same tendencies are in place. The heads of grain in verse 6 are "skinny, shriveled," whereas in verse 23 they are "sterile, skinny, and shriveled." Pharaoh's speech offers an embellished version that intensifies the negative aspect of the dream. No such developments appear in the description of either the healthy cattle or the good heads of grain. Pharaoh's dream has become even more of a nightmare as it is retold. And no Egyptian can offer an "interpretation" (v. 8) or an "explanation" (v. 24).

It is, of course, a fortuity that the chief wine steward remembers Joseph since, immediately upon hearing the dream, Joseph is able to provide an interpretation. And, consistent with his earlier claim that God is the author of such interpretations, Joseph tells Pharaoh that the doubled dreams are God's way of letting Pharaoh know what God is about to do. The deity's intention will not change. Joseph's claim is not only that God can interpret dreams but also that God is in control of what is happening to Pharaoh and the entire land of Egypt.

In interpreting Pharaoh's dreams, Joseph makes two interpretive moves. First, the number 7 refers to seven years, and the good/bad crops and herds refer to bounty and famine, respectively. The dream is treated as symbolic, similar to the one with which the Joseph story began and similar to the ones of the baker and wine steward. Second, Joseph avers that, unlike a single dream with an unhappy outcome, which some ritual might deter, the doubled dream refers to an event that cannot be avoided.

Joseph then moves beyond his role of dream interpreter to that of sage administrator. Readers never hear Pharaoh respond to the interpretation of his dreams until after Joseph proposes a way to address the situation prophesied in the dreams. Joseph offers a plan whereby food will be saved and stored during the seven good years. The plan includes a striking provision. The food should be stored in the cities (v. 35); presumably an urban environment will more likely be secure. There is a striking rationale as well, "so that the land will not be wiped out" (v. 36). Joseph's plan is grounded in an ecological concern, that the land, the source of Egyptian agricultural bounty, be preserved during the years of drought such that it can be productive again, once the seven years of famine have passed. Such concern for the land is emphasized by repetition of the noun "land" (41:29, 30 [2×], 31, 33, 34 [2×], 36 [2×]), 41, 43, 44, 45, 46, 47, 48, 52, 53, 54 [2×], 55, 56, 57 [2×].

[37–57] Pharaoh's response to Joseph is initially couched in theological language as he builds on Joseph's own claim that God is the one who will respond to Pharaoh's dream (v. 16). Pharaoh claims that Joseph possesses "the spirit of God." And when he says, "because God has informed you about all this," a statement that occurs after Joseph has presented his plan, one may assume that Pharaoh is responding to both the interpretation of his dreams and Joseph's proposal regarding the collection and storage of food. He even borrows Joseph's own diction, "savvy and wise," in describing Joseph's qualities.

From this point to the end of the chapter, Joseph's ascent to power is rapid and profound. Pharaoh's placing him "over his house" recalls Joseph's role as overseer of Potiphar's house. And just as only one thing was withheld from him, Potiphar's wife, Pharaoh gives him full responsibility over his house, withholding only one thing, the throne. To underscore his elevated status, Pharaoh grants Joseph new clothes, jewelry, and an Egyptian wife, Asenath. He is even given a new, Egyptian name (v. 45).

The overall narrative becomes more of a report than a story, and it is occasionally repetitive. Verse 44 essentially repeats the power granted to Joseph in 41:40, and 41:48 reports twice that grain is being stored in cities.

During the years of fertility and plenty, Asenath gives birth to two boys: Manasseh and Ephraim. The popular etymology of Manasseh's name is striking: "God has helped me forget all my misery." The issue of forgetting has played an important role earlier in the narrative, when the wine steward forgot about Joseph (40:23). Now Joseph attests to a God who helps one forget the difficulties he has experienced earlier. This ability of the deity to affect Joseph's memory is consistent with the interest in the inner life of characters that one finds throughout the Joseph short story. Here it is unusual since the deity is involved in that inner life. Both of the boys' names refer to Joseph's way of understanding his past life: as one made up of misery and misfortunes.

The final verses of the chapter report the end of the good years and the onset of famine, "just as Joseph said they would." The famine not only drives the story further; it also confirms Joseph's role as authoritative interpreter. His role in administering the distribution of food focuses initially on provisions to the Egyptians. But, due to the worldwide famine, others travel to Egypt to secure food. In both cases, the author makes clear that Joseph is selling the grain to both parties. This international trade sets the stage for the next chapter, in which Israelites travel to Egypt to purchase food.

A number of theological perspectives are at work in this chapter. Joseph attributes the power of dream interpretation to the deity. Through the dreams, the author maintains that God is in charge of what is happening to Pharaoh and the land of Egypt. Joseph reports experiencing a beneficent deity, one who can remove terrible memories. This beneficent deity also cares for "the land" and for "all the world" (v. 57).

Genesis 42:1–38
Joseph Recognizes His Brothers but Treats Them as Strangers

An abrupt transition back to the household of Jacob introduces a chapter in which geographic movement abounds. The brothers go down to Egypt and then return to the land of Canaan. Genesis 42 is rich in dialogue, though the characters sometimes speak past each other. It is a chapter in which deep emotions are portrayed, by Joseph, by his brothers, and by their father. And it is a chapter in which Jacob, at both beginning and end, seems to be in control. He sends his sons down to Egypt yet forbids them from taking Benjamin to that foreign land. It is also a chapter in which Joseph exerts control over his brothers just as he has already acted powerfully over the land of Egypt.

> 42:1 When Jacob discovered that there was grain in Egypt, he said to his
> sons, "Why do you keep staring at each other?" 2 He continued, "I have
> heard that there is grain in Egypt. Go down there and purchase [some]
> for us from there so that we may live and not die." 3 So ten of Joseph's
> brothers went down to buy grain from Egypt. 4 But Jacob did not send
> Benjamin, Joseph's brother, to keep something terrible from happening
> to him. 5 Jacob's sons went to buy [grain] along with the others who were
> going due to the famine in the land of Canaan.
>
> 6 Now Joseph was ruler over the land; he was the one who sold [grain]
> to all the people of the land. So Joseph's brothers came and bowed to him,
> their faces toward the ground. 7 When Joseph saw them, he recognized
> them but treated them as strangers and spoke harshly to them. He said to
> them, "From where have you come?" They responded, "From the land
> of Canaan to purchase grain." 8 Even though Joseph had recognized
> his brothers, they did not recognize him. 9 Joseph then remembered the
> dreams he had dreamed concerning them. Joseph said, "You are spies.
> You have come to discover the vulnerability of this country." 10 They
> responded, "No, my lord. Your servants have come to purchase food.
> 11 All of us are the sons of one man. We are honest. Your servants are
> not spies." 12 He said to them, "No! You have come to discover the
> vulnerability of the land." 13 They responded, "We, your servants, were
> twelve brothers, the sons of one man in the land of Canaan. The youngest

remains with his father. Another is no longer alive." 14 Joseph said to them, "It is just as I have told you, 'You are spies.' 15 Here is how you will be tested. As surely as Pharaoh lives, you shall not leave this place until your younger brother arrives here. 16 Send one of your number to bring your brother. The rest of you will remain in prison, to test whether or not your words are true. And if not, as surely as Pharaoh lives, you are spies." 17 He put them in prison for three days.

18 Then, on the third day, Joseph said to them, "Do this and you will live. I am a God-fearing person.[a] 19 If you are honest, have one of your brothers incarcerated in the prison where you have been. The rest of you go and bring grain for the famine present in your households. 20 Then you shall bring your younger brother to me. In this way, your words will be verified, and you will not die." They agreed to this. 21 They then said to one another,[b] "We are certainly suffering now because of our brother; when we saw his deep distress and when he pleaded with us, we didn't respond to him. Therefore, we are now experiencing this distress." 22 Reuben then responded to them, "Didn't I tell you, 'Don't harm the boy'? But you didn't listen to me. Now his blood is demanding a response." 23 They didn't know that Joseph understood them since there had been an interpreter for them. 24 Joseph left and wept. Then he returned and spoke with them. Next, he selected Simeon from among them and had him shackled in front of them. 25 Joseph gave an order to fill their bags with grain, to return their silver in each one's sack, and to provide them with food for the journey. And that was done for them.

26 They loaded their grain onto their donkeys and left there. 27 When one of them opened his sack to give food to his donkey where they were staying for the night, he saw his silver; it was at the top of the pack. 28 He said to his brothers, "My silver has been returned. Look, it's in my pack." Each of the brothers was shaken. They said, "What is this that God has done to us?"

29 When they came to Jacob their father in the land of Canaan, they told him everything that had happened to them, 30 "The man, a lord of the land, spoke harshly to us; he accused us of spying on the land. 31 But we said to him, 'We are honest; we are not spies. 32 We were twelve brothers, the sons of one father. One is no longer alive, and the youngest is now with our father in the land of Canaan.' 33 Then the man, a lord of the land, said to us, 'In this way I will discover whether or not you are spies, whether you are honest. Leave one of your brothers with me but go and take grain[c] on account of the famine in your households. 34 Then bring your youngest brother to me so that I may verify whether or not you are spies, whether you are honest. Then I will give your brother back to you, and you will be able to trade in the land.'"

35 When they were emptying their sacks, there was a pouch of silver
in each bag. When they and their father saw the pouches of silver, they
were terrified. 36 Jacob their father said to them, "You have robbed me
[of my children]. Joseph is no more. Simeon is no more. And now you
would take Benjamin. How can all this be happening to me?" 37 Reuben
responded to his father, "You may kill my two sons if I do not bring him
back to you. Let him come with me, and I will bring him back to you."
38 Jacob said, "My son will never go down with you. His brother is dead,
and he alone remains. Something terrible might happen to him on the trip
you are undertaking. Then you would have sent down my aged head in
sorrow to Sheol."

a. Literally, "I fear God."
b. Literally, "each to his brother."
c. "Grain" is missing in MT but present in LXX.

[42:1–5] This chapter commences with Jacob in charge of his household. He upbraids his sons for doing nothing during a time of famine. (The narrator has let the reader implicitly know that there is famine where Jacob lives by reporting at the end of Gen 41 that "the famine was severe throughout the entire world." Only in 42:5 does the narrator explicitly state that famine has reached the land of Canaan.) Moreover, Jacob, not the sons, learns how they might secure food, by going to Egypt to buy grain. Here again, the preceding chapter set the stage for this possibility by informing readers that Joseph was selling grain not only to Egyptians but to an international market. Based on this knowledge, Jacob commands his sons to go down to Egypt and purchase grain. It is a life-or-death matter. The narrator introduces a touch of irony when reporting that "ten of Joseph's brothers" leave for Egypt. In 42:1, they are called Jacob's sons. By labeling them Joseph's brothers, the author has left the door open for the recurrence of brotherly tension and strife. This fraternal relationship is further emphasized when readers discover that the one son not on his way to Egypt is Benjamin, who was, along with Joseph, Rachel's son. Jacob does not permit Benjamin to travel to Egypt for fear that something bad might happen to him. Yet again, Jacob favors one son over others: the implication of his decision regarding Benjamin is that he is willing to let harm come upon one or more of his other sons.

[6–25] The scene abruptly shifts back to Egypt. The narrator introduces a new term for Joseph's role, literally, "the ruler," a noun with a root that bears royal connotations in Gen 49:10 (but cf. Eccl 7:19). This term helps realize the imagery of the dream reported in Gen 37:8, according to which Joseph will rule over his brothers. And that sort of royal role helps explain the reason for the brothers genuflecting before Joseph after they arrive in Egypt. Readers know that Joseph treats them as strangers, speaking harshly to them. But the narrator does not imply overtly or necessarily that Joseph speaks any more harshly to them than he would to any other stranger who has come to buy grain from him. Such "harsh" speech may simply be part of his royal-like prerogative. Interestingly, the author twice uses the verb *nkr*, though with different meanings: "recognize" (v. 7) and "treat as strangers" (v. 8).

The dialogue in 42:7–16 exemplifies that harsh speech. Here Joseph clearly treats his brothers in a way different from how he treats others who come to buy grain. Within this dialogue, verses 8–9a are an aside from the omniscient narrator, making clear that the brothers do not recognize him and that Joseph is construing this interaction on the basis of the dreams reported in Gen 37. He "remembers" the dreams even as, in the preceding chapter, he is enabled to forget the onerous things that have happened to him (41:51).

The dialogue between Joseph and his brothers offers a wonder of explicit and implicit meanings. He charges them with being spies, having come to explore ways in which Egypt might be vulnerable to attack. They respond en masse that they are not spies. And they make a further claim that might at first appear odd: "All of us are sons of one man." They appeal to their familial ties as a way of defending themselves from the charge of being spies. The implicit logic seems to be that if they were spies, they would not be related in such a way. Still, the appeal to family solidarity seems ironic in a chapter where the relationship between that "one man" and his ten sons, now speaking in Egypt, is fraught with tension. Moreover, the appeal to their being sons of one man ignores the different statuses from the identity of their mothers. None of the ten sons born to three women are as favored by Jacob as much as Rachel's sons.

In their defense, the brothers claim to be "honest" (v. 11), an assertion that must have been jarring to Joseph's ears. Joseph's reiteration of his charge that they are spies leads them to say more, something about Joseph himself (and his brother Benjamin). Why they offer this background is a mystery, but perhaps it is psychologically necessary. For whatever reason, they feel compelled to comment about all the sons of that one man, not just the ten who are now in Egypt to buy grain. Joseph does not respond directly to this comment about himself, but again insists on their status as spies (he does this four times [vv. 9, 12, 14, 16] in their dialogue with him). Then he then proposes a "test," the nature of which is obscure. If their imprisonment for three days is the test, then it clearly does not accomplish its goal. If, however, the three days are intended to "soften them up," then, in the ensuing verses, Joseph learns that they will accept his plan of having one of them remain imprisoned in Egypt and that at least Reuben rues what the brothers have done to Joseph (v. 22).

Joseph announces a plan as a part of the test, that one brother remain in Egypt while the others return to the land of Canaan with food and then return with "your youngest brother." Joseph's rationales are multiple, though only one is overt: "for I fear God." It is not clear why a God-fearing person would exact the test that Joseph is promulgating. Perhaps Joseph is something akin to what his brothers have stated. They say they are "honest"; he says he fears God, which is presumably an even stronger claim than that of honesty. Whether or not he implies that they do not fear God is unclear. In any case, the brothers immediately agree to his plan. This is the last time in the chapter that Joseph's words are heard directly. There are, of course, other rationales: Joseph is sending food to his father's household in their time of need and is setting the conditions for seeing his father and his brother Benjamin.

The plan stimulates conversation among the brothers, conversation in which they psychologize what is happening to them. They allude to an unattested episode and/or mood, one in which Joseph is in deep distress and pleads with them. His "distress" now results in their "distress" (v. 21). Then one of the brothers, Reuben, chides the brothers for their earlier behavior toward Joseph. Even though he wrongly claims that Joseph's *blood* is demanding a response, the very much alive Joseph is now demanding a response.

The narrator controls the remainder of this deeply emotional scene, reporting that Joseph is, literally, moved to tears by what he has heard. After he regains control of his emotions, he enacts his plan, singling out Simeon as the brother to be incarcerated. And then comes the surprise: Joseph orders his minions to put the money, which his brothers have brought to buy grain, into their bags of grain.

[26–38] The brothers' trip back to the land of Canaan includes a startling discovery, even though the omniscient narrator has already let readers know that this will happen. One of Jacob's sons discovers that the silver with which he has bought the grain is at the top of his bag of grain. Oddly, none of his brothers are said to open their bags. That, however, does not keep them from being emotionally shaken. Moreover, the brothers attribute this happenstance to the deity: "What is this that God has done to us?" The question, unlike Reuben's rhetorical question in verse 22, does not suggest an obvious answer. It does, however, imply that the brothers impute the presence of their silver to the deity; it is not an accident. Further, for the reader, who knows that Joseph and not God has done it, Joseph has godlike power over them. Ultimately, the question is ambiguous. Do they think that what God has done to them is good or ill?

Finally, Jacob's sons return to Canaan. The redundant phrase "their father Jacob" (v. 29) signals his authority over them, just as the preceding verses have highlighted Joseph's authority over them. As a group they offer a summary of what has happened to them in Egypt. Their account has been "cleaned up." There is no reference to all of them having been imprisoned for three days. Nor do they describe Simeon's being shackled in front of them and imprisoned. But there is new information as well. They report that Joseph has said he would let them trade throughout the land of Egypt (v. 34), something not reported earlier.

The account is emotionally neutral, with none of the intensity in the original reporting. To this summary, Jacob surprisingly offers no verbal response. Only after all of them discover silver in their bags of grain does the world of overtly deep feelings return. The brothers are depressed. Jacob laments the death of Joseph and the likely demise of Simeon, and he accuses his sons of having deprived him of his children. One might have thought that Jacob would have this reaction immediately after he learns that Simeon has been imprisoned, but that response is delayed until after the silver is discovered in their bags of grain.

Just as in Egypt, only Reuben speaks out, asking Jacob to let him take Benjamin to Egypt. Yet again there is new information: he has two sons, whom he will let Jacob kill if Reuben does not bring Benjamin back alive. Jacob responds decisively, refusing to let Benjamin go. When saying, "He alone remains," Jacob diminishes the status of his other sons. Jacob, even at this stage in the story, is still showing favoritism. As in 42:4, Jacob is worried that "something terrible" might happen to Benjamin. He is also worried that such an event would result in a sorrowful death for himself. The chapter ends with Joseph's test in full play. By the end of 42:38, there is no plan for the brothers to return. From Joseph's perspective, they have, to this point, failed the test.

Genesis 43:1–34
Benjamin Comes to Egypt with His Brothers

This chapter offers action in two settings: the land of Canaan (vv. 1–14) and Egypt (vv. 15–34). The famine is now in control. Moreover, it is clear that neither Jacob nor his sons are concerned about Simeon, who remains in Egypt. Benjamin, who does not speak, is the center of attention. Only if Jacob permits him to travel to Egypt will the brothers be able to buy food. His presence in Egypt, when Joseph sees him, results in a great banquet. The chapter also gives attention to the silver that the brothers discover in their sacks. Their father and the steward of Joseph's house offer differing rationales for the presence of the silver. The chapter begins with disgruntled brothers and their father, and it concludes with profound expressions of emotion. Joseph is deeply moved when he speaks to Benjamin, characterizing him as "my son," and the brothers are astounded that they are seated at the banquet according to their birth order.

> 43:1 The famine became terrible in the land. 2 When they had finished
> eating the grain they had brought from Egypt, their father said to them,
> "Go back and buy a little more food for us." 3 But Judah said to him,
> "The man swore to us, 'You will not see me unless your brother is with
> you.' 4 If you are willing to send our brother with us, we will go down
> and buy food for you; 5 but if you are not willing, we will not go down.
> The man really did say to us, 'You will not see me unless your brother is
> with you.'" 6 Israel then said, "Why did you mistreat me by telling him
> that you had another brother?" 7 They replied, "The man interrogated us
> about those in our family: 'Is your father still alive? Do you have another
> brother?' We then gave him all this information. How could we know that
> he would say, 'Bring your brother down'?" 8 Judah then said to Israel his
> father, "Send the lad with me. We need to hurry and go so that we can
> live and not die—all of us, including you and those younger. 9 I take total
> responsibility for him; you will see him again. If I don't bring him back
> to you and put him before you, you can treat me as guilty forever. 10 If
> we had not wasted time, we would have come back twice as quickly."
>
> 11 Israel, their father, responded, "If such is necessary, then do this:
> take some of the best produce from the land in your sacks and take them

down to the man as a present—a little balsam, a little honey, rose oil,
pistachios, and almonds. 12 And take twice as much silver as before—
along with the silver that was found in the top of your sacks. Perhaps it
was a mistake. 13 Moreover, take your brother. Get up and go to the man!
14 May God Almighty[a] act graciously toward you in your interactions
with the man[b] so that he will send back your other brother along with
Benjamin. If I am deprived of children, so be it." 15 So the men took the
present and double the amount of silver along with Benjamin and went
on their way down to Egypt and appeared before Joseph.

16 When Joseph saw them along with Benjamin, he said to the person
in charge of his household, "Bring the men into the house. Slaughter an
animal and prepare it because the men will dine with me at noon." 17 The
man did as Joseph had ordered and brought the men into Joseph's house.
18 The men were afraid when they had been brought into Joseph's house
and said, "It's because of the silver, which was put back earlier in our
sacks. We've been brought here to be assaulted, captured, enslaved, and
to have our donkeys taken." 19 So they approached the man who was
in charge of Joseph's house and spoke to him at the house's entrance.
20 They said, "My lord, when we had come down earlier to buy grain,
21 and had come to a place to spend the night, we opened our sacks, and
there each man's silver was at the top of his sack—the entire amount of
silver. So we have brought it back. 22 We have now brought back even
more silver to buy grain. We don't know who put the silver back into
our sacks." 23 Then he [the man in charge] said, "It's all right. Don't
worry. Your God, the God of your father, put treasure in your sacks. I
had received your silver." He then brought out Simeon to them. 24 When
the man brought the men into Joseph's house, he gave them water so they
could wash their feet and gave them food for their donkeys. 25 Then they
prepared the gift for Joseph, who was coming at noon; they had heard
that he would dine with them there.

26 When Joseph came home, they brought him the present that they
had with them in the house and bowed down to him. 27 He asked about
their welfare and said, "Is your father all right, the old man whom you had
mentioned? Is he still alive?" 28 They replied, "Your servant, our father,
is indeed all right; he is still alive." They bowed down respectfully. 29 He
looked up and saw Benjamin, his brother, the son of his own mother. He
said, "Is this your younger brother whom you mentioned to me? May
God act graciously to you, my son." 30 Then Joseph quickly left the room
because he was overwhelmed by his love for his brother and was about
to start crying. He went into a private room and cried there. 31 Then he
washed his face and went out. When he had gotten control of himself,
he said, "Serve the meal." 32 They served him by himself and them by

themselves. (The Egyptians who were there eating with him [were served]
by themselves because Egyptians are not permitted to eat with Hebrews;
that would be a disgrace.) 33 They sat before him in the order of their
birth: the firstborn based on his birthright, on to the youngest, based on
his youth. The men looked at each other in amazement. 34 He sent some
of his food to them. The amount given to Benjamin was five times larger
than any of theirs. So they drank a great deal and had a good time with him.

a. Hebrew, *El Shaddai.*
b. Literally, "before the man."

[43:1–14] The famine has now gained control over the land of Canaan such that Jacob's family needs food. Jacob's response to this situation is flawed, however, in at least two ways. First, he orders his sons to return to Egypt and purchase "a little" food, clearly an inadequate response to the famine that they are experiencing. Moreover, his plan for them to return does not take into account the test that Joseph has created. Joseph will only release Simeon if his brothers bring Benjamin to Egypt. Though Jacob has been informed about this test (42:33–34), he has either forgotten or ignored it.

As in the case at the end of the preceding chapter, one of Jacob's sons speaks. Judah reminds Jacob of "the man's" condition: they will not be able to see him unless Benjamin comes with them to Egypt. In so doing, Judah, on behalf of his brothers, refuses to follow Jacob's orders. Judah's challenge elicits a feeble response from his father, asking why his sons "mistreat" him. His assignment of blame to them masks his own responsibility for much of what has happened. And it does not directly address what Judah has just said to him. Then the brothers as a whole respond to Jacob's question by recounting the intensity of Joseph's interrogation. Jacob offers no response to what they say. And so Judah, as did Reuben previously, asks his father to permit him to take Benjamin with them to Egypt. However, unlike Reuben, who has said that Jacob may kill his two sons if he does not bring Benjamin back with him, Judah simply says that Jacob may treat him as "guilty" forever, a less draconian vow than Reuben's. Judah even offers a subtle dig at his father, noting that they could already be back if he had not delayed in agreeing to send Benjamin with them. Clearly, the sons are now in a position to disagree with and upbraid their father.

To this offer, Jacob responds favorably. And this time, he supplements the plan of the brothers by proposing that they take a gift made up of various agricultural products produced in the land: nuts, honey, and plant extracts. (Interestingly, two of the products are those that the Ishmaelite traders take to Egypt: 37:25.) There is a certain irony that, during a severe famine, sufficient products are available for the brothers to take as gifts to Egypt. At a minimum, the gifts would be construed as especially valuable at such a time. Moreover, Jacob opens the family coffers, providing twice as much silver for the purchase of grain as for their first trip. While ordering them to take silver, Jacob offers an aside that sets the stage for dialogue about the silver later in the chapter. Jacob suggests that a mistake of some sort may account for the presence of the silver in their bags on the way home. He concludes his speech by offering a prayer that "the man" be compassionate to them by sending back Simeon, whom he does not name, and Benjamin, whom he does name. His final words, however, seem to reconcile him to his fate, even if those two individuals do not return.

[15–34] Immediately after those words, the narrator transports the brothers to Egypt, where they stand before Joseph. Oddly, the narrator refers to them as "the men" (so also v. 24), the same sort of impersonal reference as "the man," Joseph (43:3, 7, 14). The issue of concealed and revealed identity is now a driving force in the narrative. Joseph apparently recognizes Benjamin, but the narrator delays reporting his feelings about Benjamin until he meets with them just before the banquet. The revelation of Joseph's feelings and identity takes place slowly once the brothers have returned to Egypt.

That the brothers are taken to Joseph's house offers a contrast to the unstated venue in which he has met with them earlier (ch. 42). The only physical location mentioned there is the prison where Joseph incarcerates them for three days. The house, in contrast, is a less bureaucratic setting, though one in which the brothers are overtly afraid that they will be robbed and enslaved. When in the house, the brothers engage the person in charge of the residence in dialogue about the silver they have found in their sacks. After reporting their experience of finding the silver, the steward confirms that he has received the money. Unlike Jacob, who attributes the money in the sacks as a possible mistake, the steward offers a theological explanation: "Your God, the God of your father" put it there. Moreover, the steward construes the silver as "treasure." (Elsewhere in the OT, this same word can mean a treasure given by God [e.g., Isa 45:3].) It is, of course, possible to maintain that Joseph is an agent of a providential deity, who has provided treasure to Joseph's brothers. That claim would need to be tempered by the anguish that the gift has caused the brothers, as will again be the case in the next chapter.

At this point, it is appropriate to observe that Joseph has presented his brothers with a gift (their silver), and that his brothers are bringing him a gift (agricultural goods). To this extent, there is a certain symmetry since neither party has gained an advantage by giving a gift that is not more or less matched. This dual presentation of gifts underscores the complexity of the relations between Joseph and his brothers, a complexity evident even at the end of the Joseph short story.

The final scene of the chapter takes place inside Joseph's house. The brothers present their gift, and Joseph, as before, interrogates them, this time using familial diction. He asks them about the welfare of their father and then about the identity of his brother Benjamin, whom the narrator characterizes not as his brother but as "his mother's son." Perhaps the use of the word "brother" would have recalled Joseph's oppression by his brothers who were born to someone other than Rachel. In any case, Joseph offers a blessing in which he continues to use familial diction by naming Benjamin as "my son" rather than "my brother." Joseph has, in effect, taken a paternal role in his relationship with Benjamin. Simply the utterance of that blessing makes Joseph break down such that he must leave the room. The narrative is not yet ready for him to reveal himself to his brothers.

The narrative concludes with a description of the banquet, one characterized by the use of Egyptian protocol, according to which the brothers and the Egyptians eat separately. Joseph eats by himself. Joseph's separateness underscores his dual identity, a son of Jacob and an Egyptian official. Nonetheless, his knowledge of the birth order of his brothers results in their being seated according to their respective ages, Reuben to Benjamin, which astounds them. (This description is consistent with the narrator's interest in exploring overt descriptions of feelings, hence the fear of the brothers in v. 18 and Joseph's being overcome by his emotions in v. 30.) Moreover, Joseph gives extra food to his brothers, including five times as much to Benjamin. Clearly Joseph is subtly providing signals of his identity, but they are lost on his brothers, who are drinking a great deal at the banquet.

The final verse of the chapter includes overt reference to favoritism in the family. Joseph, as has his father before, shows favoritism to Benjamin in providing him with more food than that offered to his brothers. Favoritism inheres in this family's relationships.

Genesis 44:1–34
Joseph's Silver Cup Is Found in Benjamin's Bag

In this chapter, Joseph perpetrates a ruse, which involves a false theft and the threat of enslaving Benjamin. The ruse builds on the earlier gift of silver to the brothers, which is repeated. However, this time Joseph commands his steward to put a silver cup in Benjamin's sack. When that cup is discovered, the brothers are forced to return to Joseph's house, which, during the preceding evening, has been the scene of a pleasant banquet. Now, Joseph confronts them and accuses them of stealing the cup. Once they have been accused, only Judah speaks (vv. 16, 18–34). The second speech sets the stage for the story's climax at the beginning of the next chapter. Throughout the chapter, action proceeds based on the verbal responses of the primary characters. The reader does not know beforehand how the brothers will react to the false accusation, how Joseph will respond to their self-sentence, how Judah will respond to Joseph's plan that Benjamin be enslaved, and, at the beginning of the next chapter, how Joseph will respond to Judah's long speech. The human characters are very much in charge of what happens, unlike other places in the Joseph story where providence seems to be working itself out.

> 44:1 Then he ordered the person in charge of his house, "Fill the sacks
> of these men with as much food as they can carry and put each man's
> silver in the top of his bag. 2 Put my silver cup in the top of the bag of
> the youngest along with the silver for his grain." He did what Joseph told
> him to do. 3 At dawn, the men and their donkeys were sent on their way.
> 4 When they hadn't gone very far from the city, Joseph said to the person
> in charge of his house, "Get up and go after the men. When you reach
> them, say to them, 'Why have you acted badly instead of well?[a] 5 Isn't [it]
> this from which my master drinks? Moreover, he uses it for divination.
> How could you do such a wicked thing?'"
>
> 6 Upon reaching them, he said all this to them. 7 They responded to
> him, "Why does my lord speak like this to us? Your servants would never
> act like this! 8 The silver that we found in our sacks, we returned to you
> from the land of Canaan. Why would we have stolen gold or silver from
> the house of your master? 9 Whichever of your servants is found with it

should die. Moreover, we should become slaves to your master." 10 He
said, "It will be just as you have said for the one who is found with it. He
will become my slave, but the rest of you will go free." 11 Then each of
them quickly put his bag down on the ground and opened his bag. 12 He
examined [them], starting with the oldest and finishing with the youngest.
The cup was found in Benjamin's bag. 13 They tore their clothes, each
one loaded his donkey, and they returned to the city.

14 Judah and his brothers went to Joseph's house; he was still there.
They bowed down abjectly before him. 15 "What is this that you have
done? Didn't you understand that a person such as I can know things by
divination?" 16 Judah said, "What can we say to my lord? What might be
said? How can we defend ourselves? God has revealed the treachery of
your servants. We are now slaves to my lord—all of us, not just the one
who was found with the cup in his possession." 17 He said, "I wouldn't
do that. Only the one who was found with the cup in his possession will
become my slave. The rest of you may go in peace to your father."

18 Judah got up and said, "My lord, let your servant speak directly to
your lordship. May you not be angry even though you are like Pharaoh
himself. 19 My lord had asked his servants, 'Do you have a father or
brother?' 20 And we said to my lord, 'We have a father who is old, and we
have a younger brother, a son of his old age; his brother is dead. Only he
is left as a child of his mother; his father loves him.' 21 You said to your
servants, 'Bring him down to me so that I can see him.' 22 We responded
to my lord, 'The lad can't leave his father. If he were to leave, his father
would die.' 23 You said to your servants, 'If your younger brother doesn't
come down with you, you will never again see my face.' 24 When we had
gone up to your servant, my father, we told him what my lord had said.
25 Then, when our father said, 'Return and buy a little food for us,' 26 we
said, 'We can't go down. Unless our younger brother is with us, we won't
go down. We won't be able to see the face of the man unless our younger
brother is with us.' 27 Then your servant, my father, said to us, 'You know
that my wife bore two sons for me. 28 One has left me—I thought that he
had been mauled; I have never seen him again. 29 And now if you take
this one away from me, and he suffers a fatal accident, you will have
brought down my aged body in grief to Sheol.' 30 Now when I come to
your servant, my father, and the lad is not with us, then, since his life is
linked to his [youngest son's] life, 31 when he sees that the lad is not with
us, he will surely die. Your servants will have brought down the aged
body of your servant, our father, to Sheol in agony. 32 Moreover, your
servant has taken total responsibility for the lad on behalf of my father,
saying, 'If I do not bring him back to you, I will be guilty in my father's
eyes as long as I live.' 33 Now, please let your servant stay here instead of

the lad, to become a slave of my lord. Let the lad go up with his brothers.
34 How can I go up to my father without the lad with me? I am afraid that
something terrible might happen to my father."

a. LXX includes the following sentence, "Why did you steal my silver cup?"

[44:1–34] For a second time, the brothers are sold grain in exchange for the silver they have brought to Egypt. And for the second time, Joseph orders that the silver be put into the tops of their sacks. Only this time he also commands his steward to put his silver cup into Benjamin's bag. What earlier was an apparently beneficent act (one that, however, created anguish among his brothers: 42:28, 35) becomes an occasion for Joseph to accuse them of theft.

When the silver and the silver cup are found, the steward focuses only on the silver cup. He accuses them of acting "badly instead of well," of doing something wicked by taking the cup. His speech is primarily couched in the form of questions. Only the charge of acting wickedly is phrased in the indicative. Put another way, the speech that Joseph has created for the steward does not suggest what might happen to the brothers based on the theft of Joseph's cup. What will happen to them is left open. The first hint of what might happen is made by the brothers themselves. They, rather than Joseph, begin to forge their future.

After being challenged by Joseph's servant, the brothers protest their innocence. However, they also offer a potential punishment, should they be found guilty. The person who stole the cup should die, and the others should become Joseph's slaves (v. 9). The steward responds in a positive way to their self-sentence, but he also immediately revises it. The one in whose bag the cup was found shall not die but shall be "my slave." And the rest of the brothers will not be enslaved but will go free. This revision presumably means that the only crime in view is the theft of the cup, not the presence of the silver in the brothers' bags. Only after that revision does the search of the bags take place, which results in the discovery of the cup in Benjamin's sack.

After the brothers are brought back to Joseph's house, he challenges them with two questions. He refers neither to the silver nor to the cup. Instead, he opens with a general question and then moves to a more specific one about his ability to divine information. One might infer that he is, in effect, asking, "Don't you know that I can find things out by divination even without the cup that you have stolen?" And, presumably, what he is able to know by divination is that Benjamin has stolen his cup. (Divination using a drinking vessel could involve watching the liquid's surface for patterns that, when interpreted, presage the future [lecanomancy], or reading patterns in the dregs at the cup's bottom to similar effect.)

At this point Judah steps up to admit their culpability. But he does so in an unusual way. He does not report that either the steward or Joseph has found them out. Instead, he says, "God has revealed the treachery of your servants." One must ask, to what treachery is he is referring? The theft of his cup or the treachery of the brothers toward Joseph many years ago? Many interpreters have advocated for the latter option, but it makes little sense for Judah to be admitting their guilt regarding their earlier treatment of Joseph to this Egyptian official, whom they do not yet know to be Joseph. Instead, one should focus on Judah's claim that they are all guilty of stealing the cup. Such a claim revises the earlier proposal made by all of them that the one who stole the cup should die and that the others should be enslaved. Judah's admission of collective guilt is really an attempt to negotiate away from the sentence of death for the presumed thief (v. 9), which turns out to be Benjamin.

Why does Joseph perpetrate this trickery on his brothers? The narrator offers no overt evidence that the false accusation is designed as a test. At a minimum, the narrator reports that Joseph is a "just" man. He would not keep all his brothers enslaved, only the one who has been accused of stealing his cup. It is as if Joseph opens the door for a positive outcome, but much will depend upon how the brothers or, in this case, one of them responds to the false accusation and Joseph's plan to enslave Benjamin. Joseph accedes to one element of Judah's proposal, that enslavement rather than capital punishment be in play. But Joseph revises Judah's proposal by stating that only the thief should be enslaved. The others would be permitted to go back to their father, presumably with their grain and silver.

Judah now faces a new challenge. He has been successful in negotiating away the death sentence that the brothers have proposed. However, he now confronts a situation in which all the brothers may return to Jacob, though without Benjamin, a situation that he knows would be dire for his father. Jacob has earlier recognized the possibility that he might need to grieve for "my children" (43:14), but he does not come to grips with the possibility that he will have to lament the death of only Benjamin, which, as Judah will soon make clear, would kill him (v. 31).

There is a certain irony with the way in which Judah begins his speech, characterizing himself as "your servant," the same Hebrew word that Joseph has used, meaning "slave" (v. 17). Though Judah has asked, "What can we say to my lord?" (v. 16), he now formulates a speech that will move both the brothers and Joseph beyond the deadlock regarding false accusation of theft and the threat of enslavement for Benjamin. Beginning in verse 19, Judah recounts Joseph's interactions with his brothers as those were narrated in Gen 42. This rehearsal is not entirely accurate. Joseph has not posed the question quoted in 44:19. In Gen 42, the brothers simply blurted out the information about their family as a part of their defense against the accusation that they were spies. Beyond that, Judah summarizes what has taken place in Gen 42–43, including Judah's willingness to accept the blame if Benjamin does not return from the journey to Egypt. In addition, he requests that *he*, rather than Benjamin, be enslaved in Egypt to avoid causing his father to suffer. This is an exceptional speech, the longest (17 verses) in the entire Joseph short story. Judah's deeply emotional plea on behalf of his father and indeed Benjamin, who remains unnamed in the speech, sets the stage for Joseph's profoundly felt response in the ensuing verses.

Genesis 45:1–28
Joseph Reveals Himself to His Brothers: "God Sent Me to Preserve Life"

This chapter constitutes the point of climax in the Joseph story. The one whom his brothers thought to be dead reveals that he is alive, a ruler in and over Egypt. This development does not stem from a plan that Joseph has made but instead reflects his response to the speech of his brother Judah (44:18–34) and to the presence of his brothers. Judah has shown himself willing to be enslaved in place of Benjamin and to be deeply concerned about the welfare of his father. Moreover, Joseph again sees his younger brother before him. All these factors make it impossible for him to control his emotions and to continue to hide his identity.

Immediately after Joseph reveals himself to his brothers, he offers them a theological perspective on what has transpired. He maintains that, contrary to what his brothers must be thinking, God has directed Joseph's life. Though his brothers may have sold him into slavery, it was God who brought Joseph to Egypt and who has enabled him to become a ruler there. Not only that, God also has a purpose in this direction: preserving life. What has happened to Joseph is embedded in the larger narrative of an international, ecological disaster: a famine that lasts seven years. What may have appeared to be a small-scale story about one family's disarray is really a momentous narrative about how God has provided food for all those who come to Egypt to purchase it.

Once the scene in which Joseph reveals his identity to his brothers takes place, Pharaoh enters as a speaker promising that members of Joseph's family will have "the best from the land of Egypt." Following court protocol, he speaks to Joseph, who then conveys that information to his brothers. As a result of both Joseph's and Pharaoh's admonitions and assurances, the brothers return to Canaan. After Jacob's sons report to him that Joseph is alive, Jacob agrees to travel to Egypt, a course of action leading to the family's place for living that continues beyond the book of Genesis.

> **45:1** Joseph was no longer able to control himself in front of those who
> stood before him. He shouted, "Get everyone away from me!" No one
> was with him when Joseph made himself known to his brothers. **2** He
> wept so loudly that the Egyptians, including the house of Pharaoh, heard

it. 3 Joseph said to his brothers, "I am Joseph. Is my father still alive?" However, his brothers couldn't respond to him because they were terrified of him.

4 Joseph said, "Come near to me," which they did. He said, "I am your brother Joseph, whom you sold into Egypt. 5 Don't worry now or be angry with each other because you sold me here. God sent me ahead of you to preserve life. 6 There have been two years of famine throughout the country, and there will be five more years without cultivating or harvesting. 7 God sent me ahead of you to establish a remnant on earth—to keep alive many survivors for you. 8 You did not send me here, but God did. He established me as a father to Pharaoh, as lord over his entire house and ruler over all the land of Egypt. 9 Go up quickly to my father and say to him, 'Thus says Joseph your son, God has set me as lord over all Egypt. Come down to me. Don't remain there. 10 You shall live in the land of Goshen, where you will be near to me, you, your children, your grandchildren, your flocks, your herds—everything that you own. 11 I will take care of you here. Since five years of famine remain, you, your children, and all who are with you might become impoverished.' 12 Look, your own eyes and the eyes of my brother Benjamin see that I myself am speaking to you. 13 Tell my father about all the wealth in Egypt—all that you have seen. Bring my father down here immediately." 14 He embraced the neck of Benjamin his brother and wept. Benjamin also embraced him and wept. 15 He then kissed all his brothers and wept because of them. After that, his brothers conversed with him.

16 The commotion was heard in Pharaoh's house, where someone said, "Joseph's brothers have arrived." It pleased both Pharaoh and his servants. 17 Pharaoh said to Joseph, "Say to your brothers: 'Do this! Load your pack animals and return to the land of Canaan. 18 Bring your father and your household goods and come to me. I will give to you the best from the land of Egypt. You will eat the choice produce of the country.' 19 You are also ordered to say, 'Do this! Take wagons from the land of Egypt for your children and wives. Bring your father and come. 20 Don't worry about your possessions. You shall have the best from the entire land of Egypt.'"

21 The sons of Israel acted accordingly. Joseph gave them wagons just as Pharaoh had ordered. And he gave them provisions for the journey. 22 He also gave to each one a change of clothes, but to Benjamin he gave three hundred pieces of silver and five changes of clothes. 23 And to his father he sent ten donkeys carrying some of the best things from Egypt and ten female donkeys carrying grain, prepared food, and other provisions for his father's journey. 24 He sent his brothers off. As they went, he told them, "Don't quarrel on the trip!"

25 They went up from Egypt and came to the land of Canaan, to Jacob
their father. 26 Then they said to him, "Joseph is still alive! He even rules
over the entire land of Egypt." But he was stunned, unable to believe them.
27 They then told him everything that Joseph had instructed them to tell
him. When he saw the wagons that Joseph had sent to bring him, Jacob
their father came to life. 28 Israel said, "This is fantastic! My son Joseph
is still alive. I must go down and see him before I die."

[45:1–15] The Joseph in verse 1 is the same Joseph who almost wept in public in an earlier scene (43:30–31; cf. 42:24). This time, however, he does not retreat to another room but instead commands his courtiers to leave. Royal protocol is thereby maintained when Joseph decides to reveal his identity to his brothers.

In the earlier scene, Joseph was moved by his affection for Benjamin. This time concern for his father seems to be a driving force: "Is my father still alive?" The question seems odd, since Judah has just told Joseph that he is concerned about Jacob's reaction to the brothers going back to Canaan without Benjamin (44:34). One suspects that the author has molded the character of Joseph carefully such that he is not hearing all that is being said, including that his father is still alive. His deeply felt emotions are affecting his perceptions. Moreover, his emotions are matched by those of his brothers. Joseph is unable to control his feelings; they are unable to respond to what they have just heard. Joseph is losing control and shouting; they are terrified of this Egyptian ruler who claims to be their brother.

After Joseph's first self-revelatory statement, he commands his brothers to approach him, whereupon he offers a lengthy speech (45:4–13). There are several salient features in the speech. First, he regains control of his emotions and returns to his role as a ruler of Egypt. Second, he speaks in the imperative mood to his brothers: "Don't worry now," "Go up quickly," "Don't remain there," "Tell my father," "Bring my father down here." Joseph is in charge of his brothers. Third, he places his call for them to bring his father to Egypt within the context of the current famine. He sends a message to his father that he will become impoverished due to the five years of remaining famine if he remains in Canaan. The current crisis makes it imperative for Jacob to come to Egypt; it is not simply a matter of coming there to see his long-lost son. Fourth, he makes a promise to Jacob that he will take care of him and his family. Fifth, he construes his life to this point as one in which God, not his brothers, has sent him to Egypt. His brothers' prior action is simply embedded in the divine plan. It is, to be sure, a plan to assist Jacob's family, but there is a larger purpose: "to preserve life," which presumably means those in Egypt and those who have been coming to receive food available due to Joseph's careful planning: "All the world came to Joseph in Egypt to buy grain" (41:57).

The scene concludes with a return to overt emotion: Joseph and his brothers weeping and embracing. That moment of embrace is initiated by Joseph and Benjamin hugging and crying (vv. 14–15). Joseph's full brother has pride of place among his other brothers, a reality that will manifest itself in the favoritism he soon shows to Benjamin (v. 22). Benjamin is even singled out near the end of Joseph's just completed speech (v. 12). These emotional interactions finally enable his brothers to converse with Joseph; earlier they were unable to speak with him (v. 3).

[16–20] Pharaoh's speech to Joseph enfranchises what Joseph has just said. As befits a pharaoh, he issues orders, twice commanding Joseph to say to his brothers, "Do this!" And twice Pharaoh promises that Jacob and his family will enjoy "the best" that Egypt has to offer. Pharaoh's speech serves as a guarantee for what Joseph has already proclaimed.

[21–28] The omniscient narrator controls much in the final eight verses. He reports the behavior of the "sons of Israel," an odd locution that is of a piece with the transition occurring near the end of the book of Genesis: the move from familial to political diction. The diverse names for Joseph's father, Jacob (v. 27) and Israel (v. 28), enable the use of this phrase.

Joseph continues in his political role. He follows Pharaoh's order by providing his brothers with wagons. Joseph admonishes his brothers not to quarrel on their journey. He offers provisions of various kinds. When doing this, he gives Benjamin more clothes than he did to his brothers and even three hundred pieces of silver. Such gifts recall moments earlier in the story (ch. 37); the attention to clothes and the payment of silver when Joseph is sold to the Ishmaelites. Joseph is providing garments for Benjamin in a special way just as Jacob has done for Joseph.

Israel's brief speech in the chapter's final verse foreshadows moments later in the short story. He exults that Joseph is still alive and wants to see him before he dies. Though Joseph's work in Egypt will keep the sons of Israel alive, by the story's end, both Jacob and Joseph will die. The death of Jacob is reported in 49:29–33 and Joseph's in 50:22–26. It is no accident that Joseph's final speech is to "the sons of Israel" (50:25 MT), the same language used in 45:21.

Genesis 46:1–34
God Tells Jacob to Bring His Family to Egypt

Jacob travels from the land of Canaan to Egypt, where he encounters Joseph in the land of Goshen. Joseph then sets the stage for his brothers and his father to meet Pharaoh, a meeting with the goal of gaining permission for Israel to settle in the land of Goshen. The report of this journey is interrupted by a lengthy genealogy that identifies by name the sons and grandchildren of Jacob. They comprise a group of seventy people. The genealogy is noteworthy since it also refers to one of Jacob's great-grandchildren who is a member of the Davidic lineage.

46:1 Israel left with all that he had and came to Beersheba, where he
offered sacrifices to the God of his father, Isaac. 2 God said to Israel in a
dream,[a] "Jacob, Jacob." He replied, "Yes." 3 He said, "I am El,[b] the God
of your father. Do not be afraid to go down to Egypt because I will make
a great nation of you there. 4 I will go down with you to Egypt, and I will
also bring you back again. And Joseph will close your eyes."

5 So Jacob left Beersheba. The sons of Israel lifted up Jacob, their
father, their children, and their wives into the wagons that Pharaoh had
sent to carry them. 6 They took their herds and the rest of their things that
they had owned while they were in the land of Canaan. Jacob and all his
progeny arrived in Egypt: 7 his sons, his grandsons with him, his daughters and his granddaughters; he brought all his progeny with him to Egypt.

8 These are the names of the Israelites who came to Egypt, Jacob and
his children: Reuben, Jacob's firstborn; 9 the children of Reuben: Hanoch,
Pallu, Hezron, and Carmi. 10 The children of Simeon: Jemuel, Jamin,
Ohad, Jachin, Zohar, and Saul, the son of a Canaanite woman. 11 The
children of Levi: Gershon, Kohath, and Merari. 12 The children of Judah:
Er, Onan, Shelah, Perez, and Zerah (Er and Onan had died in the land of
Canaan); the children of Perez were Hezron and Hamul. 13 The children
of Issachar: Tola, Puvah, Yob,[c] and Shimron. 14 The children of Zebulun:
Sered, Elon, and Jahleel 15 (these are the children of Leah, whom she bore
to Jacob in Paddan-Aram, along with his daughter Dinah); he had thirty-
three sons and daughters in all. 16 The children of Gad: Ziphion, Haggi,

Shuni, Ezbon, Eri, Arodi, and Areli. **17** The children of Asher: Imnah, Ish-
vah, Ishvi, Beriah, and their sister Serah. The children of Beriah: Heber
and Malchiel **18** (these are the children of Zilpah [whom Laban gave to his
daughter Leah]; she bore them to Jacob, sixteen persons). **19** The children
of Rachel, Jacob's wife: Joseph and Benjamin. **20** Children were born to
Joseph in the land of Egypt; Asenath, the daughter of Potiphera, the priest
of ʾOn, bore Manasseh and Ephraim to him. **21** The children of Benjamin:
Bela, Becher, Ashbel, Gera, Naaman, Ehi, Rosh, Muppim, Huppim, and
Ard **22** (these are the children of Rachel who were born to Jacob, fourteen
persons in all). **23** The children of Dan: Hushim.[d] **24** The children of Naphtali: Jahzeel, Guni, Jezer, and Shillen **25** (these are the children of Bilhah,
whom Laban gave to his daughter Rachel; she bore them to Jacob, seven
persons in all). **26** All the people who belonged with Jacob and who came
to Egypt were, with the exception of his sons' wives, his progeny; they
numbered sixty-six persons in all. **27** The children of Joseph who were
born to him in Egypt numbered two. All the people in the house of Jacob
who came into Egypt numbered seventy.

28 He sent Judah ahead of him to Joseph so that he could tell them the
way to Goshen. When they had arrived in the land of Goshen, **29** Joseph
prepared his chariot and went up to meet his father Israel in Goshen.
When he saw him, he embraced him and wept for a while. **30** Israel said
to Joseph, "Now that I have seen your face, I can die, knowing that you
are still alive." **31** Joseph said to his brothers and to his father's household, "I will go and make a report to Pharaoh and say, 'My brothers and
my father's household from the land of Canaan have come to me. **32** The
men are shepherds, those who take care of herds. They have brought
their flocks and herds along with everything else that they own.' **33** When
Pharaoh summons you and says, 'What do you do?' **34** you should say,
'Your servants have been taking care of herds—from the time that we
were young until now, both we and our forebears,' so that you will be
able to settle in the land of Goshen. All shepherds are an abomination to
the Egyptians."

a. Literally, "a night vision."
b. Literally, "the El."
c. Cf. LXX, SP, "Yashub" (Num 26:24; 1 Chr 7:1).
d. Cf. LXX, "Hashum."

[46:1–7] According to the geography presented in the book of Genesis, Jacob has earlier been living in Bethel (35:6) but has traveled to near Ephrath/Bethlehem and then settled "beyond the tower of Eder" (35:21). That puts him in the territory of Judah. At the outset of the Joseph short story, there is reference to Shechem and Dothan, though not as a reference to Jacob's residence. Both cities are in the tribal territory of Manasseh, considerably north of Bethlehem. In sum, it is difficult to know precisely from what area Jacob is thought to be moving at the outset of Gen 46. Yet it is clear that he is on his way to Egypt at Joseph's behest. On that journey, he stops at Beersheba, where he experiences a nocturnal epiphany, one in which God assures Jacob that the deity will accompany him on his journey. (God's self-presentation as El, without any other appellation, is striking [cf. the more usual "El Elyon" or "El Elohe Israel" in Genesis].) This deity offers other assurances as well: the deity will bring Jacob back to the land of Canaan, and Joseph will conduct an important mortuary ritual, the closing of a deceased person's eyes. Interestingly, other biblical authors do not report explicitly that any of these promised acts take place.

As is often the case in the Joseph narrative, the deity acts in less than overt ways. If God does accompany Jacob to Egypt, it is a hidden act. If God brings Jacob back to the land of Canaan, it is through Joseph's doing. And if Joseph closes Jacob's eyes, it is through the agency of the Egyptian morticians. The reference to eyes and sight at two places in this chapter (vv. 4, 30) foreshadows Jacob's coming death in terms of his relationship to Joseph. Moreover, verse 3 strikes the note of transition from Israel as a family to Israel as a nation, a transition that takes place throughout the final chapters of Genesis. The phrase "sons of Israel," which can refer to Jacob's sons (so v. 5), can also signify the larger entity "Israelites" (so v. 8).

[8–27] These verses provide a genealogy that includes several notations and, at two points, moves to Jacob's grandchildren. The key feature is the organization of Jacob's sons according to their birth mothers. One may speak about the significance of the genealogy in its own right and then its role within the narrative. The significance of the genealogy rests on the varying levels of fertility among the sons and of Jacob's wives: Leah (v. 15), Zilpah (v. 18), Rachel (vv. 19, 22), Bilhah (v. 25). Of these four, Leah's sons have borne the most children, thirty-three. The sons are, in fact, listed in the order of their mothers' number of grandchildren: Leah with thirty-three, Zilpah with sixteen, Rachel with fourteen, and Bilhah with seven. Verse 10 also attests to intermarriage with the Canaanites; one of Simeon's sons was born to an unnamed Canaanite woman. The genealogy thus recognizes five of Jacob's grandchildren born to non-Israelite women (Saul, Perez, Zerah, Ephraim, Manasseh) and the latter two of those he will adopt as his sons (see ch. 48).

The genealogy includes an annotation about two deaths and a citation of several of Jacob's great-grandchildren (v. 12). These great-grandchildren are significant since one of them, Hezron, belongs in the lineage of David (see Ruth 4:18–19). In addition, reference to Rachel occurs both at the beginning (v. 19) and end (v. 22) of the section devoted to her. In the three other cases, Jacob's wives are mentioned only at the end of such sections.

The “irregular” numbers of Jacob’s grandchildren yield a round number of seventy, a number that also appears in Exod 1:5 as the population of Israelites who move to Egypt. This genealogy, placed in the narrative only after Jacob and his family enter Egypt, functions in the larger biblical narrative to emphasize the incredible growth of the people while they are in Egypt. According to Exod 12:37, the Israelites traveling within Egypt just before the exodus from the country number “six hundred thousand men.” Such numbers help sustain the claim made in Exod 1:7, “The Israelites were fruitful and prolific; they multiplied and grew exceedingly strong, so that the land was filled with them.”

[28–34] The final section of this chapter describes an intimate scene between son and father (vv. 28–30) and then a strategic dialogue between Joseph and his brothers (vv. 31–34). Jacob has already arrived in Egypt and, apparently, stopped in the land of Goshen (v. 28 is the first place in the chapter mentioning Goshen; cf. 45:10). It is apparently presumed to be the place where the family will settle. Though the precise location of Goshen remains unknown, the phrase “land of Goshen” probably refers to the eastern Nile Delta region.

Jacob and Joseph speak only after a long embrace, the same sort of embrace with which Joseph has greeted Benjamin (45:14). Moreover, Jacob expresses the same sentiment that he initially expressed when he was told that Joseph was alive: that he could die after he has seen Joseph. Once he greets his father, Joseph tells his brothers what will happen when they have an audience with Pharaoh. Joseph counsels them to avoid announcing their vocation as shepherds but rather to say that they take care of herds since shepherds are an abomination to Egyptians (46:33–34). (There is no evidence in ancient Egyptian sources for such a negative view of shepherds or, for that matter, sheep and goats, both of which are present in Egyptian paintings and sculptures.) Joseph appears to want his brothers to avoid alienating Pharaoh by telling them what they really do, with the risk that Pharaoh will deny their request to live in the land of Goshen. Oddly, however, Joseph suggests that he himself will be telling Pharaoh that his brothers are shepherds (v. 32); that may open the door for the brothers themselves to tell Pharaoh that they are shepherds, which they do later (47:3). Despite that revelation, they are granted the opportunity to live in the land of Goshen. Joseph’s admonition to his brothers seems to be more of an attempt to exercise power over them, telling them what to say and making it appear to them that he knows more about Egyptian customs than they do, rather than an accurate report about Egyptian sentiments concerning shepherds.

Genesis 47:1–31
Joseph Saves the Egyptians from Starvation

Genesis 47 addresses three distinct topics: Israel's acquiring land in Egypt, how Egyptians survived the severe famine, and Jacob's coming death. Of these, the first two are related in an inverse fashion. Due to Pharaoh's beneficence, Israel is permitted to settle in "the best part of the country." In contrast, due to the severe famine, the Egyptians lose their land to Pharaoh in return for grain to consume. Joseph is instrumental in both transactions. The transition between the first two scenes emphasizes the different impacts of the famine on the Egyptians and the Israelites. The latter have food provided to them by Joseph; the latter go hungry due to the famine. In none of the scenes is the deity mentioned by name.

> 47:1 Joseph went and made a report to Pharaoh. He said, "My father, my brothers, their herds, their flocks along with everything else that they own have come from the land of Canaan, and they are now in the land of Goshen." 2 From among all his brothers, he took five of them and introduced them to Pharaoh. 3 Pharaoh said to them, "What do you do?" They responded to Pharaoh, "Your servants are shepherds, both we and our forebears." 4 They continued, "We have come to live in the land as immigrants since there is no pastureland for the flocks of your servants. The famine is terribly severe in the land of Canaan. And now your servants would like to live in the land of Goshen." 5 Pharaoh said to Joseph, "Your father and your brothers have come to you. 6 The land of Egypt is before you. Settle your father and your brothers in the best part of the country. They may dwell in the land of Goshen. Moreover, if you know that some of them are highly competent, you can put them in charge of my herds."
>
> 7 Then Joseph brought Jacob his father and he presented him to Pharaoh, whereupon Jacob blessed Pharaoh. 8 Pharaoh said to Jacob, "How old are you?" 9 Jacob replied, "I have traveled for one hundred and thirty years—a limited and difficult life. The years of my life do not compare well with the travels of my forebears." 10 Then Jacob blessed Pharaoh and left his presence. 11 Joseph settled his father and his brothers. He gave them property in the land of Egypt, in the best part of the land, in the land

of Rameses, just as Pharaoh had ordered. 12 Joseph provided food for his
father, his brothers, and everyone else in his father's house, with special
attention to the number of children.

13 There was no food throughout the land of Egypt because the famine
was very severe. Both the land of Egypt and the land of Canaan suffered
due to the famine. 14 Joseph collected all the silver that could be found
in the land of Egypt and the land of Canaan in exchange for the grain
there. He deposited the silver in Pharaoh's household. 15 When the silver
from the land of Egypt and from the land of Canaan had been spent, all
the Egyptians came to Joseph and said, "Give us food! Why should we
die in your presence? Our silver is gone." 16 Joseph said, "Give me your
livestock, and I will sell you bread for your livestock, if your silver is
gone." 17 So they brought their livestock to Joseph. Joseph sold them
food for the horses, the livestock, the herds, flocks, and the donkeys. In
that year, he provided food for them in exchange for all their livestock.
18 When that year ended, they came to him in the next year and said, "It
is impossible to hide from my lord that the silver has been spent and the
herds and[a] cattle belong to my lord. Nothing is left before my lord except
our bodies and our land. 19 Why should we die with you looking on, both
we and our land? Purchase us and our land in exchange for food so that we
can stay alive. We, along with our land, will become slaves for Pharaoh.
Provide seed for us so that we can stay alive and not die and so that the
land won't be ruined."

20 So Joseph acquired all the land of Egypt for Pharaoh because each
Egyptian sold his field due to the severity of the famine for them. The land
became Pharaoh's. 21 As for the people, he moved them to cities[b] from
one end of Egypt to the other. 22 Only the land of the priests he did not
acquire since it [the land] was a special plot from Pharaoh. They ate food
from that special plot that Pharaoh had given to them. For that reason they
did not sell their land. 23 Joseph said to the people, "Look, I have acquired
you and your land for Pharaoh today. Here is seed for you. Plant the land.
24 At harvesttime, you shall contribute one-fifth to Pharaoh; four-fifths
shall be yours as seed to plant, as food for you and your households,
and especially as food for your children." 25 They responded, "You have
saved our lives! We have found favor with our lord and will be Pharaoh's
slaves." 26 So Joseph established a principle that holds even today: one-
fifth of the land's produce belongs to Pharaoh. Only the land allotted to
the priests does not belong to Pharaoh.

27 Israel lived in the land of Egypt, in the region of Goshen. They
acquired possessions there, had many children, and became numerous.
28 Jacob was in the land of Egypt for seventeen years. Altogether he lived
one hundred forty-seven years.

29 When the time of Jacob's death approached, he summoned his son
Joseph and said, "If I am worthy, please place your hand under my thigh
and agree to deal with me in a loving and truthful way. Do not bury me
in Egypt. 30 When I lie down with my ancestors, you should bring me up
from Egypt and bury me in their tomb." He responded, "I will do exactly
what you have said." 31 He said, "Swear to me." So he made an oath. Then
Israel slumped down at the head of his bed.

a. MT does not include "and."
b. SP and LXX read, "He enslaved them."

[47:1–12] In these verses, the author recounts three interactions with Pharaoh. In the first, Joseph reports to Pharaoh that his family has joined him in Egypt, noting that they currently reside in the land of Goshen. Immediately thereafter, Joseph selects five of his brothers to meet Pharaoh. They respond to his question about their vocation by ignoring Joseph's admonition (see 46:34) that they not reveal their livelihood as shepherds. They even emphasize that this has been their family's role for generations before requesting that they be permitted to settle as immigrants in the land of Goshen. Pharaoh does not respond directly to the brothers, but instead turns to Joseph, granting his brothers' request, repeating what Joseph has already told him (47:1). In addition, Pharaoh invites Joseph to nominate those of his brothers who are especially qualified to look after his own herd. But this never happens, according to the story.

Once the brothers have departed, Joseph introduces his father to Pharaoh. Unlike the situation with Joseph's brothers, Jacob has no request to make. Instead, readers are told that Jacob blessed Pharaoh twice (vv. 7, 10). Jacob, as one who blesses, will return to that role in chapters 48–49, though there he blesses only Israelites. Apart from the formulaic phrases about Jacob as one who blesses, he answers Pharaoh's question about his age by identifying himself as someone who has experienced a difficult life, especially when compared with his forebears. Readers do not know whether he laments the length of his life or the challenges he has encountered. (According to the book of Genesis, Abraham lived for 175 years [25:7], Isaac for 180 years [35:28], and Jacob for 147 years [47:28]). It is not surprising that Jacob characterizes himself as a "traveler," given his journeys in the land as well as in the Transjordan and now in Egypt.

Once the interactions with Pharaoh have concluded, Joseph implements Pharaoh's grant of land, in the best part of Egypt, as Pharaoh has ordered. Yet at the conclusion of the scene, the land is now known as "the land of Rameses" instead of the land of Goshen (47:11). This new label foreshadows the situation in Exod 1:11, in which Rameses is listed as a city. There and then, the Israelites no longer have the same status as they have under the earlier Pharaohs. Genesis

47:12 also highlights Joseph's ability to provide food, a key issue in the ensuing verses (in both cases, he is expressly concerned about the welfare of children, both Egyptian and Israelite).

[13–26] This report about famine in Egypt and Joseph's role in addressing it interrupts the narrative about Jacob's household early after their arrival in Egypt. The word "food" connects the foregoing section (v. 12) to this one (v. 13). Moreover, the word "famine" appears in the earlier portion as well (v. 4). The notice about the absence of food in Egypt jars the reader. There is an irony that famine exists in both Egypt and Canaan. The Israelites who have left Canaan to find food in Egypt confront the same problem there as at home. Oddly, there is no reference to difficulties faced by the Israelites in the land of Goshen. Readers are told that Joseph provides them with food (so v. 12).

The account about famine focuses on the way in which Joseph both provides food for the Egyptians and exacts an increasingly high price for that food. The provision of food is divided into three accounts based on what the people pay: (1) money, (2) livestock, and (3) land and enslavement. Based on the chronology implicit in verses 17–18, one may presume that this process takes place over the course of three years.

The common plight in Egypt and Canaan initially results in Joseph's selling grain to both areas. However, verse 15 reports a dialogue between Joseph and Egyptians, and not with him and Canaanites. Only in the first year is territory beyond Egypt in view. The author makes clear that the assets Joseph accumulates in exchange for food belong to the state-sponsored program. The silver is taken into Pharaoh's household, and the people are moved into a series of cities. Moreover, the exception of the land owned by priests is a national policy. Finally, the policy of taxing produce at 20 percent is thought to be something that "holds even today." It is not an ad hoc policy of Joseph but something that perdures.

Three distinct issues require further comment. Verse 19 introduces the topic of enslavement. In that regard, the author takes pains to portray Joseph as less than the worst kind of slave trader since the hungry Egyptians themselves suggest this option to save their lives (so also v. 25). Still, it is impossible to read this verse without seeing it as a foreshadowing: Israelites becoming enslaved in Egypt.

Verse 21 presents a difficult text-critical problem. Although the Septuagint reads, "He enslaved them," the Masoretic Text refers to forced urbanization: "He moved them to cities." Since the rest of the verse deals with geography, a move to the cities makes sense. Moreover, if Egyptians are being enslaved, some form of forced urbanization makes sense, especially since the cities throughout the land are near the land that the slaves tend.

In verse 19, the Egyptians plead not only that they might live but that the land itself might prosper. They want not only to eat but also to be able to plant so that they can grow food. The provision of grain as both seed and food continues a focus on both the land and the people; it also attests to the reality of Egypt as a breadbasket in the Mediterranean area. Joseph responds directly to their plea by stating that the grain the Egyptians may keep should be used for both seed and food. Moreover, along with Joseph's overt concern for Israelite children (v. 12), he mentions explicitly that some food should be given to Egyptian children (v. 24).

[27–31] These final verses follow directly on the initial section of Gen 47 (vv. 1–12). There is no organic connection between verses 13–26 and 27–31. They focus on Jacob as he approaches his final days and his concern for proper burial in the ancestral cemetery. Jacob makes Joseph take an oath to inter him there, an act recounted in Gen 50. Joseph will reiterate such an end-of-life request for himself, for his bones to be carried "up from here," a request made to his brothers, not to his sons (50:24–26; cf. Josh 24:32, the burial of Joseph at Shechem).

Consistent with the Priestly admonition to be fruitful and multiply, Israel flourishes in Egypt (v. 27). Unfortunately, this very fertility will soon be viewed negatively by the Egyptians (so Exod 1:9–10). Still, the language of family has faded and the new collective, Israel, is the subject of these verbs. The transition from family to people continues to take place.

Genesis 48:1–22
Jacob Blesses Joseph's Sons, Claiming Them as His Own

This chapter recounts the blessing of Joseph's two sons, yet another instance in which the younger brother achieves greater status than his older one. This time, however, the reversal is due not to trickery but to the virtual blindness of Jacob and to his foreknowledge of the future. He can hold the two boys but cannot tell them apart. Though he cannot distinguish their faces, he can foresee their fates, a capacity exercised in the following chapter: "I will tell you what will happen to you in the coming days" (49:1).

48:1 After these things took place, someone informed[a] Joseph, "Your
father is very sick." So he took his two sons, Manasseh and Ephraim, with
him. 2 When Jacob was told, "Your son Joseph has come to you," Israel
summoned his strength and sat up on his bed. 3 Jacob said to Joseph,
"God Almighty[b] revealed himself to me at Luz in the land of Canaan
and blessed me. 4 He said to me, 'I am going to make you fertile and
numerous. I will make you an assembly of peoples. I will give this land
to your progeny who succeed you as a possession forever.' 5 As of now,
your two sons who were born to you in the land of Egypt before I came
to you in Egypt—Ephraim and Manasseh—will be mine, just as Reuben
and Simeon are mine. 6 However, your other progeny who will be born
to you will be yours. They will inherit according to the status of their
brothers. 7 After I left Paddan, Rachel died in the land of Canaan on the
journey while we were still quite a way from Ephrath. So I buried her on
the way to Ephrath, otherwise known as Bethlehem."

8 Jacob looked at Joseph's sons and said, "Who are they?" 9 Joseph
responded to his father, "They are my sons whom God has given to me
in this place." Jacob[c] said, "Bring them to closer to me so that I can bless
them." 10 Due to his age, Jacob's eyes were cloudy; he could not see well.
So Joseph[d] brought them to him, whereupon he kissed and hugged them.
11 Israel said to Joseph, "Though I had not thought that I would see your
face, God has let me even see your children." 12 Joseph then took them
off his lap[e] and bowed down deeply before him. 13 Joseph presented the
two of them, with Ephraim in his right hand on Israel's left side and

Manasseh in his left hand on Israel's right side. **14** Israel extended his
right hand and put it on Ephraim's, the younger son's, head and his left
hand on Manasseh's head: he had made a mistake[f] with his hands since
Manasseh was the older one. **15** He blessed Joseph and said,

"May the God with whom my ancestors walked, Abraham and Isaac;
 the God who has shepherded me from earlier times until now,
16 the messenger, the one who has rescued me from everything evil,
 bless the lads.
May they be known by my name,
 and the name of my ancestors, Abraham and Isaac.
May they flourish[g] throughout the world."

17 When Joseph saw that his father had put his right hand on Ephraim's
head, he became upset. He grabbed his father's hand to take it away from
Ephraim and to put it on Manasseh. **18** Joseph said to his father, "No,
father, this one is the firstborn. Put your right hand on his head." **19** But
his father refused, "I know, son. He, too, will become a people, even a
great one. Nonetheless, his younger brother will become even greater
than him. His descendants will become many nations." **20** So on that day
he blessed them,

"Through you,[h] Israel will be blessed, when he said,
'May God establish you[h] like Ephraim and Manasseh.'"

So he placed Ephraim ahead of Manasseh. **21** Israel said to Joseph, "Even
though I am about to die, God will be with you[i] and will bring you[i] back
to the land of your ancestors. **22** Moreover, I grant you one mountain
pasture[j] more than your brothers, one that I captured from the Amorites
with my sword and my bow."

a. MT, "he informed."
b. Hebrew, *El Shaddai.*
c. MT, "he."
d. MT, "he."
e. Literally, "his knees."
f. The verb *śkl* in the piel can mean "to make a mockery of" (so Isa 44:25).
g. Literally, "become numerous."
h. Singular.
i. Plural.
j. MT *šəkem*. The word can mean the shoulder or back of a person. It also designates the city Shechem.

[48:1–22] Verses 1–2 feature anonymous communication. Joseph hears about the gravity of his father's illness from "someone," and Jacob is told by an unnamed party that his son has arrived. Such anonymity suggests a certain distance between Joseph and his father. In contrast to the lack of explicit names, the patriarch is known by his two names, Israel and Jacob, in the same verse, suggesting that Jacob, and not Joseph, is the focal point in this narrative. *Jacob* will make the decision about the relative statuses of the boys, and he is the one who will favor Joseph yet again. (The presence of the two names is almost certainly not evidence of different sources in this episode.)

Jacob's speech to Joseph (vv. 3–7) includes a reprise of an earlier promise and blessing and then a virtual adoption of Joseph's two sons by Jacob, as well as a clause regarding any further children that Joseph might have. (There is no record of Joseph having any more children.) As for the former, Jacob alludes to the occasion when God has blessed him (35:9) and made the dual promise of progeny and land. In both this and the earlier text, the deity construes the vast progeny in political rather than familial terms, so "a nation and an assembly of nations" (35:11) and "an assembly of peoples" (48:4). The nuance in 48:4 is important. Israel will not become just one people but an assembly of peoples, a phrase that emphasizes the national diversity that will exist within Israel. As for land, verse 4 advances the promise beyond chapter 35 by insisting that it will be in Israel's hands "forever" (the same phrase appears in 17:8, a Priestly text).

The relationship of 48:7 to the foregoing is not obvious. Paddan-Aram, which figures prominently in the Priestly material in Genesis, is mentioned in Gen 35:9 as a place Jacob leaves soon before Rachel dies. However, after departing Paddan-Aram, Jacob and Rachel reside at Bethel, where El Shaddai blesses him, before traveling south to the area around Bethlehem. Jacob's allusion to leaving Paddan-Aram in Gen 48 appears to truncate the longer report of their residences present in Gen 35. The episode involving the death of Rachel (35:16–21) appears immediately after the one in which God blesses Jacob at Bethel and may therefore simply have been included here as a part of that larger narrative.

Once the earlier promises have been affirmed, Jacob moves to the youngest generation. In so doing, he ensures that Joseph's two sons will be part of the progeny to whom the earlier promise was made, despite the fact that they were born to an Egyptian mother. The listing of Ephraim before Manasseh (v. 5) foreshadows the higher status Ephraim will receive later in the chapter. It is no accident that Jacob refers explicitly to Reuben and Simeon. Both were born to Leah, one of Jacob's primary wives (and not one of their servants). Based on this juxtaposition of Ephraim and Manasseh with Reuben and Simeon, there could be no question about the legitimacy of Jacob having "adopted" Manasseh and Ephraim. Moreover, Jacob makes clear that he is adopting only those two sons of Joseph. Any other children of Joseph will have to inherit directly through him, not through one of his aforementioned sons.

In a poignant scene, Jacob embraces and "sees" the two boys, even though they are only blurred images for him. There is some irony with Israel proclaiming that he has seen Joseph and now his sons, but it is notable that he imputes the seeing of the children as caused by God. Without God's help and with his reduced vision, he cannot have seen the lads. Joseph carefully presents the boys, with Manasseh on Jacob's right side. However, Jacob places his right hand, the hand of blessing, on Ephraim. Even though Jacob's hands are on the boys' heads, the narrator, oddly, reports that he blesses Joseph; yet in the poetic speech that follows, Jacob's calls upon the deity to bless "the lads." Jacob's speech is interesting, since it involves a doxology, characterizing God as one who has acted as a shepherd and as one who manifests Godself as a "messenger" (so Gen 31:11; 32:1). Jacob's blessing of the boys is based on what the deity has done for Jacob throughout his life, though expressed in poetic rather than "historical" terms.

When Joseph objects to Jacob's placing the hand of blessing on Ephraim, Jacob appeals to his knowledge of the future, one in which Ephraim will be "greater than" Manasseh. Another poetic phrase (v. 20) offers a blessing of both lads, though it does not elevate Ephraim over Manasseh. In fact, neither poetic element (vv. 15–16, 20) attests to the difference in their statuses, suggesting that the poetry existed before the creation of this narrative. The fact that the second-person pronoun in verse 20 is singular is consistent with this judgment.

Both of the boys will be great; their greatness is expressed in diction normally used of communities: "people," "nation." This wording is especially important at the end of Genesis: Israel is moving away from being just a family and becoming a people or nation. It remains difficult, however, to understand what the author may have in mind when referring to Ephraim's future as "many nations" (v. 19). Equally difficult is the sense in which a singular "you" (v. 20) will be the source of blessing for others. It is as if the diction of Gen 12:3; 18:18; 28:14 is being transferred to the two boys instead of one individual. (The "you" in v. 21 [2×] is plural, probably referring to Joseph and his sons.)

The chapter concludes with an unexpected blessing of Joseph, one in which Jacob grants him more land than he has to Joseph's brothers. The wordplay (so note j) suggests that this land includes the city of Shechem. Such favoritism toward Joseph at the end of the narrative is ironic, given the way that Jacob's favoring of him has earlier created such jealousy among his brothers. The favoritism of Jacob toward Ephraim, his now-adopted son, concludes with an iteration of his favoritism of Joseph, his natural son. This blessing presages the one that follows in 49:22–26.

Genesis 49:1–33
Jacob Offers His Final Words to His Sons and Dies

Based on the similarities between Gen 49 and Deut 33, one may infer a genre of poetic literature in which a "patriarch," like Jacob or Moses in these two cases, offers pronouncements about the present and future of the Israelite tribes. The sayings can be positive, such as the one for Judah (Gen 49:8–12); negative, like the one for Simeon and Levi (49:5–7); or neutral, like the one for Zebulun (49:13). Some of the utterances offer an explanation for what is foretold, such as the earlier action of Reuben (35:22), which warrants his degraded status. Some focus on the future (e.g., Gad, 49:19]); others seem to reflect the status quo (e.g., Issachar, 49:14). Since Judah is the most prominent of the brothers in the Joseph short story, it is no accident that he receives a powerfully positive blessing. The same may be said for the statement concerning Joseph and, by implication, his two sons, Ephraim and Manasseh. However, though both Judah and Joseph are treated in an affirmative way, Jacob's utterances concerning them reflect different contexts. Judah will be great in large part because of his royal future as a progenitor in the line of David. Judah is something of a cipher for the future kingdom of Judah. The blessing of Joseph does not seem to include the notion of his role as an eponymous figure for the Northern Kingdom. Rather, Joseph's blessing focuses on the agricultural fertility of the land associated with him and, even more, the fertility of his family.

The pronouncements do not appear in haphazard fashion. Instead, they are largely organized according to their mothers and by their birth order. The initial six sons are those born to Leah. The first four occur in their birth order; the next two, Zebulun and Issachar, are in reverse order. The next four sons were born to Bilhah (Dan and Naphtali) and Zilpah (Gad and Asher). They do not occur in birth order and are not organized by mother. Finally, Rachel's sons, Joseph and Benjamin, appear in their order of birth. The chapter concludes with Jacob's speech, which includes lengthy directions for his burial, and a brief report about his death.

> **49:1** Then Jacob summoned his sons and said, "Gather around and I will tell you what will happen to you in the coming days.

2 Come together and listen, sons of Jacob;
Listen to Israel your father:

3 Reuben, you are my firstborn,
my strength, the firstfruits of my virility.
4 Reckless as water, you will not have precedence
  because you mounted your father's bed;
  you profaned it, going[a] to my couch.

5 Simeon and Levi are brothers;
  their knives are violent weapons.
6 I hope I never become part of their group,
  my reputation not be linked to their company,
because they killed people when they became angry,
  they injured cattle without reason.
7 Cursed be their anger; it is truly violent,
  their anger; it is shameless.
I will scatter them in Jacob,
  I will disperse you in Israel.

8 Judah, your brothers will praise you;
  your hand will be at the throat of your enemies,
  your father's sons will bow down before you.
9 Judah is a lion's cub;
  you have gone up from the kill.
He kneels, crouching like a lion, like a lioness.
  Who would disturb him?
10 The scepter won't leave Judah,
  nor the staff from between his legs
until tribute[b] arrives,
  [until] people obey him.
11 He hitches his male donkey to the vine,
  the foal of his female donkey to a select grapevine.
He cleans his clothing with wine,
  his garments with the blood of grapes.
12 His eyes are darker than wine,
  his teeth are whiter than milk.

13 Zebulun will live at the seashore;
  he will be a harbor for ships,
  his border reaching as far as Sidon.

14 Issachar is a powerful donkey
lying down among the saddlebags.
15 He found a good resting place,
a land that was pleasant.
He lowered his shoulder to work,
he slaved at forced labor.

16 Dan will provide justice for his people
as one of Israel's tribes.
17 Dan will be a snake by the road,
a horned snake next to the path,
which will strike at the horse's hooves
so that its rider falls off.

18 I long for your salvation, LORD.

19 Gad will be robbed by robbers,
but he will rob their rear guard.[c]

20 Asher's food will be luscious,
he will provide food fit for a king.

21 Naphtali is a doe set free,
one who has beautiful antlers.[d]

22 Joseph is a young bull,[e]
a young bull near a spring,
that walks around the wall.
23 They attacked him furiously,
they fired at him, the archers assaulted him fiercely.
24 Nonetheless, his bow remained ready,
his hands and arms agile,[f]
due to the Powerful One of Jacob,
due to the Shepherd, the Rock of Israel,
25 due to God, your father, who will help you,
due to Shaddai, who will bless you:
with blessings of the heavens above,
blessings of the deep that lies below,
blessings of breasts and womb.
26 The blessings of your father
are stronger than the blessings of the eternal mountains,
than the desirable things on the everlasting hills.

May these rest on the head of Joseph,
 on the forehead of the one distinguished from his brothers.

27 Benjamin is a wolf that tears apart;
 in the morning he devours prey,
 in the evening he shares the spoil."

28 All these are the twelve tribes of Israel. This is what their father
said to them when he blessed them, each one with a blessing appropriate
for him.

29 He ordered them, "I am about to be united with my people. Bury me
with my ancestors in the cave that is in the field of Ephron, the Hittite,
30 in the cave of the field at Machpelah that is near Mamre in the land
of Canaan, the field that Abraham acquired from Ephron the Hittite as a
burial ground. 31 That is where Abraham and Sarah his wife are buried.
Moreover, Isaac and Rebekah his wife are buried there. I even buried
Leah there. 32 It is the property with the field and the cave in it that had
belonged to the Hittites." 33 Then Jacob stopped giving orders to his sons.
He lifted his feet onto his bed, took his last breath, and was united with
his people.

a. MT, "he went."
b. Some SP MSS read "Shiloh," and some LXX texts read "peace."
c. Reading *ʿăqēbām* with the mem from the beginning of v. 20.
d. Hebrew uncertain. See comments.
e. The entire verse is uncertain. See comments.
f. MT, "the arms of his hands."

[49:1–2] The prose introduction (v. 1) and conclusion (v. 28) frame the poetic pronouncements. The introduction construes them as sayings regarding individuals; the conclusion treats them as sayings regarding tribes. The latter is consistent with the move to political entities at the end of Genesis. Verse 1 does not suggest that these sayings will function as "blessings" (cf. Deut 33:1). Rather, Jacob gathers his sons so that they will learn something about what will happen to them and their descendants.

[3–4] Though Reuben was Jacob's firstborn, he will not have pride of place because he had intercourse with one of Jacob's partners (Gen 35:22). The poetry builds on the notion of the firstborn by referring to the offering of firstfruits. However, the metaphor of water flowing unpredictably underscores Reuben's uncertain future.

[5–7] Simeon and Levi are treated together. As with Reuben, their future is linked to past misdeeds, when they have revenged the treatment of their full sister, Dinah. According to Gen 34, they killed "all the males" of Shechem with their swords. The reference to injuring cattle is unclear since Gen 34 reports that their brothers took the livestock from Shechem. The first-person utterance, "I will divide them in Jacob," seems to be the deity's declaration. Levi is mentioned at length in Deut 33; Simeon receives no comment there. The pronouncement locates them in the north, though Joshua 19 locates Simeon to the south of Judah's land. The verbs "scatter/disperse," rather than the traditional translation of "divide," reflect the absence of land for both tribes. Levi does not receive an allocation of land due to its role as a tribe of priests. Simeon apparently never holds the land given to it.

[8–12] The pronouncement concerning Judah offers a remarkable admixture of images. Even though the larger literary setting for Gen 49 involves Jacob's sons bowing down to Joseph (as in 43:26, 28; 50:18), this utterance highlights the brothers bowing down to Judah. The image almost certainly reflects the political ideology, if not historical reality, of the united monarchy, a time when the tribe of Judah held authority over all the other tribes. Next the poet likens Judah to a young lion, one that has already killed, a predator of whom one must beware. The final three verses move to personification of Judah as a human, a royal figure. Now "people," not just his brothers, do obeisance to him. Finally, this figure is placed in a vineyard, hitching his donkey to a vine, cleaning (perhaps "dyeing") his clothes in red wine. His "vine" must be stronger than the typical grapevine to serve as a hitching post. The saying concludes with vivid chromatic imagery: red wine, dark eyes, white teeth. The saying about Judah in Deut 33 is in no way comparably glorious.

[13–21] The sons of Bilhah and Zilpah receive minimal treatment. Zebulun's status is simply that of the status quo, situated on or near the seashore. The saying in Deut 33 also refers to Zebulun's location near the sea and sand, even though the tribe will be to the east of Asher, on the coast. Zebulun may be associated with the sea due to goods that reach it from the coast along a trade route through the plain of Megiddo.

In Deut 33:18–19, Zebulun and Issachar receive the same pronouncement, which may reflect the fact that they share a border. In Gen 49, they receive distinct though contiguous sayings. Both are in the present tense, which is also the case in Deut 33. As in the sayings associated with Judah, Dan, Naphtali, Joseph, and Benjamin, so also Issachar is likened to an animal, a powerful donkey able to rest after hard labor. It lies among "saddlebags" (cf. Judg 5:16 for the same word) after carrying them.

The name Dan means "to judge," and the saying about him attests to that role. However, what might at first hearing strike one as a positive feature is challenged by the characterization of Dan as a dangerous snake, one that makes a horse rear and throw its rider (cf. Gen 3:15 for the image of a snake striking at the heel). Oddly, in Deut 33, Dan features as a lion cub, the image used for Judah in Gen 49:9.

Verse 18 almost certainly has been introduced into the pronouncements after they were completed. Though similar language appears in Ps 119:166, it is difficult to know how the tribal sayings might have been used in a liturgical context. It may reflect the devotional sentiment of a copyist, though again, why it appears at this place in the collection is unclear.

The name Gad is related to the Hebrew word for "raid," hence this prediction that stems from a play on words, a feature also present in the saying about Dan. Both utterances share the motif of attacking someone's heels. Gad receives much more favorable treatment in Deut 33. The saying regarding Asher predicts not only agricultural prosperity but also that it will be in service to royalty. The territory of Asher was associated with olive orchards, a fact that lies behind the reference to "oil" in Deut 33:24.

Though it is clear that Naphtali is likened to a doe that has been set free, the final two words of the saying can be translated in many ways, such as "that makes beautiful sounds" or "that gives birth to beautiful fawns." According to *The Hebrew and Aramaic Lexicon* (*HALOT* 4:1635), *ʾmr* can mean "branched antlers" or beautiful young animals; and *šeper*, a hapax legomenon, can mean "loved one" or "darling"; hence the translation "beautiful antlers."

[22–26] The saying concerning Joseph is, at the outset, difficult to translate. Many translators consider Gen 49:22 to reflect floral imagery. It seems preferable, however, to see Joseph characterized as an animal, here a bull, as has been the case in so many of the other pronouncements (so CEB). (Though using a different noun, Deut 33 also characterizes Joseph as a bull.) Genesis 49:22–23 situate the bull near a spring and soon coming under attack from archers. Then in verse 24a, the imagery switches to that of a person, Joseph himself as archer. That movement from animal to human also takes place in the saying about Judah.

In verse 24b, the poet offers a remarkable theological inventory, ways of describing the deity who has enabled Joseph to defend himself. The assemblage in verses 24–25 alludes to the deity's hands and name, to the deity who has been specially related to Jacob, to metaphors of rock and shepherd for the deity, and to the archaic notion of the deity as Shaddai. After developing that theological resource, the poet highlights the blessings that lie in Joseph's future. They are cosmic in scope, stemming from the heavenly heights and the cosmic deep. They involve human fertility as exemplified by the birth and feeding of children (womb and breast). The blessings that come from Jacob are stronger than those provided by mountains, probably a reference to crops and/or herds located on the sides of hills. The saying about Joseph in Deut 33 also refers to the heavens and cosmic deep; but unlike Gen 49, it emphasizes the produce that will stem from the mountains. In Gen 49, it is as if the poet knows that tradition in Deuteronomy but contends that the blessings from Jacob, which involve human fertility, are even greater than that promised in Deut 33:13–16. The phrase "your father," which appears twice, highlights the special relationship that Joseph has with Jacob.

[27] The final pronouncement characterizes Benjamin as a hungry wolf that at one time eats his prey and at another is willing to share it. The saying in Deut 33:12 is utterly different, absent faunal imagery.

[28] The prose verse 28 does not belong to the surrounding narrative, but instead is a concluding comment about the poetic sayings. The narrator, not Jacob, rightly emphasizes that the discourse is more about "tribes" than it is about persons. To this extent, it is consistent with the movement away from family and toward political entities that is underway at the end of Genesis. Moreover, this verse offers a construal of the sayings as "blessings," even though some of the fates Jacob has pronounced do not appear to be "blessings." (In contrast, the pronouncements in Deut 33 are introduced as "blessings"; such is not the case in Gen 49. The rhetoric of 49:1 is that of prediction, not of blessing.)

[29–33] The narrative resumes, though in its current form it does not presume the existence of the just-offered patriarchal pronouncements. Genesis 49:1 reported the convocation of Jacob's sons, and it was followed by discrete sayings for each son. Now there is a general admonition for all of them as a cohort. Some tension exists between this command to all the sons and the ensuing charge to Joseph in 50:5; but since Joseph is seeking permission from "the household of Pharaoh" to leave Egypt in order to bury his father, he refers to *his* responsibility and not that of all his brothers.

Jacob's charge is almost redundant. He offers seven ways of specifying where he wants to be buried: with his ancestors, in the cave of Ephron, in the field of Machpelah, in the land of Canaan, in the field that Abraham bought, in the place where five other people are buried, and in the cave purchased from the Hittites. Once that speech is concluded, the narrator briefly reports that Jacob then died.

The place of burial clearly appears to be more important than the fact of his death. This is likely the case since Jacob's identification of his burial site underscores the fact that Israel has a legitimate foothold in a portion of the land of Canaan. It is a claim rooted in the purchase of land described in Gen 23. That transaction not only allows for Jacob to be buried in the tract at Machpelah, but it also sets the stage for a larger claim, which occurs when the bones of Joseph are likewise buried in the land of Canaan, but at a different place (so Gen 50:24–25; Josh 24:32, at Shechem). The burial places of both Jacob and Joseph were purchased from Canaanites, thereby making at least a portion of the land a legitimate possession of the Israelites.

Genesis 50:1–26
Joseph Speaks with His Brothers and Dies

The final chapter of Genesis comprises two distinct scenes, one involving the lamentation for and burial of Jacob and another narrating the final interactions between Joseph and his brothers. Both share a concern that the respective protagonists, Jacob and Joseph, be interred in the land of Canaan, though there is greater focus on the place of Jacob's interment than there is for Joseph's. From a literary point of view, there is minimal tension in the first portion of the chapter. Early on, Pharaoh accedes to Joseph's request that he be permitted to travel to the land of Canaan to bury his father. In the second portion, however, the brothers continue to be worried about how Joseph will treat them. There is accommodation, if not reconciliation, between them. From a religious perspective, the first section attests to the importance of mourning and funerary rites at the end of a person's life. It is an oddly cross-cultural situation, involving the death and burial of the final patriarch, Jacob/Israel, yet according to Egyptian norms. The second section is more overtly theological, highlighting the claim of Joseph, and the author of the Joseph short story, that God has turned something intended as pernicious into something beneficial.

> **50:1** Joseph embraced his father's head, wept over him, and kissed him.
> **2** Then Joseph ordered his servants, the physicians, to embalm his father,
> whereupon they embalmed Israel. **3** It took forty days, the amount of
> time necessary for embalming. Moreover, the Egyptians mourned for
> him seventy days.
>
> **4** When the period of mourning for him had ended, Joseph said to
> Pharaoh's household, "If what I do is acceptable to you, please report to
> Pharaoh, **5** 'My father made me promise with an oath, "I am about to die.
> You must bury me in the tomb that I had carved out for myself in the land
> of Canaan." Now I must go up and bury my father. Then I will return.'"
> **6** Pharaoh responded, "Go up and bury your father, the one who required
> you to make this promise."
>
> **7** So Joseph went up to bury his father. All sorts of Pharaoh's servants
> went with him, the senior servants of his household along with all sorts of

other senior servants, 8 the entire household of Joseph, his brothers, and the household of his father. Only their children, flocks, and herds remained in the land of Goshen. 9 Chariots and their teams of horses also went up with him. It was a terribly large assemblage. 10 When they arrived at the threshing floor of Atad,[a] which was east of the Jordan River, they held a grief-filled and dignified service of mourning. He conducted funerary rites on behalf of his father for seven days. 11 When the inhabitants of the land, the Canaanites, observed the funerary rites at the threshing floor of Atad, they said, "This is a significant funerary rite for the Egyptians." (Therefore, that place is known as "Egyptian funerary rite," which is east of the Jordan River.) 12 His sons did this for him just as he had ordered them. 13 His sons brought him up to the land of Canaan, and they buried him in the cave of the field of Machpelah, the field near Mamre that Abraham had purchased from Ephron the Hittite to become a burial ground. 14 Then Joseph returned to Egypt after burying his father, he along with his brothers and all those who had gone up with him to bury his father.

15 When Joseph's brothers realized that their father was dead, they said to each other, "Perhaps Joseph will bear a grudge against us and retaliate against us for all the terrible things we did to him." 16 So they approached[b] Joseph and said, "Before his death, our father gave a command: 17 'Thus you must say to Joseph, "Please forgive the crime of your brothers, their sinful actions that wronged you. It is now time to forgive the crime of the servants of the God of your father."'" Joseph wept when they spoke with him. 18 His brothers came[c] and bowed down deeply before him and said, "We are your servants." 19 Joseph replied to them, "Don't be afraid! Am I like God? 20 You plotted evil against me, but God turned it into something good—to keep a great people alive, as he is doing today. 21 So don't fear now! I will take care of you and your children." He comforted them and spoke reassuringly with them.

22 So Joseph lived in Egypt, he and his father's household. Joseph was one hundred ten years old. 23 Joseph lived to see Ephraim's great-grandchildren. Moreover, the children of Machir, the son of Manasseh, were born on Joseph's knees.

24 Joseph said to his brothers, "I am about to die. God will surely protect you and bring you up from this country to the country that he promised to Abraham, Isaac, and Jacob." 25 Joseph made his brothers promise, "When God finally rescues you, you must bring up my body from this place." 26 So Joseph died when he was one hundred ten years old. They embalmed him and placed him in a coffin in Egypt.

a. MT hāʾāṭād, lit., "the Atad," which could be translated, "threshing floor of buckthorns." The word "Atad" does not occur elsewhere in the OT as a proper name. However, threshing floors are often associated with a person's name, as in the "threshing floor of Nacon" (2 Sam 6:6) and the "threshing floor of Araunah" (2 Sam 24:18).

b. So LXX; MT reads "they commanded," which is probably a dittography from the word "command" later in the sentence.

c. Some scholars have conjectured that the word should be "wept," though there is no manuscript evidence for this proposal.

[50:1–14] These verses bear a strong Egyptian coloration. The author ensures that readers know Jacob's corpse is embalmed, giving him the respect appropriate for a high-ranking Egyptian official. There is continuing emphasis on protocol at the Pharaonic court: Joseph does not speak directly to Pharaoh but instead sends a message to the royal household. The funerary cortege includes not only members of Jacob's family, but also many Egyptian officials along with their chariots. (The presence of chariots and horses foreshadows the character of the Egyptian forces that go after the Israelites: Exod 14:9; 15:1, 4.) Even the Canaanites who witness the funerary rites characterize them as Egyptian (Gen 50:11–12). However, despite the Egyptianizing character of the rituals, there is a subcurrent in the text locating responsibility for the final lamentation and the burial with Joseph and the other sons, not the Egyptians (vv. 12, 14).

Such Egyptianizing reflects more than an interest in providing local color. Mortuary rites of forty days, a mourning period of seventy days, and funerary rites of seven days highlight the elevated status of Jacob, even in the eyes of the Egyptians. Such status stands in marked contrast to the low status that Israelites will soon have in the book of Exodus. The deaths of Hebrew boys (Exod 1:22) will entail no such lamentation by the Egyptians. And even the death of Joseph (Gen 50:26) is not said to result in the sorts of mourning and mortuary rites that have been held for his father. It is as if the soon-to-be-diminished status of the Israelites has already begun with the death of Joseph.

Space and geography play a prominent role in the mourning for Jacob. He died in Egypt, presumably in the land of Goshen (47:27). However, in Joseph's speech to Pharaoh's household, readers learn that Jacob has requested that he be buried in a cave that he has carved out for himself (v. 5). This detail does not accord well with Jacob's speech to Joseph reported in 47:30, where reference is made to the ancestral burial ground, presumably that of Machpelah. It may be that this reference to a cave that Jacob has created attests to a tradition about Jacob's burial that is different from the one narrated in 50:13. (Some have suggested that the cave is evidence of a different source.) In any case, the massive funeral cortege does not proceed immediately to the land of Canaan but alights in the Transjordan, at the threshing floor of Atad (see note a). The threshing floor as a place for mourning rites is otherwise unattested in the Hebrew Bible, though it can be a place for religious performance (so 2 Sam 24:18; cf. 1 Chr 21:15–28). After the rites in the Transjordan, the cortege moves across the Jordan to the ancestral burial plot of Machpelah, near Mamre, which Abraham has acquired and used on multiple occasions since that time. Here the interment takes place. (This movement, from Egypt through the Transjordan and then into the land of Canaan, presages the route that Israel will later take as they enter the land.)

[15–26] The second section of the chapter focuses, though not exclusively, on Joseph's relationship with his brothers. The broader world of which that topic is a part involves Joseph's own family: his children and their progeny. These verses unveil the interior world in which the brothers worry about how Joseph will treat them. In expressing their worry, they decide to communicate with Joseph. The precise character of that communication remains unclear, as the translation of verse 16 and the textual note suggest. The Hebrew text records, "They commanded," which hardly fits the tone of their statement to Joseph. But to say, "They approached," does not specify the manner of approach. It could be direct, or they could have used a messenger. The text remains oblique.

Moreover, what the brothers say appears disingenuous. They manufacture a speech and put it in the mouth of their recently deceased father. If Jacob actually formulated such a speech, it would have been spoken directly to Joseph, not conveyed to him by his brothers. Several features of the fictive speech require comment. First, the mandate that Joseph forgive their sin reflects the discourse about God forgiving the sin of a human (e.g., Gen 18:24; Exod 23:21; Josh 24:19; Job 7:21; Ps 25:18). The brothers, and not Jacob, have given Joseph the status of a deity, an issue that reappears in ironic fashion in Gen 50:19. Second, the characterization of the brothers as "the servants of the God of your father" elevates them as they become God's servants. Such a status may reflect their soon-to-be-made claim that they are Joseph's servants. If Joseph functions like a deity, the brothers can claim that they are God's servants. Third, the phrase "and now" (*wəʿattâ*) reappears at the beginning of verse 21, creating an overt emphasis on the present time as it will affect the future relationship of Joseph (so also the word *kayyôm*, "today," in v. 20). Both the brothers and Joseph are focusing on "the now" and its implications.

Joseph responds by weeping, the second time he has wept in this chapter (so v. 1; cf. also 43:30; 45:2). At this point, the brothers finally approach him and submit that they are indeed Joseph's servants (or slaves), echoing the words of the speech that has just been delivered to Joseph, presumably by a messenger. The brothers are, in these verses, depicted as servants of multiple parties, both human and divine, and Joseph virtually bridges that divide.

Joseph's speech begins with a phrase that is often spoken by the deity in the OT, "Do not fear!" Here again, Joseph speaks with the voice of the deity, which makes his question "Am I like God?" answerable in the affirmative. Joseph does have preternatural power over his brothers at this point in the story. Nonetheless, unlike their fictive speech to him, the author describes his speech to them as consoling (v. 21).

Joseph's speech also attests to God's providential care. The Hebrew text uses the same verb (*ḥšb*) to refer to the brothers' earlier plotting and to the deity's eventually turning it into something good. Both parties planned something, but God's planning won out, despite the evil actions of Joseph's brothers. This claim echoes Joseph's speech to his brothers in Gen 45, though there is a difference in nuance. In chapter 45, Joseph avers three times that God "sent" Joseph to Egypt (vv. 5, 7, 8). There, God is causing behavior. In Gen 50, God's activity is less overt, more providential.

Finally, Joseph's speech underscores a major change that has taken place by the end of the book of Genesis. Earlier, he was reported to have provided food for his family (45:11; 47:12). That family has now become a different sort of entity, a great people (50:20)—more than just a family. Still, even within that large people, there is time for a summary report about Joseph's own family and his death. The focus is on Joseph and his father's household, as if Joseph is the primary descendant. He lives with his father's household; there is no specific reference to coresidence with his brothers. Rather, the author reports Joseph's progeny. The phrase "born on Joseph's knees" (v. 23) may refer to the sort of blessing that Jacob has given to Joseph's sons seated on his knees (48:12).

The final verses reflect a continuing concern about proper burial as burial in the land, a note introduced in the narrative about Abraham (ch. 23). The last of the three promises in Gen 50 (vv. 17, 21, 25) involves the brothers' task of returning Joseph's body to the land of Canaan. The final verse places him in Egypt, which means that the storyline is not yet complete. Israel the people and Joseph need to return to the land. The language of rescue (v. 24) indicates that Israel's status will change for the worse after Joseph's death. (The fate of Joseph's body is narrated in Exod 13:19 and Josh 24:32.) But when Israel does return, they do so no longer as a family but as a people.

INDEX OF SCRIPTURE AND OTHER ANCIENT SOURCES

OLD TESTAMENT

ANCIENT NEAR EASTERN TEXTS

DEAD SEA SCROLLS

NEW TESTAMENT

Galatians

INDEX OF SUBJECTS AND AUTHORS